CCSP Self-Study: Securing Cisco IOS Networks (SECUR)

John F. Roland

Cisco Press

Cisco Press
800 East 96th Street
Indianapolis, Indiana 46240 USA

CCSP Self-Study: Securing Cisco IOS Networks (SECUR)

John F. Roland

Copyright © 2004 Cisco Systems, Inc.

Published by:
Cisco Press
800 East 96th Street
Indianapolis, IN 46240 USA

Printed in the United States of America 1 2 3 4 5 6 7 8 9 0

First Printing   March   2004

Library of Congress Cataloging-in-Publication Number: 2003107993

ISBN: 1-58705-151-6

Warning and Disclaimer

This book is designed to provide information about securing Cisco IOS routers and includes security practices, protocols, software, and equipment that work on or in conjunction with Cisco IOS equipment to provide layers of security to networks. Every effort has been made to make this book as complete and as accurate as possible, but no warranty or fitness is implied.

The information is provided on an "as is" basis. The authors, Cisco Press, and Cisco Systems, Inc. shall have neither liability nor responsibility to any person or entity with respect to any loss or damages arising from the information contained in this book or from the use of the discs or programs that may accompany it.

The opinions expressed in this book belong to the author and are not necessarily those of Cisco Systems, Inc.

Trademark Acknowledgments

All terms mentioned in this book that are known to be trademarks or service marks have been appropriately capitalized. Cisco Press or Cisco Systems, Inc. cannot attest to the accuracy of this information. Use of a term in this book should not be regarded as affecting the validity of any trademark or service mark.

The Cisco Press self-study book series is as described, intended for self-study. It has not been designed for use in a classroom environment. Only Cisco Learning Partners displaying the following logos are authorized providers of Cisco curriculum. If you are using this book within the classroom of a training company that does not carry one of these logos, then you are not preparing with a Cisco trained and authorized provider. For information on Cisco Learning Partners please visit:www.cisco.com/go/authorizedtraining. To provide Cisco with any information about what you may believe is unauthorized use of Cisco trademarks or copyrighted training material, please visit: http://www.cisco.com/logo/infringement.html.

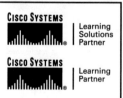

Corporate and Government Sales

Cisco Press offers excellent discounts on this book when ordered in quantity for bulk purchases or special sales. For more information, please contact: **U.S. Corporate and Government Sales**   1-800-382-3419
corpsales@pearsontechgroup.com

For sales outside of the U.S. please contact: **International Sales**   international@pearsontechgroup.com

Feedback Information

At Cisco Press, our goal is to create in-depth technical books of the highest quality and value. Each book is crafted with care and precision, undergoing rigorous development that involves the unique expertise of members from the professional technical community.

Readers' feedback is a natural continuation of this process. If you have any comments regarding how we could improve the quality of this book, or otherwise alter it to better suit your needs, you can contact us through e-mail at feedback@ciscopress.com. Please make sure to include the book title and ISBN in your message.

We greatly appreciate your assistance.

Publisher	John Wait
Editor-in-Chief	John Kane
Executive Editor	Brett Bartow
Cisco Representative	Anthony Wolfenden
Cisco Press Program Manager	Nannette M. Noble
Acquisitions Editor	Michelle Grandin
Production Manager	Patrick Kanouse
Development Editor	Dan Young
Project Editor	Ginny Bess Munroe
Copy Editor	Bill McManus
Technical Editors	Leon Katcharian, Jay Swan, and Dale Tesch Jr.
Team Coordinator	Tammi Barnett
Book and Cover Designer	Louisa Adair
Composition	Interactive Composition Corporation
Indexer	Julie Bess
Proofreader	Missy Pluta

CISCO SYSTEMS

Corporate Headquarters
Cisco Systems, Inc.
170 West Tasman Drive
San Jose, CA 95134-1706
USA
www.cisco.com
Tel: 408 526-4000
    800 553-NETS (6387)
Fax: 408 526-4100

European Headquarters
Cisco Systems International BV
Haarlerbergpark
Haarlerbergweg 13-19
1101 CH Amsterdam
The Netherlands
www-europe.cisco.com
Tel: 31 0 20 357 1000
Fax: 31 0 20 357 1100

Americas Headquarters
Cisco Systems, Inc.
170 West Tasman Drive
San Jose, CA 95134-1706
USA
www.cisco.com
Tel: 408 526-7660
Fax: 408 527-0883

Asia Pacific Headquarters
Cisco Systems, Inc.
Capital Tower
168 Robinson Road
#22-01 to #29-01
Singapore 068912
www.cisco.com
Tel: +65 6317 7777
Fax: +65 6317 7799

Cisco Systems has more than 200 offices in the following countries and regions. Addresses, phone numbers, and fax numbers are listed on the
Cisco.com Web site at www.cisco.com/go/offices.

Argentina • Australia • Austria • Belgium • Brazil • Bulgaria • Canada • Chile • China PRC • Colombia • Costa Rica • Croatia • Czech Repub
Denmark • Dubai, UAE • Finland • France • Germany • Greece • Hong Kong SAR • Hungary • India • Indonesia • Ireland • Israel • Ita
Japan • Korea • Luxembourg • Malaysia • Mexico • The Netherlands • New Zealand • Norway • Peru • Philippines • Poland • Portu
Puerto Rico • Romania • Russia • Saudi Arabia • Scotland • Singapore • Slovakia • Slovenia • South Africa • Spain • Swed
Switzerland • Taiwan • Thailand • Turkey • Ukraine • United Kingdom • United States • Venezuela • Vietnam • Zimbab

About the Author

John F. Roland, CCNA, CCDA, CCNP, CCDP, CSS-1, MCSE, is a security specialist who works for WesTek Consulting. John has worked in the IT field for more than 22 years, from COBOL programming on IBM main-frames to LAN/WAN design and implementation on U.S. military networks and, more recently, to the development of Cisco and Microsoft certification training materials. John's current assignment has him designing technical training materials for a large cable communications company.

John holds a bachelor's degree in accounting from Tiffin University, Tiffin, Ohio, with minors in math and electrical engineering from General Motors Institute, Flint, Michigan.

About the Technical Editors

Leon Katcharian is an education specialist at Cisco Systems, Inc., where he designs and develops training on Cisco network security products. Leon has more than 19 years of experience in the data-networking field, having been a technical support engineer, a technical instructor, a technical writer, and a course developer.

Jay Swan teaches Cisco courses with Global Knowledge. He is a certified Cisco Systems instructor with bachelor's and master's degrees from Stanford University. Prior to joining Global Knowledge, he worked in the ISP and higher education fields. Jay holds the CCNP and CCSP certifications. He lives in southwest Colorado, where he is an active trail runner, search and rescue volunteer, and martial arts practitioner.

Dale Tesch Jr. is an advanced technology engineer in security for Cisco Systems North East Channels Team. He holds a bachelor's in computer information systems (CIS), as well as the CCNP and CISSP certifications. Dale resides in the Seacoast region of New Hampshire with his wife Zarina and their three children, Isabella, Douglas, and Andrew. Dale's hobbies include playing softball and coaching soccer.

Dedications

This book is dedicated to my wife, Mariko, and to our son, Michael, for their continuing support. Their steady love and encouragement has helped keep me on target through the development of this book. You're the greatest!

—John F. Roland

Acknowledgments

I want to thank Michelle Grandin from Cisco Press for believing in me and for helping to get the project going. Michelle helped me in many ways during this project and was always there to lend an encouraging word or a guiding hand, and it has been a real pleasure to work with her over these few months.

Dan Young provided consistent editorial feedback, direction, support, and encouragement to keep me on track through this project. His contributions to the development and consistency of this book are innumerable, and I enjoyed working with him very much. Thank you.

I would also like to thank the technical reviewers, Leon Katcharian, Jay Swan, and Dale Tesch Jr., for their comments, suggestions, and careful attention to detail. Without their help, this book would not be the valuable resource that it has become. Thank you all.

Contents at a Glance

Table of Contents

Foreword

CCSP Self-Study: Securing Cisco IOS Networks (SECUR) is a Cisco-authorized, self-paced learning tool that helps you understand foundation concepts covered on the SECUR exam. This book was developed in cooperation with the Cisco Internet Learning Solutions Group, the team within Cisco responsible for the development of the SECUR exam. As an early-stage exam preparation product, this book teaches the knowledge needed to identify security threats and the skills necessary to work with the security features of Cisco IOS. Whether you are studying to become CCSP certified or are simply seeking to gain a better understanding of the products, services, and policies that enable you to secure Cisco IOS router networks, you will benefit from the information presented in this book.

Cisco Systems and Cisco Press present this material in text-based format to provide another learning vehicle for our customers and the broader user community in general. Although a publication does not duplicate the instructor-led or e-learning environment, we acknowledge that not everyone responds in the same way to the same delivery mechanism. It is our intent that presenting this material via a Cisco Press publication will enhance the transfer of knowledge to a broad audience of networking professionals.

Cisco Press will present other books in the Certification Self-Study Series on existing and future exams to help achieve Cisco Internet Learning Solutions Group's principal objectives: to educate the Cisco community of networking professionals and to enable that community to build and maintain reliable, scalable networks. The Cisco Career Certifications and classes that support these certifications are directed at meeting these objectives through a disciplined approach to progressive learning.

In order to succeed with Cisco Career Certifications and in your daily job as a Cisco certified professional, we recommend a blended learning solution that combines instructor-led training with hands-on experience, e-learning, and self-study training. Cisco Systems has authorized Cisco Learning Partners worldwide, which can provide you with the most highly qualified instruction and invaluable hands-on experience in lab and simulation environments. To learn more about Cisco Learning Partner programs available in your area, please go to http://www.cisco.com/go/authorizedtraining.

The books Cisco Press creates in partnership with Cisco Systems will meet the same standards for content quality demanded of our courses and certifications. It is our intent that you will find this and subsequent Cisco Press certification self-study publications of value as you build your networking knowledge base.

Thomas M. Kelly
Vice-President, Internet Learning Solutions Group
Cisco Systems, Inc.
March 2004

Preface

Network security has been a concern for most organizations for many years, and the original Managing Cisco Network Security (MCNS) course, the forerunner to this course, was very well received for that very reason. That well-written course provided critical information for "networkers" trying to keep up with the growing number of network threats and countermeasures. The MCNS course was a component of the Cisco Security Specialist (CSS-1) curriculum.

Because of the demands of customers for a professional-level security course, Cisco redesigned the original CSS-1 courses to create the new Cisco Certified Security Professional (CCSP) curriculum. The redesigned MCNS course became the Securing Cisco IOS Networks (SECUR) course, which is the basis for this book.

John F. Roland
WesTek Consulting, LLC
March 2004

Introduction

The goal of this book is to help readers implement Cisco IOS network security technologies with the goal of creating highly manageable and secure networks. This book is designed to supplement the Cisco SECUR course or act as a standalone reference.

Intended Audience

This book is written for anyone who wants to learn about Cisco network security features and technologies. The main target audience is networking professionals who need to expand their knowledge beyond routing and switching technologies and improve their ability to install, configure, monitor, and verify Cisco network security using the powerful features of Cisco IOS Software and Cisco IOS Firewall. This book assumes that you have knowledge of Cisco networking equivalent to pass the CCNA certification exam.

The secondary target audience is general users who need to understand network security threats and how to mitigate those threats. This book explains many network security concepts and technologies with a user-friendly approach that will appeal to readers who prefer less technical manuals.

The Cisco Certified Security Professional

You may be interested in pursuing professional certification through the Cisco demanding series of certification exams to provide you with a means of validating your expertise to current or prospective employers and to your peers. Many network professionals are pursuing the CCSP certification because network security has become a critical element in the overall security plan of 21st-century businesses. This book has been designed to help you attain this prestigious certification, if that is your goal.

The CCSP certification is a main certification track, beginning at the CCNA and ending at the CCIE level, as do the CCNP, CCDP, and CCIP certifications. The CCSP certification requires you to pass five exams. The prerequisite for being awarded your CCSP certification upon completion of these exams is that you hold a current CCNA certification. Table I-1 contains a list of the exams in the CCSP certification series.

Table I-1   *CCSP Certification Exams*

Exam Number	Recommended Training
642-501 SECUR	**Securing Cisco IOS Networks (SECUR) (Formerly MCNS) v1.0** This five-day course teaches the knowledge and skills needed to secure Cisco IOS router networks.
642-511 CSVPN	**Cisco Secure Virtual Private Networks (CSVPN) v3.1** This four-day course teaches the knowledge and skills needed to describe, configure, verify, and manage the Cisco VPN 3000 Concentrator, Cisco VPN Software Client, and Cisco VPN 3002 Hardware Client feature set.

Table I-1   *CCSP Certification Exams (Continued)*

Exam Number	Recommended Training
642-521 CSPFA	**Cisco Secure PIX Firewall Advanced (CSPFA) v3.1** This four-day course teaches the knowledge and skills needed to describe, configure, verify, and manage the PIX Firewall product family.
642-531 CSIDS	**Cisco Secure Intrusion Detection Systems (CSIDS) v3.0** This three-day course teaches the knowledge and skills needed to design, install, and configure a Cisco Intrusion Protection solution for small, medium-sized, and enterprise networks. Additionally, you learn how to manage, administer, and monitor your intrusion detection systems.
642-541 CSI	**Cisco SAFE Implementation (CSI) v1.1** This four-day course teaches the knowledge and skills needed to implement and use the principles and axioms presented in the "SAFE: Extending the Security Blueprint to Small, Midsize, and Remote-User Networks" whitepaper on specific devices.

The CCSP certification is valid for three years, after which you must perform the requirements for recertification. Currently, the requirement is that you retake the current version of the appropriate exams. You can find out more about the CCSP track at Cisco.com (search for "Career Certifications").

The Cisco recommended training path for the CCSP certification is to attend the instructor-led training courses offered by the Cisco training partners. Table I-1 describes the recommended courses that are designed around hours of lab work so that you can get practical experience configuring or managing the devices that you are studying.

Book Features

This book has a number of unique features that help you learn and put to work the network security topics covered in this book:

- **Concepts covered**—At the beginning of each chapter is a list of topics covered in that chapter. This provides a reference to the concepts covered and can be used as an advanced organizer.

- **Figures, examples, and tables**—This book contains figures, examples, and tables that present each chapter's content in an easy-to-use form. The figures help explain concepts and software processes, the examples provide examples of commands and output, and the tables present facts such as command syntax with descriptions.

- **Case studies**—The Future Corporation, a hypothetical enterprise, is used in each chapter to anchor configuration examples into a unified whole and to make the examples more realistic. A sample network security policy based on The Future Corporation is used throughout this book as a model of how to implement security policy directives. Case study network examples in many chapters summarize configuration information taught in the chapters based on The Future Corporation's customer environment.

- **Command summaries**—Command summaries are included with each section, making it easier to learn and apply the tasks being presented.

- **Chapter summaries**—At the end of each chapter is a summary of the concepts covered in that chapter. It provides a synopsis of the chapter and serves as a study aid.

- **Review questions**—After the summary in each chapter are 10 or more review questions that reinforce the concepts presented in that chapter. They help you test your understanding before you move on to new concepts. The answers to these questions are provided in Appendix A.

- **Comprehensive glossary of terms**—The glossary provides definitions for the key terms used throughout the book for easy reference.

Organization of This Book

This book is organized into 13 chapters, 3 appendixes, and a glossary.

- Chapter 1, "Introduction to Network Security," presents a discussion of some of the threats that endanger network security and covers the tools and procedures that can be used to mitigate these threats and their potentially destructive impact.

- Chapter 2, "Basic Cisco Router Security," presents an introduction to securing Cisco routers using proven methods for securing the physical router device, protecting the router adminis- trative interface, and implementing AAA.

- Chapter 3, "Advanced AAA Security for Cisco Router Networks," covers Cisco Secure ACS software for Windows NT or Windows 2000, UNIX (Solaris), and the new Cisco Secure ACS Appliance, as well as the security services of TACACS+, RADIUS, and Kerberos.

- Chapter 4, "Cisco Router Threat Mitigation," describes the risks associated with connecting an enterprise to the Internet and the methods used to reduce those risks.

- Chapter 5, "Cisco IOS Firewall Context-Based Access Control Configuration," provides an introduction to the Cisco IOS Firewall and discusses CBAC, global timeouts and thresholds, port-to-application mapping, and inspection rules.

- Chapter 6, "Cisco IOS Firewall Authentication Proxy," introduces the Cisco IOS Firewall authentication proxy and server and router configurations required to support authentication proxy.

- Chapter 7, "Cisco IOS Firewall Intrusion Detection System," covers information on the Cisco IOS Firewall Intrusion Detection System package for Cisco routers and how to configure it.

- Chapter 8, "Building IPSec VPNs Using Cisco Routers and Pre-Shared Keys," teaches how to configure Cisco IOS IPSec using pre-shared keys for authentication.

- Chapter 9, "Building Advanced IPSec VPNs Using Cisco Routers and Certificate Authorities," introduces configuration of Cisco IOS IPSec using a certificate authority.

- Chapter 10, "Configuring IOS Remote Access Using Cisco Easy VPN," covers the configuration of Cisco IOS remote access using the Cisco Easy Virtual Private Network (VPN) and the Cisco VPN Client.

- Chapter 11, "Securing Cisco Routers Using Security Device Manager," introduces and explains the Cisco Security Device Manager.

- Chapter 12, "Managing Enterprise VPN Routers," introduces and explains the Management Center for VPN Routers (Router MC).

- Chapter 13, "Case Study," allows you to put together most of the security elements discussed throughout this book.

- Appendix A, "Answers to Chapter Review Questions," provides the answers to the review questions at the end of each chapter.

- Appendix B, "Sample Network Security Policy," contains an example of a network security policy for The Future Corporation network.

- Appendix C, "Configuring Standard and Extended Access Lists," presents an overview of configuring standard and extended IP access lists in Cisco IOS Software.

- The Glossary provides a comprehensive glossary of terms used and introduced in this book.

Icons Used in This Book

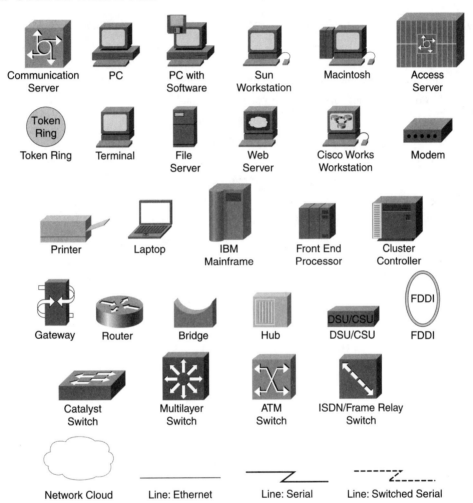

Command Syntax Conventions

The conventions used to present command syntax in this book are the same conventions used in the *Cisco IOS Command Reference*, as follows:

- **Boldface** indicates commands and keywords that are entered literally as shown. In actual configuration examples and output (not general command syntax), boldface indicates commands that are manually input by the user (such as a **show** command).

- *Italics* indicate arguments for which you supply actual values.

- Vertical bars (|) separate alternative, mutually exclusive elements.

- Square brackets ([ ]) indicate optional elements.

- Braces ({ }) indicate a required choice.

- Braces within brackets ([{ }]) indicate a required choice within an optional element.

CHAPTER 1

Introduction to Network Security

When networks first started appearing, they tended to be isolated, stand-alone networks. Securing these private networks was relatively easy: make sure critical assets were backed up regularly, keep the power on, and keep plenty of spare replacement parts in the cupboard. These networks did not provide much function, though, and they did not stay isolated for very long.

Computer installations during the 1950s consisted of stand-alone mainframes that used punch cards for data entry and magnetic tapes for data storage. These systems were mostly automated calculating machines with limited processing power and no interconnectivity.

The next step was to connect disk storage devices and dumb terminals to the central mainframe to permit direct data entry—and thus networks were born. Application development brought messaging and other online tools to improve communication and facilitate work processes. The networks were there, they were closed to external sources and were very secure, but they stood alone.

In the early 1960s, the military started looking at computers as potential tools to help improve communication and management functions. That could not happen until computers could talk to each other, so the United States Department of Defense Advanced Research Project Agency (ARPA) solicited the help of some top academic thinkers to see what they could do to solve the problem.

The task of getting computers to talk to each other was no small problem. Mainframes were being produced by half-a-dozen manufactures, each using its own proprietary operating system (OS). A protocol had to be developed that could be used by any OS to talk to any other OS. Physical connectivity was another problem altogether.

In 1969, the University of California, Los Angeles, the Stanford Research Institute in Menlo Park, California, the University of California, Santa Barbara, and the University of Utah became the first networked organizations anywhere in the world. They named the network the ARPA Network, or ARPANet, and started a communications revolution that is still rocking our world.

The protocol that resulted from these preliminary experimentations was the Internet Protocol (IP), which eventually gave the Internet its name. More and more educational and governmental organizations began tapping into the ARPANet until, in the 1980s, the military separated from the ARPANet and formed the MILNET as its own network. The

National Science Foundation (NSF) continued to promote and develop the NSFNet as the national nonmilitary network that grew into what we now know as the Internet.

The introduction of personal computers (PCs) by manufacturers, such as Apple and IBM, enabled network designers to break away from the mainframe systems. Portable network and file servers using OSs, such as UNIX, Banyan VINES, Novell Netware, Apple LocalTalk, and Microsoft Windows, began to become more and more common, allowing PCs attached to these servers to communicate with each other. Local networks could talk to other local networks by using the Transmission Control Protocol/Internet Protocol (TCP/IP), using direct connections through dedicated circuits or through the shared circuits of the Internet.

Electronic mail was one of the biggest uses of the Internet in the early days, along with file sharing using protocols such as TCP/IP's File Transmission Protocol (FTP). In 1993, a group of students at the University of Illinois released its Mosaic application, the first widely adopted web browser. Netscape and Microsoft picked up the torch and ignited the explosive growth of the Internet that is still expanding today.

The MILNET was gone by the 1990s, to be replaced by the Nonsecure Internet Protocol Network (NIPRNET) and the Secure Internet Protocol Network (SIPRNET), which grew in parallel to the Internet. The main difference between the NIPRNET and the SIPRNET was that the NIPRNET was connected to the Internet at controlled choke points located on the East and West coasts. The SIPRNET was isolated because the threat of external attacks from the Internet was well established by that time in the brief history of internetworks.

Today, isolated networks are rare and typically only used when extreme security is required. Typical networks today are interconnected through the Internet and often use portions of the public Internet as extensions of the corporate, private network. Although all networks are at some risk from internal security threats, this connection to and through the Internet creates a significant increase in potential external security threats to modern networks.

This chapter presents a discussion of some of those threats and covers the tools and procedures that you can use to mitigate these threats and their potentially destructive impact. Additionally, this chapter provides an overview of the Cisco SAFE Blueprint, a security concept for deploying network security in depth and the basis of the Cisco security product integration.

Objectives

Upon completion of this chapter, you will be able to perform the following tasks:

- Describe the need for network security
- Describe the Cisco SAFE Blueprint
- Understand network attack taxonomy
- Identify the components of a complete network security policy
- Identify Cisco network security products
- Identify Cisco network security management software applications

- Identify the security issues implicit in common management protocols and functions
- Identify the three most common methods of implementing NAT and NAT-T

Since the mid-1990s, Internet-enabled business, or e-business, has drastically improved companies' efficiency and revenue growth. E-business applications such as e-commerce, supply-chain management, and remote access enable companies to streamline processes, lower operating costs, and increase customer satisfaction. Such applications require mission-critical networks that accommodate voice, video, and data traffic, and these networks must be scalable to support increasing numbers of users and the need for greater capacity and performance. However, as networks enable more and more applications and are available to more and more users from around the world, they become ever more vulnerable to a wider range of security threats. To combat those threats and ensure that e-business transactions are not compromised, security technology must play a major role in today's networks.

A Closed Network

A closed network typically consists of a network designed and implemented in a corporate environment, and provides connectivity only to known parties and sites without connecting to public networks. In the past, networks were designed in this way and were thought to be reasonably secure because they had no outside connectivity. Figure 1-1 depicts a typical closed network.

Figure 1-1   *Closed Network*

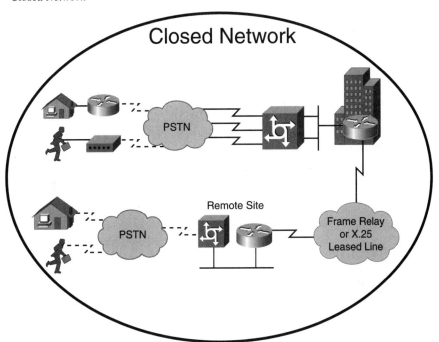

Today's Network

Today, networks are designed with availability to the Internet and public networks, which is a major requirement. Most of today's networks have several entry points to other networks both public and private; therefore, securing these networks has become fundamentally important. Figure 1-2 shows the many entry points into an open network.

Figure 1-2   *Open Network*

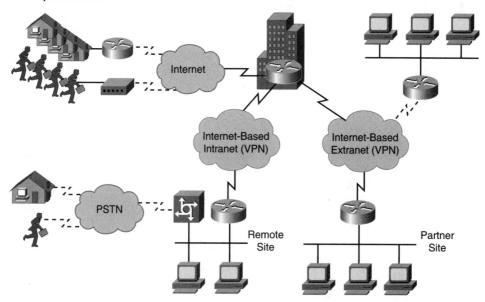

Threat Capabilities—More Dangerous and Easier to Use

With the development of large, open networks, there has been a huge increase in network security threats in the past 20 years. Attackers have discovered more network vulnerabilities, and the tools that are used to hack a network have become simpler to use and require less technical knowledge, as shown in Figure 1-3. For example, downloadable applications are available that require little or no attacking knowledge to implement. There are also vulnerability-assessment applications available for troubleshooting a network that, when used improperly, can pose severe threats.

Tools such as Computer Oracle and Password System (COPS), MacAnalysis, Security Administrator's Integrated Network Tool (SAINT), and Security Administrator's Tool for Analyzing Networks (SATAN), just to name a few, are powerful network scanners that network administrators can use to locate and correct network weaknesses. Attackers, too, can use some of these tools, but when they find weaknesses, it will not be to correct them.

Wireless access also opens networks to additional security threats. Attackers may be able to exploit weaknesses in the Wired Equivalent Privacy (WEP) protocol or exploit the fact that wireless networks provide access points that may be outside of the physical controls of an organization.

Figure 1-3 *Threat Capabilities over Time*

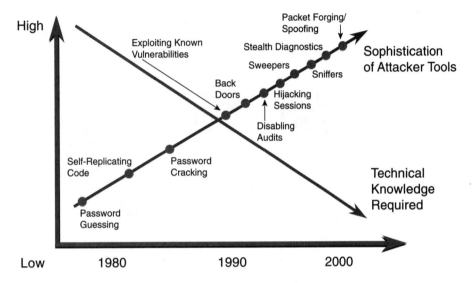

The Changing Role of Security

With so many threats to networks, security has moved to the forefront of network management and implementation. It is necessary for the survival of many businesses to allow open access to network resources, and ensure that the data and resources are as secure as possible.

The need for security is becoming more important because of the following:

- **Customer privacy**—Ensuring the security of customer financial information and profiles, privacy, and communications
- **Corporate functionality**—Ensuring the continuity and consistency of daily business functions
- **Terrorism**—Guarding against denial of service (DoS) attacks or potential infrastructure meltdowns caused by cyber-terrorists
- **Government data security**—Protecting government databases from compromise and possible misuse of information
- **Communications infrastructure**—Ensuring continuous operation of vital global and international communication links

The E-Business Challenge

The Internet has radically shifted expectations of companies' abilities to build stronger relationships with partners, suppliers, customers, and employees. Now, companies are more agile and competitive. E-business is giving birth to exciting new applications for e-commerce, supply-chain management, customer care, workforce optimization, and e-learning applications, as shown in Figure 1-4. These new applications streamline and improve processes, speed up turnaround times, lower costs, and increase user satisfaction.

Figure 1-4   *Expanded Access*

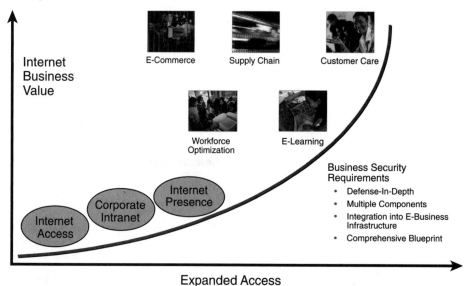

E-business requires mission-critical networks that accommodate ever-increasing constituencies and demands for greater capacity and performance. These networks also need to handle voice, video, and data traffic as networks converge into multiservice environments.

Security must be a fundamental component of any e-business strategy. As enterprise network managers open their networks to more users and applications, they also expose these networks to greater risk.

Legal and Governmental Policy Issues

The legal ramifications of breaches in data confidentiality and integrity can also be extremely costly for organizations. The U.S. government has enacted and is currently developing regulations to control the privacy of electronic information. In fact, there are currently approximately 50 bills before the U.S. Congress related to the regulation of online privacy and security. The existing and pending regulations generally stipulate that organizations in violation could face a range of penalties.

Three of the most important regulations are:

- **Gramm-Leach Bliley Act (GLBA) of 1999**—Provides that organizations in violation of this act, which includes several privacy regulations for U.S. financial institutions, might face a range of penalties from termination of their Federal Deposit Insurance Corporation (FDIC) insurance to up to $1 million in monetary penalties.

  Even if an external attacker is the perpetrator of an attack, the company storing that information can potentially be found negligent by the courts if the information was not adequately safeguarded. Furthermore, companies that suffer breaches in data integrity might be required to defend against lawsuits initiated by customers who are negatively affected by the incorrect or offensive data and seek monetary or punitive damages.

- **Government Information Security Reform Act (GISRA) of 2000**—Under this act, agencies must undergo annual self-assessments and independent assessments of their security practices and policies, which are required for submission.

- **Health Insurance Portability and Accountability Act (HIPPA) of 1996 (Public Law 104-191)**—Enacted as part of a broad Congressional attempt at incremental healthcare reform. The "administrative simplification" aspect of that law requires the U.S. Department of Health and Human Services (DHHS) to develop standards and requirements for maintenance and transmission of health information that identifies individual patients.

  These standards are designed to do the following:

  - Improve the efficiency and effectiveness of the healthcare system by standardizing the interchange of electronic data for specified administrative and financial transactions.

  - Protect the security and confidentiality of electronic health information.

The Cisco SAFE Blueprint

The details of the Cisco SAFE Blueprint are contained in several documents. The original document, titled "SAFE: A Security Blueprint for Enterprise Networks," can be found at http://www.cisco.com/go/safe. A second document, titled "SAFE: Extending the Security Blueprint to Small, Midsize, and Remote-User Networks," can be found at the same URL. This SAFE document modifies the basic principles for smaller networks, including remote-user networks, such as those used by teleworkers and mobile workers.

Additional white papers at this URL contain SAFE discussions of Internet Protocol Security (IPSec) virtual private networks (VPNs), wireless networks, telephony, and a variety of other security topics. This website is an excellent source of information on these critical security topics.

The Cisco SAFE Blueprint is a loosely structured guide, based on Cisco and Cisco partner products, which can be used when designing the security elements of a network. SAFE builds layered security by developing and deploying mitigating defenses in depth against expected threats. Using this security blueprint, a network designer can be reasonably assured that the failure of one security system will not result in a compromise of targeted network resources.

SAFE was developed around these fundamental design objectives:

- Network security policy drives the need for security and attack mitigation solutions
- Security is implemented in depth throughout the network, not just at choke points or through specialized security devices
- Security should be cost-effective to deploy
- Reporting and management must be secure
- Critical network assets require authentication, authorization, and accounting (AAA) of access by users and administrators
- Subnets and critical resources should be monitored by intrusion detection systems

SAFE concedes that attacks may be externally or internally originated. SAFE networks are designed to prevent the majority of attacks from penetrating network defenses and affecting network resources, while still providing essential network services to the organization. When attacks do succeed, SAFE networks react quickly to contain and minimize their effects. SAFE does not introduce radically new concepts; it simply describes a logical approach to integrating various security products and tools (modules) into a unified security structure.

SAFE is based on a modular concept that allows threat-mitigation efforts to be applied in a systematic manner that scales well with network growth. The basic modules are based on the following axioms:

- Routers are targets
- Switches are targets
- Hosts are targets
- Networks are targets
- Applications are targets.
- Secure management and reporting

These are not surprising concepts. The following sections explore these axioms in more depth.

Routers Are Targets

Routers control access to and from every network. They route traffic, advertise networks, and filter traffic to and from a network. Routers are critical elements in network security. Public information is readily available for probing, attacking, and gaining valuable information from routers. At a minimum, router administrators should do the following:

- Lock down Telnet access to all routers.
- Lock down Simple Network Management Protocol (SNMP) access to all routers.
- Use Terminal Access Controller Access Control System Plus (TACACS+) to control access to router management functions.

- Turn off unneeded services.   *enum all services*
- Turn on logging at appropriate levels.
- Authenticate routing table updates.

Switches Are Targets

Switches typically provide the next layer of network control, but, unlike routers, not as much information is publicly available about security risks associated with switches. Switch security includes all the elements described in the previous section for routers plus the following:

- Ports with no need to trunk should have their trunk settings configured to off instead of leaving them set at auto.
- Be sure that trunk ports use VLAN numbers that are not used anywhere else in the switch.
- Disable all unused ports on a switch to prevent unauthorized physical access.
- Use VLANs in conjunction with other methods for securing access between two subnets, but do not rely on it to be the sole security.

Hosts Are Targets

Hosts are the most frequently compromised devices on any network. Hosts come in a wide variety of hardware platforms, operating systems, and application software. Each of these elements has various levels of updates, patches, and fixes available at different times. Keeping all of these elements current in a busy network is a difficult prospect. To secure hosts, follow these steps:

- Document each component within a system, including all hardware, operating systems, and critical applications.
- Keep systems updated with the latest patches and fixes and pay attention to how these patches and fixes might affect other system components.
- To prevent the updates themselves from causing DoS attacks, use test environments to evaluate updates before applying them to production systems.

Networks Are Targets

Network attacks usually take advantage of a fundamental element of network operation. Some attacks use Address Resolution Protocol (ARP) or Media Access Control (MAC) based Layer 2 attacks. Router and switch security practices can help mitigate these kinds of attacks.

Some attacks use sniffers to gather critical access information. Access control methods can help here to some extent.

One of the most uncontrollable types of attacks on networks is the distributed denial of service (DDoS) attack. This attack uses tens or hundreds of systems to simultaneously send bogus data to an IP address with the goal of making the entire network unresponsive. DDoS is almost unstoppable. One method that can help is to have the service provider configure rate limiting on the customer's connection. Undesired traffic that exceeds a predetermined threshold will be dropped, preserving some amount of bandwidth for critical functions.

✱Use the private network ranges identified in RFC 1918 and filter them on routers using the guidelines in RFC 2827. This action will prevent systems from targeting private addresses and will help preserve the source identity of attackers.

Applications Are Targets

Attackers also specifically target applications. Applications are written by individuals who may introduce unintentional errors in the code. All software used on your systems should go through code review and extensive code testing, but that is not normally something you have any control over.

One of the best methods for protecting applications is through the use of intrusion detection systems (IDSs). IDS devices can be network IDS (NIDS) devices or software installed on a host to create a host-based IDS (HIDS) device. NIDS devices scan the entire network for suspect activity and can normally issue reports and do some basic corrective action. HIDS devices monitor specific hosts and can usually perform more extensive corrective actions against suspect activity than can NIDS devices.

False positives and negatives are a common occurrence with IDSs. Something that may look like an attack could be legitimate traffic (false positive) and something that may look like legitimate traffic could be an attack that does not get recognized (false negative). One of the first tasks when implementing an IDS is to tune the system to minimize false positives and negatives.

NIDS devices have three basic methods of responding to attacks: logging, shunning, and TCP resets. Logging is a passive response to attack recognition and allows administrators to use reporting tools to scan logs at a later date and then make considered responses to certain attacks. Shunning occurs when a NIDS recognizes an attack and sends an updated access control list (ACL) to the router blocking the address of the attacker(s). NIDS devices can also reset TCP sessions by sending TCP reset messages to the attacking devices.

SAFE recommends the deployment of both NIDS and HIDS devices in networks to provide defenses in depth. NIDS devices generally work from signature databases and look for specific matching traffic patterns. These devices are very good at catching most of the common network attacks. HIDS devices, such as the Cisco Security Agent, sometimes monitor behavior patterns instead of working from a database of known signatures. HIDS devices may be able to identify attacks that might get by NIDS devices.

Secure Management and Reporting

The final axiom in the SAFE documents discusses secure management and reporting. Knowing what to manage, when to manage it, and how to manage it seem like elementary concepts, but some careful consideration of these elements can go a long way toward helping to protect network assets.

It is important to choose the type of management you plan to deploy across the network. Out-of-band (OOB) management is most secure because each network device and host has a dedicated interface that is used strictly for management and logging functions, unconnected to the rest of the network. This type of management can be costly to deploy, however, so many organizations use in-band management, where management traffic shares the same network as normal network traffic.

Whenever possible, syslog servers should be used to keep track of logs from multiple devices. Used in conjunction with Network Time Protocol (NTP) to synchronize the time of all devices, syslog servers can collect data in one location for ease of reporting.

Change management is another critical element of network security. When an attack occurs, it is important to know the model, version, and patch level of all network devices and systems. Careful management of these elements can be a big help in mitigating network attacks.

Network Attack Taxonomy

This section provides an overview of various network attacks and effects.

Without proper protection, any part of any network can be susceptible to attacks or unauthorized activity. Professional attackers, company competitors, or even internal employees can violate all routers, switches, and hosts. In fact, according to several studies, more than half of all network attacks are waged internally.

The Computer Security Institute (CSI) in San Francisco estimates that between 60 and 80 percent of network misuse comes from inside the enterprises in which the misuse has taken place. Cisco Systems Posture Assessment Group reports that the inside network is 100 percent vulnerable to attack. To determine the best ways to protect networks against attacks, IT managers must understand the many types of attacks and the damage that these attacks can cause to e-business infrastructures. Then, they must take steps to build a more secure network.

Figure 1-5 shows that network attacks can be as varied as the systems they attempt to penetrate.

Figure 1-5   *Varied Attacks*

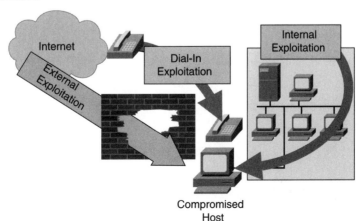

Compromised
Host

Network Security Threats

There are four general threats to network security:

- **Unstructured threats**—These threats primarily consist of random attackers using various common tools, such as malicious shell scripts, password crackers, credit card number generators, and dialer daemons. Although attackers in this category have often been motivated by malicious intent, many are more interested in the intellectual challenge of cracking safeguards than creating havoc.

- **Structured threats**—These threats are created by attackers who are highly motivated and technically competent. Typically, such attackers act alone or in small groups to understand, develop, and use sophisticated attacking techniques to penetrate unsuspecting businesses. These groups are often involved with the major fraud and theft cases reported to law enforcement agencies. Occasionally, such attackers are hired by organized crime, industry competitors, or state-sponsored intelligence-collection organizations.

- **External threats**—These threats consist of structured and unstructured threats originating from an external source. These threats can have malicious and destructive intent, or may simply be errors that generate a threat.

- **Internal threats**—These threats are typically from disgruntled current or former employees. Although internal threats may seem more ominous than threats from external sources, security measures are available for reducing vulnerabilities to internal threats and responding when attacks occur.

Types of Network Attack

There are many common attacks that can occur against a network. Any of the following can be used to compromise your system:

- Packet sniffers
- IP spoofing
- Privilege escalation
- DoS or DDoS
- Password attacks
- Man-in-the-middle attacks
- Application layer attacks
- Network reconnaissance
- Trust exploitation
- Port redirection
- Virus
- Trojan horse

- Worm
- Operator error

Packet Sniffers

Network communications is performed serially, sending one packet or cell after another until the entire message has been transmitted. The overriding reason for breaking streams into network packets is that computers have limited intermediate buffers.

Several network applications distribute network packets in clear text; that is, the information sent across the network is not encrypted. Because the network packets are not encrypted, they can be processed and understood by any application that can pick them up off the network and process them.

A network protocol specifies how packets are identified and labeled, which enables a computer to determine whether a packet is intended for it. Because the specifications for network protocols, such as TCP/IP, are widely published, a third party can easily interpret the network packets and develop a packet sniffer. (The real threat today results from the numerous freeware and shareware packet sniffers that are available, which do not require the user to understand anything about the underlying protocols.)

A packet sniffer is a software application that uses a network adapter card in promiscuous mode (a mode in which the network adapter card sends all packets received on the physical network wire to an application for processing) to capture all network packets that are sent across a LAN. The packet sniffer can only capture packets that traverse the network segment where the sniffer is connected. Some common network protocols that pass information in clear text are Telnet, FTP, SNMP, and Post Office Protocol (POP).

Packet Sniffer Types

Because several network applications distribute network packets in clear text, a packet sniffer can provide its user with meaningful and often sensitive information, such as user account names and passwords. If you use networked databases, a packet sniffer can provide an attacker with information that is queried from the database, as well as the user account names and passwords used to access the database. One serious problem with acquiring user account names and passwords is that users often reuse their login names and passwords across multiple applications.

In addition, many network administrators use packet sniffers, as shown in Figure 1-6, to diagnose and fix network-related problems. Because, in the course of their usual and necessary duties, these network administrators (such as those in a payroll department) work during regular employee hours, they can potentially examine sensitive information distributed across the network.

Many users employ a single password for access to all accounts and applications. Because attackers know and use human characteristics (attack methods known collectively as social engineering attacks), such as using a single password for multiple accounts, they are often successful in gaining access to sensitive information.

Figure 1-6 *Packet Sniffer*

Host A   Router A   Router B   Host B

Packet sniffers are available commercially, or you can find excellent packet sniffers on freeware/shareware websites. Some OSs (notably some of the Linux versions) come with built-in sniffers. Most packet sniffers are configurable to enable you to do the following:

- Capture entire packets or just the first 300 to 400 bytes of each packet
- Select the type of traffic you want to record, such as FTP, rlogin, Telnet, and HTTP
- Limit packet capture to specific source and target addresses or address ranges
- Read the packet information by translating binary data into readable text

Packet Sniffer Mitigation

To help mitigate the effect of packet sniffers, the following techniques and tools can be used:

- **Authentication**—Using strong authentication is a first option for defense against the misuse of information gained through the use of packet sniffers. Strong authentication can be broadly defined as a method of authenticating users that cannot easily be circumvented.

    A common example of strong authentication is one-time passwords (OTPs). An OTP is a type of two-factor authentication, which involves using something you posses combined with something you know. Automated teller machines (ATMs) use two-factor authentication. A customer needs both an ATM card and a personal identification number (PIN) to make transactions. With an OTP, you need a PIN and your token card to authenticate to a device or software application.

    A token card is a hardware or software device that generates new, seemingly random, passwords at specified intervals (usually 60 seconds). A user combines that random password with a PIN to create a unique password that works only for one instance of authentication. If an attacker learns that password by using a packet sniffer, the information is useless because the password has already expired.

NOTE   This mitigation technique is effective only against a packet sniffer implementation that is designed to grab passwords. Sniffers deployed to learn sensitive information (such as mail messages) would still be effective.

- **Switched infrastructure**—Another method of countering the use of packet sniffers in your network environment, is to use switched infrastructures. For example, if an entire organization deploys switched Ethernet, attackers can gain access only to the traffic that flows on the specific port to which they connect. A switched infrastructure obviously does not eliminate the threat of packet sniffers, but it can greatly reduce their effectiveness.

  Someone with access to a switch could configure the Switched Port Analyzer (SPAN) function to permit a port with a sniffer attached to monitor traffic from other ports in the switch. Additionally, an attacker could flood the switch with ARP requests, effectively converting the switch to a hub and opening it up for a packet sniffer.

- **Antisniffer tools**—A third method of countering the use of packet sniffers is to employ software and hardware designed to detect the use of sniffers on a network. Such software and hardware does not completely eliminate the threat, but, like many network security tools, they are part of the overall system. These so-called "antisniffers" detect changes in the response time of hosts to determine whether the hosts are processing more traffic than their own. One such network security software tool, which is available from Security Software Technologies, is called AntiSniff.

- **Cryptography**— The most effective method for countering packet sniffers is cryptography. Rendering packet sniffers irrelevant, cryptography is even more effective than preventing or detecting the use of packet sniffers. If a communication channel is cryptographically secure, the only data a packet sniffer will detect is cipher text (a seemingly random string of bits) and not the original message. The Cisco deployment of network-level cryptography is based on IPSec, which is a standard method for networking devices to communicate privately using IP. Other cryptographic protocols for network management include Secure Shell Protocol (SSH) and Secure Sockets Layer (SSL).

IP Spoofing

An IP spoofing attack occurs when an attacker outside your network pretends to be a trusted computer, either by using an IP address that is within the range of IP addresses for your network or by using an authorized external IP address that you trust and to which you wish to provide access to specified resources on your network.

Normally, an IP spoofing attack is limited to the injection of data or commands into an existing stream of data passed between a client and server application or a peer-to-peer (PTP) network connection. To enable bidirectional communication, the attacker must change all routing tables to point to the spoofed IP address. Another approach the attacker could take is to simply not worry about receiving any response from the applications. If an attacker is attempting to get a system to mail a sensitive file to them, application responses are unimportant.

However, if an attacker manages to change the routing tables to point to the spoofed IP address, the attacker can receive all the network packets that are addressed to the spoofed address and reply just as any trusted user can. Like packet sniffers, IP spoofing is not restricted to people who are external to the network.

IP Spoofing Mitigation

IP spoofing can yield access to user accounts and passwords, and it can also be used in other ways. For example, an attacker could emulate one of your internal users in ways that prove embarrassing for your organization, such as by sending e-mail messages to business partners that appear to have originated from someone within your organization. Such attacks are easier when an attacker has a user account and password, but they are possible by combining simple spoofing attacks with knowledge of messaging protocols.

The threat of IP spoofing can be reduced, but not eliminated, through the following measures:

- **Access control**—The most common method for preventing IP spoofing is to properly configure access control. To reduce the effectiveness of IP spoofing, configure access control to deny any traffic from the external network that has a source address that should reside on the internal network.

NOTE   Access control helps prevent spoofing attacks only if the internal addresses are the only trusted addresses. If some external addresses are trusted, this method is not effective.

- **Request For Comments (RFC) 2827 filtering**—This type of filtering prevents any outbound traffic on your network that does not have a source address in your organization's own IP range. Your Internet service provider (ISP) can also implement this type of filtering.

  This filtering denies any traffic that does not have the source address that was expected on a particular interface. For example, if an ISP is providing a connection to the IP address 15.1.1.0/24, the ISP could filter traffic so that only traffic sourced from address 15.1.1.0/24 can enter the ISP router from that interface.

NOTE   Unless all ISPs implement this type of filtering, its effectiveness is significantly reduced.

Also, the further you get from the devices that you want to filter, the more difficult it becomes to do that filtering at a granular level. For example, performing RFC 2827 filtering at the access router to the Internet requires that you allow your entire major network number (that is, 10.0.0.0/8) to traverse the access router. If you perform filtering at the distribution layer, as in this architecture, you can achieve more specific filtering (that is, 10.1.5.0/24).

RFC 2827 addresses ingress filtering, but the techniques can be applied equally to egress filtering, as well. Ingress filtering is typically used on routers to prevent targeted addresses or address ranges from entering the router. In this case, you know you do not want traffic from certain sources even entering your system, so you simply keep it out. Egress filtering is used to specify allowable ports for targeted addresses or address ranges. You may permit certain addresses to reach your Internet server, for example, but not allow them to reach your intranet server or internal network.

The most effective method for mitigating the threat of IP spoofing is the same as the most effective method for mitigating the threat of packet sniffers: namely, eliminating its effectiveness. IP spoofing can function correctly only when devices use IP address–based authentication; therefore, if you use additional authentication methods, IP spoofing attacks are irrelevant. Cryptographic authentication is the best form of additional authentication, but when that is not possible, strong two-factor authentication using OTPs can also be effective.

Privilege Escalation

During reconnaissance attacks, the attacker prefers to remain anonymous. The goal is to gain information, and the longer they can remain unobserved, the more information they can potentially gain. A user with a higher privilege level stands a better chance of remaining unobserved because they can remove or alter information to cover their tracks.

Attackers may gain access to a system with valid credentials at an unprivileged user level and then utilize known weaknesses in system applications or services to escalate their privilege level to give themselves administrative rights on the system. Once they have administrative privileges, they can probe the system for additional weaknesses or begin harvesting sensitive information with the ability to hide evidence of their presence and remain hidden from normal detection methods.

Protection against privilege escalation begins by removing unused services or applications from network devices. Attackers know the vulnerabilities of the systems they are attacking and will attempt to probe every possible avenue to reach their goal. Obscure or little used applications and services are favorite targets of opportunity because administrators tend to ignore them until the damage has been done.

The next best defense against privilege escalation is to conscientiously apply a strict password policy. Use strong passwords and change them frequently, and be sure that all access routes into a device are password protected. Educate users and administrators on the critical need to protect passwords from compromise and solicit their assistance in maintaining password integrity.

Review users accounts frequently and remove those no longer required. Be sure to disable system accounts or, at the very least, place very secure passwords on these accounts. Validate privilege levels during this process and limit administrative rights to trusted administrators.

Tighten privilege levels on applications and storage locations. Many systems default to permitting full access to anyone that has been authenticated by the system. Microsoft Windows is a good example of this open policy; permitting everyone full access to files and folders by default in many versions of this widely used operating system. Your network security policy should deny access by default, permitting access on an as-needed basis only.

You should study system log files frequently and track down the cause of unusual events. Also, periodically check system files for evidence of tampering. Record operating system directory information and system service settings on newly configured systems to use as a baseline for comparison. Any changes to system files (new files, renamed files, different date/time stamp) should be carefully checked and authenticated.

Denial of Service

DoS attacks are different from most other attacks because they are not targeted at gaining access to your network or the information on your network. These attacks focus on making a service unavailable for normal use, which is typically accomplished by exhausting some resource limitation on the network or within an OS or application.

DoS attacks are not very subtle. They are designed to "overload" your systems, denying you their service. These attacks require little effort to execute because they typically take advantage of protocol weaknesses or are carried out using traffic that would normally be allowed into a network. DoS attacks are among the most difficult to completely eliminate because of the way they use protocol weaknesses and "native" traffic to attack a network.

Distributed Denial of Service

DDoS attacks are the "next generation" of DoS attacks on the Internet. This type of attack is not new—User Datagram Protocol (UDP) and Transmission Control Protocol (TCP) SYN flooding, Internet Control Message Protocol (ICMP) echo request floods, and ICMP directed broadcasts (also known as smurf attacks) are similar—but the scope certainly is new. Victims of DDoS attacks experience packet flooding from many different sources, possibly spoofed IP source addresses, that bring their network connectivity to a grinding halt. In the past, the typical DoS attack involved a single attacker's attempt to flood a target host with packets. With DDoS tools, an attacker can conduct the same attack using thousands of systems, as shown in Figure 1-7.

In this type of attack, the attacker uses their terminal to scan for systems to hack. When the handler systems are accessed, the attacker then installs software on them to scan for, compromise, and infect agent systems. When the agent systems are accessed, the attacker then loads remote-control attack software to carry out the DoS attack.

Figure 1-7   *DDoS Attack*

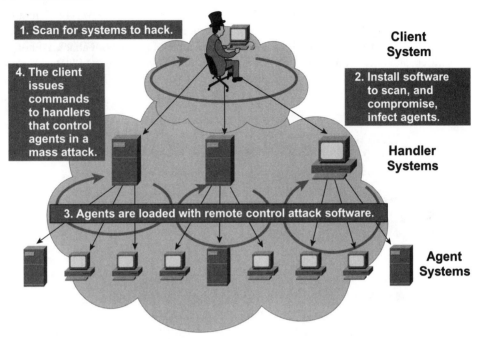

1. Scan for systems to hack.

Client System

2. Install software to scan, and compromise, infect agents.

4. The client issues commands to handlers that control agents in a mass attack.

Handler Systems

3. Agents are loaded with remote control attack software.

Agent Systems

DoS Mitigation

When involving specific network server applications, such as an HTTP server or an FTP server, these attacks can focus on acquiring and keeping open all the available connections supported by that server, effectively locking out valid users of the server or service. DoS attacks can also be implemented using common IPs, such as TCP and ICMP. Most DoS attacks exploit a weakness in the overall architecture of the system being attacked rather than a software bug or security hole. However, some attacks compromise the performance of your network by flooding the network with undesired, and often useless, network packets and by providing false information about the status of network resources.

The threat of DoS attacks can be reduced through the following two methods:

- **Antispoof features**—Proper configuration of antispoof features on your routers and firewalls can reduce your risk. This configuration includes RFC 2827 filtering at a minimum. If attackers cannot mask their identities, they might not attack.

- **Anti-DoS features**—Proper configuration of anti-DoS features on routers and firewalls can help limit the effectiveness of an attack. These features often involve limits on the amount of half-open connections that a system allows open at any given time.

Password Attacks

Password attacks can be implemented against login attempts using several different methods, including brute-force attacks, Trojan horse programs (discussed later in the chapter), IP spoofing, and packet sniffers. Figure 1-8 is an example of a password attack. Although packet sniffers and IP spoofing can yield user accounts and passwords, password attacks usually refer to repeated attempts to identify a user account, password, or both. These repeated attempts are called brute-force attacks.

Figure 1-8 *Password Attack*

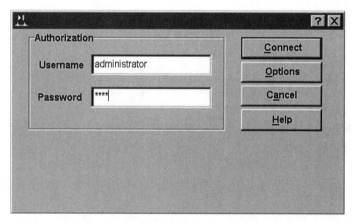

Often a brute-force attack is performed using a program that runs across the network and attempts to log in to a shared resource, such as a server. When an attacker successfully gains access to a resource, they have the same rights as the user whose account has been compromised to gain access to that resource. If this account has sufficient privileges, the attacker can create a back door for future access, without concern for any status and password changes to the compromised user account.

Password Attack Example

Just as with packet sniffers and IP spoofing attacks, a brute-force password attack can provide access to accounts that can be used to modify critical network files and services. An example that compromises your network's integrity is an attack in which the attacker modifies the routing tables for your network. By doing so, the attacker ensures that all network packets are routed to the attacker before they are transmitted to their final destination. In such a case, an attacker can monitor all network traffic, effectively becoming a "man in the middle."

The following are the two different methods for computing passwords with L0phtCrack (shown in Figure 1-9), a readily available password-cracking software tool:

- **Dictionary cracking**—The password hashes for all the words in a dictionary file are computed and compared against all the password hashes for the users. This method is extremely fast and finds very simple passwords.

- **Brute-force computation**—This method uses a particular character set, such as A–Z, or A–Z plus 0–9, and computes the hash for every possible password made up of those characters. It always computes the password if it is made up of the character set that you have selected to test. The downside is that time is required for completion of this type of attack.

Figure 1-9   *L0phtCrack*

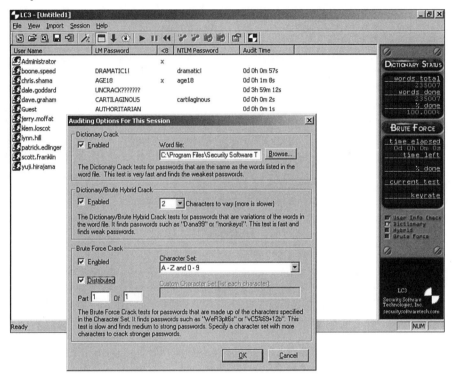

Password Attack Mitigation

The following are password attack mitigation techniques:

- **Do not allow users to have the same password on multiple systems**—Most users use the same password for each system they access, and often personal system passwords are the same as well.

- **Disable accounts after unsuccessful logins**—This helps to prevent continuous password attempts.

- **Do not use plain text passwords**—Use of either an OTP or an encrypted password is recommended.

- **Use "strong" passwords**—Many systems now provide strong password support and can restrict a user to only the use of strong passwords. Strong passwords are at least eight characters long and contain uppercase and lowercase letters, numbers, and special characters.

- **Use password aging**—System administrators can force users to change passwords periodically by using password aging. Passwords should be set to expire every 30 to 60 days to help limit the usefulness of compromised passwords.

Man-In-The-Middle Attacks

A man-in-the-middle attack, which might look something like Figure 1-10, requires that the attacker have access to network packets that come across the networks. Such attacks are often implemented by using network packet sniffers and routing and transport protocols. The possible uses of such attacks are theft of information, hijacking of an ongoing session to gain access to your internal network resources, traffic analysis to derive information about your network and its users, denial of service, corruption of transmitted data, and introduction of new information into network sessions.

Figure 1-10 *Man-In-The-Middle Attack*

In a successful man-in-the-middle attack, the middleman impersonates one end of a trusted session. As the trusted hosts initiate their session, the middleman listens in, captures the necessary authentication information, and then takes over the identity of one host. The middleman may initiate a DoS attack on the hijacked host to keep it busy while conducting a session with the other host. This kind of attack may be aimed at gathering sensitive information from the remaining host.

Man-In-The-Middle Mitigation

Man-in-the-middle attack mitigation is achieved, as shown in Figure 1-11, by encrypting traffic in an IPSec tunnel, which would allow the attacker to see only cipher text. Additional techniques for mitigating man-in-the-middle attacks include the following:

- **Static ARP**—Can be used in smaller networks to prevent an attacker from using ARP poisoning to replace a valid ARP entry with a bogus entry pointing to their MAC address.

Figure 1-11 *Mitigating Man-In-The-Middle Attacks*

- **Private VLANs**—Restrict conversations to devices that are members of the VLAN. Potential man-in-the-middle attackers would need access to one of the devices hosting the VLAN to participate in the conversation.

- **802.1x**—Allows use of Extensible Authentication Protocol (EAP) over LANs, providing a means of encapsulating the authentication conversation and keeping it hidden from a middleman.

An example of a man-in-the-middle attack could be someone who is working for your ISP, who can gain access to all network packets transferred between your network and any other network.

Application Layer Attacks

Application layer attacks can never be completely eliminated, because new vulnerabilities are always being discovered. Application layer attacks can be implemented using several different methods:

- One of the most common methods is to exploit well-known weaknesses in software commonly found on servers, such as sendmail, PostScript, and FTP. By exploiting these weaknesses, attackers can gain access to a computer with the permissions of the account running the application, which is usually a privileged, system-level account. One method of exploiting these protocols is to use the ports that are associated with the protocols (for example, TCP port 80 used in an attack against a web server behind a firewall) to penetrate defense systems.

- Trojan horse program attacks are implemented using programs that an attacker substitutes for common programs. These programs may provide all the functionality that the normal program provides, but also include other features that are known to the attacker, such as monitoring login attempts to capture user account and password information. These programs can capture sensitive information and distribute it back to the attacker. They can also modify application functionality, such as applying a blind carbon copy to all e-mail messages so that the attacker can read all of your organization's e-mail.

  One of the oldest forms of application layer attacks is a Trojan horse program that displays a screen, banner, or prompt that the user believes is the valid login sequence. The program then captures the information that the user enters and stores or e-mails it to the attacker. Next, the program either forwards the information to the normal login process (normally impossible on modern systems) or simply sends an expected error to the user (for example, Bad Username/Password Combination), exits, and starts the normal login sequence. The user, believing that they have incorrectly entered the password (a common mistake experienced by everyone), re-enters the information and is allowed access.

- Worms are another type of attack frequently used today. Worms are similar to viruses because they are computer programs that replicate themselves and that may interfere with the normal use of a computer or an application. Worms, unlike viruses, do not attach themselves to other programs or files. They are separate entities that can replicate and spread themselves automatically by using the sending and receiving features of computers.

- One of the newest forms of application layer attacks exploits the openness of several new technologies: the HTML specification, web browser functionality, and HTTP. These attacks, which include Java applets and ActiveX controls, involve passing harmful programs across the network and loading them through a user's browser.

Application Layer Attack Mitigation

The following are some measures that you can take to reduce your risks for application layer attacks:

- **Read OS and network log files or have them analyzed**—It is important to review all logs and take action accordingly.

- **Subscribe to mailing lists that publicize vulnerabilities**—Most application and OS vulnerabilities are published on the web at various sources.

- **Keep your OS and applications current with the latest patches**—Always test patches and fixes in a nonproduction environment. This prevents downtime and avoids errors from being generated unnecessarily.

- **IDSs can watch for known attacks, monitor and log attacks, and, in some cases, prevent attacks**—The use of IDSs can be essential to identifying security threats and mitigating some of those threats, and, in most cases, can be done automatically. IDSs may be either stand-alone devices that passively monitor network traffic and compare it to patterns (signatures) of known attacks, or host-based devices that specifically monitor and react to network activity to and from that host.

Network Reconnaissance

Network reconnaissance refers to the overall act of learning information about a target network by using publicly available information and applications. When attackers attempt to penetrate a particular network, they often need to learn as much information as possible about the network before launching attacks. This can take the form of DNS queries, ping sweeps, and port scans:

- **Domain Name System (DNS) queries**—Reveal such information as who owns a particular domain and what addresses have been assigned to that domain.

- **Ping sweeps**—Present a picture of the live hosts in a particular environment.
- **Port scans**—Cycle through all well-known ports to provide a complete list of all services running on the hosts.

Figure 1-12 demonstrates an example of how existing Internet tools can be used for network reconnaissance (for example, an IP address query or a DNS query).

Figure 1-12 *Reconnaissance Tools*

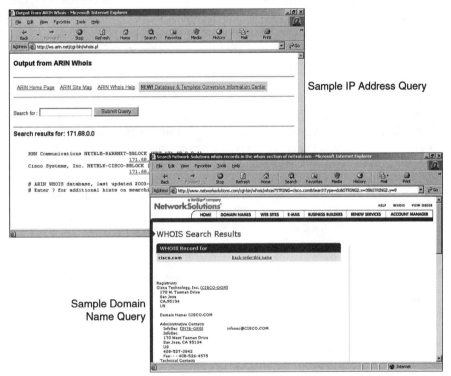

DNS queries can reveal such information as who owns a particular domain and what addresses have been assigned to that domain. Ping sweeps of the addresses that are revealed by the DNS queries can present a picture of the live hosts in a particular environment. After such a list is generated, port-scanning tools can cycle through all well-known ports to provide a complete list of all services that are running on the hosts that were discovered by the ping sweep. Finally, an attacker can examine the characteristics of the applications that are running on the hosts. This can lead to specific information that is useful when the attacker attempts to compromise that service.

IP address queries can reveal critical information, such as who owns a particular IP address or range of addresses and what domain is associated to them.

Network Reconnaissance Mitigation

If ICMP echo and echo reply are turned off on edge routers (for example, ping sweeps can be stopped, but at the expense of network diagnostic data), port scans can still be run without full ping sweeps. They simply take longer because they need to scan IP addresses that might not be live.

Network reconnaissance cannot be entirely prevented, but IDSs at the network and host levels can usually notify an administrator when a reconnaissance attack is underway. This allows the administrator to better prepare for the coming attack or to notify the ISP who is hosting the system that it is launching the reconnaissance probe.

Trust Exploitation

Although not an attack in and of itself, trust exploitation refers to an attack where an individual takes advantage of a trust relationship within a network. The classic example is a perimeter network connection from a corporation. These network segments often house DNS, Simple Mail Transfer Protocol (SMTP), and HTTP servers. Because they all reside on the same segment, a compromise of one system can lead to the compromise of other systems, because they might trust other systems that are attached to their same network. Figure 1-13 is an example of a system on the outside of a firewall that has a trust relationship with a system on the inside of a firewall. When the outside system is compromised, an attacker can leverage that trust relationship to attack the inside network.

Figure 1-13 *Exploiting Trusts*

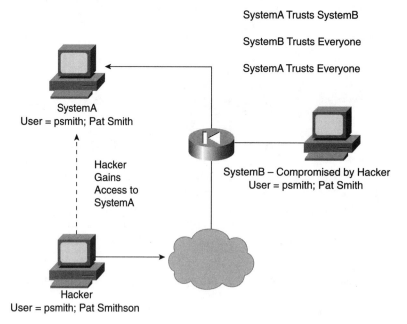

SystemA Trusts SystemB

SystemB Trusts Everyone

SystemA Trusts Everyone

SystemA
User = psmith; Pat Smith

Hacker
Gains
Access to
SystemA

SystemB – Compromised by Hacker
User = psmith; Pat Smith

Hacker
User = psmith; Pat Smithson

Several trust models exist that are susceptible to trust attacks. The following list shows some of the more common models:

- Windows
    - **Domains**—Trusts are explicitly defined between domains. Once trusts are established, access permissions can be granted for users in one domain to access resources in the other domain.
    - **Active directory**—Permissions in the Windows Active Directory (AD) control access to all network resources. The concept of domains has been replaced by functionality in the AD.
- Linux and UNIX
    - **Network File System (NFS)**—This model uses the NFS protocol to provide remote file access across Linux or UNIX networks.
    - **Network Information Service plus (NIS+)**—This model uses the NIS+ protocol to find and access NIS databases.

Trust Exploitation Mitigation

You can mitigate trust- and exploitation-based attacks through tight constraints on trust levels within a network. Systems on the outside of a firewall should never be absolutely trusted by systems on the inside of a firewall, as shown in Figure 1-14. Such trust should be limited to specific protocols and should be authenticated by something other than an IP address where possible. Additional authentication techniques might include OTP, tokens, digital certificates, or RADIUS authentication servers.

Figure 1-14 *Mitigating Trust Exploitation*

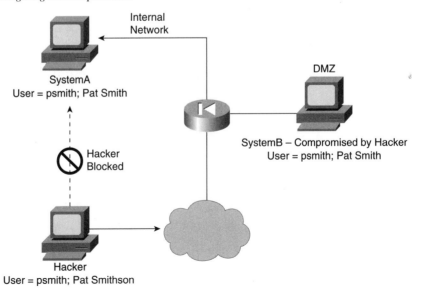

Port Redirection

Port redirection attacks, as shown in Figure 1-15, are a type of trust exploitation attack that uses a compromised host to pass traffic through a firewall that would otherwise be dropped. Consider a firewall that has three interfaces and a host on each interface. The host on the outside can reach the host on the public services segment (commonly referred to as a demilitarized zone [DMZ]), but not the host on the inside. The host on the public services segment can reach the host on both the outside and the inside. If attackers were able to compromise the public services segment host, they could install software to redirect traffic from the outside host directly to the inside host. Though neither communication violates the rules implemented in the firewall, the outside host has now achieved connectivity to the inside host through the port redirection process on the public services host. An example of an application that can provide this type of access is F-PIPE.

Figure 1-15 *Port Redirection*

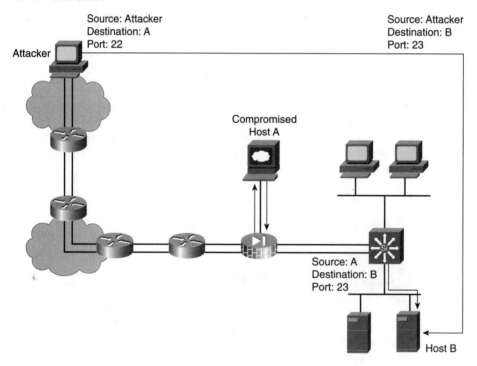

Port redirection can be mitigated primarily through the use of proper trust models, which are network specific (as mentioned earlier). Assuming that a system is under attack, a host-based IDS can help to detect the attacker and prevent them from installing such redirection utilities on the host.

Unauthorized Access

Although not a specific type of attack, unauthorized access attacks refer to the majority of attacks executed on networks today. An example is shown in Figure 1-16. In order for someone to brute-force a Telnet login, they must first get the Telnet prompt on a system. Upon connection to the Telnet port, the attacker might see the message "authorization required to use this resource." If the attacker continues to attempt access, the attacker's actions become "unauthorized." These kinds of attacks can be initiated both on the outside and on the inside of a network.

Figure 1-16 *Unauthorized Access*

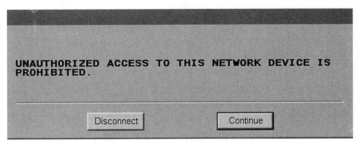

Mitigation techniques for unauthorized access attacks are very simple. They involve reducing or eliminating the ability of an attacker to gain access to a system by using an unauthorized protocol and, possibly, presenting the attacker with a message, as shown in Figure 1-16. An example would be preventing attackers from having access to the Telnet port on a server that needs to provide web services to the outside. If an attacker cannot reach that port, it is very difficult to attack it. The primary function of a firewall in a network is to prevent simple unauthorized access attacks.

Viruses, Trojan Horses, and Worms

The primary vulnerabilities for end-user workstations are attacks by viruses, Trojan horses, and worms. Viruses refer to malicious software that is attached to another program to execute a particular unwanted function on a user's workstation. An example of a virus is a program that is attached to command.com (the primary interpreter for Windows systems), which deletes certain files and infects any other versions of command.com that it can find.

A Trojan horse is different from a virus only in that the entire application is written to look like something else, when in fact it is an attack tool. An example of a Trojan horse is a software application that runs a simple game on the user's workstation. While the user is occupied with the game, the Trojan horse mails a copy of itself to every user in the user's address book. Then other users receive the game and play it, thus spreading the Trojan horse.

Worms are similar to viruses but are not embedded in other programs. Worms are stand-alone programs that live to replicate themselves to other systems and may or may not cause harm to your system. Worms need some kind of host to propagate themselves to other systems, and e-mail makes a good host. Worms can hop a ride as an attachment to other systems and then hop off and begin the replication process all over again. A worm can create its own e-mail message using address books found on the local host. Worms can act very quickly and become dangerous DoS devices by flooding e-mail systems with bogus messages that are used to carry the worm to new hosts.

These kinds of applications can be contained through the effective use of antivirus software at the user level and potentially at the network level. Antivirus software can detect most viruses and many Trojan horse applications and prevent them from spreading in the network. Keeping up-to-date with the latest developments in these sorts of attacks can also lead to a more effective posture against these attacks. As new virus and Trojan horse applications are released onto the Internet, enterprises need to keep up-to-date with the latest antivirus software and application versions.

Although antivirus software can protect systems against known viruses and can detect virus-like activity, some types of attacks can go undetected by these products. Some attacks do not follow known or identified patterns, but they do exhibit anomalous network activity. IDS sensors, both network and host-based, can compare baseline (normal) network activity with current activity. When an anomaly is detected, the event can be logged, notification can be sent to system administrators, and, in some cases, the IDS may try to terminate the activity.

Operator Error

Even the best planning and implementation of network policies cannot guard against operator errors. Well-intentioned efforts can have results as effective as planned DoS network attacks, shutting down portions of your network for a period of time.

Rushing configuration changes, fatigued administrators, and lack of planning and coordination can lead to errors in judgment and execution of tasks. Your best defense against administrator errors is careful planning.

For network device maintenance, use a scheduled maintenance window to minimize the effect on your user community in case of configuration mistakes. Be sure you backup configuration files before making any changes to them. Use a checklist so you don't skip steps.

You won't be able to do much to counter normal user errors. Regular backup of data stores can be used to restore corrupted application data. You can apply the most current system and application patches and updates to guard against some types of problems. Make sure users are properly trained and that they have only the access privileges required for them to perform their jobs.

Network Security Policy

A network security policy can be as simple as an acceptable use policy for network resources or it can be several hundred pages in length and detail every element of connectivity and associated policies.

According to the *Site Security Handbook* (RFC 2196), "A security policy is a formal statement of the rules by which people who are given access to an organization's technology and information assets must abide." It further states that "A security policy is essentially a document summarizing how the corporation will use and protect its computing and network resources."

Security policies provide many benefits and are worth the time and effort needed to develop them. Developing a security policy

- Provides a process to audit existing network security.
- Provides a general security framework for implementing network security.
- Defines which behavior is and is not allowed.
- Helps determine which tools and procedures are needed for the organization.
- Helps communicate consensus among a group of key decision makers and define responsibilities of users and administrators.
- Defines a process for handling network security incidents.
- Enables global security implementation and enforcement. Computer security is now an enterprise-wide issue and computing websites are expected to conform to the network security policy.
- Creates a basis for legal action if necessary.

The following are some key policy sections:

- **Statement of authority and scope**—Specifies who sponsors the security policy and what areas the policy covers.
- **Acceptable use policy**—Specifies what the company will and will not allow regarding its information infrastructure.
- **Identification and authentication policy**—Specifies what technologies, equipment, or combination of the two the company will use to ensure that only authorized individuals have access to its data.
- **Internet access policy**—Specifies what the company considers ethical and proper use of its Internet access capabilities.
- **Campus access policy**—Specifies how on-campus users will use the company's data infrastructure.
- **Remote access policy**—Specifies how remote users will access the company's data infrastructure.
- **Incident handling procedure**—Specifies how the company will create an incident response team and the procedures it will use during and after an incident occurs.

Cisco Network Security Products

Cisco has a wide variety of security products that adhere to the SAFE axiom of security in depth. These devices enable a wide range of security options for controlling and monitoring networks. The following list provides an overview of these products.

- **Cisco IOS Firewall**—An extension of the Cisco IOS software used on most Cisco routers, the Cisco IOS Firewall offers integrated firewall and intrusion detection capabilities. This software add-on enhances Cisco IOS authentication, encryption, and failover. The Cisco IOS Firewall turns Cisco routers into powerful all-in-one solutions for multiprotocol routing, perimeter security, intrusion detection, per-user authentication and authorization, and VPN support using protocols such as IPSec and Layer 2 Tunneling Protocol (L2TP). Some Cisco routers can be equipped with Advanced Integration Modules (AIMs) that can be used to offload the VPN encryption process from the central processor of the router.

- **Cisco Private Internet Exchange (PIX) Firewall**—An integrated hardware and software package that provides full stateful firewall protection and IPSec VPN capabilities, the Cisco PIX Firewall uses a dedicated OS and offers high performance, scalability, and redundancy. PIX Firewalls can be configured with optional VPN Acceleration Cards (VACs) to offload the IPSec encryption process from the central processor and speed up VPN functions.

- **Cisco VPN 3000 Series Concentrator**—Whereas the Cisco IOS Firewall and Cisco PIX Firewall are capable of providing VPN support for networks, the Cisco VPN 3000 Series Concentrators were specifically designed to enable enterprise-wide VPN utilization. The Cisco VPN 3000 Series Concentrators are easy to install, configure, and monitor, and they support the widest range of VPN client software implementations. These devices offer clustering and failover support and can be upgraded with multiple Scalable Encryption Processing (SEP) modules to offload the encryption processes from the main processor.

- **Cisco IDS**—Whereas the previous three products are designed to prevent or minimize network intrusion, Cisco IDS is designed to detect intrusion events that may have bypassed perimeter defenses or that may have originated from within the network itself. Cisco IDS devices provide accurate threat detection, intelligent threat investigation (to eliminate false alarms), ease of management, and flexible deployment options.

Cisco Management Software

Cisco has developed a wide range of applications that can be used to monitor and manage Cisco devices and other critical assets in your network. This section takes a look at the applications most closely associated with the security aspects of your network.

Cisco VPN Device Manager

Cisco VPN Device Manager (VDM) is a wizards-based GUI application used to manage and configure site-to-site VPNs on Cisco 7100 and 7200 routers using a web browser. VDM monitors system statistics and router health and enables easier VPN setup and troubleshooting. VDM also has graphing capabilities for quick analysis of system data such as traffic volume, tunnel counts, and system utilization. VDM is a product typically employed by service providers.

Cisco PIX Device Manager

Cisco PIX Device Manager (PDM) is a GUI-based management tool to manage and configure Cisco PIX Firewalls. While most beneficial for enterprise and service provider users, this application can be used by any organization that is looking for a tool to enhance productivity and network security. PDM can generate real-time and historical reports that can be used to analyze usage trends and security events and to develop performance baselines.

Cisco VPN Solution Center

Cisco VPN Solution Center (VPNSC) enables customers to efficiently manage IPSec VPN deployments on Cisco IOS routers, Cisco VPN 3000 Series Concentrators, and Cisco PIX Firewalls. Using VPNSC, administrators can configure Internet Key Exchange (IKE) and IPSec tunnels between any of these devices. VPNSC automates time-consuming and complex tasks, such as resolving incompatible or inconsistent IPSec and IKE policies among devices. VPNSC helps customers respond quickly to continually changing and expanding VPN requirements.

CiscoWorks VPN/Security Management Solutions

Cisco has developed a set of management tools for enterprise networks that fall under the CiscoWorks umbrella of products called CiscoWorks VPN/Security Management Solution (VMS). VMS management applications are used for configuring, monitoring, and troubleshooting VPNs and security on Cisco PIX Firewalls, Cisco VPN 3000 Series Concentrators, Cisco IOS Firewalls, and Cisco IDS devices. VMS scales well and can be employed in small- or large-scale security implementations. VMS includes the following tools:

- **CiscoWorks VPN Monitor**—A web-based management tool, CiscoWorks VPN Monitor gives network administrators the means to easily collect, store, and view VPN information from their web browser. CiscoWorks VPN Monitor provides a graphical indication of the status of VPNs and provides drill-down and graphing capabilities to aid in troubleshooting. This application works for either remote access or site-to-site configurations using PPTP, L2TP, or IPSec as the VPN protocol. CiscoWorks VPN Monitor can be used with Cisco VPN 3000 Series Concentrators and a series of VPN-capable Cisco routers, including 1700, 2600, 3600, 7100, and 7200 series routers.

- **CiscoWorks Resource Manager Essentials (RME)**—CiscoWorks RME is a suite of network management solutions for Cisco routers, switches, and access servers. RME's browser interface gives network administrators quick access to critical network information and simplifies administrative tasks. RME's applications include Inventory Manager, Change Audit, Device Configuration Manager, Software Image Manager, Availability Manager, Syslog Analyzer, and Cisco Management Connection. Optional add-on applications enhance the capabilities of this product.

- **CiscoWorks CiscoView**—CiscoView is a management application used for monitoring and configuring the broad range of Cisco internetworking products. CiscoView's graphical representation of device chassis and color-coded modules and ports allow for quick and comprehensive monitoring and management activities.

- **CiscoWorks CD One**—CiscoWorks CD One contains the CiscoWorks Server desktop that is used as a common launching point and navigational interface for the CiscoWorks family of products and for third-party tools. The CiscoWorks Server desktop gives control for securing, launching, and managing these applications.

- **CiscoWorks Common Services Software**—The CiscoWorks management and monitoring centers for PIX, VPN Routers, IDS Sensors, and QoS Policy Manager 3.0 (QPM) are given a shared application infrastructure through CiscoWorks Common Services Software. Administrative roles and Management Center access privileges can be defined through this application. CiscoWorks Common Service Software can provide data storage for CiscoWorks client applications and is included in the CiscoWorks CD One product.

- **Cisco Security Agent**—Cisco Security Agent is a HIDS that can be deployed on desktop computers and servers to defend against network attacks. Cisco Security Agent does not depend upon databases of known attack signatures. It examines the behavior of mission-critical applications and protects the network against known and unknown attacks. Cisco Security Agent not only detects suspicious behavior, it can stop it, protecting valuable network resources.

- **CiscoWorks Auto Update Server Software**—Another network management product designed to work with Cisco PIX Firewalls is the CiscoWorks Auto Update Server Software application. Supporting a pull model, this CiscoWorks product can be used to automatically update initial configurations, configuration updates, and OS updates, as well as provide configuration verification periodically.

- **CiscoWorks Management Center for IDS Sensors**—The first of the three CiscoWorks Management Center products mentioned here is the one developed to manage network

IDS and switch IDS sensors. A web-based GUI application, this software's wizards simplify the learning process. Sensors may be combined into groups for ease of administration, and the software permits the creation of new signatures to help protect against new threats and minimize false positives.

- **CiscoWorks Management Center for PIX Firewalls**—CiscoWorks Management Center for PIX Firewalls provides centralized management of access rules, Network Address Translation (NAT), intrusion detection, and Easy VPN (EZVPN) for Cisco PIX Firewalls. CiscoWorks Management Center for PIX Firewalls can provide support for up to 1000 Cisco PIX Firewalls.

- **CiscoWorks Management Center for VPN Routers (Router MC)**—Like the Management Centers for IDS Sensors and PIX Firewalls, CiscoWorks Router MC gives administrators a management tool with an intuitive GUI for the configuration and deployment of VPN connections for large-scale and site-to-site applications. Router MC enables large enterprises to define multiple administrative and operational roles by controlling individual user and deployment permissions. Router MC simplifies the management of policy definitions, offers a hierarchical inheritance model, and provides flexible deployment and reporting capabilities.

- **CiscoWorks Monitoring Center for Security**—The CiscoWorks Monitoring Center for Security provides a unified server to capture, view, correlate, and report security events from network IDS, switch IDS, host IDS, PIX Firewalls, and IOS devices. The visibility of critical events can be managed from a flexible notification engine. An alarm database provides the cause and severity of problems and suggested remedies.

Management Protocols and Functions

The protocols that you use to manage your network can also be sources of vulnerability. This section examines common management protocols and how they can be exploited.

Telnet

If the managed device does not support any of the recommended protocols, such as SSH and SSL, Telnet may have to be used (although this protocol is not highly recommended). You should recognize that the data within a Telnet session is sent as clear text, and may be intercepted by anyone with a packet sniffer located along the data path between the managed device and the management server. The data may include sensitive information, such as the configuration of the device itself, passwords, and so on.

Regardless of whether SSH, SSL, or Telnet is used for remote access to the managed device, ACLs should be configured to allow only management servers to connect to the device. All attempts from other IP addresses should be denied and logged. RFC 2827 filtering at the ingress router should also be implemented to mitigate the chance of an attacker from outside the network spoofing the addresses of the management hosts.

Simple Network Management Protocol

SNMP is a network management protocol that can be used to retrieve information from a network device (commonly referred to as read-only access) or to remotely configure parameters on the device (commonly referred to as read-write access). SNMP uses passwords, called community strings, within each message as a very simple form of security using TCP and UDP ports 161 and 162. Unfortunately, most implementations of SNMP on networking devices today send the community string in clear text along with the message. Therefore, SNMP messages may be intercepted by anyone with a packet sniffer located along the data path between the device and the management server, and the community string may be compromised.

If the community string is compromised, an attacker could reconfigure the device if read-write access via SNMP is allowed. Therefore, configure SNMP with only read-only community strings. You can further protect your network by setting up access control on the device you wish to manage via SNMP to allow only the appropriate management hosts access.

Syslog

Syslog, which is information generated by a device that has been configured for logging, is sent as clear text between the managed device and the management host on UDP port 514. Syslog has no packet-level integrity checking to ensure that the packet contents have not been altered in transit. An attacker may alter syslog data to confuse a network administrator during an attack.

Where possible, syslog traffic may be encrypted within an IPSec tunnel to mitigate the chance that it will be altered in transit. In situations where the syslog data cannot be encrypted within an IPSec tunnel because of cost or the capabilities of the device itself, you should note that there is a potential for the syslog data to be falsified by an attacker.

- When allowing syslog access from devices on the outside of a firewall, RFC 2827 filtering at the egress router should be implemented. This scenario mitigates the chance of an attacker from outside the network spoofing the address of the managed device and sending false syslog data to the management hosts.

- Access control lists should also be implemented on the firewall to allow syslog data from only the managed devices themselves to reach the management hosts. This scenario prevents an attacker from sending large amounts of false syslog data to a management server to confuse you during an attack.

Trivial File Transfer Protocol

Many network devices use TFTP to transfer configuration or system files across the network. TFTP uses port 69 for both TCP and UDP. TFTP uses UDP for the data stream between the requesting host and the TFTP server.

You should recognize that the data within a TFTP session might be intercepted by anyone with a packet sniffer located along the data path between the device and the management server. The data may include sensitive information, such as the configuration of the device itself, and so on. Where possible, TFTP traffic should be encrypted within an IPSec tunnel to mitigate the chance that it will be intercepted.

Network Time Protocol

NTP is used to synchronize the clocks of various devices across a network. Synchronization of the clocks within a network is critical for digital certificates and for correct interpretation of events within syslog data. NTP uses port 123 for both UDP and TCP connections.

A secure method of providing clocking for the network is for you to implement your own master clock for the private network that is synchronized to Coordinated Universal Time (UTC) via satellite or radio. However, clock sources are available to synchronize to via the Internet, if you do not wish to implement your own master clock because of costs or other reasons.

An attacker could attempt a DoS attack on a network by sending bogus NTP data across the Internet in an attempt to change the clocks on network devices in such a manner that digital certificates are considered invalid. Further, an attacker could attempt to confuse you during an attack by disrupting the clocks on network devices. This scenario would make it difficult for you to determine the order of syslog events on multiple devices.

Version 3 and above of NTP supports a cryptographic authentication mechanism between peers. The use of the authentication mechanism, as well as ACLs that specify which network devices are allowed to synchronize with other network devices, helps mitigate against such a scenario. You should weigh the cost benefits of pulling clock information from the Internet with the possible risk of doing so and allowing it through the firewall. Many NTP servers on the Internet do not require any authentication of peers. Therefore, you must trust that the clock itself is reliable, valid, and secure.

Network Address Translation and NAT Transversal

The IP version 4 (IPv4) addressing scheme of 32 bits, which is subdivided into classes based on the values of the first three high-order bits, must have seemed like overkill to the original pioneers of IP, because it theoretically supports over 4.2 billion unique addresses. Significant numbers of addresses are lost to the mechanics of IP, however, which renders two addresses for every subnet unusable (network and broadcast addresses). Additional addresses are lost to special classes, leaving only approximately 3.2 billion addresses available for use.

In the early days of the Internet, this was a significant number, but then the Internet started to become more and more popular, threatening to quickly use up all the available IP addresses. The IP development community came up with a new addressing scheme of 128 bits, which came to be known as IP version 6 (IPv6). This version has plenty of room, enabling a staggering 3.4×10^{38} possible addresses. IPv6 seemed like a winner, but implementation would take years and, in the meantime, Internet use continued to grow at alarming rates.

The overwhelming acceptance of the Internet initially caused a major panic in the IP community. In May 1994, Kjeld Egevang and Paul Francis submitted RFC 1631 to the Internet community. This RFC, titled "The IP Network Address Translator (NAT)," laid the foundation for NAT, which ultimately turned out to be the magic potion that would make the IPv4 lack-of-address issue disappear.

The concept of NAT stems from the way IP addresses are used. Private TCP/IP networks used by businesses or government network communities require IP addresses for every host on the network, but only a very small fraction of those hosts ever communicates across the Internet at any given time. Egevang and Francis reasoned that you could use any address you wanted (possibly the private network addresses identified in RFC 1597) as long as you did not route them out to the Internet. When one of your private hosts needs to communicate across the Internet, simply translate its private IP address into a public IP address that is routable and recognized on the Internet. When the destination host responds, simply reverse the translation process. With this stroke of genius, the impending lack of available addresses was forestalled for many years to come.

NAT has minimal impact as a security measure, but it is frequently a component of security devices. NAT is implemented on devices that buffer private networks from the public Internet; devices such as routers, firewalls, and VPN concentrators. You can configure NAT in many different ways. Take a look at the three most common:

- **Static NAT**—This form of NAT is used when public hosts need to communicate with a private host and need to always use the same IP address. This is a typical requirement for Internet servers. In this case, a one-to-one translation table is created in the device that will be performing the NAT function.

  This type of translation should be used infrequently because it does nothing to reduce the need for public IP addresses. It is sometimes necessary, however, because all private hosts must share a consistent addressing scheme. This type of NAT is usually required for any devices that are registered on external DNS servers.

- **Dynamic NAT**—A better method of using NAT is to set aside a pool of available public addresses and use them on a first-come-first-served basis whenever the need for a public address arises. As the public addresses are released, they return to the pool and become available for the next host that requires translation services.

With dynamic NAT, you start to see reductions in the number of public IP addresses required for a network community. This is a good choice if you have sufficient public addresses to form the address pools.

- **Network Address Port Translation (NAPT)**—For serious conservation of public IP addresses, NAPT, also called overloading, is the method to use. The more common term for overloading is Port Address Translation (PAT). This is a special case of static NAT in that every public address that requires translation is converted to the same public IP address. The translation occurs on the TCP or UDP port to establish a unique identifier for a specific communication. A single public IP address used with PAT can support approximately 4000 private IP addresses.

  NAT Traversal (NAT-T) lets IPSec peers connect through a NAT device by encapsulating IPSec traffic in UDP datagrams. NAT-T uses port 4500 to provide port information for the NAT devices. NAT-T auto-detects NAT devices and only encapsulates IPSec traffic when necessary. If the client is behind a NAT device, NAT-T further allows the client to learn the external IP address so that it may configure port mappings to forward packets from the external port of the NAT to the internal port used by the application.

NAT-T is performed as part of IKE Phase 2 negotiations and is transparent to the client. Some configuration may be required on the device that the client connects with (router, firewall, or VPN concentrator) to identify whether TCP or UDP port translation is used.

Chapter Summary

The need for network security has increased as networks have become more complex and interconnected.

The following are the four types of security threats:

- Unstructured
- Structured
- External
- Internal

The Cisco SAFE Blueprint provides guidelines for implementing security in depth across enterprise networks.

The following are common attack methods and techniques used by attackers:

- Packet sniffers
- IP weaknesses
- Password attacks
- DoS or DDoS attacks

- Man-in-the-middle attacks
- Application layer attacks
- Trust exploitation
- Port redirection
- Viruses
- Trojan horses
- Worms
- Operator error

The Cisco security hardware devices include IOS Firewalls, PIX Firewalls, VPN 3000 Concentrators, and IDS Sensors.

Cisco provides a wide range of security management applications that can facilitate security device configuration and policy management.

The following are possible components of a security policy:

- Statement of authority and scope
- Acceptable use policy
- Identification and authentication policy
- Internet use policy
- Campus access policy
- Remote access policy
- Incident handling procedure

Common management protocols are integral to maintaining a secure infrastructure.

NAT is a method of minimizing the requirement for public IP addresses.

VPN clients use NAT-T to discover and configure NAT settings when the VPN passes through a device performing NAT.

Chapter Review Questions

The following review questions cover some of the key facts and concepts that were introduced in this chapter. Answers to these questions can be found in Appendix A, "Answers to Chapter Review Questions."

1 List three reasons that explain why network security is becoming more important.

2 What is the Cisco SAFE Blueprint?

3 What are the four types of security threats?

4 List four common attack methods or techniques used by attackers.

5 What four methods can be used to mitigate the use of packet sniffers by network intruders?

6 List four key components of a complete security policy.

7 What four types of hardware are included in Cisco offerings of network security products?

8 Which of the Cisco network security management applications was designed specifically to manage VPNs on Cisco 7100 and 7200 routers?

9 What is the biggest security issue with using syslog servers to record system messages from network devices?

10 What are the three most common methods for implementing NAT?

Upon completion of this chapter, you will be able to perform the following tasks:

- Describe the Cisco IOS Firewall Features
- Describe How to Secure Cisco Router Physical Installations
- Secure Administrative Access for Cisco Routers
- Describe the Components of a Basic AAA Implementation
- Configure a Perimeter Router for AAA Using a Local Database
- Test the Perimeter Router AAA Implementation Using Applicable **debug** Commands

CHAPTER 2

Basic Cisco Router Security

This chapter presents an introduction to securing Cisco routers using proven methods for securing the physical router device, protecting the router administrative interface, and implementing authentication, authorization, and accounting (AAA).

This chapter includes the following topics:

- Cisco IOS Firewall features
- Securing Cisco router installations
- Securing Cisco router administrative access
- Introduction to AAA for Cisco routers
- Configuring AAA for Cisco perimeter routers

Cisco IOS Firewall Features

The optional Cisco IOS Firewall component takes advantage of corporate investment in Cisco IOS routers by adding security functions to the already versatile Cisco IOS software. Security can be very effective when correctly configured on routers because it is an inherent part of networks, not an added component.

Cisco IOS Firewall is a full-featured security product that can be used for security and policy enforcement on direct intranet or extranet connections, and on connections through the Internet, such as those used by remote users or branch offices. The Cisco IOS Firewall security product is available for a wide range of Cisco routers:

- **Small routers**—Cisco 800, URB900, and 1700 series routers that are typically used for small office/home office (SOHO) applications.
- **Midsize routers**—Cisco 2600, 3600, and 3700 series routers that are typically used for branch office or extranet applications.
- **Large-sized routers and switches**—Cisco 7100, 7200, 7400, 7500, RSM series routers, Catalyst 5000 switches, and Catalyst 6000 switches where high-throughput environments are required.

Cisco IOS Firewall Benefits

The Cisco IOS Firewall offers these values and benefits:

- **Flexibility**—When installed on a Cisco router, Cisco IOS Firewall provides a scalable, all-in-one solution. With the Cisco IOS Firewall installed, these routers can perform multiprotocol routing, perimeter security, inline intrusion detection, VPN support, and per-user authentication and authorization.

- **Investment protection**—Existing hardware, interface configurations, and protocol configurations can remain in place while the powerful security tools of the Cisco IOS Firewall are implemented. Administrators do not need to be trained on new equipment.

- **VPN support**—The Cisco IOS Firewall works with Cisco IOS software to provide encryption and quality of service (QoS) to VPN traffic. High-priority delivery can be given to mission-critical VPN traffic.

- **Scalable deployment**—Cisco IOS Firewall can be installed on a wide variety of router platforms to meet the bandwidth and performance requirements of networks of various sizes.

- **Easier provisioning**—Automated provisioning can be accomplished by combining the Cisco Intelligence Engine 2100 Series (IE2100 Series) Configuration Registrar and the Cisco IOS XML application. Using these tools, routers with little or no preconfiguration can be shipped to remote destinations and configured automatically simply by plugging the device into the network. The router then pulls the current Cisco IOS and IOS Firewall software, router configuration, and security policy configurations from the Configuration Registrar.

Cisco IOS Firewall Highlights

Some of the features of the Cisco IOS Firewall include:

- **Stateful Cisco IOS Firewall inspection engine**—This feature, also known as Context-Based Access Control (CBAC), gives per-application-based access control for all traffic across perimeters.

- **Intrusion detection**—Supporting 100 signatures, intrusion detection provides real-time monitoring, interception, and response to network misuse.

- **Firewall voice traversal**—The H.323v2 and SIP (Q1CY03) voice protocols are supported by the Cisco IOS Firewall to determine the call flow and associated channels that are opened.

- **Internet Control Message Protocol (ICMP) inspection**—ICMP traffic is frequently blocked at firewalls to prohibit attacker probes. The Cisco IOS Firewall allows responses to ICMP packets (such as echo request and echo reply) that originate from inside the firewall. The remaining ICMP traffic can be blocked.

- **Authentication proxy**—Users who originate LAN-based, HTTP, or dial-in communications can be authenticated and authorized using industry-standard authorization protocols. SSL secured user IDs and passwords can be used with HTTP Secure (HTTPS) to provide increased confidentiality. TACACS+ and RADIUS AAA protocols can be used to set individual, per-user security policies.

- **Destination URL Policy Management**—Better known as IP URL Filtering, Destination URL Policy Management permits or denies HTTP traffic to URLs based on local caching of previous requests, static URL permit and deny tables, or through external server databases provided by Websense Inc. and N2H2 Inc.

- **Per-user firewalls**—AAA servers can store per-user policies that can be downloaded to service providers after user authentication to provide firewall, ACL, and other settings, which are supported by Cisco IOS Firewall.

- **Cisco IOS router and firewall provisioning**—IE2100 enables simplified (zero touch) provisioning of the Cisco IOS software version, configuration, and security policies.

- **Denial of service (DoS) detection and prevention**—DoS detection and prevention is included to protect router resources against this type of common attack. The firewall checks packet headers and drops suspicious packets.

- **Dynamic port mapping**—Permits the Cisco IOS Firewall to use nonstandard ports for supported applications.

- **Java applet blocking**—Packets that contain unidentified, malicious Java applets are recognized and dropped to minimize potential damage from this type of attack.

- **Virtual private networks (VPNs), IP Security (IPSec) encryption, and QoS support**—The Cisco IOS Firewall supports VPN functions using the encryption, tunneling, and QoS features of the Cisco IOS Software to enable strong perimeter security and advanced bandwidth management.

- **Real-time alerts**—Use the configurable ability of the firewall to log alerts for preconfigured conditions, such as DoS attacks.

- **Audit trail**—On a per-application, per-feature basis, you can configure storage for detailed transaction audit trails. Keep track of the time stamp, source host, destination host, ports, duration, and total number of bytes transmitted for detailed reporting.

- **Advanced traffic filtering**—In addition to supporting standard and extended access control lists (ACLs), Cisco IOS Firewall also supports lock and key ACLs to grant temporary access through the firewall with proper identification.

- **Policy-based multi-interface support**—Using Cisco IOS Firewall security policies, you can control user access by IP address and interface.

- **Network Address Translation (NAT)**—NAT and Port Address Translation (PAT) let you hide internal and private network addresses from outside observers.

- **Time-based access lists**—You can set up ACLs to be effective for set periods based on the time of day and day of the week.

- **Peer router authentication**—Cisco IOS Firewall can be configured to authenticate peer routers to ensure that routing information is obtained from trusted sources.

Securing Cisco Router Installations

Insecure installation of network routers and switches is an often-overlooked security threat, which, if left unheeded, can have dire results. Software-based security measures alone cannot prevent premeditated or even accidental network damage due to poor installations. This section discusses ways to identify and remedy insecure installations.

Installation Risk Assessment

Before discussing how to secure Cisco routing and switching installations, it is important to make a distinction between low-risk and high-risk devices:

- **Low-risk devices**—These devices are typically low-end or SOHO devices, such as the Cisco 800/900/1700 series routers and Cisco switches that are found in environments where access to the physical devices and cabling does not present a high risk to the corporate network. In these types of installations, it may be physically impossible and even too costly to provide a locked wiring closet for physical device security. In these situations, the IT manager must make a decision on what devices can and cannot be physically secured and at what risk.

- **High-risk (mission-critical) devices**—These devices are typically found in larger offices or corporate campuses where tens, hundreds, or even thousands of employees reside, or where the same large numbers of employees remotely access corporate data. These are usually Cisco Internet routers, Catalyst switches, firewalls, and management systems used to route and control large amounts of data, voice, and video traffic. These devices represent a much higher security threat if physically accessed by disgruntled employees or affected by negative environmental conditions.

Figure 2-1 depicts some of the factors that distinguish low-risk devices from high-risk devices. This section concentrates on identifying and physically securing those mission-critical devices while keeping in mind that some physical security resolutions may be easily applied to some low-risk installations as well.

Figure 2-1   *Installation Risk Assessment*

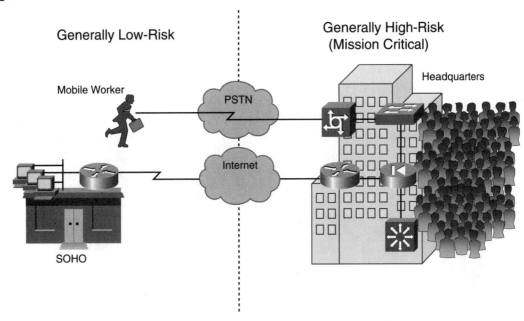

Common Threats to Cisco Router and Switch Physical Installations

Insecure installations or "physical access" threats can be generally classified as follows:

- **Hardware threats**—Threats of physical damage to the router or switch hardware.
- **Environmental threats**—Threats such as temperature extremes (too hot or too cold) or humidity extremes (too wet or too dry).
- **Electrical threats**—Threats such as voltage spikes, insufficient supply voltage (brownouts), unconditioned power (noise), and total power loss.
- **Maintenance threats**—Threats such as poor handling of key electronic components (electrostatic discharge), lack of critical spares, poor cabling, poor labeling, and so on.

The sections that follow describe how to mitigate these four common threat types.

Hardware Threat Mitigation

Mission-critical Cisco routing and switching equipment should be located in wiring closets or computer or telecommunications rooms that meet the following minimum requirements:

- Authorized personnel must lock the room and allow limited access only.
- The room should not be accessible via a dropped ceiling, raised floor, window, ductwork, or point of entry other than the secured access point.

- If possible, electronic access control should be used, with all entry attempts logged by security systems and monitored by security personnel.

- If possible, security personnel should monitor security cameras with automatic log recording.

Locate the blueprints of the room, as shown in the example in Figure 2-2, to ensure that you have identified all possible access points.

Figure 2-2 *Hardware Threat Mitigation*

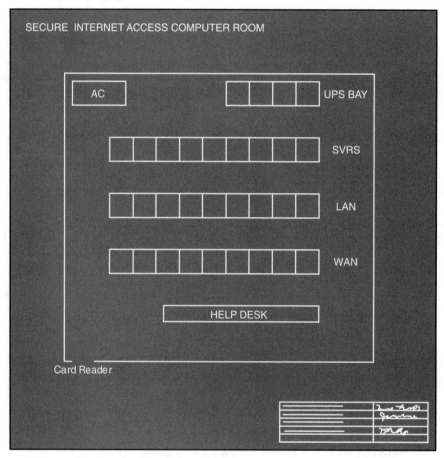

Environmental Threat Mitigation

The following items should be used to limit environmental damage to Cisco router and switching devices:

- The room must be supplied with dependable systems for temperature and humidity control and provide positive airflow, as shown in Figure 2-3. Always verify the recommended environmental parameters of the Cisco routing and switching equipment with the supplied product documentation.

- If possible, the room environmental parameters should be remotely monitored and alarmed.
- The room must be free from electrostatic and magnetic interferences.

Figure 2-3   *Environmental Threat Mitigation*

Electrical Threat Mitigation

Electrical supply problems can be limited by adhering to the following:

- Install uninterrupted power supply (UPS) systems for mission-critical Cisco routing and switching devices.
- Install backup generator systems for mission-critical power supplies.
- Plan for and initiate regular UPS or generator testing and maintenance procedures based on the manufacturer's suggested preventative maintenance schedule.
- Use filtered power.
- Install redundant power supplies on critical devices.
- Monitor and alarm power-related parameters at the supply and device levels.

Maintenance Threat Mitigation

Maintenance threats are a broad category that covers many items. The following general rules should be adhered to in order to prevent these types of threats:

- All equipment cabling should be clearly labeled and secured to equipment racks to prevent accidental damage or disconnection or incorrect termination.

- Cable runs, raceways, or both should be used to traverse rack-to-ceiling or rack-to-rack connections.

- Always follow electrostatic discharge (ESD) procedures when replacing or working inside Cisco router and switch devices. An environment free of interferences is ideal, but not always obtainable; therefore, the use of ESD grounding mechanisms such as wrist or ankle straps should be used.

- Maintain a stock of critical spares for emergency use.

- Do not leave a console connected to and logged in to any console port. Always log out of administrative interfaces when leaving.

- Always disconnect unused modems or connections from the Aux port(s) of network devices.

Always remember that no room is ever totally secure and should not be relied upon to be the sole protector of device access. Once inside a secure room, there is nothing to stop an intruder from connecting a terminal to the console port of a Cisco router or switch.

Securing Cisco Router Administrative Access

Configuring secure administrative access is an extremely important security task. If an unauthorized person were to gain administrative access to a router, the person could alter routing parameters, disable routing functions, or discover and gain access to other systems in the network.

Connecting to the Router Console Port

One way to perform initial router configuration tasks is to access the router console port with a console. A console is a terminal that is connected to a router console port and can either be a dumb terminal or a PC running terminal-emulation software, as shown in Figure 2-4. Consoles are only one way network administrators obtain administrative access to configure and manage routers. Other ways to gain administrative access include Secure Shell (SSH), Telnet, HTTP, and Simple Network Management Protocol (SNMP).

Figure 2-4   *Connect to Router Console Port*

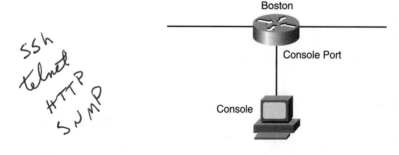

The first step in securing Cisco router administrative access is to configure secure system passwords. These passwords are either stored in the router itself (local) or on remote AAA servers, such as the Cisco Secure Access Control Server (ACS). This section contains information on configuring local passwords only. Password authentication using AAA will be discussed in an upcoming section of this chapter titled "Introduction to AAA for Cisco Routers."

Password Creation Rules

When creating passwords for Cisco routers, always keep the following rules in mind:

- Passwords must be anywhere from 1 to 25 characters in length and may include the following:
    - Any alphanumeric characters
    - Uppercase characters, lowercase characters, or both
- Passwords cannot have a number as the first character.
- Password-leading spaces are ignored, but all spaces after the first character are not ignored.
- Passwords should be changed based on the schedule detailed in the organization's security policy.

Cisco recommends using a strong password policy for protection from dictionary attacks. Cisco's recommendation for strong passwords includes the following characteristics:

- A minimum of 10 characters
- A mixture of uppercase and lowercase letters
- At least one numeric character (0 to 9) or nonalphanumeric character (example:!#@&)
- No form of the user's name or user ID
- A word that is not found in the dictionary (domestic or foreign)
- Randomly generated passwords

need pswd generator

Initial Configuration Dialog

If you are working on a new router (from the factory) or an existing router that has been reset (possibly using the Cisco password-recovery procedure), you will be asked if you want to enter the initial configuration dialog, which is partially shown in Example 2-1.

Example 2-1 *Router Initial Configuration Dialog*

```
--- System Configuration Dialog ---
Would you like to enter the initial configuration dialog? [yes/no] y
Configuring global parameters:
Enter host name [Router]: Boston
The enable secret is a password used to protect access to
privileged EXEC and configuration modes. This password, after
entered, becomes encrypted in the configuration.
Enter enable secret: CantGessMe
The enable password is used when you do not specify an enable
secret password, with some older software versions, and some boot
images.
Enter enable password: WontGessMe
The virtual terminal password is used to protect access to the
router over a network interface.
Enter virtual terminal password: CantGessMeVTY
.
.
```

Within the first few questions of the initial configuration dialog can be found several Cisco router password requirements:

- What will be this router's enable secret password?
- What will be this router's enable password?
- What will be the password used to access the router using virtual terminal (Telnet)?

The enable secret password is used to enter enable mode (sometimes referred to as *privileged* or *privileged EXEC* mode). You can set the enable secret password by entering a password during the initial configuration dialog or by using the **enable secret** command in global configuration mode. The enable secret password is always hashed inside the router configuration using a message digest algorithm 5 (MD5) hashing algorithm.

The enable password is also used to enter enable mode but is a holdover from older versions of Cisco IOS Software. If you try to enter the same password for the enable password that you used for the enable secret password, the System Configuration Dialog will present an error message telling you that they are the same. If you try a second time, the system will permit the duplicate password. This is not good practice and should be avoided.

By default, the enable password is not hashed in the router configuration. The global command **service password-encryption** causes Cisco IOS to hash clear-text passwords, rendering them unreadable to someone who may be viewing the router's configuration with an administrator.

Cisco decided to keep the older **enable password** command in later versions of Cisco IOS even though **enable secret password** is a safer way to store privileged EXEC passwords. The thinking was that if you downgraded the router to a version of Cisco IOS that did not support **enable secret password**, you would still have the enable password protecting the privileged EXEC password.

Be sure to use different passwords for the enable secret password and the enable password. The System Configuration Dialog makes it easy for you to keep them different by presenting a warning when they are the same. Although there is no automated method of ensuring their difference, your security policy should make it very clear that these two passwords must be different. When both passwords are configured on a router, the enable secret password overrides the enable password.

The virtual terminal password is the user-level password entered when connecting to the router using Telnet. You can set this password during the initial configuration dialog or by using the **password** command in vty line configuration mode.

Configuring Minimum Password Length

Cisco IOS Software Release 12.3(1) and later allow administrators to set the minimum character length for all router passwords using the **security passwords** global configuration command. This command provides enhanced security access to the router by allowing you to specify a minimum password length, eliminating common passwords that are prevalent on most networks, such as "lab" and "cisco." This command affects user passwords, the enable password, the enable secret password, and line passwords created after the command was executed (existing router passwords remain unaffected).

The syntax for the **security passwords** command is as follows:

```
security passwords min-length length
```

- *length*—Minimum length of a configured password (choose a length from 0 to 16). A minimum length of 8 characters is recommended.

NOTE   Cisco recommends that you set your minimum password length to at least 10 characters. Never use a length of 0.

After this command is enabled, any attempt to create a new password that is less than the specified length will fail. Any attempt to create a shorter password will result in an error message similar to the following:

```
% Password too short - must be at least 8 characters. Password configuration
  failed.
```

Configuring the Enable Secret Password

If you did not use the initial configuration dialog to configure your enable secret password, you must use the **enable secret** command in global configuration mode. The **enable secret** command uses a one-way hash based on MD5 to hash the password in the router configuration file. MD5 hashing is considered irreversible by most cryptographers. That being said, it should be noted that even this type of encryption is still vulnerable to brute-force or dictionary attacks.

MD5 creates a 128-bit hash. Current processors, techniques, and cracking programs can identify the hash within 30 days. That is a fairly long time and requires a serious commitment to bypassing the MD5 hash, but it can be done. You need to be diligent in changing your passwords frequently to make it more difficult to compromise your passwords.

Use the **enable secret** command in global configuration mode.

The syntax for the **enable secret** command is as follows:

enable secret *password*

The following example shows the configuration of the enable secret password on a router named Boston:

Boston(config)# **enable secret Curium96**

Looking at the running configuration in Example 2-2 after this command has been issued shows that the enable secret password has been hashed with the MD5 hashing algorithm (indicated by the number 5 in the configuration for the password and by the cryptic representation of the password).

Example 2-2 *Running Configuration Indicates the Enable Secret Password Is Hashed with MD5*

```
Boston# show running-config
!
hostname Boston
!
no logging console
enable secret 5 $1$ptCj$vRErS/tehv53JjaqFMzBT/
!
```

NOTE If you forget the enable secret password, you have no alternative but to replace it using the Cisco router password-recovery procedure.

Configuring the Console Port User-Level Password

By default, the console port does not require a password for console administrative access.

NOTE Cisco routers bypass normal configuration startup if the Break key is pressed within 60 seconds of power up or reboot, leaving the console user in ROM Monitor (ROMMON) mode in full control of the router. This capability is used for maintenance purposes, such as when running the Cisco router password-recovery procedure. Even though this Break-key scenario is always available to someone who has physical access to the router console port, it is still important to set a user-level password for users who might try to gain console access remotely.

Always configure a console port user-level password. Complete the following steps to create a new user-level password for the console line from global configuration mode:

Step 1 Enter console 0 line configuration mode:

```
Boston(config)# line console 0
```

[handwritten: vty 0 4   aux 0]

Step 2 Enable password checking on login:

```
Boston(config-line)# login
```

Step 3 Enter the new console user-level password (in this example, ConUser1):

```
Boston(config-line)# password ConUser1
```

If you were to view the router configuration using the **show run** command, you would see the following for the console line configuration:

```
line con 0
login
password ConUser1
```

Notice that the password is seen in clear text (unencrypted). Passwords left in clear text pose a serious threat to router security if the router is physically compromised, someone gains access to the EXEC privilege level, or a listing of the configuration is compromised. The upcoming section in this chapter titled "Encrypting Passwords Using the **service password-encryption** Command" discusses a method for applying additional security to router passwords.

Configuring a vty User-Level Password

Cisco routers support multiple Telnet sessions each serviced by a logical vty connection. Five vty connections are supported by default, but you can configure up to 100 by simply entering the command **line vty 0 99** instead of the default command **line vty 0 4**.

By default, Cisco routers do not have any user-level passwords configured for these vty connections. If you enable password checking, you must also configure a vty user-level password before attempting to access the router using Telnet. If you fail to configure a vty user-level password, and password checking is enabled for vty connections, you will encounter an error message similar to that in Example 2-3.

Example 2-3 *Indication That vty User-Level Password Is Not Configured*

```
Telnet 10.0.1.2
Trying…
Connected to 10.0.1.2.
Escape character is '^]'.
Password required, but none set
Connection closed by remote host.
```

There are two ways to configure a user-level vty password: enter the password during the initial configuration dialog (virtual terminal password), or use the **password** command in vty line configuration mode. Always configure passwords for all the vty ports in this manner:

Step 1 Enter vty line configuration mode for the range of 5 vty lines, 0 through 4:

```
Boston(config)# line vty 0 4
```

Step 2 Enable password checking on login (vty lines default to this command):

```
Boston(config-line)# login
```

Step 3 Enter the new vty user-level password (in this example, "CantGessMevty"):

```
Boston(config-line)# password CantGessMevty
```

NOTE An enable password must also be configured if Telnet is to gain access to the privileged EXEC (enable) mode of the router. Use either the **enable** *password* or **enable secret** *password* command to set the enable password for your routers.

In the example, vty lines 0 to 4 are configured simultaneously to look for the password specified. Just like console user-level passwords, vty passwords are not encrypted in the router configuration.

The following are a few more items to keep in mind when securing Telnet connections to a Cisco router:

- If you do not set an enable password for the router, you will not be able to access privileged EXEC mode using Telnet. That may sound like a good thing, preventing Telnet users from entering privileged EXEC mode, but the lack of an enable password means that anyone connecting through the console port can enter privileged EXEC mode without any password requirement whatsoever. Use either the **enable** *password* or **enable secret** *password* command to set the enable password for your routers.

- Telnet access should be limited to only specified systems by building an ACL that does the following (ACLs are covered in depth in Chapter 4, "Cisco Router Threat Mitigation"):
  — Allows Telnet access from specific hosts only (allows certain IP addresses)
  — Blocks Telnet access from specific "trouble" hosts (disallows certain IP addresses)
  — Ties the ACL to the vty connections by using the **access-class** command

Example 2-4 shows ACL 30 restricting Telnet access to host 10.0.1.1 for vty connections 0 to 4.

Example 2-4 *ACL Restricting Telnet Access to vty Connections 0 to 4*

```
Boston(config)# access-list 30 permit 10.0.1.1
Boston(config)# line vty 0 4
Boston(config-line)# access-class 30 in
```

TIP	Make sure that you configure passwords for all the vty lines on the router. Remember that you can add more vty lines to the router, but they must be protected as well as the default 0 to 4 lines.

Configuring an Auxiliary User-Level Password

By default, Cisco router auxiliary ports do not require a password for remote administrative access. Administrators sometimes use this port to remotely configure and monitor the router using a dialup modem connection.

Unlike enable and vty user-level passwords, the auxiliary password is not configured during the initial configuration dialog and must be configured using the **password** command in auxiliary line configuration mode.

NOTE	If you want to prevent someone from accessing privileged EXEC mode from an auxiliary port, use the **no exec** command within the auxiliary line configuration mode.

Setting the auxiliary user-level password is only one of several steps you must complete when configuring a router auxiliary port for remote dial-in access. The following example shows other important commands that are used when configuring an auxiliary port.

Step 1   Permit incoming and outgoing modem calls on this line:

```
Boston(config)# line aux 0
Boston(config-line)# modem inout
```

Step 2   Specify the line speed that should be used to communicate with the modem:

```
Boston(config-line)# speed 9600
```

Step 3   Allow all protocols to use the line:

```
Boston(config-line)# transport input all
```

Step 4   Enable RTS/CTS flow control:

```
Boston(config-line)# flowcontrol hardware
```

Step 5   Authenticate incoming connections using the password configured on the line (the password is configured in Step 6):

```
Boston(config-line)# login
% Login disabled on line 65, until 'password' is set
```

Step 6   Configure a password to authenticate incoming calls on this line:

```
Boston(config-line)# password NeverGessMeAux
```

For more information on configuring router auxiliary ports, see Cisco.com. Just like console and vty user-level passwords, auxiliary passwords are not encrypted in the router configuration. This is why it is important to use the **service password-encryption** command, which is covered in the next section.

Encrypting Passwords Using the service password-encryption Command

With the exception of the enable secret password, all Cisco router passwords are by default stored in clear text within the router configuration. These passwords can be clearly seen by performing a **show running-config** command. Sniffers can also see the passwords if your Trivial File Transfer Protocol (TFTP) router configuration files traverse an unsecured intranet or Internet connection. If an intruder were to gain access to the TFTP server where the router configuration files are stored, the intruder would be able to obtain these passwords.

The **service password-encryption** command encrypts all passwords (except the previously encrypted enable secret password) in the router configuration file using a proprietary Cisco algorithm based on a Vigenere cipher (indicated by the number 7 when viewing the configuration). This method is not as safe as MD5, which is used with the **enable secret password** command, but it will slow down the discovery of the router's user-level passwords.

The Vigenere cipher is a simple character-replacement method of obscuring clear text and was developed in the 16th century. This type of encryption can be easily broken using simple scripting programs in very short order. The **service password-encryption** command would not prevent a committed attacker from obtaining your passwords, but it would prevent a person from looking over your shoulder and reading the passwords in clear text from the screen or from a printed copy. MD5, with its resultant 128-bit hash, is a much more secure method, but it is no longer considered an unbreakable method of securing information.

NOTE	The encryption algorithm in the **service password-encryption** command is considered relatively weak by most cryptographers, and several Internet sites already post mechanisms for cracking this cipher. This only shows that relying on encrypted passwords alone is not sufficient security for your Cisco routers. You need to ensure that the communications link between the console and the routers, or between the TFTP or management server and the routers, is a secured connection. Securing this connection is discussed in a later section of this chapter titled, "Apply Authentication Commands to Lines and Interfaces."

The syntax for the **service password-encryption** command is as follows:

```
service password-encryption
```

There are no arguments for this command.

After all of your passwords have been configured for the router, you should run the **service password-encryption** command in global configuration mode as follows:

```
Boston(config)# service password-encryption
```

Use the **show running-config** command to see the results of the **service password-encryption** command, as demonstrated in Example 2-5.

Example 2-5   *Displaying Results of the* **service password-encryption** *Command*

```
Boston# show running-config
enable password 7 06020026144A061E
!
line con 0
password 7 0956F57A109A
!
line vty 0 4
password 7 034A18F366A0
!
line aux 0
password 7 7A4F5192306A
```

Enhanced Username Password Security

Starting with Cisco IOS Software Release 12.0(18)S, system administrators can choose to use an MD5 hashing mechanism to encrypt username passwords. MD5 hashing of passwords is a much better encryption scheme than the standard type 7 encryption found in the **service password-encryption** command. The added layer of MD5 encryption is useful in environments in which the password crosses the network or is stored on a TFTP server.

MD5 hashing of Cisco IOS username passwords is accomplished by using the **username secret** command in global configuration mode. Administrators can choose to enter either a clear-text password for MD5 hashing by the router (option 0) or a previously encrypted MD5 secret (option 5).

The syntax for the **username secret** command is as follows:

```
username name secret {[0] password | 5 encrypted-secret}
```

- *name*—The username.
- **0** (Optional)—Indicates that the following clear text *password* is to be hashed using MD5.
- *password*—Clear-text password to be hashed using MD5.
- **5**—Indicates that the following *encrypted-secret* password was hashed using MD5.
- *encrypted-secret*—The MD5 encrypted-secret password that will be stored as the encrypted user password.

NOTE   MD5 encryption is a strong encryption method that is not retrievable; therefore, you cannot use MD5 encryption with protocols that require clear-text passwords, such as Challenge Handshake Authentication Protocol (CHAP).

Securing ROMMON with no service password-recovery

By default, Cisco IOS routers allow a break sequence during power up, forcing the router into ROMMON mode. Once the router is in ROMMON mode, anyone can choose to enter a new enable secret password using the well-known Cisco password-recovery procedure. This procedure, if performed correctly, leaves the router configuration intact. This scenario presents a potential security breach in that anyone who gains physical access to the router console port can enter ROMMON, reset the enable secret password, and discover the router configuration.

This potential security breach can be mitigated by using the **no service password-recovery** global configuration command.

NOTE   The **no service password-recovery** command is a hidden Cisco IOS command and is not shown when requesting command-line help.

The syntax for the **no service password-recovery** command is as follows:

```
no service password-recovery
```

This command has no arguments or keywords.

CAUTION   If a router is configured with **no service password-recovery**, all access to ROMMON is disabled. If the router's Flash memory does not contain a valid Cisco IOS image, you will not be able to use the **rommon xmodem** command to load a new Flash image. To repair the router, you must obtain a new Cisco IOS image on a Flash SIMM, or on a PCMCIA card (3600 only). See Cisco.com for more information regarding backup Flash images.

Example 2-6 shows the process of entering the **no service password-recovery** command and the resultant warning message issued by the router in response to the command.

Example 2-6 *Bootup with* **no service password-recovery** *Enabled*

```
Boston(config)# no service password-recovery
WARNING:
Executing this command will disable password recovery mechanism. Do not execute this
  command without another plan for password recovery.
Are you sure you want to continue? [yes/no]: yes
Boston(config)#
```

Once the **no service password-recovery** command is executed, the router boot sequence will
look similar to the sequence shown in Example 2-7.

Example 2-7   *Bootup with* **no service password-recovery** *Enabled*

```
System Bootstrap, Version 11.3(2)XA4, RELEASE SOFTWARE (fc1)
Copyright (c) 1999 by cisco Systems, Inc.
C2600 platform with 65536 Kbytes of main memory

PASSWORD RECOVERY FUNCTIONALITY IS DISABLED
program load complete, entry point: 0x80008000, size: 0xed9ee4
```

Also, after the **no service password-recovery** command is executed, a show running
configuration listing will contain the **no service password-recovery** statement, as shown
in Example 2-8.

Example 2-8   *Bootup with* **no service password-recovery** *Enabled*

```
!
version 12.0
service tcp-keepalives-in
service timestamps debug datetime localtime show-timezone
service timestamps log datetime localtime show-timezone
service password-encryption
no service password-recovery
!
hostname Boston
```

Authentication Failure Rate with Logging

Starting with Cisco IOS Software Release 12.3(1), system administrators can configure the
number of allowable unsuccessful login attempts by using the **security authentication failure
rate** global configuration command. By default, the router allows ten login failures before
initiating a 15-second delay. A syslog message will be generated every time the rate is
exceeded.

When the number of failed login attempts reaches the configured rate, two events occur:

- A TOOMANY_AUTHFAILS event message is sent by the router to the configured syslog
server.
- A 15-second delay timer starts.

Once the 15-second delay has passed, the user may continue to attempt to login to the
router.

The syntax for the security authentication failure rate command is as follows:

```
security authentication failure rate threshold-rate log
```

- *threshold-rate*—Number of allowable unsuccessful login attempts. The default is 10
(range: 2 to 1024).

NOTE	The **log** keyword is required. This command must result in a generated syslog event.

Setting Timeouts for Router Lines

You can provide an extra safety factor when an administrator walks away from an active console session by terminating an unattended console connection after a period of inactivity. By default, an administrative interface stays active (and logged on) for 10 minutes after the last session activity. After that, the interface times out and logs out of the session. It is recommended that you adjust these timers to limit the amount of time to within 2 to 3 minutes maximum to minimize the window of opportunity for someone to gain access to an open console session.

You can adjust these timers by using the **exec-timeout** command in line configuration mode for each of the line types used.

The syntax for the **exec-timeout** command is as follows:

```
exec-timeout minutes [seconds]
```

Example 2-9 shows how you might set timeouts of 3 minutes and 30 seconds for the console and auxiliary lines.

Example 2-9 *Setting Router Timeouts for Console/Auxiliary Lines*

```
Boston(config)# line console 0
Boston(config-line)# exec-timeout 3 30
Boston(config)# line aux 0
Boston(config-line)# exec-timeout 3 30
```

Setting Privilege Levels

Cisco routers enable you to configure various privilege levels for your administrators. Different passwords can be configured to control who has access to the various privilege levels. This is especially helpful in a help desk environment where certain administrators are allowed to configure and monitor every part of the router (level 15) while other administrators may be restricted to only monitoring (customized levels 2 to 14). The 16 levels (numbered 0 to 15) are designated as follows:

- Level 0 is seldom used, but it places the user at the **router>** prompt and includes five commands: **disable**, **enable**, **exit**, **help**, and **logout**.
- Level 1 is predefined for user-level access privileges and places the user at the **router>** prompt.
- Levels 2 to 14 may be customized for user-level privileges.
- Level 15 is predefined for enable mode (**enable** command) and places the user at the **router#** prompt.

Privileges are assigned to levels 2 to 14 using the **privilege** command from global configuration mode. The syntax for the **privilege** command is as follows:

```
privilege mode {level level command | reset command}
```

- *mode*—Specifies the configuration mode. See the list after this table for options for this argument.
- **level** (Optional)—Enables setting a privilege level with a specified command.
- *level* (Optional)—Indicates the privilege level associated with a command. You can specify up to 16 privilege levels, using numbers 0 through 15.
- *command* (Optional)—Indicates the command to which the privilege level is associated.
- **reset** (Optional)—Resets the privilege level of a command.
- *command* (Optional)—Indicates the command for which you want to reset the privilege level.

For example, to set a command privilege for level 2 users and then set the enable secret password for those users, you would enter the following:

```
Boston(config)# privilege exec level 2 ping
Boston(config)# enable secret level 2 Patriot
```

The following list contains all the router configuration modes that can be configured using the **privilege** command:

- **accept-dialin**—VPDN group accept dial-in configuration mode
- **accept-dialout**—VPDN group accept dial-out configuration mode
- **address-family**—Address family configuration mode
- **atm-bm-config**—ATM bundle member configuration mode
- **atm-bundle-config**—ATM bundle configuration mode
- **atm-vc-config**—ATM virtual circuit configuration mode
- **atmsig_e164_table_mode**—ATMSIG E164 Table configuration mode
- **cascustom**—Channel-associated signaling (CAS) custom configuration mode
- **configure**—Global configuration mode
- **controller**—Controller configuration mode
- **dhcp**—DHCP pool configuration mode
- **dspfarm**—DSP farm configuration mode
- **exec**—EXEC mode
- **flow-cache**—Flow aggregation cache configuration mode
- **interface**—Interface configuration mode
- **interface-dlci**—Frame Relay DLCI configuration mode

- **ip-vrf**—IP VRF parameters configuration mode
- **line**—Line configuration mode
- **map-class**—Map class configuration mode
- **map-list**—Map list configuration mode
- **null-interface**—Null interface configuration mode
- **preaut**—AAA Preauth definitions configuration mode
- **request-dialin**—VPDN group request dial-in configuration mode
- **request-dialout**—VPDN group request dial-out configuration mode
- **route-map**—Route map configuration mode
- **router**—Router configuration mode
- **tdm-conn**—TDM connection configuration mode
- **vc-class**—VC class configuration mode
- **vpdn-group**—VPDN group configuration mode
- **rsvp_policy_local**—RSVP protocol local policy configuration moded
- **alps-ascu**—ALPS ASCU configuration mode
- **alps-circuit**—ALPS circuit configuration mode
- **config-rtr-http**—RTR HTTP raw request configuration mode
- **crypto-map**—Crypto map configuration mode
- **crypto-transform**—Crypto transform configuration mode
- **gateway**—Gateway configuration mode
- **ipenacl**—IP named extended access-list configuration mode
- **ipsnacl**—IP named simple access-list configuration mode
- **lane**—ATM LAN emulation LECS configuration mode
- **mpoa-client**—MPOA Client configuration mode
- **mpoa-server**—MPOA Server configuration mode
- **rtr**—RTR entry configuration mode
- **sg-radius**—RADIUS server group definition mode
- **sg-tacacs+**—TACACS+ server group mode
- **sip-ua**—SIP UA configuration mode
- **subscriber-policy**—Subscriber policy configuration mode
- **tcl**—Tcl mode
- **template**—Template configuration mode

- **translation-rule**—Translation rule configuration mode
- **voiceclass**—Voice class configuration mode
- **voiceport**—Voice configuration mode
- **voipdialpeer**—Dial peer configuration mode

Configuring Banner Messages

Banner messages should be used to warn would-be intruders that they are not welcome on your network. Banners are very important, especially from a legal perspective.

Choosing what to place in your banner messages is extremely important and should be reviewed by legal counsel before placing them on your routers. Never use the word "welcome" or any other familiar greeting that may be misconstrued as an invitation to use the network.

You should specify what is considered "proper use" of the system. You should also state that the system is being monitored and that privacy should not be expected while using the system.

Banners are disabled by default and must be explicitly enabled by the administrator. The banner command is really made up of five distinct commands:

- **banner exec**—Specifies and enables a message to be displayed when an EXEC process is created on the router (an EXEC banner)
- **banner incoming**—Specifies and enables a banner to be displayed when there is an incoming connection to a terminal line from a host on the network
- **banner login**—Specifies and enables a customized banner to be displayed before the username and password login prompts
- **banner motd**—Specifies and enables a message-of-the-day (MOTD) banner
- **banner slip-ppp**—Specifies and enables a banner to be displayed when a Serial Line Interface Protocol (SLIP) or PPP connection is made

Use the **banner** command to specify appropriate messages from global configuration mode. An example of setting the MOTD banner is as follows:

```
Boston(config)# banner motd #
WARNING: You are connected to $(hostname) on the Cisco Systems, Incorporated
    network.
Unauthorized access and use of this network will be vigorously prosecuted. #
```

The syntax for the **banner** command is as follows:

```
banner {exec | incoming | login | motd | slip-ppp} d message d
```

- *d*—Represents the delimiting character of your choice (for example, a pound sign, #). You cannot use the delimiting character in the banner message.

- *message*—represents the message text. You can include tokens in the form $(token) in the message text. Tokens will be replaced with the corresponding configuration variable.

The following list contains valid tokens for use within the **banner** command:

- **$(hostname)**—Displays the host name for the router
- **$(domain)**—Displays the domain name for the router
- **$(line)**—Displays the vty or tty (asynchronous) line number
- **$(line-desc)**—Displays the description attached to the line

Securing SNMP Access

SNMP systems may gain administrative access to Cisco routers by communicating with the router's internal SNMP agent and Management Information Base (MIB).

An SNMP agent is responsible for reading and formatting all SNMP messages between the router and an SNMP network management system (NMS). An SNMP MIB is a tree-like list of objects within the router that point the SNMP agent to various router configuration parameters and statistics. After the SNMP agent on the router is configured, SNMP systems may perform some or all of the following tasks:

- Read certain configuration parameters and statistics found in the router SNMP agent MIB (read-only mode)
- Write certain configuration parameters to the router SNMP agent MIB (read-write mode)
- Receive SNMP traps (router events) from the router SNMP agent

SNMP systems use a community string as a type of password to access router SNMP agents. SNMP agents accept commands and requests only from SNMP systems that use the correct community string. By default, most SNMP systems use a community string of "public." If you were to configure your router SNMP agent to use this commonly known community string, anyone with an SNMP system would be able to—at a minimum—read the router MIB. Because router MIB variables can point to things such as routing tables and other security-critical parts of the router configuration, it is extremely important to create your own custom SNMP community strings.

You must consider the following questions when developing SNMP access for Cisco routers:

- Which community strings will have read-only access?
- Which community strings will have read-write access?
- Which SNMP systems are permitted to access the router SNMP agents (limiting host IP addresses using ACLs)?

To configure a router SNMP community string, use the **snmp-server community** command in global configuration mode. You may configure multiple community strings for your Cisco router by repeating this command for each string. Cisco recommends using different community strings for requests and trap messages, which reduces the likelihood of subsequent attacks if one or the other is compromised.

The syntax for the **snmp-server community** command is as follows:

```
snmp-server community string [ro | rw] [number]
```

- *string*—Represents the community string that acts like a password and permits access to the SNMP protocol.

- **ro** (Optional)—Specifies read-only access. Authorized management stations are only able to retrieve MIB objects.

- **rw** (Optional)—Specifies read-write access. Authorized management stations are able to both retrieve and modify MIB objects.

- *number* (Optional)—Represents an integer from 1 to 99 that specifies an ACL of IP addresses that are allowed to use the community string to gain access to the router.

Use the **ro** option to limit a community string to read-only access (only SNMP get-requests and get-next-requests are allowed); for example:

```
PR1(config)# snmp-server community readSNMP ro
```

Use the **rw** option to allow read and write access (SNMP get-requests, get-next-requests, and set-requests are allowed) for the designated community string; for example:

```
PR1(config)# snmp-server community ReadWriteSNMP rw
```

ACLs can be used for both read-only and read-write modes. Figure 2-5 shows a network in which administrators at the two management systems require read-write SNMP permission on router PR1.

Figure 2-5   *Securing SNMP Access*

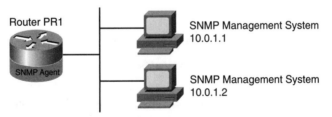

Use the **snmp-server** command in association with ACLs to limit which hosts are allowed access to the router SNMP agent. Example 2-10 shows a read-write mode community string.

Example 2-10 *Limiting Host Access to the Router SNMP Agent*

```
PR1(config)# access-list 10 permit 10.0.1.1
PR1(config)# access-list 10 permit 10.0.1.2
PR1(config)# snmp-server community string RWSNMP rw 10
```

SNMP traps and informs are router events that are automatically sent to one or more SNMP systems by a router SNMP agent. Traps are sent out to designated SNMP systems regardless of whether the host is there or not. Informs always require an acknowledgment from the designated SNMP system to verify that the message was received. Because traps and informs can contain critical routing and configuration information, it is important that you designate exactly where you want the traps and informs sent.

The following list contains types of router SNMP traps that are enabled (sent) by default (all other types of traps must be specifically enabled to be sent):

- **Interface traps**—Sent whenever an interface goes active or inactive
- **Reload traps**—Sent whenever a router reload occurs
- **Configuration change traps**—Sent whenever a change is made to the router configuration

There are two ways to specifically enable traps and informs to be generated by the router:

- **Enable global traps and informs**—Use the **snmp-server enable traps** command to enable all SNMP traps and informs to be sent by the router.
- **Enable host**—Use the **snmp-server host** command to specify which traps and informs to send while simultaneously specifying the SNMP system host where the traps and informs are to be sent.

Use the **snmp-server enable traps** command from global configuration mode to enable the sending of all traps and informs by the router.

NOTE   The **snmp-server enable traps** command only enables traps and informs. It does not specify the SNMP system host to which the traps and informs are to be sent.

The syntax for the **snmp-server enable traps** command is as follows:

```
snmp-server enable traps [notification-type]
```

The optional *notification-type* argument represents the type of notification (trap or inform) to enable or disable. If no type is specified, all notifications available on your device are enabled or disabled. The notification type can be one of the following keywords:

- **config**—Controls configuration notifications, as defined in the CISCO-CONFIG-MAN-MIB (enterprise 1.3.6.1.4.1.9.9.43.2). The notification type is (1) ciscoConfigManEvent.
- **ds0-busyout**—Sends notification whenever the busyout of a DS0 interface changes state (Cisco AS5300 platform only). This is from the CISCO-POP-MGMT-MIB (enterprise 1.3.6.1.4.1.9.10.19.2) and the notification type is (1) cpmDS0BusyoutNotification.

- **ds1-loopback**—Sends notification whenever the DS1 interface goes into loopback mode (Cisco AS5300 platform only). This notification type is defined in the CISCO-POP-MGMT-MIB (enterprise 1.3.6.1.4.1.9.10.19.2) as (2) cpmDS1LoopbackNotification.

- **entity**—Controls Entity MIB modification notifications. This notification type is defined in the ENTITY-MIB (enterprise 1.3.6.1.2.1.47.2) as (1) entConfigChange.

- **hsrp**—Controls Hot Standby Routing Protocol (HSRP) notifications, as defined in the CISCO-HSRP-MIB (enterprise 1.3.6.1.4.1.9.9.106.2). The notification type is (1) cHsrpStateChange.

- **modem-health**—Controls modem-health notifications.

- **rsvp**—Controls Resource Reservation Protocol (RSVP) notifications.

- **tty**—Controls TCP connection notifications.

- **xgcp**—Sends External Media Gateway Control Protocol (XGCP) notifications. This notification is from the XGCP-MIB-V1SMI.my and the notifications are enterprise 1.3.6.1.3.90.2 (1) xgcpUpDownNotification.

Once you have globally enabled SNMP traps with the **snmp-server enable traps** command, you can enable traps for a wide variety of different protocols and system variables by using specific **snmp-server enable traps** commands. You can find a complete list of these commands on Cisco.com.

A more efficient way of enabling traps and informs is to use the **snmp-server host** command, because it accomplishes two tasks at once:

- Specifies which SNMP system host is to be sent the traps and informs

- Specifies which traps and informs are to be enabled

You must specify which SNMP systems (host-addr) are to receive SNMP traps by entering the **snmp-server host** command in global configuration mode.

The syntax for the **snmp-server host** command is as follows:

```
snmp-server host host-addr [traps | informs] [version {1 | 2c | 3 [auth |
   noauth | priv]}] i-string [udp-port port] [notification-type]
   [vrf vrf-name]
```

- *host-addr*—Name or Internet address of the SNMP system host (the targeted recipient).

- **traps**—(Optional) Sends SNMP traps to this host. This is the default.

- **informs**—(Optional) Sends SNMP informs to this host.

- **version**—(Optional) Version of SNMP used to send the traps. Version 3 is the most secure model, because it allows packet encryption with the **priv** keyword. If you use the **version** keyword, one of the following must be specified:

- **1**—SNMPv1. This option is not available with informs.
- **2c**—SNMPv2C. Specifies SNMP version 2C.
- **3**—SNMPv3. The following three optional keywords can follow the **version 3** keyword:
    - **auth** (Optional)—Enables MD5 and Secure Hash Algorithm (SHA) packet authentication.
    - **noauth** (Default.)—The noAuthNoPriv security level. This is the default if the [**auth** | **noauth** | **priv**] keyword choice is not specified.
    - **priv** (Optional)—Enables Data Encryption Standard (DES) packet encryption (also called "privacy").
- *community-string*—Password-like community string sent with the notification operation. Though you can set this string using the **snmp-server host** command by itself, recommended practice is to define this string using the **snmp-server community** command prior to using the **snmp-server host** command.
- **udp-port** *port*—(Optional) UDP port of the host to use. The default is 162.
- *notification-type*—(Optional) Type of notification to be sent to the host. If no type is specified, all notifications are sent. The notification type can be one or more of the following keywords:
    - **bgp**—Sends Border Gateway Protocol (BGP) state change notifications
    - **calltracker**—Sends Call Tracker call-start/call-end notifications
    - **config**—Sends configuration notifications
    - **dspu**—Sends downstream physical unit (DSPU) notifications
    - **entity**—Sends Entity MIB modification notifications
    - **envmon**—Sends Cisco enterprise-specific environmental monitor notifications when an environmental threshold is exceeded
    - **frame-relay**—Sends Frame Relay notifications
    - **hsrp**—Sends Hot Standby Routing Protocol notifications
    - **ipmobile**—Sends Mobile IP notifications
    - **ipsec**—Sends IP Security notifications
    - **isdn**—Sends ISDN notifications
    - **llc2**—Sends Logical Link Control, type 2 (LLC2) notifications
    - **mpls-ldp**—Sends MPLS Label Distribution Protocol (LDP) notifications indicating status changes in LDP sessions

- **mpls-traffic-eng**—Sends MPLS traffic engineering notifications indicating changes in the status of MPLS traffic engineering tunnels
- **mpls-vpn**—Sends MPLS VPN notifications
- **pim**—Sends Protocol Independent Multicast (PIM) notifications
- **repeater**—Sends standard repeater (hub) notifications
- **rsrb**—Sends remote source-route bridging (RSRB) notifications
- **rsvp**—Sends Resource Reservation Protocol notifications
- **rtr**—Sends SA Agent (RTR) notifications
- **sdlc**—Sends Synchronous Data Link Control (SDLC) notifications
- **sdllc**—Sends SDLC Logical Link Control (SDLLC) notifications
- **snmp**—Sends any enabled RFC 1157 SNMP linkUp, linkDown, authenticationFailure, warmStart, and coldStart notifications
- **srp**—Sends Spatial Reuse Protocol (SRP) notifications
- **stun**—Sends serial tunnel (STUN) notifications
- **syslog**—Sends error message notifications (Cisco Syslog MIB); specify the level of messages to be sent with the **logging history level** command
- **tty**—Sends Cisco enterprise-specific notifications when a TCP connection closes
- **voice**—Sends SNMP poor quality of voice traps, when used with the **snmp enable peer-trap poor qov** command
- **vsimaster**—Sends VSI Master notifications
- **x25**—Sends X.25 event notifications
- **vrf** *vrf-name*—(Optional) Specifies the virtual private network (VPN) routing and forwarding (VRF) table that should be used to send SNMP notifications.

The following is an example of using the **snmp-server host** command to limit where the router will send SNMP traps:

```
PR1(config)# snmp-server host 10.0.1.1 traps
```

The following is an example of using the **snmp-server host** command to limit where TCP connection close traps will be sent by the router:

```
PR1(config)# snmp-server host 10.0.1.2 traps tty
```

One final SNMP-related command is the **snmp-server trap-source** command. This command specifies which interface on the router (and, hence, the corresponding IP address) will be the source for all SNMP traps and informs generated by the router. The loopback0 interface makes an excellent choice for the source interface because it is always considered to be active.

Use the **snmp-server trap-source** command from global configuration mode.

The syntax for the **snmp-server trap-source** command is as follows:

```
snmp-server trap-source interface
```

The following is an example of using the **snmp-server trap-source** command for the Loopback0 interface:

```
PR1(config)# snmp-server trap-source loopback0
```

There are several more **snmp-server** commands available to you in the *Cisco IOS Command Reference* at Cisco.com.

Enhanced Features of SNMP Version 3

SNMP Version 3 (SNMPv3) is an interoperable standards-based protocol for network management that provides secure access to devices by using a combination of authenticating and encrypting packets over the network. SNMPv3 provides message integrity, authentication, and encryption capabilities to SNMP.

SNMPv3 uses both security models and security levels:

- **Security model**—An authentication strategy that is set up for a user and the group in which the user resides.
- **Security level**—The permitted level of security within a security model.

A combination of a security model and a security level determines which security mechanism is employed when handling an SNMP packet. Three security models are available: SNMPv1, SNMPv2c, and SNMPv3. Security models SNMPv1 and SNMPv2c use a community string match for access control and do not provide encryption or authentication services.

SNMPv3 uses a username match for access control, HMAC-MD5 or HMAC-SHA for authentication, and DES 56-bit encryption for privacy. Data can be collected securely from SNMP devices without fear of the data being compromised. Confidential information such as SNMP **set** command packets that change a router's configuration can be encrypted to prevent their contents from being exposed on the network.

SNMPv3 defines the following concepts:

- **Principal**—A user or application that requires SNMP services.
- **Group**—A collection of principals that requires like SNMP access and services. Groups define the access policy, security model, and security level for a set of principals. Groups also determine the list of notifications its principals can receive.
- **Engine**—A host that runs a copy of SNMP to perform the SNMP functions for sending and receiving messages, authenticating and encrypting/decrypting messages, and controlling access to managed objects.

- **Context**—An access policy that defines collection of SNMP managed objects that can be accessed for reading, writing, and creating.
- **View**—A combination of SNMP characteristics that defines the level of access and services that an SNMP principal can request from an SNMP engine.

In addition to enabling traps, as discussed in the previous section, enabling SNMPv3 requires five additional steps:

Step 1   **Configure the SNMP server engine ID**—Identifies the location and identity of the copy of SNMP to use.

Step 2   **Configure the SNMP server views**—Names or modifies a list of SNMP object identifiers (OIDs) that should be included or excluded.

Step 3   **Configure the SNMP server group names**—Defines the table that maps SNMP users to SNMP views.

Step 4   **Configure the SNMP server hosts**—Specifies the recipient of an SNMP notification operation.

Step 5   **Configure the SNMP server users**—Identifies a principal and attaches them to a group.

Configure SNMP-Server EngineID

The SNMP engine ID is a unique string that is used to identify the device for administration purposes. You do not need to specify an engine ID for the local device because it will default to a generated string using Cisco's enterprise number (1.3.6.1.4.1.9) and the MAC address of the first interface on the device.

When you specify an ID, you do not need to specify the entire 24-character engine ID if it contains trailing zeros. Specify only the portion of the engine ID up until the point where only zeros remain in the value. For example, to configure an engine ID of 123400000000000000000000, you can specify **snmp-server engineID local 1234**.

Changing the value of the local engine ID once it has been used invalidates the security digests of SNMPv3 users, and the users will have to be reconfigured. A user's password is converted to an MD5 or SHA security digest, which is based on both the password and the local engine ID. If the local value of the engine ID changes, the security digests of SNMPv3 users will be invalid.

Community strings are also affected when the engine ID changes. A remote engine ID is required when an SNMPv3 inform is configured. The remote engine ID is used to compute the security digest for authenticating and encrypting packets sent to a user on the remote host.

To configure a name for either the local or remote SNMP engine on the router, use the **snmp-server engineID** command in global configuration mode.

The syntax for the **snmp-server engineID** command is as follows:

```
snmp-server engineID [local engineid-string] | [remote ip-address
[udp-port udp-port-number] [vrf vrf-name] engineid-string]
```

- **local**—Specifies the SNMP engine ID on the local device.
- *engineid-string*—The character string that identifies the engine ID. Consists of up to 24 characters.
- **remote**—Specifies the SNMP engine ID on the remote device.
- *ip-address*—The IP address of the device that contains the remote copy of SNMP.
- **udp-port**—(Optional) Specifies a User Datagram Protocol (UDP) port of the host to use.
- *udp-port-number*—(Optional) The socket number on the remote device that contains the remote copy of SNMP. The default is 161.
- **vrf**—(Optional) Instance of a routing table.
- *vrf-name*—(Optional) Name of the VPN routing/forwarding (VRF) table to use to store data.

The following example shows how you could use the **snmp-server engineID** command to specify the SNMP engine ID for a remote engine. This example also configures the VRF name traps-vrf for SNMP communications with the remote device at 172.16.44.129.

```
router(config)# snmp-server engineID remote 172.16.44.129 vrf traps-vrf
80000009030000B064EFE100
```

Configure SNMP-Server Views

Group definitions identify views that permit or deny read, write, notify, and access functions. Views are simply lists of SNMP MIB OIDs based on the Abstract Syntax Notation One (ASN.1) tree.

There are two standard predefined views, **everything** and **restricted**, which can be used when a view is required. Use **everything** to indicate that the user can see all objects. Use **restricted** to indicate that the user can see three groups: system, snmpStats, and snmpParties.

To create or update a view entry, use the **snmp-server view** command in global configuration mode.

The syntax for the **snmp-server view** command is as follows:

```
snmp-server view view-name oid-tree {included | excluded}
```

- *view-name*—Label for the view record that you are updating or creating. The name is used to reference the record.

- *oid-tree*—OID of the ASN.1 subtree to be included or excluded from the view. To identify the subtree, specify a text string consisting of numbers, such as 1.3.6.2.4, or a word, such as system. Replace a single subidentifier with the asterisk (*) wildcard to specify a subtree family; for example, 1.3.*.4.

- **included** | **excluded**—Type of view. You must specify either **included** or **excluded**.

The following example of using the **snmp-server view** command creates a view named allmib2 that includes all objects in the MIB-II subtree:

```
router(config)# snmp-server view allmib2 mib-2 included
```

The following example of using the **snmp-server view** command creates a view named syscisco that includes all objects in the MIB-II system group and all objects in the Cisco enterprise MIB:

```
router(config)# snmp-server view syscisco system included
router(config)# snmp-server view syscisco cisco included
```

The following example of using the **snmp-server view** command creates a view named sysifsevn that includes all objects in the MIB-II system group except for sysServices (System 7) and all objects for interface 1 in the MIB-II interfaces group:

```
router(config)# snmp-server view sysifsevn system included
router(config)# snmp-server view sysifsevn system.7 excluded
router(config)# snmp-server view sysifsevn ifEntry.*.1 included
```

Configure SNMP-Server Group Names

SNMP groups identify the security levels and permissions that members of the group will be able to use. Group definitions include:

- Selection of the security model to use

- Whether packets will be authenticated

- Whether packets will be encrypted

- Which views to use for read, write, notify, and access usage levels

To configure a new SNMP group, or a table that maps SNMP users to SNMP views, use the **snmp-server group** command in global configuration mode.

The syntax for the **snmp-server group** command is as follows:

```
snmp-server group group-name {v1 | v2c | v3 {auth | noauth | priv}} [read read-view]
  [write write-view] [notify notify-view ] [access access-list]
```

- *group-name*—The name of the group.

- **v1**—Specifies SNMPv1, the least secure of the possible security models.

- **v2c**—Specifies SNMPv2c, the second least secure of the possible security models. It allows for the transmission of informs and counter 64, which allows for integers twice the width of what is normally allowed.

- **v3**—Specifies SNMPv3, the most secure of the possible security models.

- **auth**—Specifies authentication of a packet without encrypting it.

- **noauth**—Specifies no authentication of a packet.

- **priv**—Specifies authentication of a packet with encryption.

- **read**—(Optional) The option that allows you to specify a read view.

- read-view—A string (not to exceed 64 characters) that is the name of the view that enables you only to view the contents of the agent.

- **write**—(Optional) The option that allows you to specify a write view.

- *write-view*—A string (not to exceed 64 characters) that is the name of the view that enables you to enter data and configure the contents of the agent.

- **notify**—(Optional) The option that allows you to specify a notify view.

- *notify-view*—A string (not to exceed 64 characters) that is the name of the view that enables you to specify a notify, inform, or trap.

- **access**(—Optional) The option that enables you to specify an access list.

- *access-list*—A string (not to exceed 64 characters) that is the name of the access list.

The following example of using the **snmp-server group** command creates a group named supadmin that uses SNMPv3, authenticates and encrypts all packets, and uses the standard view **everything** for reading, writing, and notifying:

```
router(config)# snmp-server group supadmin v3 priv read everything write
    everything notify everything
```

The following example of using the **snmp-server group** command creates a group named genuser that uses SNMPv3, authenticates all packets, and uses specific views for reading, writing, and notifying:

```
router(config)# snmp-server group genuser v3 auth read genread write genwrite
    notify gennote
```

Configure SNMP-Server Hosts

SNMP notifications can be sent as traps or inform requests. Traps are not as reliable as informs because traps are not acknowledged by the receiving host, whereas informs are acknowledged. If an SNMP engine sends an inform that is not acknowledged, the SNMP engine will resend the notification.

Informs consume more resources in the agent and in the network. An inform request must be held in memory until a response is received or the request times out. Additionally, informs may be retried several times to achieve successful delivery, increasing traffic and contributing to a higher overhead on the network.

If you do not enter an **snmp-server host** command, no notifications are sent. To send notifications to multiple hosts, you must use a separate **snmp-server host** command for each host. You can specify multiple notification types in the command for each host.

When multiple **snmp-server host** commands are given for the same host and type of notification, each succeeding command overwrites the previous command and only the last **snmp-server host** command will be in effect. For example, if you enter two **snmp-server host inform** commands for the same host, only settings from the second command will be activated.

The **snmp-server host** command is used in conjunction with the **snmp-server enable** command, which specifies the SNMP notifications to send globally. Setting at least one **snmp-server enable** command and the **snmp-server host** command for that host will permit the host to receive most notifications.

The **snmp-server enable** command does not control all types of notifications. Some notification types are always enabled and others are enabled by different commands. For example, the linkUpDown notifications are controlled by the **snmp trap link-status** command and do not require an **snmp-server enable** command.

The **snmp-server host** command is used to identify the recipients of SNMP trap notifications. By default, no notifications are sent. You can enter this command with no keywords to send all notifications as traps to the host. In this case, no informs will be sent to this host.

The default is SNMPv1, if no **version** keyword is present. If version 3 is specified, but no security level is specified, the default security level is **noauth**.

The **no snmp-server host** command with no keywords will disable traps, but not informs. To disable informs, use the **no snmp-server host informs** command.

NOTE   If the community string is not defined using the **snmp-server community** command prior to using this command, the default form of the **snmp-server community** command will automatically be inserted into the configuration. The password (community string) used for this automatic configuration of the SNMP server community will be the same as specified in the **snmp-server host** command. This is the default behavior for Cisco IOS Release 12.0(3) and later.

To specify the recipient of an SNMP notification operation, use the **snmp-server host** command in global configuration mode.

The syntax for the **snmp-server host** command is as follows:

```
snmp-server host host-address [traps | informs] [version {1 | 2c | 3 [auth |
   noauth | priv]}] community-string [udp-port port] [notification-type]
   [vrf vrf-name]
```

- *host-address*—Name or Internet address of the host (the targeted recipient).
- **traps**—(Optional) Specifies that notifications should be sent as traps. This is the default.
- **informs**—(Optional) Specifies that notifications should be sent as informs.
- **version**—(Optional) Version of the SNMP used to send the traps. Version 3 is the most secure model, because it allows packet encryption with the **priv** keyword. If you use the **version** keyword, one of the following keywords must be specified:
  - **1**—SNMPv1. This option is not available with informs.
  - **2c**—SNMPv2C.
  - **3**—SNMPv3. One of the following three optional keywords can follow the version 3 keyword:
    - — **auth**—Enables MD5 and SHA packet authentication.
    - — **noauth**—Specifies that the noAuthNoPriv security level applies to this host. This is the default security level for SNMPv3.
    - — **priv**—Enables DES packet encryption (also called "privacy").
- *community-string*—Password-like community string sent with the notification operation. Though you can set this string using the **snmp-server host** command by itself, it is recommended that you define this string using the **snmp-server community** command prior to using the **snmp-server host** command.
- **udp-port** *port*—(Optional) UDP port of the host to use. The default is 162.
- *notification-type*—(Optional) Type of notification to be sent to the host. If no type is specified, all available notifications are sent. The notification type can be one or more of the following keywords:
  - **bgp**—Sends BGP state change notifications
  - **calltracker**—Sends Call Tracker call-start/call-end notifications
  - **config**—Sends configuration change notifications
  - **director**—Sends DistributedDirector-related notifications
  - **dspu**—Sends DSPU notifications

- **entity**—Sends Entity MIB modification notifications
- **envmon**—Sends Cisco enterprise-specific environmental monitor notifications when an environmental threshold is exceeded
- **frame-relay**—Sends Frame Relay notifications
- **hsrp**—Sends HSRP notifications
- **ipmobile**—Sends Mobile IP notifications
- **ipsec**—Sends IPSec notifications
- **isdn**—Sends ISDN notifications
- **llc2**—Sends LLC2 notifications
- **mpls-ldp**—Sends MPLS LDP notifications indicating status changes in LDP sessions
- **mpls-traffic-eng**—Sends MPLS traffic engineering notifications indicating changes in the status of MPLS traffic engineering tunnels
- **mpls-vpn**—Sends MPLS VPN notifications
- **pim**—Sends PIM notifications
- **repeater**—Sends standard repeater (hub) notifications
- **rsrb**—Sends RSRB notifications
- **rsvp**—Sends RSVP notifications
- **rtr**—Sends Service Assurance Agent (RTR) notifications
- **sdlc**—Sends SDLC notifications
- **sdllc**—Sends SDLLC notifications
- **snmp**—Sends any enabled RFC 1157 SNMP linkUp, linkDown, authenticationFailure, warmStart, and coldStart notifications

---

NOTE   To enable RFC 2233 compliant link up/down notifications, you should use the **snmp server link trap** command.

- **srp**—Sends SRP notifications
- **stun**—Sends STUN notifications
- **syslog**—Sends error message notifications (Cisco Syslog MIB); specify the level of messages to be sent with the **logging history level** command

- **tty**—Sends Cisco enterprise-specific notifications when a TCP connection closes

- **voice**—Sends SNMP poor quality of voice traps, when used with the **snmp enable peer-trap poor qov** command

- **vsimaster**—Sends VSI Master notifications

- **x25**—Sends X.25 event notifications

- **vrf** *vrf-name*—(Optional) Specifies the VRF table that should be used to send SNMP notifications.

You can use access lists with the **snmp-server community** command to control the capabilities of community strings. The following example could be used if you want to configure a unique SNMP community string named comaccess for traps, preventing SNMP polling access with this string:

```
router(config)# snmp-server community comaccess ro 10
router(config)# snmp-server host 172.20.2.160 comaccess
router(config)# access-list 10 deny any
```

You can enable all traps globally with the **snmp-server enable** command and control which traps get sent to specific hosts by attaching specific keywords to the **snmp-server host** command. The following example shows how you could send just SNMP traps using the community string comaccess:

```
router(config)# snmp-server enable traps
router(config)# snmp-server host myhost.cisco.com comaccess snmp
```

The following example sends the SNMP and Cisco environmental monitor enterprise-specific traps to address 172.30.44.87:

```
router(config)# snmp-server enable traps snmp
router(config)# snmp-server enable traps envmon
router(config)# snmp-server host 172.30.44.87 public snmp envmon
```

Configure SNMP-Server Users

The **snmp-server user** command identifies a user, assigns the user to a group, and identifies security parameters for that user.

To configure a new user to an SNMP group, use the **snmp-server user** command in global configuration mode. The syntax for the **snmp-server user** command is as follows:

```
snmp-server user username group-name [remote host [udp-port port]] {v1 | v2c | v3
    [encrypted] [auth {md5 | sha} auth-password]} [access access-list]
```

- *username*—The name of the user on the host that connects to the agent.

- *group-name*—The name of the group to which the user belongs.

- **remote** *host*—(Optional) Specifies a remote SNMP entity to which the user belongs, and the host name or IP address of that entity.

- **udp-port** *port*—(Optional) Specifies the UDP port number of the remote host. The default is UDP port 162.

- **v1**—Specifies that SNMPv1 should be used.

- **v2c**—Specifies that SNMPv2c should be used.

- **v3**—Specifies that the SNMPv3 security model should be used. Allows the use of the **encrypted** or **auth** keywords.

- **encrypted**—(Optional) Specifies whether the password appears in encrypted format (a series of digits, masking the true characters of the string).

- **auth**—(Optional) Specifies which authentication level should be used.

- **md5**—The HMAC-MD5-96 authentication level.

- **sha**—The HMAC-SHA-96 authentication level.

- *auth-password*—A string (not to exceed 64 characters) that enables the agent to receive packets from the host.

- **access** *access-list*—(Optional) Specifies an access list to be associated with this SNMP user. The *access-list* argument represents a value from 1 to 99 that is the identifier of the standard IP access list.

The following example adds user pjadams to the group supadmin, sets the security to SNMPv3 with encryption and SHA authentication, and sets the authentication password to "pqr732ni9f":

```
router(config)# snmp-server user pjadams supadmin v3 encrypted auth sha pqr732ni9f
```

Introduction to AAA for Cisco Routers

Authentication, authorization, and accounting (AAA) services are used to authenticate router administrators and users who wish to access the corporate LAN through dial-in or Internet connections.

AAA services provide higher degrees of scalability than the user-level and privileged EXEC authentication you have learned so far.

Unauthorized access and repudiation in campus, dialup, and Internet environments creates the potential for network intruders to gain access to sensitive network equipment and services. The Cisco AAA services enable systematic and scalable access security.

AAA Model: Network Security Architecture

Network and administrative access security in the Cisco environment—whether it involves campus, dialup, or Internet access—is based on a modular architecture that has three functional components:

- **Authentication**—Requires users and administrators to prove that they really are who they say they are, using a username and password, challenge and response, token cards, and other methods: "I am user *student* and my password *validateme* proves it."

- **Authorization**—After authenticating the user and administrator, authorization services decide which resources the user and administrator are allowed to access and which operations the user and administrator are allowed to perform: "User *student* can access host *2000_Server* with *Telnet*."

- **Accounting and auditing**—Accounting records what the user and administrator actually did, what they accessed, and how long they accessed it for accounting and auditing purposes. Accounting keeps track of how network resources are used: "User *student* accessed host *2000_Server* with *Telnet 15 times*."

The AAA model can be thought of as a series of questions and answers:

- Authentication
  - Q: Who are you?
  - A: I am user *student* and my password *validateme* proves it.
- Authorization
  - Q: What can you do? What can you access?
  - A: I can access host 2000_Server with Telnet.
- Accounting
  - Q: What did you do? How long did you do it? How often did you do it?
  - A: I accessed host 2000_Server with Telnet 15 times.

Implementing AAA

Cisco networking products support AAA access control using either a local security database or a remote security server database. A local security database is configured in the router for a small group of network users. A remote security database is a separate server running an AAA security protocol that provides AAA services for multiple network devices and large numbers of network users.

Cisco provides several ways to implement AAA services for Cisco routers and switch equipment, as shown in Figure 2-6:

- **Self-contained AAA**—AAA services may be self-contained in the router/NAS itself (also known as local authentication).

- **Cisco Secure ACS**—AAA services on the router or network access server (NAS) contact an external Cisco Secure ACS system for user and administrator authentication.

- **Cisco Secure ACS Solution Engine**—AAA services on the router or NAS contact an external Cisco Secure ACS Solution Engine for user and administrator authentication.

- **Third-party ACS**—(Not shown in Figure 2-6.) AAA services on the router or NAS contact an external, Cisco-approved, third-party ACS system for user and administrator authentication.

Figure 2-6   *Implementing Cisco AAA*

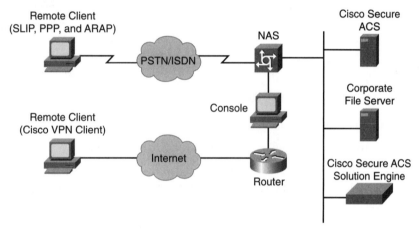

You can use AAA to manage and monitor:

- **Administrative access**—Console, Telnet, and Aux access
- **Remote user network access**—Async, group-async, BRI, and serial (PRI) access

Implementing AAA Using Local Services

If you have one or two NASs or routers providing access to your network, you probably want to store username and password security information locally on the Cisco NASs or routers. This is referred to as local authentication on a local security database. Local authentication characteristics are as follows:

- Used for small networks
- Username and password are stored in the Cisco router
- User authenticates against the local security database in the Cisco router
- Does not require an external database

The system administrator must populate the local security database by specifying username profiles for each user that might log in.

TIP | You can store hundreds of users in local databases, and local AAA implementations can be used to good advantage if the end-user requirement for remote access is low, if there is not a dedicated administrator, or if there is a low availability of network resources.

Local authentication typically works as shown in Figure 2-7.

Figure 2-7 *Implementing AAA Using Local Services*

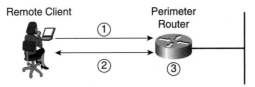

In Figure 2-7, the sequence of event occurs as follows:

1   The client establishes connection with the router.

2   The router prompts the user for her username and password.

3   The router authenticates the username and password in the local database. The connection is established and the user is authorized to access the network based on information in the local database.

Implementing AAA Using External Servers

The problem with local implementations of AAA is that it does not scale well. Most corporate environments have multiple Cisco routers and NASs with hundreds or thousands of users vying for access to the corporate LAN. Maintaining local databases for each Cisco router and NAS for this size network is just not feasible.

As shown in Figure 2-8, one or more Cisco Secure ACS systems (server or engine) can manage all user and administrative access needs for an entire corporate network using one or more databases.

Figure 2-8 *Implementing AAA Using External Servers*

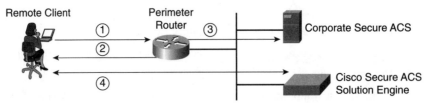

The sequence of events shown in Figure 2-8 is as follows:

1 The client establishes a connection with the router.

2 The router prompts the user for her username and password.

3 The router passes the username and password to the Cisco Secure ACS (server or engine).

4 The Cisco Secure ACS authenticates the user. The user is authorized to access the network based on information found in the Cisco Secure ACS database.

External AAA systems, such as the Cisco Secure ACS server or Cisco Secure ACS Solution Engine, communicate with Cisco routers and NASs using AAA protocols. These protocols are discussed in the next section.

The TACACS+ and RADIUS AAA Protocols

Shown in Figure 2-9, TACACS+ and RADIUS are the two predominant security server protocols used for AAA with Cisco firewalls, routers, and NASs. TACACS+ remains more secure than RADIUS, while RADIUS has a robust API and strong accounting. Cisco developed the Cisco Secure ACS family of AAA servers to support both TACACS+ and RADIUS.

Figure 2-9   *TACACS+ and RADIUS AAA Protocols*

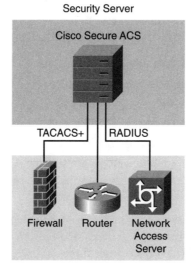

TACACS+ is considered to be more versatile, but RADIUS is preferred for enterprise ISPs because it uses fewer CPU cycles and is less memory-intensive. Some other differences between the protocols are described in Table 2-1.

Table 2-1   *TACACS+ Versus RADIUS*

TACACS+	RADIUS
Uses TCP.	Uses UDP.
Encrypts the entire body of the packet; more secure.	Encrypts only the password in the access-request packet; less secure.
Uses the AAA architecture, which separates authentication, authorization, and accounting.	Combines authentication and authorization.
Cisco proprietary.	Industry standard (created by Livingston Enterprises, Inc.).
Provides two ways to control the authorization of router commands: on a per-user or per-group basis.	Does not allow users to control which commands can be executed on a router.
Useful for router management.	Not useful for router management.
Database supports storage of encrypted passwords.	Database does not support storage of encrypted passwords.

The Cisco Secure ACS family is a comprehensive and flexible platform for securing access to the network. Cisco Secure ACS secures network access for the following:

- Dialup via Cisco NAS and routers
- Router and switch console and vty port access for administrators
- Cisco PIX Firewall access
- VPN 3000 Series Concentrators (RADIUS only)
- Wireless LAN (WLAN) support using Cisco Light Extensible Authentication Protocol (LEAP) and Protected Extensible Authentication Protocol (PEAP)
- Wireless 802.1x authentication for switches

Cisco Secure ACS works closely with the NAS, router, VPN 3000 Concentrator, and PIX Firewall to implement a comprehensive security policy via the AAA architecture. It also works with industry-leading token cards and servers.

The Cisco Secure ACS server is easily managed via standard browsers, enabling simple moves, adds, and changes to usernames, passwords, and network devices. It is implemented on both the UNIX and Windows NT/2000 Server platforms.

The Cisco Secure ACS Solution Engine performs the same functions as the Cisco Secure ACS server products, but in a single rack-unit (RU) mounted, dedicated hardware platform.

NOTE   This Cisco Secure ACS Solution Engine is only available in V3.2 or later.

You will learn more about using these remote AAA alternatives in Chapter 3, "Advanced AAA Security for Cisco Router Networks."

Authentication Methods and Ease of Use

The most common user authentication method is the use of usernames and passwords. Username and password methods range from weak to strong in authentication power. Simple authentication methods use a database of usernames and passwords, while methods that are more complex use one-time passwords (OTPs).

Figure 2-10 shows the strength and ease of use for the various authentication methods.

Figure 2-10 *Authentication Methods and Ease of Use*

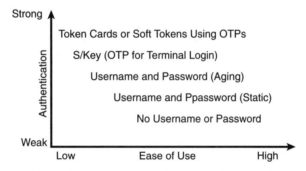

Consider each of the authentication methods listed in Figure 2-10 from the bottom of the list up:

- **No username or password**—Some system administrators and users decide not to use the username and password capabilities of their NASs. This is the least secure option. A network intruder only has to discover the access method to gain access to the networked system.

- **Username and password (static)**—Stays the same until changed by the system administrator or user. Susceptible to playback attacks, eavesdropping, theft, and password-cracking programs.

- **Username and password (aging)**—Expires after a set time (usually 30 to 60 days) and must be reset, usually by the user, before network access is granted. Susceptible to playback attacks, eavesdropping, theft, and password cracking, but to a lesser degree than static username and password pairs.

- **OTPs**—A stronger method, providing the most secure username and password method. Most OTP systems are based on a "secret pass-phrase," which is used to generate a list of passwords. OTPs are only good for one login and are, therefore, not useful to anyone who manages to eavesdrop and capture them. Some systems use a portion of the previous password to generate the next password, making it that much more difficult to trick the system into generating a usable password.

- **Token cards and soft tokens**—Based on something you have (token card) and something you know (token card PIN). Token cards are typically small electronic devices about the size and complexity of a credit card–sized calculator. There are many token card vendors, and each has its own token card server. The PIN is entered into the card, which generates a secure password. A token server receives and validates the password. The password interplay usually consists of a remote client computer, a NAS, and a security server running token security software. This presents a problem if you want to dial in with Point-to-Point Protocol (PPP) using dial-on-demand routing (DDR) or multilink. In this case, a static password is assigned for the PPP connection and an ACL restricts the user to Telnet to the access server. Once connected to the line vty number, the user can use the lock-and-key feature to "open the ACL" or can merge their interface configuration with a virtual template from a TACACS+ server to replace the ACL. This is also known as "double authentication."

The authentication method should be chosen and implemented based on the guidelines established in the network security policy.

Authentication: Remote PC Username and Password

A typical example of dialup authentication using usernames and password authentication is shown in Figure 2-11. On the client end, the Windows 2000 LAN connection prompts the user for their username and password, which is sent over communication lines using TCP/IP and PPP to a remote NAS or a security server for authentication. As a matter of policy and for security reasons, do not allow users to check the Save Password check box.

Figure 2-11 *Authentication: Remote PC Username and Password*

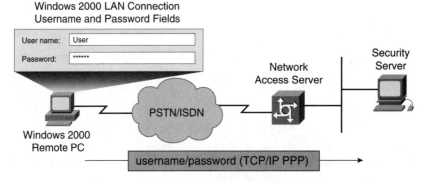

Authentication of usernames and passwords is commonly used with secure Internet applications. For example, some Cisco Connection Online (CCO) applications require a user to be registered and to possess a username and password assigned by CCO. When the user accesses a secure CCO application using a web browser, the application causes the web browser to display a window requesting a username and password. The username and password can be validated using an AAA security server.

Authentication: One-Time Passwords, S/Key

Remote logins can allow passwords to be sent as clear text over networks. An eavesdropper could capture passwords and use them to gain unauthorized access to systems. One way to create passwords that can be safely sent over remote connections is to use a one-way hashing algorithm to create an OTP scheme, which is what S/Key does.

S/Key provides a list of OTPs that are generated by an S/Key program hash function. The passwords are sent in clear text over the network. S/Key cannot be used unless the server supports S/Key.

S/Key uses either message digest algorithm 4 (MD4) or MD5 (one-way hashing algorithms developed by Ron Rivest) to create an OTP system. In this system, passwords are sent clear text over the network; however, after a password has been used, it is no longer useful to the eavesdropper. The biggest advantage of S/Key is that it protects against eavesdroppers without modification of client software and imposes only marginal inconvenience to the users.

As Figure 2-12 illustrates, the S/Key system involves three main pieces:

- **The client**—The client is responsible for providing the login shell to the user. It does not contain any persistent storage for password information.

- **The host**—The host is responsible for processing the user's login request. It stores the current OTP and the login sequence number in a file. It is also responsible for providing the client with a seed value.

- **A password calculator**—The password calculator is a one-way hashing function, which is defined as a function that loses information each time that it is applied.

Figure 2-12 *Authentication: One-Time Passwords, S/Key*

The network protocol between the client and the host is completely independent of the scheme. Cisco Secure ACS supports S/Key authentication.

Authentication: Token Cards and Servers

Another OTP authentication method that adds a new layer of security is accomplished with a token card (or smart card) and a token server. Each token card, about the size of a credit card, is programmed to a specific user and each user has a unique PIN that can generate a password keyed strictly to the corresponding card. OTP authentication takes place between the specified token server with a token card database and the user.

Token cards and servers generally work as shown in Figure 2-13.

Figure 2-13 *Authentication—Token Cards and Servers*

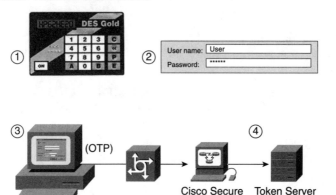

The list that follows describes the transactions listed by number in Figure 2-13:

1 The user generates an OTP with the token card by using a security algorithm.

2 The user enters the OTP into the authentication window generated by the remote client (in this example, the Windows Dial-Up Networking window).

3 The remote client sends the OTP to the token server via the network and a NAS.

4 The token server uses the same algorithm to verify that the password is correct and authenticates the remote user.

Token cards are credit card–sized electronic devices that contain the same password-generating algorithm as the token authentication server. Both the token card and the token server use the same seed to generate the same OTP, or token. The card-generated token is sent to the token server. If this token matches the one that the token server generated, the user is authenticated. Two token card and server methods are used:

- **Time-based**—In this system, the token card contains a cryptographic key and generates a password (or token) using a PIN entered by the user. The password is entered into the remote client, which sends it to the token server. The password is loosely synchronized in time to the token server. The server compares the token received to a token generated internally. If they match, the user is authenticated and allowed access.

- **Challenge-response**—In this system, the token card stores a cryptographic key. The token server generates a random string of digits and sends it to the remote client that is trying to access the network. The remote user enters the random string, and the token card computes a cryptographic function using the stored key and random string. The result is sent back to the token server, which has also computed the function. If the results match, the user is authenticated.

Token cards are now implemented in software for installation on the remote client. SofToken, which generates single-use passwords without the associated cost of a hardware token, is one example of software token cards. Cisco Secure ACS 3.2 for Windows supports authentication from the following token-card servers:

- ActivCard Token Server 3.1
- CRYPTOCard CRYPTOAdmin 5.16
- PassGo (formerly AXENT) Defender version 4.1.3
- RSA ACE/Server version 5.1 and ACE Agent version 5.5 for Windows 2000
- Secure Computing PremierAccess Server version 3.1

Cisco Secure ACS 2.3(6) for UNIX supports authentication with token-card servers from the following companies:

- CRYPTOCard
- Secure Computing
- Security Dynamics, Inc.

AAA Example: Authentication via PPP Link

An important component to consider in remote access security, as shown in Figure 2-14, is support for authentication accomplished with Password Authentication Protocol (PAP), CHAP, and Microsoft CHAP (MS-CHAP). PPP is a standard encapsulation protocol for the transport of different network-layer protocols (including, but not limited to, IP) across serial, point-to-point links. PPP enables authentication between remote clients and servers using PAP, CHAP, or MS-CHAP.

Figure 2-14 *AAA Example: Authentication via PPP Link*

PAP

PAP provides a simple method for the remote client to establish its identity using a two-way handshake. The handshake is done only after initial PPP link establishment. After the link establishment phase is complete, a username and password pair is repeatedly sent by the peer to the authenticator until authentication is acknowledged or the connection is terminated. Disadvantages of PAP include:

- PAP uses a clear text, repeated password.
- PAP is subject to eavesdropping and replay attacks.

CHAP

CHAP is used to periodically verify the identity of the peer using a three-way handshake. The handshake is done upon initial link establishment, and may be repeated anytime after the link has been established. Features of CHAP include:

- CHAP uses a unique secret password for every remote user.

- A random-number challenge is sent upon linkup and may be repeated periodically to prevent session hijacking.

- The CHAP response is an MD5 hash of the challenge plus the secret password, providing authentication.

- CHAP is a robust method of countering sniffing and replay attacks.

CHAP provides protection against playback attack by using a variable challenge value that is unique and unpredictable. The use of repeated challenges is intended to limit the time of exposure to any single attack. The NAS (or a security server such as Cisco Secure ACS) is in control of the frequency and timing of the challenges. A major advantage of the constantly changing challenge string is that the line cannot be sniffed and played back later to gain unauthorized access to the network.

This authentication method depends upon a secret known only to the authenticator and that remote client. The secret is not sent over the link. Although the authentication is only one-way, by negotiating CHAP in both directions, the same secret set may easily be used for mutual authentication.

CHAP requires that the secret be available in plain-text form. Irreversibly encrypted password databases that are commonly available, such as the Windows NT SAM hive, cannot be used.

MS-CHAP

MS-CHAP is Microsoft's version of CHAP. MS-CHAP is an extension of the CHAP described in RFC 1994. MS-CHAP enables PPP authentication between a PC using Microsoft Windows and a NAS. PPP authentication using MS-CHAP can be used with or without AAA security services.

MS-CHAP differs from standard CHAP as follows:

- MS-CHAP is enabled while the remote client and the NAS negotiate PPP parameters after link establishment.

- The MS-CHAP Response packet is in a format designed for compatibility with Microsoft Windows networking products.

- MS-CHAP version 2 enables the network security server (authenticator) to control retry and password-changing mechanisms. MS-CHAP allows the remote client to change the MS-CHAP password.

- MS-CHAP version 2 defines a set of reason-for-failure codes returned to the remote client by the NAS.

Cisco routers support MS-CHAP version 1 in Cisco IOS Release 11.3 and later with the **ppp authentication ms-chap** command. MS-CHAP version 2 is supported in Cisco IOS Release 12.2 and later.

Cisco NASs and routers are configured to perform authorization using the **aaa authorization** commands.

You can configure Cisco Secure ACS to perform authorization tasks with NAS and routers. The per-user security policy determines how authorization is configured.

You can configure Cisco NAS and routers to capture and display accounting data by using the **aaa accounting** commands, including the following: **exec** commands; network services such as SLIP, PPP, and AppleTalk Remote Access (ARA); and system-level events not associated with users.

Configuring AAA for Cisco Perimeter Routers

The remainder of this chapter describes how to configure a Cisco perimeter router to perform AAA using a local database.

Authenticating Perimeter Router Access

Following the Cisco SAFE axiom that all routers are targets, it is important that you secure your network access servers and Internet routers at all interfaces.

As Figure 2-15 illustrates, you must configure the perimeter router to secure administrative access and remote LAN network access using AAA commands.

Figure 2-15 *Authenticating Perimeter Router Access*

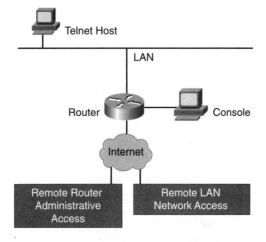

Table 2-2 compares the router access modes, port types, and AAA command elements.

Table 2-2   *Comparison of Router Access Modes, Port Types, and AAA Command Elements*

Access Type	Modes	NAS Ports	AAA Command Element
Remote administrative access	Character (line/exec mode)	tty, vty, aux, and cty	login, exec, NASI connection, ARAP, and enable
Remote network access	Packet (interface mode)	async, group-async BRI, and serial (PRI)	PPP, network, and ARAP

Perimeter Router AAA Configuration Process

The following are the general steps required to configure the perimeter router for AAA:

Step 1   Secure access to privileged EXEC and configuration mode on vty, asynchronous, auxiliary, and tty ports.

Step 2   Enable AAA globally on the perimeter router by using the **aaa new-model** command.

Step 3   Configure AAA authentication lists.

Step 4   Configure AAA authorization for use after the user has passed authentication.

Step 5   Configure the AAA accounting options for how you want to write accounting records.

Step 6   Verify the configuration.

Secure Access to Privileged EXEC and Configuration Mode

Two methods for securing privileged EXEC mode for Cisco routers are as follows:

```
router(config)# enable password changeme
router(config)# service password-encryption
!
router(config)# enable secret supersecret
```

The use of the **enable password** command should be coupled with the use of the **service password-encryption** command.

This method of securing privileged EXEC mode is not as secure as the use of the **enable secret** command with its MD5 hashing.

Always use one of these methods to secure privileged EXEC mode. It is recommended that you use the **enable secret** command whenever possible because it has a stronger hashing algorithm than the **service password-encryption** command and because **enable password** is written to the configuration file in clear text.

An enable password is defined as follows:

- Must contain from 1 to 25 upper- and lowercase alphanumeric characters
- Must not have a number as the first character
- Can have leading, intermediate, and trailing spaces

Enabling AAA Globally Using the aaa new-model Command

The first step to configure a NAS or router to use the AAA process is to establish an AAA section in the configuration file by using the **aaa new-model** command.

The **aaa new-model** command forces the router to override every other authentication method previously configured for the router lines. If an administrative Telnet or console session is lost while enabling AAA on a Cisco router, and no local AAA user authentication account and method exists, the administrator will be locked out of the router. Therefore, it is important that you configure a local database account to help prevent administrative access lockout while configuring AAA.

At a minimum, the following commands should be entered, in the order shown:

```
Router(config)# aaa new-model
Router(config)# username username password password
Router(config)# aaa authentication login default local
```

Specifying the "local" authentication method enables you to re-establish your Telnet or console session and use the locally defined authentication list to access the router once more. If you fail to do this and you then become locked out of the router, physical access to the router is required (console session), with a minimum of having to perform a password-recovery sequence. At worst, the entire configuration saved in NVRAM can be lost.

The **aaa authentication login** command is covered in more detail in the upcoming section titled, "**aaa authentication login** Command."

aaa authentication Commands

A complete list of the available **aaa authentication** commands and their syntax for Cisco IOS release 12.3 or later can be obtained at Cisco.com. It is important that you learn three of these commands and how to implement them in an AAA environment:

- **aaa authentication login**—Determines which authentication steps to use when users attempt to log in to the router.

- **aaa authentication ppp**—Determines which authentication steps to use for user sessions on serial interfaces that use PPP, a common situation for dial-in users.

- **aaa authentication enable default**—Determines which authentication steps to use when someone tries to enter privileged EXEC mode with the **enable** command.

After enabling AAA globally on the access server, you need to define the authentication method lists and apply them to lines and interfaces. These authentication method lists are security profiles that indicate the service (PPP, AppleTalk Remote Access Protocol (ARAP), NetWare Access Server Interface (NASI), or login) and authentication method (local, TACACS+, RADIUS, login, or Enable password). Up to four authentication methods may be applied to a line or interface. A good security practice is to have local authentication as a last method to recover from a severed link to the chosen method's server.

Complete the following steps to define an authentication method list using the **aaa authentication** command:

Step 1 Specify the service (PPP, ARAP, or NASI) or login authentication.

Step 2 Identify a list name or default. A list name is any alphanumeric string you choose. You assign different authentication methods to different named lists. You can specify only one dial-in protocol per authentication method list. However, you can create multiple authentication method lists with each of these options. You must give each list a different name.

Step 3 Specify the authentication method and how the router should handle requests when one of the methods is not operating (for example, the AAA server is down). You can specify up to four methods for AAA to try before stopping the authentication process.

Step 4 After defining these authentication method lists, apply them to one of the following:

  - **Lines**—tty, vty, console, aux, and async lines or the console port for login and asynchronous lines (in most cases) for ARA

- **Interfaces**—Interfaces sync, async, and virtual configured for PPP, SLIP, NASI, or ARAP

Step 5   Use the **aaa authentication** command in global configuration mode to enable the AAA authentication processes.

aaa authentication login Command

Use the **aaa authentication login** command in global configuration mode to set AAA authentication at login. Three possible configurations for **aaa login authentication** that you could use are as follows:

```
router(config)# aaa authentication login default enable
router(config)# aaa authentication login console-in local
router(config)# aaa authentication login tty-in line
```

In these examples, **console-in** and **tty-in** are simply method list names created by the administrator. The following is the syntax for the **aaa authentication login** command:

```
aaa authentication login {default | list-name} method1 [method2…]
```

- **default**—Uses the listed authentication methods that follow this argument as the default list of methods when a user logs in.
- *list-name*—Character string used to name the list of authentication methods activated when a user logs in.
- *method*—Specifies at least one of the following keywords:
  - **enable**—Uses the enable password for authentication
  - **krb5**—Uses Kerberos 5 for authentication
  - **krb5-telnet**—Uses Kerberos 5 Telnet authentication protocol when using Telnet to connect to the router
  - **line**—Uses the line password for authentication
  - **local**—Uses the local username database for authentication
  - **local-case**—Uses case-sensitive local username authentication
  - **none**—Uses no authentication
  - **group radius**—Uses the list of all RADIUS servers for authentication
  - **group tacacs+**—Uses the list of all TACACS+ servers for authentication
  - **group** *group-name*—Uses a subset of RADIUS or TACACS+ servers for authentication as defined by the **aaa group server radius** or **aaa group server tacacs+** commands

aaa authentication ppp Command

You can use the **aaa authentication ppp** command in global configuration mode to specify one or more AAA authentication methods for use on serial interfaces running PPP, as these examples show:

```
router(config)# aaa authentication ppp default local
router(config)# aaa authentication ppp dial-in local none
```

The second example uses **dial-in** as a list name. The following is the syntax for the **aaa authentication ppp** command:

```
aaa authentication ppp {default | list-name} method1 [method2…]
```

- **default**—Uses the listed authentication methods that follow this argument as the default list of methods when a user logs in.

- *list-name*—Character string used to name the list of authentication methods activated when a user logs in.

- *method*—Specifies at least one of the following keywords:

  - **if-needed**—Does not authenticate if user has already been authenticated on a tty line

  - **krb5**—Uses Kerberos 5 for authentication (can only be used for PAP authentication)

  - **local**—Uses the local username database for authentication

  - **local-case**—Uses case-sensitive local username authentication

  - **none**—Uses no authentication

  - **group** *group-name*—Uses a subset of RADIUS or TACACS+ servers for authentication as defined by the **aaa group server radius** or **aaa group server tacacs+** commands

aaa authentication enable default Command

Use the **aaa authentication enable default** command in global configuration mode to enable AAA authentication to determine whether a user can access the privileged command level, as this example shows:

```
router(config)# aaa authentication enable default group tacacs+
```

The following is the syntax for the **aaa authentication enable default** command:

```
aaa authentication enable default method1 [method2…]
```

- *method*—Specifies at least one of the following keywords:

  - **enable**—Uses the enable password for authentication

- **line**—Uses the line password for authentication
- **none**—Uses no authentication
- **group radius**—Uses the list of all RADIUS servers for authentication
- **group tacacs+**—Uses the list of all TACACS+ servers for authentication
- **group** *group-name*—Uses a subset of RADIUS or TACACS+ servers for authentication as defined by the **aaa group server radius** or **aaa group server tacacs+** commands

Apply Authentication Commands to Lines and Interfaces

Authentication commands can be applied to router lines and interfaces as shown in Example 2-11.

Example 2-11 *Applying Authentication Commands to Router Lines/Interfaces*

```
router(config)# aaa new-model
router(config)# aaa authentication login default enable
router(config)# aaa authentication login console-in group tacacs+ local
router(config)# aaa authentication login dial-in group tacacs+
router(config)# username ConAdmin1 password 87*(rTYgom)
router(config)# line console 0
router(config-line)# login authentication console-in
router(config)# int s3/0
router(config-if)# ppp authentication chap dial-in
```

The following is a brief explanation of the lines in Example 2-11:

- **aaa new-model**—Enables AAA on the router.
- **aaa authentication login default enable**—Establishes the enable password as the default login method.
- **aaa authentication login console-in group tacacs+ local**—Establishes the use of TACACS+ authentication whenever the list named console-in is used. If TACACS+ authentication fails, then authenticate with a local login name and password.
- **aaa authentication login dial-in group tacacs+**—Establishes the use of TACACS+ authentication whenever the list named dial-in is used.
- **username ConAdmin1 password 87*(rTYgom)**—Establishes a local username and password, most likely to use with the console-in login method list.
- **line console 0**—Enters line console configuration mode.

- **login authentication console-in**—Uses the console-in list for login authentication on console port 0.

- **int s3/0**—Specifies port 0 of serial interface slot number 3.

- **ppp authentication chap dial-in**—Uses the dial-in list for PPP CHAP authentication on the interface specified in the previous line.

NOTE   Recommended practice is that you always use a default list for AAA last-resort authentication.

---

aaa authorization Command

Use the **aaa authorization** command in global configuration mode to set parameters that restrict user access to a network. The following is the syntax for the **aaa authorization** command:

```
aaa authorization {network | exec | commands level | reverse-access | configuration}
{default | list-name} method1 [method2…]
```

- **network**—Runs authorization for all network-related service requests, including SLIP, PPP, PPP NCPs, and ARA.

- **exec**—Runs authorization to determine whether the user is allowed to run an EXEC shell. This facility might return user profile information such as **autocommand** information.

- **commands**—Runs authorization for all commands at the specified privilege level.

- *level*—Specific command level that should be authorized. Valid entries are 0 to 15.

- **reverse-access**—Runs authorization for reverse access connections, such as reverse Telnet.

- **configuration**—Downloads the configuration from the AAA server.

- **default**—Uses the listed authentication methods that follow this argument as the default list of methods for authorization.

- *list-name*—Character string used to name the list of authentication methods.

- *method*—Specifies at least one of the following keywords:

  - **group** *group-name*—Uses a subset of RADIUS or TACACS+ servers for authentication as defined by the **aaa group server radius** or **aaa group server tacacs+** commands

- **if-authenticated**—Allows the user to access the requested function if the user is authenticated
- **krb5-instance**—Uses the instance defined by the **kerberos instance map** command
- **local**—Uses the local database for authorization
- **none**—No authorization is performed

There is a provision for naming the authorization list after specifying the service, just like there is for naming an authentication list. Also, the list of methods is not limited to just a single method, but rather may have up to four methods listed for failing over to, just as the **aaa authentication** command could.

Named authorization lists allow you to define different methods for authorization and accounting and apply those methods on a per-interface or per-line basis. Example 2-12 demonstrates some possible uses of the **aaa authorization** command.

Example 2-12 *Different Implementations of the* **aaa authorization** *Command*

```
router(config)# enable secret level 1 Patriot
router(config)# enable secret level 15 334tTjP9#a
router(config)# aaa new-model
router(config)# aaa authentication login default enable
router(config)# aaa authentication login console-in group tacacs+ local
router(config)# aaa authentication login dial-in group tacacs+
router(config)# username ConAdmin1 password 87*(rTYgom
router(config)# aaa authorization commands 1 alpha local
router(config)# aaa authorization commands 15 bravo if-authenticated group TacPlus local
router(config)# aaa authorization network charlie local none
router(config)# aaa authorization exec delta if-authenticated group TacPlus
router(config)# privilege exec level 1 ping
router(config)# line console 0
router(config-line)# login authentication console-in
router(config)# int s3/0
router(config-if)# ppp authentication chap dial-in
```

The list that follows briefly describes each line in Example 2-12:

- **enable secret level 1 Patriot**—Establishes an enable secret password for level 1 users.
- **enable secret level 15 334tTjP9#a**—Establishes an enable secret password for level 15 users.
- **aaa new-model**—Enables AAA on the router.
- **aaa authentication login default enable**—Establishes the enable password as the default login method.

- **aaa authentication login console-in group tacacs+ local**—Establishes the use TACACS+ authentication whenever the list named console-in is used. If TACACS+ authentication fails, then authenticate with a local login name and password.

- **aaa authentication login dial-in group tacacs+**—Establishes the use of TACACS+ authentication whenever the list named dial-in is used.

- **username ConAdmin1 password 87*(rTYgom**—Establishes a local username and password, most likely to use with the console-in login method list.

- **aaa authorization commands 1 alpha local**—Uses local username database to authorize the use of all level 1 commands.

- **aaa authorization commands 15 bravo if-authenticated group TacPlus local**—Lets the user run level 15 commands if the user is already authenticated. If the user is not already authenticated, the user must authenticate against one of the TACACS+ servers in group TacPlus before being allowed to run level 15 commands.

- **aaa authorization network charlie local none**—Uses the local database to authorize the use of all network services, such as SLIP, PPP, and ARAP. If the local server is not available, this command performs no authorization, and the user can use all network services.

- **aaa authorization exec delta if-authenticated group TacPlus**—Lets the user run the EXEC process if the user is already authenticated. If the user is not already authenticated, the user must authenticate against one of the TACACS+ servers in group TacPlus before being allowed to run EXEC commands.

- **privilege exec level 1 ping**—Enables ping for level 1 users.

- **line console 0**—Enters line console configuration mode.

- **login authentication console-in**—Uses the console-in list for login authentication on console port 0.

- **int s3/0**—Specifies port 0 of serial interface slot number 3.

- **ppp authentication chap dial-in**—Uses the dial-in list for PPP CHAP authentication on the interface specified in the previous line.

aaa accounting Commands

The AAA accounting feature lets you track the services that users are accessing and the amount of network resources they are consuming.

You use the **aaa accounting** global configuration command to set parameters that record what a user is doing or has done. You use accounting commands in global configuration mode for auditing and billing purposes. The following is the syntax for the **aaa accounting** command:

```
aaa accounting {auth-proxy | system | network | exec | connection | commands level}
  {default | list-name} [vrf vrf-name] {start-stop | stop-only | none} [broadcast]
  [method1 [method2]]
```

- **auth-proxy**—Provides information about all authenticated-proxy user events.

- **system**—Performs accounting for all system-level events not associated with users, such as reloads.

- **network**—Runs accounting for all network-related service requests, including SLIP, PPP, PPP Network Control Protocols (NCPs), and ARAP.

- **exec**—Runs accounting for EXEC shell session. This keyword might return user profile information such as what is generated by the **autocommand** command.

- **connection**—Provides information about all outbound connections made from the NAS, such as Telnet, local-area transport (LAT), TN3270, packet assembler and disassembler (PAD), and rlogin.

- **commands** *level*—Runs accounting for all commands at the specified privilege level. Valid privilege level entries are integers from 0 through 15.

- **default**—Uses the listed accounting methods that follow this argument as the default list of methods for accounting services.

- *list-name*—Character string used to name the list accounting methods.

- **vrf** *vrf-name*—(Optional) Specifies a VRF configuration. Note that VRF is used only with system accounting.

- **start-stop**—Sends a "start" accounting notice at the beginning of a process and a "stop" accounting notice at the end of a process. The "start" accounting record is sent in the background. The requested user process begins regardless of whether the "start" accounting notice was received by the accounting server.

- **stop-only**—Sends a "stop" accounting notice at the end of the requested user process.

- **none**—Disables accounting services on this line or interface.

- **broadcast**—(Optional) Enables sending accounting records to multiple AAA servers. Simultaneously sends accounting records to the first server in each group. If the first server is unavailable, failover occurs using the backup servers defined within that group.

- *method*—Specifies at least one of the following keywords:

    - **group radius**—Uses the list of all RADIUS servers for accounting as defined by the **aaa group server radius** command

- **group tacacs+**—Uses the list of all TACACS+ servers for accounting as defined by the **aaa group server tacacs+** command

- **group** *group-name*—Uses a subset of RADIUS or TACACS+ servers for accounting as defined by the server group *group-name*

At a minimum, you should enable the following accounting commands on your router:

- **aaa accounting system wait-start local**—Audits system events using the wait-start accounting method.

- **aaa accounting network stop-only local**—Sends stop record notices when network services terminate.

- **aaa accounting exec start-stop local**—Sends a start record notice when the EXEC process begins and a stop record when the EXEC process ends.

- **aaa accounting commands 15 wait-start local**—Sends a start record notice and waits for acknowledgement before any level 15 command can begin. Sends a stop record notice when the command terminates.

Troubleshooting AAA

You can troubleshoot AAA using the **debug** commands, including **debug aaa authentication**, **debug aaa authorization**, and **debug aaa accounting**.

You can use the following **debug** commands on the NAS to trace TACACS+ packets and monitor authentication, authorization, or accounting activities:

- **debug aaa authentication**—Displays debugging messages on authentication functions

- **debug aaa authorization**—Displays debugging messages on authorization functions

- **debug aaa accounting**—Displays debugging messages on accounting functions

debug aaa authentication Command

Use the **debug aaa authentication** privileged EXEC command to display information on AAA and TACACS+ authentication. Use the **no debug aaa authentication** form of the command to disable this debug mode.

You would use the **debug aaa authentication** command when AAA does not appear to be working correctly and you suspect a problem in the authentication. When reviewing output from the **debug aaa authentication** command, you would be looking for any words or phrases that indicate a problem. Words such as fail, denied, and refused indicate some kind of problem worthy of your attention.

Example 2-13 provides sample debug output for a successful AAA authentication using a TACACS+ server and providing the following information (highlighted in the output):

- A single EXEC login that uses the "default" method list and the first method, TACACS+, is displayed.

- The TACACS+ server sends a GETUSER request to prompt for the username.

- Once the username has been received, the TACACS+ server sends a GETPASS request to prompt for the password.

- Upon successful authentication, the TACACS+ server sends a PASS response to indicate a successful login.

- The number 32177624 is the session ID, which is unique for each authentication. Use this ID number to distinguish between different authentications if several are occurring concurrently.

Example 2-13 debug aaa authentication *Output*

```
router# debug aaa authentication
10:18:12: AAA/AUTHEN: create_user user='' ruser='' port='tty19'
 rem_addr='172.31.60.15' authen_type=1 service=1 priv=1
10:18:12: AAA/AUTHEN/START (0): port='tty19' list='' action=LOGIN service=LOGIN
10:18:12: AAA/AUTHEN/START (0): using "default" list
10:18:12: AAA/AUTHEN/START (32177624): Method=TACACS+
10:18:12: TAC+ (32177624): received authen response status = GETUSER
10:18:12: AAA/AUTHEN (32177624): status = GETUSER
10:18:15: AAA/AUTHEN/CONT (32177624): continue_login
10:18:15: AAA/AUTHEN (32177624): status = GETUSER
10:18:15: AAA/AUTHEN (32177624): Method=TACACS+
10:18:15: TAC+: send AUTHEN/CONT packet
10:18:15: TAC+ (32177624): received authen response status = GETPASS
10:18:15: AAA/AUTHEN (32177624): status = GETPASS
10:18:20: AAA/AUTHEN/CONT (32177624): continue_login
10:18:20: AAA/AUTHEN (32177624): status = GETPASS
10:18:20: AAA/AUTHEN (32177624): Method=TACACS+
10:18:20: TAC+: send AUTHEN/CONT packet
10:18:20: TAC+ (32177624): received authen response status = PASS
10:18:20: AAA/AUTHEN (32177624): status = PASS
```

debug aaa authorization Command

Use the **debug aaa authorization** privileged EXEC command to display information on AAA and TACACS+ authorization. Use the **no debug aaa authorization** form of the command to disable this debug mode. Example 2-14 provides a sample of the use of this command.

Example 2-14 debug aaa authorization *Output*

```
router# debug aaa authorization
2:23:21: AAA/AUTHOR (0): user='carrel'
2:23:21: AAA/AUTHOR (0): send AV service=shell
2:23:21: AAA/AUTHOR (0): send AV cmd*
2:23:21: AAA/AUTHOR (342885561): Method=TACACS+
2:23:21: AAA/AUTHOR/TAC+ (342885561): user=carrel
2:23:21: AAA/AUTHOR/TAC+ (342885561): send AV service=shell
2:23:21: AAA/AUTHOR/TAC+ (342885561): send AV cmd*
2:23:21: AAA/AUTHOR (342885561): Post authorization status = FAIL
```

Example 2-14 shows output from the **debug aaa authorization** command where an EXEC authorization for user carrel is performed:

- On the first line, the username carrel is authorized.

- On the second and third lines, the attribute value (AV) pairs are authorized.

- The debug output displays a line for each AV pair that is authenticated.

- The display indicates the authorization method used.

- The final line in the display indicates the status of the authorization process, which, in this case, has failed.

The **aaa authorization** command causes a request packet containing a series of AV pairs to be sent to the TACACS+ daemon as part of the authorization process. The daemon responds in one of the following three ways:

- Accepts the request as is

- Makes changes to the request

- Refuses the request, thereby refusing authorization

The AV pairs associated with the **debug aaa authorization** command that may appear in the debug output are described as follows:

- **service=arap**—Authorization for the ARA protocol is being requested.

- **service=shell**—Authorization for EXEC startup and command authorization is being requested.

- **service=ppp**—Authorization for PPP is being requested.

- **service=slip**—Authorization for SLIP is being requested.

- **protocol=lcp**—Authorization for LCP is being requested (lower layer of PPP).

- **protocol=ip**—Used with service=slip and service=slip to indicate which protocol layer is being authorized.

- **protocol=ipx**—Used with service=ppp to indicate which protocol layer is being authorized.

- **protocol=atalk**—Used with service=ppp or service=arap to indicate which protocol layer is being authorized.

- **protocol=vines**—Used with service=ppp for VINES over PPP.

- **protocol=unknown**—Used for undefined or unsupported conditions.

- **cmd=x**—Used with service=shell, if cmd=NULL, this is an authorization request to start an EXEC session. If cmd is not NULL, this is a command authorization request and will contain the name of the command being authorized (for example, cmd=telnet).

- **cmd-arg=x**—Used with service=shell. When performing command authorization, the name of the command is given by a cmd=x pair for each argument listed (for example, cmd-arg=archie.sura.net).

- **acl=x**—Used with service=shell and service=arap. For ARA, this pair contains an access list number. For service=shell, this pair contains an access class number (for example, acl=2).

- **inacl=x**—Used with service=ppp and protocol=ip. Contains an IP input access list for SLIP or PPP/IP (for example, inacl=2).

- **outacl=x**—Used with service=ppp and protocol=ip. Contains an IP output access list for SLIP or PPP/IP (for example, outacl=4).

- **addr=x**—Used with service=slip, service=ppp, and protocol=ip. Contains the IP address that the remote host should use when connecting via SLIP or PPP/IP (for example, addr=172.30.23.11).

- **routing=x**—Used with service=slip, service=ppp, and protocol=ip. Equivalent in function to the /routing flag in SLIP and PPP commands. Can either be true or false (for example, routing=true).

- **timeout=x**—Used with service=arap. The number of minutes before an ARA session disconnects (for example, timeout=60).

- **autocmd=x**—Used with service=shell and cmd=NULL. Specifies an autocommand to be executed at EXEC startup (for example, autocmd=telnet yxz.com).

- **noescape=x**—Used with service=shell and cmd=NULL. Specifies a noescape option to the username configuration command. Can be either true or false (for example, noescape=true).

- **nohangup=x**—Used with service=shell and cmd=NULL. Specifies a nohangup option to the username configuration command. Can be either true or false (for example, nohangup=false).

- **priv-lvl=x**—Used with service=shell and cmd=NULL. Specifies the current privilege level for command authorization as a number from 0 to 15 (for example, priv-lvl=15).

- **zonelist=x**—Used with service=arap. Specifies an AppleTalk zonelist for ARA (for example, zonelist=5).

- **addr-pool=x**—Used with service=ppp and protocol=ip. Specifies the name of a local pool from which to get the address of the remote host.

debug aaa accounting Command

Use the **debug aaa accounting** privileged EXEC command to display information on accountable events as they occur. Use the **no debug aaa accounting** form of the command to disable this debug mode. Example 2-15 shows some sample output from the **debug aaa accounting** command.

The primary reason for using **debug** commands of any kind is to help you troubleshoot a problem. Debug output from normal activity should be gathered to use as a baseline of comparison. When you are experiencing a problem, you can then run another debug of similar activity and compare it to a "normal" baseline, looking for words in the output that indicate a problem exists or that something happened out of sequence.

Example 2-15 debug aaa accounting *Output*

```
router# debug aaa accounting
16:49:21: AAA/ACCT: EXEC acct start, line 10
16:49:32: AAA/ACCT: Connect start, line 10, glare
16:49:47: AAA/ACCT: Connection acct stop:
task_id=70 service=exec port=10 protocol=telnet address=172.31.3.78 cmd=glare
  bytes_in=308 bytes_out=76 paks_in=45 paks_out=54 elapsed_time=14
```

The information displayed by the **debug aaa accounting** command is independent of the accounting protocol used to transfer the accounting information to a server. Use the **debug tacacs** and **debug radius** protocol-specific commands to get more detailed information about protocol-level issues.

You can also use the **show accounting** command to step through all active sessions and to print all the accounting records for actively accounted functions. The **show accounting** command enables you to display the active accountable events on the system. It provides systems administrators a quick look at what is happening, and may also be useful for collecting information in the event of data loss on the accounting server. The **show accounting** command displays additional data on the internal state of the AAA security system if **debug aaa accounting** is active as well.

Chapter Summary

The following list summarizes what you have learned in this chapter:

- In the local AAA server, the local router performs AAA services.
- Administrative and remote LAN access modes can be secured with AAA.
- Cisco router AAA configuration should follow an orderly progression.
- Use the **aaa new-model** command to add AAA to a Cisco router.
- Use **aaa** commands to specify authentication, authorization, and accounting processes and methods.
- Use **debug aaa** commands selectively to troubleshoot AAA.

Review of Cisco IOS Commands

Many Cisco IOS version 12.3 commands were discussed or referenced in this chapter. These commands can be found in the *Command Reference* online at http://www.cisco.com/univercd/cc/td/doc/product/software/ios123/123mindx/crgindx.htm.

Chapter Review Questions

The following review questions cover some of the key facts and concepts that were introduced in this chapter. Answers to these questions can be found in Appendix A, "Answers to Chapter Review Questions."

1   What are the four general classifications used to group physical threats to network security?

2   List four methods that can be used to mitigate hardware threats to mission-critical routing and switching equipment located in a telecommunications room.

3   What is the biggest difference between the enable password and the enable secret password?

4   Assuming that all network ports have been connected, configured, and enabled properly, what must be present to permit Telnet access to a router?

5   What Cisco IOS command can you use to encrypt vty passwords?

6   What three services are provided by AAA servers, such as the Cisco Secure ACS system?

7   What are the two predominant security server protocols used for AAA with Cisco devices?

8   What three elements are required in S/Key systems?

9   What command is used to globally enable the AAA service on a Cisco IOS router?

10   What AAA command would you use to establish local authentication as the default method to use in case the AAA server is not reachable via the network?

11   After you have configured AAA authentication and authorization commands globally, what must you do to complete the AAA configuration process?

12   List the three **debug** commands that you can use to troubleshoot AAA activities on your Cisco IOS router.

Case Study

Throughout the remainder of this book, each chapter contains a "Scenario" section that is designed to reinforce the material presented in the chapter. Each scenario uses a fictitious company, The Future Corporation, to practice the topics presented in the particular chapter.

This chapter's "Scenario" section introduces The Future Corporation and begins the process of securing the network. Details of The Future Corporation's network will be supplied as needed in the following chapters.

The Future Corporation

The Future Corporation is a multinational company with corporate headquarters in Dallas, Texas, and overseas headquarters in London, England. Figure 2-16 shows a general diagram of the corporate network. The corporation has six branch offices similar to the Austin, Texas, office and ten small sales offices that are similar to the Waco, Texas, office.

Figure 2-16 *The Future Corporation*

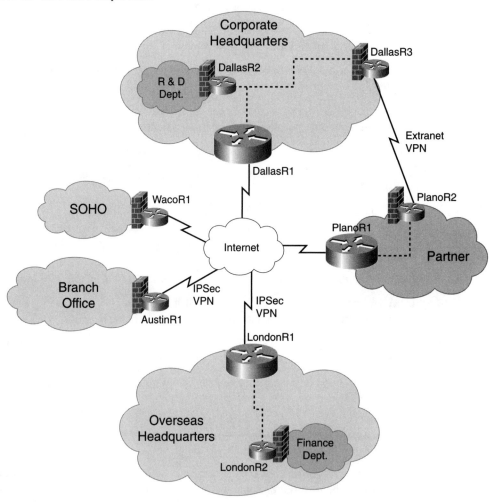

Table 2-3 shows the types of routers that are deployed. DallasR1, PlanoR1, and LondonR1 are all border routers with PIX Firewalls behind them to protect their networks. The PlanoR1 and PlanoR2 routers belong to Plastics, Incorporated, one of several business partners to which The Future Corporation has established extranet VPN connections. Configuration of PlanoR1 and PlanoR2 is done by administrators of Plastics, Incorporated.

Table 2-3   *Routers of The Future Corporation*

Facility	Router Name	Router Type
Dallas Corporate Headquarters	DallasR1	Cisco 7200 Router
	DallasR2	Cisco 3600 Router with Cisco IOS Firewall
	DallasR3	Cisco 2650 Router with Cisco IOS Firewall
Plano office of Plastics, Incorporated	PlanoR1	Cisco 3600 Router
	PlanoR2	Cisco 2650 Router with Cisco IOS Firewall
London Overseas Headquarters	LondonR1	Cisco 3600 Router
	LondonR2	Cisco 2600 Router with Cisco IOS Firewall
Austin Branch Office	AustinR1	Cisco 2600 Router with Cisco IOS Firewall
Waco Sales Office	WacoR1	Cisco 1700 Router with Cisco IOS Firewall

Security Policy Compliance

As the network administrator for The Future Company, you have been involved in developing a security policy for your organization. The policy has been finalized and now you must begin ensuring that the policy is implemented correctly throughout your network.

The network policy includes these requirements:

1 All routers will use the following enable password: GreenH2O

2 All routers will use the following enable secret password: BlueH2O

3 All routers will use this vty password for all vty lines: WhiteH2O

4 All routers will use the following console password: BlackH2O

5 All routers will use the following auxiliary password: Gr8Life

6 Level 2 administrators will use the following enable secret password: BigRapids

7 Level 2 administrators may execute only the **ping** command.

8 Terminate unattended console and auxiliary connections on all routers after 4 minutes and 20 seconds of no activity.

9 Force encryption of all passwords on all routers.

10 Each router will display the following banner for connections made to the system through the Internet:

WARNING: You are connected to $(hostname) on The Future Corporation network. Unauthorized access and use of this network will be vigorously prosecuted.

11 The SNMP read-only community string for all routers is ROSNMP.

12 The SNMP read-write community string for all routers is RWSNMP using standard access list number 88 for all administrative workstations (192.168.44.121, 192.168.44.122, 192.168.64.123, 142.16.18.121, 142.16.18.122, and 142.16.18.123).

13 Use AAA TACACS+ authentication for login; default to a local username of aaadmin and a password of aaaisdown. The ACS server is located at 192.168.44.200 for the Dallas headquarters and at 142.16.18.200 for other parts of the network. The TACACS server key is future123key.

Scenario 1

Execute the commands on router DallasR1 that will ensure that these security policy requirements are satisfied.

Scenario 2

Modify the configuration settings to use TACACS+ authentication on the console port of router DallasR1. If the ACS server is not active, console login should default to the enable password.

Solutions

In some cases your answers may differ from the solutions shown here. Cisco devices may have several different methods of accomplishing the intended results.

Scenario 1

Execute the following commands on router DallasR1:

1 Enable password: GreenH2O

— Set the enable password:

DallasR1(config)#**enable password GreenH2O**

2 Enable secret password: BlueH2O

— Set the enable secret password:

DallasR1(config)#**enable secret BlueH2O**

3 vty password: WhiteH2O

  — Set up vty lines 0 to 4 to use passwords and set the password:

  DallasR1(config)#**line vty 0 4**

  DallasR1(config-line)#**login**

  DallasR1(config-line)#**password WhiteH2O**

4 Console password: BlackH2O

  — Set up the console port to use passwords and set the password:

  DallasR1(config)#**line console 0**

  DallasR1(config-line)#**login**

  DallasR1(config-line)#**password BlackH2O**

5 AUX password: Gr8Life

  — Set up the auxiliary port to use passwords and set the password:

  DallasR1(config)#**line aux 0**

  DallasR1(config-line)#**login**

  DallasR1(config-line)#**password Gr8Life**

6 Level 2 enable secret password: BigRapids

  — Set the enable secret password for level 2 users:

  DallasR1(config)#**enable secret level 2 BigRapids**

7 Level 2 users may execute only the **ping** command.

  — Set **ping** as the available command for level 2 users:

  DallasR1(config)#**privilege exec level 2 ping**

8 Terminate unattended console and auxiliary connections after 4 minutes and 20 seconds of no activity.

  — Set the inactivity timeout on the console port to 4 minutes and 20 seconds:

  DallasR1(config)#**line console 0**

  DallasR1(config-line)#**exec-timeout 4 20**

  — Set the inactivity timeout on the auxiliary port to 4 minutes and 20 seconds:

  DallasR1(config)#**line aux 0**

  DallasR1(config-line)#**exec-timeout 4 20**

9 Force encryption of all passwords.

  — Set up password encryption for all passwords:

  DallasR1(config)#**service password-encryption**

10 Each router will display the following banner for connections made to the system through the Internet:

WARNING: You are connected to $(hostname) on The Future Corporation network. Unauthorized access and use of this network will be vigorously prosecuted.

— Set up the message of the day banner:

DallasR1(config)#**banner motd #**

WARNING: You are connected to $(hostname) on The Future Corporation network. Unauthorized access and use of this network will be vigorously prosecuted. #

11 The SNMP read-only community string is ROSNMP.

— Set the read-only community string:

DallasR1(config)#**snmp-server community ROSNMP ro**

12 The SNMP read-write community string is RWSNMP using standard access list number 88 for all administrative workstations (192.168.44.121, 192.168.44.122, 192.168.64.123, 142.16.18.121, 142.16.18.122, and 142.16.18.123).

— Create the standard ACL containing the permissible IP addresses of the administrative workstations (note that IP address 192.168.64.123 is located in the overseas headquarters):

DallasR1(config)#**access-list 88 permit 192.168.44.121**

DallasR1(config)#**access-list 88 permit 192.168.44.122**

DallasR1(config)#**access-list 88 permit 192.168.64.123**

DallasR1(config)#**access-list 88 permit 142.16.18.121**

DallasR1(config)#**access-list 88 permit 142.16.18.122**

DallasR1(config)#**access-list 88 permit 142.16.18.123**

— Set the read-write SNMP community string and provide the list of allowable device addresses:

DallasR1(config)#**snmp-server community RWSNMP rw 88**

13 Use AAA TACACS+ authentication for login; default to a local username of aaadmin and a password of aaaisdown. The ACS server is located at 192.168.44.200 for the Dallas headquarters and at 142.16.18.200 for other parts of the network. The TACACS server key is future123key.

— Enable AAA service:

DallasR1(config)#**aaa new-model**

— Set the default login method to TACACS+ with local authentication for backup:

DallasR1(config)#**aaa authentication login default group tacacs+ local**

— Establish a local username and password:

DallasR1(config)#**username aaadmin password aaaisdown**

— Provide the location of the AAA server:

DallasR1(config)#**tacacs-server host 142.16.18.200**

— Define the key to use with TACACS+ traffic:

DallasR1(config)#**tacacs-server key future123key**

Scenario 2

Modify the configuration settings to use TACACS+ authentication on the console port of router DallasR1.

— Create a new authentication entry for the console port:

DallasR1(config)#**aaa authentication login console-in group tacacs+ enable**

— Set up the console port to use the new authentication entry:

DallasR1(config)#**line console 0**

DallasR1(config-line)#**login authentication console-in**

— Remove the console password:

DallasR1(config)#**line console 0**

DallasR1(config-line)#**no password BlackH2O**

Upon completion of this chapter, you will be able to perform the following tasks:

- Describe the Features and Architecture of Cisco Secure ACS 3.0 for Windows 2000/NT Servers (Cisco Secure ACS for Windows)
- Configure Cisco Secure ACS for Windows to Perform AAA Functions
- Describe the Features and Architecture of Cisco Secure ACS 2.3 for UNIX
- Configure the Perimeter Router to Enable AAA Processes to Use a TACACS Remote Service

CHAPTER 3

Advanced AAA Security for Cisco Router Networks

This chapter covers Cisco Secure ACS 3.0 for Windows 2000/NT Servers (Cisco Secure ACS for Windows) and Cisco Secure ACS for UNIX (Solaris). The Windows 2000 version has the most coverage in this chapter. The configuration of the Windows 2000 product is covered as a high-level overview. This chapter also covers the security services of TACACS+, RADIUS, and Kerberos.

This chapter includes the following topics:

- Introduction to Cisco Secure ACS for Windows
- Product overview: Cisco Secure ACS for Windows
- Product overview: Cisco Secure ACS for UNIX (Solaris)
- Installing Cisco Secure ACS for Windows
- Administering and troubleshooting Cisco Secure ACS for Windows
- TACACS+ overview and configuration
- Verifying TACACS+
- RADIUS configuration overview
- Kerberos overview

Cisco Secure ACS Introduction

This section presents an introduction to the Cisco Secure ACS offerings shown in Figure 3-1, including the following products:

- Cisco Secure ACS for Windows
- Cisco Secure ACS for UNIX

The next three sections discuss each of the Cisco Secure ACS product offerings.

Figure 3-1 *Cisco Secure ACS Servers*

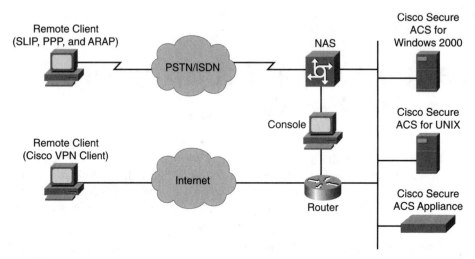

Cisco Secure ACS for Windows

Cisco Secure ACS for Windows is a network security software application that helps you control access to the campus network, dial-in access, and the Internet. Cisco Secure ACS for Windows operates as Windows NT or Windows 2000 services and controls authentication, authorization, and accounting (AAA) of users accessing the network.

This section presents an overview of the product and prepares you to install and configure Cisco Secure ACS for Windows.

Cisco Secure ACS for Windows provides AAA services to network devices that function as AAA clients, such as routers, network access servers, PIX Firewalls, and VPN 3000 Concentrators. An AAA client is any device that provides AAA client functionality and uses one of the AAA protocols supported by Cisco Secure ACS for Windows. It also supports third-party devices that can be configured to use TACACS+ or RADIUS protocols. Cisco Secure ACS for Windows treats all such devices as AAA clients. Cisco Secure ACS for Windows uses the TACACS+ and RADIUS protocols to provide AAA services that ensure a secure environment.

Cisco Secure ACS for Windows helps to centralize access control and accounting, in addition to router and switch access management. With Cisco Secure ACS for Windows, network administrators can quickly administer accounts and globally change levels of service offerings for entire groups of users. Although the use of an external user database is optional, support for many popular user repository implementations enables companies to use the working knowledge gained from and the investment already made in building the corporate user repositories.

Cisco Secure ACS for Windows is an easy-to-use ACS that is simple to install and administer. It runs on the popular Windows NT Server 4.0 (SP5 or 6) or 2000 Server (SP 1 or 2) Microsoft operating systems. The Cisco Secure ACS for Windows administration interface is viewed using supported web browsers, making it easy to administer.

Cisco Secure ACS for Windows authenticates usernames and passwords against the Windows NT or Windows 2000 user database, the Cisco Secure ACS for Windows database, a token server database, or Novell NetWare Directory Service (NDS).

Different levels of security can be used with Cisco Secure ACS for Windows for different requirements. The basic user-to-network security level is Password Authentication Protocol (PAP). Although it does not represent the highest form of encrypted security, PAP does offer convenience and simplicity for the client. PAP allows authentication against the Windows NT or Windows 2000 database. With this configuration, users need to log in only a single time. Challenge Handshake Authentication Protocol (CHAP) allows a higher level of security for encrypting passwords when communicating from a client to the network access server. You can use CHAP with the Cisco Secure ACS for Windows user database. Microsoft CHAP (MS-CHAP) is a version of CHAP that was developed by Microsoft to work more closely with the Microsoft Windows operating system.

PAP, CHAP, and MS-CHAP are authentication protocols that are used to encrypt passwords. However, each protocol provides a different level of security:

- **PAP**—Uses clear-text passwords and is the least sophisticated authentication protocol. If you are using the Windows NT or Windows 2000 user database to authenticate users, you must use PAP password encryption.

- **CHAP**—Uses a challenge-response mechanism with one-way encryption on the response. CHAP lets Cisco Secure ACS for Windows negotiate downward from the most secure to the least secure encryption mechanism, and it protects passwords transmitted in the process. CHAP passwords are reusable. If you are using the Cisco Secure ACS for Windows user database for authentication, you can use either PAP or CHAP.

- **MS-CHAP**—Cisco Secure ACS for Windows supports MS-CHAP for user authentication. The differences between MS-CHAP and standard CHAP follow:

  — The MS-CHAP response packet is in a format that is compatible with Microsoft Windows and LAN Manager 2.x. The MS-CHAP format does not require the authenticator to store a clear-text or reversibly encrypted password.

  — MS-CHAP provides an authenticator-controlled authentication retry mechanism.

  — MS-CHAP version 2 provides additional failure codes in the Failure Packet Message field.

General Features

Cisco Secure ACS for Windows, depicted in Figure 3-2, has the following general features:

- Simultaneous TACACS+ and RADIUS support between Cisco Secure ACS for Windows and the NAS or perimeter router

Figure 3-2   *General Features*

- Windows NT or Windows 2000 user database support:
  - Leverages and consolidates Windows NT or Windows 2000 username and password management
  - Enables single login to network and Windows NT or Windows 2000 domains
  - Runs on Windows NT or Windows 2000 standalone, primary domain controller (PDC), and backup domain controller (BDC) server configurations

---

NOTE   Although Cisco Secure ACS for Windows can function on a BDC or PDC, Cisco SAFE practices recommend placing the application on a standalone server to separate the services of one authentication server from another. Doing so will improve the security posture by making it potentially more difficult for an attacker to penetrate multiple devices.

- Supports the use of external user database:
  - External token card servers
  - NDS
  - ACS databases
  - Others
- Supports the following, leading authentication protocols:
  - ASCII/PAP
  - CHAP
  - MS-CHAP
  - LEAP
  - EAP-CHAP
  - EAP-TLS
  - ARAP
- Network access server callback feature supported for increased security

AAA Services

Cisco Secure ACS for Windows supports the following AAA features:

- TACACS+ support for:
  - Access lists, named or numbered
  - Time-of-day and day-of-week access restrictions
  - AppleTalk Remote Access (ARA) support
  - Enable-privilege support levels
  - Authentication to an LDAP server
  - One-time password (OTP) for enable passwords
- RADIUS versions:
  - IETF RADIUS
  - Cisco RADIUS Attribute-Value pairs
  - Proprietary RADIUS extensions (Lucent)
- Single TACACS+/RADIUS database for simultaneous support

Other AAA product features are as follows:

- VPN and Virtual Private Dialup Network (VPDN) support is available at the origination and termination of VPN (L2F) tunnels
- User restrictions can be based on remote address Calling Line Identification (CLID)
- Can disable an account on a specific date or after "n" failed attempts

Administration Features

Cisco Secure ACS for Windows has many user-friendly administration features, such as:

- Browser-based GUI allows management from a web browser via a LAN or by dialing in. Simplifies and distributes configuration for ACS, user profiles, and group profiles:
  - Help and online documentation is included for quick problem solving and access from a web browser (The browser does not use SSL; it uses CSAdmin running as a Windows service to provide the website for ACS)
  - Permits group administration of users for maximum flexibility and to facilitate enforcement and changes of security policies
  - Remote administration can be permitted/denied by using a unique administration username/password
  - Remote administrator session has a timeout value
  - Can view a logged-in user list for a quick view of who is connected
- Creates separate TACACS+ and RADIUS files stored in comma-separated value (CSV) spreadsheet format for easy import into databases and spreadsheet applications

- Has import utility to rapidly import a large number of users

- Hash-indexed flat-file database support for high-speed transaction processing (Cisco Secure ACS for Windows user database)

Distributed System Features

As shown in Figure 3-3, Cisco Secure ACS for Windows can be used in a distributed system. Multiple Cisco Secure ACS for Windows servers and AAA servers can be configured to communicate with one another as masters, clients, or peers. Cisco Secure ACS for Windows also recognizes network access restrictions of other Cisco Secure ACS for Windows servers on the distributed network.

Figure 3-3   *Distributed System Features*

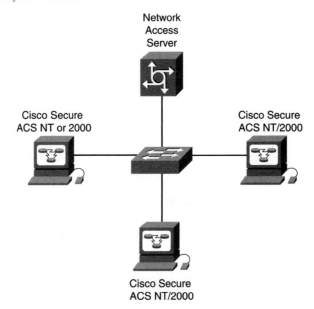

Network
Access
Server

Cisco Secure
ACS NT or 2000

Cisco Secure
ACS NT/2000

Cisco Secure
ACS NT/2000

Cisco Secure ACS for Windows allows you to use powerful features, such as:

- **Authentication forwarding**—Authentication forwarding allows the Cisco Secure ACS for Windows to automatically forward an authentication request from a network access server to another Cisco Secure ACS for Windows. After authentication, authorization privileges are applied to the network access server for that user authentication.

- **Fallback on failed connection**—You can configure the order in which Cisco Secure ACS for Windows checks the remote Cisco Secure ACS for Windows servers if the network connection to the primary Cisco Secure ACS for Windows server fails. If an authentication request cannot be sent to the first listed server, the next listed server is checked, in order down the list, until a Cisco Secure ACS for Windows server handles the authentication. If Cisco Secure ACS for Windows cannot connect to any of the servers on the list, authentication fails.

- **Remote and centralized accounting**—Cisco Secure ACS for Windows can be configured to point to a centralized Cisco Secure ACS for Windows that is used as the accounting server. The centralized Cisco Secure ACS for Windows will still have all the capabilities that a Cisco Secure ACS for Windows server has, with the addition of being a central repository for all accounting logs that are sent.

External Database Support

You can configure Cisco Secure ACS for Windows to forward authentication of users to one or more external user databases. Support for external user databases means that Cisco Secure ACS for Windows does not require that you create duplicate user entries in the Cisco Secure user database. Users can be authenticated using any of the following:

- Windows NT or Windows 2000 user database
- LDAP
- NDS
- Open Database Connectivity (ODBC)—compliant relational databases
- LEAP Proxy RADIUS servers
- Symantec (AXENT) Defender token servers
- Secure Computing SafeWord token servers
- RSA SecurID token servers
- RADIUS-based token servers, including:
  - ActivCard token servers
  - CRYPTOCard token servers
  - VASCO token servers
  - Generic RADIUS token servers

Regardless of which database is used to authenticate users, the Cisco Secure user database, internal to Cisco Secure ACS for Windows, authorizes requested network services.

Cisco Secure ACS for Windows requires an application program interface (API) for third-party authentication support. Cisco Secure ACS for Windows communicates with the external user database using the API. For Windows NT or Windows 2000, Generic LDAP, and Novell NDS authentication, the API for the external authentication is local to the Cisco Secure ACS for Windows system and is provided by the local operating system. In these cases, no further components are required.

In the case of ODBC authentication sources, in addition to the Windows ODBC interface, the third-party ODBC driver must be installed on the Cisco Secure ACS for Windows server.

To communicate with each traditional token server, you must have software components provided by the OTP vendors installed, in addition to the Cisco Secure ACS for Windows components. You must also specify in User Setup that a token card server be used.

For RADIUS-based token servers, such as those from ActivCard, CRYPTOCard, and VASCO, the standard RADIUS interface serves as the third-party API.

Database Management Features

Two utilities, Database Replication and Relational Database Management System (RDBMS) Synchronization, are provided with Cisco Secure ACS for Windows. These utilities help automate the process of keeping your Cisco Secure ACS for Windows database and network configuration current. A third utility, CSUtil.exe, allows for database backup and restore functionality.

Figure 3-4 shows a typical installation that can support Database Replication, RDBMS Synchronization, and ODBC import. These three topics will be discussed in the following sections.

Figure 3-4   *Database Management Features*

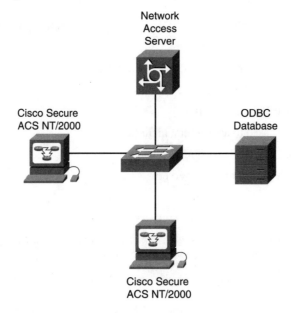

Database Replication

Database Replication is a powerful feature that is designed to simplify the construction of a fault-tolerant AAA service environment based on the Cisco Secure ACS for Windows. The primary purpose of Database Replication is to provide the facility to replicate various parts of the setup on a Cisco Secure ACS for Windows master server to one or more Cisco Secure ACS for Windows client systems, allowing the administrator to automate the creation of mirror systems. These mirror systems can then be used to provide server redundancy as fallback or secondary servers to support fault-tolerant operation if the master or primary system fails.

Do not confuse Database Replication with database/system backup. Database Replication is not a complete replacement for database backup. You should still have a reliable database backup strategy to ensure data integrity.

RDBMS Synchronization

RDBMS Synchronization is an integration feature designed to simplify integration of Cisco Secure ACS for Windows with a third-party RDBMS application. RDBMS Synchronization automates synchronization with an SQL, Oracle, or Sybase RDBMS data source by providing the following functions:

- Specification of an ODBC data source to use for synchronization data that is shared by Cisco Secure ACS for Windows and the other RDBMS application and to provide control of the Cisco Secure ACS for Windows updates to an external application

- Control of the timing of the import/synchronization process, including the creation of schedules

- Control of which systems are to be synchronized

The RDBMS Synchronization feature has two components:

- **CSDBSync**—CSDBSync is a dedicated Windows NT or Windows 2000 service that performs automated user and group account management services for Cisco Secure ACS for Windows.

- **ODBC data store (table)**—This table specifies the record format. Each record holds user or group information that corresponds with the data stored for each user in the Cisco Secure ACS for Windows database. Additionally, each record contains other fields, including an action code for the record. Any application can write to this table, and CSDBSync reads from it and takes actions on each record that it finds in the table (for example, add user, delete user, and so on) as determined by the action code.

ODBC Import Definitions

Cisco Secure ACS for Windows supports the import of data from ODBC-compliant databases, such as Microsoft Access or Oracle. Importing is done with a single table to import user/group information into one or more ACS servers.

The CSAccupdate service processes the table and updates local/remote ACS installations according to its configuration.

Windows Architecture

Cisco Secure ACS for Windows provides AAA services to multiple NASs or perimeter routers. It includes seven service modules, as shown in Figure 3-5.

Figure 3-5   *Windows Architecture*

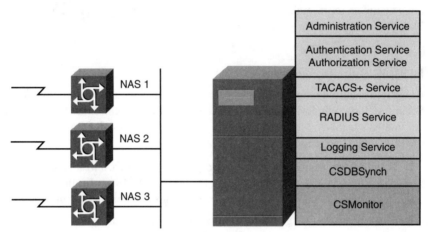

Each module can be started and stopped individually from within the Microsoft Service Control Panel or as a group from within the Cisco Secure ACS for Windows browser interface.

Cisco Secure ACS for Windows installs the following Windows services on your server:

- **Administration service (CSAdmin)**—Cisco Secure ACS for Windows is equipped with its own internal web server. After Cisco Secure ACS for Windows is installed, you must configure it from its HTML/Java interface, which requires CSAdmin to always be enabled.

- **Authentication and authorization service (CSAuth)**—The primary responsibility of Cisco Secure ACS for Windows is the authentication and authorization of requests from devices to permit or deny access to a specified user. CSAuth is the service that is responsible for determining whether access should be granted and for defining the privileges associated with that user. CSAuth is the database manager.

- **TACACS service (CSTacacs) and RADIUS service (CSRadius)**—These services communicate between the CSAuth module and the access device that is requesting the authentication and authorization services. CSTacacs is used to communicate with TACACS+ devices and CSRadius is used to communicate with RADIUS devices. Both services can run simultaneously. When only one security protocol is used, only the respective service needs to be running.

- **Logging service (CSLog)**—CSLog is the service that is used to capture and place logging information. CSLog gathers data from the TACACS+ or RADIUS packet and CSAuth and manipulates the data to be put into the CSV files. The CSV files are created daily starting at midnight.

- **CSDBSync service**—This service performs automated user and group account management services for Cisco Secure ACS for Windows. CSDBSync is the service that is used to synchronize the Cisco Secure ACS for Windows database with third-party RDBMSs and is an alternative to using the ODBC dynamic link library (DLL). Starting with Version 2.4, CSDBSync synchronizes AAA client, AAA server, network device groups (NDGs), and Proxy Table information with data from an external relational database.

- **CSMon**—CSMon is the Cisco Secure ACS for Windows self-monitoring and self-correcting service. CSMon works for both TACACS+ and RADIUS and automatically detects which protocols are in use. CSMon facilitates minimum downtime in a remote access network environment by performing four basic activities:

  - **Monitoring**—Monitors the overall status of Cisco Secure ACS for Windows and the host server on which it is running. CSMon monitors the generic host system state, application-specific performance, and system resource consumption by Cisco Secure ACS for Windows.

  - **Recording**—Records and reports all exceptions to the CSMon Log or the Windows Event Log.

  - **Notification**—Alerts the administrator to potential problems and real events regarding Cisco Secure ACS for Windows and records the activity. CSMon can be configured to send messages concerning exception events, responses, and the outcomes of response actions.

  - **Response**—Attempts to automatically and intelligently fix detected problems. CSMon can respond to warning events and failure events by taking either predefined actions or customer-definable actions.

Using the ACS Database

Using either the TACACS+ or the RADIUS protocol, the network access server directs all dial-in user access requests to Cisco Secure ACS for Windows for authentication and authorization of privileges, which verifies the username and password. Cisco Secure ACS for Windows then returns a success or failure response to the network access server, which permits or denies user access. When the user has been authenticated, Cisco Secure ACS for Windows sends a set of authorization attributes to the network access server, and then the accounting functions take effect.

Referring to the numbers shown in Figure 3-6, when the Cisco Secure ACS for Windows user database is selected, the following service and database interaction occurs:

1 TACACS+ or RADIUS service directs the request to the Cisco Secure ACS Authentication and Authorization Windows NT or Windows 2000 service.

2 The request is authenticated against the Cisco Secure ACS for Windows user database, associated authorizations are assigned, and accounting information is logged to the Cisco Secure ACS Logging service.

3 The Windows NT or Windows 2000 user database does not authenticate the user to permit dial. The user must log in to Windows NT or Windows 2000 once the dialup AAA process is complete.

Figure 3-6 *Using the ACS Database*

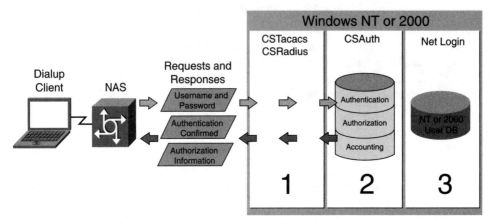

Cisco Secure ACS for Windows uses a built-in user database that is a hash-indexed flat file. This type of file is not searched from the top of a text file as typically associated with the term flat file, but instead is indexed like a database. The hash-indexed flat file builds an index and tree structure so that searches can occur exponentially, which enables the Cisco Secure ACS for Windows user database to rapidly authenticate users.

Using the Cisco Secure ACS for Windows user database requires you to manually enter the usernames. However, after the usernames exist in the Cisco Secure ACS for Windows user database, administration is easier than using the Windows NT or Windows 2000 user database. The Cisco Secure ACS for Windows user database supports authentication for PAP, CHAP, and MS-CHAP.

Using Windows User Database

Figure 3-7 shows the flow of the steps used when you elect to use the Windows NT or Windows 2000 user database for authentication and authorization.

Following the numbers shown in Figure 3-7, when Cisco Secure ACS for Windows uses the Windows NT or Windows 2000 user database for AAA, the following service and database interaction occurs:

1   TACACS+ or RADIUS service directs the request to the Cisco Secure ACS Authentication and Authorization service.

2   The username and password are sent to the Windows NT or Windows 2000 user database for authentication.

3   If approved, Windows NT or Windows 2000 grants dial permission as a local user.

4   A response is returned to Cisco Secure ACS for Windows and authorizations are assigned.

5   Confirmation and associated authorizations assigned in Cisco Secure ACS for Windows for that user are sent to the network access server. Accounting information is logged.

Figure 3-7   *Using Windows User Database*

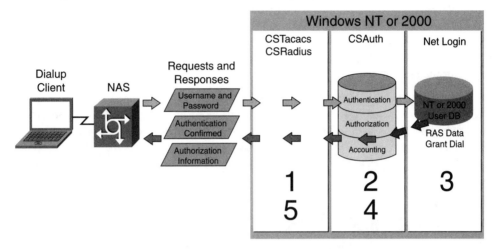

An added benefit of using the Windows NT or Windows 2000 user database is that the username and password that are used for authentication are the same that are used for network login. As such, you can require users to enter their username and password once, for the convenience of a simple, single login.

Token Card Support

Cisco Secure ACS for Windows supports several third-party token servers, such as RSA SecurID, Secure Computing SafeWord, Symantec (AXENT) Defender, and any hexadecimal X.909 token card such as CRYPTOCard. As shown in Figure 3-8, for some token servers, Cisco Secure ACS for Windows acts as a client to the token server.

Figure 3-8   *Token Card Support*

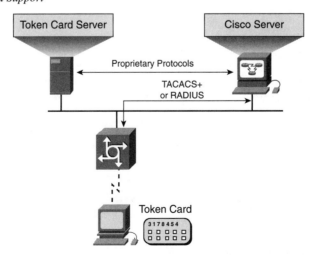

For others, it uses the token server's RADIUS interface for authentication requests. As with the Windows NT or Windows 2000 database, after the username is located in the Cisco Secure user database, CSAuth can check the selected token server to verify the username and token-card password. The token server then provides a response, approving or denying validation. If the response is approved, CSAuth knows that authentication should be granted for the user.

Cisco Secure ACS for Windows can support token servers using the RADIUS server that is built into the token server. Rather than using the vendor's proprietary API, Cisco Secure ACS for Windows sends standard RADIUS authentication requests to the RADIUS authentication port on the token server. The token servers that are supported through their RADIUS servers are those from ActivCard, CRYPTOCard, VASCO, PassGo Technologies, RSA Security, and Secure Computing.

NOTE   Before Cisco Secure ACS 3.0.1, support for CRYPTOCard token servers used the vendor-proprietary interface provided with the CRYPTOCard token server.

Beginning with Cisco Secure ACS 3.0.1, Cisco supports CRYPTOCard token servers using a standard RADIUS interface.

Cisco Secure ACS for Windows also supports any token server that is a RADIUS server compliant with IETF RFC 2865. So, in addition to the RADIUS-enabled token server vendors that are explicitly supported, this enables you to use any token server that supports RADIUS-based authentication.

You can create multiple instances of each of these token server types in Cisco Secure ACS for Windows.

Versions 3.1 and 3.2 Enhancements

Cisco is constantly upgrading and enhancing hardware and software products, and Cisco Secure ACS for Windows is no exception. You can always find the latest version information at Cisco's website. This section looks at some of the important new features that have been added to Cisco Secure ACS for Windows by versions 3.1 and 3.2.

The following are the Cisco Secure ACS for Windows version 3.1 product enhancements:

- **Protected Extensible Authentication Protocol (PEAP) support**—Nonproprietary PEAP for wireless user authentication provides stronger security, greater extensibility, and support for one-time token authentication and password aging.

- **SSL support for administrative access**—SSL can be used to secure administrative access to the Cisco Secure ACS for Windows HTML interface.

- **Change Password (CHPASS) improvements**—Cisco Secure ACS for Windows allows you to control whether network administrators can change passwords during Telnet sessions that are hosted by TACACS+ AAA clients.

- **Improved IP pool addressing**—To reduce the possibility of allocating an IP address that is already in use, Cisco Secure ACS for Windows uses the IETF RADIUS Class attribute as an additional index for user sessions.

- **Network device search**—New search capabilities let you search for a configured network device based on the device name, IP address, type (AAA client or AAA server), and network device group.

- **Improved Public Key Infrastructure (PKI) support**—During Extensible Authentication Protocol Transport Layer Security (EAP-TLS) authentication, Cisco Secure ACS for Windows can perform binary comparison of the certificate received from an end-user client to user certificates stored in Lightweight Directory Access Protocol (LDAP) directories.

- **Extensible Authentication Protocol (EAP) proxy enhancements**—Cisco Secure ACS for Windows supports Light Extensible Authentication Protocol (LEAP) and EAP-TLS proxy to other RADIUS or external databases using EAP over standard RADIUS.

- **CiscoWorks Management Center application support**—Cisco Secure ACS for Windows provides a consolidated administrative TACACS+ control framework for many Cisco security management tools, such as CiscoWorks VPN/Security Management Solution (VMS) and the suite of CiscoWorks Management Centers.

The following are the Cisco Secure ACS for Windows version 3.2 product enhancements:

- **PEAP support for Microsoft Windows clients**—Support for Microsoft PEAP supplicants that are available for Windows 98, NT, 2000, and XP was added in this update.

- **LDAP multithreading**—To improve performance in task-intensive environments such as wireless deployments, Cisco Secure ACS for Windows Server Version 3.2 is now capable of processing multiple LDAP authentication requests in parallel.

- **EAP-TLS enhancements**—New EAP-TLS enhancements have been brought in Cisco Secure ACS for Windows Server Version 3.2 that further extend Cisco Secure ACS PKI capabilities.

- **Machine authentication support**—Machine authentication allows pulling down machine group policies from Windows Active Directory independently of a subsequent interactive user authentication session.

- **EAP mixed configurations**—Cisco Secure ACS for Windows Server Version 3.2 supports the following EAP types:
  - PEAP (EAP-GTC)
  - PEAP (EAP-MSCHAPv2)
  - EAP-TLS
  - EAP-MD5
  - Cisco EAP wireless

- **Flexible EAP settings allowed**—One or several EAP types can be selected concurrently.

- **Accounting support for Aironet**—Cisco Secure ACS for Windows Server Version 3.2 supports user-based accounting from Cisco Aironet wireless access.

- **Downloadable access control lists for VPN users**—Cisco Secure ACS for Windows Server Version 3.2 extends per-user ACL support to Cisco VPN solutions.

Cisco Secure ACS for UNIX (Solaris)

Cisco Secure ACS for UNIX is used to authenticate users and determine which internal networks and services they may access. By authenticating users against a database of user and group profiles, Cisco Secure ACS for UNIX effectively secures private enterprise and service provider networks from unauthorized access.

Cisco Secure ACS for UNIX incorporates a multiuser, web-based Java configuration and management tool that simplifies server administration and enables multiple system administrators to simultaneously manage security services from multiple locations. The GUI supports Microsoft and Netscape web browsers, providing multiplatform compatibility and offering secure administration via the industry-standard SSL communication mechanism.

Token cards from CRYPTOCard, Secure Computing Corporation, and RSA Security are supported. Token cards are the strongest available method to authenticate users dialing in and to prevent unauthorized users from accessing proprietary information. Cisco Secure ACS for UNIX now supports industry-leading relational database technologies from Sybase, Inc. and Oracle Corporation. Traditional scalability, redundancy, and nondistributed architecture limitations are removed with the integration of relational database technologies, such as Sybase's SQLAnywhere. Storage and management of user and group profile information is greatly simplified.

General Features

Security is an increasingly important aspect of the growth and proliferation of LANs and WANs. You want to provide easy access to information on your network, but you also want to prevent access by unauthorized personnel. Cisco Secure ACS for UNIX is designed to help ensure the security of your network and track the activity of people who successfully connect to your network. Cisco Secure ACS for UNIX uses the TACACS+ protocol to provide this network security and tracking.

TACACS+ uses AAA to provide network access security and enable you to control access to your network from a central location. Each facet of AAA significantly contributes to the overall security of your network, as follows:

- Authentication determines the identity of users and whether they should be allowed access to the network.

- Authorization determines the level of network services available to authenticated users once they are connected.

- Accounting keeps track of each user's network activity.

- AAA within a client or server architecture (in which transaction responsibilities are divided into two parts: client [front end], and server [back end]) allows you to store all ecurity information in a single, centralized database instead of distributing the information around the network in many different devices.

For further information on AAA, see the section titled "Introduction to AAA for Cisco Routers" in Chapter 2, "Basic Cisco Router Security."

You can use Cisco Secure ACS for UNIX to make changes to the database that administers security on your network on a few security servers instead of making changes to every NAS in your network.

Using Cisco Secure ACS for UNIX, you can expand your network to accommodate more users and provide more services without overburdening system administrators with security issues. As new users are added, system administrators can make a small number of changes in a few places and still ensure network security.

Cisco Secure ACS for UNIX can be used with the TACACS+ protocol, the RADIUS protocol, or both. Some features are common to both protocols, while other features are protocol-dependent.

Cisco Secure ACS for UNIX has the following features when used with either the TACACS+ or RADIUS protocol:

- Support for use of common token card servers, including those from CRYPTOCard, Secure Computing (formerly Enigma Logic), and RSA Security

- Relational database support for Oracle Enterprise, Sybase Enterprise, and Sybase SQLAnywhere (supplied with Cisco Secure ACS for UNIX)

- Encrypted protocol transactions so that passwords are never subject to unauthorized monitoring

- Supported on SPARC Solaris version 2.51 or greater

- Support for group membership

- Support for accounting

- Support for S/Key authentication

- Ability to specify the maximum number of sessions per user

- Ability to disable an account after *n* failed attempts

- Web-based interface for easy administration of network security

Customers can upgrade to any 2.x version of Cisco Secure ACS for UNIX from existing versions, gaining access to the many user-friendly features of the latest version of Cisco Secure ACS for UNIX.

Cisco Secure ACS for UNIX 2.3 adds the Distributed Systems Manager (DSM), which enables system administrators to

- Limit the number of concurrent sessions that are available to a specific user, group, or VPDN (DSM enabled)
- Set per-user session limits for individual users or groups of users (limited support without DSM enabled)

Installing Cisco Secure ACS 3.0 for Windows 2000/NT Servers

Cisco Secure ACS 3.0 for Windows 2000/NT Servers is easy to install and configure. This section presents a brief overview of the essential installation steps. The following discussion is based on a Point-to-Point Protocol (PPP) dialup user being authenticated against Cisco Secure ACS for Windows using the Windows NT or Windows 2000 user database, via the TACACS+ protocol.

The Cisco Secure ACS for Windows installation can be condensed to the following steps:

Step 1   Configure the Windows NT or Windows 2000 server to work with Cisco Secure ACS for Windows.

Step 2   Verify a basic network connection from the Windows NT or Windows 2000 server to the network access server using ping and Telnet.

Step 3   Install Cisco Secure ACS for Windows on the Windows NT or Windows 2000 server following the Windows NT or Windows 2000 installation shield.

Step 4   Configure Cisco Secure ACS for Windows via the web browser interface.

Step 5   Configure the network access server for AAA.

Step 6   Verify correct installation and operation.

Configuring the Server

The first step to follow when installing Cisco Secure ACS for Windows is to configure Windows NT or Windows 2000 for Cisco Secure ACS for Windows by performing the following steps:

Step 1   Determine whether the host server is a domain controller or a member server. This decision must be made based on the design of the Windows NT or Windows 2000 server architecture of your company.

Step 2   Configure Windows NT or Windows 2000 User Manager.

Step 3   Use Windows NT or Windows 2000 services to control ACS.

Cisco does not recommend that you install Cisco Secure ACS for Windows on PDCs or BDCs. These Windows authentication devices can become very busy and are frequent targets of network attacks. Placing Cisco Secure ACS for Windows on one of these devices exposes it to potential compromise and possible service delays.

Verifying Connections Between Windows Server and Other Network Devices

Verify that the NAS or router can ping the Windows NT or Windows 2000 server that will host Cisco Secure ACS for Windows. This verification will simplify installation and eliminate problems when configuring Cisco Secure ACS for Windows and devices that interface with it.

Cisco Secure ACS for Windows is easy to install from a CD-ROM. It installs like any other Windows application, using an InstallShield template. Before you begin the installation, ensure that you have the network access server information, such as host name, IP address, and TACACS+ key. Be sure that the version of Java that is identified in the installation manual is installed on the server before you begin the installation process.

NOTE   Beginning with Cisco Secure ACS for Windows version 3.1, Cisco no longer supports running Cisco Secure ACS for Windows on a Windows NT 4.0 server.

Installing Cisco Secure ACS for Windows on the Server

Follow the InstallShield template instructions as listed below:

Step 1   Select and configure the database.

Step 2   Configure Cisco Secure ACS for Windows for the NAS or router using the web browser.

Step 3   Configure the NAS or router for Cisco Secure ACS for Windows.

Configuring Cisco Secure ACS for Windows Using the Web Browser

After you successfully install Cisco Secure ACS for Windows, an ACS Admin icon appears on the Windows NT or 2000 desktop. You configure and manage Cisco Secure ACS for Windows through the web-based GUI. The GUI is designed using frames, so you must view it with a supported web browser.

Cisco Secure ACS for Windows supports only HTML; a web browser is the only way to configure it. Cisco Secure ACS for Windows supports the following browsers:

— Microsoft Internet Explorer version 5.0 and above for Microsoft Windows

— Netscape Communicator version 4.76 and above for Microsoft Windows

Continue the initial configuration of Cisco Secure ACS for Windows as follows:

Step 1   Select the icon to launch the browser with the address http://127.0.0.1:2002/.

  - http://*ip address*:2002/ and http://*host name*:2002/ also work.

Step 2   Perform required tasks to establish users and groups, and to configure network and system settings as outlined in the section of this chapter titled, "Administering and Troubleshooting Cisco Secure ACS for Windows."

Configuring Remaining Devices for AAA

You must configure the NAS, routers, and switches to work with Cisco Secure ACS for Windows. Router configuration is described in Chapter 6, "Cisco IOS Firewall Authentication Proxy."

You may also need to configure a token card server to work with Cisco Secure ACS for Windows to perform AAA.

The following are some of the possible configuration combinations in which Cisco Secure ACS for Windows is used to perform AAA. In each configuration, each of the devices must be configured to work with Cisco Secure ACS for Windows.

  - Dialup using the Windows NT or Windows 2000 user database with TACACS+
  - Dialup using the Cisco Secure ACS for Windows user database with TACACS+
  - Dialup using a token card server with TACACS+
  - Dialup using the Cisco Secure ACS for Windows user database with RADIUS (Cisco)
  - Dialup for an AppleTalk Remote Access Protocol (ARAP) client using the Cisco Secure ACS for Windows user database with TACACS+
  - Router management using the Cisco Secure ACS for Windows user database with TACACS+
  - PIX Firewall authentication/authorization using the Windows NT or Windows 2000 user database with TACACS+

Verify Correct Installation and Operation

Verification of correct installation begins by checking to see whether Cisco Secure ACS services are running or stopped by accessing the Service Control page. You can do that by following these steps:

Step 1   In the navigation bar, click **System Configuration**.

Step 2   Click **Service Control** to display the status of the Cisco Secure ACS for Windows services.

Next, you need to test authentication and authorization from one of your devices that has been configured to use the server. A good test is to use a Telnet connection to a router that has been configured for AAA on its VTY lines.

Step 1   Connect to the router though Telnet.

Step 2   Enter your username and password when prompted by the system.

Step 3   Verify that you are granted the level of access control you expected to receive based on the username you used.

Step 4   If there are any problems, verify the configuration on the router and double-check the Cisco Secure ACS for Windows settings that you established for the test user.

Administering and Troubleshooting Cisco Secure ACS for Windows

The Cisco Secure ACS for Windows web browser interface makes administration of AAA features easy. Each of the buttons on the navigational bar (listed next in top-to-bottom order as shown in Figure 3-9) represents a particular area or function that you can configure. Depending on your configuration, you may not need to configure all the areas.

- **User Setup**—Add, edit, and delete user accounts, and list users in databases
- **Group Setup**—Create, edit, and rename groups, and list all users in a group

Figure 3-9   *Main Window*

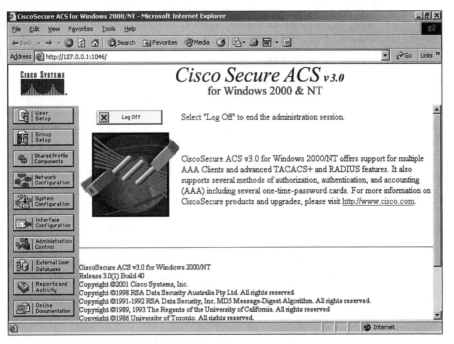

- **Shared Profile Components**—Develop and name reusable, shared sets of authorization components that may be applied to one or more users or groups of users and referenced by name within individual profiles. Components include network access restrictions (NARs), command authorization sets, and downloadable PIX ACLs.

- **Network Configuration**—Configure and edit network access server parameters, add and delete network access servers, and configure AAA server distribution parameters

- **System Configuration**—Start and stop Cisco Secure ACS for Windows services, configure logging, control Database Replication, and control RDBMS Synchronization

- **Interface Configuration**—Configure user-defined fields that will be recorded in accounting logs, configure TACACS+ and RADIUS options, and control display of options in the user interface

- **Administration Control**—Control administration of Cisco Secure ACS for Windows from any workstation on the network

- **External User Databases**—Configure the unknown user policy, configure authorization privileges for unknown users, and configure external database types

- **Reports and Activity**—View the following information, which is a partial list of the types of reports available to you when you select this button. You can import these files into most database and spreadsheet applications.

  — **TACACS+ Accounting Report**—Lists when sessions stop and start, records network access server messages with username, provides CLID information, and records the duration of each session

  — **RADIUS Accounting Report**—Lists when sessions stop and start, records network access server messages with username, provides CLID information, and records the duration of each session

  — **Failed Attempts Report**—Lists authentication and authorization failures with an indication of the cause

  — **Logged in Users**—Lists all users who are currently receiving services for a single network access server or all network access servers with access to Cisco Secure ACS for Windows

  — **Disabled Accounts**—Lists all user accounts that are currently disabled

  — **Admin Accounting Report**—Lists configuration commands entered on a TACACS+ (Cisco) network access server

- **Online Documentation**—Provides more detailed information about the configuration, operation, and concepts of Cisco Secure ACS for Windows

As previously stated, the preceding list represents the order in which the buttons appear on the navigational bar, not the order that you want to follow for configuration. The order to follow for configuration depends on your preferences and needs. One typical order of configuration is as follows:

Step 1 **Administration Control**—Configure access for remote administrators.

Step 2   **Network Configuration**—Configure and verify connectivity to a network access server.

Step 3   **Group Setup**—Configure available options and parameters for specific groups. All users must belong to a group.

Step 4   **User Setup**—Add users to a group that is configured.

Step 5   **Additional configuration**—Verify or configure settings in all other necessary areas.

Start troubleshooting Cisco Secure ACS for Windows–related AAA problems by examining the Failed Attempts Report under Reports and Activity, as shown in Figure 3-10. The report shows several types of failures.

Figure 3-10 *Troubleshooting Grid*

Date ↓	Time	Message-Type	User Name	Group Name	Caller-ID	Authen-Failure-Code	Authen-Failure-Code	Author-Data	NAS-Port	NAS-IP-Address
12/06/2002	12:59:46	Author Failed	aaauser	Default Group	10.1.2.12	..	Service denied	service=auth-proxy cmd*	Ethernet0/0	10.0.2.2
12/06/2002	12:58:31	Author Failed	aaauser	Default Group	10.1.2.12	..	Service denied	service=auth-proxy cmd*	Ethernet0/0	10.0.2.2
12/06/2002	12:38:10	Authen Failed	andy	is-in	async	CS password invalid	..	..	tty0	10.0.2.2

Cisco Secure ACS for Windows has debug capabilities that uses a combination of logging files to record debug information. You can view these logging files as reports in order to check for system problems. You can also run CSTacacs, CSRadius, and CSAuth from a DOS command line to see debug information for those services. See the Cisco Tech Notes article at http://www.cisco.com/en/US/products/sw/secursw/ps2086 /products_tech_note09186a00800afec1.shtml for more information on setting debug log levels and using the debug command-line capabilities of the Cisco Secure ACS for Windows service modules.

Authentication Failure

Assuming that Cisco Secure ACS for Windows and the router are communicating and that you are authenticating against the Windows NT or Windows 2000 user database, check the following items if you encounter an authentication failure:

- Are the username and password being entered correctly? (The password is case sensitive.)

- Do the username and password exist in the Windows NT or Windows 2000 user database? (Use the Windows 2000 User Manager administration tool to verify the user entry and to reset passwords, if necessary.)

- Is the dial-in interface on the network access server configured with **ppp authentication pap**?

- Is the User Must Change Password at Next Login check box checked in Windows NT or Windows 2000? (Uncheck the check box it if it is checked.)

- Does the username have the rights to log on locally in the Windows NT or Windows 2000 Server window (Trust Relationship/Domain)?

- Is Cisco Secure ACS for Windows configured to authenticate against the Windows NT or Windows 2000 user database?

- Is Cisco Secure ACS for Windows configured to grant dial-in permission to the user?

- If the username was able to authenticate before and is unable to now, is the account disabled on Windows NT or Windows 2000 or Cisco Secure ACS for Windows?

- Has the password expired on Windows NT or Windows 2000?

- Does the username contain an illegal character?

Windows NT or Windows 2000 will send the domain name and username for authentication when a user attempts to access the network through Dial-Up Networking (DUN).

Authorization Failure

If the dial-in user is authenticating, but authorization is failing, check the following:

- Are the proper network services checked in the Group Settings?

- If IP is checked, how is the dial-in user obtaining an IP address?

- Is there an IP pool configured on the network access server?

- Is the name of the IP pool entered in the Group Settings? (Leave this blank if a default IP pool has been configured.)

- If authorizing commands, has the **aaa authorization** *commands* **1 tacacs+** command been entered into the Cisco IOS configuration? (You can substitute any privilege level from 0 to 15 for the **1** in this command.)

- Has the radio button for the command been selected?

- Has the radio button for the argument been selected?

Accounting Failure

If AAA is not working, yet there is no entry in the report, there is an invalid setup between Cisco Secure ACS for Windows and the router. Check the following items to troubleshoot this problem:

- Can the router ping the Windows NT or Windows 2000 server?

- Can the Windows NT or Windows 2000 server ping the router?

- Is the TACACS+ host IP address correctly configured in the router?

- Is the identical TACACS+ host key entered on both the router and Cisco Secure ACS for Windows?

- Is TACACS+ accounting configured on the router?

Troubleshooting Dial-In Client PC Problems

If the dial-in user is a Windows 95 or Windows 98 PC using DUN, here are some things to check:

- Is the proper version of DUN installed? It should be DUN version 1.3.
- Are connection properties configured to use Require Encrypted Password under Server Type?
- Is the connection configured to use the correct protocol?
- Is the selected Dial-Up Server type PPP: Windows 95/98, Windows NT 3.5, Internet?
- Is the user authorized to use a specific command?

Other problems may be encountered with remote administration. Check the following:

- Ensure that the web browser is correctly configured—enough cache is allocated and Java is enabled.
- Ensure that Remote Administration is configured to allow remote web browser access (IP address and username/password).

Troubleshooting Using Cisco IOS Commands

The following Cisco IOS debug commands are useful for troubleshooting:

```
debug aaa authentication
debug aaa authorization
debug tacacs
debug radius
```

TACACS+ Overview

TACACS+ is an improved version of TACACS. TACACS+ forwards username and password information to a centralized security server. Figure 3-11 shows a typical TACACS+ topology.

Figure 3-11 *General Features*

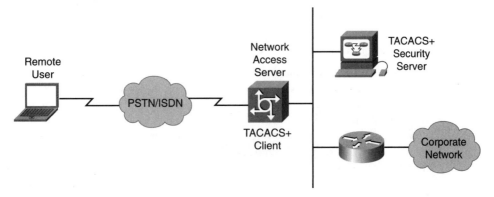

General Features

TACACS+ has the following features:

- **TCP packets for reliable data transport**—TACACS+ uses TCP as the communication protocol between the remote client and security server.

    — Supports the AAA architecture

- **Link is encrypted**—The data payload of IP packets (TCP packets) is encrypted for security and is stored in encrypted form in the remote security database.

    — Supports PAP, CHAP, and MS-CHAP authentication

    — Useful for both LAN and WAN security

- **Serial Line Internet Protocol (SLIP), PPP, and ARA supported for dialup security**—SLIP is TCP/IP over direct connections and modems, which allows one computer to connect to another or to a whole network. PPP is more robust than SLIP, supporting multiple protocols with built-in security. ARA provides to Macintosh users direct access to information and resources at a remote AppleTalk site. TN3270 and X.121 addresses used with X.25 are also supported.

    — Auto-command supported

    — Callback supported

    — Per-user access lists can be assigned in authorization phase

There are at least three versions of TACACS:

- **TACACS**—An industry-standard protocol specification (RFC 1492) that forwards username and password information to a centralized server. The centralized server can be either a TACACS database or a database such as the UNIX password file with TACACS protocol support. For example, the UNIX server with TACACS passes requests to the UNIX database and sends an accept or reject message back to the access server.

- **XTACACS**—Defines the extensions that Cisco added to the TACACS protocol to support new and advanced features. XTACACS is multiprotocol and can authorize connections with SLIP, PPP (IP or Internet Packet Exchange [IPX]), ARA, EXEC, and Telnet. XTACACS supports multiple TACACS servers, syslog for sending accounting information to a UNIX host, connects where the user is authenticated into the access server "shell," and can Telnet or initiate SLIP, PPP, or ARA after initial authentication. XTACACS is essentially obsolete concerning Cisco AAA features and products.

- **TACACS+**—Enhanced and continually improved version of TACACS that allows a TACACS+ server to provide the services of AAA independently. Each service can be tied into its own database or can use the other services available on that server or on the network. TACACS+ was introduced in Cisco IOS Release 10.3. This protocol is a completely new version of the TACACS protocol referenced by RFC 1492 and developed by Cisco. It is not compatible with XTACACS. TACACS+ has been submitted to the IETF as a draft proposal.

The rich feature set of the TACACS+ client/server security protocol is fully supported in Cisco Secure ACS for Windows software.

The first steps in configuring the router are as follows:

Step 1   Enable TACACS+.

Step 2   Specify the list of Cisco Secure ACS for Windows servers that will provide AAA services for the router.

Step 3   Configure the encryption key that is used to encrypt the data transfer between the router and the Cisco Secure ACS for Windows server.

The **aaa new-model** command forces the router to override every other authentication method previously configured for the router lines. If an administrative Telnet or console session is lost while enabling AAA on a Cisco router, and no enable password is specified, the administrator may be locked out of the router and may need to perform the password-recovery process specific to that router to regain access to the device.

CAUTION   When using the Cisco IOS **aaa new-model** command, always provide for an enable password login method. This guards against the risk of being locked out of the router if the administrative session fails while you are in the process of enabling AAA, or if the TACACS+ server becomes unavailable.

Configuring TACACS+

When configuring a NAS to support AAA, as shown in Figure 3-12, at a minimum the following commands should be entered, in the order shown:

```
Router(config)# aaa new-model
Router(config)# aaa authentication login default tacacs+ enable
```

Figure 3-12   *Globally Enabling AAA*

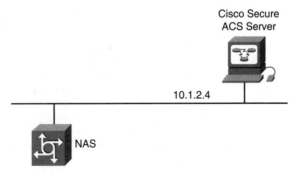

Specifying the "enable" authentication method enables you to reestablish your Telnet or console session and use the enable password to access the router once more. If you fail to do this, and you become locked out of the router, physical access to the router is required (console session), with a minimum of having to perform a password-recovery sequence. At worst, the entire configuration saved in nonvolatile random-access memory (NVRAM) can be lost.

To begin global configuration, enter the following commands, using the correct IP address of the Cisco Secure ACS for Windows servers and your own encryption key:

```
router(config)# tacacs-server key 2bor!2b@?
router(config)# tacacs-server host 10.1.2.4
```

Or use the following:

```
router(config)# tacacs-server host 10.1.2.4 key 2bor!2b@?
```

In this example, the 2bor!2b@? key is the encryption key that is shared between the router and the Cisco Secure ACS for Windows server. The encryption key you choose for your environment should be kept secret to protect the privacy of passwords that are sent between the Cisco Secure ACS for Windows server and the router during the authentication process.

When configuring a TACACS+ key for use on multiple TACACS+ servers, remember that the key must be the same for all TACACS+ servers listed for a given router.

You can specify multiple Cisco Secure ACS for Windows servers by repeating the **tacacs-server** host command.

After you enable AAA globally on the access server, define the authentication method lists, and then apply them to lines and interfaces. These authentication method lists are security profiles that indicate the protocol (ARAP or PPP) or login and authentication method (TACACS+, RADIUS, or local authentication).

To define an authentication method list using the **aaa authentication** command, complete the following steps:

Step 1 Specify the dial-in protocol (ARAP, PPP, or NetWare Access Server Interface [NASI]) or login authentication.

Step 2 Identify a list name or default. A list name is any alphanumeric string you choose. You assign different authentication methods to different named lists. You can specify only one dial-in protocol per authentication method list. However, you can create multiple authentication method lists with each of these options. You must give each list a different name.

Step 3 Specify the authentication method. You can specify up to four methods. For example, you could specify TACACS+, followed by local. This would permit you to log in with a local username and password in case a TACACS+ server is not available on the network.

After defining these authentication method lists, apply them to one of the following:

- **Lines**—tty lines or the console port for login and asynchronous lines (in most cases) for ARA
- **Interfaces**—Interfaces (synchronous or asynchronous) configured for PPP

Use the **aaa authentication** command, as described in Chapter 2, in global configuration mode to enable AAA authentication processes.

The NAS configuration in Example 3-1 shows only commands important to AAA security.

Example 3-1   *Important AAA Security Commands*

```
aaa new-model
aaa authentication login default tacacs+ enable
aaa authentication ppp default tacacs+
aaa authorization exec tacacs+
aaa authorization network tacacs+
aaa accounting exec start-stop tacacs+
aaa accounting network start-stop tacacs+
enable secret 5 $1$x1EE$33AXd2VTVvhbWL0A37tQ3.
enable password 7 15141905172924
!
username admin password 7 094E4F0A1201181D19
!
interface Serial2
 ppp authentication pap
!
tacacs-server host 10.1.1.4
tacacs-server key ciscosecure
!
line con 0
 login authentication no_tacacs
```

Referring to this configuration, the meanings of the configuration entries are as follows:

- **aaa new-model**—Enables the AAA access control model. Use of the **no** form of this command disables this functionality. You can subsequently restore previously configured AAA commands by reissuing the command.

  You could use the **aaa authentication login default tacacs+ enable** command to specify that if your TACACS+ server fails to respond, you can log in to the access server by using your enable password. If you do not have an enable password set on the router, you will not be able to log in to it until you have a functioning TACACS+ UNIX daemon or Windows NT or Windows 2000 server process configured with usernames and passwords. The enable password in this case is a last-resort authentication method. You also can specify **none** as the last-resort method, which means that no authentication is required if all other methods failed.

- **aaa authentication login default tacacs+ enable**—Sets AAA authentication at login using the default list against the TACACS+ server. For this code, the enable password would be used if the TACACS+ server became unavailable.

- **aaa authentication ppp default tacacs+**—Sets AAA authentication for PPP connections using the default list against the TACACS+ database.

- **aaa authorization exec tacacs+**—Sets AAA authorization to determine if the user is allowed to run an EXEC shell on the NAS against the TACACS+ database.

- **aaa authorization network tacacs+**—Sets AAA authorization for all network-related service requests, including SLIP, PPP, PPP NCPs, and ARA protocols, against the TACACS+ database. The TACACS+ database and the NAS must be configured to specify the authorized services.

- **aaa accounting exec start-stop tacacs+**—Sets AAA accounting for EXEC processes on the NAS to record the start and stop time of the session against the TACACS+ database.

- **aaa accounting network start-stop tacacs+**—Sets AAA accounting for all network-related service requests, including SLIP, PPP, PPP NCPs, and ARA protocols, to record the start and stop time of the session against the TACACS+ database.

- **username admin password 7 094E4F0A1201181D19**—Sets a username and password in the local security database for use with the **aaa authentication local-override** command.

NOTE   This command shows the password after it has been encrypted, as it would be shown in a display of the router's configuration as a result of the **service password-encryption** command. The password would be entered as clear text and Cisco IOS would take care of the encryption.

- **ppp authentication pap**—Sets PPP authentication to use PAP, CHAP, or both CHAP and PAP. MS-CHAP could also be specified. The **ppp authentication if-needed** command causes the NAS to not perform CHAP or PAP authentication if the user has already provided authentication. This option is available only on asynchronous interfaces.

- **tacacs-server host 10.1.1.4**—Provides the IP address of the TACACS+ server.

- **tacacs-server key ciscosecure**—Provides the shared-secret key that authenticates the router on the TACACS+ server. This password permits AAA communications between the router and the TACACS+ server.

The following are the first steps in configuring the router:

Step 1   Enable TACACS+.

Step 2   Specify the list of Cisco Secure ACS for Windows servers that will provide AAA services for the router.

Step 3   Configure the encryption key that is used to encrypt the data transfer between the router and the Cisco Secure ACS for Windows server.

The **tacacs-server** command is described as follows:

- **tacacs-server host** (*hostname* | *ip-address*)—Specifies the IP address or the host name of the remote TACACS+ server host. This host is typically a UNIX system running TACACS+ software.

- **tacacs-server key** *shared-secret-text-string*—Specifies a shared secret text string used between the access server and the TACACS+ server. The access server and TACACS+ server use this text string to encrypt passwords and exchange responses. The shared key set with the **tacacs-server key** command is a default key to be used if a per-host key was not set. It is a better practice to set specific keys per **tacacs-server host**.

It is possible to configure TACACS+ without a shared key at both the client device (that is, NAS) and the security server (that is, Cisco Secure) if you do not want the connection to be encrypted. This might be useful for a lab or training environment but is strongly discouraged in a production environment.

NOTE

A router can have only one **tacacs-server key** command even though it might have multiple **tacacs-server host** commands to configure multiple TACACS+ servers for continuity of service. Therefore, the password that is assigned to the router on each of the TACACS+ servers must be identical and will be the password used in the **tacacs-server key** command on the router.

On the other hand, the TACACS+ server can communicate with multiple host routers, each of which can use a unique key. The TACACS+ server associates the key with the individual router identities in its database.

The following command specifies that the AAA authentication list called no_tacacs is to be used on the console:

```
line con 0
 login authentication no_tacacs
```

Verifying TACACS+

This section explains how to verify AAA TACACS+ operations using the following Cisco IOS debug commands:

```
debug aaa authentication
debug tacacs
debug tacacs events
```

Use the **debug tacacs** command on the router to trace TACACS+ packets and display debugging messages for TACACS+ packet traces.

The output listing below shows part of the **debug aaa authentication** command output for a TACACS login attempt that was successful. The information indicates that TACACS+ is the authentication method used.

```
14:01:17: AAA/AUTHEN (567936829): Method=TACACS+
14:01:17: TAC+: send AUTHEN/CONT packet
14:01:17: TAC+ (567936829): received authen response status = PASS
14:01:17: AAA/AUTHEN (567936829): status = PASS
```

Also, note that the AAA/AUTHEN status indicates that the authentication has passed.

There are three possible results of an AAA session:

- Pass
- Fail
- Error

Pass is the desired output. If you see a Fail or Error result in the **debug aaa authentication** output, it could be the result of a configuration or hardware error. Check the configuration on the router first to make sure the TACACS+ server information is correct, and then check connectivity to the server. If you find no problems, it could indicate a misconfiguration of the TACACS+ server.

Troubleshooting follows a basic tenant—look for what changed last. If you made a configuration change and the AAA process quit working, double-check the configuration, going so far as to restore the configuration that you saved before making the change (You did do that, didn't you?) to see if AAA service is restored. If your router and AAA server have been communicating with no problems, no configuration changes have been made, and no new users have been added, then that points toward a hardware or circuit problem.

The next two sections examine the debug output for successful and failed attempts.

debug tacacs Command Example Output—Failure

Example 3-2 shows part of the **debug tacacs** command output for a TACACS+ login attempt that was unsuccessful as indicated by the status FAIL. The status fields are probably the most useful part of the **debug tacacs** command.

Example 3-2 **debug tacacs** *Command Output for a TACACS Unsuccessful Login Attempt*

```
13:53:35: TAC+: Opening TCP/IP connection to 10.1.1.4/49
13:53:35: TAC+: Sending TCP/IP packet number 416942312-1 to 10.1.1.4/49
(AUTHEN/START)
13:53:35: TAC+: Receiving TCP/IP packet number 416942312-2 from 10.1.1.4/49
13:53:35: TAC+ (416942312): received authen response status = GETUSER
13:53:37: TAC+: send AUTHEN/CONT packet
13:53:37: TAC+: Sending TCP/IP packet number 416942312-3 to 10.1.1.4/49
```

Example 3-2 **debug tacacs** *Command Output for a TACACS Unsuccessful Login Attempt (Continued)*

```
(AUTHEN/CONT)
13:53:37: TAC+: Receiving TCP/IP packet number 416942312-4 from 10.1.1.4/49
13:53:37: TAC+ (416942312): received authen response status = GETPASS
13:53:38: TAC+: send AUTHEN/CONT packet
13:53:38: TAC+: Sending TCP/IP packet number 416942312-5 to 10.1.1.4/49
(AUTHEN/CONT)
13:53:38: TAC+: Receiving TCP/IP packet number 416942312-6 from 10.1.1.4/49
13:53:38: TAC+ (416942312): received authen response status = FAIL
13:53:40: TAC+: Closing TCP/IP connection to 10.1.1.4/49
```

debug tacacs Command Example Output—Pass

Example 3-3 shows part of the **debug tacacs** command output for a TACACS login attempt that was successful, as indicated by the status PASS.

Example 3-3 **debug tacacs** *Command Output for a TACACS Successful Login Attempt*

```
14:00:09: TAC+: Opening TCP/IP connection to 10.1.1.4/49
14:00:09: TAC+: Sending TCP/IP packet number 383258052-1 to 10.1.1.4/49 (AUTHEN/START)
14:00:09: TAC+: Receiving TCP/IP packet number 383258052-2 from 10.1.1.4/49
14:00:09: TAC+ (383258052): received authen response status = GETUSER
14:00:10: TAC+: send AUTHEN/CONT packet
14:00:10: TAC+: Sending TCP/IP packet number 383258052-3 to 10.1.1.4/49 (AUTHEN/CONT)
14:00:10: TAC+: Receiving TCP/IP packet number 383258052-4 from 10.1.1.4/49
14:00:10: TAC+ (383258052): received authen response status = GETPASS
14:00:14: TAC+: send AUTHEN/CONT packet
14:00:14: TAC+: Sending TCP/IP packet number 383258052-5 to 10.1.1.4/49 (AUTHEN/CONT)
14:00:14: TAC+: Receiving TCP/IP packet number 383258052-6 from 10.1.1.4/49
14:00:14: TAC+ (383258052): received authen response status = PASS
14:00:14: TAC+: Closing TCP/IP connection to 10.1.1.4/49
```

debug tacacs events Output

Example 3-4 shows sample **debug tacacs events** command output.

Example 3-4 **debug tacacs events** *Command Output*

```
router# debug tacacs events
%LINK-3-UPDOWN: Interface Async2, changed state to up
00:03:16: TAC+: Opening TCP/IP to 10.1.1.4/49 timeout=15
00:03:16: TAC+: Opened TCP/IP handle 0x48A87C to 10.1.1.4/49
00:03:16: TAC+: periodic timer started
00:03:16: TAC+: 10.1.1.4 req=3BD868 id=-1242409656 ver=193 handle=0x48A87C (ESTAB)
expire=14 AUTHEN/START/SENDAUTH/CHAP queued
00:03:17: TAC+: 10.1.1.4 ESTAB 3BD868 wrote 46 of 46 bytes
00:03:22: TAC+: 10.1.1.4 CLOSEWAIT read=12 wanted=12 alloc=12 got=12
00:03:22: TAC+: 10.1.1.4 CLOSEWAIT read=61 wanted=61 alloc=61 got=49
00:03:22: TAC+: 10.1.1.4 received 61 byte reply for 3BD868
00:03:22: TAC+: req=3BD868 id=-1242409656 ver=193 handle=0x48A87C (CLOSEWAIT) expire=9
AUTHEN/START/SENDAUTH/CHAP processed
00:03:22: TAC+: periodic timer stopped (queue empty)
```

continues

Example 3-4 **debug tacacs events** *Command Output (Continued)*

```
00:03:22: TAC+: Closing TCP/IP 0x48A87C connection to 10.1.1.4/49
00:03:22: TAC+: Opening TCP/IP to 10.1.1.4/49 timeout=15
00:03:22: TAC+: Opened TCP/IP handle 0x489F08 to 10.1.1.4/49
00:03:22: TAC+: periodic timer started
00:03:22: TAC+: 10.1.1.4 req=3BD868 id=299214410 ver=192 handle=0x489F08 (ESTAB)
expire=14 AUTHEN/START/SENDPASS/CHAP queued
00:03:23: TAC+: 10.1.1.4 ESTAB 3BD868 wrote 41 of 41 bytes
00:03:23: TAC+: 10.1.1.4 CLOSEWAIT read=12 wanted=12 alloc=12 got=12
00:03:23: TAC+: 10.1.1.4 CLOSEWAIT read=21 wanted=21 alloc=21 got=9
00:03:23: TAC+: 10.1.1.4 received 21 byte reply for 3BD868
00:03:23: TAC+: req=3BD868 id=299214410 ver=192 handle=0x489F08 (CLOSEWAIT) expire=13
AUTHEN/START/SENDPASS/CHAP processed
00:03:23: TAC+: periodic timer stopped (queue empty)
```

In this example, the opening and closing of a TCP connection to a TACACS+ server are shown, and also the bytes read and written over the connection and the connection's TCP status.

The TACACS messages are intended to be self-explanatory or for consumption by service personnel only. However, the following two messages that may be shown require a brief explanation:

- **00:03:16: TAC+: Opening TCP/IP to 10.1.1.4/49 timeout=15**—Indicates that a TCP open request to host 10.1.1.4 on port 49 will time out in 15 seconds if it gets no response.

- **00:03:16: TAC+: Opened TCP/IP handle 0x48A87C to 10.1.1.4/49**—Indicates a successful open operation and provides the address of the internal TCP "handle" for this connection.

There is certainly more information provided in the output than there is time or space to address in this book. For more detailed information, refer to the *Debug Command Reference* on the documentation CD-ROM, the Cisco.com website, or in printed form.

You can get more meaningful output from debug commands if you first configure the router using the **service timestamps** *type* **[uptime] datetime [msec] [localtime] [show-timezone]** command. The following describes the **service timestamps** command parameters (the parameters in brackets in the preceding sentence are optional):

- *type*—Type of message to time-stamp; debug or log.
- **uptime**—Time-stamp with time since the system was rebooted.
- **datetime**—Time-stamp with the date and time.
- **msec**—Include milliseconds in the date and timestamp.
- **localtime**—Time-stamp relative to the local time zone.
- **show-timezone**—Include the time zone name in the timestamp.

RADIUS Overview

RADIUS is an access server AAA protocol developed by Livingston Enterprises, Inc. (now part of Lucent Technologies). It is a system of distributed security that secures remote access to networks and network services against unauthorized access. RADIUS is composed of three components:

- Protocol with a frame format that uses UDP/IP
- Server
- Client

The server runs on a central computer, typically at the customer's site, while the clients reside in the dial-up access servers and can be distributed throughout the network. Cisco incorporated the RADIUS client into Cisco IOS, starting with Cisco IOS Release 11.1.

Client/Server Model

A router operates as a client of RADIUS. The client is responsible for passing user information to designated RADIUS servers, and then acting on the response that is returned. RADIUS servers are responsible for receiving user connection requests, authenticating the user, and then returning all configuration information that is necessary for the client to deliver service to the user. The RADIUS servers can act as proxy clients to other kinds of authentication servers.

Network Security

Transactions between the client and RADIUS server are authenticated using a shared secret, which is never sent over the network. In addition, any user passwords are sent encrypted between the client and RADIUS server to eliminate the possibility that someone who is snooping on an unsecured network could determine a user's password.

Flexible Authentication Mechanisms

The RADIUS server supports a variety of methods to authenticate a user. When it is provided with the username and original password given by the user, it can support PPP, PAP, CHAP, or MS-CHAP UNIX login, and other authentication mechanisms.

Configuring RADIUS

RADIUS configuration is a three-step process:

Step 1 Configure communication between the router and the RADIUS server.

Step 2 Use the AAA global configuration commands to define authentication and authorization method lists containing RADIUS. Method lists include the keywords as follows:

   — **enable**—Uses the enable password for authentication

— **line**—Uses the line password for authentication

— **local**—Uses the local username database for authentication

— **none**—Uses no authentication

— **radius**—Uses RADIUS authentication

— **tacacs+**—Uses TACACS+ authentication

Step 3 Use line and interface commands to cause the defined method lists to be used.

Use the following **radius-server** command to configure router to RADIUS server communication:

```
radius-server key keystring
radius-server host {host-name | ipaddress}
```

You can also accomplish the same thing by combining these two commands into the following single command:

```
radius-server host ipaddress key keystring
```

Examples of using these three commands are shown here:

```
router(config)# radius-server key 2bor!2b@?
router(config)# radius-server host 10.1.2.4
!
router(config)# radius-server host 10.1.2.4 key 2bor!2b@?
```

NOTE   The **radius-server** global command is analogous to **tacacs-server** global commands.

RADIUS is a fully open protocol, distributed in source code format that can be modified to work with any security system that is currently available on the market. Cisco supports RADIUS under its AAA security paradigm. RADIUS can be used with other AAA security protocols, such as TACACS+, Kerberos, or local username lookup. Cisco Secure ACS for Windows supports RADIUS.

RADIUS has been implemented in a variety of network environments that require high levels of security while maintaining network access for remote users. RADIUS combines authentication and authorization. The protocol is specified in RFCs 2138 and 2139.

As of this writing, three major versions of RADIUS are available:

- **IETF, with approximately 63 attributes**—Developed and proposed to IETF by Livingston Enterprises, now a division of Lucent Technologies. The RADIUS protocol is specified in RFC 2138, and RADIUS accounting in RFC 2139.

- **Cisco implementation, supporting approximately 58 attributes**—Starting in Cisco IOS Release 11.2, an increasing number of attributes and functionality are included in each release of Cisco IOS software and Cisco Secure ACS for Windows.

- **Lucent implementation, supporting over 254 attributes**—Lucent is constantly changing and adding vendor-specific attributes, such as token caching and password changing. An API enables rapid development of new extensions, making competing vendors work hard to keep up. Although Livingston Enterprises developed RADIUS originally, it was championed by Ascend.

Vendors have implemented proprietary extensions to RADIUS features. TACACS+ is considered superior because:

- TACACS+ encrypts the entire TACACS+ packet (RADIUS only encrypts the shared-secret password portion).

- TACACS+ separates authentication and authorization, making possible distributed security services.

- RADIUS has limited "name space" for attributes.

Figure 3-13 shows a typical network configuration that uses both TACACS+ and RADIUS.

Figure 3-13 *Comparison of TACACS+ and RADIUS*

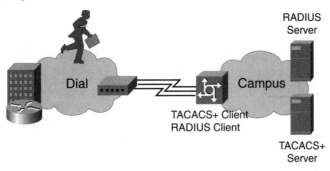

There are several differences between TACACS+ and RADIUS:

- **Functionality**—TACACS+ separates AAA functions according to the AAA architecture, allowing modularity of the security server implementation. RADIUS combines authentication and authorization and separates accounting, thus allowing less flexibility in implementation.

- **Transport protocol**—TACACS+ uses TCP. RADIUS uses UDP, which was chosen for simplification of client and server implementation, yet UDP makes the RADIUS protocol less robust and requires the server to implement reliability measures, such as packet retransmission and timeouts, instead having them built into the TCP protocol.

- **Challenge/response**—TACACS+ supports bidirectional challenge and response as used in CHAP between two routers. RADIUS supports unidirectional challenge and response from the RADIUS security server to the RADIUS client.

- **Protocol support**—TACACS+ provides more complete dial-up and WAN protocol support than RADIUS.

- **Data integrity**—TACACS+ encrypts the entire packet body of every packet. RADIUS only encrypts the Password Attribute portion of the Access-Request packet, which makes TACACS+ more secure.

- **Customization**—The flexibility provided in the TACACS+ protocol allows many things to be customized on a per-user basis (that is, customizable username and password prompts). RADIUS lacks flexibility and therefore many features that are possible with TACACS+ are not possible with RADIUS (that is, message catalogs).

- **Authorization process**—With TACACS+, the server accepts or rejects the authentication request based on the contents of the user profile. The client (router) never knows the contents of the user profile. With RADIUS, all reply attributes in the user profile are sent to the router. The router accepts or rejects the authentication request based on the attributes that are received.

- **Accounting**—TACACS+ accounting includes a limited number of information fields. RADIUS accounting can contain more information than TACACS+ accounting records, which is RADIUS's key advantage over TACACS+.

RADIUS Attribute Enhancements

Cisco has introduced enhancements in the latest releases of the Cisco IOS software to support RADIUS attribute capabilities. Some of the more important ones are discussed here.

ACL Default Direction (RADIUS Attribute 11)

The ACL Default Direction feature permits you to configure access lists that dynamically change the RADIUS packet filter direction upon successful RADIUS user authentication. Default filter direction without the application of the RADIUS Attribute 11 capability is outbound, which means that packets must enter the router and be filtered before being sent to the outbound interface.

With RADIUS Attribute 11, you can set the default direction and override that setting as RADIUS authentication occurs. Setting the direction to filter inbound packets causes the router to filter the packets before they are allowed to enter the router.

The following steps are required to implement RADIUS Attribute 11 on a Cisco IOS router:

Step 1   Set the default direction of filters from RADIUS to inbound or outbound using the global **radius-server attribute 11** command. The command format is

```
radius-server attribute 11 direction default [inbound | outbound]
```

Step 2   Attach the **Filter-Id** attribute to the clients on the RADIUS server. Use the format **Filter-Id = "myfilter.out"** to override the default direction to outbound. Use the format **Filter-ID = "myfilter.in"** to override the default direction to inbound. A typical RADIUS user configuration might look like this:

```
Client Password = "mypasswd"
        Service-Type = Framed,
        Framed-Protocol = PPP,
        Filter-Id = "myfilter.out"
```

Accounting Input Gigawords (RADIUS Attribute 52)

Enabled by default, RADIUS Attribute 52 allows the router to maintain a running count of how many times the Acct-Input-Octets counter has wrapped around 2^{32} (4,294,967,296) while providing RADIUS service. The counter resets to 0 at 2^{32} and RADIUS Attribute 52 simply keeps track of how many times the counter refreshed in order to provide an accurate packet count when viewing service statistics. This attribute does not require any configuration.

Accounting Output Gigawords (RADIUS Attribute 53)

Enabled by default, RADIUS Attribute 53 allows the router to maintain a running count of how many times the Acct-Output-Octets counter has wrapped around 2^{32} (4,294,967,296) while providing RADIUS service. The counter resets to 0 at 2^{32} and RADIUS Attribute 52 simply keeps track of how many times the counter refreshed in order to provide an accurate packet count when viewing service statistics. This attribute does not require any configuration.

Tunnel Client Endpoint (Radius Attribute 66)

The Tunnel Client Endpoint capability allows the user to specify the host name of the network access server, rather than having to remember the IP address of the NAS. A typical client configuration might look like the following example:

```
Cisco.com Password = "cisco"
Service-Type = Outbound-User,
Tunnel-Type = :1:L2F,
Tunnel-Medium-Type = :1:IP,
Tunnel-Client-Endpoint = :1:"cisco2"
Tunnel-Server-Endpoint = :1:"172.21.135.4",
Tunnel-Assignment-Id = :1:"nas1",
Tunnel-Password = :1:"cisco"
```

Connection Information (RADIUS Attribute 77)

This attribute is enabled by default and keeps track of the upstream and downstream speeds of connecting clients. You can view these speeds by using the **debug radius** command on the router. You can tell whether the modem connection speed was renegotiated to a lower speed after the connection was made.

Kerberos Overview

Kerberos is a secret-key network authentication protocol, developed at the Massachusetts Institute of Technology (MIT), that uses the Data Encryption Standard (DES) cryptographic algorithm for encryption and authentication. Kerberos was designed to authenticate requests for network resources. Kerberos, like other secret-key systems, is based on the concept of a trusted third party that performs secure verification of users and services.

In the Kerberos protocol, this trusted third party is called the Key Distribution Center (KDC). It performs the same function as a certification authority (CA), which is discussed in Chapter 9, "Building Advanced IPSec VPNs Using Cisco Routers and Certificate Authorities." The following lists some of the distinguishing characteristics of Kerberos:

- Secret-key authentication protocol
- Authenticates users and network services that they use
- Uses 40- or 56-bit DES for encryption and authentication (weak by today's standards)
- Relies on a trusted third party (KDC) for key distribution
- Embodies "single login" concept
- Expensive to administer—labor intensive

Cisco IOS Release 12.0 includes Kerberos 5 support, which allows organizations that are already deploying Kerberos 5 to use an existing KDC (similar to a CA in IP Security [IPSec]) with their routers and NAS. The following network services are Kerberized in Cisco IOS software:

- **Telnet**—Logs a client (from router to another host) into a server (from another host to router) to permit interactive Telnet sessions
- **rlogin**—Logs a user in to a remote UNIX host for an interactive session similar to Telnet
- **rsh**—Logs a user in to a remote UNIX host and allows execution of one UNIX command
- **rcp**—Logs a user in to a remote UNIX host and allows copying of files from the host

---

NOTE   You can use the **connect** EXEC command with the **/telnet** or **/rlogin** keyword to log in to a host that supports Telnet or rlogin, respectively. You can use the **/encrypt kerberos** keyword to establish an encrypted Telnet session from a router to a remote Kerberos host. Alternatively, you can use the **telnet** EXEC command with the **/encrypt kerberos** keyword to establish an encrypted Telnet session.

NOTE   You can use the **rlogin** and **rsh** EXEC commands to initiate rlogin and rsh sessions.

NOTE   You can use the **copy rcp** EXEC command or configuration command to enable obtaining configuration or image files from an RCP server.

Chapter Summary

This chapter discussed Cisco Secure ACS for Windows and Cisco Secure ACS for UNIX. The following list identifies important points that were described for each of these management products:

- Cisco Secure ACS for Windows has the following characteristics:
  - Runs as a service on Windows NT or 2000 Server.
  - Authenticates using TACACS+ or RADIUS.
  - Cisco NAS, PIX, VPN 3000 or routers can authenticate against Cisco Secure ACS for Windows.
  - Can use usernames and passwords in the Windows NT or 2000 user database, ACS user database, token server, or NDS.
  - Installation is similar to other Windows applications (InstallShield).
  - Management is done via a web browser.
  - Supports distributed ACS systems.
  - With a remote security server for AAA, the server performs AAA, enabling easier management.
  - TACACS+, RADIUS, and Kerberos are the security server protocols supported by Cisco.
  - Troubleshooting tools include debug commands for TACACS+.
- Cisco Secure ACS for UNIX has the following characteristics:
  - Provides AAA security for enterprise networks.
  - Supports both TACACS+ and RADIUS.
  - Uses the Sybase SQLAnywhere database by default and can interface with Sybase Enterprise SQL and Oracle Enterprise databases.
  - Customers can upgrade any 2.x version of Cisco Secure ACS for UNIX to the most current release.
  - Is easy to install and has a web-based GUI.
  - RADIUS databases can be imported into Cisco Secure ACS for UNIX.

Cisco IOS Commands Presented in This Chapter

Many Cisco IOS version 12.2 commands were discussed or referenced in this chapter. These commands can be found in the *Command Reference* online at http://www.cisco.com/univercd /cc/td/doc/product/software/ios123/123mindx/crgindx.htm.

Chapter Review Questions

The following review questions cover some of the key facts and concepts that were introduced in this chapter. Answers to these questions can be found in Appendix A, "Answers to Chapter Review Questions."

1 What authentication protocols are supported by Cisco Secure ACS for Windows?

2 Cisco Secure ACS for Windows can communicate with other ACS servers as masters, clients, or peers to enable what three strong distributed system features?

3 Which Windows NT service module has the primary responsibility for determining whether access should be granted and for defining the privileges associated with each user?

4 List the six steps required to install Cisco Secure ACS for Windows?

5 What protocol must you use to perform the configuration of Cisco Secure ACS for Windows?

6 When you want to configure reusable sets of authorization components to apply to one or more users or groups of users, which option from the Cisco Secure ACS for Windows main menu would you choose?

7 What system administration capabilities does the Cisco Secure ACS for UNIX enable for UNIX 2.3 DSM?

8 What operating system supports Cisco Secure ACS for Unix 2.3?

9 What are the first steps that are required to configure a Cisco IOS router to use TACACS+ with a Cisco Secure ACS for Windows server?

10 You will be configuring your Cisco IOS router for access to three different Cisco Secure ACS for Windows servers using TACACS+. What must you keep in mind as you prepare to configure the router for AAA service?

11 Which Cisco IOS command can you use to get a more meaningful output from debug commands?

Case Study

Continuing with the case study for The Future Corporation, the system administrator now needs to continue the configuration of the DallasR1 router shown in Figure 3-14.

Scenario

Complete the following configuration tasks on the DallasR1 router:

1 Identify the TACACS+ server whose IP address is 142.16.18.200 using a preshared key of future123key.

2 To make it easier to track logging events and to make debug output more useable, set up the router to time-stamp logging and debug entries using local time. Record debug times to the millisecond.

3 Set up accounting to record all start and stop times for EXEC processes and network processes on the ACS server.

Figure 3-14 *The Future Corporation*

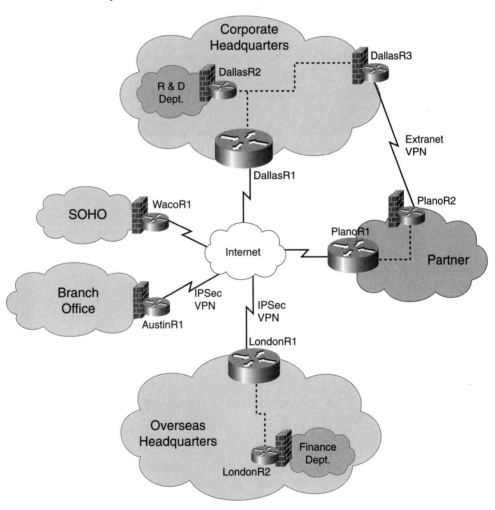

Solutions

The following commands will accomplish the required configuration:

1 Identify the TACACS+ server whose IP address is 142.16.18.200 using a preshared key of future123key:

```
DallasR1(config)# tacacs-server host 142.16.18.200
DallasR1(config)# tacacs-server key future123key
```

2 To make it easier to track logging events and to make debug output more useable, set up the router to time-stamp logging and debug entries using local time. Record debug times to the millisecond.

```
DallasR1(config)# service timestamps debug datetime localtime msec
DallasR1(config)# service timestamps log datetime localtime
```

3 Set up accounting to record all start and stop times for EXEC processes and network processes on the ACS server:

```
DallasR1(config)# aaa accounting exec start-stop tacacs+
DallasR1(config)# aaa accounting network start-stop tacacs+
```

Once these commands have been entered, the configuration for router DallasR1 (excluding interface entries) looks like Example 3-5.

Example 3-5 *DallasR1 Final Configuration*

```
version 12.2
service timestamps debug datetime localtime msec
service timestamps log datetime localtime
service password-encryption
!
hostname DallasR1
!
aaa new-model
aaa authentication login default group tacacs+ local
aaa authentication login console-in group tacacs+ enable
aaa accounting exec start-stop tacacs+
aaa accounting network start-stop tacacs+
enable secret 5 $1$ES4r$tA1rlg0beW/Kvk6jGIj2f.
enable secret level 2 5 $1$mCGe$.1fTlJ.fcR8NHqa0AMR2F/
enable password 7 09611E1C171113171C
!
username aaadmin password 7 1531035C147F3F752B38
!
access-list 88 permit 192.168.44.121
access-list 88 permit 192.168.44.122
access-list 88 permit 192.168.64.123
access-list 88 permit 142.16.18.121
access-list 88 permit 142.16.18.122
access-list 88 permit 142.16.18.123
```

Example 3-5 *DallasR1 Final Configuration (Continued)*

```
snmp-server community ROSNMP ro
snmp-server community RWSNMP rw 88
tacacs-server host 142.16.18.200
tacacs-server key future123key
privilege exec level 2 ping
!
banner motd #
WARNING: You are connected to $(hostname) on The Future Corporation network.
Unauthorized access and use of this network will be vigorously prosecuted. #
!
line con 0
 login authentication console-in
 exec-timeout 4 20
line aux 0
 login
 password 7 112A115507471F5D0721
 exec-timeout 4 20
line vty 0 4
 login
 password 7 05280E5F31195A581A0E
!
end
```

Upon completion of this chapter, you will be able to perform the following tasks:

- Disable Unused Router Services and Interfaces
- Describe the Differences Between Various Types of Cisco Access Control Lists
- Design and Build Both Standard and Extended Access Control Lists
- Use Access Control Lists to Mitigate Common Router Security Threats
- Implement Syslog Logging
- Design Secure Management and Reporting for Router Networks
- Use AutoSecure to Secure Cisco Routers

CHAPTER 4

Cisco Router Threat Mitigation

This chapter describes the risks associated with connecting an enterprise to the Internet and the methods used to reduce those risks. It includes the following topics:

- Using routers to secure the network
- Disabling unused security-related router services
- Disabling unused router interfaces
- Implementing Cisco access control lists
- Mitigating security threats using access control lists
- Filtering router service traffic
- Filtering network traffic
- Mitigating distributed denial of service (DDoS)
- Configuring a sample router
- Implementing syslog logging

Using Routers to Secure the Network

This section considers different router topologies that can be used to secure a network, including a standalone perimeter router; a perimeter router and firewall; a perimeter router with integrated firewall; and a perimeter router, firewall, and internal firewall.

Standalone Perimeter Router

The most basic routed network consists of a corporate LAN connected to the Internet using a single perimeter router. This router must secure the corporate network (trusted network) from malicious activity originating on the Internet (untrusted network). Installations of this type, shown in Figure 4-1, are typical of small enterprises.

The perimeter router, being the only line of defense for the enterprise, is relied upon to both authenticate Internet users and prevent as many attacks as possible.

Figure 4-1 *Standalone Perimeter Router*

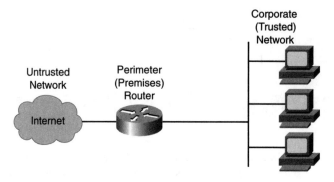

Perimeter Router and Firewall

Midsize networks typically employ a firewall appliance behind the perimeter router, as shown in Figure 4-2.

Figure 4-2 *Perimeter Router and Firewall*

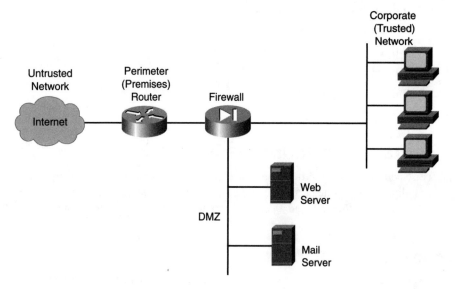

In this scenario, the perimeter router now acts as a screening device, passing all packets destined for the corporate network to the firewall for further processing. The firewall, with its additional security features, can perform user authentication as well as more in-depth packet filtering.

Firewall installations also make it possible to build a demilitarized zone (DMZ) where hosts (that are commonly accessed from the Internet) are placed.

Perimeter Router with Integrated Firewall

Cisco offers an alternative to a dedicated firewall by incorporating many firewall features in the perimeter router itself. Figure 4-3 shows an example of this type of installation.

Figure 4-3   *Perimeter Router with Integrated Firewall*

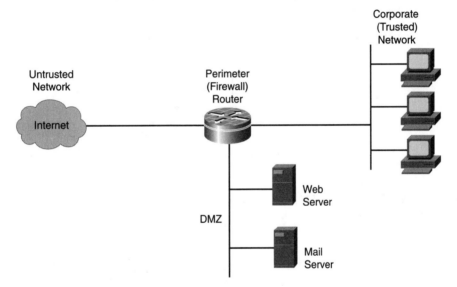

Although this approach does not provide the same security features that a Cisco PIX Firewall appliance offers, a router with an integrated firewall feature set may solve many small to midsize business perimeter security requirements.

Perimeter Router, Firewall, and Internal Router

Finally, many midsize to large enterprises use internal (local network) routers along with perimeter (premises) routers and firewall appliances, as shown in Figure 4-4.

Internal routers provide even more security to the network by screening traffic to various parts of the protected corporate network.

Sometimes, internal (local network) routers are replaced by high-end Cisco Catalyst series switches, which contain their own security features.

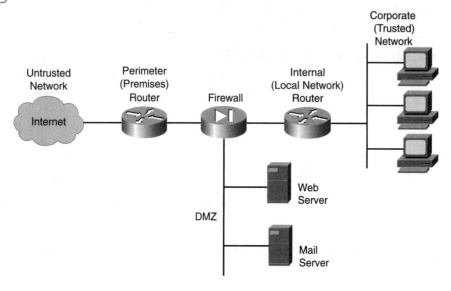

Figure 4-4   *Perimeter Router, Firewall, and Internal Router*

Securing Router Services and Interfaces

This section discusses Cisco router network services and interfaces and how to secure them.

Cisco routers support many network services that may or may not be required in certain enterprise networks. Turning off or restricting access to these services greatly improves network security by providing only those services that the network requires, and no more. Leaving unused network services enabled increases the possibility of those services being used maliciously.

The following sections discuss the services that have been chosen for their security-related features. These are the router services that are most likely to be used in network attacks.

Disabling BOOTP Server

BOOTP is a UDP service that can be used by Cisco routers to access copies of Cisco IOS on another Cisco router running the BOOTP service. In this scenario, one Cisco router acts as a Cisco IOS server that can download Cisco IOS to other Cisco routers acting as BOOTP clients, as shown in Figure 4-5.

In reality, this service is rarely used and can allow an attacker to download a copy of a router's configuration. This service is enabled by default.

Figure 4-5 *BOOTP Server*

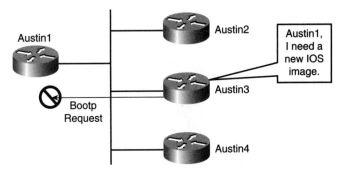

To disable the BOOTP service, use the **no ip bootp server** command from global configuration mode. The syntax for the **no ip bootp server** command is as follows:

```
no ip bootp server
```

This command has no arguments or keywords.

Disabling CDP Service

CDP is a device discovery protocol that runs over Layer 2 on all Cisco-manufactured devices (routers, bridges, access servers, and switches) and allows network management applications to discover Cisco devices that are neighbors of already known devices. CDP is media- and protocol-independent and can be used to show information about the interfaces that your router uses. This service is enabled by default.

With CDP, network management applications can learn the device type and the SNMP agent address of neighboring devices running lower-layer, transparent protocols. This feature enables applications to send SNMP queries to neighboring devices, as shown in Figure 4-6.

Figure 4-6 *CDP Service*

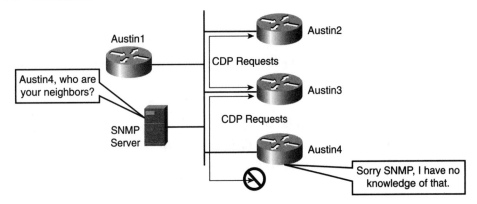

If a router has SNMP enabled and has used CDP to discover its neighbors, an attacker may be able to access important routing information by using an SNMP server.

Disable the CDP server by using the **no cdp run** command in global configuration mode. The syntax for the **no cdp run** command is as follows:

```
no cdp run
```

This command has no arguments or keywords.

If you need to use CDP, restrict its use to only those interfaces that require it. Otherwise, use the **no cdp enable** command in interface configuration mode to disable it, as shown here:

```
Austin4(config)# interface e0/1
Austin4(config-if)# no cdp enable
```

Disabling Configuration Autoloading Service

Cisco routers may load their startup configuration from a network server as well as from their local memory. Loading router configurations across a network, as shown in Figure 4-7, can be dangerous and should only be considered for fully trusted networks (as in a standalone test network). This service is disabled by default.

Figure 4-7 *Configuration Autoloading Service*

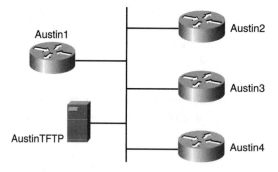

Disable the configuration autoloading service by using the **no boot network** and **no service config** commands in global configuration mode. The syntax for the **no boot network** command is as follows:

```
no boot network remote-url
```

- *remote-url*—Location of the configuration file. Use the following syntax:
    - ftp:[[[//[*username*[:*password*]@]*location*]/*directory*]/*filename*]
    - rcp:[[[//[*username*@]*location*]/*directory*]/*filename*]
    - tftp:[[[//*location*]/*directory*]/*filename*]

The syntax for the **no service config** command is as follows:

```
no service config
```

This command has no arguments or keywords.

Restricting DNS Service

By default, the Cisco router DNS service sends name queries to the 255.255.255.255 broadcast address. You should avoid using this broadcast address because it may allow an attacker to emulate one of your DNS servers. Figure 4-8 shows a router requesting DNS services.

Figure 4-8   *Requesting DNS Service*

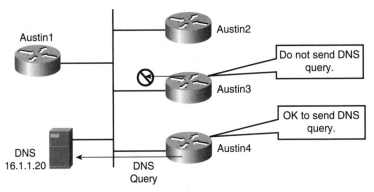

This service is enabled by default. If your routers need to use this service, ensure that you explicitly set the name of your DNS servers in the router configuration.

Set the DNS server names using the **ip name-server** command in global configuration mode. The syntax for the **ip name-server** command is as follows:

```
ip name-server server-address1 [server-address2...server-address6]
```

- *server-address1* — IP address of the name server.

- *server-address2...server-address6* (Optional) — IP addresses of additional name servers (a maximum of six name servers is allowed).

NOTE   Always disable the DNS service when it is not in use.

When the DNS service is not required by your network, disable it by using the **no ip domain-lookup** command in global configuration mode. The syntax for this command is as follows:

```
no ip domain-lookup
```

This command has no arguments or keywords.

Disabling FTP Server

The FTP server feature configures a router to act as an FTP server. FTP clients can copy files to and from certain directories on the router. In addition, the router can perform many other standard FTP server functions. This feature first became available in Cisco IOS Software Release 11.3 AA.

FTP can be used to gain access to the router file system and therefore can be used to attack the network or the router itself. Unless your routers are being used as FTP servers, you should always disable the FTP server feature.

Starting in Cisco IOS Software Release 12.3, the router FTP service is disabled by default using the **no ftp-server write-enable** command. This can be seen in any Cisco IOS Software Release 12.3 or greater by using the **show running-config** command as shown in Example 4-1 (this example shows only a small portion of the **show running-config** command output).

Example 4-1   **no ftp-server write-enable** *Command Usage Example*

```
Austin4# show running-config
!
!
no ftp-server write-enable
!
```

Routers that are operating with Cisco IOS Software Release 12.3 or earlier should have their FTP servers disabled using the **no ftp-server enable** command, as shown in Figure 4-9.

Figure 4-9   *Disabling FTP Server*

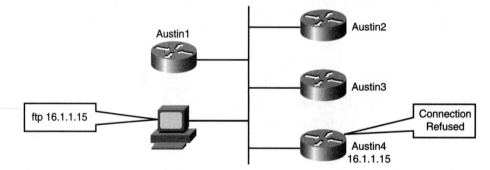

Routers that are operating with Cisco IOS Software Release 12.3 or later, where the FTP server has been manually enabled, should have the FTP server disabled using the **no ftp-server write-enable** command, as shown in Figure 4-9.

The syntax for the commands is as follows:

```
no ftp-server enable
no ftp-server write-enable
```

These commands have no arguments or keywords.

Disabling Finger Service

The Finger protocol (port 79) allows users throughout the network to get a list of the users currently using a particular routing device. The information displayed includes the processes running on the system, the line number, connection name, idle time, and terminal location. This information is provided through the Cisco Internet over Satellite IOS software **show users** EXEC command. Although this information is not usually sensitive in nature, unauthorized persons can use this information to plan malicious damage. This service is enabled by default. Figure 4-10 shows how to disable finger service.

Figure 4-10 *Disabling Finger Service*

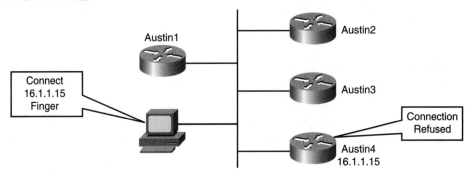

Disable the finger service when not a network requirement by using the **no ip finger** or **no service finger** commands in global configuration mode, as shown in the configuration in Example 4-2 for router Austin4 from Figure 4-11.

Example 4-2 **no service finger** *Command Usage Example*

```
Austin4(config)# no ip finger
Austin4(config)# no service finger
Austin4(config)# exit
Austin4# connect 16.1.1.15 finger
Trying 16.1.1.15, 79 ...
% Connection refused by remote host
```

NOTE   The **service finger** command has been replaced by the **ip finger** command. However, the **service finger** and **no service finger** commands continue to function to maintain backward compatibility with older versions of Cisco IOS software.

The syntax for the **no ip finger** command is as follows:

```
no ip finger
```

This command has no arguments or keywords.

The syntax for the **no service finger** command is as follows:

```
no service finger
```

This command has no arguments or keywords.

Disabling Gratuitous ARPs

Most Cisco routers (by default) send out a gratuitous Address Resolution Protocol (ARP) message whenever a client connects and negotiates an IP address over a PPP connection. Exploiting gratuitous ARP messages is the main mechanism used in ARP poisoning attacks. You should disable gratuitous ARP messages on each router interface unless they are otherwise needed.

NOTE   Cisco routers generate a gratuitous ARP transmission even when the client receives the address from a local address pool.

Starting with Cisco IOS Software Release 11.3, system administrators can disable gratuitous ARP transmissions by using the **no ip gratuitous-arps** command in global configuration mode, as shown in Figure 4-11.

Figure 4-11 *Disabling Proxy ARP*

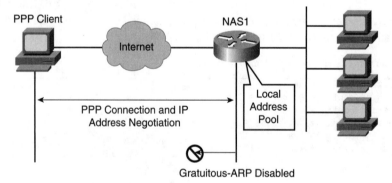

The syntax for the **no ip gratuitous-arps** command is as follows:

```
no ip gratuitous-arps
```

This command has no arguments or keywords.

Disabling HTTP Service

Most recent Cisco IOS software versions support remote configuration and monitoring using the World Wide Web's HTTP protocol. In general, HTTP access is equivalent to interactive access to the router. The authentication protocol used for HTTP is equivalent to sending a clear-text password across the network, and, unfortunately, there is no effective provision in HTTP for challenge-based or one-time passwords (OTPs). This makes HTTP a relatively risky choice for use across the public Internet. The default setting for this service is Cisco device dependent.

NOTE   The Cisco Security Device Manager (SDM) uses HTTP to access the router. Do not disable the router HTTP service if SDM is to be used to manage the router.

If you choose to use HTTP for management, you should restrict access to appropriate IP addresses by using the **ip http access-class** command. You should also configure authentication by using the **ip http authentication** command. As with interactive logins, the best choice for HTTP authentication is to use a TACACS+ or RADIUS server. It is usually wisest to avoid using the "enable" password as an HTTP password.

If web-based administration is not required, disable the HTTP service by using the **no ip http server** command in global configuration mode. Figure 4-12 shows an example of disabling HTTP service.

Figure 4-12 *Disabling HTTP Service*

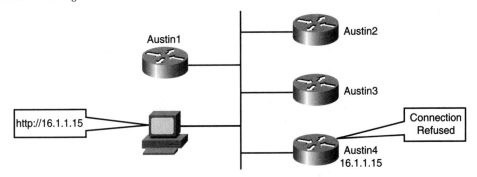

The syntax for the **no ip http server** command is as follows:

```
no ip http server
```

This command has no arguments or keywords.

If web-based administration is a requirement for your network, make sure to implement the following:

- Configure usernames and passwords as described in Chapter 3, "Advanced AAA Security for Cisco Router Networks."

- Use authentication, authorization, and accounting (AAA; external AAA servers preferred) whenever possible.

- Use IP access control lists (ACLs) to restrict which hosts have web server access to the routers (presented in the section of this chapter titled "Implementing Cisco Access Control Lists").

- Use syslog logging to track who accesses the routers and when (presented in the section of this chapter titled "Implementing Syslog Logging").

Disabling IP Classless Routing Service

At times the router may receive packets destined for a subnet of a network that has no network default route. If the IP classless service is enabled, the Cisco IOS software will forward such packets to the best supernet route possible. This service is enabled by default. This service can be used by various attacks and thus, unless it is a requirement of your network, should be disabled.

To disable IP classless routing, use the **no ip classless** command in global configuration mode. The syntax for the **no ip classless** command is as follows:

```
no ip classless
```

This command has no arguments or keywords.

Disabling IP Directed Broadcasts

IP directed broadcasts are used in the extremely common and popular smurf and fraggle DoS attacks. This service is enabled in Cisco IOS versions earlier than Release 12.0 and is disabled in Cisco IOS Release 12.0 and later.

An IP directed broadcast is a datagram that is sent to the broadcast address of a subnet to which the sending machine is not directly attached. The directed broadcast is routed through the network as a unicast packet until it arrives at the target subnet, where it is converted into a link-layer broadcast. Because of the nature of the IP addressing architecture, only the last router in the chain, the one that is connected directly to the target subnet, can conclusively identify a directed broadcast.

In a smurf attack, the attacker sends ICMP echo requests from a falsified source address to a directed broadcast address, causing all the hosts on the target subnet to send replies to the falsified source. By sending a continuous stream of such requests, the attacker can create a much larger stream of replies, which can completely inundate the host whose address is being falsified.

If a Cisco interface is configured with the **no ip directed-broadcast** command, as shown in Figure 4-13, directed broadcasts that would otherwise be converted into link-layer broadcasts at that interface are dropped instead.

Figure 4-13 *Disabling IP Directed Broadcasts*

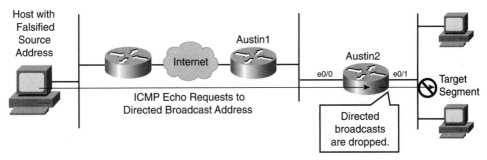

Disable IP directed broadcasts by using the **no ip directed-broadcast** command in interface configuration mode, as demonstrated in Example 4-3.

Example 4-3 **no ip directed-broadcast** *Command Usage Example*

```
Austin2(config)# interface e0/1
Austin2(config-if)# no ip directed-broadcast
Austin2(config-if)# exit
```

The syntax for the **no ip directed-broadcast** command is as follows:

```
no ip directed-broadcast
```

This command has no arguments or keywords.

Disabling IP Identification

IP identification support allows you to query a TCP port for identification. This feature enables RFC 1413, an unsecure protocol, for reporting the identity of a client that is initiating a TCP connection and a host that is responding to the connection.

With IP identification support, an attacker can connect to a TCP port on a host, issue a simple text string to request information, and get back a simple text-string reply. No attempt is made to protect against unauthorized queries. This data can provide network information to an attacker. The service should be explicitly disabled.

Disable RFC 1413 identification by using the **no ip identd** global configuration command. The syntax for the **no ip identd** command is as follows:

```
no ip identd
```

This command has no arguments or keywords.

Disabling ICMP Mask Replies

Mask replies are disabled in Cisco IOS by default. When mask replies are enabled, the Cisco IOS software responds to ICMP mask requests by sending ICMP mask reply messages containing the interface's IP address mask. These messages can provide an attacker with information about the subnet masks that are used by a network. This information can be gathered during reconnaissance attacks and used in creating a network diagram to be used for subsequent attacks. As shown in Figure 4-14, automatic replies must be disabled on all router interfaces, especially those pointing to untrusted networks.

Figure 4-14 *Disabling ICMP Mask Replies*

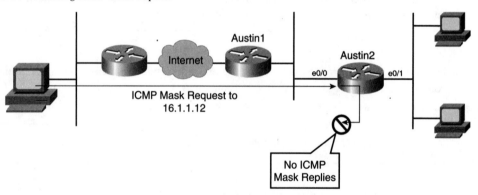

Disable IP mask replies by using the **no ip mask-reply** command in interface configuration mode, as demonstrated in Example 4-4.

Example 4-4 **no ip mask-reply** *Command Usage Example*

```
Austin2(config)# interface e0/0
Austin2(config-if)# no ip mask-reply
Austin2(config-if)# exit
```

The syntax for the **no ip mask-reply** command is as follows:

```
no ip mask-reply
```

This command has no arguments or keywords.

Disabling ICMP Redirects

Redirect messages are enabled in Cisco IOS by default. An ICMP redirect message instructs an end node to use a specific router as its path to a particular destination. In a properly functioning IP network, a router sends redirects only to hosts on its own local subnets, no end node ever sends a redirect, and no redirect is ever sent more than one network hop away. However, an attacker may violate these rules.

IP redirects enable the sending of redirect messages if the router is forced to resend packets through the same interface on which they were received. This can be used to map the network and thus should be explicitly disabled on interfaces to untrusted networks.

As shown in Figure 4-15, disable IP redirects using the **no ip redirect** command in interface configuration mode.

Figure 4-15 *Disabling IP Redirects*

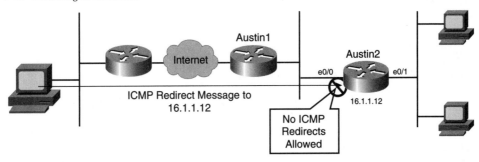

You can use the **no ip redirect** command in interface configuration mode, as demonstrated in Example 4-5.

Example 4-5 **no ip redirect** *Command Usage Example*

```
Austin2(config)# interface e0/0
Austin2(config-if)# no ip redirect
Austin2(config-if)# exit
```

The syntax for the **no ip redirect** command is as follows:

```
no ip redirect
```

This command has no arguments or keywords.

TIP   It is a good idea to filter out incoming ICMP redirects at the input interfaces of any router that lies at a border between administrative domains. It is also not unreasonable for any ACL that is applied on the input side of a Cisco router interface to filter out all ICMP redirects. This will cause no operational impact in a correctly configured network. Note that this filtering prevents only redirect attacks launched by remote attackers. It is still possible for attackers to cause significant trouble using redirects if their host is directly connected to the same segment as a host that is under attack.

Disabling IP Source Routing

The IP protocol supports source routing options that allow the sender of an IP datagram to control the route that datagram will take toward its ultimate destination, and generally the route that any reply will take on the return trip. These options are rarely used for legitimate purposes in real networks. Some older IP implementations do not process source-routed packets properly, and it may be possible to crash machines running these implementations by sending them datagrams with source routing options. Source routing is enabled in Cisco IOS by default.

A Cisco router with **no ip source-route** set will never forward an IP packet that carries a source routing option. You should use this command unless you know that your network needs source routing.

Disable IP source routing by using the **no ip source-route** command in global configuration mode. The syntax for the **no ip source-route** command is as follows:

```
no ip source-route
```

This command has no arguments or keywords.

Disabling ICMP Unreachable Messages

Attackers can use ICMP unreachable messages to map your network because they notify the sender of incorrect (unreachable) IP addresses. These messages are enabled in Cisco IOS by default and should be disabled on all interfaces, especially those interfaces that are connected to untrusted networks.

Disable IP unreachable messages by using the **no ip unreachable** command in interface configuration mode, as demonstrated in Example 4-6.

Example 4-6 **no ip unreachable** *Command Usage Example*

```
Austin2(config)# interface e0/0
Austin2(config-if)# no ip unreachable
Austin2(config-if)# exit
```

The syntax for the **no ip unreachable** command is as follows:

```
no ip unreachable
```

This command has no arguments or keywords.

NOTE   Using the **no ip unreachable** command can complicate system-troubleshooting efforts. It is important to know when addresses are unreachable. When you use the **no ip unreachable** command, keep in mind that you may need to temporarily disable the command to perform comprehensive troubleshooting of your network.

Disabling MOP Service

The Digital Equipment Corporation Maintenance Operation Protocol (MOP) service is enabled, by default, on most Cisco router Ethernet interfaces. MOP presents a potential attack vector on the router and therefore should be explicitly disabled at all interfaces that do not require it.

Disable the MOP service by using the **no mop enabled** command in interface configuration mode, as shown in Figure 4-16.

Figure 4-16 *Disabling MOP*

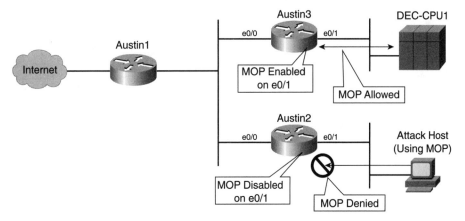

The syntax for the **no mop enabled** command is as follows:

```
no mop enabled
```

This command has no arguments or keywords.

Disabling NTP Service

The Network Time Protocol (NTP) is used to synchronize time on multiple devices. A vulnerability has been discovered (and publicly announced) in the NTP daemon query-processing functionality. By sending a crafted NTP control packet, it is possible to trigger a buffer overflow in the NTP daemon.

This vulnerability can be exploited remotely. The successful exploitation may cause arbitrary code to be executed on the target machine. This vulnerability is difficult to exploit and would require significant engineering skill and a thorough knowledge of the internal operation of Cisco IOS software or the SUN Solaris operating system. Both NTP server and client devices are vulnerable.

When enabled, the router acts as a time server for other network devices. When NTP is properly configured and protected, it can be a valuable troubleshooting aid because it synchronizes logging time stamps across network devices. NTP service is enabled by default. Router Austin4 in Figure 4-17 has NTP service disabled.

Figure 4-17 *Disabling NTP Service*

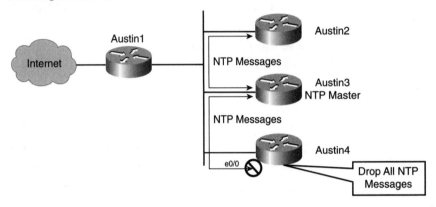

If you need to use NTP, it is important that you do the following:

- Configure a trusted time source and configure all routers as part of an NTP hierarchy.
- Use proper authentication.
- Use an ACL to drop NTP messages at the router interfaces (more information about writing ACLs is given later in this chapter under the section titled "Implementing Cisco Access Control Lists").

NOTE   When using ACLs to drop NTP messages, keep in mind that disabling NTP messages on one router interface does not prevent NTP messages from other parts of the router.

To prevent an interface from receiving NTP packets, use the **ntp disable** interface configuration command, as demonstrated in Example 4-7.

Example 4-7   **ntp disable** *Command Usage Example*

```
Austin4(config)# interface e0/0
Austin4(config-if)# ntp disable
Austin4(config-if)# exit
```

The syntax for the **ntp disable** command is as follows:

```
ntp disable
```

This command has no arguments or keywords.

Disabling PAD Service

The packet assembler/disassembler (PAD) service is, by default, enabled on most Cisco routers. This service is used to enable X.25 connections between the routers and other network devices. One example of where the PAD service is used is when a router must process traffic between a remote IP user and an X.25 host. In this scenario, the remote IP user communicates with the enterprise router PAD service, which then performs any IP-to-X.25 protocol translation and X.25 message forwarding.

Once a connection to the router PAD service is established, an attacker could use the PAD interface to cause disruptions to both route processing and device stability. Therefore, the PAD service should be explicitly disabled when not required for X.25 network operations.

Disable the PAD service by using the **no service pad** global configuration command, as shown in Figure 4-18.

Figure 4-18 *Disabling PAD Service*

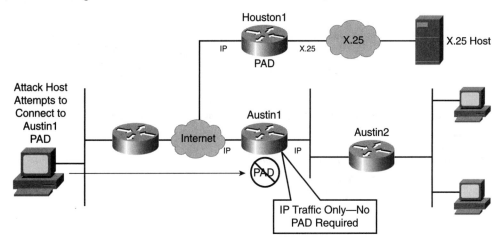

The syntax for the **no service pad** command is as follows:

```
no service pad
```

This command has several arguments and keywords but they are not required to disable the PAD service and therefore are not described here.

Disabling Proxy ARP

When proxy ARP is enabled on a Cisco router, it allows that router to extend the network (at Layer 2) across multiple interfaces (LAN segments) by configuring the router to act as a proxy for Layer 2 (the data link layer) address resolution. Cisco routers enable proxy ARP on all interfaces by default.

Because proxy ARP allows hosts from different LAN segments to look like they are on the same segment, proxy ARP is only safe when used between trusted LAN segments. Attackers can take advantage of the trusting nature of proxy ARP by spoofing a trusted host and then intercepting packets. Because of this inherent security weakness, you should always disable proxy ARP on router interfaces that do not require it, especially those connected to untrusted networks, as shown in Figure 4-19.

Figure 4-19 *Disabling Proxy ARP*

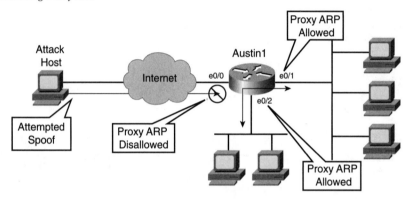

Disable proxy ARP by using the **no ip proxy-arp** command in interface configuration mode, as demonstrated in Example 4-8.

Example 4-8 **no ip proxy-arp** *Command Usage Example*

```
Austin1(config)# interface e0/0
Austin1(config-if)# no ip proxy-arp
Austin1(config-if)# exit
```

The syntax for the **no ip proxy-arp** command is as follows:

    no ip proxy-arp

This command has no arguments or keywords.

Disabling SNMP Service

The SNMP service (enabled by default) allows a router to respond to remote SNMP queries and configuration changes. If you plan to use SNMP, you should restrict which SNMP systems have access to the routers by using ACLs. When you decide not to use SNMP for a router, you must make sure that you complete several steps to ensure that SNMP is truly unavailable to an attacker. Disabling the SNMP service alone does not fully protect the router. Be sure to fully disable SNMP access as shown in Figure 4-20.

Figure 4-20 *Disabling SNMP*

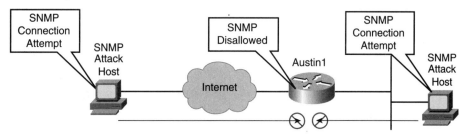

You should complete the following steps on a Cisco router to fully disable SNMP access to that router:

Step 1 Remove any existing SNMP community strings by using the **no snmp-server community** command in global configuration mode as shown in the following example:

```
Austin1(config)# no snmp-server community public ro
Austin1(config)# no snmp-server community config rw
```

The syntax for the **no snmp-server community** command is as follows:

```
no snmp-server community string [ro | rw]
```

- *string*—Indicates the community string that you wish to remove.

- **ro**—Specifies that the string to be removed has read-only access.

- **rw**—Specifies that the string to be removed has read-write access.

Step 2 Create an ACL that explicitly denies all traffic as follows (more information about writing ACLs is given later in this chapter, under "Implementing Cisco Access Control Lists"):

```
Austin1(config)# access-list 60 deny any
Austin1(config)# access-list 60 permit any
```

Step 3 Create a new, difficult-to-crack, read-only SNMP community string and make it subject to the new ACL you created in Step 2:

```
Austin1(config)# snmp-server community dj1973 ro 60
```

Step 4 Disable all SNMP trap functions by using the **no snmp-server enable traps** command in global configuration mode:

```
Austin1(config)# no snmp-server enable traps
```

The syntax for the **no snmp-server enable traps** command is as follows:

```
no snmp-server enable traps [notification-type]
```

- *notification-type* (Optional)—Indicates the type of notification (trap or inform) to disable. If no type is specified (most secure form of the command), all notifications available on the router are disabled.

Step 5 Disable the SNMP system shutdown function by using the **no snmp-server system-shutdown** command in global configuration mode:

```
Austin1(config)# no snmp-server system-shutdown
```

This prevents an SNMP system-shutdown request (from an SNMP manager) from resetting the Cisco SNMP agent on the router.

The syntax for the **no snmp-server system-shutdown** command is as follows:

```
no snmp-server system-shutdown
```

This command has no arguments or keywords.

Step 6 Disable the SNMP service using the **no snmp-server** command in global configuration mode:

```
Austin1(config)# no snmp-server
```

The syntax for the **no snmp-server** command is as follows:

```
no snmp-server
```

This command has no arguments or keywords.

Example 4-9 shows how you would apply this series of steps on router Austin1.

Example 4-9 *Disabling SNMP Services*

```
Austin1(config)# no snmp-server community public ro
Austin1(config)# no snmp-server community config rw
Austin1(config)# access-list 60 deny any
Austin1(config)# snmp-server community dj1973 ro 60
Austin1(config)# no snmp-server enable traps
Austin1(config)# no snmp-server system-shutdown
Austin1(config)# no snmp-server
```

Disabling Small Servers

By default, Cisco devices up through Cisco IOS Release 11.3 offer the "small services": echo, chargen, daytime, and discard. Small services are enabled by default in Cisco IOS versions earlier than Release 11.3 and are disabled in Cisco IOS Release 11.3 and later. These services, especially their UDP versions, can be used to launch DoS and other attacks that would otherwise be prevented by packet filtering.

For example, an attacker might send a DNS packet, falsifying the source address to be a DNS server that would otherwise be unreachable, and falsifying the source port to be the DNS service port (port 53). If such a packet were sent to the Cisco router UDP echo port, the result would be the router sending a DNS packet to the server in question. No outgoing ACL checks would be applied to this packet, because it would be considered locally generated by the router itself.

NOTE   This book frequently refers to TCP and UDP port numbers. If you would like to see the most current and complete list of these numbers, visit IANA's website at http://www.iana.org /assignments/port-numbers.

Although most abuses of the small services can be avoided or made less dangerous by using antispoofing ACLs, the services should almost always be disabled in any router that is part of a firewall or lies in a security-critical part of the network. Because the services are rarely used, the best policy is usually to disable them on all routers of any description.

The small services are disabled by default in Cisco IOS Software Release 12.0 and later. In earlier software, small services may be disabled by using the commands **no service tcp-small-servers** and **no service udp-small-servers** in global configuration mode, as follows:

```
Austin2(config)# no service tcp-small-servers
Austin2(config)# no service udp-small-servers
```

TCP Servers

TCP small servers service is enabled in Cisco IOS versions earlier than Release 11.3 and disabled in Cisco IOS Release 11.3 and later. The small servers are servers (daemons) running in the router that are sometimes useful for diagnostics, but are rarely used. Disable this service explicitly.

The syntax for the **no service tcp-small-servers** command is as follows:

```
no service tcp-small-servers
```

This command has no arguments or keywords.

UDP Servers

UDP small servers service is enabled in Cisco IOS versions earlier than Release 11.3 and disabled in Cisco IOS Release 11.3 and later. The small servers are servers (daemons) running in the router that are sometimes useful for diagnostics, but are rarely used. Disable this service explicitly.

The syntax for the **no service udp-small-servers** command is as follows:

```
no service udp-small-servers
```

This command has no arguments or keywords.

Enabling TCP Keepalives

By default, Cisco routers do not continually test whether a previously connected TCP endpoint is still reachable. If one end of a TCP connection idles out or terminates abnormally (crashes, reloads, and so on), the opposite end of the connection may still believe the session is available. These "orphaned" sessions use up valuable router resources. Attackers have been known to take advantage of this weakness to attack Cisco routers.

To remedy this situation, Cisco routers can be configured to send periodic keepalive messages to ensure that the remote end of a session is still available. If the remote device fails to respond to the keepalive message, the sending router will clear the connection. This action immediately frees router resources for other, more important tasks. Keepalives are important because they help guard against orphaned sessions.

Use the **service tcp-keepalives-in** global configuration command to detect and delete inactive incoming interactive sessions initiated by a remote host, as shown in Figure 4-21.

Figure 4-21 *TCP Keepalives*

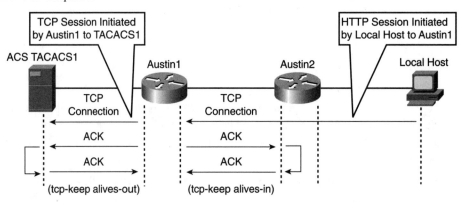

Use the **service tcp-keepalives-out** global configuration command to detect and delete inactive outgoing interactive sessions initiated by a local user, as shown in Figure 4-21.

The syntax for the **service tcp-keepalives** commands is as follows:

```
service tcp-keepalives-in
service tcp-keepalives-out
```

These commands have no arguments or keywords.

Disabling TFTP Server

The TFTP server feature configures a router to act as a TFTP server host. As a TFTP server host, the router responds to TFTP Read Request messages by sending a copy of the system image contained in ROM or one of the system images contained in Flash memory to the requesting host. The TFTP Read Request message must use one of the filenames that are specified in the configuration.

Flash memory can be used as a TFTP file server for other routers on the network. This feature allows you to boot a remote router with an image that resides in the Flash server memory. Some

Cisco devices allow you to specify one of the various Flash memory locations (bootflash:, slot0:, slot1:, slavebootflash:, slaveslot0:, or slaveslot1:) as the TFTP server.

TFTP access to your routers can be used to gain access to the router file system and therefore can be used to attack the network or the router itself. Unless your routers are being used as TFTP servers, you should always disable the TFTP server feature.

NOTE   The steps required to disable the TFTP server vary across different Cisco router product lines. Always consult the configuration guide for your particular Cisco router model before continuing.

Disable the TFTP server for Flash memory by using the **no tftp-server flash** global configuration command, as shown in Figure 4-22.

Figure 4-22 *Disabling the TFTP Server*

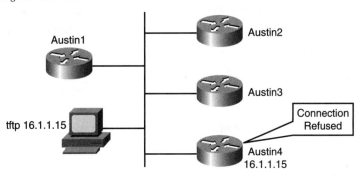

The syntax for the **no tftp-server flash** command for Cisco 1600 and 3600 series routers is as follows:

```
no tftp-server flash [device:][partition-number:]filename
```

The syntax for the **no tftp-server flash:** command for Cisco 7000 family routers is as follows:

```
no tftp-server flash device:filename
```

The syntax for the **no tftp-server flash:** command for other Cisco routers is as follows:

```
no tftp-server {flash [partition-number:]filename1 | rom alias filename2}
```

The following shows the explanation of the keywords for these **no tftp-server flash** command formats:

- **flash**—Specifies the TFTP service of a file in Flash memory. Use **flash** with no other keywords to disable the TFTP server for all files in Flash memory.

- **rom**—Specifies the TFTP service of a file in ROM.

- *filename1*—Name of a file in Flash or in ROM that the TFTP server uses in answering TFTP Read Requests.

- **alias**—Specifies an alternate name for the file that the TFTP server uses in answering TFTP Read Requests.

- *filename2*—Alternate name of the file that the TFTP server uses in answering TFTP Read Requests. A client of the TFTP server can use this alternate name in its Read Requests.

- *partition-number* (Optional)—Specifies the TFTP service of a file in the specified partition of Flash memory. If the partition number is not specified, the file in the first partition is used. For the Cisco 1600 series and Cisco 3600 series routers, you must enter a colon after the partition number if a filename follows it.

- *device:* (Optional)—Specifies the TFTP service of a file on a Flash memory device in the Cisco 1600 series, Cisco 3600 series, and Cisco 7000 family routers. The colon is required. Valid devices are as follows:

  - **flash**—Internal Flash memory on the Cisco 1600 series and Cisco 3600 series routers. This is the only valid device for the Cisco 1600 series routers.

  - **bootflash**—Internal Flash memory on the Cisco 7000 family routers.

  - **slot0**—First PCMCIA slot on the Cisco 3600 series and Cisco 7000 family routers.

  - **slot1**—Second PCMCIA slot on the Cisco 3600 series and Cisco 7000 family routers.

  - **slavebootflash**—Internal Flash memory on the slave RSP card of a Cisco 7507 or Cisco 7513 router configured for HSA.

  - **slaveslot0**—First PCMCIA slot of the slave RSP card on a Cisco 7507 or Cisco 7513 router configured for HSA.

  - **slaveslot1**—Second PCMCIA slot of the slave RSP card on a Cisco 7507 or Cisco 7513 router configured for HSA.

- *filename*—Name of the file on a Flash memory device that the TFTP server uses in answering a TFTP Read Request. Use this argument only with the Cisco 1600 series, Cisco 3600 series, Cisco 7000 series, or Cisco 7500 series routers.

Disabling Unused Router Interfaces

Unused open router interfaces invite unauthorized access to the router and the network. You can limit this type of attack by disabling the unused interfaces on all routers, as shown in Figure 4-23.

Always disable unused router interfaces by using the **shutdown** command in interface configuration mode, as demonstrated in Example 4-10.

Figure 4-23 *Disabling Unused Router Interfaces*

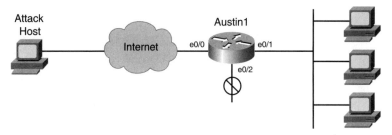

Example 4-10 *Disabling an Unused Router Interface*

```
Austin1(config)# interface e0/2
Austin1(config-if)# shutdown
Austin1(config-if)# exit
```

The syntax for the **shutdown** command is as follows:

> **shutdown**

This command has no keywords or arguments.

Once an interface is shut down, the router requires administrative privileges to open the interface to new network connections.

Implementing Cisco Access Control Lists

This section provides a review of basic Cisco ACL design and implementation.

Cisco routers use ACLs as packet filters to decide which packets to allow across an interface. Packets that are allowed across an interface are called permitted packets. Packets that are not allowed across an interface are called denied packets. ACLs contain one or more rules or statements that determine what data is to be permitted or denied across an interface.

ACLs are designed to enforce one or more corporate security policies. For example, suppose that one of your corporate security policies is to allow only one SNMP server to access the SNMP agents on your routers. Once this policy is written, you can develop an ACL that includes certain statements that, when applied to a router interface, can implement this policy.

Cisco router security depends strongly on well-written ACLs to restrict access to router network services and to filter packets as they traverse the router.

Identifying Access Control Lists

Either a number or a name can identify Cisco ACLs and the protocols they filter.

For numbered ACLs, the number of the ACL determines what protocol is being filtered. Table 4-1 lists access list numbers and their associated protocol types.

Table 4-1   *Access List Number Ranges*

Access List Number Range	Type
1–99	IP standard ACL
100–199	IP extended ACL
200–299	Ethernet type-code ACL Or Transparent bridging (protocol type) ACL Or Source-route bridging (protocol type) ACL
300–399	DECnet and extended DECnet ACL
400–499	Xerox Network Systems (XNS) standard ACL
500–599	XNS extended ACL
600–699	AppleTalk ACL
700–799	Ethernet address ACL Or Transparent bridging (vendor code) ACL Or Source-route bridging (vendor code) ACL
800–899	IPX standard ACL
900–999	IPX extended ACL
1000–1099	Internetwork Packet Exchange (IPX) Service Advertising Protocol (SAP) ACL
1100–1199	Extended transparent bridging ACL
1200–1299	IPX summary address ACL
1300–1999	IP standard ACL (expanded range)
2000–2699	IP extended ACL (expanded range)
1100–1199	Extended transparent bridging ACL

Starting with Cisco IOS Release 11.2, you can identify ACLs with an alphanumeric string (a name) rather than a number. Named ACLs allow you to configure more ACLs in a router than if you were to use numbered ACLs alone. If you identify your ACL with a name rather than a number, the mode and command syntax are slightly different. Currently, only packet and route filters can use a named list.

ACL names use alphanumeric characters. Names cannot contain spaces or punctuation and must begin with an alphabetic character.

NOTE	Named ACLs will not be recognized by any software release prior to Cisco IOS Release 11.2.

Types of IP Access Control Lists

Cisco routers support two types of IP ACLs:

- **Standard IP ACLs**—Can filter IP packets based on the source address only.
- **Extended IP ACLs**—Can filter IP packets based on several attributes, including the following:
  - Source IP address
  - Destination IP address
  - Source TCP/UDP ports
  - Destination TCP/UDP ports
  - ICMP and Internet Group Management Protocol (IGMP) message types
  - Optional protocol type information for finer granularity of control

NOTE	Cisco IOS Release 11.1 introduced substantial changes to IP ACLs. These extensions are backward compatible; migrating from a release earlier than Release 11.1 to the current image will convert your ACLs automatically. However, previous releases are not forward compatible with these changes. Thus, if you save an ACL with the current image and then use older software, the resulting ACL will not be interpreted correctly. This could cause you severe security problems, so be sure that you save your old configuration file before booting Release 11.1 or later images.

Standard Numbered ACL Format

The syntax for the standard numbered **access-list** command is as follows:

```
access-list access-list-number {deny | permit} source [source-wildcard]
```

- *access-list-number*—This number serves a dual purpose:
  - It is the number of the ACL.
  - It specifies that this is a standard IP protocol ACL (range 1 to 99 and 1300 to 1999).
- **deny**—Drops all packets that match the specified source address.
- **permit**—Allows packets that match the specified source address to flow through the interface.
- *source*—Specifies the IP address of a host or group of hosts (if a wildcard mask is also specified) whose packets are to be examined.

- *source-wildcard*—The wildcard mask applied to the source to determine a source group of hosts whose packets are to be examined. Note that when no mask is specified, the default mask becomes **0.0.0.0**.

Create a standard numbered ACL by using the **access-list** command, as demonstrated in Example 4-11.

Example 4-11 *Configuring a Standard ACL*

```
Austin2(config)# access-list 2 permit 36.48.0.3
Austin2(config)# access-list 2 deny 36.48.0.0 0.0.255.255
Austin2(config)# access-list 2 permit 36.0.0.0 0.255.255.255
```

In this example, network 36.0.0.0 is a Class A network whose second octet specifies a subnet; that is, its subnet mask is 255.255.0.0. The third and fourth octets of a network 36.0.0.0 address specify a particular host. Using ACL 2, the Cisco IOS software would accept address 36.48.0.3 on subnet 48 and reject all others on that subnet. The last line of the list shows that the software would accept addresses on all other network 36.0.0.0 subnets.

When using wildcard masks in ACLs, a 0 in the mask indicates a portion of the address that must match, and a 255 indicates a portion of the address that does not need to match. In the second line of Example 4-11, the wildcard mask is 0.0.255.255, indicating that a match of the first two octets is all that is required to trigger this statement. Any packet with a source address of **36.48.anything.anything** will be denied by this list.

In the third line of Example 4-11, the wildcard mask is 0.255.255.255, indicating that it requires a match only on the first octet. Any packet with a source address of **36.anything.anything.anything** will be permitted by this entry.

ACLs are processed sequentially. The first entry that is satisfied ends the matching process. Remember that an implicit **deny any** always completes an ACL. It is actually good practice to explicitly enter this command so that you don't forget about it.

NOTE   When building either standard or extended ACLs, by default, the end of the ACL contains an implicit **deny any** statement. Further, with standard ACLs, if you omit the mask from the ACL entry, the mask defaults to 0.0.0.0.

The syntax for the standard numbered **access-list** command is as follows:

```
access-list access-list-number {deny | permit} source [source-wildcard]
```

- *access-list-number*—This number serves a dual purpose:
    - It is the number of the ACL.
    - It specifies that this is a standard IP protocol ACL (range 1 to 99 and 1300 to 1999).
- **deny**—Drops all packets that match the specified source address.

- **permit**—Allows packets that match the specified source address to flow through the interface.
- *source*—Specifies the IP address of a host or group of hosts (if a wildcard mask is also specified) whose packets are to be examined.
- *source-wildcard*—The wildcard mask applied to the source to determine a source group of hosts whose packets are to be examined. Note that when no mask is specified, the default mask becomes **0.0.0.0**.

In addition to the keywords specified above, standard numbered IP ACLs also support the following keywords:

- **any**—Specifies any host. This is the same as using an IP address and wildcard mask of **0.0.0.0 255.255.255.255**.
- **host**—Specifies an exact host match. This is the same as specifying a wildcard mask of **0.0.0.0**.
- **log**—Enables logging of packets that match the deny or permit statements (Cisco IOS Release 11.3 or later).

Starting with Cisco IOS Release 11.3, standard ACLs can provide logging messages about packets permitted or denied by a standard IP ACL. That is, any packet that matches the ACL will cause an informational logging message about the packet to be sent to the console. The level of messages logged to the console is controlled by the **logging console** command. This capability was previously only available in extended IP ACLs.

The first packet that triggers the ACL causes an immediate logging message. Subsequent packets are collected over 5-minute intervals before they are displayed or logged. The logging message includes the ACL number, whether the packet was permitted or denied, the source IP address of the packet, and the number of packets from that source permitted or denied in the prior 5-minute interval.

NOTE   The router logging facility might drop some logging message packets if there are too many to be handled or if there is more than one logging message to be handled in 1 second. This behavior prevents the router from crashing due to too many logging packets. Therefore, the logging facility should not be solely relied upon as a security tool because it may not be an accurate source of the number of matches to an ACL.

Standard Named ACL Format

Complete the following steps to create a standard named ACL:

Step 1   Enter the **ip access-list standard** command in global configuration mode as shown in the following example:

```
Austin2(config)# ip access-list standard protect
```

The syntax for the **ip access-list standard** command is as follows:

```
ip access-list standard access-list-name
```

- *access-list-name*—Name of the ACL. Names cannot contain a space or quotation mark, and must begin with an alphabetic character to prevent ambiguity with numbered ACLs.

Step 2   Enter the **deny** or **permit** command in standard named ACL mode:

```
Austin2(config-std-nacl)# deny 36.48.0.0 0.0.255.255
Austin2(config-std-nacl)# permit 36.0.0.0 0.255.255.255
Austin2(config-std-nacl)# exit
```

The syntax for the standard named ACL **deny** and **permit** commands are as follows:

```
{deny | permit} source [source-wildcard]
```

- **deny**—Drops all packets that match the specified source address.
- **permit**—Allows packets that match the specified source address to flow through the interface.
- *source*—Specifies the IP address of a host or group of hosts (if a wildcard mask is also specified) whose packets are to be examined.
- *source-wildcard*—The wildcard mask applied to the source to determine a source group of hosts whose packets are to be examined.

NOTE   When building either standard or extended ACLs, by default, the end of the ACL contains an implicit deny all statement. Further, with standard ACLs, if you omit the mask from the ACL entry, the mask defaults to **0.0.0.0**.

In addition to the keywords specified above, standard named IP ACLs also support the following keywords:

- **any**—Specifies any host. This is the same as using an IP address and wildcard mask of **0.0.0.0 255.255.255.255**.
- **host**—Specifies an exact host match. This is the same as specifying a wildcard mask of **0.0.0.0**.
- **log**—Enables logging of packets that match the deny or permit statements (Cisco IOS Release 11.3 or later).

NOTE   Named ACLs will not be recognized by any software release prior to Cisco IOS Release 11.2.

Starting with Cisco IOS Release 11.3, standard ACLs can provide logging messages about packets permitted or denied by a standard IP ACL. That is, any packet that matches the ACL will cause an informational logging message about the packet to be sent to the console. The level of messages logged to the console is controlled by the **logging console** command. This capability was previously only available in extended IP ACLs.

The first packet that triggers the ACL causes an immediate logging message. Subsequent packets are collected over 5-minute intervals before they are displayed or logged. The logging message includes the ACL number, whether the packet was permitted or denied, the source IP address of the packet, and the number of packets from that source permitted or denied in the prior 5-minute interval.

Extended Numbered ACL Format

Extended ACLs allow packet filtering on source and destination addresses, protocol type, source and destination port, as well as several protocol-dependent options. Figure 4-24 shows where an extended numbered ACL could be applied.

Figure 4-24 *Network for Extended Numbered ACL*

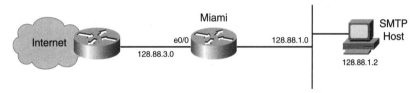

Referring to the sample network shown in Figure 4-24, create an extended numbered ACL for router Miami by using the **access-list** command in global configuration mode and apply it to the appropriate interface. The resulting numbered ACL should look very much like the list demonstrated in Example 4-12.

Example 4-12 *Number ACL Example*

```
Miami(config)# access-list 103 permit tcp any 128.88.0.0 0.0.255.255 established
Miami(config)# access-list 103 permit tcp any host 128.88.1.2 eq smtp
Miami(config)# interface e0/0
Miami(config-if)# ip access-group 103 in
```

In this example, the Miami router interface e0/0 is part of a Class B network with the 128.88.0.0 address. The mail server, with the 128.88.1.2 address, delivers Internet mail. The **established** keyword within the ACL is used only for TCP datagrams to indicate an established connection. A match occurs if the TCP datagram has the acknowledgment (ACK) code or reset (RST) bits set, indicating that the packet belongs to an existing connection. In this scenario, if the ACK bit is not set and the synchronize (SYN) bit is set, then someone on the Internet has initialized the session and the packet is denied.

NOTE   When building either standard or extended ACLs, by default, the end of the ACL contains an implicit deny all statement.

The syntax for the **access-list** command is as follows:

```
access-list access-list-number {deny | permit} {protocol-number | protocol-keyword}
  {source source-wildcard | any | host} {source-port} {destination destination-
  wildcard | any | host} {destination-port} [established] [log | log-input]
```

- *access-list-number*—This number serves a dual purpose:
  — It is the number of the ACL.
  — It specifies that this is a extended IP protocol ACL (range 100 to 199 and 2000 to 2699).
- **deny**—Drops all packets that match the specified source address.
- **permit**—Allows packets that match the specified source address to flow through the interface.
- *protocol-number*—Integer in the range of 0 to 255 that represents an IP protocol.
- *protocol-keyword*—Name of an IP protocol. Can be one of the following: **eigrp**, **gre**, **icmp**, **igmp**, **igrp**, **ip**, **ipinip**, **nos**, **ospf**, **tcp**, or **udp**.
- *source*—IP address of the host or network where the packet originated.
- *source-wildcard*—The wildcard mask applied to the source IP address.
- *source-port*—Specifies the port that the packet originated from. This can be the actual port number (for example, **80**) or the common name (for example, **http**). For TCP and UDP packets, **source-port** also supports the following operators: **gt** (greater than), **lt** (less than), **eq** (equal), and **neq** (not equal).
- *destination*—IP address of the host or network where the packet is being sent.
- *destination-wildcard*—The wildcard mask applied to the destination IP address.
- *destination-port*—Specifies the port number to which the packet is being sent. This can be the actual port number (for example, **80**), or the common name (for example, **http**). For TCP and UDP packets, **source-port** also supports the following operators: **gt**, **lt**, **eq**, and **neq**.
- **established** (TCP only)—Verifies whether either the RST or ACK bit is set. If either of these bits is set, the packet is part of a previously established connection. This can be used

to restrict TCP responses to one direction when sessions are initiated from the opposite direction.

- **log**—Enables logging of packets that match the deny or permit statements (Cisco IOS Release 11.3 and later).

- **log-input**—Includes the input interface, source MAC address, or virtual circuit (VC) in the logging output.

- **any**—Specifies any host. This is the same as using an IP address and wildcard mask of **0.0.0.0 255.255.255.255**.

- **host**—Specifies an exact host match. This is the same as specifying a wildcard mask of **0.0.0.0**.

Extended Named ACL Format

Referring to router Miami in Figure 4-24, complete the following steps to create an extended named ACL:

Step 1 Enter the **ip access-list extended** command in global configuration mode as shown in the following example:

```
Miami(config)# ip access-list extended mailblock
```

The syntax for the **ip access-list extended** command is as follows:

```
ip access-list extended access-list-name
```

- *access-list-name*—Name of the ACL. Names cannot contain a space or quotation mark, and must begin with an alphabetic character to prevent ambiguity with numbered ACLs.

NOTE   Named ACLs will not be recognized by any software release prior to Cisco IOS Release 11.2.

Step 2 Enter the **deny** or **permit** command in extended named ACL mode:

```
Miami(config-ext-nacl)# permit tcp any 128.88.0.0 0.0.255.255 established
Miami(config-ext-nacl)# permit tcp any host 128.88.1.2 eq smtp
Miami(config-ext-nacl)# exit
```

The syntax for the extended named ACL **deny** and **permit** commands are as follows:

```
{deny | permit} {protocol-number | protocol-keyword} {source source-wildcard |
    any | host} {source-port} {destination destination-wildcard | any | host}
    {destination-port} [established] [log | log-input]
```

- **deny**—Drops all packets that match the specified source address.

- **permit**—Allows packets that match the specified source address to flow through the interface.
- *protocol-number*—Integer in the range of 0 to 255 that represents an IP protocol.
- *protocol-keyword*—Name of an IP protocol. Can be one of the following: **eigrp**, **gre**, **icmp**, **igmp**, **igrp**, **ip**, **ipinip**, **nos**, **ospf**, **tcp**, or **udp**.
- *source*—IP address of the host or network where the packet originated.
- *source-wildcard*—The wildcard mask applied to the source IP address.
- *source-port*—Specifies the port that the packet originated from. This can be the actual port number (for example, **80**) or the common name (for example, **http**). For TCP and UDP packets, **source-port** also supports the following operators: **gt** (greater than), **lt** (less than), **eq** (equal), and **neq** (not equal).
- *destination*—IP address of the host or network where the packet is being sent.
- *destination-wildcard*—The wildcard mask applied to the destination IP address.
- *destination-port*—Specifies the port number to which the packet is being sent. This can be the actual port number (for example, **80**) or the common name (for example, **http**). For TCP and UDP packets, **source-port** also supports the following operators: **gt**, **lt**, **eq**, and **neq**.
- **established** (TCP only)—Verifies whether either the RST or ACK bit is set. If either of these bits is set, the packet is part of a previously established connection. This can be used to restrict TCP responses to one direction when sessions are initiated from the opposite direction.
- **log**—Enables logging of packets that match the deny or permit statements (Cisco IOS Release 11.3 or later).
- **log-input**—Includes the input interface, source MAC address, or VC in the logging output.
- **any**—Specifies any host. This is the same as using an IP address and wildcard mask of **0.0.0.0 255.255.255.255**.
- **host**—Specifies an exact host match. This is the same as specifying a wildcard mask of **0.0.0.0**.

NOTE   When building either standard or extended ACLs, by default, the end of the ACL contains an implicit deny all statement.

In addition to the keywords specified above, both extended numbered IP ACLs and extended named IP ACLs also support the following keywords:

- *icmp-type*—Specifies that the ACL perform filtering based on the ICMP message type (0 to 255).

- *icmp-message*—Specifies that the ACL perform filtering based on the ICMP message symbolic name (for example, **echo-reply**).

- **precedence** *precedence*—Specifies that the ACL perform filtering based on the precedence level name or number (0 to 7).

- **remark**—Used to add remarks (up to 100 characters long) to ACLs (Cisco IOS Release 12.0 or later).

Commenting IP ACL Entries

You should get into the habit of annotating your ACLs (especially large and complex ACLs) with remarks as an aid to troubleshooting problems. To write a helpful comment (remark) for an entry in an IP ACL, use the **remark** ACL configuration command in global configuration mode, as follows:

```
Miami(config)# access-list 102 remark Allow traffic to file server
Miami(config)# access-list 102 permit ip any host 128.88.1.6
```

The syntax for the **remark** command is as follows:

```
remark message
```

- *message*—The remark to add to the ACL (100-character maximum).

Developing ACL Rules

Before you start to develop any ACLs, consider the following basic rules:

- **Rule #1: Write it out**—Never sit down at a router and start to develop an ACL without first spending some time in design. The best ACL developers suggest that you write out a list of things that you want the ACL to accomplish. Starting with something as simple as the following will do: "This ACL must block all SNMP access to the router except for the SNMP host at 16.1.1.15."

- **Rule #2: Set up a development system**—Whether this is your laptop PC or a dedicated server, you need a place to develop and store your ACLs. Word processors or text editors of any kind will do, as long as you can save the files in ASCII text format. Build yourself a library of your most commonly used ACLs and use them as sources for new files. ACLs can be pasted into the router's running configuration (requires console or Telnet access) or stored in a router configuration file. The system you choose should support Trivial File Transfer Protocol (TFTP) to make it easy to transfer any resulting configuration files to the router.

NOTE   Attackers love to gain access to router configuration development
systems or TFTP servers that store ACLs. An attacker can discover a
lot about your network from looking at these easily read text files,
such as addresses of the subnets directly connected to the router,
which routing protocols are used, which protocols are routed, AAA
configuration and host information, passwords and password hashes,
default routes, VPN information, peer addresses, and a variety of
other information that could lead to further attacks on different
network assets. For this reason, it is imperative that the system on
which you choose to develop and store your router files be a secure
system.

- **Rule #3: Test**—If at all possible, test your ACLs in a secure environment before placing them into production. This is a commonsense approach to any router configuration changes, and most enterprises maintain their own network test beds. Yes, testing costs money, but it can save a lot more time and money in the long run.

ACL Directional Filtering

ACLs must be applied to a router interface to take effect. It is important to note that ACLs are applied to an interface based on the direction of the data flow, as shown in Figure 4-25:

- **Inbound (in)**—The ACL applies to packets flowing toward the router interface.
- **Outbound (out)**—The ACL applies to packets flowing away from the router interface.

Figure 4-25 *ACL Directional Filtering*

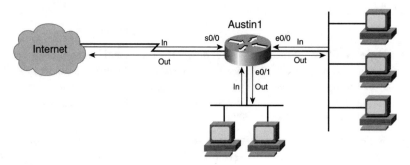

Applying ACLs to Interfaces

Before you apply an ACL to a router interface, make sure that you know which direction it will be filtering.

Apply ACLs to router interfaces by using the **ip access-group** command in interface configuration mode, as demonstrated in Example 4-13.

Example 4-13 *Applying ACLs to Interfaces*

```
Tulsa(config)# interface e0/1
Tulsa(config-if)# ip access-group 2 in
Tulsa(config)# interface e0/2
Tulsa(config-if)# ip access-group mailblock out
Tulsa(config-if)# exit
```

The syntax for the **ip access-group** command is as follows:

```
ip access-group {access-list-number | access-list-name} {in | out}
```

- *access-list-number*—Number of the IP standard numbered or IP extended numbered ACL. This is a decimal number from 1 to 199 or from 1300 to 2699.
- *access-list-name*—Name of the IP standard named or IP extended named ACL as specified by the **ip access-list** command.
- **in**—Filters on inbound (flowing toward router interface) packets.
- **out**—Filters on outbound (flowing away from router interface) packets.

Displaying ACLs

Display current router ACLs by using the **show access-lists** command in privileged EXEC mode, as demonstrated in Example 4-14.

Example 4-14 *Viewing an ACL*

```
Miami# show access-lists
Extended IP access list 102
    permit ip any host 128.88.1.6

Extended IP access list mailblock
    permit tcp any 128.88.0.0 0.0.255.255
    established

Miami#
```

The syntax for the **show access-list** command is as follows:

```
show access-lists {access-list-number | access-list-name}
```

- *access-list-number*—Number of the IP standard numbered or IP extended numbered ACL. This is a decimal number from 1 to 199 or from 1300 to 2699.
- *access-list-name*—Name of the IP standard named or IP extended named ACL as specified by the **ip access-list** command.

Optionally, you may use the **show ip interface** command to view the ACLs that are bound to router interfaces.

The syntax for the **show ip interface** command is as follows:

```
show ip interface [type number]
```

- *type* (Optional)—Specifies the interface type.
- *number* (Optional)—Specifies the interface number.

Enabling Turbo ACLs

Cisco IOS Release 12.0(6)S and later supports the compiling of ACLs into Turbo ACLs for Cisco 7200 series and Cisco 7500 series routers. ACLs are normally searched sequentially to find a matching rule and are ordered specifically to take this factor into account. Because of the increasing needs and requirements for security filtering and packet classification, ACLs can expand to the point that searching the ACL adds a significant amount of time and memory when packets are being forwarded. Moreover, the time that the router takes to search the list is not always consistent, adding a variable latency to the packet forwarding. A high CPU load is necessary for searching an ACL with several entries.

The Turbo ACL feature compiles the ACLs into a set of lookup tables, while maintaining the first matching requirements. Packet headers are used to access these tables in a small, fixed number of lookups, independently of the existing number of ACL entries. The benefits of this feature include the following:

- For ACLs larger than three entries, the CPU load required to match the packet to the predetermined packet-matching rule is lessened. The CPU load is fixed, regardless of the size of the ACL, allowing for larger ACLs without incurring any CPU overhead penalties. The larger the ACL, the greater the benefit.
- The time taken to match the packet is fixed, so that latency of the packets is smaller (significantly in the case of large ACLs) and, more importantly, consistent, allowing better network stability and more accurate transit times.

You should use the **access-list compiled** command in global configuration mode as follows whenever you develop ACLs with more than three statements:

```
R2(config)# access-list compiled
R2(config)# exit
```

The syntax for the **access-list compiled** command is as follows:

```
access-list compiled
```

This command has no keywords or arguments.

To view the status of your Turbo ACLs, use the **show access-list compiled** command in privileged EXEC mode. Example 4-15 demonstrates the use of the **show access-list compiled** command and shows a partial listing of the resultant output.

Example 4-15 show access-list compiled *Command Output Example*

```
R2# show access-list compiled
Compiled ACL statistics:
12 ACLs loaded, 12 compiled tables
 ACL         State     Tables  Entries  Config  Fragment  Redundant  Memory
1           Operational   1       2       1       0         0        1Kb
2           Operational   1       3       2       0         0        1Kb
3           Operational   1       4       3       0         0        1Kb
4           Operational   1       3       2       0         0        1Kb
5           Operational   1       5       4       0         0        1Kb
9           Operational   1       3       2       0         0        1Kb
20          Operational   1       9       8       0         0        1Kb
21          Operational   1       5       4       0         0        1Kb
101         Operational   1      15       9       7         2        1Kb
102         Operational   1      13       6       6         0        1Kb
120         Operational   1       2       1       0         0        1Kb
199         Operational   1       4       3       0         0        1Kb
First level lookup tables:
Block    Use              Rows      Columns   Memory used
 0    TOS/Protocol         6/16     12/16      66048
 1    IP Source (MS)      10/16     12/16      66048
 2    IP Source (LS)      27/32     12/16     132096
 3    IP Dest (MS)         3/16     12/16      66048
 4    IP Dest (LS)         9/16     12/16      66048
 5    TCP/UDP Src Port     1/16     12/16      66048
 6    TCP/UDP Dest Port    3/16     12/16      66048
 7    TCP Flags/Fragment   3/16     12/16      66048
```

The syntax for the **show access-list compiled** command is as follows:

```
show access-list compiled
```

This command has no keywords or arguments.

Enhanced ACLs

So far, this chapter has discussed two basic types of Cisco ACLs:

- Standard
- Extended

However, these are not the only types of ACLs that are supported by Cisco routers. Enhanced types of ACLs have been designed to better secure routers and their networks.

These enhanced ACLs are described as follows:

- **Dynamic**—Dynamic ACLs (also known as lock and key) create specific, temporary openings in response to a user authentication. The syntax for dynamic ACLs is very similar to the syntax for extended ACLs. Dynamic ACLs are available in Cisco IOS Release 11.1 and later.

Here is an example of using a dynamic ACL:

— A user originates a Telnet session with a router.

— The router authenticates the user with a username and password lookup.

— The router closes the Telnet session and creates in the ACL a dynamic entry that permits packets with the authenticated user source IP address.

— Once the user closes the session, the dynamic entry goes away.

- **Time based**—These ACLs are really just numbered or named ACLs that are implemented based upon the time of day or the day of the week. They make it easier to implement changes to your routing plans after hours, on weekends, or during other time- and day-related organizational events. Time-based ACLs are available in Cisco IOS Release 12.0 and later.

- **Reflexive**—Also called IP session filtering, these ACLs create dynamic entries for IP traffic on one interface of the router based upon sessions that originate from a different interface of the router. This allows you to control connections on the untrusted side of a router when a connection is initiated from the trusted side. These ACLs are actually modified extended IP named ACLs. Reflexive ACLs are available in Cisco IOS Release 11.3 and later.

- **Context-Based Access Control (CBAC)**—Whereas reflexive ACLs can only secure single-channel applications such as Telnet, CBAC can secure multichannel operations based on upper-layer information. Found in the Firewall Feature Set, CBAC examines packets as they enter or leave router interfaces, and determines what application protocols to allow. CBAC ACLs are available in Cisco IOS Release 12.0T and later.

For now, it is important that you understand how to use standard and extended ACLs. CBAC will be covered in more depth in Chapter 5, "Cisco IOS Firewall Context-Based Access Control Configuration."

There are several caveats to consider when working with ACLs:

- **Implicit deny all**—All Cisco ACLs end with an implicit deny all statement. Although you may not actually see this statement in your ACLs, rest assured that it exists.

- **Standard ACL limitation**—Because standard ACLs are limited to packet filtering on source addresses only, you may need to create extended ACLs to implement your security policies.

- **Statement evaluation order**—ACL statements are evaluated in a sequential (top down) order starting with the first entry in the list. This means that it is very important that you consider the order in which you place statements in your ACLs.

- **Specific statements**—Certain ACL statements are more specific than others and therefore should be placed higher in the ACL. For example, blocking all UDP traffic at the top of the list negates the blocking of SNMP packets lower in the list. You must make sure that statements at the top of the ACL do not negate any statements found lower in the list.

- **Directional filtering**—Cisco ACLs have a directional filter that determines whether they examine inbound packets (toward the interface) or outbound packets (away from the interface). Always double-check the direction of data that your ACL is filtering.

- **Adding statements**—New statements added to an existing ACL will always be appended to the bottom of the ACL. Because of the inherent top-down statement evaluation order of ACLs, these new entries may render the ACL unusable. In these cases, you will need to create a new ACL (with the correct statement ordering), delete the old ACL, and assign the new ACL to the router interface.

- **Special packets**—Router-generated packets, such as routing table updates, are not subject to outbound ACL statements on the source router, because that router trusts information that it generates itself. If filtering these types of packets is part of your security policy, then they must be acted upon by other router inbound ACLs.

- **Extended ACL placement**—Extended ACLs that are placed too far from the source being filtered can adversely impact packets flowing to other interfaces. Always consider placing extended ACLs as close as possible to the source being filtered.

- **Standard ACL placement**—Because standard ACLs filter packets based on the source address, placing these ACLs too close to the source can adversely impact packets destined to other destinations. Always place standard ACLs as close to the destination as possible.

Mitigating Security Threats by Using ACLs

This section explains how to use ACLs to mitigate common perimeter router security threats.

As a review, always apply the following general rules when deciding how to handle router services, ports, and protocols:

- **Disable unused services, ports, or protocols**—If no one, including the router itself, needs to use an enabled service, port, or protocol, disable that service, port, or protocol.

- **Limit access to services, ports, or protocols**—If a limited number of users or systems require access to an enabled router service, port, or protocol, limit access to that service, port, or protocol by using ACLs.

Filtering Traffic

ACLs are important because they act as traffic filters between the corporate (trusted) network and the Internet (untrusted network), as shown in Figure 4-26. Using ACLs, the router enforces corporate security policies by rejecting protocols and restricting port usage.

Table 4-2 contains a list of common router services that can be used to gather information about your network or, worse, to attack your network. Unless your network configuration specifically requires one of these services, they should not be allowed to traverse the router. Block these services inbound to the protected network and outbound to the Internet by using ACLs.

Figure 4-26 *Traffic Filtering*

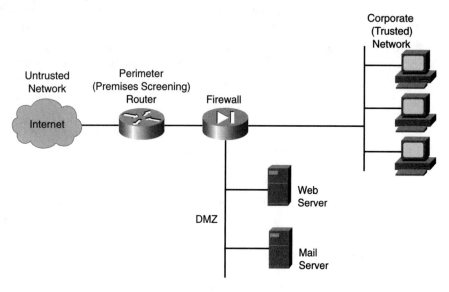

Table 4-2 *Common Router Services*

Service	Port	Transport
tcpmux	1	TCP and UDP
echo	7	TCP and UDP
discard	9	TCP and UDP
daytime	13	TCP and UDP
chargen	19	TCP and UDP
time	37	TCP and UDP
whois	43	TCP
bootp	67	UDP
tftp	69	UDP
dcp	93	TCP and UDP
sunrpc	111	TCP and UDP
epmap	135	TCP and UDP
netbios-ns	137	TCP and UDP
netbios-dgm	138	TCP and UDP
netbios-ssn	139	TCP and UDP
xdmcp	177	UDP

Table 4-2   *Common Router Services (Continued)*

Service	Port	Transport
Microsoft-ds	445	TCP
exec	512	TCP
printer	515	TCP
talk	517	UDP
ntalk	518	UDP
uucp	540	TCP
Microsoft UPnP SSDP	1900 and 5000	TCP and UDP
nfs	2049	UDP
X Window System	6000–6063	TCP
ircu	6665–6669	TCP
italk	12345	TCP
Back Orifice	31337–31338	TCP and UDP

Table 4-3 contains a list of common services that reside either on the corporate protected network or on the router itself. These services should be denied to Internet clients by using ACLs.

Table 4-3   *Additional Services*

Service	Port	Transport
finger	79	TCP
snmp	161	TCP and UDP
snmptrap	162	TCP and UDP
rlogin	513	TCP
who	513	UDP
shell	514	TCP
syslog	514	UDP
New-who	550	TCP and UDP

There are two ways to control access to router services:

- **Disable the service itself**—Once a router service is disabled, no one can use that service. Disabling a service is safer, and more reliable, than attempting to block all access to the service using an ACL.

- **Restrict access to the service using ACLs**—If your situation requires limited access to a service, then build and test appropriate ACLs.

Theoretical Network

Figure 4-27 depicts a theoretical network that will be referenced throughout the remainder of this chapter.

Figure 4-27 *Theoretical Network*

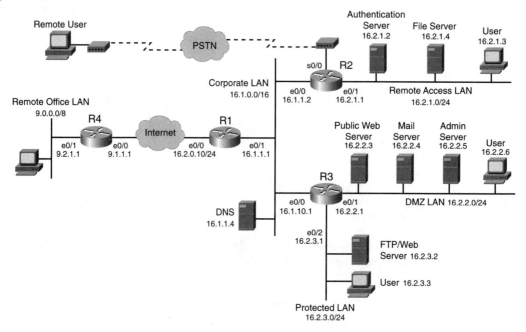

NOTE   For the sake of clarity, the ACLs contained in the following sections are depicted as individual ACLs. Generally, you will not build many small ACLs as shown here. Most likely, you would build at least one ACL for the outside router interface, one for the inside router interface, and one or more for general router use. Do not attempt to combine the small examples shown here into these larger lists, as the statements will tend to contradict one another. A sample router configuration is shown in the section of this chapter titled, "Sample Router Configuration," which details how these functions are combined into logical ACLs.

Filtering Router Service Traffic

This section explains how to implement ACLs to filter IP traffic that is destined for the following router services:

- Telnet
- SNMP
- Routing protocols

Telnet Service

Telnet (vty) is typically used by systems administrators to access the router for configuration and maintenance. Figure 4-28 shows a portion of the theoretical network from Figure 4-27.

Figure 4-28 *Telnet Service Filtering*

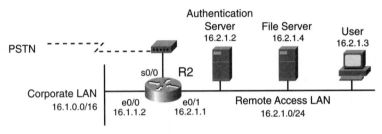

You should restrict which hosts have access to the vty lines of the router by using an ACL, as demonstrated in Example 4-16.

Example 4-16 *Filtering Telnet Service*

```
R2(config)# access-list 105 permit host 16.2.1.3 eq 23 any log
R2(config)# access-list 105 permit host 16.2.1.2 eq 23 any log
R2(config)# access-list 105 deny any log
R2(config)# line vty 0 4
R2(config-line)# access-class 105 in
R2(config-line)# end
```

In this example, IP extended ACL 105 allows only hosts 16.2.1.3 and 16.2.1.2 to access router R2 using Telnet (port 23). All other hosts are denied Telnet access to R2. This ACL is also designed to log all successful and unsuccessful attempts to access R2 using Telnet.

SNMP Service

Because of the inherent lack of authentication, SNMP should be used only on protected, internal networks. You should limit access to a router's SNMP agent by using an ACL as follows that applies to router R2 in Figure 4-28:

```
R2(config)# access-list 80 permit host 16.2.1.3
R2(config)# snmp-server community snmp-host1 ro 80
```

In this example, only the SNMP host with IP address 16.2.1.3 may access router R2's SNMP agent. It further specifies that the SNMP host must use a community string of snmp-host1.

Routing Protocols

Cisco routers share routing table update information to provide directions on where to route traffic. Attackers can use routing table information to map out a potential victim's network to locate possible targets of opportunity. To minimize the possibility of a router sharing routing table information with an attacker who is masquerading as a trusted peer, ACLs should be used to limit what routes a router will accept (take in) or advertise (send out) to its counterparts.

NOTE   Several routing protocols are available on Cisco IOS routers, including (but not limited to) Open Shortest Path First (OSPF), Border Gateway Protocol (BGP), Interior Gateway Routing Protocol (IGRP), Enhanced Interior Gateway Routing Protocol (EIGRP), Intermediate System-to-Intermediate System (IS-IS), and Routing Information Protocol (RIP). These protocols each handle routing table updates differently, and not all of them accept standard ACLs as a method of filtering updates. OSPF, for example, only permits the use of this type of filter for outbound updates on autonomous system boundary routers (ASBRs). Be sure to check the capabilities of the protocol that you use. Almost all the protocols have some method of filtering updates and all of them have authentication capabilities so that table updates will be shared only with trusted peers.

Figure 4-29 shows a portion of the theoretical network of Figure 4-27.

Figure 4-29 *OSPF Route Filtering*

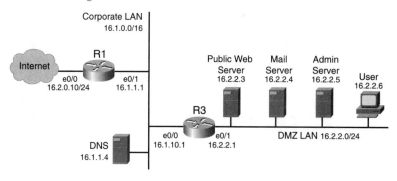

Example 4-17 demonstrates a standard IP ACL as it is applied to the OSPF routing protocol, area 1. In this example, router R3 will not advertise out interface e0/0 any routes of the 16.2.2.0 DMZ network.

Example 4-17 *Filtering OSPF Service*

```
R1(config)# access-list 12 deny 16.2.2.0 0.0.0.255
R1(config)# access-list 12 permit any
R1(config)# router ospf 1
R1(config-router)# distribute-list 12 out
R1(config-router)# end
```

Filtering Network Traffic

This section explains how to implement ACLs for mitigating the following threats:

- IP address spoofing—inbound
- IP address spoofing—outbound
- DoS TCP SYN attacks—blocking external attacks
- DoS TCP SYN attacks—using TCP intercept
- DoS smurf attacks
- Filtering ICMP messages—inbound
- Filtering ICMP messages—outbound
- Filtering traceroute

IP Address Spoof Mitigation

One method that attackers frequently use to gain information from a network is to try to appear as a trusted member of the network under attack. This is done by spoofing the source IP address in packets that are destined to the internal network under attack. The attacker simply changes the source IP address in the packet to an address that belongs to the internal network subnet.

Inbound

As a rule, you should not allow any IP packets inbound to a private network that contain the source address of any internal hosts or networks. Router R2 in Figure 4-30 will be used for the examples in this section.

Figure 4-30 *IP Address Spoof Mitigation*

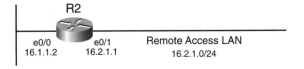

Example 4-18 shows the ACL 150 for router R2.

Example 4-18 *Access List 150 for Router R2*

```
R2(config)# access-list 150 deny ip 16.2.1.0 0.0.0.255 any log
R2(config)# access-list 150 deny ip 127.0.0.0 0.255.255.255 any log
R2(config)# access-list 150 deny ip 0.0.0.0 0.255.255.255 any log
R2(config)# access-list 150 deny ip 10.0.0.0 0.255.255.255 any log
R2(config)# access-list 150 deny ip 172.16.0.0 0.15.255.255 any log
R2(config)# access-list 150 deny 192.168.0.0 0.0.255.255 any log
```

continues

Example 4-18 *Access List 150 for Router R2 (Continued)*

```
R2(config)# access-list 150 deny 224.0.0.0 15.255.255.255 any log
R2(config)# access-list 150 deny ip host 255.255.255.255 any log
R2(config)# access-list 150 permit ip any 16.2.1.0 0.0.0.255
R2(config)# interface e0/0
R2(config-if)# ip access-group 150 in
R2(config-if)# exit
```

This ACL denies any packets from the following sources:

- Any addresses from the internal 16.2.1.0 network.

- Any local host addresses (127.0.0.0/8).

- Any reserved private addresses (RFC 1918).

- Any addresses in the IP multicast address range (224.0.0.0/4).

This ACL is applied to the external interface (e0/0) of router R2.

Outbound

As a rule, you should not allow any outbound IP packets with a source address other than a valid IP address of the internal network.

Example 4-19 shows the configuration of ACL 105 for router R2 of Figure 4-30. This ACL permits only those packets that contain source addresses from the 16.2.1.0/24 network and denies all others.

Example 4-19 *Filtering the Source Address on Outbound Packets*

```
R2(config)# access-list 105 permit ip 16.2.1.0 0.0.0.255 any
R2(config)# access-list 105 deny ip any any log
R2(config)# interface e0/1
R2(config-if)# ip access-group 105 in
R2(config-if)# end
```

This ACL is applied to the inside interface (e0/1) of router R2.

DoS TCP SYN Attack Mitigation

You can accomplish DoS TCP SYN attack mitigation in either of two ways: block external access or use TCP intercept.

Blocking External Access

TCP SYN DoS attacks involve sending large numbers of packets into the internal network in an attempt to flood the connection queues of the receiving nodes.

The ACL in Example 4-20 for router R2 of Figure 4-30 is designed to prevent inbound packets, with only the SYN flag set, from traversing the router.

Example 4-20 *Blocking External TCP SYN DoS Packets*

```
R2(config)# access-list 109 permit tcp any 16.2.1.0 0.0.0.255 established
R2(config)# access-list 109 deny ip any any log
R2(config)# interface e0/0
R2(config-if)# ip access-group 109 in
R2(config-if)# end
```

It does allow responses from the outside network for requests that originated on the inside network. It also denies any connection from the outside network from initiating a TCP connection.

Using TCP Intercept

TCP intercept is a tool for protecting internal network hosts from external TCP SYN attacks. The ACL in Example 4-21 blocks packets from unreachable hosts by allowing only reachable external hosts to initiate TCP connections to internal hosts. This ACL applies to router R2 of Figure 4-30.

Example 4-21 *Using TCP Intercept*

```
R2(config)# ip tcp intercept list 110
R2(config)# access-list 110 permit tcp any 16.2.1.0 0.0.0.255
R2(config)# access-list 110 deny ip any any log
R2(config)# interface e0/0
R2(config-if)# ip access-group 110 in
R2(config-if)# end
```

Using TCP intercept, the router examines each inbound TCP connection attempt to determine whether the source address is from an external, reachable host. The software establishes a connection with the client on behalf of the destination server and, if successful, establishes the connection with the server on behalf of the client; it then knits the two half connections together transparently. If the host is reachable, the connection is allowed. If the host is unreachable, the connection attempt is dropped.

NOTE   Because it examines every TCP connection attempt, TCP intercept can impose a performance burden on your routers. Always test for any performance problems before using TCP intercept in a production environment.

DoS Smurf Attack Mitigation

Smurf attacks consist of sending large numbers of ICMP packets to a router subnet broadcast address using a spoofed IP address from that same subnet. Some routers may be configured to forward these broadcasts to other routers in the protected network, causing degraded performance. The ACL shown in Example 4-22 for router R2 of Figure 4-30 is used to prevent this forwarding from occurring and halting the smurf attack.

Example 4-22 *Filtering Smurf Attacks*

```
R2(config)# access-list 111 deny ip any host 16.2.1.255 log
R2(config)# access-list 111 deny ip any host 16.2.1.0 log
R2(config)# interface e0/0
R2(config-if)# ip access-group 111 in
R2(config-if)# end
```

This ACL blocks all IP packets originating from any host destined for the broadcast addresses specified (16.2.1.255 and 16.2.1.0).

NOTE   Cisco IOS Release 12.0 and later now have **no ip directed-broadcast** on by default, preventing this type of ICMP attack. Therefore, you may not need to build an ACL as shown here.

Filtering ICMP Messages

Filtering inbound, outbound, and traceroute ICMP messages is critical to the security of your network.

Inbound

There are several types of ICMP message types that can be used against your network. Programs use some of these messages; others are used for network management and so are automatically generated by the router.

ICMP Echo packets can be used to discover subnets and hosts on the protected network and can also be used to generate DoS floods. ICMP redirect messages can be used to alter host routing tables. Both ICMP echo and redirect messages should be blocked inbound by the router.

The ACL shown in Example 4-23 for router R2 of Figure 4-30 blocks all ICMP echo and redirect messages.

Example 4-23 *Filtering Inbound ICMP Messages*

```
R2(config)# access-list 112 deny icmp any any echo log
R2(config)# access-list 112 deny icmp any any redirect log
R2(config)# access-list 112 deny icmp any any mask-request log
R2(config)# access-list 112 permit icmp any 16.2.1.0 0.0.0.255
R2(config)# interface e0/0
R2(config-if)# ip access-group 112 in
R2(config-if)# end
```

As an added safety measure, this ACL also blocks mask-request messages. All other ICMP messages inbound to the 16.2.1.0/24 network are allowed.

Outbound

The following ICMP messages are recommended for network management and should be allowed outbound:

- **Echo**—Allows users to ping external hosts
- **Parameter problem**—Informs host of packet header problems
- **Packet too big**—Required for packet Maximum Transfer Unit (MTU) discovery
- **Source quench**—Throttles down traffic when necessary

As a rule, you should block all other ICMP message types outbound.

The ACL shown in Example 4-24 for router R2 of Figure 4-30 permits all the required ICMP messages outbound while denying all others.

Example 4-24 *ACL that Permits and Denies ICMP Messages*

```
R2(config)# access-list 114 permit icmp 16.2.1.0 0.0.0.255 any echo
R2(config)# access-list 114 permit icmp 16.2.1.0 0.0.0.255 any parameter-problem
R2(config)# access-list 114 permit icmp 16.2.1.0 0.0.0.255 any packet-too-big
R2(config)# access-list 114 permit icmp 16.2.1.0 0.0.0.255 any source-quench
R2(config)# access-list 114 deny icmp any any log
R2(config)# interface e0/1
R2(config-if)# ip access-group 114 in
R2(config-if)# end
```

Traceroute

The traceroute feature uses some of the ICMP message types to accomplish its tasks. Traceroute displays the IP addresses of routers that a packet encounters along its path (hops) from source to destination. Attackers can use responses to the traceroute ICMP messaging to discover subnets and hosts on the protected network.

As a rule, you should block all inbound and outbound traceroute UDP messages, as shown in Example 4-25, for router R2 of Figure 4-30 (UDP ports 33400 to 34400).

Example 4-25 *Block All Inbound and Outbound Traceroute UDP Messages*

```
R2(config)# access-list 120 deny udp any any range 33400 34400 log
R2(config)# interface e0/0
R2(config-if)# ip access-group 120 in
R2(config-if)# end
R2(config)# access-list 121 permit udp 16.2.1.0 0.0.0.255 any range 33400 34400 log
R2(config)# interface e0/1
R2(config-if)# ip access-group 121 in
R2(config-if)# end
```

DDoS Mitigation

This section explains how to configure your routers to help reduce the effect of DDoS attacks.

Generally, routers cannot prevent all DDoS attacks, but they can help reduce the number of occurrences by building ACLs that filter known attack ports.

This section explains how to block the following DDoS agents:

- TRIN00
- Stacheldraht
- TrinityV3
- Subseven

NOTE   Blocking these ports may have an impact on regular network users as they block some high port numbers that may be used by legitimate network clients. You may wish to wait to block these port numbers until a particular threat presents itself.

The following ACL rules are generally applied to inbound and outbound traffic between the protected network and the Internet.

TRIN00

The following example for router R2 of Figure 4-30 shows an example of blocking the TRIN00 DDoS attack by blocking traffic on the following ports:

- TCP—1524 (Ingress Lock)
- TCP—27665 (Unassigned)
- UDP—31335 (Unassigned)
- UDP—27444 (Unassigned)

```
R2(config)# access-list 190 deny tcp any any eq 1524 log
R2(config)# access-list 190 deny tcp any any eq 27665 log
R2(config)# access-list 190 deny udp any any eq 31335 log
R2(config)# access-list 190 deny udp any any eq 27444 log
```

Stacheldraht

The following example for router R2 of Figure 4-30 shows an example of blocking the Stacheldraht DDoS attack by blocking traffic on the following ports:

- TCP—16660 (Unassigned)
- TCP—65000 (Unassigned)

```
R2(config)# access-list 190 deny tcp any any eq 16660 log
R2(config)# access-list 190 deny tcp any any eq 65000 log
```

The Stacheldraht DDoS uses ICMP Echo Request and Echo Reply messages for communications to set up, control, and monitor the attack. You can stop the actual attack by blocking TCP ports 16660 and 65000, but if you want to prevent an attacker from setting up back doors on your system, you may want to block ICMP Echo Request (TCP port 8) and ICMP Echo Reply (TCP port 0) as shown in the following commands:

```
R2(config)# access-list 190 deny icmp any any echo
R2(config)# access-list 190 deny icmp any any echo-reply
```

Remember that blocking these ICMP ports will prevent the use of the ping command and may not be desirable for your network.

TrinityV3

The following example for router R2 of Figure 4-30 shows an example of blocking the TrinityV3 DDoS attack by blocking traffic on the following ports:

- TCP—33270 (Unassigned)
- TCP—39168 (Unassigned)

```
R2(config)# access-list 190 deny tcp any any eq 33270 log
R2(config)# access-list 190 deny tcp any any eq 39168 log
```

Subseven

The following example for router R2 of Figure 4-30 shows an example of blocking the Subseven DDoS attack by blocking traffic on the following ports:

- TCP—Range 6711 to 6712 (Unassigned)
- TCP—6776 (Unassigned)
- TCP—6669 (IRCU)
- TCP—2222 (Rockwell CSP1)
- TCP—7000 (AFS3 Fileserver)

```
R2(config)# access-list 190 deny tcp any any range 6711 6712 log
R2(config)# access-list 190 deny tcp any any eq 6776 log
R2(config)# access-list 190 deny tcp any any eq 6669 log
R2(config)# access-list 190 deny tcp any any eq 2222 log
R2(config)# access-list 190 deny tcp any any eq 7000 log
```

Sample Router Configuration

This section contains a sample router configuration for the theoretical network router R2. This partial configuration file contains several ACLs that contain most of the ACL features already explained in this chapter. View this partial configuration as an example of how to integrate multiple ACL policies into a few main router ACLs.

Theoretical Network—Sample Configuration for Router R2

Example 4-26 is a partial configuration file for router R2 of Figure 4-30 that shows how to combine many ACL functions into two or three larger ACLs.

Example 4-26 *Combining ACL Functions into Two or Three Larger ACLs*

```
!
hostname R2
!
interface Ethernet0/0
   ip address 16.1.1.2 255.255.0.0
   ip access-group 126 in
!
interface Ethernet0/1
   ip address 16.2.1.1 255.255.255.0
   ip access-group 128 in
!
router ospf 44
network 16.1.0.0 0.0.255.255 area 0
network 16.2.1.0 0.0.0.255 area 1
!
! Access list 80 applies to SNMP hosts allowed to access this router
no access-list 80
access-list 80 permit host 16.2.1.2
access-list 80 permit host 16.2.1.3
!
! Access list 126 applies to traffic flowing from external networks to the
! internal network or to the router itself
no access-list 126
access-list 126 deny ip 16.2.1.0 0.0.0.255 any log
access-list 126 deny ip host 16.1.1.2 host 16.1.1.2 log
access-list 126 deny ip 127.0.0.0 0.255.255.255 any log
access-list 126 deny ip 0.0.0.0 0.255.255.255 any log
access-list 126 deny ip 10.0.0.0 0.255.255.255 any log
access-list 126 deny ip 172.16.0.0 0.15.255.255 any log
access-list 126 deny ip 192.168.0.0 0.0.255.255 any log
access-list 126 deny ip 224.0.0.0 15.255.255.255 any log
access-list 126 deny ip any host 16.2.1.255 log
access-list 126 deny ip any host 16.2.1.0 log
access-list 126 permit tcp any 16.2.1.0 0.0.0.255 established
access-list 126 deny icmp any any echo log
access-list 126 deny icmp any any redirect log
access-list 126 deny icmp any any mask-request log
access-list 126 permit icmp any 16.2.1.0 0.0.0.255
access-list 126 permit ospf 16.1.0.0 0.0.255.255 host 16.1.1.2
access-list 126 deny tcp any any range 6000 6063 log
access-list 126 deny tcp any any eq 6667 log
```

Example 4-26 *Combining ACL Functions into Two or Three Larger ACLs (Continued)*

```
access-list 126 deny tcp any any range 12345 12346 log
access-list 126 deny tcp any any eq 31337 log
access-list 126 permit tcp any eq 20 16.2.1.0 0.0.0.255 gt 1023
access-list 126 deny udp any any eq 2049 log
access-list 126 deny udp any any eq 31337 log
access-list 126 deny udp any any range 33400 34400 log
access-list 126 permit udp any eq 53 16.2.1.0 0.0.0.255 gt 1023
access-list 126 deny tcp any range 0 65535 any range 0 65535 log
access-list 126 deny udp any range 0 65535 any range 0 65535 log
access-list 126 deny ip any any log
!
! Access list 128 applies to traffic flowing from the internal network to external
! networks or to the router itself
no access-list 128
access-list 128 deny ip host 16.2.1.1 host 16.2.1.1 log
access-list 128 permit icmp 16.2.1.0 0.0.0.255 any echo
access-list 128 permit icmp 16.2.1.0 0.0.0.255 any parameter-problem
access-list 128 permit icmp 16.2.1.0 0.0.0.255 any packet-too-big
access-list 128 permit icmp 16.2.1.0 0.0.0.255 any source-quench
access-list 128 deny tcp any any range 1 19 log
access-list 128 deny tcp any any eq 43 log
access-list 128 deny tcp any any eq 93 log
access-list 128 deny tcp any any range 135 139 log
access-list 128 deny tcp any any eq 445 log
access-list 128 deny tcp any any range 512 518 log
access-list 128 deny tcp any any eq 540 log
access-list 128 permit tcp 16.2.1.0 0.0.0.255 gt 1023 any lt 1024
access-list 128 permit udp 16.2.1.0 0.0.0.255 gt 1023 any eq 53
access-list 128 permit udp 16.2.1.0 0.0.0.255 any range 33400 34400 log
access-list 128 deny tcp any range 0 65535 any range 0 65535 log
access-list 128 deny udp any range 0 65535 any range 0 65535 log
access-list 128 deny ip any any log
!
! Access list 85 applies to remote access for the specified hosts to the router
! itself
no access-list 85
access-list 85 permit tcp host 16.2.1.10 host 0.0.0.0 eq 23 log
access-list 85 permit tcp host 16.2.1.11 host 0.0.0.0 eq 23 log
access-list 85 permit tcp host 16.2.1.12 host 0.0.0.0 eq 23 log
access-list 85 deny ip any any log
!
snmp-server community snmp-host1 ro 80
!
```

Implementing Syslog Logging

This section provides an overview of syslog logging and how to configure your routers to support this function.

Implementing a router logging facility is an important part of any network security policy. Cisco routers can log information regarding configuration changes, ACL violations, interface status, and many other types of events.

Cisco routers can direct log messages to several different facilities. You should configure the router to send log messages to one or more of the following:

- **Console**—Console logging is used when modifying or testing the router while connected to the console. Messages sent to the console are not stored by the router, and therefore are not very valuable as security events.

- **Terminal lines**—Enabled EXEC sessions can be configured to receive log messages on any terminal lines. Like console logging, this type of logging is not stored by the router and therefore is only valuable to the user on that line.

- **Memory buffer**—You may direct a router to store log messages in router memory. Buffered logging is a bit more useful as a security tool because messages are instantly available, but it has the drawback of having its events cleared whenever the router is booted.

- **SNMP traps**—Certain router events may be processed by the router SNMP agent and forwarded as SNMP traps to an external SNMP host. This is a viable security logging facility, but it requires the configuration and maintenance of an SNMP system.

- **Syslog**—Cisco routers can be configured to forward log messages to an external syslog service. This service may reside on any number of servers, including Windows and UNIX-based systems. This is the most popular message logging facility because of its long-term log storage capabilities and because it provides a central location for all router messages.

NOTE   Performing forensics on router logs can become very difficult if your router clocks are not running the correct time. Cisco recommends that you use an NTP facility to ensure that all of your routers are operating at the correct time, as long as you use ACLs to control which devices can use the protocol.

Syslog Systems

Syslog implementations contain two types of systems, as shown in Figure 4-31:

- **Syslog servers**—Also known as destination hosts, these systems accept and process log messages from syslog clients

- **Syslog clients**—Routers or other types of Cisco equipment that generate and forward log messages to syslog servers

Figure 4-31 *Syslog Systems*

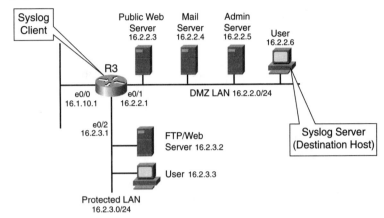

Cisco Log Severity Levels

Cisco router log messages fall into one of eight levels, as shown in Table 4-4. The lower the level number, the higher the severity level.

Table 4-4   *Log Message Levels*

Level	Name	Description
0	Emergencies	Router unusable
1	Alerts	Immediate action required
2	Critical	Condition is critical
3	Errors	Error condition
4	Warnings	Warning condition
5	Notifications	Normal but important event
6	Informational	Informational message
7	Debugging	Debug message

NOTE   When entering logging levels in commands beginning with Cisco IOS Release 11.3, you must specify the level name. Beginning with Cisco IOS Release 12.0, the **logging level** command supports using both the level number and the level name.

Here are some examples of different level messages:

- **0**—%TCPIP-0-PANIC : panic[[chars]@[dec]] in [chars]: [chars]
  - **Explanation**—An unexpected internal error has occurred in the TCP/IP stack.

- **1**—%ENV_MON-1-SHUTDOWN : Environmental Monitor initiated shutdown
    - **Explanation**—The system has reached a shutdown temperature level, and the router is being shut down to avoid any damage.
- **2**—%SYS-2-GETBUFFFAIL : [chars] buffer allocation ([dec] bytes) failed from [hex]
    - **Explanation**—An operation could not be accomplished because of a low-memory condition. The router memory has been exhausted or fragmented. This condition may be caused by the current system configuration, the network environment, or a software error.
- **3**—%SYS-3-NOELEMENT : [chars]:Ran out of buffer elements for enqueue
    - **Explanation**—The process has run out of buffer elements and is unable to enqueue data.
- **4**—%CRYPTO-4-ENC_METHOD_NOT_SUPPORTED : Invalid encryption method for IKE policy [int]
    - **Explanation**—The configured encryption method is not supported.
- **5**—%SYS-5-CONFIG_I : Configured from [chars] by [chars]
    - **Explanation**—The router configuration has been changed.
- **6**—%SYS-6-BOOTTIME : Time taken to reboot after reload = [dec] seconds
    - **Explanation**—This informational message provides the time taken for the router to come up after a reload or crash. The time is actually the difference between the last crash and a successive boot. If autoboot was not set and the router is in ROM Monitor mode for a long time, the reload time shown could be a large number.
- **7**—%SPANTREE-7-BLOCK_PORT_TYPE : Blocking [chars] on [chars]. Inconsistant port type.
    - **Explanation**—The specified interface has an inconsistent port type and is being held in a spanning-tree blocking state until the port type inconsistency is resolved.

Log Message Format

Cisco router log messages contain three main parts. The following is an example of a log message:

```
Oct 29 10:00:01 EST:  #SYS-5-CONFIG_I:  Configured from console by vty0 (16.2.2.6)
```

The three main parts of the message are

- **Timestamp**—Oct 29 10:00:01 EST
- **Log message name and severity level**—#SYS-5-CONFIG_I
- **Message text**—Configured from console by vty0 (16.2.2.6)

NOTE	The log message name is not the same thing as a message level name.

Syslog Router Commands

Complete the following steps to implement syslog for your Cisco routers:

Step 1 Configure destination host(s).

You must configure the router to send log messages to one or more syslog servers (also known as destination hosts or logging hosts). There is no maximum number of destination hosts supported by Cisco routers, but usually only one or two are needed. Destination hosts are identified by their host name or IP address.

Use the **logging** command in global configuration mode to set the destination (logging) hosts.

The syntax for the **logging** command is as follows:

```
logging [host-name | ip-address]
```

- *host-name*—Name of the host to be used as a syslog server.
- *ip-address*—IP address of the host to be used as a syslog server.

Step 2 (Optional) Set the log severity (trap) level.

This limits the logging of error messages sent to syslog servers to only those messages at the specified level.

Use the **logging trap** command in global configuration mode to set the severity (trap) level.

The syntax for the **logging trap** command is as follows:

```
logging trap level
```

- *level*—Limits the logging of messages to the syslog servers to a specified level. You can enter the level number (0 to 7) or level name.

Step 3 (Optional) Set the syslog facility.

You must configure the syslog facility to which error messages are sent. The eight commonly used syslog facility names for Cisco routers are local0 to local7.

Use the **logging facility** command in global configuration mode to set the syslog facility.

The syntax for the **logging facility** command is as follows:

```
logging facility facility-type
```

- *facility-type*—The syslog facility type (local0 to local7).

Step 4 (Optional) Set the source interface.

You must specify the source IP address of syslog packets, regardless of through which interface the packets actually exit the router. Use the router interface on the same network as the syslog server, or the one with the least number of hops to the syslog server.

Use the **logging source-interface** command in global configuration mode to set the source interface.

The syntax for the **logging source-interface** command is as follows:

```
logging source-interface interface-type interface-number
```

- *interface-type*—The interface type (for example, Ethernet).
- *interface-number*—The interface number (for example, 0/1).

Step 5 Enable logging.

Make sure that the router logging process is enabled by using the **logging on** command in global configuration mode.

The syntax for the **logging on** command is as follows:

```
logging on
```

This command has no arguments or keywords.

You can implement syslog as shown in Figure 4-32.

Figure 4-32 *Implementing Syslog*

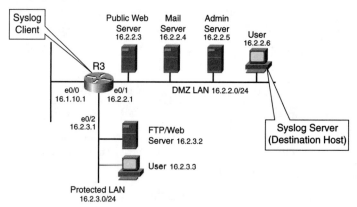

Example 4-27 demonstrates configuring syslog for router R3 of Figure 4-32 using the commands previously specified.

Example 4-27 *Configuring Syslog for Router R3*

```
R3(config)# logging 16.2.2.6
R3(config)# logging trap informational
R3(config)# logging on
```

Designing Secure Management and Reporting for Enterprise Networks

This section provides an overview of the Cisco "SAFE: Extending the Security Blueprint to Small, Midsize, and Remote-User Networks" (SAFE SMR) secure management and reporting design specification.

The principal goal of SAFE is to provide best-practice information on designing and implementing secure networks. The SAFE SMR specification contains design and implementation information that is specific to the management and reporting portion of your network. The SAFE blueprint refers to the design of the management and reporting systems as the "management module."

NOTE   This topic discusses only a small portion of the SAFE blueprint. For more detailed information regarding the SAFE blueprint, go to Cisco.com and search on "SAFE" or attend the Cisco SAFE Implementation (CSI) course.

In the preceding section, "Syslog Router Commands," you learned how to configure logging for your Cisco routers. This is a fairly straightforward operation when your network contains only a few Cisco routers. However, logging and reading information from hundreds of devices can prove to be a challenging proposition and can raise several important questions:

- Which logs are most important?
- How do you separate important messages from mere notifications?
- How do you ensure that logs are not tampered with in transit?
- How do you ensure that your time stamps match each other when multiple devices report the same alarm?
- What information is needed if log data is required for a criminal investigation?
- How do you deal with the volume of messages that can be generated by a large network?

In the first half of this chapter you also learned about the basics of router management. You learned about securing administrative access and device configurations. Like device logging, this is a fairly straightforward operation for smaller Cisco router networks. However, managing administrative access and device configurations for many more devices can raise a different set of questions:

- How do you securely manage many devices in many locations?
- How can you track changes on devices to troubleshoot when attacks or network failures occur?

SAFE Architectural Perspective

As can be seen in Figure 4-33, the SAFE enterprise management module has two network segments that are separated by a Cisco IOS router that acts as a firewall and a virtual private network (VPN) termination device. The segment outside the firewall connects to all the devices that require management. The segment inside the firewall contains the management hosts themselves and the Cisco IOS routers that act as terminal servers.

Figure 4-33 *SAFE Enterprise Management*

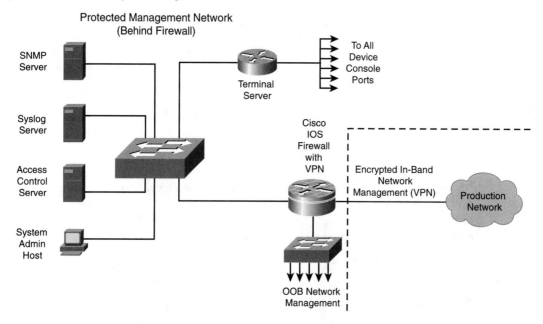

Information flow between management hosts and the managed devices can take two paths:

- **Out of band (OOB)** — Information flows within a network on which no production traffic resides.

- **In band** — Information flows across the enterprise production network or the Internet (or both).

The connection to the production network is only provided for selective Internet access, limited in-band management traffic, and IPSec-protected management traffic from predetermined hosts. In-band management occurs only when a management application itself does not function OOB or when the Cisco device being managed does not physically have enough interfaces to support the normal management connection. It is this latter case that employs IPSec tunnels. The Cisco IOS Firewall is configured to allow syslog information into the management segment, as well as Telnet, Secure Shell (SSH), and SNMP if these are first initiated by the inside network.

Both management subnets operate under an address space that is completely separate from the rest of the production network. This practice ensures that the management network will not be advertised by any routing protocols. It also enables the production network devices to block any traffic from the management subnets that appears on the production network links.

Any in-band management or Internet access occurs through a Network Address Translation (NAT) process on the Cisco IOS router that translates the nonroutable management IP addresses to previously determined production IP address ranges.

The management module provides configuration management for nearly all devices in the network through the use of two primary technologies:

- **Cisco IOS routers acting as terminal servers**—The routers provide a reverse Telnet function to the console ports on the Cisco devices throughout the enterprise.

- **Dedicated management network segment**—More extensive management features (software changes, content updates, log and alarm aggregation, and SNMP management) are provided through the dedicated management network segment.

Because the management network has administrative access to nearly every area of the network, it can be a very attractive target to hackers. The management module has been built with several technologies that are designed to mitigate those risks. The first primary threat is a hacker attempting to gain access to the management network itself. This threat can be mitigated only through the effective deployment of security features in the remaining modules in the enterprise. All the remaining threats assume that the primary line of defense has been breached. To mitigate the threat of a compromised device, access control is implemented at the firewall, and at every other possible device, to prevent exploitation of the management channel. A compromised device cannot even communicate with other hosts on the same subnet because private VLANs on the management segment switches force all traffic from the managed devices directly to the Cisco IOS Firewall, where filtering takes place. Password sniffing reveals only useless information because of the OTP environment.

SNMP management has its own set of security needs. Keeping SNMP traffic on the management segment allows it to traverse an isolated segment when pulling management information from devices. With SAFE, SNMP management can pull information from devices but is not allowed to push changes. To ensure this, each device is configured with a "read-only" string.

Proper aggregation and analysis of the syslog information is critical to the proper management of a network. From a security perspective, syslog provides important information about security violations and configuration changes. Depending on the device in question, different levels of syslog information might be required. Having full logging with all messages sent might provide too much information for an individual or syslog analysis algorithm to sort. Logging for the sake of logging does not improve security. You may configure SNMP "read-write" when using an OOB network, but be aware of the increased security risk of a clear text string allowing modification of device configurations.

Information Paths

The primary goal of SAFE SMR is to facilitate the secure management of all devices and hosts within the enterprise architecture, as shown in Figure 4-34. Logging and reporting information flow from the devices to the management hosts, while content, configurations, and new software flow to the devices from the management hosts.

Figure 4-34 *SAFE Protected Management Network*

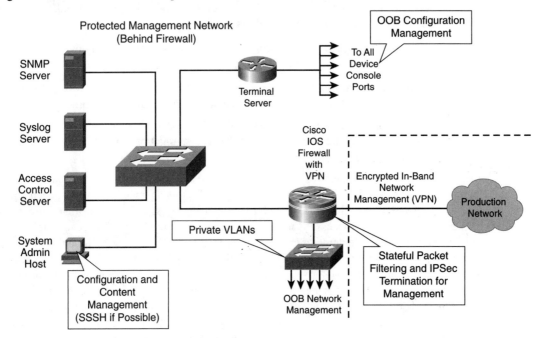

From an architectural perspective, providing OOB management of network systems is the best first step in any management and reporting strategy. Devices should have a direct local connection to such a network where possible, and where impossible (because of geographic or system-related issues), the device should connect via a private encrypted tunnel over the production network. Such a tunnel should be preconfigured to communicate only across the specific ports required for management and reporting. The tunnel should also be locked down so that only appropriate hosts can initiate and terminate tunnels.

After you have implemented an OOB management network, dealing with logging and reporting becomes more straightforward. Most networking devices can send syslog data, which can be invaluable when troubleshooting network problems or security threats. Send this data to one or more syslog analysis hosts on the management network. Depending on the device involved, you can choose various logging levels to ensure that the correct amount of data is sent to the logging devices. To ensure that log message times are comparable to one another, clocks on hosts and network devices must be synchronized. For devices that support it, NTP provides a way to ensure that accurate time is kept on all devices. When you are dealing with an attack, seconds matter, because it is important to identify the order in which a specified attack took place.

NOTE   OOB management is not always desirable. Often the decision depends on the type of management application that you are running and the protocols that are required. For example, consider a management tool whose goal is to determine reachability of all the devices on the production network. If a critical link fails between two core switches, you would want this management console to alert an administrator. If this management application is configured to use an OOB network, it may never determine that the link has failed, because the OOB network makes all devices appear to be attached to a single network. With management applications such as these, it is preferred to run the management application in-band. In-band management needs to be configured in as secure a manner as possible. Often in-band and OOB management can be configured from the same management network, provided that there is a firewall between the management hosts and the devices needing management.

When in-band management of a device is required, you should consider the following questions, in order:

1   **What management protocols does the device support?**—Devices with IPSec should be managed by simply creating a tunnel from the management network to the device. This setup allows many insecure management protocols to flow over a single encrypted tunnel. When IPSec is not possible because it is not supported on a device, other, less-secure options must be chosen. For configuration of the device, SSH or Secure Sockets Layer (SSL) can often be used instead of Telnet to encrypt any configuration modifications made to a device. These protocols can sometimes also be used to push and pull data to a device instead of insecure protocols such as TFTP and FTP. Often, however, TFTP is required on Cisco equipment to back up configurations or to update software versions. This fact leads to the second question.

2   **Does this management channel need to be active at all times?**—If not, holes can be placed temporarily in a firewall while the management functions are performed and then later removed. This process does not scale with large numbers of devices, however, and should be used sparingly, if at all, in enterprise deployments. If the channel needs to be active at all times, such as with SNMP, the third question should be considered.

3   **Do you really need this management tool?**—Often, SNMP managers are used on the inside of a network to ease troubleshooting and configuration. However, SNMP should be treated with the utmost care because the underlying protocol has its own set of security vulnerabilities. If SNMP is required, consider providing read-only access to devices via SNMP, and treat the SNMP community string with the same care you might use for a root password on a critical UNIX host. Know that by introducing SNMP into your production network, you are introducing a potential vulnerability into your environment.

Configuration change management is another issue related to secure management. When a network is under attack, it is important to know the state of critical network devices and when the last known modifications took place. Creating a plan for change management should be a part of your comprehensive security policy, but, at a minimum, you should record changes using authentication systems on the devices and archive configurations via FTP or TFTP.

General Guidelines for Out-of-Band Management

The following are OOB secure management guidelines for the architecture:

- It should provide the highest level of security; it should mitigate the risk of passing insecure management protocols over the production network.
- It should keep clocks on hosts and network devices synchronized.
- It should record changes and archive configurations.

The following are in-band secure management guidelines:

- Decide if the device really needs to be managed or monitored.
- Use IPSec when possible.
- Use SSH or SSL instead of Telnet.
- Decide whether the management channel needs to be open at all times.
- Keep clocks on hosts and network devices synchronized.
- Record changes and archive configurations.

Even though OOB management is recommended for devices in SAFE enterprises, SAFE SMR recommends in-band management, because the goal is cost-effective security deployment.

In the SAFE SMR architecture, management traffic flows in-band in all cases and is made as secure as possible by using tunneling protocols and secure variants to insecure management protocols (for example, SSH is used whenever possible instead of Telnet). With management traffic flowing in-band across the production network, it becomes very important to follow more closely the axioms mentioned earlier in the lesson.

To ensure that log messages are time-synchronized to one another, clocks on hosts and network devices must be synchronized. For devices that support it, NTP provides a way to ensure that accurate time is kept on all devices.

When you are dealing with an attack, seconds matter, because it is important to identify the order in which a specified attack occurred.

NTP is used to synchronize the clocks of various devices across a network. Synchronization of the clocks within a network is critical for digital certificates and for correct interpretation of events within syslog data. A secure method of providing clocking for the network is for network administrators to implement their own master clocks. The private network should then be synchronized to Universal Time Coordinate (UTC) via satellite or radio. However, clock sources are available that synchronize via the Internet for network administrators who do not wish to implement their own master clocks because of cost or other reasons.

An attacker could attempt a DoS attack on a network by sending bogus NTP data across the Internet in an attempt to change the clocks on network devices in such a manner that digital certificates are considered invalid. Further, an attacker could attempt to confuse a network administrator during an attack by disrupting the clocks on network devices. This scenario would make it difficult for the network administrator to determine the order of syslog events on multiple devices.

NTP version 3 and above supports a cryptographic authentication mechanism between peers. The use of the authentication mechanism, as well as the use of ACLs that specify which network devices are allowed to synchronize with other network devices, is recommended to help mitigate such an attack.

The network administrator should weigh the cost benefits of pulling the clock from the Internet with the possible risk of doing so and allowing it through the firewall. Many NTP servers on the Internet do not require any authentication of peers. Therefore, the network administrator must trust that the clock itself is reliable, valid, and secure. NTP uses UDP port 123.

Logging and Reporting

Logging and reading information from many devices can be very challenging. To make this information more usable, perform the following:

- Identify which logs are most important.
- Separate important messages from notifications.
- Ensure that logs are not tampered with in transit.
- Ensure that time stamps match each other when multiple devices report the same alarm.
- Identify what information is needed if log data is required for a criminal investigation.
- Identify how to deal with the volume of messages that can be generated when a system is under attack.

Each of these issues is company-specific and requires input from management, as well as from the network and security teams, to identify the priorities of reporting and monitoring. The implemented security policy should also play a large role in answering these questions.

From a reporting standpoint, most networking devices can send syslog data, which can be invaluable when you are troubleshooting network problems or security threats. You can send this data to your syslog analysis host from any devices whose logs you wish to view. This data can be viewed in real time or on demand and in scheduled reports. Depending on the device involved, you can choose various logging levels to ensure that the correct amount of data is sent to the logging device. You also need to flag device log data within the analysis software to permit granular viewing and reporting. For example, during an attack, the log data provided by Layer 2 switches might not be as interesting as the data provided by the intrusion detection system (IDS).

To ensure that log messages are time-synchronized to one another, clocks on hosts and network devices must be synchronized. For devices that support it, NTP provides a way to ensure that accurate time is kept on all devices. When you are dealing with an attack, seconds matter, because it is important to identify the order in which a specified attack occurred.

Configuration change management is another issue related to secure management. When a network is under attack, it is important to know the state of critical network devices and when the last known modifications occurred. Creating a plan for change management should be a part of your comprehensive security policy, but, at a minimum, you should record changes using authentication systems on the devices and archive configurations via FTP or TFTP.

Configuring SSH Servers

Whenever possible, you should use SSH instead of Telnet to manage your Cisco routers. SSH version 1 is supported in Cisco IOS Release 12.1(1)T and later (Cisco currently does not support SSH version 2). Cisco routers that are configured for SSH act as SSH servers. You will need to provide an SSH client such as PuTTY, OpenSSH, or Tera Term for the administrator workstation you wish to use to configure and manage your routers using SSH.

NOTE   Cisco routers operating at Cisco IOS Release 12.1(3)T or later can act as SSH clients and as SSH servers. This means that you could initiate an SSH client-to-server session from your router to a central SSH server system. The SAFE SMR design does not typically use this functionality, because it is more likely that you will be accessing the router from an SSH client system, not the other way around.

SSH employs strong encryption to protect the SSH client-to-SSH server session. Unlike Telnet, which allows anyone with a sniffer to see exactly what you are sending and receiving to and from your routers, SSH encrypts the entire session.

Complete the following tasks before configuring your routers for SSH server operations:

- Ensure that the target routers are running a Cisco IOS software image 12.1(1)T or later and the IPSec feature set. Only Cisco IOS software images that contain the IPSec feature set support SSH servers.
- Ensure that the target routers are configured for either local authentication or AAA for username/password authentication.
- Ensure that each of the target routers has a unique host name.
- Ensure that each of the target routers is using the correct domain name of your network.

Complete the following steps to configure your Cisco router to support SSH server:

Step 1   Configure the IP domain name using the **ip domain-name** global configuration command, as shown in the following example:

```
Austin2(config)# ip domain-name cisco.com
```

Step 2   Generate the RSA keys using the **crypto key generate rsa** global configuration command, as shown in the following example:

```
Austin2(config)# crypto key generate rsa general-keys modulus 1024
```

> **NOTE**   It is recommended that you use a minimum key length of modulus 1024.

Step 3   Configure the time that the router waits for the SSH client to respond by using the **ip ssh time-out** global configuration command, as shown in the following example:

```
Austin2(config)# ip ssh time-out 120
```

Step 4   Configure the SSH retries by using the **ip ssh authentication-retries** global configuration command, as shown in the following example:

```
Austin2(config)# ip ssh authentication-retries 4
```

> **CAUTION**   Be sure to disable Telnet transport input on all the router vty lines or else the router will continue to allow insecure Telnet sessions.

Step 5   Disable vty inbound Telnet sessions, as shown in the following example:

```
Austin2(config)# line vty 0 4
Austin2(config-line)# no transport input telnet
```

Step 6   Enable vty inbound SSH sessions, as shown in the following example:

```
Austin2(config-line)# transport input ssh
Austin2(config-line)# end
Austin2#
```

The SSH protocol is automatically enabled once you generate the SSH keys. Once the keys are created, you may access the router SSH server using your SSH client software.

The procedure for connecting to a Cisco router SSH server varies depending on the SSH client application that you are using. Generally, the SSH client passes your username to the router SSH server. The router SSH server will then prompt you for the correct password. Once the password has been verified, you can configure and manage the router as if you were a standard vty user.

Securing SNMP Access

SNMP systems may gain administrative access to Cisco routers by communicating with the router's internal SNMP agent and Management Information Base (MIB).

An SNMP agent is responsible for reading and formatting all SNMP messages between the router and an SNMP network management system (NMS). An SNMP MIB is a tree-like list of objects within the router that point the SNMP agent to various router configuration parameters and statistics. After the SNMP agent on the router is configured, SNMP systems may perform some or all of the following tasks:

- Read certain configuration parameters and statistics found in the router SNMP agent MIB (read-only mode)

- Write certain configuration parameters to the router SNMP agent MIB (read-write mode)

- Receive SNMP traps (router events) from the router SNMP agent

SNMP systems use a community string as a type of password to access router SNMP agents. SNMP agents accept commands and requests only from SNMP systems using the correct community string. By default, most SNMP systems use a community string of "public." If you were to configure your router SNMP agent to use this commonly known community string, anyone with an SNMP system would be able to—at a minimum—read the router MIB. Because router MIB variables can point to things like routing tables and other security-critical parts of the router configuration, it is extremely important that you create your own custom SNMP community strings.

You must consider the following questions when developing SNMP access for Cisco routers:

- Which community strings will have read-only access?

- Which community strings will have read-write access?

- Which SNMP systems will be permitted to access the router SNMP agents (limiting host IP addresses using ACLs)?

To configure a router SNMP community string, use the **snmp-server community** command in global configuration mode. You may configure multiple community strings for your Cisco router by repeating this command for each string.

The syntax for the **snmp-server community** command is as follows:

```
snmp-server community string [ro | rw] [number]
```

- *string*—Community string that acts like a password and permits access to the SNMP protocol.

- **ro** (Optional)—Specifies read-only access. Authorized management stations are only able to retrieve MIB objects.

- **rw** (Optional)—Specifies read-write access. Authorized management stations are able to both retrieve and modify MIB objects.

- *number* (Optional)—Integer from 1 to 99 that specifies an ACL of IP addresses that are allowed to use the community string to gain access to the router.

The following example shows how to configure SNMP for the partial network shown in Figure 4-35.

Figure 4-35 *SNMP Network Management*

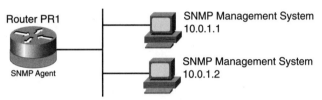

Use the **ro** option to limit a community string to read-only access (only SNMP get-requests and get-next-requests are allowed):

```
PR1(config)# snmp-server community readSNMP ro
```

Use the **rw** option to allow read and write access (SNMP get-requests, get-next-requests, and set-requests are allowed) for the designated community string:

```
PR1(config)# snmp-server community ReadWriteSNMP rw
```

NOTE   SNMP management systems can query a managed agent's SNMP MIB information using get and get-next requests. Get requests retrieve specific MIB information, while get-next requests retrieve successive MIB information. SNMP management systems can manipulate MIB information using set requests.

ACLs can be used for both read-only and read-write modes. Use the **snmp-server** command in association with ACLs to limit which hosts are allowed access to the router SNMP agent (this example shows a read-write mode community string):

```
PR1(config)# access-list 10 permit 10.0.1.1
PR1(config)# access-list 10 permit 10.0.1.2
PR1(config)# snmp-server community string RWSNMP rw 10
```

SNMP traps and informs are router events that are automatically sent to one or more SNMP systems by a router SNMP agent. Traps are sent to designated SNMP systems regardless of whether the host is there or not. Informs always require an acknowledgment from the designated SNMP system to verify that the message was received. Because traps and informs can contain critical routing and configuration information, it is important that you designate exactly where you want the traps and informs sent.

The following list contains types of router SNMP traps that are enabled (sent) by default (all other types of traps must be specifically enabled to be sent):

- **Interface traps**—Sent whenever an interface becomes active or inactive.

- **Reload traps**—Sent whenever a router reload occurs.

- **Configuration change traps**—Sent whenever a change is made to the router configuration.

There are two ways to specifically enable traps and informs to be generated by the router:

- **Enable global traps and informs**—Use the **snmp-server enable traps** command to enable all SNMP traps and informs to be sent by the router.

- **Enable host**—Use the **snmp-server host** command to specify which traps and informs to send while simultaneously specifying the SNMP system host to which the traps and informs are to be sent.

Use the **snmp-server enable traps** command from global configuration mode to enable the sending of all traps and informs by the router. Note that this command only enables traps and informs; it does not specify the SNMP system host to which the traps and informs are to be sent.

The syntax for the **snmp-server enable traps** command is as follows:

```
snmp-server enable traps [notification-type]
```

- *notification-type* (Optional)—Type of notification (trap or inform) to enable or disable. If no type is specified, all notifications available on your device are enabled or disabled. The notification type can be one of the following keywords:

  — **config**—Controls configuration notifications, as defined in the CISCO-CONFIG-MAN-MIB (enterprise 1.3.6.1.4.1.9.9.43.2). The notification type is (1) ciscoConfigManEvent.

  — **dlsw [circuit | tconn]**—Controls DLSw notifications, as defined in the CISCO-DLSW-MIB (enterprise 1.3.6.1.4.1.9.10.9.1.7). When the **dlsw** keyword is used, you can specify the specific notification types you wish to enable or disable. If no keyword is used, all DLSw notification types are enabled. The option can be one of the following keywords:

    — **circuit**—Enables DLSw circuit traps:

      (1) ciscoDlswTrapCircuitUp

      (2) ciscoDlswTrapCircuitDown

    — **tconn**—Enables DLSw peer transport connection traps:

      (1) ciscoDlswTrapTConnPartnerReject

      (2) ciscoDlswTrapTConnProtViolation

      (3) ciscoDlswTrapTConnUp

      (4) ciscoDlswTrapTConnDown

  — **ds0-busyout**—Sends notification whenever the busyout of a DS0 interface changes state (Cisco AS5300 platform only). This is from the CISCO-POP-MGMT-MIB (enterprise 1.3.6.1.4.1.9.10.19.2) and the notification type is (1) cpmDS0BusyoutNotification.

— **ds1-loopback**—Sends notification whenever the DS1 interface goes into loopback mode (Cisco AS5300 platform only). This notification type is defined in the CISCO-POP-MGMT-MIB (enterprise 1.3.6.1.4.1.9.10.19.2) as (2) cpmDS1LoopbackNotification.

— **entity**—Controls Entity MIB modification notifications. This notification type is defined in the ENTITY-MIB (enterprise 1.3.6.1.2.1.47.2) as (1) entConfigChange.

— **hsrp**—Controls Hot Standby Routing Protocol (HSRP) notifications, as defined in the CISCO-HSRP-MIB (enterprise 1.3.6.1.4.1.9.9.106.2). The notification type is (1) cHsrpStateChange.

— **ipmulticast**—Controls IP multicast notifications.

— **modem-health**—Controls modem-health notifications.

— **rsvp**—Controls Resource Reservation Protocol (RSVP) notifications.

— **rtr**—Controls Service Assurance Agent/Response Time Reporter (RTR) notifications.

— **syslog**—Controls error message notifications (Cisco Syslog MIB). Specify the level of messages to be sent with the **logging history level** command.

— **xgcp**—Sends External Media Gateway Control Protocol (XGCP) notifications. This notification is from the XGCP-MIB-V1SMI.my and the notifications are enterprise 1.3.6.1.3.90.2 (1) xgcpUpDownNotification.

A more efficient way of enabling traps and informs is to use the **snmp-server host** command because it accomplishes two tasks at once:

- Specifies which SNMP system host is to be sent the traps and informs
- Specifies which traps and informs are to be enabled

You must specify which SNMP systems (host-addr) are to receive SNMP traps by entering the **snmp-server host** command in global configuration mode.

The syntax for the **snmp-server host** command is as follows:

```
snmp-server host host-addr [traps | informs] [version {1 | 2c | 3 [auth |
   noauth | priv]}] community-string [udp-port port] [notification-type]
```

- *host-addr*—Name or Internet address of the SNMP system host (the targeted recipient).
- **traps** (Optional)—Sends SNMP traps to this host. This is the default.
- **informs** (Optional)—Sends SNMP informs to this host.
- **version** (Optional)—Version of SNMP used to send the traps. Version 3 is the most secure model, because it allows packet encryption with the **priv** keyword. If you

use the **version** keyword, one of the following must be specified:

- **1**—SNMPv1. This option is not available with informs.
- **2c**—SNMPv2C. Specifies SNMP version 2C.
- **3**—SNMPv3. The following three optional keywords can follow the version 3 keyword:
    - **auth** (Optional)—Enables message digest algorithm 5 (MD5) and Secure Hash Algorithm (SHA) packet authentication.
    - **noauth** (Default)—The noAuthNoPriv security level. This is the default if the [**auth** | **noauth** | **priv**] keyword choice is not specified.
    - **priv** (Optional)—Enables Data Encryption Standard (DES) packet encryption (also called "privacy").

- *community-string*—Password-like community string sent with the notification operation. Though you can set this string by using the **snmp-server host** command by itself, it is recommended that you define this string using the **snmp-server community** command prior to using the **snmp-server host** command.

- **udp-port** *port* (Optional)—UDP port of the host to use. The default is 162.

- *notification-type* (Optional)—Type of notification to be sent to the host. If no type is specified, all notifications are sent. The notification type can be one or more of the following keywords:
    - **bgp**—Sends Border Gateway Protocol (BGP) state change notifications.
    - **calltracker**—Sends Call Tracker call-start/call-end notifications.
    - **config**—Sends configuration notifications.
    - **dspu**—Sends downstream physical unit (DSPU) notifications.
    - **entity**—Sends Entity MIB modification notifications.
    - **envmon**—Sends Cisco enterprise-specific environmental monitor notifications when an environmental threshold is exceeded.
    - **frame-relay**—Sends Frame Relay notifications.
    - **hsrp**—Sends HSRP notifications.
    - **isdn**—Sends ISDN notifications.
    - **llc2**—Sends Logical Link Control, type 2 (LLC2) notifications.
    - **repeater**—Sends standard repeater (hub) notifications.
    - **rsrb**—Sends remote source-route bridging (RSRB) notifications.
    - **rsvp**—Sends RSVP notifications.
    - **rtr**—Sends SA Agent (RTR) notifications.
    - **sdlc**—Sends Synchronous Data Link Control (SDLC) notifications.
    - **sdllc**—Sends SDLC over Logical Link Control (SDLLC) notifications.

- **snmp**—Sends any enabled RFC 1157 SNMP linkUp, linkDown, authenticationFailure, warmStart, and coldStart notifications.
- **stun**—Sends serial tunnel (STUN) notifications.
- **syslog**—Sends error message notifications (Cisco Syslog MIB). Specify the level of messages to be sent with the **logging history level** command.
- **tty**—Sends Cisco enterprise-specific notifications when a TCP connection closes.
- **voice**—Sends SNMP traps when the quality of voice (qov) traffic becomes degraded, when used with the **snmp enable peer-trap poor qov** command.
- **x25**—Sends X.25 event notifications.

The following shows an alternate example of using the **snmp-server host** command to limit where the router will send SNMP traps for the partial network shown in Figure 4-35:

```
PR1(config)# snmp-server host 10.0.1.1 traps
```

The following is an example of using the **snmp-server host** command to limit where TCP connection close traps will be sent by the router:

```
PR1(config)# snmp-server host 10.0.1.2 traps tty
```

One final SNMP-related command is the **snmp-server trap-source** command. This command specifies which interface on the router (and, hence, the corresponding IP address) will be the source for all SNMP traps and informs generated by the router. The loopback0 interface makes an excellent choice for the source interface because it is always considered to be active.

Use the **snmp-server trap-source** command from the global configuration mode.

The syntax for the **snmp-server trap-source** command is as follows:

```
snmp-server trap-source interface
```

The following is an example of using the **snmp-server trap-source** command for the loopback 0 interface:

```
PR1(config)# snmp-server trap-source loopback0
```

There are several more **snmp-server** commands available to you that are described in the *Cisco IOS Command Reference* at Cisco.com.

Using AutoSecure to Secure Cisco Routers

This section explains how to use the Cisco IOS Release 12.3 AutoSecure feature to secure Cisco routers.

The AutoSecure feature is found in Cisco IOS Release 12.3 and subsequent 12.3T releases for Cisco 800, 1700, 2600, 3600, 3700, 7200, and 7500 series routers.

AutoSecure is a single privileged EXEC command that allows you to quickly and easily eliminate many of the potential security threats already covered in this book. AutoSecure helps to make you more efficient at securing Cisco routers.

AutoSecure performs the following tasks on the target router:

- Disables certain potentially insecure global services
- Enables certain security-based global services
- Disables certain potentially insecure interface services
- Enables appropriate security-related logging
- Takes steps to secure administrative access to the router
- Takes steps to secure the router forwarding plane

AutoSecure allows two modes of operation:

- **Interactive mode**—Prompts you to choose the way you want to configure router services and other security-related features
- **Noninteractive mode**—Configures your router's security-related features based on a set of Cisco defaults

Obviously, interactive mode provides greater control than noninteractive mode over the router security-related features. However, there may be occasions when you want to quickly secure a router without much human intervention. In these latter cases, noninteractive mode becomes the better choice.

Getting Started

AutoSecure is initiated using the **auto secure** command in privileged EXEC mode. The syntax for this command is as follows:

```
auto secure [management | forwarding] [no-interact]
```

- **management** (Optional)—Only the management plane will be secured.
- **forwarding** (Optional)—Only the forwarding plane will be secured.
- **no-interact** (Optional)—The user will not be prompted for any interactive configurations. No interactive dialog parameters will be configured, including usernames or passwords.

Example 4-28 shows how this portion of the AutoSecure dialog appears.

Example 4-28 *AutoSecure Initial Dialog*

```
Router# auto secure
     --- AutoSecure Configuration ---
*** AutoSecure configuration enhances the security of
the router but it will not make router absolutely secure
from all security attacks ***
```

Example 4-28 *AutoSecure Initial Dialog (Continued)*

```
All the configuration done as part of AutoSecure will be
shown here. For more details of why and how this configuration
is useful, and any possible side effects, please refer to Cisco
documentation of AutoSecure.
At any prompt you may enter '?' for help.
Use ctrl-c to abort this session at any prompt.

Gathering information about the router for AutoSecure
```

Interface Selection

As shown in Example 4-29, the first questions that AutoSecure asks you are directly related to how the router is connected to the Internet. AutoSecure needs to know the following:

- Is the router going to be connected to the Internet?
- How many interfaces are connected to the Internet?
- What are the names of the interfaces connected to the Internet?

Example 4-29 *AutoSecure Internet Questions*

```
Is this router connected to internet? [no]: y
Enter the number of interfaces facing internet [1]: 1
Interface      IP-Address       OK? Method Status  Protocol
Ethernet0/0    10.0.2.2         YES NVRAM  up       up
Ethernet0/1    172.30.2.2       YES NVRAM  up       up

Enter the interface name that is facing internet: Ethernet0/1
```

Securing Management Plane Services

Next, AutoSecure disables the most common attack vectors by shutting down their associated global router services. The following global services have been designated as high-risk attack vectors and will be disabled by AutoSecure:

- **Finger**—Disabling this service keeps intruders from seeing who is logged in to the router and from where they are logged in.
- **PAD**—Disabling this service prevents intruders from accessing the X.25 PAD command set on the router.
- **Small servers**—Disabling the UDP and TCP small servers prevents attackers from using those services in DoS attacks.
- **CDP**—Disabling this service prevents attackers from exploiting a recently discovered CDP security threat.
- **BOOTP** —Disabling this service prevents attackers from using it to generate DoS attacks.

- **HTTP**—Disabling this service prevents attackers from accessing the HTTP router administrative access interface.

- **Identification**—Disabling this service prevents attackers from querying TCP ports for identification.

- **NTP**—Disabling this service prevents attackers from corrupting router time bases.

- **Source routing**—Disabling this service prevents attackers from exploiting older Cisco IOS software–based routers that do not process source routing properly.

- **Gratuitous ARPs**—Disabling gratuitous ARPs prevents the router from broadcasting the IP address of its interfaces.

AutoSecure enables the following router global services:

- **Service password encryption**—Automatically encrypts all passwords in the router configuration

- **TCP keepalives in/out**—Allows the router to quickly clean up idle TCP sessions

Example 4-30 shows how this portion of the AutoSecure dialog appears.

Example 4-30 *AutoSecure Disabling Common Attack Vectors*

```
Securing Management plane services..

Disabling service finger
Disabling service pad
Disabling udp & tcp small servers
Enabling service password encryption
Enabling service tcp-keepalives-in
Enabling service tcp-keepalives-out
Disabling the cdp protocol

Disabling the bootp server
Disabling the http server
Disabling the finger service
Disabling source routing
Disabling gratuitous arp
```

Creating Security Banner

Next, AutoSecure prompts you to create a banner to be shown every time someone accesses the router. This is the same as using the **banner** command in global configuration mode.

Example 4-31 shows how this portion of the AutoSecure dialog appears.

Example 4-31 *AutoSecure Banner Creation*

```
Here is a sample Security Banner to be shown
at every access to device. Modify it to suit your
enterprise requirements.
```

Example 4-31 *AutoSecure Banner Creation (Continued)*

```
Authorised Access only
 This system is the property of So-&-So-Enterprise.
 UNAUTHORISED ACCESS TO THIS DEVICE IS PROHIBITED.
 You must have explicit permission to access this
 device. All activities performed on this device
 are logged and violations of of this policy result
 in disciplinary action.

Enter the security banner {Put the banner between
k and k, where k is any character}:
#This system is the property of Cisco Systems, Inc.
UNAUTHORIZED ACCESS TO THIS DEVICE IS PROHIBITED.#
```

NOTE   Remember to place the banner between two delimiting characters of your choice. In this example, pound (#) characters are used as delimiters.

Configuring Passwords, AAA, SSH Server, and Domain Name

Next, AutoSecure prompts you to configure the following:

- **Enable secret**—AutoSecure checks to see if the router's enable secret password is the same as the enable password or if it is not configured at all. If either is true, you are prompted to enter a new enable secret password.

- **AAA local authentication**—AutoSecure checks to see if AAA local authentication is enabled and if a local user account exists. If neither is true, you are prompted to enter a new username and password. Then, AAA local authentication is enabled. AutoSecure also configures the router console, aux, and vty lines for local authentication, EXEC timeouts, and transport.

- **SSH server**—AutoSecure asks you whether you want to configure the SSH server. If you answer "yes," AutoSecure automatically configures the SSH timeout to 60 seconds and the number of SSH authentication retries to 2.

- **Host name**—If you configured a host name for this router prior to starting the AutoSecure procedure, you will not be prompted to enter one here. However, if the router is currently using the factory default host name of **Router**, you will be prompted to enter a unique host name. This is important because SSH requires a unique host name for key generation.

- **Domain name**—AutoSecure prompts you for the domain to which this router belongs. Like the host name parameter, a domain name is important for SSH key generation.

Example 4-32 shows how this portion of the AutoSecure dialog appears.

Example 4-32 *AutoSecure Password Configuration*

```
Enable secret is either not configured or is same as enable password
Enter the new enable secret: Curium96

Configuration of local user database
Enter the username: student1
Enter the password: student1
Configuring aaa local authentication
Configuring console, Aux and vty lines for
local authentication, exec-timeout, transport

Configure SSH server? [yes]: y
Enter the domain-name: cisco.com
```

Configuring Interface-Specific Services

Next, AutoSecure automatically disables the following services on all router interfaces:

- IP redirects
- IP proxy ARP
- IP unreachables
- IP directed broadcasts
- IP mask replies

Example 4-33 shows how this portion of the AutoSecure dialog appears.

Example 4-33 *AutoSecure Disabling Specific Interface Services*

```
Configuring interface specific AutoSecure services
Disabling the following ip services on all interfaces:

 no ip redirects
 no ip proxy-arp
 no ip unreachables
 no ip directed-broadcast
 no ip mask-reply
```

Configuring Cisco Express Forwarding and Ingress Filters

Next, AutoSecure secures the router forwarding plane by completing the following:

- Enables Cisco Express Forwarding (CEF). AutoSecure enables CEF (or Distributed CEF) if the router platform supports this type of caching. Routers configured for CEF perform better under SYN flood attacks (directed at hosts, not the routers themselves) than routers configured using a standard cache.
- Builds the following three extended named ACLs for ingress filtering (antispoofing):
    - **autosec_iana_reserved_block**—Blocks all IANA reserved IP address blocks

— **autosec_private_block**—Blocks RFC 1918 private IP address blocks

— **autosec_complete_block**—Blocks multicast, Class E, and other IP addresses prohibited for source address (and all addresses blocked by the first two ACLs listed here)

NOTE   Although the AutoSecure user interface refers to the third ACL as autosec_complete_block, in reality, the router creates it as autosec_complete_bogon.

Example 4-34 shows how this portion of the AutoSecure dialog appears.

Example 4-34 *AutoSecure Configuring CEF and Ingress Filters*

```
Securing Forwarding plane services..

Enabling CEF (it might have more memory requirements on some low end platforms)

Configuring the named acls for Ingress filtering

autosec_iana_reserved_block: This block may subject to
change by iana and for updated list visit
www.iana.org/assignments/ipv4-address-space.
1/8, 2/8, 5/8, 7/8, 23/8, 27/8, 31/8, 36/8, 37/8, 39/8,
41/8, 42/8, 49/8, 50/8, 58/8, 59/8, 60/8, 70/8, 71/8,
72/8, 73/8, 74/8, 75/8, 76/8, 77/8, 78/8, 79/8, 83/8,
84/8, 85/8, 86/8, 87/8, 88/8, 89/8, 90/8, 91/8, 92/8, 93/8,
94/8, 95/8, 96/8, 97/8, 98/8, 99/8, 100/8, 101/8, 102/8,
103/8, 104/8, 105/8, 106/8, 107/8, 108/8, 109/8, 110/8,
111/8, 112/8, 113/8, 114/8, 115/8, 116/8, 117/8, 118/8,
119/8, 120/8, 121/8, 122/8, 123/8, 124/8, 125/8, 126/8,
197/8, 201/8

autosec_private_block:
10/8, 172.16/12, 192.168/16

autosec_complete_block: This is union of above two and
the addresses of source multicast, class E addresses
and addresses that are prohibited for use as source.
source multicast (224/4), class E(240/4), 0/8, 169.254/16,
192.0.2/24, 127/8.
```

Configuring Ingress Filtering and CBAC

Next, AutoSecure performs the following steps:

- **Configures ingress filtering on edge interfaces**—AutoSecure asks if you want to apply ingress filtering on the router edge (connected to Internet) interfaces. If you answer "yes,"

AutoSecure prompts you to choose which one of the three previously configured antispoofing ACLs to apply.

- **Enables Unicast RPF**—AutoSecure automatically configures strict Unicast RPF on all interfaces connected to the Internet. This helps drop any source-spoofed packets.

- **Configures CBAC Firewall feature**—AutoSecure asks if you want to enable generic CBAC inspection rules on all interfaces connected to the Internet. If you answer "yes," a set of generic inspect rules is assigned to Internet-facing router interfaces.

Example 4-35 shows how this portion of the AutoSecure dialog appears.

Example 4-35 *AutoSecure Configuring CEF and Ingress Filters*

```
Configure Ingress filtering on edge interfaces? [yes]: y

[1] Apply autosec_iana_reserved_block acl on all edge interfaces
[2] Apply autosec_private_block acl on all edge interfaces
[3] Apply autosec_complete_bogon acl on all edge interfaces
Enter your selection [3]: 1
Enabling unicast rpf on all interfaces connected to internet

Configure CBAC Firewall feature? [yes/no]: y
```

Checking Configuration and Applying It to Running Configuration

Finally, AutoSecure displays the changes as they will be applied to the router that is running the configuration. If you now wish to apply these changes, answer "yes" to the "Apply this configuration to running-config?" question.

The following code listing shows how this portion of the AutoSecure dialog appears.

NOTE   Notes have been inserted into this listing to help you understand what AutoSecure is doing at various points. These notes are not part of the router AutoSecure command-line interface (CLI) output.

NOTE   In the beginning of the listing, AutoSecure disables several router global services that are considered possible attack vectors and enables other global services that help protect the router and the network.

```
no service finger
no service pad
no service udp-small-servers
```

```
no service tcp-small-servers
service password-encryption
service tcp-keepalives-in
service tcp-keepalives-out
no cdp run
no ip bootp server
no ip http server
no ip finger
no ip source-route
no ip gratuitous-arps
This is the configuration generated:
```

NOTE   Next, AutoSecure creates a banner to be displayed upon any access to the router. This banner message contains the text that you provided during the AutoSecure script.

```
banner #This system is the property of Cisco Systems, Inc.
UNAUTHORIZED ACCESS TO THIS DEVICE IS PROHIBITED.#
```

NOTE   Next, AutoSecure sets a minimum password length of six characters. You are not prompted to set this minimum in the AutoSecure script. This is performed automatically by AutoSecure.

```
security passwords min-length 6
```

NOTE   Next, AutoSecure configures an authentication failure rate of ten. This allows a user ten failed login attempts before the router sends an authentication failure event to the logger (router log or syslog server). You are not prompted to specify this rate in the AutoSecure script. This is performed automatically by AutoSecure.

```
security authentication failure rate 10 log
```

NOTE   Next, AutoSecure configures the enable secret password that you specified during the AutoSecure script. Enable secret uses an MD-5 hashing mechanism (denoted by the number 5).

```
enable secret 5 $1$D5gC$4X79guFOe4rTOTqJgngZ0.
```

NOTE	Next, AutoSecure configures the local user account that you specified during the AutoSecure script. Notice that this password is encrypted using a Cisco-proprietary Vigenere-based cipher (denoted by the number 7). This is the result of AutoSecure automatically running the **service password-encryption** command earlier.

```
username student1 password 7 0832585B0D1C0B0343
```

NOTE	Next, AutoSecure enables AAA local authentication.

```
aaa new-model
aaa authentication login local_auth local
```

NOTE	Next, AutoSecure configures console line 0 for local authentication, an EXEC session timeout after 5 minutes of idle time, and outgoing Telnet connections.

```
line console 0
 login authentication local_auth
 exec-timeout 5 0
 transport output telnet
```

NOTE	Next, AutoSecure configures auxiliary line 0 for local authentication, an EXEC session timeout after 10 minutes of idle time, and outgoing Telnet connections.

```
line aux 0
 login authentication local_auth
 exec-timeout 10 0
 transport output telnet
```

NOTE	Next, AutoSecure configures vty lines 0 through 4 for local authentication and incoming Telnet connections.

```
line vty 0 4
 login authentication local_auth
 transport input telnet
```

NOTE	Next, AutoSecure configures the router host name that you specified in the AutoSecure script.

```
hostname R2
```

NOTE	Next, AutoSecure configures the router domain name that you specified in the AutoSecure script.

```
ip domain-name cisco.com
```

NOTE	Next, AutoSecure generates a pair of general-purpose RSA keys. These keys will are used by SSH.

```
crypto key generate rsa general-keys modulus 1024
```

NOTE	Next, AutoSecure sets the SSH timeout timer to 60 seconds. This setting applies to the SSH negotiation phase and determines how long the router waits for an SSH client to respond. Once the EXEC session starts, the standard timeouts configured for the vty lines apply.

```
ip ssh time-out 60
```

NOTE	Next, AutoSecure configures the SSH authentication retries for two failed attempts, after which the interface will be reset.

```
ip ssh authentication-retries 2
```

NOTE	Next, AutoSecure configures vty lines 0 through 4 to support both SSH and Telnet incoming connections. Note that Telnet was previously configured for the vty lines. This step simply adds SSH to the list of possible incoming connection types.

```
line vty 0 4
 transport input ssh telnet
```

Next, AutoSecure configures the router logging facility for more detailed security logging than is typically found in Cisco routers.

```
service timestamps debug datetime localtime show-timezone msec
service timestamps log datetime localtime show-timezone msec
logging facility local2
logging trap debugging
service sequence-numbers
logging console critical
logging buffered
```

NOTE Next, AutoSecure disables services that are considered security threats on all router interfaces.

```
int Ethernet0/0
 no ip redirects
 no ip proxy-arp
 no ip unreachables
 no ip directed-broadcast
 no ip mask-reply

int Ethernet0/1
 no ip redirects
 no ip proxy-arp
 no ip unreachables
 no ip directed-broadcast
 no ip mask-reply
```

NOTE Next, AutoSecure enables CEF to aid router performance during SYN flood attacks.

```
ip cef
```

NOTE Next, AutoSecure configures an extended named ACL that is called autosec_iana_reserved_block. Once assigned to the inbound direction of an Internet-facing router interface, this ACL will block all IANA reserved IP addresses (currently known to this version of AutoSecure). Please note the remark at the end of this ACL regarding updates to the IANA list of reserved addresses. If you wish to block any IANA reserved addresses that are not included in this list, you need to update the ACL manually after running the AutoSecure script.

```
ip access-list extended autosec_iana_reserved_block
 deny ip 1.0.0.0 0.255.255.255 any
 deny ip 2.0.0.0 0.255.255.255 any
 deny ip 5.0.0.0 0.255.255.255 any
 deny ip 7.0.0.0 0.255.255.255 any
 deny ip 23.0.0.0 0.255.255.255 any
 deny ip 27.0.0.0 0.255.255.255 any
 deny ip 31.0.0.0 0.255.255.255 any
 deny ip 36.0.0.0 0.255.255.255 any
 deny ip 37.0.0.0 0.255.255.255 any
 deny ip 39.0.0.0 0.255.255.255 any
 deny ip 41.0.0.0 0.255.255.255 any
 deny ip 42.0.0.0 0.255.255.255 any
 deny ip 49.0.0.0 0.255.255.255 any
 deny ip 50.0.0.0 0.255.255.255 any
 deny ip 58.0.0.0 0.255.255.255 any
 deny ip 59.0.0.0 0.255.255.255 any
 deny ip 60.0.0.0 0.255.255.255 any
 deny ip 70.0.0.0 0.255.255.255 any
 deny ip 71.0.0.0 0.255.255.255 any
 deny ip 72.0.0.0 0.255.255.255 any
 deny ip 73.0.0.0 0.255.255.255 any
 deny ip 74.0.0.0 0.255.255.255 any
 deny ip 75.0.0.0 0.255.255.255 any
 deny ip 76.0.0.0 0.255.255.255 any
 deny ip 77.0.0.0 0.255.255.255 any
 deny ip 78.0.0.0 0.255.255.255 any
 deny ip 79.0.0.0 0.255.255.255 any
 deny ip 83.0.0.0 0.255.255.255 any
 deny ip 84.0.0.0 0.255.255.255 any
 deny ip 85.0.0.0 0.255.255.255 any
 deny ip 86.0.0.0 0.255.255.255 any
 deny ip 87.0.0.0 0.255.255.255 any
 deny ip 88.0.0.0 0.255.255.255 any
 deny ip 89.0.0.0 0.255.255.255 any
 deny ip 90.0.0.0 0.255.255.255 any
 deny ip 91.0.0.0 0.255.255.255 any
 deny ip 92.0.0.0 0.255.255.255 any
 deny ip 93.0.0.0 0.255.255.255 any
 deny ip 94.0.0.0 0.255.255.255 any
 deny ip 95.0.0.0 0.255.255.255 any
 deny ip 96.0.0.0 0.255.255.255 any
 deny ip 97.0.0.0 0.255.255.255 any
 deny ip 98.0.0.0 0.255.255.255 any
 deny ip 99.0.0.0 0.255.255.255 any
 deny ip 100.0.0.0 0.255.255.255 any
 deny ip 101.0.0.0 0.255.255.255 any
 deny ip 102.0.0.0 0.255.255.255 any
 deny ip 103.0.0.0 0.255.255.255 any
 deny ip 104.0.0.0 0.255.255.255 any
 deny ip 105.0.0.0 0.255.255.255 any
 deny ip 106.0.0.0 0.255.255.255 any
 deny ip 107.0.0.0 0.255.255.255 any
 deny ip 108.0.0.0 0.255.255.255 any
 deny ip 109.0.0.0 0.255.255.255 any
```

```
   deny ip 110.0.0.0 0.255.255.255 any
   deny ip 111.0.0.0 0.255.255.255 any
   deny ip 112.0.0.0 0.255.255.255 any
   deny ip 113.0.0.0 0.255.255.255 any
   deny ip 114.0.0.0 0.255.255.255 any
   deny ip 115.0.0.0 0.255.255.255 any
   deny ip 116.0.0.0 0.255.255.255 any
   deny ip 117.0.0.0 0.255.255.255 any
   deny ip 118.0.0.0 0.255.255.255 any
   deny ip 119.0.0.0 0.255.255.255 any
   deny ip 120.0.0.0 0.255.255.255 any
   deny ip 121.0.0.0 0.255.255.255 any
   deny ip 122.0.0.0 0.255.255.255 any
   deny ip 123.0.0.0 0.255.255.255 any
   deny ip 124.0.0.0 0.255.255.255 any
   deny ip 125.0.0.0 0.255.255.255 any
   deny ip 126.0.0.0 0.255.255.255 any
   deny ip 197.0.0.0 0.255.255.255 any
   deny ip 201.0.0.0 0.255.255.255 any
   permit ip any any
   remark This acl might not be up to date. Visit www.iana.org/assignments/ipv4-add
   ress-space for update list
   exit
```

NOTE   Next, AutoSecure configures an extended named ACL called autosec_private_block. Once it has been assigned to the inbound direction of an Internet-facing router interface, this ACL will block all RFC 1918 private addresses (currently known to this version of AutoSecure).

```
   ip access-list extended autosec_private_block
    deny ip 10.0.0.0 0.255.255.255 any
    deny ip 172.16.0.0 0.15.255.255 any
    deny ip 192.168.0.0 0.0.255.255 any
    permit ip any any
    exit
```

NOTE   Next, AutoSecure configures an extended named ACL called autosec_complete_bogon (a union of the previous two ACLs plus some extra address restrictions). Once assigned to the inbound direction of an Internet-facing router interface, this ACL will block all IANA reserved IP addresses, RFC 1918 private addresses, source multicast addresses, and Class E addresses (currently known to this version of AutoSecure). Please note the remark at the end of this ACL regarding updates to the IANA list of reserved addresses. If you wish to block any IANA reserved addresses that are not included in this list, you need to update the ACL manually after running the AutoSecure script.

```
ip access-list extended autosec_complete_bogon
 deny ip 1.0.0.0 0.255.255.255 any
 deny ip 2.0.0.0 0.255.255.255 any
 deny ip 5.0.0.0 0.255.255.255 any
 deny ip 7.0.0.0 0.255.255.255 any
 deny ip 23.0.0.0 0.255.255.255 any
 deny ip 27.0.0.0 0.255.255.255 any
 deny ip 31.0.0.0 0.255.255.255 any
 deny ip 36.0.0.0 0.255.255.255 any
 deny ip 37.0.0.0 0.255.255.255 any
 deny ip 39.0.0.0 0.255.255.255 any
 deny ip 41.0.0.0 0.255.255.255 any
 deny ip 42.0.0.0 0.255.255.255 any
 deny ip 49.0.0.0 0.255.255.255 any
 deny ip 50.0.0.0 0.255.255.255 any
 deny ip 58.0.0.0 0.255.255.255 any
 deny ip 59.0.0.0 0.255.255.255 any
 deny ip 60.0.0.0 0.255.255.255 any
 deny ip 70.0.0.0 0.255.255.255 any
 deny ip 71.0.0.0 0.255.255.255 any
 deny ip 72.0.0.0 0.255.255.255 any
 deny ip 73.0.0.0 0.255.255.255 any
 deny ip 74.0.0.0 0.255.255.255 any
 deny ip 75.0.0.0 0.255.255.255 any
 deny ip 76.0.0.0 0.255.255.255 any
 deny ip 77.0.0.0 0.255.255.255 any
 deny ip 78.0.0.0 0.255.255.255 any
 deny ip 79.0.0.0 0.255.255.255 any
 deny ip 83.0.0.0 0.255.255.255 any
 deny ip 84.0.0.0 0.255.255.255 any
 deny ip 85.0.0.0 0.255.255.255 any
 deny ip 86.0.0.0 0.255.255.255 any
 deny ip 87.0.0.0 0.255.255.255 any
 deny ip 88.0.0.0 0.255.255.255 any
 deny ip 89.0.0.0 0.255.255.255 any
 deny ip 90.0.0.0 0.255.255.255 any
 deny ip 91.0.0.0 0.255.255.255 any
 deny ip 92.0.0.0 0.255.255.255 any
 deny ip 93.0.0.0 0.255.255.255 any
 deny ip 94.0.0.0 0.255.255.255 any
 deny ip 95.0.0.0 0.255.255.255 any
 deny ip 96.0.0.0 0.255.255.255 any
 deny ip 97.0.0.0 0.255.255.255 any
 deny ip 98.0.0.0 0.255.255.255 any
 deny ip 99.0.0.0 0.255.255.255 any
 deny ip 100.0.0.0 0.255.255.255 any
 deny ip 101.0.0.0 0.255.255.255 any
 deny ip 102.0.0.0 0.255.255.255 any
 deny ip 103.0.0.0 0.255.255.255 any
 deny ip 104.0.0.0 0.255.255.255 any
 deny ip 105.0.0.0 0.255.255.255 any
 deny ip 106.0.0.0 0.255.255.255 any
 deny ip 107.0.0.0 0.255.255.255 any
 deny ip 108.0.0.0 0.255.255.255 any
 deny ip 109.0.0.0 0.255.255.255 any
```

```
      deny ip 110.0.0.0 0.255.255.255 any
      deny ip 111.0.0.0 0.255.255.255 any
      deny ip 112.0.0.0 0.255.255.255 any
      deny ip 113.0.0.0 0.255.255.255 any
      deny ip 114.0.0.0 0.255.255.255 any
      deny ip 115.0.0.0 0.255.255.255 any
      deny ip 116.0.0.0 0.255.255.255 any
      deny ip 117.0.0.0 0.255.255.255 any
      deny ip 118.0.0.0 0.255.255.255 any
      deny ip 119.0.0.0 0.255.255.255 any
      deny ip 120.0.0.0 0.255.255.255 any
      deny ip 121.0.0.0 0.255.255.255 any
      deny ip 122.0.0.0 0.255.255.255 any
      deny ip 123.0.0.0 0.255.255.255 any
      deny ip 124.0.0.0 0.255.255.255 any
      deny ip 125.0.0.0 0.255.255.255 any
      deny ip 126.0.0.0 0.255.255.255 any
      deny ip 197.0.0.0 0.255.255.255 any
      deny ip 201.0.0.0 0.255.255.255 any

      deny ip 10.0.0.0 0.255.255.255 any
      deny ip 172.16.0.0 0.15.255.255 any
      deny ip 192.168.0.0 0.0.255.255 any

      deny ip 224.0.0.0 15.255.255.255 any
      deny ip 240.0.0.0 15.255.255.255 any
      deny ip 0.0.0.0 0.255.255.255 any
      deny ip 169.254.0.0 0.0.255.255 any
      deny ip 192.0.2.0 0.0.0.255 any
      deny ip 127.0.0.0 0.255.255.255 any
      permit ip any any
      remark This acl might not be up to date. Visit www.iana.org/assignments/ipv4-add
      ress-space for update list
      exit
```

NOTE   Next, AutoSecure applies the ACL that you selected via the AutoSecure script to the Internet-facing router interface or interfaces. Here, the autosec_iana_reserved_block (option 1) ACL is applied on the inbound side of the Ethernet0/1 interface.

```
      interface Ethernet0/1
       ip access-group autosec_iana_reserved_block in
      exit
```

NOTE   Next, AutoSecure creates an extended numbered ACL (100). This ACL permits UDP Bootstrap Protocol client (bootpc) packets from any source to any destination. This ACL is used by Unicast RPF on Internet-facing router interfaces.

```
ip access-list extended 100
 permit udp any any eq bootpc
```

NOTE   Next, AutoSecure enables Unicast RPF strict checking mode using ACL 100 on all Internet-facing router interfaces. Because ACL 100 permits bootpc packets, spoofed bootpc packets will be forwarded to the destination address. The forwarded bootpc packets are counted in the interface statistics.

```
interface Ethernet0/1
 ip verify unicast source reachable-via rx 100
```

NOTE   Next, AutoSecure enables CBAC audit-trail logging to provide a record of network access through the Cisco IOS Firewall, including illegitimate access attempts, and inbound and outbound services.

```
ip inspect audit-trail
```

NOTE   Next, AutoSecure configures the DNS idle timeout for 7 seconds.

```
ip inspect dns-timeout 7
```

NOTE   Next, AutoSecure configures the TCP idle timeout for 14,400 seconds (240 minutes).

```
ip inspect tcp idle-time 14400
```

NOTE   Next, AutoSecure configures the UDP idle timeout to 1800 seconds (30 minutes).

```
ip inspect udp idle-time 1800
```

NOTE   Next, AutoSecure configures the CBAC autosec_inspect inspection rules set.

```
ip inspect name autosec_inspect cuseeme timeout 3600
ip inspect name autosec_inspect ftp timeout 3600
ip inspect name autosec_inspect http timeout 3600
ip inspect name autosec_inspect rcmd timeout 3600
ip inspect name autosec_inspect realaudio timeout 3600
ip inspect name autosec_inspect smtp timeout 3600
ip inspect name autosec_inspect tftp timeout 30
ip inspect name autosec_inspect udp timeout 15
ip inspect name autosec_inspect tcp timeout 3600
```

NOTE   Next, AutoSecure creates the autosec_firewall_acl extended named ACL. This ACL permits UDP bootpc packets from any source to any destination while denying all other packets.

```
ip access-list extended autosec_firewall_acl
 permit udp any any eq bootpc
 deny ip any any
```

NOTE   Next, AutoSecure applies the CBAC autosec_inspect inspection rule set to the outbound side of all Internet-facing router interfaces. Here, the inspection rule set is applied on the outbound side of Ethernet0/1.

```
interface Ethernet0/1
 ip inspect autosec_inspect out
 !
 end
```

NOTE   Finally, AutoSecure asks you if you want to apply these changes to the router running configuration.

```
Apply this configuration to running-config? [yes]: y
```

NOTE   If you chose to configure the SSH server, AutoSecure now generates the RSA keys using the host name and domain name you configured during the AutoSecure script. Please note that the factory default router name of Router will cause errors during key generation.

```
Applying the config generated to running-config
The name for the keys will be: R2.cisco.com
% The key modulus size is 1024 bits
% Generating 1024 bit RSA keys …[OK]
```

Example: Typical Router Configuration Before AutoSecure

Example 4-36 shows the router configuration just prior to applying the AutoSecure
configuration changes.

Example 4-36 *AutoSecure Configuring CEF and Ingress Filters*

```
router# show running-config
!
version 12.3
service timestamps debug uptime
service timestamps log uptime
no service password-encryption
!
hostname Router
!
no logging console
enable password cisco
!
memory-size iomem 15
ip subnet-zero
!
!
no ip domain lookup
!
ip audit notify log
ip audit po max-events 100
!
!
!
!
no voice hpi capture buffer
no voice hpi capture destination
!
!
interface Ethernet0/0
 ip address 10.0.2.2 255.255.255.0
 half-duplex
!
interface Ethernet0/1
 ip address 172.30.2.2 255.255.255.0
 half-duplex
!
router eigrp 1
 network 10.0.0.0
```

continues

Example 4-36 *AutoSecure Configuring CEF and Ingress Filters (Continued)*

```
 network 172.30.0.0
 no auto-summary
 !
no ip http server
no ip http secure-server
ip classless
 !
 !
line con 0
line aux 0
line vty 0 4
 password cisco
 login
 !
 !
 !
end
```

Example: Typical Router Configuration After AutoSecure

Example 4-37 shows the result of applying this configuration to the running configuration.

Example 4-37 *AutoSecure Configuring CEF and Ingress Filters*

```
router# show running-config
!
version 12.3
no service pad
service tcp-keepalives-in
service tcp-keepalives-out
service timestamps debug datetime msec localtime show-timezone
service timestamps log datetime msec localtime show-timezone
service password-encryption
service sequence-numbers
!
hostname R2
!
security authentication failure rate 10 log
security passwords min-length 6
logging buffered 4096 debugging
logging console critical
enable secret 5 $1$O4np$y8yIPRJ07h2.bZzPngIDC.
enable password 7 00071A150754
!
username student1 password 7 095F5A1C1D0019065A
memory-size iomem 15
aaa new-model
!
!
```

Example 4-37 *AutoSecure Configuring CEF and Ingress Filters (Continued)*

```
aaa authentication login local_auth local
aaa session-id common
ip subnet-zero
no ip source-route
no ip gratuitous-arps
ip cef
!
!
no ip domain lookup
ip domain name cisco.com
!
no ip bootp server
ip inspect audit-trail
ip inspect udp idle-time 1800
ip inspect dns-timeout 7
ip inspect tcp idle-time 14400
ip inspect name autosec_inspect cuseeme timeout 3600
ip inspect name autosec_inspect ftp timeout 3600
ip inspect name autosec_inspect http timeout 3600
ip inspect name autosec_inspect rcmd timeout 3600
ip inspect name autosec_inspect realaudio timeout 3600
ip inspect name autosec_inspect smtp timeout 3600
ip inspect name autosec_inspect tftp timeout 30
ip inspect name autosec_inspect udp timeout 15
ip inspect name autosec_inspect tcp timeout 3600
ip audit notify log
ip audit po max-events 100
ip ssh time-out 60
ip ssh authentication-retries 2
!
!
!
no voice hpi capture buffer
no voice hpi capture destination
!
!
interface Ethernet0/0
 ip address 10.0.2.2 255.255.255.0
 no ip redirects
 no ip unreachables
 no ip proxy-arp
 half-duplex
!
interface Ethernet0/1
 ip address 172.30.2.2 255.255.255.0
 ip access-group autosec_iana_reserved_block in
 ip verify unicast source reachable-via rx 100
 no ip redirects
 no ip unreachables
```

continues

Example 4-37 *AutoSecure Configuring CEF and Ingress Filters (Continued)*

```
 no ip proxy-arp
 ip inspect autosec_inspect out
 half-duplex
!
router eigrp 1
 network 10.0.0.0
 network 172.30.0.0
 no auto-summary
!
no ip http server
no ip http secure-server
ip classless
!
!
ip access-list extended autosec_complete_bogon
 deny    ip 1.0.0.0 0.255.255.255 any
 deny    ip 2.0.0.0 0.255.255.255 any
 deny    ip 5.0.0.0 0.255.255.255 any
 deny    ip 7.0.0.0 0.255.255.255 any
 deny    ip 23.0.0.0 0.255.255.255 any
 deny    ip 27.0.0.0 0.255.255.255 any
 deny    ip 31.0.0.0 0.255.255.255 any
 deny    ip 36.0.0.0 0.255.255.255 any
 deny    ip 37.0.0.0 0.255.255.255 any
 deny    ip 39.0.0.0 0.255.255.255 any
 deny    ip 41.0.0.0 0.255.255.255 any
 deny    ip 42.0.0.0 0.255.255.255 any
 deny    ip 49.0.0.0 0.255.255.255 any
 deny    ip 50.0.0.0 0.255.255.255 any
 deny    ip 58.0.0.0 0.255.255.255 any
 deny    ip 59.0.0.0 0.255.255.255 any
 deny    ip 60.0.0.0 0.255.255.255 any
 deny    ip 70.0.0.0 0.255.255.255 any
 deny    ip 71.0.0.0 0.255.255.255 any
 deny    ip 72.0.0.0 0.255.255.255 any
 deny    ip 73.0.0.0 0.255.255.255 any
 deny    ip 74.0.0.0 0.255.255.255 any
 deny    ip 75.0.0.0 0.255.255.255 any
 deny    ip 76.0.0.0 0.255.255.255 any
 deny    ip 77.0.0.0 0.255.255.255 any
 deny    ip 78.0.0.0 0.255.255.255 any
 deny    ip 79.0.0.0 0.255.255.255 any
 deny    ip 83.0.0.0 0.255.255.255 any
 deny    ip 84.0.0.0 0.255.255.255 any
 deny    ip 85.0.0.0 0.255.255.255 any
 deny    ip 86.0.0.0 0.255.255.255 any
 deny    ip 87.0.0.0 0.255.255.255 any
 deny    ip 88.0.0.0 0.255.255.255 any
 deny    ip 89.0.0.0 0.255.255.255 any
 deny    ip 90.0.0.0 0.255.255.255 any
```

Example 4-37 *AutoSecure Configuring CEF and Ingress Filters (Continued)*

```
deny   ip 91.0.0.0 0.255.255.255 any
deny   ip 92.0.0.0 0.255.255.255 any
deny   ip 93.0.0.0 0.255.255.255 any
deny   ip 94.0.0.0 0.255.255.255 any
deny   ip 95.0.0.0 0.255.255.255 any
deny   ip 96.0.0.0 0.255.255.255 any
deny   ip 97.0.0.0 0.255.255.255 any
deny   ip 98.0.0.0 0.255.255.255 any
deny   ip 99.0.0.0 0.255.255.255 any
deny   ip 100.0.0.0 0.255.255.255 any
deny   ip 101.0.0.0 0.255.255.255 any
deny   ip 102.0.0.0 0.255.255.255 any
deny   ip 103.0.0.0 0.255.255.255 any
deny   ip 104.0.0.0 0.255.255.255 any
deny   ip 105.0.0.0 0.255.255.255 any
deny   ip 106.0.0.0 0.255.255.255 any
deny   ip 107.0.0.0 0.255.255.255 any
deny   ip 108.0.0.0 0.255.255.255 any
deny   ip 109.0.0.0 0.255.255.255 any
deny   ip 110.0.0.0 0.255.255.255 any
deny   ip 111.0.0.0 0.255.255.255 any
deny   ip 112.0.0.0 0.255.255.255 any
deny   ip 113.0.0.0 0.255.255.255 any
deny   ip 114.0.0.0 0.255.255.255 any
deny   ip 115.0.0.0 0.255.255.255 any
deny   ip 116.0.0.0 0.255.255.255 any
deny   ip 117.0.0.0 0.255.255.255 any
deny   ip 118.0.0.0 0.255.255.255 any
deny   ip 119.0.0.0 0.255.255.255 any
deny   ip 120.0.0.0 0.255.255.255 any
deny   ip 121.0.0.0 0.255.255.255 any
deny   ip 122.0.0.0 0.255.255.255 any
deny   ip 123.0.0.0 0.255.255.255 any
deny   ip 124.0.0.0 0.255.255.255 any
deny   ip 125.0.0.0 0.255.255.255 any
deny   ip 126.0.0.0 0.255.255.255 any
deny   ip 197.0.0.0 0.255.255.255 any
deny   ip 201.0.0.0 0.255.255.255 any
deny   ip 10.0.0.0 0.255.255.255 any
deny   ip 172.16.0.0 0.15.255.255 any
deny   ip 192.168.0.0 0.0.255.255 any
deny   ip 224.0.0.0 15.255.255.255 any
deny   ip 240.0.0.0 15.255.255.255 any
deny   ip 0.0.0.0 0.255.255.255 any
deny   ip 169.254.0.0 0.0.255.255 any
deny   ip 192.0.2.0 0.0.0.255 any
deny   ip 127.0.0.0 0.255.255.255 any
permit ip any any
remark This acl might not be up to date. Visit www.iana.org/assignments/ipv4-ad
dress-space for update list
```

continues

Example 4-37 *AutoSecure Configuring CEF and Ingress Filters (Continued)*

```
ip access-list extended autosec_firewall_acl
 permit udp any any eq bootpc
 deny   ip any any
ip access-list extended autosec_iana_reserved_block
 deny   ip 1.0.0.0 0.255.255.255 any
 deny   ip 2.0.0.0 0.255.255.255 any
 deny   ip 5.0.0.0 0.255.255.255 any
 deny   ip 7.0.0.0 0.255.255.255 any
 deny   ip 23.0.0.0 0.255.255.255 any
 deny   ip 27.0.0.0 0.255.255.255 any
 deny   ip 31.0.0.0 0.255.255.255 any
 deny   ip 36.0.0.0 0.255.255.255 any
 deny   ip 37.0.0.0 0.255.255.255 any
 deny   ip 39.0.0.0 0.255.255.255 any
 deny   ip 41.0.0.0 0.255.255.255 any
 deny   ip 42.0.0.0 0.255.255.255 any
 deny   ip 49.0.0.0 0.255.255.255 any
 deny   ip 50.0.0.0 0.255.255.255 any
 deny   ip 58.0.0.0 0.255.255.255 any
 deny   ip 59.0.0.0 0.255.255.255 any
 deny   ip 60.0.0.0 0.255.255.255 any
 deny   ip 70.0.0.0 0.255.255.255 any
 deny   ip 71.0.0.0 0.255.255.255 any
 deny   ip 72.0.0.0 0.255.255.255 any
 deny   ip 73.0.0.0 0.255.255.255 any
 deny   ip 74.0.0.0 0.255.255.255 any
 deny   ip 75.0.0.0 0.255.255.255 any
 deny   ip 76.0.0.0 0.255.255.255 any
 deny   ip 77.0.0.0 0.255.255.255 any
 deny   ip 78.0.0.0 0.255.255.255 any
 deny   ip 79.0.0.0 0.255.255.255 any
 deny   ip 83.0.0.0 0.255.255.255 any
 deny   ip 84.0.0.0 0.255.255.255 any
 deny   ip 85.0.0.0 0.255.255.255 any
 deny   ip 86.0.0.0 0.255.255.255 any
 deny   ip 87.0.0.0 0.255.255.255 any
 deny   ip 88.0.0.0 0.255.255.255 any
 deny   ip 89.0.0.0 0.255.255.255 any
 deny   ip 90.0.0.0 0.255.255.255 any
 deny   ip 91.0.0.0 0.255.255.255 any
 deny   ip 92.0.0.0 0.255.255.255 any
 deny   ip 93.0.0.0 0.255.255.255 any
 deny   ip 94.0.0.0 0.255.255.255 any
 deny   ip 95.0.0.0 0.255.255.255 any
 deny   ip 96.0.0.0 0.255.255.255 any
 deny   ip 97.0.0.0 0.255.255.255 any
 deny   ip 98.0.0.0 0.255.255.255 any
 deny   ip 99.0.0.0 0.255.255.255 any
 deny   ip 100.0.0.0 0.255.255.255 any
 deny   ip 101.0.0.0 0.255.255.255 any
```

Example 4-37 *AutoSecure Configuring CEF and Ingress Filters (Continued)*

```
 deny    ip 102.0.0.0 0.255.255.255 any
 deny    ip 103.0.0.0 0.255.255.255 any
 deny    ip 104.0.0.0 0.255.255.255 any
 deny    ip 105.0.0.0 0.255.255.255 any
 deny    ip 106.0.0.0 0.255.255.255 any
 deny    ip 107.0.0.0 0.255.255.255 any
 deny    ip 108.0.0.0 0.255.255.255 any
 deny    ip 109.0.0.0 0.255.255.255 any
 deny    ip 110.0.0.0 0.255.255.255 any
 deny    ip 111.0.0.0 0.255.255.255 any
 deny    ip 112.0.0.0 0.255.255.255 any
 deny    ip 113.0.0.0 0.255.255.255 any
 deny    ip 114.0.0.0 0.255.255.255 any
 deny    ip 115.0.0.0 0.255.255.255 any
 deny    ip 116.0.0.0 0.255.255.255 any
 deny    ip 117.0.0.0 0.255.255.255 any
 deny    ip 118.0.0.0 0.255.255.255 any
 deny    ip 119.0.0.0 0.255.255.255 any
 deny    ip 120.0.0.0 0.255.255.255 any
 deny    ip 121.0.0.0 0.255.255.255 any
 deny    ip 122.0.0.0 0.255.255.255 any
 deny    ip 123.0.0.0 0.255.255.255 any
 deny    ip 124.0.0.0 0.255.255.255 any
 deny    ip 125.0.0.0 0.255.255.255 any
 deny    ip 126.0.0.0 0.255.255.255 any
 deny    ip 197.0.0.0 0.255.255.255 any
 deny    ip 201.0.0.0 0.255.255.255 any
 permit ip any any
 remark This acl might not be up to date. Visit www.iana.org/assignments/ipv4-ad
dress-space for update list
ip access-list extended autosec_private_block
 deny    ip 10.0.0.0 0.255.255.255 any
 deny    ip 172.16.0.0 0.15.255.255 any
 deny    ip 192.168.0.0 0.0.255.255 any
 permit ip any any
logging trap debugging
logging facility local2
access-list 100 permit udp any any eq bootpc
no cdp run
!
radius-server authorization permit missing Service-Type
!
!
!
!
banner motd ^CThis system is the property of Cisco Systems, Inc.
UNAUTHORIZED ACCESS TO THIS DEVICE IS PROHIBITED.^C
!
line con 0
 exec-timeout 5 0
```

continues

Example 4-37 *AutoSecure Configuring CEF and Ingress Filters (Continued)*

```
 login authentication local_auth
 transport output telnet
line aux 0
 login authentication local_auth
 transport output telnet
line vty 0 4
 password 7 14141B180F0B
 login authentication local_auth
 transport input telnet ssh
!
!
!
end
```

Chapter Summary

The following list summarizes what you have learned in this chapter:

- Unused router services and interfaces should be disabled.

- There are several different types of Cisco ACLs and it is important that you know where and when they should be used.

- ACLs are used to mitigate many common router security threats.

- Syslog logging is a very helpful tool to have in your security toolkit.

Cisco IOS Commands Presented in This Chapter

Many Cisco IOS version 12.3 commands were discussed or referenced in this chapter. These commands can be found in the *Command Reference* online at http://www.cisco.com/univercd /cc/td/doc/product/software/ios123/123mindx/crgindx.htm.

Chapter Review Questions

The following review questions cover some of the key facts and concepts that were introduced in this chapter. Answers to these questions can be found in Appendix A, "Answers to Chapter Review Questions."

1 List six network services that you might want to disable on your Cisco IOS Firewall router.

2 What command would you use to disable BOOTP service on your Cisco IOS Firewall, and where would the command be applied?

3 You can disable CDP either globally or by individual interface on a Cisco IOS device. What global and interface commands would you use in each case?

4 What are the major differences between a standard IP ACL and an extended IP ACL on a Cisco IOS device?

5 What is the key feature of the Turbo ACL feature of Cisco IOS Firewalls?

6 What are the four types of enhanced ACLs within the Cisco IOS Firewall product?

7 You have created a standard ACL with the following entry:

access-list 84 permit 168.41.0.0 0.0.255.255

You have applied the list to inbound traffic on your Cisco IOS Firewall's external interface. What will be the effect of this ACL?

8 Create a standard named ACL and apply it to serial interface 3/4 on your Cisco IOS Firewall, AustinHQ1, for inbound traffic. The ACL should permit all addresses from network 203.43.18.0 except for hosts 203.43.18.47 and 203.43.18.123. Additionally, this ACL should prevent traffic from all other sources. Name the ACL EastAustin. Show the commands that would be required to complete this assignment.

9 What are the three basic rules that you should follow when developing ACLs?

10 What are the two ways to control access to router services?

11 Configure an ACL and apply it to the appropriate line(s) to restrict Telnet access to router AustinHQ3 to the management workstations at 172.17.19.44 and 172.17.19.73.

12 Why might you want to filter ICMP messages on your Cisco IOS Firewall router?

13 When you set up logging on your Cisco IOS device, you can send the log message to one or more facilities. What are the five most common facilities that can be used for this purpose?

14 Cisco router log messages fall into one of eight levels from 0 to 7. Which of these level numbers indicates the most severe error condition?

15 You have set up a syslog server at 172.16.19.47. You want to begin sending log messages to that device for error messages indicating a critical condition on router AustinHQ7. What commands would you enter on the router to set up this new logging requirement?

Case Study

The Future Corporation's network structure is shown in Figure 4-36.

Figure 4-36 *The Future Corporation*

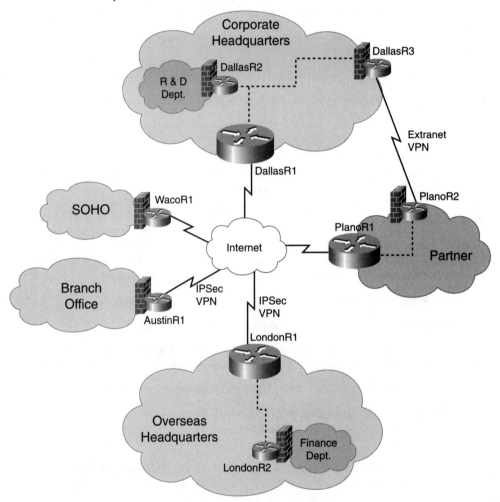

The public and private interface IP addresses are shown in Table 4-5. Remember that RFC 1597 IP addresses are not routed across the public network.

Table 4-5 *The Future Corporation IP Addresses*

Router	Public Interface	IP Address/Mask	Private Interface	IP Address/Mask
DallasR1	S3/0	203.14.17.1/24	FE4/0	172.16.10.1/24
DallasR2	FE0/0	172.16.10.2/24	FE0/1	192.168.10.1/24

Table 4-5   *The Future Corporation IP Addresses (Continued)*

Router	Public Interface	IP Address/Mask	Private Interface	IP Address/Mask
DallasR3	S1/0	207.118.14.30/24	FE0/0	172.16.10.3/24
WacoR1	S1/0	193.122.19.82/24	FE0/0	192.168.20.1/24
AustinR1	S1/0	195.147.231.47/24	FE0/0	192.168.30.1/24
LondonR1	S1/0	205.18.26.34/24	FE0/0	172.16.20.1/24
LondonR2	FE0/0	172.16.20.2/24	FE0/1	192.168.40.1/24
PlanoR1	S1/0	202.24.38.14/24	FE0/0	172.16.10.1/24
PlanoR2	S1/0	207.118.14.35/24	FE0/0	172.16.10.2/24

The DNS server for The Future Corporation is located at the Dallas corporate headquarters with a public NAT IP address of 203.14.17.13.

Scenario

Using the information from Figure 4-36 and Table 4-5, show the commands you would use when configuring router AustinR1 to disable the following common services:

- Disable BOOTP service
- Disable CDP service
- Disable IP classless routing service
- RestrictDNS service
- Disable finger service
- Disable HTTP service
- Disable IP directed broadcasts
- Disable IP mask replies
- Disable IP redirects
- Disable IP source routing
- Disable IP unreachable messages (for interfaces connected to untrusted networks)
- Disable NTP service
- Disable proxy ARP
- Disable SNMP
- Disable small servers
- Disable unused router interfaces

Solutions

The commands required to disable the specified services on AustinR1 follow:

- Disable BOOTP service

```
AustinR1(config)# no ip bootp server
```

- Disable CDP service

```
AustinR1(config)# no cdp run
AustinR1(config)# interface s1/0
AustinR1(config-if)# no cdp enable
AustinR1(config-if)# exit
```

- Disable IP classless routing service

```
AustinR1(config)# no ip classless
```

- Restrict DNS service

```
AustinR1(config)# ip name-server 203.14.17.13
AustinR1(config)# no ip domain-lookup
```

- Disable finger service

```
AustinR1(config)# no ip finger
AustinR1(config)# no service finger
```

- Disable HTTP service

```
AustinR1(config)# no ip http server
```

- Disable IP directed broadcasts

```
AustinR1(config)# interface s1/0
AustinR1(config-if)# no ip directed-broadcast
AustinR1(config-if)# exit
AustinR1(config)# interface fe0/0
AustinR1(config-if)# no ip directed-broadcast
AustinR1(config-if)# exit
```

- Disable IP mask replies

```
AustinR1(config)# interface s1/0
AustinR1(config-if)# no ip mask-reply
AustinR1(config-if)# exit
AustinR1(config)# interface fe0/0
AustinR1(config-if)# no ip mask-reply
AustinR1(config-if)# exit
```

- Disable IP redirects

```
AustinR1(config)# interface s1/0
AustinR1(config-if)# no ip redirect
AustinR1(config-if)# exit
```

- Disable IP source routing

```
AustinR1(config)# no ip source-route
```

- Disable IP unreachable messages (for interfaces connected to untrusted networks)

```
AustinR1(config)# interface s1/0
AustinR1(config-if)# no ip unreachable
AustinR1(config-if)# exit
```

- Disable NTP service

```
AustinR1(config)# interface s1/0
AustinR1(config-if)# ntp disable
AustinR1(config-if)# exit
AustinR1(config)# interface fe0/0
AustinR1(config-if)# ntp disable
AustinR1(config-if)# exit
```

- Disable proxy ARP

```
AustinR1(config)# interface s1/0
AustinR1(config-if)# no ip proxy-arp
AustinR1(config-if)# exit
```

- Disable SNMP

```
AustinR1 (config)# no snmp-server community public ro
AustinR1 (config)# no snmp-server community config rw
AustinR1 (config)# access-list 60 deny any
AustinR1 (config)# snmp-server community m44s36b5 ro 60
AustinR1 (config)# no snmp-server enable traps
AustinR1 (config)# no snmp-server system-shutdown
AustinR1 (config)# no snmp-server
```

- Disable small servers

```
AustinR1 (config)# no service tcp-small-servers
AustinR1 (config)# no service udp-small-servers
```

Assuming that you have performed the scenario configurations from Chapters 1 and 2 on AustinR1, after you have completed the configuration steps from this chapter, performing a **show running-config** on AustinR1 will display the results in Example 4-38.

Example 4-38 *Displaying the Running Configuration*

```
AustinR1# show running-config
version 12.2
service timestamps debug datetime localtime msec
service timestamps log datetime localtime
service password-encryption
no service tcp-small-servers
no service udp-small-servers
!
hostname AustinR1
!
aaa new-model
aaa authentication login default group tacacs+ local
aaa authentication login console-in group tacacs+ enable
```
continues

Example 4-38 *Displaying the Running Configuration (Continued)*

```
aaa accounting exec start-stop tacacs+
aaa accounting network start-stop tacacs+
enable secret 5 $1$ES4r$tA1rlg0beW/Kvk6jGIj2f.
enable secret level 2 5 $1$mCGe$.1fTlJ.fcR8NHqa0AMR2F/
enable password 7 09611E1C171113171C
!
no ip source-route
no ip bootp server
ip name-server 203.14.17.13
no cdp run
no ip classless
no ip domain-lookup
no ip finger
no service finger
no ip http server
no ip proxy-arp
!
interface FastEthernet0/0
 ip address 192.168.30.1 255.255.255.0
 no ip directed-broadcast
 no ip mask-reply
 ntp disable
!
interface Serial1/0
 ip address 195.147.231.47 255.255.255.0
 no cdp enable
 no ip directed-broadcast
 no ip mask-reply
 no ip redirect
 no ip unreachable
 ntp disable
!
username aaadmin password 7 1531035C147F3F752B38
!
access-list 60 deny any
access-list 88 permit 192.168.44.121
access-list 88 permit 192.168.44.122
access-list 88 permit 192.168.64.123
access-list 88 permit 142.16.18.121
access-list 88 permit 142.16.18.122
access-list 88 permit 142.16.18.123
no snmp-server community public ro
no snmp-server community config rw
snmp-server community m44s36b5 ro 60
no snmp-server enable traps
no snmp-server system-shutdown
no snmp-server
tacacs-server host 142.16.18.200
tacacs-server key future123key
privilege exec level 2 ping
```

Example 4-38 *Displaying the Running Configuration (Continued)*

```
!
banner motd #
WARNING: You are connected to $(hostname) on The Future Corporation network.
Unauthorized access and use of this network will be vigorously prosecuted. #
!
line con 0
 login authentication console-in
 exec-timeout 4 20
line aux 0
 login
 password 7 112A115507471F5D0721
 exec-timeout 4 20
line vty 0 4
 login
 password 7 05280E5F31195A581A0E
!
end
```

Upon completion of this chapter, you will be able to perform the following tasks:

- Define the Cisco IOS Firewall
- Define CBAC
- Configure CBAC

CHAPTER 5

Cisco IOS Firewall Context-Based Access Control Configuration

Cisco IOS routers are usually located in perfect positions to provide firewall support to organizations. Traffic must pass through one or more routers to get to destinations on the private enterprise network.

For many years, Cisco IOS only provided rudimentary firewall support in the form of access control lists and network address translation. While these are important components of any firewall, they didn't offer the degree of control necessary in business networks today.

With the release of Cisco IOS version 11.3, Cisco greatly enhanced the capabilities of the Cisco IOS Firewall feature set by including Context-Based Access Control (CBAC) and additional firewall capabilities to the powerful operating system. Additional software releases have brought further enhancements to the firewall capabilities of Cisco IOS. This chapter discusses the Cisco IOS Firewall and includes the following topics:

- Introduction to the Cisco IOS Firewall
- Context-Based Access Control
- Global timeouts and thresholds
- Port-to-application mapping (PAM)
- Inspection rules
- Inspection rules and access control lists (ACLs) applied to router interfaces
- Configuration Testing and verification

Cisco IOS Firewall Introduction

This section introduces the features of the Cisco IOS Firewall, which adds a robust set of firewall control and monitoring capabilities to Cisco IOS routers. Many of these capabilities overlap those found on the Cisco PIX Firewall. Some of these features can only be found in the Cisco IOS Firewall feature set. As you review the material in this chapter, keep in mind that routers are designed primarily to route and switch data packets. Every other CPU-intensive function that is added to the router, such as firewall support, can diminish the responsiveness of the router.

You should not, as a general rule, implement extensive firewall features on core or distribution layer routers whose primary function is to move data as quickly as possible from point A to point B. Whenever possible, restrict firewall support to access-layer routers that connect directly to user subnets. You can take advantage of the routing hardware you have in place and add a high degree of firewall support by using the Cisco IOS Firewall feature set.

Cisco PIX Firewall devices were designed originally as single-purpose firewall systems. They did not do packet routing and they did not do intrusion detection. Now, of course, they do some routing and intrusion detection, but they are primarily still firewall tools. When you need dedicated, extensive firewall protection, choose the Cisco PIX Firewall over the Cisco IOS Firewall, or use them in conjunction with one another to provide security in depth for your network.

The Cisco IOS Firewall Feature Set

The Cisco IOS Firewall is a security-specific option for Cisco IOS software. It integrates robust firewall functionality, authentication proxy, and intrusion detection for every network perimeter, and enriches existing Cisco IOS security capabilities. It adds greater depth and flexibility to existing Cisco IOS security solutions, such as authentication, encryption, and failover, by delivering state-of-the-art security features, such as stateful, application-based filtering; dynamic per-user authentication and authorization; defense against network attacks; Java blocking; and real-time alerts. When combined with Cisco IOS IPSec software and other Cisco IOS software-based technologies, such as Layer 2 Tunneling Protocol (L2TP) tunneling and quality of service (QoS), the Cisco IOS Firewall provides a complete, integrated virtual private network (VPN) solution.

The Cisco IOS Firewall feature set is a suite of features for Cisco IOS routers that provides network protection on multiple levels using the following:

- **Context-Based Access Control** — The Cisco IOS Firewall CBAC engine provides secure, per-application access control across network perimeters.

- **Authentication proxy** — Network administrators can create specific security policies for each user with Cisco IOS Firewall LAN-based, dynamic, per-user authentication and authorization.

- **Intrusion detection** — Cisco IOS Firewall intrusion detection systems (IDSs) provide a level of protection beyond the firewall by protecting the network from internal and external attacks and threats.

Understanding CBAC

CBAC enhances security for TCP and UDP applications that use well-known ports, such as FTP and e-mail traffic, by scrutinizing source and destination addresses. CBAC allows network administrators to implement firewall intelligence as part of an integrated, single-box solution.

For example, sessions with an extranet partner involving Internet applications, multimedia applications, or Oracle databases would no longer need to open a network doorway accessible via weaknesses in a partner's network. CBAC enables tightly secured networks to run today's basic application traffic, as well as advanced applications, such as multimedia and videoconferencing, securely through a router.

CBAC intelligently filters TCP and UDP packets based on application layer protocol session information. It can inspect traffic for sessions that originate on any interface of the router. CBAC inspects traffic that travels through the firewall to discover and manage state information for TCP and UDP sessions. This state information is used to create temporary openings in the firewall's ACLs to allow return traffic and additional data connections for permissible sessions.

Inspecting packets at the application layer and maintaining TCP and UDP session information provides CBAC with the ability to detect and prevent certain types of network attacks, such as SYN flooding. CBAC also inspects packet sequence numbers in TCP connections to see if they are within expected ranges—CBAC drops any suspicious packets. Additionally, CBAC can detect unusually high rates of new connections and issue alert messages. CBAC inspection can help protect against certain denial of service (DoS) attacks that involve fragmented IP packets.

Working with TCP and UDP packets, as shown in Figure 5-1, CBAC has the following characteristics:

- Packets are inspected entering the firewall by CBAC if they are not specifically denied by an ACL.
- CBAC permits or denies specified TCP and UDP traffic through a firewall.
- A state table is maintained with session information.
- ACLs are dynamically created or deleted.
- CBAC protects against DoS attacks.

Figure 5-1   *Context-Based Access Control*

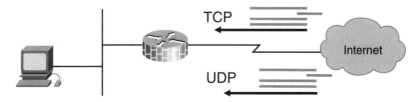

Understanding Authentication Proxy

The Cisco IOS Firewall authentication proxy feature enables network administrators to apply specific security policies on a per-user basis. Previously, user identity and related authorized access was associated with a user's IP address, or a single security policy had to be applied to an entire user group or subnet. Now, users can be identified and authorized on the basis of the per-user policy, and access privileges that are tailored on an individual basis are possible, as opposed to general policy applied across multiple users.

With the authentication proxy feature, users can log in to the network or access the Internet via HTTP, and their specific access profiles are automatically retrieved and applied from a Cisco Secure Access Control Server (CSACS) or other RADIUS or TACACS+ authentication server. The user profiles are active only when there is active traffic from the authenticated users.

Appropriate dynamic, individual access privileges are available as required, protecting the network against more general policies that are applied across multiple users. Authentication and authorization can be applied to the router interface in either direction to secure inbound or outbound extranet, intranet, and Internet usage.

The authentication proxy is compatible with other Cisco IOS security features, such as Network Address Translation (NAT), IPSec encryption, and VPN client software.

Understanding Intrusion Detection

Firewall IDS technology enhances perimeter firewall protection by taking appropriate actions on packets and flows that violate the security policy or represent malicious network activity.

Cisco IOS Firewall intrusion detection capabilities are ideal for providing additional visibility at intranet, extranet, and branch-office Internet perimeters. Network administrators now enjoy more robust protection against attacks on the network, and can automatically respond to threats from internal or external hosts.

The Cisco IOS Firewall now offers intrusion detection technology for midrange and high-end router platforms with firewall support. It is ideal for any network perimeter, and especially for locations in which a router is being deployed and additional security between network segments is required. It also can protect intranet and extranet connections where additional security is mandated, and branch-office sites that connect to the corporate office or Internet.

The Cisco IOS Firewall's IDS identifies nearly 100 common attacks by using signatures to detect patterns of misuse in network traffic. The intrusion detection signatures of the Cisco IOS Firewall were chosen from a broad cross-section of intrusion detection signatures. The signatures represent severe breaches of security and the most common network attacks and information-gathering scans.

The intrusion detection support permits Cisco IOS Firewalls to perform the following functions:

- Act as an inline intrusion detection sensor
- Perform any of the following configurable actions when a packet or packets match a signature:
  - **Alarm**—Send an alarm to a Cisco Secure IDS Director or syslog server
  - **Drop**—Drop the packet
  - **Reset**—Send TCP resets to terminate the session
- Identify nearly 100 common attacks

Using CBAC to Protect Users from Attack

This section describes the limitations of Cisco IOS ACLs and explains how CBAC better protects users from attack. It also lists the protocols that are supported by CBAC and describes the added alert and audit trail features. Finally, the CBAC configuration tasks are listed.

Cisco IOS ACLs

Before delving into CBAC, some basic ACL concepts need to be covered briefly. An ACL provides packet filtering: it has an implied "deny all" at the end of the ACL, and if the ACL is not configured, it permits all connections. Without CBAC, traffic filtering is limited to ACL implementations that examine packets at the network layer or, at most, the transport layer. Cisco IOS ACLs Provide traffic filtering by:

- Source and destination IP addresses.
- Source and destination ports.

For applications that do not negotiate ports dynamically, Cisco IOS ACLs can be used to implement a filtering firewall by controlling access to ports that may have been opened permanently to allow traffic, thereby creating a security vulnerability.

How CBAC Works

With CBAC, you specify which protocols you want to have inspected, and you specify an interface and interface direction (in or out) where the inspection originates. Only specified protocols will be inspected by CBAC. For these protocols, packets flowing through the firewall in any direction are inspected, as long as they flow through the interface where inspection is configured. Packets entering the firewall are inspected by CBAC only if they first pass the inbound ACL at the interface. If a packet is denied by the ACL, the packet is simply dropped and not inspected by CBAC.

CBAC inspects and monitors only the control channels of connections; the data channels are not inspected. For example, during FTP sessions, both the control and data channels (which are created when a data file is transferred) are monitored for state changes, but only the control channel is inspected (that is, the CBAC software parses the FTP commands and responses).

CBAC inspection recognizes application-specific commands in the control channel, and detects and prevents certain application-level attacks. CBAC inspection tracks sequence numbers in all TCP packets, and drops those packets with sequence numbers that are not within expected ranges. CBAC inspection recognizes application-specific commands, such as illegal Simple Mail Transfer Protocol (SMTP) commands, in the control channel. When CBAC suspects an attack, the DoS feature can take several actions:

- Generate alert messages
- Protect system resources that could impede performance
- Block packets from suspected attackers

CBAC uses timeout and threshold values to manage session state information, helping to determine when to drop sessions that do not become fully established. Setting timeout values for network sessions helps prevent DoS attacks by freeing system resources, dropping sessions after a specified amount of time. Setting threshold values for network sessions helps prevent DoS attacks by controlling the number of half-opened sessions, which limits the amount of system resources that are applied to half-opened sessions. When a session is dropped, CBAC sends a reset message to the devices at both endpoints (source and destination) of the session. When the system under DoS attack receives a reset command, it releases, or frees, processes and resources related to that incomplete session.

CBAC provides three thresholds against DoS attacks:

- The total number of half-opened TCP or UDP sessions
- The number of half-opened sessions based on time
- The number of half-opened TCP-only sessions per host

If a threshold is exceeded, CBAC has two options:

- Send a reset message to the endpoints of the oldest half-opened session, making resources available to service newly arriving SYN packets.
- In the case of half-opened TCP-only sessions, CBAC blocks all SYN packets temporarily for the duration configured by the threshold value. When the router blocks a SYN packet, the TCP three-way handshake is never initiated, which prevents the router from using the memory and processing resources that are needed for valid connections.

DoS detection and prevention requires that you create a CBAC inspection rule and apply that rule on an interface. The inspection rule must include the protocols that you want to monitor against DoS attacks. For example, if you have TCP inspection enabled on the inspection rule, then CBAC can track all TCP connections to watch for DoS attacks. If the inspection rule includes FTP inspection but not TCP inspection, CBAC tracks only FTP connections for DoS attacks.

A state table maintains session state information. Whenever a packet is inspected, a state table is updated to include information about the state of the packet's connection. Return traffic is permitted back through the firewall only if the state table contains information indicating that the packet belongs to a permissible session. Inspection controls the traffic that belongs to a valid session and forwards the traffic it does not know. When return traffic is inspected, the state table information is updated as necessary.

UDP sessions are approximated. With UDP, there are no actual sessions, so the software approximates sessions by examining the information in the packet and determining if the packet is similar to other UDP packets, such as similar source or destination addresses and port numbers, and if the packet was detected soon after another, similar UDP packet ("soon" in this context means within the configurable UDP idle timeout period).

ACL entries are dynamically created and deleted. CBAC dynamically creates and deletes ACL entries at the firewall interfaces, according to the information maintained in the state tables. These ACL entries are applied to the interfaces to examine traffic flowing back into the internal network.

These entries create temporary openings in the firewall to permit only traffic that is part of a permissible session. The temporary ACL entries are never saved to nonvolatile RAM (NVRAM).

Using a Cisco IOS Firewall similar to that shown in Figure 5-2, CBAC performs four essential steps:

Step 1   The CBAC rule inspects control traffic.

Step 2   CBAC inserts a temporary access list entry at the beginning of the external interface's inbound extended access list. This temporary access list entry permits inbound packets that are part of the same connection as the outbound packet just inspected.

Step 3   CBAC continues to inspect control traffic and dynamically creates and removes ACL entries as required by the application. It also monitors and protects against application-specific attacks.

Step 4   CBAC detects when an application terminates or times out and removes all dynamic ACL entries for that session.

Figure 5-2   *How CBAC Works*

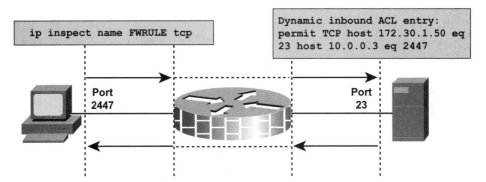

Supported Protocols

You can configure CBAC to inspect the following types of sessions:

- All TCP sessions, regardless of the application layer protocol (sometimes called single-channel or generic TCP inspection)

- All UDP sessions, regardless of the application layer protocol (sometimes called single-channel or generic UDP inspection)

You can also configure CBAC to specifically inspect certain application layer protocols. The following application layer protocols can all be configured for CBAC:

- Remote Procedure Call (RPC) (Sun RPC and not DCE RPC)

- FTP

- Trivial File Transfer Protocol (TFTP)
- UNIX R-commands, such as **rlogin**, **rexec**, and **rsh**
- SMTP
- HTTP (Java blocking)
- Oracle SQL*Net
- RealNetworks RealAudio
- Real Time Streaming Protocol (RTSP) (such as RealNetworks)
- H.323, such as Microsoft NetMeeting and Intel ProShare
- Microsoft NetShow
- StreamWorks
- VDOLive
- CUSeeMe (only White Pine version)

When a protocol is configured for CBAC, that protocol traffic is inspected, state information is maintained, and, in general, packets are allowed back through the firewall only if they belong to a permissible session.

Alerts and Audit Trails

CBAC also generates real-time alerts and audit trails based on events tracked by the firewall. Enhanced audit trail features use syslog to track all network transactions, recording time stamps, source host, destination host, ports used, and the total number of transmitted bytes, for advanced, session-based reporting.

Real-time alerts send syslog error messages to central management consoles upon detecting suspicious activity. Using CBAC inspection rules, you can configure alerts and audit trail information on a per-application-protocol basis. For example, if you want to generate audit trail information for HTTP traffic, you can specify that in the CBAC rule that covers HTTP inspection.

Configuring CBAC

The following are the tasks that are used to configure CBAC:

1 Set audit trails and alerts.

2 Set global timeouts and thresholds.

3 Define port-to-application mapping (PAM).

4 Define inspection rules.

5 Apply inspection rules and ACLs to interfaces.

6 Test and verify.

Enabling Audit Trail and Alert

Turn on logging and audit trail to provide a record of network access through the firewall, including illegitimate access attempts and inbound and outbound services.

Use the **ip inspect audit-trail** and **no ip inspect alert-off** commands to enable audit trail and alert, respectively. The following example shows how you might configure logging on a router and enable the syslog server with the **ip inspect audit-trail** command:

```
Router(config)# logging on
Router(config)# logging 10.0.0.3
Router(config)# ip inspect audit-trail
```

The syntax for the **ip inspect audit-trail** commands is as follows:

```
ip inspect audit-trail
no ip inspect audit-trail
```

The syntax for the **no ip inspect alert-off** commands is as follows:

```
ip inspect alert-off
no ip inspect alert-off
```

No other arguments or keywords are used with either command.

Global Timeouts and Thresholds

This section discusses how to configure the following global timeouts and thresholds:

- TCP, SYN, and FIN wait times
- TCP, UDP, and Domain Name System (DNS) idle times
- TCP flood DoS protection

TCP, SYN, and FIN Wait Times

CBAC uses timeouts and thresholds to determine how long to manage state information for a session, and to determine when to drop sessions that do not become fully established. These timeouts and thresholds apply globally to all sessions.

You can use the default timeout and threshold values, or you can change to values that are more suitable to your security requirements. You should make any changes to the timeout and threshold values before you continue configuring CBAC.

Use the **ip inspect tcp synwait-time** global configuration command to define how long the software will wait for a TCP session to reach the established state before dropping the session. Use the **no** form of this command to reset the timeout to the default.

The syntax of the **ip inspect tcp synwait-time** command is as follows, where *seconds* specifies how long the software will wait for a TCP session to reach the established state before dropping the session (the default is 30 seconds):

```
ip inspect tcp synwait-time seconds
no ip inspect tcp synwait-time
```

Use the **ip inspect tcp finwait-time** global configuration command to define how long a TCP session will still be managed after the firewall detects a FIN exchange. Use the **no** form of this command to reset the timeout to the default.

The syntax of the **ip inspect tcp finwait-time** command is as follows, where *seconds* specifies how long a TCP session will be managed after the firewall detects a FIN exchange (the default is 5 seconds):

```
ip inspect tcp finwait-time seconds
no ip inspect tcp finwait-time
```

TCP, UDP, and DNS Idle Times

Use the **ip inspect tcp idle-time** global configuration command to specify the TCP idle timeout (the length of time a TCP session will still be managed after no activity). Use the **no** form of this command to reset the timeout to the default.

Use the **ip inspect udp idle-time** global configuration command to specify the UDP idle timeout (the length of time a UDP session will still be managed after no activity). Use the **no** form of this command to reset the timeout to the default.

The syntax for the **ip inspect {tcp | udp} idle-time** commands is as follows, where *seconds* specifies the length of time a TCP or a UDP session will still be managed after no activity (for TCP sessions, the default is 3600 seconds, or 1 hour; for UDP sessions, the default is 30 seconds):

```
ip inspect {tcp | udp} idle-time seconds
no ip inspect {tcp | udp} idle-time
```

Use the **ip inspect dns-timeout** global configuration command to specify the DNS idle timeout (the length of time a DNS name lookup session will still be managed after no activity). Use the **no** form of this command to reset the timeout to the default.

The syntax for the **ip inspect dns-timeout** command is as follows, where *seconds* specifies the length of time a DNS name lookup session will still be managed after no activity (the default is 5 seconds):

```
ip inspect dns-timeout seconds
no ip inspect dns-timeout
```

Global Half-Opened Connection Limits

An unusually high number of half-opened sessions (either absolute or measured as the arrival rate) could indicate that a DoS attack is occurring. For TCP, *half-opened* means that the session has not reached the established state—the TCP three-way handshake has not yet been completed. For UDP, *half-opened* means that the firewall has detected no return traffic.

CBAC measures both the total number of existing half-opened sessions and the rate of session establishment attempts. Both TCP and UDP half-opened sessions are counted in the total number and rate measurements. Measurements are made once a minute.

When the number of existing half-opened sessions rises above a threshold (the **max-incomplete high** *number*), CBAC will go into aggressive mode and delete half-opened sessions as required to accommodate new connection requests. The software continues to delete half-opened requests as necessary, until the number of existing half-opened sessions drops below another threshold (the **max-incomplete low** *number*).

Use the **ip inspect max-incomplete high** command in global configuration mode to define the number of existing half-opened sessions that will cause the software to start deleting half-opened sessions. Use the **no** form of this command to reset the threshold to the default.

The syntax for the **ip inspect max-incomplete high** command is as follows, where **high** *number* specifies the number of existing half-opened sessions that will cause the software to start deleting half-opened sessions (the default is 500 half-opened sessions):

```
ip inspect max-incomplete high number
no ip inspect max-incomplete high number
```

Use the **ip inspect max-incomplete low** command in global configuration mode to define the number of existing half-opened sessions that will cause the software to stop deleting half-opened sessions. Use the **no** form of this command to reset the threshold to the default.

The syntax for the **ip inspect max-incomplete low** command is as follows, where **low** *number* specifies the number of existing half-opened sessions that will cause the software to stop deleting half-opened sessions (the default is 400 half-opened sessions):

```
ip inspect max-incomplete low number
no ip inspect max-incomplete low number
```

When the rate of new connection attempts rises above a threshold (the **one-minute high** *number*), the software will delete half-opened sessions as required to accommodate new connection attempts. The software continues to delete half-opened sessions as necessary, until the rate of new connection attempts drops below another threshold (the **one-minute low** *number*). The rate thresholds are measured as the number of new session connection attempts detected in the last one-minute sample period. The firewall router reviews the one-minute rate on an ongoing basis, meaning that the router reviews the rate more frequently than one minute and does not keep deleting half-opened sessions for one minute after a DoS attack has stopped—it will be less time.

Use the **ip inspect one-minute high** command in global configuration mode to define the rate of new unestablished sessions that will cause the software to start deleting half-opened sessions. Use the **no** form of this command to reset the threshold to the default.

The syntax for the **ip inspect one-minute high** command is as follows, where **high** *number* specifies the rate of new unestablished TCP sessions that will cause the software to start deleting half-opened sessions (the default is 500 half-opened sessions):

```
ip inspect one-minute high number
no ip inspect one-minute high
```

Use the **ip inspect one-minute low** command in global configuration mode to define the rate of new unestablished TCP sessions that will cause the software to stop deleting half-opened sessions. Use the **no** form of this command to reset the threshold to the default.

The syntax for the **ip inspect one-minute low** command is as follows, where **low** *number* specifies the number of new unestablished half-opened sessions that will cause the software to stop deleting half-opened sessions (the default is 400 half-opened sessions):

```
ip inspect one-minute low number
no ip inspect one-minute low
```

Half-Opened Connection Limits by Host

An unusually high number of half-opened sessions with the same destination host address could indicate that a DoS attack is being launched against the host. Whenever the number of half-opened sessions with the same destination host address rises above a threshold (the **max-incomplete host** *number*), the software will delete half-opened sessions according to one of the following methods:

- If the **block-time** *minutes* timeout is 0 (the default), the software deletes the oldest existing half-opened session for the host for every new connection request to the host. This ensures that the number of half-opened sessions to a given host will never exceed the threshold.

- If the **block-time** *minutes* timeout is greater than 0, the software deletes all existing half-opened sessions for the host, and then blocks all new connection requests to the host. The software will continue to block all new connection requests until the block time expires.

The software also sends syslog messages whenever the **max-incomplete host** *number* is exceeded, and when blocking of connection initiations to a host starts or ends. The **max-incomplete host** error messages include the following:

- **%FW-2-BLOCK_HOST : Blocking new TCP connections to host [IP_address] for [dec] minute[chars] (half-open count [dec] exceeded)**.

  Explanation: Any subsequent new TCP connection attempts to the specified host will be denied because the **max-incomplete host** threshold of half-open TCP connections is exceeded, and the blocking option is configured to block the subsequent new connections. The blocking will be removed when the configured block time expires.

  Recommended action: This message is for informational purposes only, but it may indicate that a SYN flood attack was attempted.

- **%FW-4-HOST_TCP_ALERT_ON : Max tcp half-open connections ([dec]) exceeded for host [IP_address]**.

  Explanation: The **max-incomplete host** limit of half-open TCP connections has been exceeded. This message indicates that a high number of half-open connections is coming to the protected server, and it may indicate that a SYN flood attack is in progress and is targeted to the specified server host.

  Recommended action: This message is for informational purposes only, but it may indicate that a SYN flood attack was attempted. If this alert is issued frequently and identified to be mostly false alarms, then the **max-incomplete**

host threshold value is probably set too low, and there is a significant amount of legitimate traffic coming into that server. In this case, the **max-incomplete host** parameter should be set to a higher number to avoid false alarms.

The global values specified for the threshold and blocking time apply to all TCP connections inspected by CBAC.

Use the **ip inspect tcp max-incomplete host** global configuration command to specify threshold and blocking time values for TCP host-specific DoS detection and prevention. Use the **no** form of this command to reset the threshold and blocking time to the default values.

The syntax for the **ip inspect tcp max-incomplete host** command is as follows:

```
ip inspect tcp max-incomplete host number block-time minutes
no ip inspect tcp max-incomplete host
```

- **host** *number*—Specifies how many half-opened TCP sessions with the same host destination address can exist at a time before the software starts deleting half-opened sessions to the host. Use a number from 1 to 250 (the default is 50 half-opened sessions).

- **block-time** *minutes*—Specifies how long the software will continue to delete new connection requests to the host (the default is 0 minutes).

Port-To-Application Mapping

This section discusses the configuration of port numbers for application protocols.

PAM enables you to customize TCP or UDP port numbers for network services or applications. PAM uses this information to support network environments that run services using ports that are different from the registered or well-known ports associated with an application.

Using the port information, PAM establishes a table of default PAM information at the firewall. The information in the PAM table enables CBAC-supported services to run on nonstandard ports. Previously, CBAC was limited to inspecting traffic using only the well-known or registered ports associated with an application. Now, PAM allows network administrators to customize network access control for specific applications and services.

PAM also supports host- or subnet-specific port mapping, which enables you to apply PAM to a single host or subnet using standard ACLs. Host- or subnet-specific port mapping is done using standard ACLs.

PAM creates a table, or database, of system-defined mapping entries using the well-known or registered port mapping information set up during the system startup. The system-defined entries comprise all the services supported by CBAC, which requires the system-defined mapping information to function properly.

NOTE   The system-defined mapping information cannot be deleted or changed; that is, you cannot map HTTP services to port 21 (FTP) or FTP services to port 80 (HTTP).

Table 5-1 shows the default system-defined services and applications found in the PAM table.

Table 5-1 *Default PAM Table Entries*

Application	Port
cuseeme	7648
exec	512
ftp	21
http	80
h323	1720
login	513
mgcp	2427
msrpc	135
netshow	1755
realmedia	7070
rtsp	554
rtsp	8554
shell	514
sip	5060
smtp	25
sql-net	1521
streamworks	1558
sunrpc	111
telnet	23
tftp	69
vdolive	7000

User-Defined Port Mapping

Network services or applications that use nonstandard ports require user-defined entries in the PAM table. For example, your network might run HTTP services on the nonstandard port 8000 instead of on the system-defined default port 80. In this case, you can use PAM to map port 8000 with HTTP services. If HTTP services run on other ports, use PAM to create additional port mapping entries. After you define a port mapping entry, you can overwrite that entry at a later time by simply mapping that specific port with a different application.

NOTE	If you try to map an application to a system-defined port, a message appears warning you of a mapping conflict.

User-defined port mapping information can also specify a range of ports for an application by establishing a separate entry in the PAM table for each port number in the range.

User-defined entries are saved with the default mapping information when you save the router configuration.

Use the **ip port-map** configuration command to establish PAM. Use the **no** form of this command to delete user-defined PAM entries.

The syntax for the **ip port-map** command is as follows:

```
ip port-map appl_name port port_num [list acl_num]
```

- *appl_name*—Specifies the name of the application with which to apply the port mapping. Use one of the following application names: cuseeme, dns, exec, finger, ftp, gopher, h323, http, imap, kerberos, ldap, login, lotusnote, mgcp, msrpc, ms-sql, netshow, nfs, nntp, pop2, pop3, realmedia, rtsp, sap, shell, sip, smtp, snmp, sql-net, streamworks, sunrpc, sybase-sql, tacacs, telnet, tftp, or vdolive.
- **port** *port_num*—Identifies a port number in the range 1 to 65535.
- **list** *acl_num*—Identifies the standard ACL number used with PAM for host- or network-specific port mapping.

User-defined entries in the mapping table can include host- or network-specific mapping information, which establishes port mapping information for specific hosts or subnets. In some environments, it might be necessary to override the default port mapping information for a specific host or subnet.

With host-specific port mapping, you can use the same port number for different services on different hosts. This means that you can map port 8000 with HTTP services for one host, while mapping port 8000 with Telnet services for another host.

Host-specific port mapping also enables you to apply PAM to a specific subnet when that subnet runs a service that uses a port number that is different from the port number defined in the default mapping information. For example, hosts on subnet 192.168.0.0 might run HTTP services on nonstandard port 8000, while other traffic through the firewall uses the default port 80 for HTTP services.

Host- or network-specific port mapping enables you to override a system-defined entry in the PAM table. For example, if CBAC finds an entry in the PAM table that maps port 25 (the system-defined port for SMTP) with HTTP for a specific host, CBAC identifies port 25 as HTTP protocol traffic on that host.

NOTE   If the host-specific port mapping information is the same as existing system- or user-defined default entries, host-specific port changes have no effect.

Use the **list** option for the **ip port-map** command to specify an ACL for a host or subnet that uses PAM. Example 5-1 shows how to apply the **list** option for the **ip port map** command.

Example 5-1   *Apply the* **list** *Option for the* **ip port map** *Command*

```
access-list 10 permit 192.168.3.4
access-list 15 permit 192.168.33.43
access-list 20 permit 192.168.5.6
access-list 50 permit 192.168.92.0
ip port-map http port 8000 list 10
ip port-map http port 25 list 15
ip port-map http ftp 8000 list 20
ip port-map http 8080 list 50
```

Displaying PAM Configurations

Use the **show ip port-map** privileged EXEC command to display the PAM information, as shown in Example 5-2, for the FTP application.

Example 5-2   *Use the* **show ip port-map** *Privileged EXEC Command to Display the PAM Information*

```
Router# sh ip port-map ftp
Default mapping: ftp    port 21    system defined
Host specific:   ftp    port 1000 in list 10 user
```

The syntax for the **show ip port-map** command is as follows:

```
show ip port-map [appl_name | port port_num]
```

- *appl_name*—Specifies the application for which to display information.

- **port** *port_num*—Specifies the alternative port number that maps to the application for which to display information.

Defining Application Protocols Inspection Rules

This section discusses how to configure the rules used to define the application protocols for inspection.

Application Protocols Inspection Rules

Inspection rules must be defined to specify what IP traffic (which application layer protocols) will be inspected by CBAC at an interface. Normally, you define only one inspection rule. The only exception might occur if you want to enable CBAC in two directions at a single firewall interface. In this case, you must configure two rules, one for each direction.

An inspection rule should specify each desired application layer protocol, as well as generic TCP or generic UDP, if desired. The inspection rule consists of a series of statements, each listing a protocol and specifying the same inspection rule name.

Inspection rules include options for controlling alert and audit trail messages and for checking IP packet fragmentation.

Use the **ip inspect name** command in global configuration mode to define a set of inspection rules. Use the **no** form of this command to remove the inspection rule for a protocol or to remove the entire set of inspection rules. The following example shows the configuration of inspection rules for SMTP and FTP:

```
Router(config)# ip inspect name FWRULE smtp alert on audit-trail on timeout 300
Router(config)# ip inspect name FWRULE ftp alert on audit-trail on timeout 300
```

The syntax for the **ip inspect name** command is as follows:

```
ip inspect name inspection-name protocol [alert {on | off}] [audit-trail {on | off}]
   [timeout seconds]
no ip inspect name inspection-name protocol
no ip inspect name
```

- **name** *inspection-name*—Names the set of inspection rules. If you want to add a protocol to an existing set of rules, use the same **inspection-name**.

- *protocol*—The protocol to inspect. Use any of the following keywords: **tcp, udp, cuseeme, ftp, http, h323, netshow, rcmd, realaudio, rpc, smtp, sqlnet, streamworks, tftp,** or **vdolive**.

- **alert** {**on** | **off**}(Optional.)—For each inspected protocol, the generation of alert messages can be set to on or off. If no option is selected, alerts are generated based on the setting of the **ip inspect alert-off** command.

- **audit-trail** {**on** | **off**}(Optional.)—For each inspected protocol, **audit-trail** can be set to on or off. If no option is selected, audit trail messages are generated based on the setting of the **ip inspect audit trail** command.

- **timeout** *seconds* (Optional.)—Specifies the number of seconds for a different idle timeout to override the global TCP or UDP idle timeouts for the specified protocol. This timeout overrides the global TCP and UDP timeouts, but will not override the global DNS timeout.

Java Inspection Rules

Java inspection enables Java applet filtering at the firewall. Java applet filtering distinguishes between trusted and untrusted applets by relying on a list of external sites that you designate as friendly. If an applet is from a friendly site, the firewall allows the applet through. If the applet is not from a friendly site, the applet will be blocked. Alternately, you could permit applets from all sites except for sites specifically designated as hostile.

Example 5-3 shows the configuration of Java applet filtering.

Example 5-3   *The Configuration of Java Applet Filtering*

```
Router(config)# ip access-list 10 deny 172.26.26.0 0.0.0.255
Router(config)# ip access-list 10 permit 172.27.27.0 0.0.0.255
Router(config)# ip inspect name FWRULE http java-list 10 alert on audit-trail on
   timeout 300
```

NOTE   If you do not configure an ACL, but use a "placeholder" ACL in the **ip inspect name inspection-name http** command, all Java applets will be blocked.

NOTE   CBAC does not detect or block encapsulated Java applets. Therefore, Java applets that are wrapped or encapsulated, such as applets in ZIP or JAR format, are not blocked at the firewall. CBAC also does not detect or block applets that are loaded via FTP or HTTP on a nonstandard port.

The syntax for the **ip inspect name** command for Java applet filtering inspection is as follows:

```
ip inspect name inspection-name http java-list acl-num [alert {on | off}] [audit-
   trail {on | off}] [timeout seconds]
no ip inspect name inspection-name http
```

- **name** *inspection-name*—Names the set of inspection rules. If you want to add a protocol to an existing set of rules, use the same *inspection-name* as the existing set of rules.

- **http**—Specifies the HTTP protocol used.

- **java-list** *acl-num*—Specifies the ACL (name or number) to use to determine "friendly" sites. This keyword is available only for the HTTP protocol for Java applet blocking. Java blocking only works with standard ACLs.

- **alert** {**on** | **off**} (Optional.)—For each inspected protocol, the generation of alert messages can be set to on or off. If no option is selected, alerts are generated based on the setting of the **ip inspect alert-off** command.

- **audit-trail** {**on** | **off**} (Optional.)—For each inspected protocol, **audit-trail** can be set to on or off. If no option is selected, audit trail messages are generated based on the setting of the **ip inspect audit-trail** command.

- **timeout** *seconds* (Optional.)—Specifies the number of seconds for a different idle timeout to override the global TCP or UDP idle timeouts for the specified protocol. This timeout overrides the global TCP and UDP timeouts, but will not override the global DNS timeout.

RPC Applications Inspection Rules

RPC inspection enables the specification of various program numbers. You can define multiple program numbers by creating multiple entries for RPC inspection, each with a different program number. If a program number is specified, all traffic for that program number will be permitted. If a program number is not specified, all traffic for that program number will be blocked. For example, if you create an RPC entry with the NFS program number, all NFS traffic will be allowed through the firewall.

The syntax of the **ip inspect name** command for RPC applications is as follows:

```
ip inspect name inspection-name rpc program-number number [wait-time minutes]
    [alert {on | off}] [audit-trail {on | off}] [timeout seconds]
no ip inspect name inspection-name protocol
```

- *inspection-name*—Names the set of inspection rules. If you want to add a protocol to an existing set of rules, use the same *inspection-name* as the existing set of rules.

- **rpc program_number** *number*—Specifies the program number to permit.

- **wait-time** *minutes* (Optional.)—Specifies the number of minutes to keep the connection opened in the firewall, even after the application terminates, allowing subsequent connections from the same source address and to the same destination address and port. The default **wait-time** is zero minutes.

- **alert {on | off}** (Optional.)—For each inspected protocol, the generation of alert messages can be set to on or off. If no option is selected, alerts are generated based on the setting of the **ip inspect alert-off** command.

- **audit-trail {on | off}** (Optional.)—For each inspected protocol, **audit-trail** can be set to on or off. If no option is selected, audit trail messages are generated based on the setting of the **ip inspect audit-trail** command.

- **timeout** *seconds* (Optional.)—Specifies the number of seconds for a different idle timeout to override the global TCP or UDP idle timeouts for the specified protocol. This timeout overrides the global TCP and UDP timeouts, but will not override the global DNS timeout.

SMTP Applications Inspection Rules

SMTP inspection causes SMTP commands to be inspected for illegal commands. Any packets with illegal commands are dropped, and the SMTP session hangs and eventually times out. An illegal command is any command except for the following legal commands: **data**, **expn**, **helo**, **help**, **mail**, **noop**, **quit**, **rcpt**, **rset**, **saml**, **send**, **soml**, and **vrfy**. If SMTP inspection is disabled, all SMTP commands are allowed through the firewall and potential mail server vulnerabilities are exposed.

The syntax for the **ip inspect name** command for SMTP application inspection is as follows:

```
ip inspect name inspection-name smtp [alert {on | off}] [audit-trail {on | off}]
    [timeout seconds]
no ip inspect name inspection-name smtp
```

- **name** *inspection-name*—Names the set of inspection rules. If you want to add a protocol to an existing set of rules, use the same *inspection-name* as the existing set of rules.

- **smtp**—Specifies the SMTP protocol for inspection.

- **alert** {**on** | **off**} (Optional.)—For each inspected protocol, the generation of alert messages can be set to on or off. If no option is selected, alerts are generated based on the setting of the **ip inspect alert-off** command.

- **audit-trail** {**on** | **off**} (Optional.)—For each inspected protocol, **audit-trail** can be set to on or off. If no option is selected, audit trail messages are generated based on the setting of the **ip inspect audit-trail** command.

- **timeout** *seconds* (Optional.)—Specifies the number of seconds for a different idle timeout to override the global TCP or UDP idle timeouts for the specified protocol. This timeout overrides the global TCP and UDP timeouts, but will not override the global DNS timeout.

IP Packet Fragmentation Inspection Rules

CBAC inspection rules can help protect hosts against certain DoS attacks involving fragmented IP packets. Even though the firewall keeps an attacker from making actual connections to a given host, the attacker may still be able to disrupt services provided by that host. This is done by sending many noninitial IP fragments, or by sending complete fragmented packets through a router with an ACL that filters the first fragment of a fragmented packet. These fragments can tie up resources on the target host as it tries to reassemble the incomplete packets.

Using fragmentation inspection, the firewall maintains an interfragment state (structure) for IP traffic. Noninitial fragments are discarded unless the corresponding initial fragment was permitted to pass through the firewall. Noninitial fragments received before the corresponding initial fragments are discarded.

NOTE   Fragmentation inspection can have undesirable effects in certain cases, because it can result in the firewall discarding any packet whose fragments arrive out of order. There are many circumstances that can cause out-of-order delivery of legitimate fragments. Apply fragmentation inspection in situations where legitimate fragments, which are likely to arrive out of order, might have a severe performance impact.

Because routers that are running Cisco IOS software are used in a very large variety of networks, and because the CBAC feature is often used to isolate parts of internal networks from one another, the fragmentation inspection feature is not enabled by default. Fragmentation detection must be explicitly enabled for an inspection rule using the **ip inspect name** (global) command. Unfragmented traffic is never discarded because it lacks a fragment state. Even when the system is under heavy attack with fragmented packets, legitimate fragmented traffic, if any, will still get some fraction of the firewall's fragment state resources, and legitimate, unfragmented traffic can flow through the firewall unimpeded.

The syntax of the **ip inspect name** command for IP packet fragmentation is as follows:

```
ip inspect name inspection-name fragment max number timeout seconds
no ip inspect name inspection-name fragment
```

- *inspection-name*—Names the set of inspection rules. If you want to add a protocol to an existing set of rules, use the same **inspection-name** as the existing set of rules.

- **fragment**—Specifies fragment inspection for the named rule.

- **max** *number*—Specifies the maximum number of unassembled packets for which state information (structures) is allocated by the software. Unassembled packets are packets that arrive at the router interface before the initial packet for a session. The acceptable range is 50 to 10000. The default is 256 state entries.

  Memory is allocated for the state structures, and setting this value to a larger number may cause memory resources to be exhausted.

- **timeout** *seconds*—Configures the number of seconds that a packet state structure remains active. When the timeout value expires, the router drops the unassembled packet, freeing that structure for use by another packet. The default timeout value is 1 second.

  If this number is set to a value greater than 1 second, it will be automatically adjusted by the software when the number of free state structures goes below certain thresholds: when the number of free states is less than 32, the timeout will be divided by 2; when the number of free states is less than 16, the timeout will be set to 1 second.

Router Interface Inspection Rules and ACLs

This section discusses the application of inspection rules and ACLs to router interfaces.

Use the **ip inspect** interface configuration command to apply a set of inspection rules to an interface. Use the **no** form of this command to remove the set of rules from the interface. The following example shows the application of inspection rule FWRULE to interface e0/0:

```
Router(config)# interface e0/0
Router(config-if)# ip inspect FWRULE in
```

The syntax for the **ip inspect** command is as follows:

```
ip inspect inspection-name {in | out }
no ip inspect inspection-name {in | out}
```

- *inspection-name*—Names the set of inspection rules.

- **in**—Applies the inspection rules to inbound traffic.

- **out**—Applies the inspection rules to outbound traffic.

Rules for Applying Inspection Rules and ACLs

For the Cisco IOS Firewall to be effective, both inspection rules and ACLs must be strategically applied to all the router's interfaces. The following is the general rule of thumb for applying inspection rules and ACLs on the router:

- On the interface where traffic initiates:
  - Apply the ACL on the inward direction that only permits wanted traffic.
  - Apply the rule on the inward direction that inspects wanted traffic.
- On all other interfaces, apply the ACL on the inward direction that denies all traffic, except traffic (such as ICMP) that is not inspected by CBAC.

Two-Interface Firewall Example

As an example, configure the router to be a firewall between two networks: inside and outside, as shown in Figure 5-3. The following is the security policy to implement:

- For traffic initiated on the inside (outbound):
  - Allow all general TCP and UDP traffic that is initiated on the inside (outbound) from network 10.0.0.0 to access the Internet.
  - Allow ICMP traffic from network 10.0.0.0.
  - Deny other networks on the inside that are not defined.
- For traffic initiated on the outside (inbound):
  - Allow everyone to access only ICMP and HTTP to host 10.0.0.3.
  - Deny any other traffic.

Outbound Traffic

Complete the following steps to implement the security policy of the previous example for outbound traffic on interface Ethernet 0/0 of Figure 5-4:

Step 1   Write a rule to inspect TCP and UDP traffic:

```
Router(config)# ip inspect name OUTBOUND tcp
Router(config)# ip inspect name OUTBOUND udp
```

Step 2   Write an ACL that permits IP traffic from the 10.0.0.0 network to any destination:

```
Router(config)# access-list 101 permit ip 10.0.0.0 0.0.0.255 any
Router(config)# access-list 101 deny ip any any
```

Step 3   Apply the inspection rule and ACL to the inside interface on the inward direction:

```
Router(config)# interface e0/0
Router(config-if)# ip inspect OUTBOUND in
Router(config-if)# ip access-group 101 in
```

Figure 5-3   *Two-Interface Firewall*

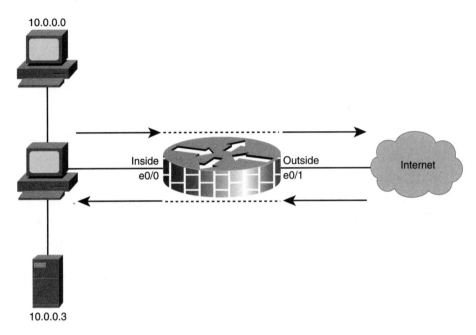

Figure 5-4   *Outbound Traffic*

Inbound Traffic

Complete the following steps to implement the security policy of the previous example for inbound traffic on interface Ethernet 0/1 of Figure 5-5:

Step 1   Write an ACL that permits ICMP- and HTTP-only traffic from the Internet to the 10.0.0.3 host:

```
Router(config)# access-list 102 permit icmp any host 10.0.0.3
Router(config)# access-list 102 permit tcp any host 10.0.0.3 eq www
Router(config)# access-list 102 deny ip any any
```

Step 2   Apply the inspection rule and ACL to the outside interface in the inward direction:

```
Router(config)# interface e0/1
Router(config-if)# ip inspect OUTBOUND in
Router(config-if)# ip access-group 102 in
```

Figure 5-5 *Inbound Traffic*

Three-Interface Firewall Example

As an example, configure the router to be a firewall between three networks, inside, outside, and DMZ, as shown in Figure 5-6. The following is the security policy to implement:

- For traffic initiated on the inside (outbound):

  - Allow all general TCP and UDP traffic initiated on the inside (outbound) from network 10.0.0.0 to access the Internet and the DMZ host 172.16.0.2.

  - ICMP traffic will also be allowed from the same network to the Internet and the DMZ host.

  - Other networks on the inside, which are not defined, must be denied.

- For traffic initiated on the outside (inbound):

  - Allow everyone to access only ICMP and HTTP to host 172.16.0.2.

  - Deny any other traffic.

Figure 5-6 *Three-Interface Firewall*

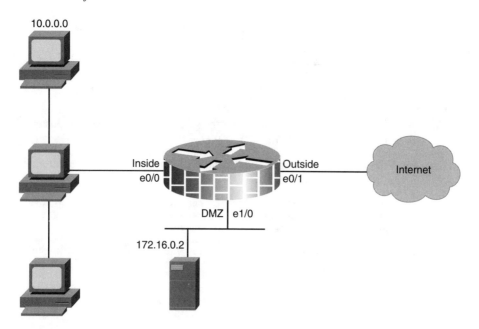

Outbound Traffic

Complete the following steps to implement the security policy of the previous example for outbound traffic on interface Ethernet 0/0 of Figure 5-7:

Step 1   Write a rule to inspect TCP and UDP traffic:

```
Router(config)# ip inspect name OUTBOUND tcp
Router(config)# ip inspect name OUTBOUND udp
```

Step 2   Write an ACL that permits IP traffic from the 10.0.0.0 network to any destination:

```
Router(config)# access-list 101 permit ip 10.0.0.0 0.0.0.255 any
Router(config)# access-list 101 deny ip any any
```

Step 3   Apply the inspection rule and ACL to the inside interface in the inward direction:

```
Router(config)# interface e0/0
Router(config-if)# ip inspect OUTBOUND in
Router(config-if)# ip access-group 101 in
```

Figure 5-7   *Configuring Inbound and Outbound Traffic*

Inbound Traffic

Complete the following steps to implement the security policy of the previous example for inbound traffic on interface Ethernet 0/1 of Figure 5-7:

Step 1   Write a rule to inspect TCP traffic:

```
Router(config)# ip inspect name INBOUND tcp
```

Step 2   Write an ACL that permits ICMP- and HTTP-only traffic from the Internet to the 172.16.0.2 host:

```
Router(config)# access-list 102 permit icmp any host 172.16.0.2
Router(config)# access-list 102 permit tcp any host 172.16.0.2 eq www
Router(config)# access-list 102 deny ip any any
```

Step 3   Apply the inspection rule and ACL to the outside interface in the inward direction:

```
Router(config)# interface e0/1
Router(config-if)# ip inspect INBOUND in
Router(config-if)# ip access-group 102 in
```

DMZ-Bound Traffic

Complete the following steps to implement the security policy of the previous example for inbound traffic on interface Ethernet 1/0 of Figure 5-7:

Step 1 Write an ACL to permit only ICMP traffic to initiate from the DMZ host:

```
Router(config)# access-list 103 permit icmp host 172.16.0.2 any
Router(config)# access-list 103 deny ip any any
```

Step 2 Write an ACL that permits ICMP- and HTTP-only traffic from any network to the 172.16.0.2 host:

```
Router(config)# access-list 104 permit icmp any host 172.16.0.2
Router(config)# access-list 104 permit tcp any host 172.16.0.2 eq www
Router(config)# access-list 104 deny ip any any
```

Step 3 Apply the ACLs to the DMZ interface:

```
Router(config)# interface e1/0
Router(config-if)# ip access-group 103 in
Router(config-if)# ip access-group 104 out
```

Testing and Verifying CBAC

This section discusses the commands available to help test and verify CBAC.

show Commands

Example 5-4 shows how you can use the **show ip inspect** command to view session information.

Example 5-4 *Use the* **show ip inspect** *Command to View Session Information*

```
Router# sh ip inspect session
Established Sessions
 Session 6155930C (10.0.0.3:35009)=>(172.30.0.50:34233) tcp SIS_OPEN
 Session 6156F0CC (10.0.0.3:35011)=>(172.30.0.50:34234) tcp SIS_OPEN
 Session 6156AF74 (10.0.0.3:35010)=>(172.30.0.50:5002) tcp SIS_OPEN
```

The **show ip inspect** command has other options as well, including the option to show the complete CBAC inspection configuration. The syntax for the **show ip inspect** command is as follows:

```
show ip inspect name inspection-name | config | interfaces | session [detail] | all
```

- *inspection-name*—Shows the configured **inspection rule** for *inspection-name*.

- **config**—Shows the complete CBAC inspection configuration.

- **interfaces**—Shows interface configuration with respect to applied inspection rules and ACLs.

- **session [detail]**—Shows existing sessions that are currently being tracked and inspected by CBAC. The optional **detail** keyword shows additional details about these sessions.

- **all**—Shows the complete CBAC configuration and all existing sessions that are currently being tracked and inspected by CBAC.

debug Commands

Use the **debug ip inspect** EXEC command to display messages about CBAC events. The **no** form of this command disables debugging output.

The syntax for the **debug ip inspect** command is as follows:

```
debug ip inspect {function-trace | object-creation | object-deletion | events |
   timers |protocol | detailed}
no debug ip inspect
```

- **function-trace**—Displays messages about software functions called by CBAC.

- **object-creation**—Displays messages about software objects being created by CBAC. Object creation corresponds to the beginning of CBAC-inspected sessions.

- **object-deletion**—Displays messages about software objects being deleted by CBAC. Object deletion corresponds to the closing of CBAC-inspected sessions.

- **events**—Displays messages about CBAC software events, including information about CBAC packet processing.

- **timers**—Displays messages about CBAC timer events, such as when a CBAC idle timeout is reached.

- *protocol*—Displays messages about CBAC-inspected protocol events, including details about the protocol's packets. Allowable protocol keywords include: **icmp, tcp, udp, cuseeme, ftp-cmd, ftp-tokens, h323, http, netshow, realaudio, rpc, rtsp, sip, smtp, skinny, sqlnet, streamworks, tftp, rcmd**, and **vdolive**.

- **detailed**—Use this form of the command in conjunction with other CBAC debugging commands. This displays detailed information for all other enabled CBAC debugging.

Removing CBAC Configuration

Use the **no ip inspect** command to remove the entire CBAC configuration, reset all global timeouts and thresholds to their defaults, delete all existing sessions, and remove all associated dynamic ACLs. This command has no other arguments, keywords, default behavior, or values.

Chapter Summary

The Cisco IOS Firewall feature set is a suite of features for Cisco IOS routers that provides network protection on multiple levels using the following:

- **Context-Based Access Control**—The Cisco IOS Firewall CBAC engine provides secure, per-application access control across network perimeters. CBAC protects networks by controlling access through a Cisco router and protecting against DoS attacks.

- **Authentication proxy**—Network administrators can create specific security policies for each user with Cisco IOS Firewall LAN-based, dynamic, per-user authentication and authorization.

- **Intrusion detection**—Cisco IOS Firewall intrusion detection systems (IDSs) provide a level of protection beyond the firewall by protecting the network from internal and external attacks and threats.

CBAC intelligently filters TCP and UDP packets based on application layer protocol session information. Working with TCP and UDP packets, CBAC has the following characteristics:

- Packets are inspected entering the firewall by CBAC if they are not specifically denied by an ACL.

- CBAC permits or denies specified TCP and UDP traffic through a firewall.

- A state table is maintained with session information.

- ACLs are dynamically created or deleted.

- CBAC protects against DoS attacks.

CBAC inspection recognizes application-specific commands in the control channel, and detects and prevents certain application-level attacks. CBAC uses timeout and threshold values to manage session state information, helping to determine when to drop sessions that do not become fully established.

A state table maintains session state information. Whenever a packet is inspected, a state table is updated to include information about the state of the packet's connection. CBAC also generates real-time alerts and audit trails based on events tracked by the firewall.

You can configure CBAC to inspect the following types of sessions:

- All TCP sessions, regardless of the application layer protocol (sometimes called single-channel or generic TCP inspection)

- All UDP sessions, regardless of the application layer protocol (sometimes called single-channel or generic UDP inspection)

You can also configure CBAC to specifically inspect certain application layer protocols, including RPC, FTP, TFTP, SMTP, and HTTP, to name a few.

The Cisco IOS Firewall authentication proxy feature enables network administrators to apply specific security policies on a per-user basis. Now, users can be identified and authorized on the basis of the per-user policy, and access privileges that are tailored on an individual basis are possible, as opposed to general policy applied across multiple users.

The Cisco IOS Firewall's IDS identifies nearly 100 common attacks by using signatures to detect patterns of misuse in network traffic.

The intrusion detection support permits Cisco IOS Firewalls to perform the following functions:

- Act as an inline intrusion detection sensor
- Perform any of the following configurable actions when a packet or packets match a signature:
  - **Alarm**—Send an alarm to a Cisco Secure IDS Director or syslog server
  - **Drop**—Drop the packet
  - **Reset**—Send TCP resets to terminate the session
- Identify nearly 100 common attacks

Cisco IOS Commands Presented in This Chapter

Many Cisco IOS version 12.3 commands were discussed or referenced in this chapter. These commands can be found in the *Command Reference* online at http://www.cisco.com/univercd/cc/td/doc/product/software/ios123/123mindx/crgindx.htm.

Chapter Review Questions

The following review questions cover some of the key facts and concepts that were introduced in this chapter. Answers to these questions can be found in Appendix A, "Answers to Chapter Review Questions."

1 What three features does the Cisco IOS Firewall feature set add to Cisco IOS routers to provide network protection on multiple levels?

2 What is the key feature of CBAC?

3 What is the key feature of the Cisco IOS Firewall authentication proxy?

4 When the Cisco IOS Firewall IDS detects a signature match on a packet, what are the three configurable actions that can be taken?

5 CBAC guards against DoS attacks by keeping track of which three thresholds?

6 How does CBAC keep track of session information?

7 List six application layer protocols that can be configured for CBAC.

8 What device does CBAC use to control the flow of allowable session traffic through an interface?

9 What six basic tasks are required to configure CBAC on a Cisco IOS Firewall router?

10 What command would you use to specify how long the software will wait for a TCP session to reach the established state before dropping the session?

11 You want to specify the number of allowable half-opened sessions that your Cisco IOS Firewall router will maintain before it begins to drop sessions at 350 half-opened sessions. What command would you use to accomplish this requirement?

12 What command would you use to define a set of CBAC inspection rules on a Cisco IOS Firewall?

Case Study

The Future Corporation's network structure is shown in Figure 5-8.

Figure 5-8 *The Future Corporation*

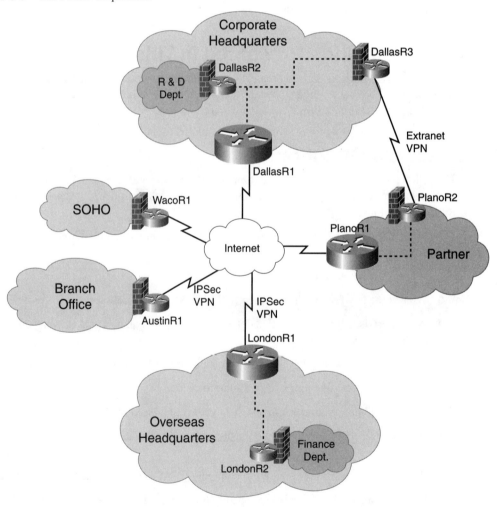

The public and private interface IP addresses are shown in Table 5-2. Remember that RFC 1597 IP address are not routed across the public network.

Table 5-2   *The Future Corporation IP Addresses*

Router	Public Interface	IP Address/Mask	Private Interface	IP Address/Mask
DallasR1	S3/0	203.14.17.1/24	FE4/0	172.16.10.1/24
DallasR2	FE0/0	172.16.10.2/24	FE0/1	192.168.10.1/24
DallasR3	S1/0	207.118.14.30/24	FE0/0	172.16.10.3/24
WacoR1	S1/0	193.122.19.82/24	FE0/0	192.168.20.1/24
AustinR1	S1/0	195.147.231.47/24	FE0/0	192.168.30.1/24
LondonR1	S1/0	205.18.26.34/24	FE0/0	172.16.20.1/24
LondonR2	FE0/0	172.16.20.2/24	FE0/1	192.168.40.1/24
PlanoR1	S1/0	202.24.38.14/24	FE0/0	172.16.10.1/24
PlanoR2	S1/0	207.118.14.35/24	FE0/0	172.16.10.2/24

The DNS server for The Future Corporation is located at the Dallas corporate headquarters with a public NAT IP address of 203.14.17.13. The syslog server is located on the same subnet with an IP address of 203.14.17.32.

Scenario

Using the information from Figure 5-8 and Table 5-2, show the commands that you would use when configuring router AustinR1 for the following common requirements:

1 Turn on logging and enable audit trail and alert to provide a record of network access through the firewall.

2 Configure CBAC to wait 45 seconds for a TCP session to reach the established state before dropping the session.

3 Configure CBAC to manage TCP sessions for 7 seconds after the firewall detects a FIN exchange.

4 Configure CBAC to manage TCP sessions for 50 minutes after no activity.

5 Configure CBAC to manage UDP sessions for 40 seconds after no activity.

6 Configure CBAC to manage a DNS name lookup session for 10 seconds after no activity.

7 Configure CBAC to permit 600 existing half-opened sessions before starting to delete half-opened sessions.

8 Configure CBAC to stop deleting half-opened sessions when the number of existing half-opened sessions reaches 350.

9 Configure CBAC to start deleting half-opened sessions when the number of new unestablished TCP sessions reaches 450.

10 Configure CBAC to stop deleting half-opened sessions when the number of new unestablished TCP sessions reaches 350.

Solutions

1 Turn on logging and enable audit trail and alert:

```
AustinR1(config)# logging on
AustinR1(config)# logging 203.14.17.32
AustinR1(config)# ip inspect audit-trail
AustinR1(config)# no ip inspect alert-off
```

2 Configure CBAC to wait 45 seconds for a TCP session to reach the established state before dropping the session:

```
AustinR1(config)# ip inspect tcp synwait-time 45
```

3 Configure CBAC to manage TCP sessions for 7 seconds after the firewall detects a FIN exchange:

```
AustinR1(config)# ip inspect tcp finwait-time 7
```

4 Configure CBAC to manage TCP sessions for 50 minutes after no activity:

```
AustinR1(config)# ip inspect tcp idle-time 3000
```

5 Configure CBAC to manage UDP sessions for 40 seconds after no activity:

```
AustinR1(config)# ip inspect udp idle-time 40
```

6 Configure CBAC to manage a DNS name lookup session for 10 seconds after no activity.

```
AustinR1(config)# ip inspect dns-timeout 10
```

7 Configure CBAC to permit 600 existing half-opened sessions before starting to delete half-opened sessions:

```
AustinR1(config)# ip inspect max-incomplete high 600
```

8 Configure CBAC to stop deleting half-opened sessions when the number of half-opened sessions reaches 350:

```
AustinR1(config)# ip inspect max-incomplete low 350
```

9 Configure CBAC to start deleting half-opened sessions when the number of new unestablished TCP sessions reaches 450:

```
AustinR1(config)# ip inspect one-minute high 450
```

10 Configure CBAC to stop deleting half-opened sessions when the number of new unestablished TCP sessions reaches 350:

```
AustinR1(config)# ip inspect one-minute low 350
```

Upon completion of this chapter, you will be able to perform the following tasks:

- Define an Authentication Proxy
- Describe How Users Authenticate to a Cisco IOS Firewall
- Describe How Authentication Proxy Technology Works
- Name the AAA Protocols Supported by the Cisco IOS Firewall
- Configure AAA on a Cisco IOS Firewall

CHAPTER 6

Cisco IOS Firewall Authentication Proxy

Trust is the defining element for most security requirements. As an administrator, you permit access for those you trust and deny access for those you distrust. It would be best if you could choose to trust authenticated individuals, but Cisco IOS access control lists permit or deny network access based on network or host addresses, not by individual user identity.

The Cisco IOS Firewall authentication proxy feature now gives you a tool to assign trust to authenticated individuals. This capability gives you much more control at the router to manage access to your network assets. This chapter includes the following topics:

- Introduction to the Cisco IOS Firewall authentication proxy
- Configuring the AAA server
- Configuring the Cisco IOS Firewall with an AAA server
- Configuring the authentication proxy
- Testing and verifying the configuration

Introduction to the Cisco IOS Firewall Authentication Proxy

This section introduces the Cisco IOS Firewall authentication proxy and describes the process of initiating an HTTP, HTTPS, FTP, or Telnet session with authentication proxy. Additional topics in this section include a discussion of the authentication proxy process, supported AAA protocols and servers, and applying and configuring the authentication proxy.

Defining the Authentication Proxy

The Cisco IOS Firewall authentication proxy feature enables network administrators to apply specific security policies on a per-user basis. Previously, user identity and related authorized access were associated with a user's IP address, or a single security policy had to be applied to an entire user group or subnet. Now, users can be identified and authorized on the basis of their per-user policy, and access privileges can be tailored on an individual basis, as opposed to a general policy applied across multiple users.

With the authentication proxy feature, users can log in to the network or access the Internet via HTTP, HTTPS, FTP, or Telnet and their specific access profiles are automatically retrieved and applied from a Cisco Secure Access Control Server (CSACS), or other RADIUS or TACACS+ authentication server. The user profiles are active only when there is active traffic from the authenticated users.

The authentication proxy is compatible with other Cisco IOS security features, such as Network Address Translation (NAT), Context-Based Access Control (CBAC), IPSec encryption, and Cisco VPN Client. NAT protects private addresses from reaching the public network, but it must be used in conjunction with CBAC to support the authentication proxy. CBAC ensures that the original host address is associated with the translated address for the session. Using the authentication proxy with IPSec provides another layer of security and access control.

Cisco IOS Release 12.3 Firewall authentication proxy has the following characteristics:

- HTTP, HTTPS, FTP, and Telnet-based authentication to retrieve a username and password from the user. HTTPS uses Secure Sockets Layer (SSL) to ensure the confidentiality of user information that is passing between the router and the client.

- Dynamic, per-user authentication and authorization via TACACS+ and RADIUS protocols, permitting administrator's authorization control at the individual level.

- Valid for all types of application traffic once authentication occurs. Individual authorization rules determine whether or not the traffic is allowable.

- Works on any interface type for inbound or outbound traffic to provide authentication services for clients that are internal or external to the router.

Supported AAA Protocols and Servers

The Cisco IOS Firewall authentication proxy supports the following AAA protocols and servers:

- TACACS+
  - Cisco Secure ACS for Windows 2000/NT Server (Cisco Secure ACS for Windows)
  - Cisco Secure ACS for UNIX
  - TACACS+ Freeware
- RADIUS
  - Cisco Secure ACS for Windows
  - Cisco Secure ACS for UNIX
  - Lucent Technologies Ascend RADIUS Server
  - Lucent Technologies Livingston RADIUS Server
  - Other standard RADIUS servers

Initiating a Session

When a user initiates an HTTP, HTTPS, FTP, or Telnet session through the firewall, it triggers the authentication proxy. The authentication proxy first checks to see if the user has been authenticated. If a valid authentication entry exists for the user, the session is allowed and the authentication proxy requires no further intervention.

If no entry exists, the authentication proxy responds to the HTTP connection request by prompting the user for a username and password, as shown in Figure 6-1.

Figure 6-1   *User Login*

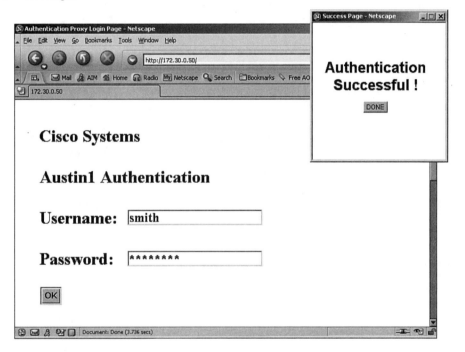

Operation with JavaScript

Users should enable JavaScript on the browser prior to initiating an HTTP connection. With JavaScript enabled on the browser, secure authentication is done automatically, and the user sees the authentication message shown in Figure 6-1. The HTTP connection is completed automatically for the user.

Operation Without JavaScript

You can use the authentication proxy without enabling JavaScript on the browser, but this poses a potential security risk if users do not properly establish network connections. If the client browser does not support JavaScript, or if site security policy prevents users from enabling JavaScript, any login attempt generates a popup window with instructions for manually completing the connection as follows:

WARNING JavaScript should be enabled in your web browser for secure authentication.

- Follow the instructions of your web browser to enable JavaScript if you would like to have JavaScript enabled for secure authentication.

OR

- Follow these steps if you want to keep JavaScript disabled or if your browser does not support JavaScript:

  1 Close this web browser window.

  2 Click the **Reload** button of the original web browser window.

After closing the popup window, the user should click Reload (Refresh for Microsoft Internet Explorer) on the browser window in which the authentication login page is displayed. If the user's last authentication attempt succeeds, clicking Reload brings up the web page that the user is trying to retrieve. If the user's last attempt fails, clicking Reload causes the authentication proxy to intercept the client HTTP traffic again, prompting the user with another login page that solicits the user's username and password.

Authentication Proxy Process

Users must successfully authenticate with the authentication server by entering a valid username and password. If the authentication succeeds, the user's authorization profile is retrieved from the authentication, authorization, and accounting (AAA) server. The authentication proxy uses the information in this profile to create dynamic access control entries (ACEs) and add them to the inbound (input) access control list (ACL) of an input interface, and to the outbound (output) ACL of an output interface if an output ACL exists at the interface. By doing this, the firewall allows authenticated users access to the network as permitted by the authorization profile. For example, a user can initiate a Telnet connection through the firewall if Telnet is permitted in the user's profile.

If the authentication fails, the authentication proxy reports the failure to the user and prompts the user with multiple retries. If the user fails to authenticate after five attempts, the user must wait 2 minutes and initiate another session to trigger the authentication proxy.

The authentication proxy sets up an inactivity (idle) timer for each user profile. As long as there is activity through the firewall, new traffic initiated from the user's host does not trigger the authentication proxy, and all authorized user traffic is permitted access through the firewall.

If the idle timer expires, the authentication proxy removes the user's profile information and dynamic ACL entries. When this happens, traffic from the client host is blocked. The user must initiate another connection to trigger the authentication proxy. The authentication proxy process is shown in Figure 6-2.

Figure 6-2   *Authentication Proxy Process*

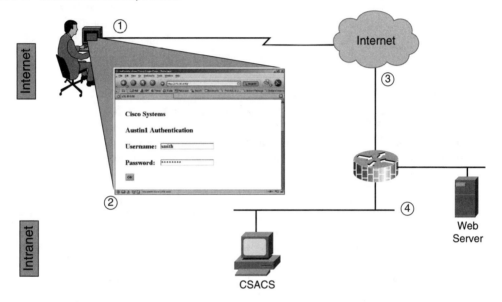

The operation of the authentication proxy includes the following steps:

1   The proxy intercepts the client's HTTP, HTTPS, FTP, or Telnet request before any ACLs. For HTTP and HTTPS traffic, the proxy saves the target URL.

2   The proxy replies to the client and asks the user to enter their username and password (and remote username and password in the case of FTP).

3   The proxy authenticates the username and password with the AAA server, downloads the authorization profile, and creates dynamic ACLs.

4   For HTTP or HTTPS, the proxy refreshes the client's browser with the saved target URL. For FTP, the proxy connects with the target server and presents the remote username and password to the server. For Telnet, the proxy connects with the target server and acts as the proxy for the authentication process to the Telnet server.

For FTP login, the client host will be prompted (by the authentication proxy router) for the username and password of the router; the client must respond with the username and password in the following format: "login: *proxy_username@ftp_username*" and "password: *proxy_passwd@ftp_passwd*:". The authentication proxy will use the proxy username and password to verify the client's profile against the AAA server's user database. After the client is successfully authenticated with the AAA server, the authentication proxy will pass the FTP (remote) username and password to the FTP server (destination server) for the application server authentication.

For Telnet login, the client host will be prompted (by the authentication proxy router) for the username, followed by the password; the client must respond with the username and password in the following format: "login: *proxy_username*:" and "password: *proxy_passwd*):". The username and password will be verified against the AAA server's user database. After the client is successfully authenticated with the AAA server, the Telnet server (destination server) will prompt the client for the username and password of the Telnet server.

Applying the Authentication Proxy

Apply the authentication proxy in the inward direction at any interface on the router where you want per-user authentication and authorization. Applying the authentication proxy inward at an interface causes it to intercept a user's initial connection request before that request is subjected to any other processing by the firewall. If the user fails to authenticate with the AAA server, the connection request is dropped.

How you apply the authentication proxy depends on your security policy. For example, you can block all traffic through an interface, and enable the authentication proxy feature to require authentication and authorization for all user-initiated HTTP, HTTPS, FTP, or Telnet connections. Users are authorized for services only after successful authentication with the AAA server. The authentication proxy feature also enables you to use standard ACLs to specify a host or group of hosts whose initial HTTP, HTTPS, FTP, or Telnet traffic triggers the proxy.

Figure 6-3 shows how you might apply the Cisco IOS Firewall authentication proxy on inside and outside interfaces.

Figure 6-3 *Authentication Proxy Configuration*

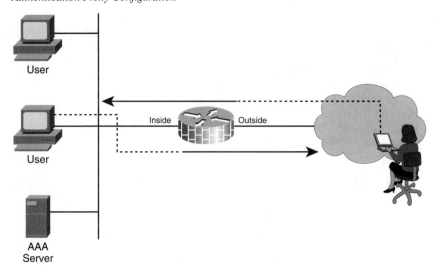

Configuring the Authentication Proxy

You can configure the Cisco IOS Firewall authentication proxy on inside and outside interfaces.

- Inside:
  - Typical uses include:
    - Manage local user privileges on an individual basis.
    - Authenticate and authorize local users who want access to Internet or intranet services.
    - Generate AAA accounting "start" and "stop" records for billing, security, or resource allocation.
  - Add an ACL to block inward traffic from the inside, except from the AAA server.
  - Outbound—Enable the authentication proxy to intercept inward HTTP, HTTPS, FTP, or Telnet traffic from the inside.
- Outside:
  - Typical uses include:
    - Manage remote user privileges on an individual basis.
    - Authenticate and authorize remote users who want access to Internet or intranet services.
    - Control access for special extranet users, giving them VIP status.
    - Use the authentication proxy with VPN clients to provide another layer of security.
  - Add an ACL to block inward traffic from the outside. Inbound—Enable the authentication proxy to intercept inward HTTP, HTTPS, FTP, or Telnet traffic from the outside.

You can configure the authentication proxy by following these steps:

Step 1 Configure the AAA server.

Step 2 Configure AAA on the router:
  - Enable AAA.
  - Specify AAA protocols.
  - Define AAA servers.
  - Allow AAA traffic.
  - Enable the router's HTTP server for AAA.

Step 3 Authenticate the proxy configuration on the router:
  - Set the default idle time.
  - Create and apply the authentication proxy rules.

Step 4   Verify the configuration.

These steps are fully described in the following sections.

Configuring the AAA Server

This section discusses how to configure the AAA server to provide authentication and authorization for the Cisco IOS Firewall authorization proxy.

Creating the auth-proxy Service on the Cisco Secure ACS

To support the authentication proxy, configure the AAA authentication proxy authorization service on the AAA server. This creates a new section in the Group Setup frame in which user profiles can be created. This does not interfere with other types of services that the AAA server may have. The Cisco Secure ACS interface configuration is shown in Figure 6-4.

Figure 6-4   *Cisco Secure ACS—Interface Configuration*

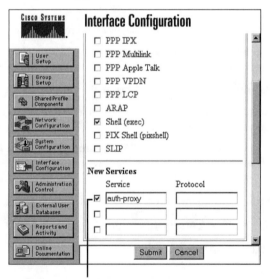

Enter the new service: auth-proxy.

Complete the following steps to add authorization rules for specific services in the Cisco Secure ACS:

Step 1   In the navigation bar, click **Interface Configuration**. The Interface Configuration frame opens.

Step 2   Click TACACS+ (Cisco IOS).

Step 3   Scroll down in the TACACS+ Services frame until you find the New Services group box.

Step 4   Select the check box closest to the Service field.

NOTE   Depending on what options your Cisco Secure ACS is running, there may be one or two check boxes in front of the Service fields. Make sure that you select the check box closest to the Service field (group column) and not the left check box (user column). If there is only one check box, then select it (as shown in Figure 6-4).

Step 5   Enter **auth-proxy** in the first empty Service field next to the check box you just selected.

NOTE   Cisco uses the term **auth-proxy** when configuring authentication proxy services or settings on the Cisco Secure ACS and Cisco IOS routers. Other ACS vendors may use different terminology.

Step 6   Click **Submit** when you are finished.

Creating User Authorization Profiles in the Cisco Secure ACS

Most ACS servers permit administrators to set up AAA for groups and individuals. A default group is typically set up first and all other groups inherit its properties, which can be modified to suit the requirements of the new group. After the groups have been created, individual accounts are established and can be associated with specific groups.

The Cisco Secure ACS server handles groups in this manner. Figure 6-5 shows the TACACS+ section of the group setup.

Follow these steps to complete the configuration of the authentication proxy:

Step 1   In the navigation bar, click **Group Setup**. The Group Setup frame opens.

Step 2   Choose your group from the drop-down list and click **Edit Settings**.

Step 3   Scroll down in the Group Setup frame until you find the newly created auth-proxy service.

Step 4   Select the **auth-proxy** check box.

Step 5   Select the **Custom Attributes** check box.

Step 6   Enter ACLs in the field below the Custom Attributes check box using the format shown in the next section, "Using proxyacl#n Attribute When Creating User Authorization Profiles." These ACLs will be applied after the user authenticates.

Step 7   Enter the privilege level of the user (must be 15 for all users) using the format shown in the next section.

Step 8   Click **Submit** and then click **Restart** when finished.

Figure 6-5   *Cisco Secure ACS—Group Configuration*

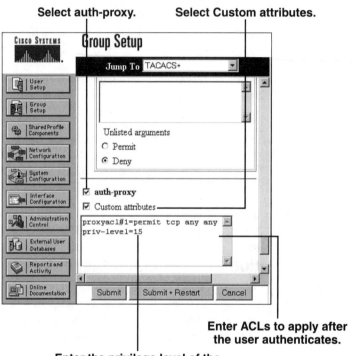

Using proxyacl#n Attribute When Creating User Authorization Profiles

Use the **proxyacl#n** attribute when you are configuring the ACLs in the profile. The **proxyacl#n** attribute is for both RADIUS and TACACS+ attribute-value pairs. The ACLs in the user profile on the AAA server must have **permit** access commands only. Set the source address to **any** in each of the user profile ACL entries. The source address in the ACLs is replaced with the source IP address of the host that is making the authentication proxy request when the user profile is downloaded to the firewall.

The syntax of the ACLs used to enter in the Custom Attributes field is as follows:

```
proxyacl#n=permit protocol any any | host ip_addr | ip_addr wildcard_mask [eq
    auth_service]
```

- *protocol*—Keyword that indicates the protocol to allow users to access: **tcp**, **udp**, or **icmp**.

- **any**—Indicates any hosts. The first **any** after *protocol* is mandatory. This indicates any source IP address, which is actually replaced with the IP address of the user that requests authorization in the ACL applied in the router.
- **host** *ip_addr*—IP address of a specific host that users can access.
- *ip_addr wildcard mask*—IP address and wildcard mask for a network that users can access.
- **eq** *auth_service*—Specific service that users are allowed to access.

Use **priv-lvl=15** to configure the privilege level of the authenticated user. The privilege level must be set to 15 for all users.

Example 6-1 shows proxy ACL definitions.

Example 6-1 *Proxy ACL Definitions*

```
proxyacl#1=permit tcp  any any eq 26
proxyacl#2=permit icmp  any host 172.30.0.50
proxyacl#3=permit tcp  any any eq ftp
proxyacl#4=permit tcp  any any eq ftp-data
proxyacl#5=permit tcp  any any eq smtp
proxyacl#6=permit tcp  any any eq telnet
priv-lvl=15
```

Configuring the Cisco IOS Firewall with an AAA Server

This section discusses how to configure the Cisco IOS Firewall to work with an AAA server and enable the authentication proxy feature.

Enabling AAA

Use the **aaa new-model** global configuration command to enable the AAA access control system. Use the **no** form of this command to disable the AAA access control model.

NOTE   After you have enabled AAA, TACACS and extended TACACS commands are no longer available. If you initialize AAA functionality and later decide to use TACACS or extended TACACS, issue the **no** form of this command and then enable the version of TACACS that you want to use.

The syntax of the **aaa new-model** command is as follows:

```
aaa new-model
no aaa new-model
```

This command has no arguments.

By default, **aaa new-model** is not enabled.

Specifying Authentication Protocols

To set AAA authentication, use the **aaa authentication login** global configuration command. Use the **no** form of this command to disable AAA authentication. The following is an example of the **aaa authentication login** command:

```
Router(config)# aaa authentication login default group tacacs+ radius
```

The syntax of the **aaa authentication login** command is as follows:

```
aaa authentication login default group method1 [method2]
no aaa authentication login default group method1 [method2]
```

- *method1*, *method2*—The following are the authentication protocols to use: **tacacs+**, **radius**, or both.

Specifying Authorization Protocols

To set AAA authorization, use the **aaa authorization auth-proxy** global configuration command. Use the **no** form of this command to disable AAA authorization. Use the **auth-proxy** keyword to enable authorization proxy for AAA methods. You can choose TACACS+, RADIUS, or both as authorization methods. The following example shows a sample **aaa authorization auth-proxy** command entry:

```
Router(config)# aaa authorization auth-proxy default group tacacs+ radius
```

The syntax of the **aaa authorization auth-proxy** command is as follows:

```
aaa authorization auth-proxy default group method1 [method2]
no aaa authorization auth-proxy default group method1 [method2]
```

- *method1*, *method2*—The following are the authorization protocols to use: **tacacs+**, **radius**, or both.

Defining TACACS+ Server and Its Key

To specify the IP address of a TACACS+ server, use the **tacacs-server host** global configuration command. Use the **no** form of this command to delete the specified IP address. You can use multiple **tacacs-server host** commands to specify additional servers. The Cisco IOS Firewall software searches for servers in the order in which you specify them. The following example shows the use of the **tacacs-server host** command:

```
Router(config)# tacacs-server host 10.0.0.3
```

The syntax of the **tacacs-server host** command is as follows:

```
tacacs-server host ip_addr
no tacacs-server host ip_addr
```

- *ip_addr*—IP address of the TACACS+ server.

To set the authentication encryption key used for all TACACS+ communications between the Cisco IOS Firewall router and the AAA server, use the **tacacs-server key** global configuration command. Use the **no** form of this command to disable the key. The following example shows the use of the **tacacs-server key** command:

```
Router(config)# tacacs-server key secretkey
```

<table>
<tr><td>**NOTE**</td><td>The key entered must match the key used on the AAA server. All leading spaces are ignored; spaces within and at the end of the key are not ignored. If you use spaces in your key, do not enclose the key in quotation marks unless the quotation marks themselves are part of the key.</td></tr>
</table>

The syntax of the **tacacs-server key** command is as follows:

```
tacacs-server key string
no tacacs-server key string
```

- *string*—Key used for authentication and encryption.

Defining a RADIUS Server and Its Key

To specify the IP address of a RADIUS server, use the **radius-server host** global configuration command. Use the **no** form of this command to delete the specified IP address. You can use multiple **radius-server host** commands to specify additional servers. The Cisco IOS Firewall software searches for servers in the order in which you specify them. The following example shows the use of the **radius-server host** command:

```
Router(config)# radius-server host 10.0.0.3
```

The syntax of the **radius-server host** command is as follows:

```
radius-server host ip_addr
no radius-server host ip_addr
```

- *ip_addr*—IP address of the RADIUS server.

To set the authentication encryption key used for all RADIUS communications between the Cisco IOS Firewall router and the AAA server, use the **radius-server key** global configuration command. Use the **no** form of this command to disable the key. The following example shows the use of the **radius-server key** command:

```
Router(config)# radius-server key secretkey
```

> **NOTE**   The key entered must match the key used on the AAA server. All leading spaces are ignored; spaces within and at the end of the key are not ignored. If you use spaces in your key, do not enclose the key in quotation marks unless the quotation marks themselves are part of the key.

The syntax of the **radius-server key** command is as follows:

```
radius-server key string
no radius-server key string
```

- *string* — Key used for authentication and encryption.

Allowing AAA Traffic to the Router

At this point you need to configure and apply an ACL to permit TACACS+ and RADIUS traffic from the AAA server to the firewall.

Use the following guidelines when writing the ACL:

- The source address is the AAA server.

- The destination address is the interface where the AAA server resides.

- You may want to permit ICMP traffic to specific management servers or workstations for administrative support.

- Deny all other traffic.

- Apply the ACL to the interface on the side where the AAA server resides.

The configuration in Example 6-2 shows an ACL that permits AAA traffic to the firewall.

Example 6-2   *ACL that Permits AAA Traffic to the Firewall*

```
Router(config)# access-list 111 permit tcp host 10.0.0.3 eq tacacs host 10.0.0.1
Router(config)# access-list 111 permit udp host 10.0.0.3 eq 1645 host 10.0.0.1
Router(config)# access-list 111 permit icmp any host 10.0.19.36
Router(config)# access-list 111 deny ip any any
Router(config)# interface ethernet0/0
Router(config-if)# ip access-group 111 in
```

> **NOTE**   UDP port 1645 in the second line of this example permits RADIUS traffic between the router and the RADIUS server.

Enabling the Router's HTTP Server

To use the authentication proxy, use the **ip http server** command to enable the HTTP server on the router and use the **ip http authentication aaa** command to make the HTTP server use AAA for authentication. The following example shows the use of the **ip http server** and **ip http authentication aaa** commands:

```
Router(config)# ip http server
Router(config)# ip http authentication aaa
```

The syntax of the **ip http server** command, which has no arguments, is as follows:

```
ip http server
```

The syntax of the **ip http authentication aaa** command, which also has no arguments, is as follows:

```
ip http authentication aaa
```

You can stop there, or you can include two additional commands to enable HTTPS service. Those commands are the **ip http secure-server** command to enable HTTPS and the **ip http secure-trustpoint** command to identify the certification authority (CA). The following example shows the use of the **ip http secure-server** and the **ip http secure-trustpoint** commands:

```
Router(config)# ip http secure-server
Router(config)# ip http secure-trustpoint netCA
```

The syntax of the **ip http secure-server** command is as follows:

```
ip http secure-server
```

This command has no arguments.

The syntax of the **ip http secure-trustpoint** command is as follows:

```
ip http secure-trustpoint trustpoint-name
```

- *trustpoint-name*—Name of a configured trustpoint. Use the same trustpoint name that was used in the associated **crypto ca trustpoint command**.

Configuring the Authentication Proxy

This section discusses how to configure the authentication proxy settings on a Cisco router.

Setting Default Idle Time

To set the authentication proxy idle timeout value (the length of time an authentication cache entry, along with its associated dynamic user ACL, is managed after a period of inactivity), use the **ip auth-proxy inactivity-timer** global configuration command. To set the default value, use the **no** form of this command. The following example demonstrates the use of the **ip auth-proxy inactivity-timer** command to set the inactivity time to 50 minutes:

```
Router(config)# ip auth-proxy inactivity-timer 50
```

NOTE   Set the **inactivity-timer** option for any authentication proxy rule to a higher value than the idle timeout value for any CBAC inspection rule. When the authentication proxy removes an authentication cache along with its associated dynamic user ACL, there might be some idle connections monitored by CBAC, and removal of user-specific ACLs could cause those idle connections to hang. If CBAC has a shorter idle timeout, CBAC resets these connections when the idle timeout expires; that is, before the authentication proxy removes the user profile.

The syntax of the **ip auth-proxy inactivity-timer** command is as follows:

```
ip auth-proxy {inactivity-timer min | absolute-timer min}
no ip auth-proxy {inactivity-timer min | absolute-timer min}
```

- **inactivity-timer** *min*—Specifies the length of time in minutes that an authentication cache entry, along with its associated dynamic user ACL, is managed after a period of inactivity. Enter a value in the range 1 to 2,147,483,647. The default value is 60 minutes.

- **absolute-timer** *min*—Specifies a window in which the authentication proxy on the enabled interface is active. Enter a value in the range 1 to 65,535 minutes (45 and a half days). The default value is 0 minutes.

Defining the Optional Authentication Proxy Banner

To display a banner, such as the router name, in the authentication proxy login page, use the **ip auth-proxy auth-proxy-banner** command in global configuration mode. To disable display of the banner, use the **no** form of this command. The syntax of the **ip auth-proxy auth-proxy-banner** command is as follows:

```
ip auth-proxy auth-proxy-banner {ftp | http | telnet} [banner-text]
no ip auth-proxy auth-proxy-banner {ftp | http | telnet}
```

- *banner-text* (Optional.)—A text string that replaces the default banner.

The **ip auth-proxy auth-proxy-banner** command allows administrators to configure one of two possible solutions:

- The **ip auth-proxy auth-proxy-banner** command is enabled but no *banner-text* argument has been supplied.

  A default banner that says "Cisco Systems, *router's hostname* Authentication" will be displayed in the authentication proxy login page.

- The **ip auth-proxy auth-proxy-banner** command with the *banner-text* argument is enabled.

  In this scenario, the administrator can supply text that will be converted to HTML by the auth-proxy parser code. The supplied banner text will be displayed in the authentication proxy login page.

NOTE   If the **ip auth-proxy auth-proxy-banner** command is not enabled, there will not be any banner configuration and no banner will be displayed to the user. Simple text boxes will be displayed for the user to enter their username and password.

The following example displays the default banner with the router name in the authentication proxy login page:

```
Router(config)# ip auth-proxy auth-proxy-banner ftp
```

The following example displays the custom banner "Access to this network is for authorized users only. Please supply your username and password." in the authentication proxy login page:

```
Router(config)# ip auth-proxy auth-proxy-banner telnet #Access to this network is
    for authorized users only. Please supply your username and password.#
```

NOTE   In the last example, the # placed before and after the banner text is used to delimit the text. You can use any character you want, as long as it is not contained within the body of the banner text.

Defining and Applying Authentication Proxy Rules

To create an authentication proxy rule, use the **ip auth-proxy name** global configuration command. To remove the authentication proxy rules, use the **no** form of this command.

The syntax of the **ip auth-proxy name** command is as follows:

```
ip auth-proxy name auth-proxy-name {ftp | http | telnet} [inactivity-timer min]
[absolute-timer min] [list {acl | acl-name}]
no ip auth-proxy name auth-proxy-name
```

- *auth-proxy-name*—Associates a name with an authentication proxy rule. Enter a name of up to 16 alphanumeric characters.
- **ftp**—Specifies FTP to trigger the authentication proxy.
- **http**—Specifies HTTP to trigger the authentication proxy.
- **telnet**—Specifies Telnet to trigger the authentication proxy.
- **inactivity-timer** *min* (Optional.)—Overrides the global authentication proxy cache timer for a specific authentication proxy name, offering more control over timeout values. Enter a value in the range 1 to 2,147,483,647. The default value is equal to the value set with the **ip auth-proxy** command.
- **absolute-timer** *min* (Optional.)—Specifies a window in which the authentication proxy on the enabled interface is active. Enter a value in the range 1 to 65,535 minutes (45 and a half days). The default value is 0 minutes.

- **list** {*acl* | *acl-name*} (Optional.)—Specifies a standard (1-99), extended (1-199), or named IP access list to use with the authentication proxy. With this option, the authentication proxy is applied only to those hosts in the access list. If no list is specified, all connections initiating HTTP, FTP, or Telnet traffic arriving at the interface are subject to authentication.

To apply an authentication proxy rule at a firewall interface, use the **ip auth-proxy** interface configuration command. To remove the authentication proxy rules, use the **no** form of this command. For outbound authentication, apply the rule to the inside interface. For inbound authentication, apply the rule to the outside interface. Example 6-3 shows the use of the global **ip auth-proxy name** and interface **ip auth-proxy** commands.

Example 6-3 *Using* **ip auth-proxy name** *and* **ip auth-proxy** *Commands*

```
Router(config)# ip auth-proxy name aprule http
Router(config)# interface ethernet0
Router(config-if)# ip auth-proxy aprule
```

The syntax of the **ip auth-proxy** command is as follows:

```
ip auth-proxy auth-proxy-name
no ip auth-proxy auth-proxy-name
```

- *auth-proxy-name*—Specifies the name of the authentication proxy rule to apply to the interface configuration. The authentication proxy rule is established with the **authentication proxy name** command.

Associating Authentication Proxy Rules with ACLs

You can associate an authentication proxy rule with an ACL, providing control over which hosts use the authentication proxy. To create an authentication proxy rule with ACLs, use the **ip auth-proxy name** global configuration command with the **list** *std-acl-num* option. To remove the authentication proxy rules, use the **no** form of this command. The following examples show the use of the **ip auth-proxy name** command with an ACL list:

```
Router(config)# ip auth-proxy name aprule http list 10
Router(config)# access-list 10 permit 10.0.0.0 0.0.0.255
Router(config)# interface ethernet0
Router(config-if)# ip auth-proxy aprule
```

Testing and Verifying the Configuration

This section discusses the procedures for testing and verifying the authentication proxy configuration.

show Commands

Use the **show ip auth-proxy** command to display the authentication proxy entries, the running authentication proxy configuration, or the authentication proxy statistics.

The syntax of the **show ip auth-proxy** command is as follows:

```
show ip auth-proxy {cache | configuration}
```

- **cache**—Displays the current list of the authentication proxy entries.
- **configuration**—Displays the running authentication proxy configuration.

debug Commands

The syntax of the **debug ip auth-proxy** command is as follows:

```
debug ip auth-proxy {detailed | ftp | function-trace | http | object-creation |
    object-deletion | telnet | timers}
```

- **detailed**—Displays details of the TCP events during an authentication proxy process. The details are generic to all FTP, HTTP, and Telnet protocols.
- **ftp**—Displays FTP events related to the authentication proxy.
- **function-trace**—Displays the authentication proxy functions.
- **http**—Displays HTTP events related to the authentication proxy.
- **object-creation**—Displays additional entries to the authentication proxy cache.
- **object-deletion**—Displays deletion of cache entries for the authentication proxy.
- **telnet**—Displays Telnet-related authentication proxy events.
- **timers**—Displays authentication proxy timer-related events.

Clearing the Authentication Proxy Cache

To clear authentication proxy entries from the router, use the **clear ip auth-proxy cache** command. The syntax of the **clear ip auth-proxy cache** command is as follows:

```
clear ip auth-proxy cache {* | ip_addr}
```

- *****—Clears all authentication proxy entries, including user profiles and dynamic ACLs.
- *ip_addr*—Clears the authentication proxy entry, including user profiles and dynamic ACLs, for the specified IP address.

Chapter Summary

The Cisco IOS Firewall authentication proxy feature enables network administrators to apply specific security policies on a per-user basis. Users can be identified and authorized on the basis of their per-user policy, and access privileges can be tailored on an individual basis, as opposed to a general policy applied across multiple users.

The authentication proxy is compatible with other Cisco IOS security features, such as Network Address Translation (NAT), Context-Based Access Control (CBAC), IPSec encryption, and Cisco VPN Client.

Cisco IOS Release 12.3 Firewall authentication proxy has the following characteristics:

- HTTP, HTTPS, FTP, and Telnet-based authentication to retrieve a username and password from the user.

- Dynamic, per-user authentication and authorization via TACACS+ and RADIUS protocols.

- Valid for all types of application traffic once authentication occurs.

- Works on any interface type for inbound or outbound traffic to provide authentication services for clients that are internal or external to the router.

The Cisco IOS Firewall authentication proxy supports the following AAA protocols and servers:

- TACACS+
  - Cisco Secure ACS for Windows
  - Cisco Secure ACS for UNIX
  - TACACS+ Freeware

- RADIUS
  - Cisco Secure ACS for Windows
  - Cisco Secure ACS for UNIX
  - Lucent Technologies Ascend RADIUS Server
  - Lucent Technologies Livingston RADIUS Server
  - Other standard RADIUS servers

You can configure the authentication proxy by following these steps:

Step 1   Configure the AAA server.

Step 2   Configure AAA on the router:

- Enable AAA.
- Specify AAA protocols.
- Define AAA servers.
- Allow AAA traffic.
- Enable the router's HTTP server for AAA.

Step 3   Authenticate the proxy configuration on the router:

  — Set the default idle time.

  — Create and apply the authentication proxy rules.

Step 4   Verify the configuration.

Cisco IOS Commands Presented in This Chapter

Many Cisco IOS version 12.3 commands were discussed or referenced in this chapter. These commands can be found in the *Command Reference* online at http://www.cisco.com/univercd/cc/td/doc/product/software/ios123/123mindx/crgindx.htm.

Chapter Review Questions

The following review questions cover some of the key facts and concepts that were introduced in this chapter. Answers to these questions can be found in Appendix A, "Answers to Chapter Review Questions."

  1 What is the key feature of the Cisco IOS Firewall authentication proxy?

  2 When using the Cisco IOS Firewall authentication proxy to apply per-user policies, where are the policies for the users stored?

  3 How does a Cisco IOS Firewall apply policies from each user's profile when performing authentication proxy functions?

  4 How does the authentication proxy handle failed login attempts?

  5 What happens when the idle timer expires for a user of authentication proxy services?

  6 Which TACACS+ AAA protocols and servers does the Cisco IOS Firewall authentication proxy support?

  7 Which RADIUS AAA protocols and servers does the Cisco IOS Firewall authentication proxy support?

  8 List the tasks that are required to configure the authentication proxy.

  9 What commands would you use to enable the HTTP server service on your router and then force AAA authentication for this service?

Case Study

The Future Corporation's network structure is shown in Figure 6-6.

The public and private interface IP addresses are shown in Table 6-1. Remember that RFC 1597 IP addresses are not routed across the public network.

Figure 6-6 *The Future Corporation*

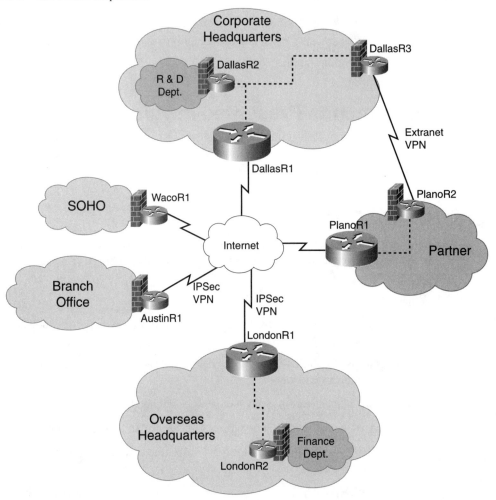

Table 6-1 *The Future Corporation IP Addresses*

Router	Public Interface	IP Address/Mask	Private Interface	IP Address/Mask
DallasR1	S3/0	203.14.17.1/24	FE4/0	172.16.10.1/24
DallasR2	FE0/0	172.16.10.2/24	FE0/1	192.168.10.1/24
DallasR3	S1/0	207.118.14.30/24	FE0/0	172.16.10.3/24
WacoR1	S1/0	193.122.19.82/24	FE0/0	192.168.20.1/24
AustinR1	S1/0	195.147.231.47/24	FE0/0	192.168.30.1/24
LondonR1	S1/0	205.18.26.34/24	FE0/0	172.16.20.1/24

Table 6-1   *The Future Corporation IP Addresses (Continued)*

Router	Public Interface	IP Address/Mask	Private Interface	IP Address/Mask
LondonR2	FE0/0	172.16.20.2/24	FE0/1	192.168.40.1/24
PlanoR1	S1/0	202.24.38.14/24	FE0/0	172.16.10.1/24
PlanoR2	S1/0	207.118.14.35/24	FE0/0	172.16.10.2/24

The DNS server for The Future Corporation is located at the Dallas corporate headquarters with a public NAT IP address of 203.14.17.13. The syslog server is located on the same subnet with an IP address of 203.14.17.32. The ACS server is located on the same subnet with an IP address of 203.14.17.34.

Scenario

Using the information from Figure 6-6 and Table 6-1, show the commands you would use when configuring router AustinR1 for the following common requirements:

1 Allow AAA service to the router. Do not permit ICMP.

2 Configure HTTP services for the authentication proxy on the router.

3 Configure the router to manage authentication cache entries for 90 minutes after a period of inactivity.

4 Define and apply an authentication proxy rule called APHTTP to the serial interface.

Solutions

1 Allow AAA service to the router, but do not permit ICMP:

```
AustinR1(config)# access-list 124 permit tcp host 203.14.17.34 eq tacacs host
   203.14.17.1
AustinR1(config)# access-list 124 permit udp host 203.14.17.34 eq 1645 host
   203.14.17.1
AustinR1(config)# access-list 124 deny ip any any
AustinR1(config)# interface s1/0
AustinR1(config-if)# ip access-group 124 in
```

2 Configure HTTP services for the authentication proxy on the router:

```
AustinR1(config)# ip http server
AustinR1(config)# ip http authentication aaa
```

3 Configure the router to manage authentication cache entries for 90 minutes after a period of inactivity:

```
AustinR1(config)# ip auth-proxy auth-cache-time 90
```

4 Define and apply an authentication proxy rule called APHTTP to the serial interface:

```
AustinR1(config)# ip auth-proxy name APHTTP http
AustinR1(config)# interface s1/0
AustinR1(config-if)# ip auth-proxy APHTTP
```

Upon completion of this chapter, you will be able to perform the following tasks:

- Describe the Cisco IOS IDS Package
- Name the Two Types of Signature Implementations Used by Cisco IOS IDS
- Name the Response Options Available with Cisco IOS IDS
- Initialize a Cisco IOS IDS Router
- Configure Protections and Disable and Exclude Signatures
- Create and Apply Audit Rules
- Verify the Configuration
- Add a Cisco IOS IDS Router to Security Monitor
- Add a Cisco IOS IDS Router to a Syslog Server

CHAPTER 7

Cisco IOS Firewall Intrusion Detection System

This chapter covers the Cisco IOS Firewall Intrusion Detection System (IDS) package for Cisco routers and how to configure it.

This chapter includes the following topics:

- Cisco IOS IDS introduction
- Initializing the Cisco IOS IDS router
- Configuring protection and disabling and excluding signatures
- Creating and applying audit rules
- Verifying the configuration
- Adding a Cisco IOS IDS router to CiscoWorks Monitoring Center for Security

Cisco IOS IDS Introduction

This section introduces the Cisco IOS Firewall IDS feature for Cisco IOS routers.

Cisco offers several nonrouter-based products to monitor your network, including the following:

- **Cisco IDS 4200 Series Sensors**—The Cisco IDS 4200 Series sensors are purpose-built, high-performance network security "appliances" that protect against unauthorized, malicious activity traversing the network, such as that found in random or orchestrated attacks on networks. Cisco IDS 4200 Series Sensors analyze traffic in real time, enabling users to quickly respond to security breaches.

- **CiscoWorks Monitoring Center for Security (Security Monitor)**—This management application centrally monitors the activity of multiple Cisco IDS 4200 Series sensors located on local or remote network segments. It is designed to address the increased requirements for security visibility, denial of service (DoS) protection, and antihacking detection.

NOTE   CiscoWorks Monitoring Center for Security is only available in VPN/Security Management Solution (VMS).

- **Cisco Threat Response (CTR)**—When monitoring network IDSs, it is important to discover whether the attack was successful and, if so, what can be done about it. Cisco's IDS appliances with CTR technology quickly verify and analyze alarms and gather critical evidence without the need for a big investment in additional manpower. CTR technology does this in a five-step approach:

    1 Analyzes the vulnerability of the target operating system or device by dispatching an agent to the device under attack.

    2 Verifies the patch level on the system under attack to determine whether corrective patches have been applied that counter the current threat.

    3 Performs a detailed system investigation, which may include:

        - An analysis of registry entries, system files, and log files

        - A search for specific files or directories, looking for traces of the attack

        - Additional measures to verify the success or failure of an attack with a high degree of certainty

    4 Collects forensic evidence and copies it to a secure location for offline analysis.

    5 Sends alerts to the system administrator, explaining the nature of the attack, details of the investigation, and copies of the forensic evidence.

- **Cisco IDS Event Viewer (IEV)**—IEV is a Java-based application that enables you to view and manage alarms for up to five sensors. You can connect to sensors and view alarms in real time, or download data for later analysis. IEV lets you view alarm status and details and even provides graphing capabilities for statistical analysis of alarms. IEV also provides access to the Network Security Database (NSDB) for signature descriptions.

- **Cisco IDS Device Manager (IDM)**—The IDM is a web-based management application that is preinstalled and enabled on Cisco IDS 4200 Series Sensors. Accessible with a variety of browsers and using SSL, IDM lets administrators configure and manage all aspects of the IDS sensors. The IDM lets administrators manage device, configuration, monitoring, and administration features of the sensor.

Cisco IOS IDS provides firewall and intrusion detection capabilities within a variety of Cisco IOS routers. It acts just like a Cisco IDS 4200 Series sensor from an intrusion detection point-of-view, and can be added to the CiscoWorks Monitoring Center for Security map as another icon, to provide a consistent view of all sensors throughout a network. Cisco IOS IDS contains an enhanced reporting mechanism that permits logging to the router's syslog service in addition to Security Monitor.

Cisco IOS IDS provides a level of protection beyond the firewall by protecting the network from internal and external attacks and threats, as shown in Figure 7-1.

This technology enhances perimeter firewall protection by taking appropriate action on packets and flows that violate the security policy or represent malicious network activity.

Administrators can configure Cisco IOS IDS to respond to security events by performing one or more of these three available actions:

- Send an alarm to a syslog server or a centralized management interface.
- Drop the packet with no notification to the source.
- For TCP sessions, reset the TCP connection.

Figure 7-1 *Cisco IOS IDS*

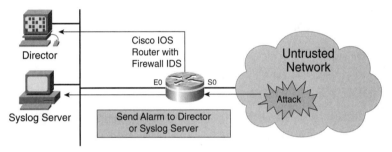

Network Visibility

The Cisco IOS IDS capabilities are ideal for providing additional visibility at intranet, extranet, and branch-office Internet perimeters, as shown in Figure 7-2. Network administrators now have more robust protection against attacks on the network and can automatically respond to threats from internal or external hosts. IDS signatures can be deployed alongside or independently of other Cisco IOS Firewall features. Existing Cisco IDS customers can deploy the Cisco IOS Firewall software-based IDS signatures to complement their current protection. This enables intrusion detection to be deployed to areas that may not be capable of supporting a sensor.

Figure 7-2 *Cisco IOS IDS Network Visibility*

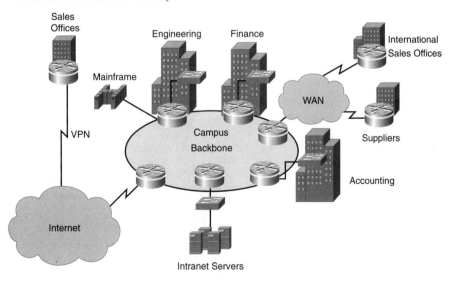

Cisco IOS IDS is intended to satisfy the security goals of all Cisco customers, and is particularly appropriate for the following:

- Enterprise customers who are interested in a cost-effective method of extending their perimeter security across all network boundaries (specifically branch-office), intranet, and extranet perimeters.

- Small- and medium-sized businesses that are looking for a cost-effective router that has an integrated firewall with intrusion detection capabilities.

- Service provider customers who want to set up managed services, providing firewall and intrusion detection to their customers, all housed within the necessary function of a router.

Supported Router Platforms

As of this writing, the Cisco routers listed in Table 7-1 support the Cisco IOS IDS feature.

Table 7-1   *Cisco Routers Supporting Cisco IOS IDS*

Product Name	Description
Cisco 1710	Dual-Ethernet Security Access Router, VPN module, IP, 3DES, Firewall
Cisco 1711-VPN/K9	1711 Security Router with VPN Module, 32 MB Flash, 64 MB DRAM
Cisco 1712-VPN/K9	1712 Security Router with VPN Module, 32 MB Flash, 64 MB DRAM
Cisco 1721	10/100BASE-T Modular Router with 2 WAN slots, 16 MB Flash, 32 MB DRAM
Cisco 1721-VPN/K9	1721 VPN bundle with VPN module, 48MB DRAM, IP Plus, Firewall, 3DES
Cisco 1751	10/100 Modular Router with 3 slots, Cisco IOS IP, 16 MB Flash, 32 MB DRAM
Cisco 1751-V	10/100 Modular Router with Voice, Cisco IOS IP/VOICE Plus, 32F/64D
Cisco 1751-VPN/K9	1751 VPN bundle with VPN module, 64 MB DRAM, IP Plus, Firewall, 3DES
Cisco 1760	10/100 Modular Router with 2WIC/VIC, 2VIC slots, 19-inch chassis
Cisco 1760-V3PN/K9	V3PN bundle with 1760-V/96 MB DRAM/VPN module/4-Ch. DSP
Cisco 1760-VPN/K9	1760 VPN bundle with VPN module, 64 MB DRAM, IP Plus, Firewall, 3DES

Table 7-1   *Cisco Routers Supporting Cisco IOS IDS (Continued)*

Product Name	Description
Cisco 1760-V	10/100 Modular Router with Voice IP/VOICE Plus, 19-inch chassis
Cisco 2610XM	10/100 Ethernet Router with Cisco IOS IP
Cisco 2610XM-DC	10/100 Ethernet Router with Cisco IOS IP—DC power
Cisco 2610XM-RPS	10/100 Ethernet Router with Cisco IOS IP—use with external RPS
Cisco 2611XM	Dual 10/100 Ethernet Router with Cisco IOS IP
Cisco 2611XM-DC	Dual 10/100 Ethernet Router with Cisco IOS IP—DC
Cisco 2611XM-RPS	Dual 10/100 Ethernet Router with Cisco IOS IP—use with external RPS
Cisco 2612	Ethernet/Token-Ring Modular Router with Cisco IOS IP
Cisco 2620XM	Mid-Performance 10/100 Ethernet Router with Cisco IOS IP
Cisco 2620XM-DC	Mid-Performance 10/100 Ethernet Router with Cisco IOS IP—DC
Cisco 2620XM-RPS	Mid-Performance 10/100 Ethernet Router with Cisco IOS IP—RPS ADPT
Cisco 2621XM	Mid-Performance Dual 10/100 Ethernet Router with Cisco IOS IP
Cisco 2621XM-DC	Mid-Performance Dual 10/100 Ethernet Router with Cisco IOS IP—DC
Cisco 2621XM-RPS	Mid-Performance Dual 10/100 Ethernet Router with Cisco IOS IP—RPS ADPT
Cisco 2650XM	High-Performance 10/100 Modular Router with Cisco IOS IP
Cisco 2650XM-DC	High-Performance 10/100 Modular Router with Cisco IOS IP—DC NEBs
Cisco 2650XM-RPS	High-Performance 10/100 Modular Router with Cisco IOS IP—RPS ADPT
Cisco 2651XM	High-Performance Dual 10/100 Modular Router with Cisco IOS IP
Cisco 2651XM-DC	High-Performance Dual 10/100 Modular Router with Cisco IOS IP—DC NEB
Cisco 2651XM-RPS	High-Performance Dual 10/100 Modular Router with IP—RPS ADPT

continues

Table 7-1 *Cisco Routers Supporting Cisco IOS IDS (Continued)*

Product Name	Description
Cisco 2651XM-V	2651XM, AIM-VOICE-30, IP Plus, 96 MB DRAM, 32 MB Flash
Cisco 2691	High-Performance 10/100 Dual Ethernet Router with 3 WIC slots, 1 network module
Cisco 2691-RPS	High-Performance 10/100 Dual Ethernet Router with 3 WIC slots, 1 NM—RPS ADPT
Cisco 3620	Cisco 3600 2-Slot Modular Router—AC with Cisco IOS IP
Cisco 3620-DC	Cisco 3600 2-Slot Modular Router—DC with Cisco IOS IP
Cisco 3661-AC	10/100 E Cisco 3660 6-Slot Modular Router—AC with Cisco IOS IP
Cisco 3661-DC	10/100 E Cisco 3660 6-Slot Modular Router—DC with Cisco IOS IP
Cisco 3662	Dual 10/100 Ethernet Cisco 3660 6-Slot Modular Router—AC with Cisco IOS IP
Cisco 3662-AC-CO	Dual 10/100 Ethernet Cisco 3660 6-Slot CO Modular Router—AC with Telco software
Cisco 3662-DC	Dual 10/100 Ethernet Cisco 3660 6-Slot Modular Router—DC with Cisco IOS IP
Cisco 3662-DC-CO	Dual 10/100 Ethernet Cisco 3660 6-Slot CO Modular Router 2xDC power supply, Telco software
Cisco 3725	Cisco 3700 Series 2-Slot Application Service Router
Cisco 3725-DC-U	3725 Router with universal power supply 24/48 volts
Cisco 3745	Cisco 3700 Series 4-Slot Application Service Router
Cisco 7204VXR-CH	Cisco 7204VXR, 4-slot chassis, 1 AC supply with Cisco IOS IP
Cisco 7206VXR-CH	Cisco 7206VXR, 6-slot chassis, 1 AC supply with Cisco IOS IP
Cisco 7304	4-Slot Chassis, NSE100, 1 power supply, Cisco IOS IP
Cisco 7401ASR-CP	7401ASR, 128 MB SDRAM, Cisco IOS IP
Cisco 831	Cisco 831 Ethernet Router
Cisco 836	Cisco 836 ADSL over ISDN Router
Cisco 837	Cisco 837 ADSL Router

For up-to-date information regarding Cisco IOS IDS feature support, use the Cisco Product Advisor at Cisco.com.

Implementation Issues

The following are issues to consider when implementing Cisco IOS IDS:

- **Memory usage and performance impact**—The performance impact of intrusion detection depends on the number of signatures enabled, the level of traffic on the router, the router platform, and other individual features enabled on the router (such as encryption and source route bridging). Because this router is being used as a security device, no packet is allowed to bypass the security mechanisms. The IDS process in the router sits directly in the packet path and thus searches each packet for signature matches. In some cases, the entire packet needs to be searched, and state information and the router must maintain even application state and awareness.

- **Updated signature coverage**—Cisco IOS IDS now identifies nearly 100 of the most common attacks by using signatures to detect patterns of misuse in network traffic. The intrusion detection signatures were chosen from a broad cross-section of intrusion detection signatures. The signatures represent severe breaches of security and the most common network attacks and information-gathering scans. On the other hand, the dedicated sensor audits over 300 signatures, providing the most comprehensive coverage on network attacks.

Signature Implementations

Cisco IDS 4200 Series sensors and Cisco IOS IDS use signature-based technology to detect network attacks. A signature is a set of rules that define the characteristics of some of the most common attacks in use, such as port scanning and DoS attacks. As Cisco IOS IDS monitors network packets, it tries to match packet behavior or content against the signatures of known attacks.

When a match is found, Cisco IOS IDS "triggers on" the event (meaning that the IDS router performs some predefined action based on the severity or type of event). Cisco IOS IDS routers can send alerts to administrators, drop the offending packets, or send TCP reset packets for some TCP events.

Some IDS devices allow modifications to some types of signatures. Administrators may even be able to create new signatures to accommodate variations in attack profiles. Cisco IOS IDS does not have signature update capability, but Cisco reviews and updates signatures on a regular basis for these devices.

Well-designed attacks try to mirror normal activity as much as possible so that attack packets hide more readily in the flood of packets being monitored. Signature-based IDSs are said to generate false-positives when they identify normal activity as an attack. These IDS devices may generate false-negatives when they fail to flag a valid attack. False-positives tend to clutter reporting mechanisms and may drop valid traffic. False-negatives are scarier in that the IDS device fails to recognize anything at all. False-negatives are almost impossible to track.

Signatures can be classified according to complexity as either atomic or compound:

- **Atomic signatures**—Signatures that trigger on a single packet. For auditing atomic signatures, there is no traffic-dependent memory requirement.

- **Compound signatures**—Signatures that trigger on multiple packets. For auditing compound signatures, Cisco IOS IDS allocates memory to maintain the state of each session for each connection. Memory is also allocated for the configuration database and for internal caching.

Cisco IOS IDS signatures are also categorized by severity as either info or attack:

- **Information signatures**—Detect information-gathering activities, such as port sweeps. While these appear as benign attacks, the information gathered from this type of attack can be used to effect malicious attacks at some time in the future.

- **Attack signatures**—Detect malicious activities, such as illegal FTP commands. These signatures detect ongoing attacks that could be attempting to disable portions of your network.

Response Options

Cisco IOS IDS acts as an inline sensor, watching packets as they traverse the router's interfaces, and acting upon them in a definable fashion. When a packet, or a number of packets in a session, matches a signature, Cisco IOS IDS may perform the following configurable actions:

- **Alarm**—Sends alarms to the CiscoWorks Management Center for IDS Sensors (MC IDS), syslog server, or router console, and then forwards the packet through.

- **Reset**—Sends packets with a reset flag to both session participants if it is a TCP session.

- **Drop**—Immediately drops the packet.

NOTE   Cisco recommends that you use the drop and reset actions together to ensure that the attack is terminated.

Configuring Cisco IOS IDS

To configure Cisco IOS IDS on a router and to have it report alarms to CiscoWorks Monitoring Center for Security, complete the following tasks:

Step 1   **Initialize Cisco IOS IDS on the router**—This includes setting the notification type, the router's PostOffice parameters, Security Monitor's PostOffice parameters, the protected network definition, and the router's maximum queue size for holding alarms.

Step 2   **Configure, disable, or exclude signatures**—This includes setting the spam attack threshold, disabling signatures globally, and excluding signatures by host or network.

Step 3   **Create and apply audit rules**—This includes creating an audit rule for information or attack signatures and then applying it to an interface. Another option is to create an audit rule that excludes hosts or networks and then apply it to an interface.

Step 4   **Verify the configuration**—This includes using available **show**, **clear**, and **debug** commands for Cisco IOS IDS.

Step 5   **Add Cisco IOS IDS to the CiscoWorks Monitoring Center for Security's map**—The IDS-enabled router appears as another sensor on the Cisco IDS Home map.

Step 1—Initializing the Cisco IOS IDS Router

This section covers the commands to set the notification type, the router's PostOffice parameters, Security Monitor's PostOffice parameters, the protected network definition, and the router's maximum queue size for holding alarms.

Setting the Notification Type

Use the **ip audit notify** global configuration command to specify the methods of alarm notification. Use the **no** form of this command to disable event notifications. The following example shows how you might apply this command:

```
Router(config)# ip audit notify nr-director
Router(config)# ip audit notify log
```

The syntax for the **ip audit notify** command is as follows:

```
ip audit notify {nr-director | log}
no ip audit notify {nr-director | log}
```

- **nr-director**—Send messages in PostOffice format to Security Monitor or Sensor.
- **log**—Send messages in syslog format to the router's console or a remote syslog server.

Setting the Protected Network

Use the **ip audit po protected** global configuration command to specify whether an IP address is on a protected network. Use the **no** form of this command to remove network addresses from the protected network list. If you specify an IP address for removal, that address is removed from the list. If you do not specify an address, then all IP addresses are removed from the list. The following example shows how you might apply this command:

```
Router(config)# ip audit po protected 10.0.0.1 to 10.0.0.254
```

The syntax for the **ip audit po protected** command is as follows:

```
ip audit po protected ip-addr [to ip-addr]
no ip audit po protected [ip-addr]
```

- **to**—Specifies a range of IP addresses.

- *ip-addr*—IP address of a network host.

Setting the Notification Queue Size

Use the **ip audit po max-events** global configuration command to specify the maximum number of event notifications that are placed in the router's event queue. Use the **no** version of this command to set the number of recipients to the default setting. The following example shows how you might apply this command:

```
Router(config)# ip audit po max-events 300
```

The syntax for the **ip audit po max-events** command is as follows:

```
ip audit po max-events number-of-events
no ip audit po max-events
```

CAUTION   The router has limited persistent storage; if the queue fills, alarms are lost on a FIFO basis. The reliability versus memory trade-off is that each alarm uses 32 KB of memory.

- *number-of-events*—Integer in the range of 1 to 65535 that designates the maximum number of events allowable in the event queue. Use with the **max-events** keyword. The default number of events is 100.

Step 2—Configuring Protection and Disabling and Excluding Signatures

This section covers the commands to set the spam attack threshold, disable signatures globally, and exclude signatures by host or network.

Configuring Spam Attack Protection

Use the **ip audit smtp spam** global configuration command to specify the number of recipients in a mail message over which a spam attack is suspected (signature identification is 3106). Use the **no** version of this command to set the number of recipients to the default setting. The following example shows how you might apply this command:

```
Router(config)# ip audit smtp spam 350
```

The syntax for the **ip audit smtp spam** command is as follows:

```
ip audit smtp spam number-of-recipients
no ip audit smtp spam
```

- *number-of-recipients*—Integer in the range of 1 to 65535 that designates the maximum number of recipients in a mail message before a spam attack is suspected. Use with the **spam** keyword. The default number of recipients is 250.

Disabling Signatures Globally

Use the **ip audit signature** global configuration command to globally disable a signature. Use the **no** form of this command to re-enable the signature. Example 7-1 shows how you might apply this command:

Example 7-1 *Applying the* **ip audit signature** *Global Configuration Command*

```
Router(config)# ip audit signature 1004 disable
Router(config)# ip audit signature 1006 disable
Router(config)# ip audit signature 3102 disable
Router(config)# ip audit signature 3104 disable
```

The syntax for the **ip audit signature** command is as follows:

```
ip audit signature sig-id disable
no ip audit signature sig-id
```

- *sig-id*—Unique integer that specifies a signature as defined in the Cisco IDS NSDB.

- **disable**—Globally disables a signature from being audited by the Cisco IOS IDS router. All 100 signatures are enabled.

Excluding Signatures by Host or Network

Use the **ip audit signature** and the **access-list** global configuration commands to attach a signature to an ACL and stop the signature from triggering when generated from a given host or network. Use the **no** form of this command to remove the signature from the ACL. Example 7-2 shows how you might apply this command.

Example 7-2 *Using the* **ip audit signature** *and the* **access-list** *Global Configuration Commands*

```
Router(config)# access-list 91 deny host 10.0.0.33
Router(config)# access-list 91 deny 10.1.1.0 255.255.255.0
Router(config)# access-list 91 permit any
Router(config)# ip audit signature 3100 list 91
Router(config)# ip audit signature 3102 list 91
```

The syntax for the **ip audit signature** command is as follows:

```
ip audit signature sig-id list acl-num
no ip audit signature sig-id
```

- *sig-id*—Unique integer that specifies a signature as defined in the NSDB.

- **list**—Specifies an ACL to associate with the signature.

- *acl-num*—Unique integer that specifies a configured ACL on the router. Use with the **list** keyword.

The syntax for the **access-list** command is as follows:

```
access-list acl-num deny [host] ip-addr [wildcard]
no access-list acl-num
```

- *acl-num*—Number of an ACL. This is a decimal number from 1 to 99.
- **deny**—Denies signature trigger if the conditions are matched.
- **host**—Identifies that the following IP address is that of a host.
- *ip-addr*—IP address of the network or host from which the packet is being sent. There are two alternative ways to specify the source:
  - Use a four-octet, dotted-decimal IP address.
  - Use the keyword **any** as an abbreviation for an IP address and wildcard of 0.0.0.0 255.255.255.255.
- *wildcard*—Wildcard bits to be applied to the IP address. There are two alternative ways to specify the source wildcard:
  - Use a four-octet, dotted-decimal format. Place 1's in the bit positions that you want to ignore.
  - Use the keyword **any** as an abbreviation for an IP address and wildcard of 0.0.0.0 255.255.255.255.

Step 3—Creating and Applying Audit Rules

This section covers the commands to create the Cisco IOS IDS audit rules and apply them to an interface.

Understanding the Packet Auditing Process

The following describes the packet auditing process with Cisco IOS IDS:

Step 1   Set the default actions for both information and attack signatures.

Step 2   Create an audit rule that specifies the signatures that should be applied to packet traffic and the actions to take when a match is found. An audit rule can apply information and attack signatures to network packets.

Step 3   Apply the audit rule to an interface on the router, specifying a traffic direction (in or out):

- If the audit rule is applied to the inbound direction of the interface, packets passing through the interface are audited before any inbound ACL has a chance to discard them. This enables an administrator to be alerted if an attack or reconnaissance activity is underway even if the router would normally reject the activity.

- If the audit rule is applied to the outbound direction on the interface, packets are audited after they enter the router through another interface. In this case, the inbound ACL of the other interface may discard packets before they are audited. This may result in the loss of IDS alarms even though the attack or reconnaissance activity was thwarted.

Step 4   Packets that are going through the interface that match the audit rule are audited by a series of modules, starting with IP; then either Internet Control Message Protocol (ICMP), TCP, or User Data Protocol (UDP) (as appropriate); and finally, the application level.

Step 5   If a signature match is found in a module, then the user-configured actions occur. Recall that Cisco IOS IDS can be configured to send an alarm, drop the offending packets, or issue TCP reset packets.

The following sections explain each of the preceding steps.

Setting the Default Actions for Information and Attack Signatures

Use the **ip audit info** global configuration command to specify the default actions for info signatures. Use the **no** form of this command to set the default action for info signatures. The following example shows how you might apply this command:

```
Router(config)# ip audit info action alarm
```

Use the **ip audit attack** global configuration command to specify the default actions for attack signatures. Use the **no** form of this command to set the default action for attack signatures. The following example shows how you might apply this command:

```
Router(config)# ip audit attack action alarm drop reset
```

The syntax for the **ip audit info** command is as follows:

```
ip audit info {action [alarm] [drop] [reset]}
no ip audit info
```

The syntax for the **ip audit attack** command is as follows:

```
ip audit attack {action [alarm] [drop] [reset]}
no ip audit attack
```

- **action**—Sets an action for the information signature to take in response to a match. The default action is to alarm.
- **alarm**—Sends an alarm to the console, Security Monitor, or to a syslog server. Use with the **action** keyword.
- **drop**—Drops the packet. Use with the **action** keyword.
- **reset**—Resets the TCP session. Use with the **action** keyword.

Creating and Applying an IDS Audit

Use the **ip audit name** global configuration command to create audit rules for information and attack signature types. Use the **no** form of this command to delete an audit rule. The following example shows how you might apply this command:

```
Router(config)# ip audit name AUDIT1 info action alarm
Router(config)# ip audit name AUDIT1 attack action alarm drop reset
```

Use the **ip audit name** command at the interface configuration prompt to apply an audit specification to a specific interface and for a specific direction. Use the **no** version of this command to disable auditing of the interface for the specified direction. The following example shows how you might apply this command:

```
Router(config)# interface e0
Router(config-if)# ip audit AUDIT1 in
```

The syntax for the **ip audit name** command is as follows:

```
ip audit name audit-name {info | attack} [action [alarm] [drop] [reset]]
no ip audit name audit-name {info | attack}
```

- *audit-name*—Name for an audit specification.
- **info**—Specifies that the audit rule is for information signatures.
- **attack**—Specifies that the audit rule is for attack signatures.
- **action**—Specifies an action or actions to take in response to a match. If an action is not specified, the default action is to alarm.
- **alarm**—Sends an alarm to the console, Security Monitor, or to a syslog server. Use with the **action** keyword.
- **reset**—Resets the TCP session. Use with the **action** keyword.
- **drop**—Drops the packet. Use with the **action** keyword.

The syntax for the **ip audit** command is as follows:

```
ip audit audit-name {in | out}
no ip audit audit-name {in | out}
```

- *audit-name*—Name for an audit specification. No audit specifications are applied to an interface or direction.
- **in**—Apply to inbound traffic.
- **out**—Apply to outbound traffic.

Creating an IDS Audit with Excluded Addresses

The **ip audit name** and **access-list** global configuration commands can be used to create audit rules for information and attack signature types that you want to exclude from triggering when generated by a particular host or network. Use the **no** form of this command to delete an audit rule. Example 7-3 shows how you might apply this command.

Example 7-3   *Using the* **ip audit name** *and* **access-list** *Global Configuration Commands*

```
Router(config)# ip audit name AUDIT2 info list 93 action alarm
Router(config)# ip audit name AUDIT2 attack list 93 action alarm drop reset
Router(config)# access-list 93 deny host 10.1.1.16
Router(config)# access-list 93 permit any
Router(config)# interface e0
Router(config-if)# ip audit AUDIT2 in
```

The syntax for the **ip audit name** command is as follows:

```
ip audit name audit-name {info | attack} [list acl-num] [action [alarm]
   [drop] [reset]]
no ip audit name audit-name {info | attack}
```

- *audit-name*—Name for an audit specification.

- **info**—Specifies that the audit rule is for information signatures.

- **attack**—Specifies that the audit rule is for attack signatures.

- **list**—Specifies an ACL to attach to the audit rule.

- *acl-num*—Unique integer that specifies a configured ACL on the router. Use with the **list** keyword.

- **action**—Specifies an action or actions to take in response to a match. If an action is not specified, the default action is to alarm.

- **alarm**—Sends an alarm to the console, Security Monitor, or to a syslog server. Use with the **action** keyword.

- **reset**—Resets the TCP session. Use with the **action** keyword.

- **drop**—Drops the packet. Use with the **action** keyword.

Step 4—Verifying the Configuration

This section covers the commands that allow you to verify that the configuration is correct. These include the **show**, **clear**, and **debug** commands.

show Commands

Use the **show ip audit statistics** command to display the number of packets audited and the number of alarms sent, among other information. The syntax for the **show ip audit statistics** command is as follows:

```
show ip audit statistics
```

Use the **show ip audit configuration** command to display additional configuration information, including default values that may not be displayed using the **show run** command. The syntax for the **show ip audit configuration** command is as follows:

```
show ip audit configuration
```

Example 7-4 shows the output of the **show ip audit configuration** command.

Example 7-4 *Output of the* **show ip audit configuration** *Command*

```
Event notification through syslog is enabled
Event notification through Security Monitor is enabled
Default action(s) for info signatures is alarm
Default action(s) for attack signatures is alarm drop reset
Default threshold of recipients for spam signature is 25
PostOffice:HostID:55 OrgID:123 Msg dropped:0
        :Curr Event Buf Size:100  Configured:100
HID:14 OID:123 S:1 A:2 H:82 HA:49 DA:0 R:0 Q:0
 ID:1 Dest:10.1.1.99:45000 Loc:172.16.58.99:45000 T:5 S:ESTAB *

Audit Rule Configuration
 Audit name AUDIT.1
    info actions alarm
    attack actions alarm drop reset
```

Use the **show ip audit interface** command to display the interface configuration. The syntax for the **show ip audit interface** command is as follows:

```
show ip audit interface
```

Example 7-5 shows the output of the **show ip audit interface** command:

Example 7-5 *Output of the* **show ip audit interface** *Command*

```
Interface Configuration
 Interface Ethernet0
  Inbound IDS audit rule is AUDIT.1
    info actions alarm
    attack actions alarm drop reset
  Outgoing IDS audit rule is not set
 Interface Ethernet1
  Inbound IDS audit rule is AUDIT.1
    info actions alarm
    attack actions alarm drop reset
  Outgoing IDS audit rule is not set
```

Use the **show ip audit debug** command to display the enabled debug flags. The syntax for the **show ip audit debug** command is as follows:

```
show ip audit debug
```

Example 7-6 shows the output of the **show ip audit interface** command:

Example 7-6 *Output of the* **show ip audit interface** *Command*

```
Interface Configuration
 Interface Ethernet0
  Inbound IDS audit rule is AUDIT.1
    info actions alarm
  Outgoing IDS audit rule is not set
```

Example 7-6 *Output of the* **show ip audit interface** *Command (Continued)*

```
Interface Ethernet1
 Inbound IDS audit rule is AUDIT.1
   info actions alarm
 Outgoing IDS audit rule is AUDIT.1
   info actions alarm
```

clear Commands

Use the **clear ip audit statistics** command to reset statistics on packets analyzed and alarms sent. The syntax for the **clear ip audit statistics** command is as follows:

```
clear ip audit statistics
```

Use the **clear ip audit configuration** command to disable Cisco IOS IDS, remove all intrusion detection configuration entries, and release dynamic resources. The syntax for the **clear ip audit configuration** command is as follows:

```
clear ip audit configuration
```

Step 5—Adding a Cisco IOS IDS Router to CiscoWorks Monitoring Center for Security

Cisco has two management and monitoring tools for IDSs: CiscoWorks Monitoring Center for Security (Security Monitor), and CiscoWorks Management Center for IDS Sensors (MC IDS). Cisco has issued an end-of-life notification for a previous tool, the Net Ranger Director.

CiscoWorks Monitoring Center for Security

CiscoWorks Monitoring Center for Security provides the following:

- Capability to capture, view, organize (with manual configuration), and report events from:
  - Network IDS sensors
  - Switch IDS sensors
  - IDS network modules for routers
  - Host-based IDSs
  - PIX Firewalls
  - Cisco IOS IDSs
- Notification of administrator-selected critical events
- Extensive database of alarms:
  - Explains cause and severity of problems
  - Suggests possible remedies

CiscoWorks Monitoring Center for Security can accept messages from Cisco IOS IDS routers using either syslog or PostOffice. Security Monitor looks at all syslog traffic on the UDP port; therefore, you do not need to add any Cisco IOS IDS routers to Security Monitor if they are sending event data using syslog. These devices will be listed in Security Monitor by their IP addresses. If you want to see them listed by their syslog device name, you need to add them to Security Monitor.

For those Cisco IOS IDS routers that use PostOffice that you want to add to Security Monitor, collect the following information before you begin this process:

- Host ID
- Organization name
- Organization ID
- PostOffice port
- Heartbeat interval

To add a Cisco IOS IDS device to Security Monitor, perform the following steps:

Step 1   Log in to CiscoWorks.

Step 2   Choose **VPN/Security Management Solution > Monitoring Center > Security Monitor**.

Step 3   Select the **Devices** tab and click **Add**.

Step 4   Select **IOS IDS** as the type of device to monitor, then click **Next** to open the Enter Device Information page.

Step 5   Enter the IP address for the device you are adding.

Step 6   If using Network Address Translation (NAT), enter the NAT address for the device.

Step 7   Enter a name for the device.

Step 8   Enter a comment about the device (optional).

Step 9   If using PostOffice, check the **Uses PostOffice** check box and enter the following:

    (a)   Host ID

    (b)   Organization name

    (c)   Organization ID

      (d) PostOffice port

      (e) Heartbeat interval

Step 10 Click **Finish** to complete the process.

If you are using the IDS MC to manage additional sensors, you can import device configurations into Security Monitor from there. The IDS MC and Security Monitor are both featured components of VMS.

CiscoWorks Management Center for IDS Sensors

The CiscoWorks Management Center for IDS Sensors provides the following:

- Management and configuration of hardware IDS devices:
  - Network IDS sensors
  - Switch IDS sensors
  - IDS network modules for routers
- Management of multiple sensors using sensor groups
- Web interface and wizards for ease of management
- Ability to create new signatures
- Automated Signature updates
- Automated Software upgrade utility

NOTE   CiscoWorks Management Center for IDS Sensors does not work with Cisco IOS IDS.

Chapter Summary

The following list summarizes what you learned in this chapter:

- The Cisco IOS IDS package is a smaller version of the IDS sensor located within IOS routers.
- The two types of signature implementations used by Cisco IOS IDS are atomic and compound.
- You need to create and apply audit rules to the IDS configuration.
- You need to select the attack signatures for IDS monitoring.
- You need to verify the Cisco IOS IDS configuration using **debug** commands.
- You may add a Cisco IOS IDS router to Security Monitor.
- You may add a Cisco IOS IDS router to a syslog server.

Signatures Used By Cisco IOS IDS

Cisco IOS IDS uses 100 of the most common attack signatures to detect patterns of misuse in network traffic. Fifty-nine of these IDS signatures were provided in Cisco IOS Firewall in versions prior to Release 12.2(11)YU. These signatures identify the most severe breaches of security, common network attacks, and information-gathering scans commonly found in an active network.

Cisco IOS IDS signatures are categorized by severity and complexity:

- Severity
  - **Info signatures**—Detect information-gathering activities such as port sweeps. There are 39 of these.
  - **Attack signatures**—Detect malicious activity, such as illegal FTP commands. There are 61 of these.
- Complexity
  - **Atomic signatures**—Detect simple patterns, such as an attempt on a specific host. There are 73 of these.
  - **Compound signatures**—Detect complex patterns, such as an attack on multiple hosts, over extended time periods with multiple packets. There are 27 of these.

Table 7-2 is a list of the signatures that are contained in Cisco IOS IDS since release 12.2(11)YU. For the most up-to-date list of signatures, visit the Cisco website at http://www.cisco.com/en/US/products/sw/secursw/ps2113/products_data_sheets_list.html.

Table 7-2   *List of Signatures Used By Cisco IOS IDS*

Signature	Title	Severity	Complexity	Timeframe
1000	IP Options-Bad Option List	Info	Atomic	Original 59
1001	IP Options-Record Packet Route	Info	Atomic	Original 59
1002	IP Options-Timestamp	Info	Atomic	Original 59
1003	IP Options-Provide s, c, h, and tcc	Info	Atomic	Original 59
1004	IP Options-Loose Source Route	Info	Atomic	Original 59
1005	IP Options-SATNET ID	Info	Atomic	Original 59
1006	IP Options-Strict Source Route	Info	Atomic	Original 59
1100	IP Fragment Attack	Attack	Atomic	Original 59
1101	Unknown IP Protocol	Info	Atomic	Original 59

Table 7-2   *List of Signatures Used By Cisco IOS IDS (Continued)*

Signature	Title	Severity	Complexity	Timeframe
1102	Impossible IP Packet	Attack	Atomic	Original 59
1104	IP Localhost Source Spoof	Attack	Atomic	Additional 41
1105	Broadcast Source Address	Attack	Atomic	Additional 41
1106	Multicast IP Source Address	Attack	Atomic	Additional 41
1107	RFC 1918 Addresses Seen	Info	Atomic	Additional 41
1202	IP Fragment Overrun— Datagram Too Long	Attack	Atomic	Additional 41
1206	IP Fragment Too Small	Attack	Atomic	Additional 41
2000	ICMP Echo Reply	Info	Atomic	Original 59
2001	ICMP Host Unreachable	Info	Atomic	Original 59
2002	ICMP Source Quench	Info	Atomic	Original 59
2003	ICMP Redirect	Info	Atomic	Original 59
2004	ICMP Echo Request	Info	Atomic	Original 59
2005	ICMP Time Exceeded for a Datagram	Info	Atomic	Original 59
2006	ICMP Parameter Problem on Datagram	Info	Atomic	Original 59
2007	ICMP Timestamp Request	Info	Atomic	Original 59
2008	ICMP Timestamp Reply	Info	Atomic	Original 59
2009	ICMP Information Request	Info	Atomic	Original 59
2010	ICMP Information Reply	Info	Atomic	Original 59
2011	ICMP Address Mask Request	Info	Atomic	Original 59
2012	ICMP Address Mask Reply	Info	Atomic	Original 59
2150	Fragmented ICMP Traffic	Attack	Atomic	Original 59
2151	Large ICMP Traffic	Attack	Atomic	Original 59

continues

Table 7-2 *List of Signatures Used By Cisco IOS IDS (Continued)*

Signature	Title	Severity	Complexity	Timeframe
2154	Ping of Death Attack	Attack	Atomic	Original 59
3038	Fragmented NULL TCP Packet	Attack	Atomic	Additional 41
3039	Fragmented Orphaned FIN Packet	Attack	Atomic	Additional 41
3040	NULL TCP Packet	Attack	Atomic	Original 59
3041	SYN/FIN Packet	Attack	Atomic	Original 59
3042	Orphaned Fin Packet	Attack	Atomic	Original 59
3043	Fragmented SYN/FIN Packet	Attack	Atomic	Additional 41
3050	Half-open SYN Attack	Attack	Compound	Original 59
3100	Smail Attack	Attack	Compound	Original 59
3101	Sendmail Invalid Recipient	Attack	Compound	Original 59
3102	Sendmail Invalid Sender	Attack	Compound	Original 59
3103	Sendmail Reconnaissance	Attack	Compound	Original 59
3104	Archaic Sendmail Attacks	Attack	Compound	Original 59
3105	Sendmail Decode Alias	Attack	Compound	Original 59
3106	Mail Spam	Attack	Compound	Original 59
3107	Majordomo Execute Attack	Attack	Compound	Original 59
3150	FTP Remote Command Execution	Attack	Compound	Original 59
3151	FTP SYST Command Attempt	Info	Compound	Original 59
3152	FTP CWD ~root	Info	Compound	Original 59
3153	FTP Improper Address Specified	Attack	Atomic	Original 59
3154	FTP Improper Port Specified	Attack	Atomic	Original 59
3215	IIS DOT DOT EXECUTE Attack	Attack	Compound	Additional 41

Table 7-2   *List of Signatures Used By Cisco IOS IDS (Continued)*

Signature	Title	Severity	Complexity	Timeframe
3229	Website Win-C-Sample Buffer Overflow	Attack	Compound	Additional 41
3233	WWW count-cgi Overflow	Attack	Compound	Additional 41
4050	UDP Bomb	Attack	Atomic	Original 59
4051	Snork	Attack	Atomic	Additional 41
4052	Chargen DoS	Attack	Atomic	Additional 41
4100	Tftp Passwd File	Attack	Compound	Original 59
4600	IOS UDP Bomb	Attack	Atomic	Additional 41
5034	WWW IIS newdsn Attack	Attack	Compound	Additional 41
5035	HTTP cgi HylaFAX Faxsurvey	Attack	Compound	Additional 41
5041	WWW Anyform Attack	Attack	Compound	Additional 41
5043	WWW ColdFusion Attack	Attack	Compound	Additional 41
5044	WWW Webcom.se Guestbook Attack	Attack	Compound	Additional 41
5045	WWW xterm Display Attack	Attack	Compound	Additional 41
5050	WWW IIS .htr Overflow Attack	Attack	Compound	Additional 41
5055	HTTP Basic Authentication Overflow	Attack	Compound	Additional 41
5071	WWW msacds.dll Attack	Attack	Compound	Additional 41
5081	WWW WinNT cmd.exe Access	Attack	Atomic	Additional 41
5090	WWW FrontPage htimage.exe Access	Attack	Atomic	Additional 41
5114	WWW IIS Unicode Attack	Attack	Atomic	Additional 41
5116	Endymion MailMan Remote Command Execution	Attack	Atomic	Additional 41

continues

Table 7-2 *List of Signatures Used By Cisco IOS IDS (Continued)*

Signature	Title	Severity	Complexity	Timeframe
5117	phpGroupWare Remote Command Exec	Attack	Atomic	Additional 41
5118	eWave ServletExec 3.0C File Upload	Attack	Atomic	Additional 41
5123	WWW Host: Field Overflow	Attack	Atomic	Additional 41
6050	DNS HINFO Request	Info	Atomic	Additional 41
6051	DNS Zone Transfer	Info	Atomic	Additional 41
6052	DNS Zone Transfer from High Port	Attack	Atomic	Additional 41
6053	DNS Request for All Records	Attack	Atomic	Additional 41
6054	DNS Version Request	Attack	Atomic	Additional 41
6055	DNS Inverse Query Buffer Overflow	Attack	Atomic	Additional 41
6056	DNS NXT Buffer Overflow	Attack	Compound	Additional 41
6057	DNS SIG Buffer Overflow	Attack	Compound	Additional 41
6062	DNS Authors Request	Info	Atomic	Additional 41
6063	DNS Incremental Zone Transfer	Info	Atomic	Additional 41
6100	RPC Port Registration	Info	Atomic	Original 59
6101	RPC Port Unregistration	Info	Atomic	Original 59
6102	RPC Dump	Info	Atomic	Original 59
6103	Proxied RPC Request	Attack	Atomic	Original 59
6150	ypserv Portmap Request	Info	Atomic	Original 59
6151	ypbind Portmap Request	Info	Atomic	Original 59
6152	yppasswdd Portmap Request	Info	Atomic	Original 59
6153	ypupdated Portmap Request	Info	Atomic	Original 59
6154	ypxfrd Portmap Request	Info	Atomic	Original 59

Table 7-2   *List of Signatures Used By Cisco IOS IDS (Continued)*

Signature	Title	Severity	Complexity	Timeframe
6155	Mountd Portmap Request	Info	Atomic	Original 59
6175	rexd Portmap Request	Info	Atomic	Original 59
6180	rexd Attempt	Info	Atomic	Original 59
6190	statd Buffer Overflow	Attack	Atomic	Original 59
8000	FTP Retrieve Password File	Attack	Atomic	Original 59

Cisco IOS Commands Presented in This Chapter

Many Cisco IOS version 12.3 commands were discussed or referenced in this chapter. These commands can be found in the *Command Reference* online at http://www.cisco.com/univercd/cc/td/doc/product/software/ios123/123mindx/crgindx.htm.

Chapter Review Questions

The following review questions cover some of the key facts and concepts that were introduced in this chapter. Answers to these questions can be found in Appendix A, "Answers to Chapter Review Questions."

1 What are two important issues to consider when implementing Cisco IOS IDS?

2 What are the two types of signature implementations used by Cisco IOS IDS?

3 What three response options are available when using Cisco IOS IDS?

4 What five steps must be completed to initialize Cisco IOS IDS?

5 What command would you use on a Cisco IOS IDS to set 134.14.15.0 through 134.14.37.0 as addresses on protected networks?

6 What command would you use to set the spam attack threshold to 120 messages on a Cisco IOS IDS?

7 You have set up your Cisco IOS IDS router to discard packets for certain types of attack activities. You would still like to be notified when the router sees the specific attack profiles. Where would you place the audit rule and what direction of traffic would you monitor to see alarms for these attack profiles?

8 Create an audit rule named AUDIT5 that presents alarms for information and attack signatures. The rule should also drop offending attack packets and reset TCP sessions when they present an attack profile.

9 Which **show** command would you use to display the interface settings for the interfaces of your Cisco IOS IDS router?

10 Which command would you use to configure you Cisco IOS IDS router to send alarm notifications to a syslog server?

11 When using PostOffice to send alerts from your Cisco IOS IDS router to your Security Monitor, what additional information must you supply that is not required when using syslog?

Case Study

The Future Corporation's network structure is shown in Figure 7-3.

Figure 7-3 *The Future Corporation*

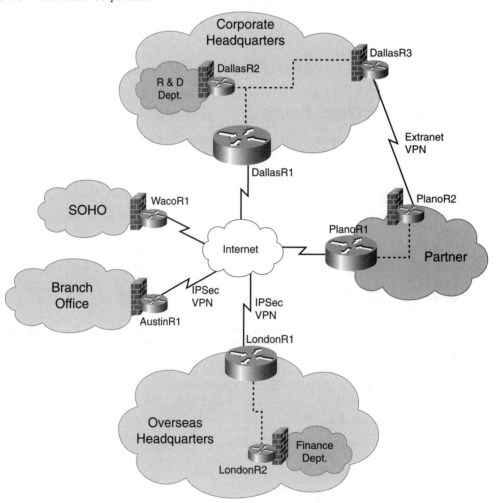

Scenario

One of the axioms of good security is to "trust, but verify." Although The Future Corporation trusts its business partner, Plastics Incorporated, its security policy requires the application of an intrusion detection sensor at border routers between all business partners. Use the following instructions to configure the IDS on Cisco IOS router DallasR3:

Step 1   Set the IDS to use syslog for alarm notifications. Messages will be sent to the syslog server located at 172.16.10.47.

Step 2   Protect the entire 172.16.10.0 network.

Step 3   Set the Cisco IOS IDS router to support a maximum of 250 notifications in the router's event queue.

Step 4   To help guard against e-mail spam attacks, set the maximum number of e-mail recipients to 120.

Step 5   From past experience, you know that your business partner uses an application that will trigger large numbers of false alarms for signature 1234. Disable this signature to help minimize the false alarms generated by your Cisco IOS IDS.

Step 6   PlanoR2 is using NAT and has a static mapping of 207.118.14.92 for a host from which you expect numerous false alarms on signature 2233. Set up an ACL to prevent Cisco IOS IDS from checking for signature 2233 for this specific address.

Step 7   Create and apply an audit rule to incoming traffic on DallasR3's S1/0 interface by using the following guidelines:

- Set the default action for packets matching informational signatures to generate alarms only.

- Set the default action for packets matching attack signatures to generate alarms, be dropped, and trigger TCP reset packets.

- Name the audit rule PLASTIC1.

- Enable the audit rule on the interface.

Step 8   Perform the following functions to verify the configuration of DallasR3:

- Display the number of packets audited and the number of alarms sent.

- Display audit configuration information.

- Display the audit information for the s1/0 interface.

- Check whether any **audit debug** commands are active.

- Reset the auditing statistics.

Solutions

The correct commands that can be used to configure the DallasR3 IOS firewall router for IDS support are as follows:

Step 1 Set the IDS to use syslog for alarm notifications. Messages will be sent to the syslog server located at 172.16.10.47.

ip audit notify log

Step 2 Protect the entire 172.16.10.0 network:

ip audit po protected 172.16.10.1 to 172.16.10.254

Step 3 Set the Cisco IOS IDS router to support a maximum of 250 notifications in the router's event queue:

ip audit po max-events 250

Step 4 To help guard against e-mail spam attacks, set the maximum number of e-mail recipients to 120:

ip audit smtp spam 120

Step 5 From past experience, you know that your business partner uses an application that will trigger large numbers of false alarms for signature 1234. Disable this signature to help minimize the false alarms generated by your Cisco IOS IDS:

ip audit signature 1234 disable

Step 6 PlanoR2 is using NAT and has a static mapping of 207.118.14.92 for a host from which you expect numerous false alarms on signature 2233. Set up an ACL to prevent Cisco IOS IDS from checking for signature 2233 for this specific address:

access-list 80 deny host 207.118.14.92
access-list 80 permit any
ip audit signature 2233 list 80

Step 7 Create and apply an audit rule to incoming traffic on DallasR3's S1/0 interface using the following guidelines:

- Set the default action for packets matching informational signatures to generate alarms only:

ip audit info action alarm

- Set the default action for packets matching attack signatures to generate alarms, be dropped, and trigger TCP reset packets:

ip audit attack action alarm drop reset

- Name the audit rule PLASTIC1:

ip audit name PLASTIC1 info
ip audit name PLASTIC1 attack

(The audit rule will use the default actions for info and attack that were set above.)

- Enable the audit rule on the interface:

int s1/0
**   ip audit PLASTIC1 in**

Step 8   Perform the following functions to verify the configuration of DallasR3:

- Display the number of packets audited and the number of alarms sent:

show ip audit statistics

- Display audit configuration information:

show ip audit configuration

- Display the audit information for the s1/0 interface:

show ip audit interface

- Check whether any **audit debug** commands are active:

show ip audit debug

- Reset the auditing statistics:

clear ip audit statistics

Upon completion of this chapter, you will be able to perform the following tasks:

- Define Two Types of Cisco Router VPN Solutions
- Describe the Cisco VPN Router Product Family
- Identify the IPSec and Other Open Standards Supported by Cisco VPN Routers
- Identify the Component Technologies of IPSec
- Explain How IPSec Works
- Configure a Cisco Router for IKE Using Pre-Shared Keys
- Configure a Cisco Router for IPSec Using Pre-Shared Keys
- Verify the IKE and IPSec Configuration
- Explain the Issues Regarding Configuring IPSec Manually and Using RSA-Encrypted Nonces
- Use IPSec with Network Address Translation

CHAPTER 8

Building IPSec VPNs Using Cisco Routers and Pre-Shared Keys

This chapter teaches you how to configure Cisco IOS IPSec using pre-shared keys for authentication. After presenting an overview of the process, this chapter shows you each major step of the configuration. It includes the following topics:

- How Cisco routers enable secure VPNs
- IPSec overview
- IPSec protocol framework
- How IPSec works
- Configuring IPSec encryption
- Overview of configuring IPSec manually
- Overview of configuring IPSec for RSA-encrypted nonces

Cisco Routers Enable Secure VPNs

Cisco routers support the latest in virtual private network (VPN) technology. A VPN is a service that offers secure, reliable connectivity over a shared public network infrastructure.

Defining VPNs

Cisco defines a VPN as an encrypted connection between private networks over a public network, such as the Internet. A VPN is a *virtual network* because the network's information is transported among network members over a public network, the Internet. A VPN is *private* because the data that is sent over the Internet is encrypted to keep it confidential. Figure 8-1 depicts a VPN environment.

Figure 8-1 *VPN Definition*

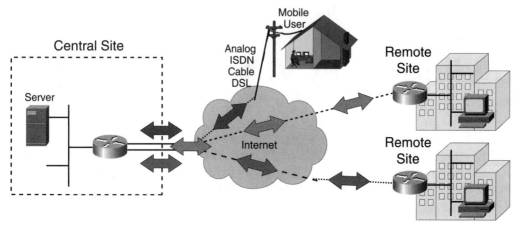

There are two types of router-based VPN networks:

- Remote access
- Site-to-site

The sections that follow describe these two types in more detail.

Remote Access VPNs

Remote access VPNs are targeted to mobile users and home telecommuters. In the past, corporations supported remote users via dial-in networks. This typically necessitated a toll or toll-free call to access the corporation. With the advent of VPNs, a mobile user can make a local call to their ISP to access the corporation via the Internet wherever they may be. As shown in Figure 8-2, remote access VPNs are an evolution of dial-in networks. Remote access VPNs can support the needs of telecommuters, mobile users, extranet consumer-to-business, and so on.

Figure 8-2 *Remote Access VPNs*

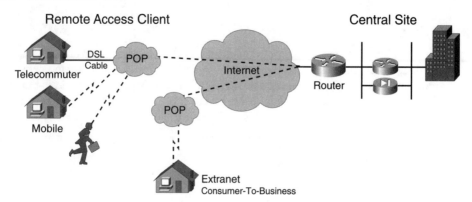

Site-To-Site VPNs

Site-to-site VPNs provide cost benefits relative to private WANs and also enable new applications such as extranets. However, site-to-site VPNs are still end-to-end networks and are subject to the same requirements that exist in private WANs, such as scalability, reliability, security, multiprotocol, and so on. In fact, because VPNs are built on a public network infrastructure, they have additional requirements, such as heightened security and advanced quality of service (QoS) capabilities, and a set of policy management tools to manage these additional features.

Cisco provides a suite of VPN-optimized routers, as shown in Figure 8-3. Cisco IOS software that is running in Cisco routers combines rich VPN services with industry-leading routing, thus delivering a comprehensive solution. Cisco routing software adds the following to site-to-site applications: scalability; reliability; multiprotocol; multiservice; management; SLA monitoring; and QoS. The Cisco VPN software adds strong security via encryption and authentication. These Cisco VPN-based products provide high performance for site-to-site, intranet, and extranet VPN solutions.

Figure 8-3   *Site-To-Site VPNs*

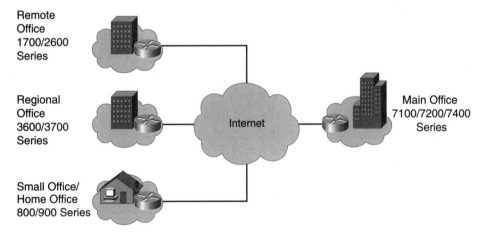

Cisco VPN Router Portfolio

Cisco provides a suite of VPN-optimized routers. These routers run the range of VPN applications, from telecommuter applications with the Cisco 800 router; to small branch office connectivity with the Cisco 1700 router; to enterprise branch office connectivity with the Cisco 1760 router; to the large branch office connectivity with the Cisco 3600 and 3725 routers; and to enterprise headquarters with the Cisco 3745 router. VPN-optimized routers provide VPN solutions for hybrid VPN environments where modularity, port density, and flexibility are required for private WAN aggregation and other classic WAN applications.

Cisco VPN Routers for Large Environments

The Cisco VPN Router portfolio adds high-end VPN connectivity with Cisco 7100, 7200, and 7400 series routers, as well as the Cisco Catalyst 6500 IPSec VPN Services Module. VPN-optimized routers and the Cisco Catalyst 6500 IPSec VPN Services Module provide VPN solutions for large-scale hybrid VPN environments where modularity, high performance, and flexibility are required.

Cisco VPN Routers for Small to Midsize Environments

You can use Table 8-1 to determine which model is best for your small to midsize environment. The table identifies router platforms, their related hardware accelerator card, and maximum throughput. Lab performance numbers are based on the following configuration: Triple Data Encryption Standard (3DES) with Hashed Message Authentication Code (HMAC)–Secure Hash Algorithm 1 (SHA-1), 100 percent CPU use, and no other services running, such as QoS, NAT, generic routing encapsulation (GRE), and so on. Actual network performance varies, depending on the services running in each router.

Table 8-1   *Cisco VPN Routers for Small to Midsize Environments*

Cisco Router	Maximum Tunnels	Performance (Mbps)	Hardware Encryption
830	<50	6	None
900	<50	6	Yes
1700	100	8	VPN module
2600XM	800	14	AIM-VPN/BP
2691	1000	80	AIM-VPN/BP
3725	2000	150	AIM-VPN/BP

Hardware encryption accelerator cards provide high-performance, hardware-assisted encryption, and key generation suitable for VPN applications. Hardware encryption accelerator cards improve overall system performance by offloading encryption and decryption processing, thus freeing main system resources for other tasks, such as route processing, QoS, and other network services. In midsize routers, there are four modules available:

- **AIM-VPN/BP (Base Performance)**—This Advanced Integration Module (AIM) can be added to all Cisco 2600 routers.

- **AIM-VPN/EP (Enhanced Performance)**—This AIM can be added to all current Cisco 2600 router models but is specifically designed to take advantage of the Cisco 2650 series high-performance routers.

- **AIM-VPN/HP (High Performance)**—High-performance AIM is for Cisco 3660 and Cisco 3745 routers.

- **NM-VPN/MP (Mid Performance)** — This network module is supported on all Cisco 3620 and 3640 routers.

Cisco VPN Routers for Enterprise-Size Environments

You can use Table 8-2 to determine which enterprise model is best for your environment. The table identifies router platforms, their related hardware encryption accelerator card, and maximum throughput. Lab performance numbers are based on the following configuration: 3DES with HMAC–SHA-1, 100 percent CPU use, and no other services running, such as QoS, NAT, GRE, and so on. Actual network performance varies depending on the services running in each router.

Table 8-2   *Cisco VPN Routers for Enterprise-Size Environments*

Cisco Router	Maximum Tunnels	Performance (Mbps)	Hardware Encryption
3745	2000	180	ISM
7120	2000	50	ISM
7140	2000	90	ISM
7200	5000	225	VAM
7400	5000	120	VAM
CAT 6500	8000	1.9G	Yes

Hardware encryption accelerator cards provide high-performance, hardware-assisted encryption, and key generation suitable for VPN applications. For the enterprise routers, there are three versions:

- **VPN Acceleration Module (VAM)** — The VAM for Cisco 7200 and 7100 series routers provides high-performance, hardware-assisted encryption, and key generation. VAM also supports IP payload Lempel-Ziv-Stac (LZS) compression services for VPN applications. There are two versions: VAM Service Adapter and VAM Service Module.

- **Integrated Service Module (ISM)** — ISM uses a special slot created for offloading encryption and key-generating services within the Cisco 7100 series routers (maximum of one ISM per Cisco 71XX series router).

- **Integrated Service Adapter (ISA)** — ISA is a service adapter that inserts in any open port adapter slot in any Cisco 7200 router and can be used within the single port adapter of the Cisco 7140 router (up to one ISA per Cisco 7140 router or two per Cisco 7200 series router, and not available on Cisco 7120 router).

The Cisco IPSec VPN Services Module is a high-speed module for the Cisco Catalyst 6500 Series Switch. Incorporating the latest in encryption hardware acceleration technology, the Cisco IPSec VPN Services Module can deliver up to 1.9 Gbps of 3DES traffic and can terminate 8000 IPSec tunnels.

What Is IPSec?

IPSec acts at the network layer, protecting and authenticating IP packets between participating IPSec devices (peers), such as PIX Firewalls, Cisco routers, Concentrators, Cisco VPN Clients, and other IPSec-compliant products. IPSec is not bound to any specific encryption or authentication algorithms, keying technology, or security algorithms. IPSec is a framework of open standards. By not binding IPSec to specific algorithms, IPSec allows for newer and better algorithms to be implemented without patching the existing IPSec standards. IPSec provides data confidentiality, data integrity, and origin authentication between participating peers at the IP layer. IPSec is used to secure a path between a pair of gateways, a pair of hosts, or a gateway and host. Figure 8-4 shows a typical IPSec deployment for a multisite organization with a mobile workforce.

Figure 8-4   *IPSec Deployment*

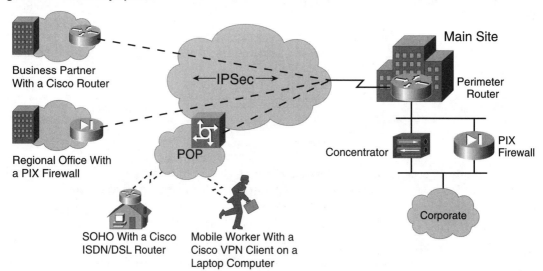

IPSec services provides four critical functions:

- **Confidentiality (encryption)**—The sender can encrypt the packets before transmitting them across a network. By doing so, no one can eavesdrop on the communication. If intercepted, the communications cannot be read.

- **Data integrity**—The receiver can verify that the data was transmitted through the Internet without being changed or altered in any way.

- **Origin authentication**—The receiver can authenticate the source of the packet, guaranteeing and certifying the source of the information.

- **Antireplay protection**—Antireplay protection verifies that each packet is unique, not duplicated.

Confidentiality (Encryption)

The good news is that the Internet is a public network. The bad news is that the Internet is a public network. Clear-text data that is transported over the Internet can be intercepted and read, as shown in Figure 8-5. To keep the data private, the data can be encrypted. By digitally scrambling the data, the data is rendered unreadable.

Figure 8-5 *Intercepting and Reading Clear-Text Data*

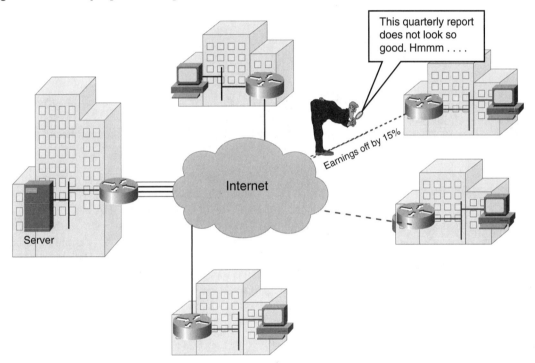

Types of Encryption

For encryption to work, both the sender and receiver need to know the rules that are used to transform the original message into its coded form. Rules are based on an algorithm and a key. An algorithm is a mathematical function, which combines a message, text, digits, or all three with a string of digits called a key. The output is an unreadable cipher string. Decryption is extremely difficult or impossible without the correct key.

In the example in Figure 8-6, someone wants to send a financial document across the Internet. At the local end, the document is combined with a key and run through an encryption algorithm. The output is undecipherable cipher text. The cipher text is then sent through the Internet. At the remote end, the message is recombined with a key and sent back through the encryption algorithm. The output is the original financial document.

Figure 8-6   *Types of Encryption*

There are two types of encryption keys: symmetric and asymmetric. With symmetric key encryption, each peer uses the same key to encrypt and decrypt the data. With asymmetric key encryption, the local end uses one key to encrypt the traffic, and the remote end uses another key to decrypt the traffic.

DH Key Exchange

DES, 3DES, HMAC–message digest algorithm 5 (MD5), and HMAC-SHA require a symmetric shared secret key to perform encryption and decryption. The question is, how does the encrypting and decrypting devices get the shared secret key? You can send the keys by e-mail, courier, overnight express, or public key exchange. The easiest method is the Diffie-Hellman (DH) public key exchange. The DH key agreement is a public key exchange method that provides a way for two peers to establish a shared secret key, which only they know, although they are communicating over an insecure channel. Figure 8-7 shows an example of a DH key.

Figure 8-7   *DH Key Exchange*

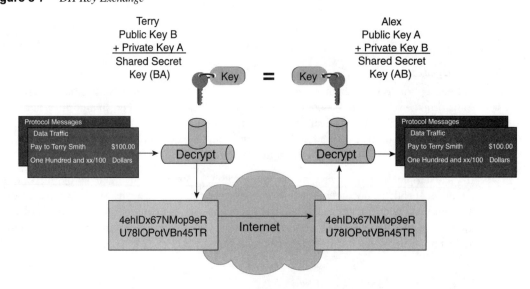

Public key cryptosystems rely on a two-key system: a public key, which is exchanged between end users, and a private key, which is kept secret by the original owners. The DH public key algorithm states that if user A and user B exchange public keys and a calculation is performed on their individual private key and one another's public key, the end result of the process is an identical shared key. The shared key is used to derive encryption and authentication keys. DH key exchange is covered in more depth in the "DH Key Exchange Process" section.

There are variations of the DH key exchange algorithm, known as DH group 1 through 7. During tunnel setup, VPN peers negotiate which DH group to use. The following is a list of some of the capabilities and uses of these algorithms:

- DH groups 1, 2, and 5 support exponentiation over a prime modulus with a key size of 768, 1024, and 1536, respectively.
- Cisco VPN Clients support DH groups 1, 2, and 5.
- DES and 3DES encryption support DH groups 1 and 2.
- Advanced Encryption Standard (AES) encryption supports DH groups 2 and 5.
- The Certicom wireless VPN Client supports group 7.
- Group 7 supports elliptical curve cryptography that reduces the time that is needed to generate keys.

Security is not an issue with the DH key exchange. Although someone may know a user's public key, the shared secret cannot be generated because the private key never becomes public.

The following lists the sequence of events that occurs during the DH process:

1 To start the DH process, each of the two peers generates a large prime integer, p and q. Each peer sends the other its prime integer over the insecure channel. For example, peer A sends p to peer B and peer B sends q to peer A. Each peer then uses the p and q values to generate g, a primitive root of p.

2 Each peer generates a private DH key (peer A: X_a, peer B: X_b).

3 Each peer generates a public DH key. The local private key is combined with the prime number p and the primitive root g in each peer to generate a public key, Y_a for peer A and Y_A for peer B. The formula for peer A is $Y_a = g^{X_a} \bmod p$. The formula for peer B is $Y_b = g^{X_b} \bmod p$. The exponentiation is computationally expensive. Mod denotes modulus.

4 The public keys Y_a and Y_b are exchanged in public.

5 Each peer generates a shared secret number (ZZ) by combining the public key received from the opposite peer with its own private key. The formula for peer A is $ZZ = (Y_b X_a) \bmod p$. The formula for peer B is $ZZ = (Y_a X_b) \bmod p$. The ZZ values are identical in each peer. Anyone who knows p or g, or the DH public keys, cannot guess or easily calculate the shared secret value—largely because of the difficulty in factoring large prime numbers.

6 Shared secret number ZZ is used in the derivation of the encryption and authentication symmetrical keys.

Encryption Algorithms

Of the encryption algorithms discussed in this section, DES, 3DES, and AES are used to encrypt IPSec packets. Rivest, Shamir, and Adleman (RSA) is used for peer authentication. For IPSec encryption, 3DES and AES are more secure than DES, but require more processing power and may not be acceptable on busy systems. AES is the newest standard, providing superior security and performance when compared to DES and 3DES.

The degree of security depends on the length of the key. If someone tries to hack the key through a brute-force attack, which tries to guess every possible combination, the number of possibilities is a function of the length of the key. The time to process all the possibilities is a function of the computing power of the computer. Therefore, the shorter the key, the easier it is to break. A 64-bit key with a relatively sophisticated computer can take approximately 1 year to break. A 128-bit key with the same machine can take roughly 10^{19} years to decrypt. Figure 8-8 shows examples of encryption algorithms.

Figure 8-8   *Encryption Algorithms*

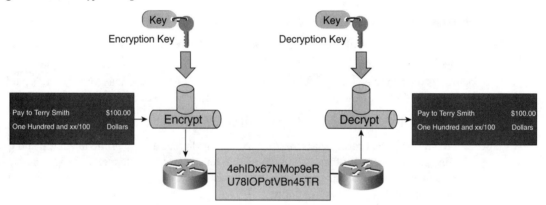

Some of the encryption algorithms that use processes similar to those shown in Figure 8-8 are as follows:

- **DES**—Developed by IBM, DES uses a 56-bit key, ensuring high-performance encryption. DES is a symmetric key cryptosystem.

- **3DES**—The 3DES algorithm is a variant of the 56-bit DES. 3DES operates similarly to DES, in that data is broken into 64-bit blocks. 3DES then processes each block three times, each time with an independent 56-bit key. 3DES effectively doubles encryption strength over 56-bit DES. DES is a symmetric key cryptosystem.

- **AES**—The National Institute of Standards and Technology (NIST) has recently adopted the new algorithm AES to replace existing DES encryption in cryptographic devices. AES provides stronger security than DES and is computationally more efficient than 3DES. AES offers three different key strengths: 128-, 192-, and 256-bit keys.

- **RSA**—RSA is an asymmetrical key cryptosystem. It uses a key length of 512, 768, and 1024 or longer. IPSec does not use RSA for data encryption. Internet Key Exchange (IKE) only uses RSA encryption during the peer authentication phase.

    RSA encryption uses asymmetric keys for encryption and decryption. Each end, local and remote, generates two encryption keys: a private and public key. They keep their private key and exchange their public key with people with whom they wish to communicate.

    To send an encrypted message, the local end encrypts the message by using the remote end's public key and the RSA encryption algorithm. The result is an unreadable cipher text, which is sent over the Internet. The remote end uses its private key and the RSA algorithm to decrypt the cipher text. The result is the original message. The only host that can decrypt the message is the destination that owns the private key.

    With RSA encryption, shown in Figure 8-9, the opposite also holds true. The remote end can encrypt a message by using its own private key. The receiver can decrypt the message by using the sender's public key. This RSA encryption technique is used for digital signatures.

Figure 8-9   *RSA Encryption*

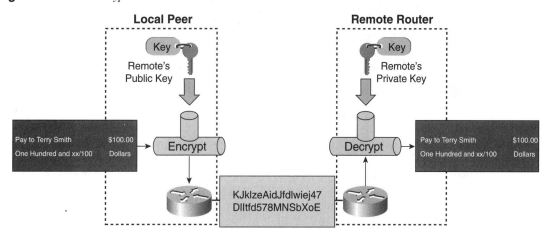

RSA encryption and peer authentication are discussed further in the upcoming section "Origin Authentication."

Data Integrity

The next VPN-critical function is data integrity. VPN data is transported over the Internet. Potentially, this data could be intercepted and modified. To guard against this, each message has a hash attached to the message. A hash guarantees the integrity of the original message. If the transmitted hash matches the received hash, the message has not been tampered with. However, if there is no match, then the message was altered.

In the example in Figure 8-10, someone is trying to send Terry Smith a check for $100. At the remote end, Alex Jones is trying to cash the check for $1000. As the check progressed through the Internet, it was altered. Both the recipient and dollar amounts were changed. In this case, the hashes do not match. The transaction is no longer valid.

Figure 8-10 *Data Integrity*

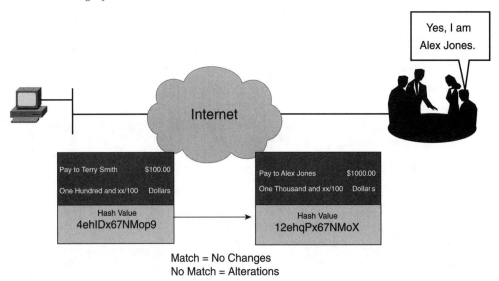

Match = No Changes
No Match = Alterations

HMAC and Its Algorithms

HMAC, shown in Figure 8-11, guarantees the integrity of the message. At the local end, the message and a shared secret key are sent through a hash algorithm, which produces a hash value. Basically, a hash algorithm is a formula used to convert a variable-length message into a single string of digits of a fixed length. It is a one-way algorithm. A message can produce a hash, but a hash cannot produce the original message. The message and hash are sent over the network.

At the remote end, there is a two-step process. First, the received message and shared secret key are sent through the hash algorithm, resulting in a recalculated hash value. Second, the receiver compares the recalculated hash with the hash that was attached to the message. If the original hash and recalculated hash match, the integrity of the message is guaranteed. If any of the original message is changed while in transit, the hash values are different.

Figure 8-11 *HMAC*

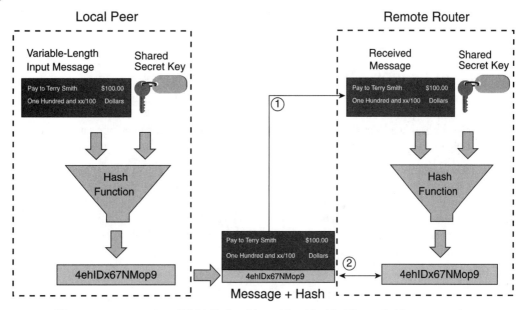

There are two common HMAC algorithms identified in Figure 8-12:

- **HMAC-MD5**—Uses a 128-bit shared secret key. The variable-length message and 128-bit shared secret key are combined and run through the HMAC-MD5 hash algorithm. The output is a 128-bit hash. The hash is appended to the original message and forwarded to the remote end.

- **HMAC-SHA-1**—Uses a 160-bit secret key. The variable-length message and the 160-bit shared secret key are combined and run through the HMAC-SHA-1 hash algorithm. The output is a 160-bit hash. The hash is appended to the original message and forwarded to the remote end.

Figure 8-12 *HMAC Algorithms*

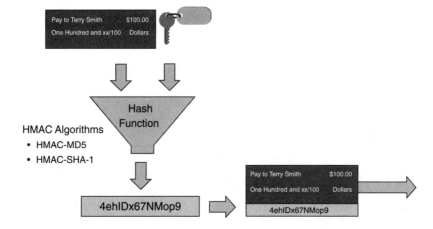

HMAC-SHA-1 is considered cryptographically stronger than HMAC-MD5. HMAC-SHA-1 is recommended when the slightly superior security of HMAC-SHA-1 over HMAC-MD5 is important.

Origin Authentication

Another critical function is origin authentication. In the middle ages, a seal guaranteed the authenticity of an edict. In modern times, a signed document is notarized with a seal and a signature. In the electronic era, a document is signed using the sender's private encryption key—a digital signature. Decrypting the signature with the sender's public key authenticates a signature.

In the example in Figure 8-13, the local device derives a hash and encrypts it with its private key. The encrypted hash—digital signature—is attached to the message and forwarded to the remote end. At the remote end, the encrypted hash is decrypted using the local end's public key. If the decrypted hash matches the recomputed hash, the signature is genuine. A digital signature ties a message to a sender. The sender is authenticated. It is used during the initial establishment of a VPN tunnel to authenticate both ends to the tunnel.

Figure 8-13 *Digital Signatures*

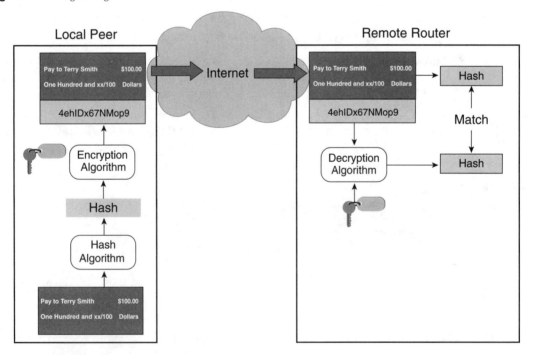

There are two common digital signature algorithms: RSA and Directory System Agent (DSA). RSA is used commercially and is the more common of the two. DSA is used by U.S. government agencies and is not as common.

Peer Authentication

When conducting business long distance, such as between the remote and corporate offices of Figure 8-14, it is necessary to know who is at the other end of the phone, e-mail, or fax. The same is true of VPN networking. The device on the other end of the VPN tunnel must be authenticated before the communication path is considered secure. There are three peer authentication methods:

- **Pre-shared keys**—A secret key value is provided to each peer prior to tunnel negotiations. The pre-shared key is entered into each peer manually and is then used to authenticate the peers.

- **RSA signatures**—Uses the exchange of digital certificates to authenticate the peers.

- **RSA-encrypted nonces**—Nonces (a random number that is generated by each peer) are encrypted and then exchanged between peers. The two nonces are used during the peer authentication process.

Figure 8-14 *Peer Authentication*

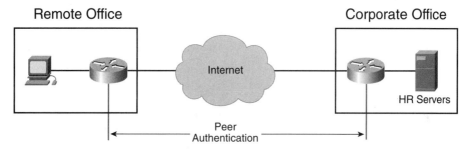

Pre-Shared Keys

With pre-shared keys, the same pre-shared key is configured on each IPSec peer. At each end, the pre-shared key is combined with other information to form the authentication key. Starting at the local end, the authentication key and the identity information (device-specific information) are sent through a hash algorithm to form hash_I. The local IKE peer provides one-way authentication by sending hash_I to the remote peer. If the remote peer is able to independently create the same hash, the local peer is authenticated, as shown in Figure 8-15.

The authentication process continues in the opposite direction. The remote peer combines its identity information with the pre-shared-based authentication key and sends them through a hash algorithm to form hash_R. Hash_R is sent to the local peer. If the local peer is able to independently create the same hash from its stored information and pre-shared-based authentication key, the remote peer is authenticated. Each peer must authenticate its opposite peer before the tunnel is considered secure.

Figure 8-15 *Pre-Shared Keys*

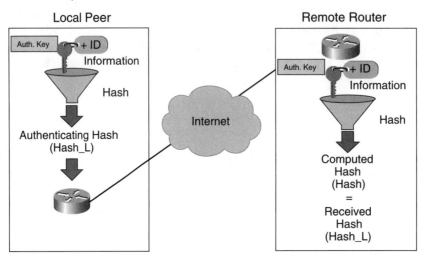

Pre-shared keys are easy to configure manually, but do not scale well. Each IPSec peer must be configured with the pre-shared key of every other peer with which it communicates.

RSA Signatures

With RSA signatures, hash_I and hash_R are not only authenticated, but also digitally signed. Starting at the local end, the authentication key and identity information (device-specific information) are sent through a hash algorithm to form hash_I. The hash_I is then encrypted using the local peer's private encryption key. The result is a digital signature. The digital signature and a digital certificate are forwarded to the remote peer. (The public encryption key for decrypting the signature is included in the digital certificate exchanged between peers.)

At the remote peer, local peer authentication is a two-step process. First, the remote peer verifies the digital signature by decrypting it using the public encryption key enclosed in the digital certificate. The result is hash_I. Next, the remote peer independently creates hash_I from stored information. If the calculated hash_I equals the decrypted hash_I, the local peer is authenticated, as shown in Figure 8-16. Digital signatures and certificates are discussed in more detail in Chapter 9, "Building Advanced IPSec VPNs Using Cisco Routers and Certificate Authorities."

After the remote peer authenticates the local peer, the authentication process begins in the opposite direction. The remote peer combines its identity information with the authentication key and sends them through a hash algorithm to form hash_R. Hash_R is encrypted using the remote peer's private encryption key, a digital signature. The digital signature and certificate are sent to the local peer. The local peer performs two tasks: it creates the hash_R from stored information, and it decrypts the digital signature. If the calculated hash_R and the decrypted hash_R match, the remote peer is authenticated. Each peer must authenticate its opposite peer before the tunnel is considered secure.

Figure 8-16 *RSA Signatures*

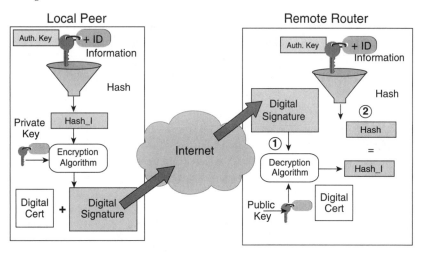

RSA-Encrypted Nonces

RSA-encrypted nonces require that each party generate a nonce—a pseudorandom number. The nonces are then encrypted and exchanged. Upon receipt of the nonce, each end formulates an authentication key made up of the initiator and responder nonces, the DH key, and the initiator and responder cookies. The nonce-based authentication key is combined with device-specific information and run through a hash algorithm. The output then becomes hash_L. The local IKE peer provides one-way authentication by sending hash_L to the remote peer. If the remote peer is able to independently create the same hash from stored information and its nonce-based authentication key, the local peer is authenticated as shown in Figure 8-17.

Figure 8-17 *RSA-Encrypted Nonces*

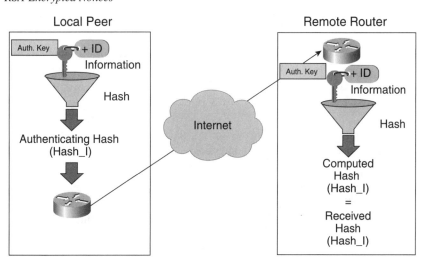

After the remote end authenticates the local peer, authentication process begins in the opposite direction. The remote peer combines its identity information with the nonce-based authentication key and sends them through a hash algorithm to form hash_R. Hash_R is sent to the local peer. If the local peer is able to independently create the same hash from stored information and the nonce-based key, the remote peer is authenticated. Each peer must authenticate its opposite peer before the tunnel is considered to be secure.

Antireplay Protection

Both types of IPSec packets, AH and ESP, contain a 32-bit sequence number that is used to provide protection against an attacker eavesdropping on an IPSec session, stealing packets, modifying them, and reinserting them into a session at a later time. IPSec does this by comparing the sequence number of the received packets against a sliding window on the destination host, or security gateway. Packets that have sequence numbers that are before the sliding window are considered late, or duplicates. Late and duplicate packets are dropped.

The sequence number is incrementally increased (starting from 1) for each established SA. The sequence number cannot repeat for the life of the SA. It is the responsibility of the receiver to perform the antireplay sequence number check.

IPSec Protocol Framework

This section explains how encryption, integrity, and authentication are applied to the IPSec protocol suite.

IPSec Protocols

IPSec is a framework of open standards. IPSec spells out the messaging to secure the communications but relies on existing algorithms, such as DES and 3DES, to implement the encryption and authentication. The two main IPSec framework protocols are as follows:

- **Authentication Header (AH)**—AH is the appropriate protocol when confidentiality is not required or permitted. It provides data authentication and integrity for IP packets that are passed between two systems. It is a means of verifying that any message that is passed from router A to router B has not been modified during transit. It verifies that the origin of the data was either router A or router B. AH does not provide data confidentiality (encryption) of packets. No encryption occurs, which means that AH packets are transported in the clear, exposing transmitted data to potential compromise.

- **Encapsulating Security Payload (ESP)**—A security protocol may be used to provide confidentiality (encryption) and authentication. ESP provides confidentiality by performing encryption at the IP packet layer. IP packet encryption conceals the data payload and the identities of the ultimate source and destination. ESP provides authentication for the inner IP packet and ESP header. Authentication provides data origin authentication, and data integrity. Although both encryption and authentication are optional in ESP, at a minimum, one of them must be selected.

Authentication Header

Authentication is achieved by applying a keyed one-way hash function to the packet to create a hash or message digest. The hash is combined with the text and transmitted. Changes in any part of the packet that occur during transit are detected by the receiver when it performs the same one-way hash function on the received packet, and compares the value of the message digest that the sender has supplied. The fact that the one-way hash also involves the use of a symmetric key between the two systems means that authenticity is guaranteed.

Authentication Header has the following characteristics:

- Ensures data integrity
- Provides origin authentication (ensures packets definitely came from the peer router)
- Uses keyed-hash mechanism
- Does not provide confidentiality (no encryption)
- Provides antireplay protection

AH Authentication and Integrity

The AH function is applied to the entire datagram, except for any mutable IP header fields that change in transit (for example, Time to Live [TTL] fields that are modified by the routers along the transmission path). AH authentication and integrity is shown in Figure 8-18.

Figure 8-18 *AH Authentication and Integrity*

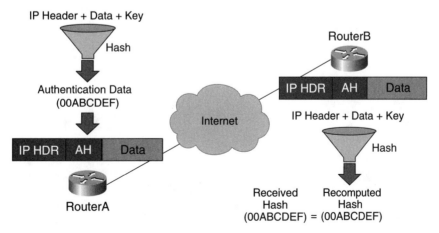

AH works as follows:

1 The IP header and data payload are hashed.

2 The hash is used to build an AH header, which is appended to the original packet.

3 The new packet is transmitted to the IPSec peer router.

4 The peer router hashes the IP header and data payload.

5 The peer router extracts the transmitted hash from the AH header.

6 The peer router compares the two hashes. The hashes must exactly match. Even if one bit is changed in the transmitted packet, the hash output on the received packet will change and the AH header will not match.

AH supports HMAC-MD5 and HMAC-SHA-1 algorithms.

Encapsulating Security Payload

ESP provides confidentiality by encrypting the payload. It supports a variety of symmetric encryption algorithms. The default algorithm for IPSec is 56-bit DES. Cisco products also support the use of 3DES for stronger encryption.

ESP can be used alone or in combination with AH. ESP with AH also provides integrity and authentication of the datagrams. First, the payload is encrypted. Then, the encrypted payload is sent through a hash algorithm: HMAC-MD5 or HMAC-SHA-1. The hash provides origin authentication and data integrity for the data payload.

Alternatively, ESP may also enforce antireplay protection by requiring that a receiving host set the Replay bit in the header to indicate that the packet has been seen.

Between two security gateways, the original payload is well protected because the entire original IP datagram is encrypted, as shown in Figure 8-19. An ESP header and trailer are added to the encrypted payload. With ESP authentication, the encrypted IP datagram and the ESP header or trailer are included in the hashing process. Last, a new IP header is appended to the front of the authenticated payload. The new IP address is used to route the packet over the Internet.

Figure 8-19 *ESP Protocol*

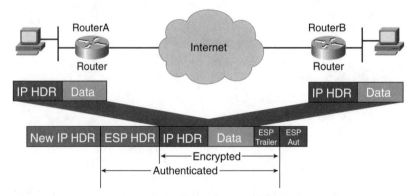

When both ESP authentication and encryption are selected, encryption is performed first before authentication. One reason for this order of processing is that it facilitates rapid detection and rejection of replayed or bogus packets by the receiving node. Prior to decrypting the packet, the receiver can authenticate inbound packets. By doing this, it can detect the problems and potentially reduce the impact of DoS attacks.

Modes of Use: Tunnel Mode Versus Transport Mode

ESP and AH can be applied to IP packets in two different ways, which are referred to as modes, as shown in Figure 8-20:

- **Tunnel mode**—ESP tunnel mode is used when either end of the tunnel is a security gateway, a Concentrator, a VPN optimized router, or a PIX Firewall. Tunnel mode is used when the final destination is not a host, but a VPN gateway. The security gateway encrypts and authenticates the original IP packet. Then, a new IP header is appended to the front of the encrypted packet. The outside, new, IP address is used to route the packet across the Internet to the remote end security gateway. Tunnel mode provides security for the whole original IP packet.

- **Transport mode**—Transport mode protects the payload of the packet, higher-layer protocols, but leaves the original IP address in the clear. The original IP address is used to route the packet across the Internet. ESP transport mode is used between two hosts. Transport mode provides security to the higher-layer protocols only.

Figure 8-20 *Modes of Use: Transport Mode Versus Tunnel Mode*

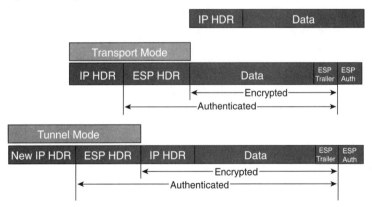

Tunnel Mode

ESP tunnel mode is used between a host and a security gateway or between two security gateways. For gateway-to-gateway applications, rather than load IPSec on all the computers at the remote and corporate offices, it is easier to have the security gateways perform the IP-in-IP encryption and encapsulation. IP-in-IP encapsulation is accomplished by adding a new IP header to existing IP packets. The original header is retained and will be used by the tunnel endpoint once the extra IP header has been removed. The original IP packet may be encrypted to provide additional security.

In the IPSec remote access application, ESP tunnel mode is used. At a home office, there may be no router to perform the IPSec encapsulation and encryption. In the example shown in Figure 8-21, the IPSec client that is running on the PC performs the IPSec IP-in-IP encapsulation and encryption. At the corporate office, the router de-encapsulates and decrypts the packet.

Figure 8-21 *Tunnel Mode*

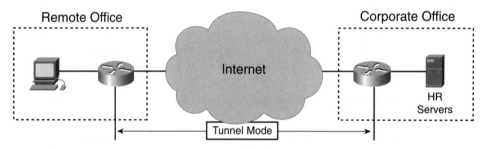

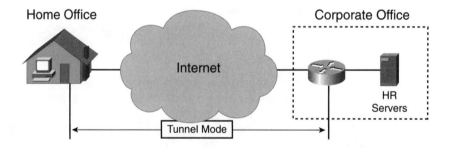

Transport Mode

Transport mode is primarily used for end-to-end connections between hosts or devices that are acting as hosts. Tunnel mode is used for everything else. An IPSec gateway (that is, a Cisco IOS router, Cisco PIX Firewall, or Cisco VPN 3000 Series Concentrator) might act as a host when being accessed by an administrator for configuration or other management operations.

For AH, transport mode is accomplished by shifting the original IP header to the left and inserting the AH header. The entire resulting packet is then hashed to provide authentication. These new packets do not support NAT because changing the IP address in the header would cause authentication to fail. You can use NAT before IPSec AH encapsulation, but not after.

ESP transport mode occurs by shifting the original IP packet header to the left, inserting an ESP header before the data, inserting an ESP trailer after the data, and adding some control information at the end of the new packet. If encryption is required, only the data and ESP trailer are encrypted. Authentication uses the ESP header, data portion, and ESP trailer from the new packet and does not use the IP header, permitting the use of NAT on these packets.

DF Bit Override Functionality with IPSec Tunnels

The Don't Fragment (DF) Bit Override Functionality with IPSec Tunnels feature allows customers to specify whether their router can clear, set, or copy the DF bit from the encapsulated header. The DF bit in the IP header tells a router whether it is allowed to fragment a packet.

Some hosts set the DF bit in the IP header of tunnel mode IPSec packets to prevent fragmentation of the packets. The DF Bit Override Functionality with IPSec Tunnels feature permits administrators to configure the setting of the DF bit when encapsulating tunnel mode IPSec traffic on a global or per-interface level. If the DF bit is set to clear, routers can fragment packets regardless of the original DF bit setting.

A significant performance impact can occur at high data rates when fragmentation is permitted, because each packet must be reassembled at the process level. Additionally, the reassemble queue can fill up and force fragments to be dropped, and the traffic is slower because of the process switching.

Interfaces that are sharing the same crypto map by using the local address feature must share the same DF bit setting. The DF Bit Override Functionality with IPSec Tunnels feature is available only for IPSec tunnel mode because IPSec transport mode does not use an encapsulating IP header.

The DF Bit Override Functionality with IPSec Tunnels feature runs on all platforms that support IPSec. The **crypto ipsec df-bit** command may be applied globally to affect the IPSec characteristics of all interfaces or it may be configured on specific interfaces to limit the effects of the command to IPSec traffic on that interface. The syntax of the command follows:

```
crypto ipsec df-bit {clear | set | copy}
```

- **Clear**—Specifies that the outer IP header will have the DF bit cleared and that the router may fragment the packet to add the IPSec encapsulation.

- **Set**—Specifies that the outer IP header will have the DF bit set; however, the router may fragment the packet if the original packet had the DF bit cleared.

- **Copy**—Specifies that the router will look in the original packet for the outer DF bit setting.

IPSec Framework

IPSec is a framework of open standards. IPSec spells out the rules for secure communications. IPSec, in turn, relies on existing algorithms to implement the encryption, authentication, and key exchange. Some of the standard algorithms are as follows:

- **DES**—DES is used to encrypt and decrypt packet data
- **3DES**—3DES effectively triples encryption strength over 56-bit DES through the use of cipher blocking
- **MD5**—MD5 is used to authenticate packet data
- **SHA-1**—SHA authenticates packet data
- **DH**—DH is a public-key cryptography protocol that allows two parties to establish a shared secret key used by encryption and hash algorithms (for example, DES and MD5) over an insecure communications channel

In the example in Figure 8-22, there are four IPSec framework squares to be filled.

Figure 8-22 *IPSec Protocol—Framework*

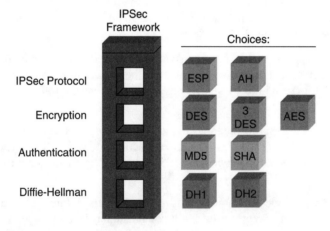

When configuring security services to be provided by an IPSec gateway, use the following steps:

Step 1   Choose an IPSec protocol: ESP or ESP with AH.

Step 2   Choose the encryption algorithm that is appropriate for the level of security desired: DES or 3DES. (The second square is an encryption algorithm.)

Step 3   Choose an authentication algorithm to provide data integrity: MD5 or SHA. (The third square is authentication.)

Step 4   Choose which group to use: DH1 or DH2. (The last square is the DH algorithm group.)

IPSec provides the framework, and the administrator chooses the algorithms that are used to implement the security services within that framework.

Five Steps of IPSec

The goal of IPSec is to protect the desired data with the needed security services. IPSec's operation can be broken down into five primary steps:

Step 1   **Identifying interesting traffic**—The VPN device recognizes that the traffic you want to send needs to be protected.

Step 2   **IKE phase 1**—Between peers, a basic set of security services is negotiated and agreed upon. This basic set of security services protects all subsequent communications between the peers. IKE phase 1 sets up a secure communications channel between peers.

Step 3   **IKE phase 2**—IKE negotiates IPSec security association (SA) parameters and sets up matching IPSec SAs in the peers. These security parameters are used to protect data and messages exchanged between endpoints. You can find more information in the "Security Association" section later in this chapter.

Step 4   **Data transfer**—Data is transferred between IPSec peers based on the IPSec parameters and keys stored in the SA database.

Step 5   **IPSec tunnel termination**—IPSec SAs terminate through deletion or by timing out.

Step 1 of IPSec: Interesting Traffic

Determining what traffic needs to be protected is done as part of formulating a security policy for use of a VPN.

The policy is used to determine what traffic needs to be protected and what traffic can be sent in the clear. For every inbound and outbound datagram, there are two choices: apply IPSec, or bypass IPSec and send the datagram in clear text. For every datagram protected by IPSec, the system administrator must specify the security services that are applied to the datagram. The security policy database specifies the IPSec protocols, modes, and algorithms that are applied to the traffic. The services are then applied to traffic destined to each particular IPSec peer. With the VPN Client, you use menu windows to select connections that you want secured by IPSec. When interesting traffic transits the IPSec client, the client initiates the next step in the process: negotiating an IKE phase 1 exchange.

Step 2 of IPSec: IKE Phase 1

In this step, you negotiate IKE policy sets, authenticate the peers, and set up a secure channel between the peers.

IKE phase 1 occurs in two modes: Main Mode and Aggressive Mode. Main Mode has three two-way exchanges between the initiator and receiver, resulting in a total of six message transfers for the process:

- **First exchange**—The algorithms and hashes that are used to secure the IKE communications are negotiated and agreed upon between peers, resulting in the Internet Security Association and Key Management Protocol (ISAKMP) policy to be used by the peers.

- **Second exchange**—Uses a DH exchange to generate shared secret keys and pass nonces to the other party, signed, and returned to prove their identity. The shared secret key is used to generate all the other encryption and authentication keys.

- **Third exchange**—Verifies the other side's identity. It is used to authenticate the remote peer. The main outcome of Main Mode is a secure communication path for subsequent exchanges between the peers. Without proper authentication, it is possible to establish a secure communication channel with an attacker who is now stealing all your sensitive material.

In Aggressive Mode, fewer exchanges are done and with fewer packets. This mode does not provide identity protection because the exchanges are made in clear text.

- **First exchange**—On the first exchange, almost everything is squeezed in: the IKE policy set negotiation; the DH public key generation; a nonce, which the other party signs; and an identity packet, which can be used to verify their identity via a third party.

- **Second exchange**—The receiver sends everything back that is needed to complete the exchange.

- **Third exchange**—The only thing left is for the initiator to confirm the exchange.

IKE Transform Sets

When trying to make a secure connection between Hosts A and B through the Internet, IKE security proposals are exchanged between Routers A and B. The proposals identify the IPSec protocol being negotiated, such as ESP. Under each proposal, the originator must delineate which algorithms are employed in the proposal, such as DES with MD5. Rather than negotiate each algorithm individually, the algorithms are grouped into sets, an IKE transform set. A transform set delineates which encryption algorithm, authentication algorithm, mode, and key length are proposed. These IKE proposals and transform sets are exchanged during the IKE Main Mode first exchange phase. If a transform set match is found between peers, the Main Mode continues. If no match is found, the tunnel is torn down.

In the example in Figure 8-23, Router A sends IKE transform sets 10 and 20 to Router B. Router B compares its set, transform set 15, with those received from Router A. In this instance, there is a match: Router A's transform set 10 matches Router B's transform set 15.

Figure 8-23 *IKE Transform Sets*

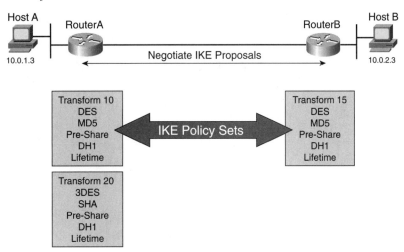

In a point-to-point application, each end may only need a single IKE policy set defined. However, in a hub-and-spoke environment, the central site may require multiple IKE policy sets to satisfy all the remote peers.

DH Key Exchange Process

DH key exchange, shown earlier in Figure 8-7, is a public key exchange method that provides a way for two peers to establish a shared secret key over an insecure communications path. With DH, there are several different DH algorithms, or groups, defined: DH groups 1 to 7. A group number defines an algorithm and unique values. For instance, group 1 defines exponentiation over a prime modulus (MODP) algorithm with a 768-bit prime number. Group 2 defines a MODP algorithm with a 1024-bit prime number. During IKE phase 1, the group is negotiated between peers. Between Cisco VPN devices, either group 1 or 2 is supported.

After the group negotiations are completed, the shared secret key is calculated (SKEYID). The SKEYID is used in the derivation of three other keys: SKEYID_a, SKEYID_e, and SKEYID_d. Each key has a separate purpose:

- **SKEYID_a**—The keying material used during the authentication process.
- **SKEYID_e**—The keying material used in the encryption process.
- **SKEY_d**—The keying material used to derive keys for non-ISAKMP SAs.

All four keys are calculated during IKE phase 1.

Authenticate Peer Identity

When conducting business over the Internet, it is necessary to know who is at the other end of the tunnel. The device on the other end of the VPN tunnel must be authenticated before the communications path is considered secure. The last exchange of IKE phase 1 is used to authenticate the remote peer.

There are three data origin authentication methods:

- **Pre-shared keys**— A secret key value is provided to each peer prior to tunnel negotiations. The pre-shared key is entered into each peer manually and is then used to authenticate the peers.

- **RSA signatures**—Digital certificates are exchanged to authenticate the peers.

- **RSA-encrypted nonces**—Nonces are encrypted and then exchanged between peers. Each peer uses the nonce from the other peer during the authentication process.

Step 3 of IPSec: IKE Phase 2

In this step, the IPSec parameters that are used to secure the IPSec tunnel are negotiated. IKE phase 2 performs the following functions:

- Negotiates IPSec parameters, IPSec transform sets

- Establishes IPSec SAs

- Periodically renegotiates IPSec SAs to ensure security

- Optionally performs an additional DH exchange when using perfect forward secrecy (PFS)

IKE phase 2 has one mode, called Quick Mode. Quick Mode occurs after IKE has established the secure tunnel in IKE phase 1. It negotiates a shared IPSec transform, derives shared secret keying material that is used for the IPSec algorithms, and establishes IPSec SAs. Quick Mode exchanges nonces that are used to generate new shared secret key material and prevent replay attacks from generating bogus SAs.

Quick Mode is also used to renegotiate a new IPSec SA when the IPSec SA lifetime expires. Quick Mode uses the keying material that is derived from the DH exchange in IKE phase 1 to refresh the keying material that is used to create the shared secret key.

IPSec Transform Sets

The ultimate goal of IKE phase 2 is to establish a secure IPSec session between endpoints. Before that can happen, each pair of endpoints negotiates the level of security required, such as encryption and authentication algorithms for the session. Rather than negotiate each protocol individually, the protocols are grouped into sets, an IPSec transform set. A transform set is a combination of algorithms and protocols that enacts a security policy for traffic. IPSec transform sets are exchanged between peers during Quick Mode. If a match is found between sets, IPSec session-establishment continues. If no match is found, the session is torn down.

In the example in Figure 8-24, Router A sends IPSec transform set 30 and 40 to Router B. Router B compares its set, transform set 55, with those received from Router A. In this instance, there is a match. Router A's transform set 30 matches Router B's transform set 55. These encryption and authentication algorithms form an SA.

Figure 8-24 *IPSec Transform Sets*

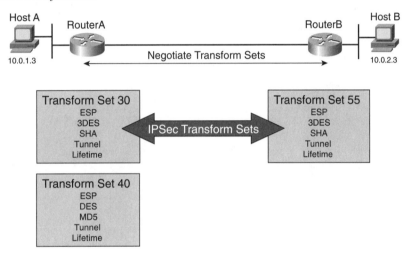

Security Association

When the security services are agreed upon between peers, each VPN peer device enters the information in a security policy database (SPD). The information includes the encryption and authentication algorithm, destination IP address, transport mode, key lifetime, and so on. This information is referred to as the SA. An SA is a one-way logical connection that provides security to all traffic that is traversing the connection. Because most traffic is bidirectional, two SAs are required: one for inbound traffic and one for outbound traffic. The VPN device indexes the SA with a number, a security parameter index (SPI). Rather than send the individual parameters of the SA through the tunnel, the source gateway, or host, inserts the SPI into the ESP header. When the IPSec peer receives the packet, it looks up the destination IP address, IPSec protocol, and SPI in its SA database (SAD), and then processes the packet according to the algorithms listed under the SPD.

The IPSec SA is a compilation of the SAD and SPD. The SAD is used to identify the SA destination IP address, IPSec protocol, and SPI number. The SPD defines the security services that are applied to the SA, encryption and authentication algorithms, and mode and key lifetime. For example, in the corporate-to-bank connection shown in Figure 8-25, the security policy provides a very secure tunnel by using 3DES, SHA, tunnel mode, and a key lifetime of 28800. The SAD value is 192.168.2.1, ESP, and SPI-12. For the remote user who is accessing e-mails, a less secure policy is negotiated using DES, MD5, tunnel mode, and a key lifetime of 28800. The SAD values are a destination IP address of 192.169.12.1, ESP, and an SPI-39.

Figure 8-25 *Security Associations*

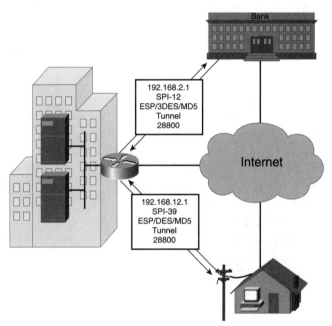

SA Lifetime

Like passwords on your company PC, the longer you keep your keys and SAs, the more vulnerable they become. The same thing is true of keys and SAs. For good security, the SA and keys should be changed periodically. There are two parameters. The first parameter is lifetime type. How is the lifetime measured? Is it measured by the number of bytes transmitted or the amount of time transpired? The second parameter is the unit of measure: kilobytes of data or seconds of time? For example, a lifetime could be based on 10,000 kilobytes of data transmitted or 28,800 seconds of time expired. The keys and SAs remain active until their lifetime expires or until some external event—for example, the client drops the tunnel—causes them to be deleted.

Step 4 of IPSec: Data Transfer

Interesting traffic is encrypted and decrypted according to the security services that are specified in the IPSec SA. After IKE phase 2 is complete and Quick Mode has established IPSec SAs, traffic is exchanged between Hosts A and B via a secure tunnel.

Step 5 of IPSec: Tunnel Termination

The final step of the IPSec process is the termination of the tunnel. IPSec SAs terminate through deletion or by timing out. An SA can time out when a specified number of seconds has elapsed or when a specified number of bytes has passed through the tunnel. When the SAs terminate, the keys are also discarded. When subsequent IPSec SAs are needed for a flow, IKE performs a new phase 2 and, if necessary, a new phase 1 negotiation. A successful negotiation results in new SAs and new keys. New SAs are usually established before the existing SAs expire, so that a given flow can continue uninterrupted.

IPSec and Dynamic Virtual Private Networks

Hub-and-spoke configurations can be complex to configure when spoke routers need to establish VPNs with other spokes on either a temporary or permanent basis. Fortunately, the Dynamic Multipoint VPN (DMVPN) feature allows administrators to better scale large and small IPSec VPNs by combining GRE tunnels, IPSec encryption, and Next Hop Resolution Protocol (NHRP).

Some of the major benefits of DMVPN include the following:

- **Hub router configuration reduction**—The DMVPN feature allows administrators to configure a single multipoint GRE tunnel interface and a single IPSec profile, with no crypto access lists on the hub router to handle all spoke routers. This keeps the size of the configuration on the hub router constant even if new spoke routers are added to the network.

- **Automatic IPSec encryption initiation**—With DMVPN, NHRP configures or resolves the peer source and destination address for GRE. This allows IPSec to be immediately triggered for point-to-point GRE tunneling. For multipoint GRE tunnels, IPSec will be triggered when the GRE peer address is resolved via NHRP.

- **Support for dynamically addressed spoke routers**—When configuring point-to-point GRE and IPSec hub-and-spoke VPN networks on the hub router, the physical interface IP address of the spoke routers must be known, because the IP address must be configured as the GRE tunnel destination address.

  DMVPN works with spoke routers that have dynamic physical interface IP addresses (common for cable and DSL connections). When spoke routers come online, they send registration packets to the hub router that contains their current physical interface IP address.

- **Dynamic tunnel creation for spoke-to-spoke tunnels**—DMVPN eliminates the need to configure direct tunnels from spoke to spoke. When a spoke router wants to transmit a packet to another spoke router, it uses NHRP to dynamically determine the required destination address of the target spoke router.

  The hub router acts as the NHRP server, handling the request for the source spoke router. The two spoke routers dynamically create an IPSec tunnel between them so that data can be directly transferred.

DMVPN relies on the following Cisco technologies:

- **NHRP**—Client/server protocol where the hub is the server and the spokes are the clients. The hub maintains an NHRP database of the public interface addresses of each spoke. Each spoke registers its real address with the hub when it boots. Spokes query the NHRP database for real addresses of destination spokes to build direct tunnels.

- **mGRE Tunnel Interface**—Allows a single GRE interface to support multiple IPSec tunnels and simplifies the size and complexity of the configuration.

Figure 8-26 shows a typical hub-and-spoke technology. The network in the diagram has the following characteristics:

- Each spoke has a permanent IPSec tunnel to the hub, not to the other spokes within the network. Each spoke registers as a client of the NHRP server.

- When a spoke needs to send a packet to a destination (private) subnet on another spoke, it queries the NHRP server for the real (outside) address of the destination (target) spoke.

- After the originating spoke learns the peer address of the target spoke, it can initiate a dynamic IPSec tunnel to the target spoke.

- The spoke-to-spoke tunnel is built over the multipoint GRE interface.

- The spoke-to-spoke links are established on demand whenever there is traffic between the spokes.

Figure 8-26 *mGRE and IPSec Integration Topology*

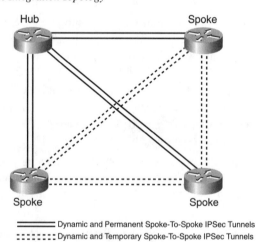

IPSec profiles are maintained on the routers, condensing IPSec policy information into a single configuration entity, which can be referenced by name from other parts of the configuration. By using the IPSec profile, administrators can configure IPSec features with a single line of configuration without having to configure an entire crypto map. IPSec profiles contain only IPSec information. They do not contain any access list or peering information.

DMVPN Configuration

Enabling mGRE and IPSec tunneling for hub-and-spoke routers requires that you configure a crypto map that uses a global IPSec policy template. You must also configure your mGRE tunnel for IPSec encryption. To configure DMVPN on your router, complete the following steps:

Step 1   Configure an IPSec Profile (required).

Step 2   Configure the hub for DMVPN (required).

Step 3   Configure the spoke for DMVPN (required).

Step 4   Verify DMVPN (optional).

These steps are discussed more fully in the following sections.

Configure an IPSec Profile

The IPSec profile shares a subset of the crypto map configuration commands. Only commands that pertain to an IPSec policy can be issued under an IPSec profile. You cannot specify the IPSec peer address or the ACL to identify the packets that are to be encrypted.

Complete the following steps to configure an IPSec profile on the hub router:

Step 1   Use the **crypto ipsec profile** command to enter crypto map configuration mode, in which you can begin defining the IPSec parameters that are to be used for IPSec encryption between spoke-and-hub and spoke-and-spoke routers. The format of the command is as follows:

  crypto ipsec profile *name*

  - *name*—Specifies the name of the IPSec profile.

Step 2   Use the **set transform-set** command to specify which transform sets can be used with the IPSec profile. The format of the command is as follows:

  set transform-set *transform-set-name* [*transform-set-name2…transform-set-name6*]

  - *transform-set-name*—Specifies the name of the transform set.

Step 3   (Optional) Use the **set identity** command to specify identity restrictions to be used with the IPSec profile. The format of the command is as follows:

  self-identity [*address* | *fqdn* | **user-fqdn** *user-fqdn*]

  - *address*—The IP address of the local endpoint.

  - *fqdn*—The fully qualified domain name (FQDN) of the host.

  - **user-fqdn** *user-fqdn*—The user FQDN that is sent to the remote endpoint.

Step 4 (Optional) Use the **set security association lifetime** command to override the global lifetime value for the IPSec profile. The format of the command is as follows:

```
set security association lifetime {seconds seconds | kilobytes kilobytes}
```

- **seconds** *seconds*—Specifies the number of seconds an SA will live before expiring.

- **kilobytes** *kilobytes*—Specifies the volume of traffic that can pass between IPSec peers using a given SA before that SA expires.

Step 5 (Optional) Use the **set pfs** command to specify that IPSec should ask for PFS when requesting new SAs for this IPSec profile. If this command is not specified, or if neither group is specified, the default (group1) will be enabled. The format of the command is as follows:

```
set pfs [group1 | group2]
```

- **group1**—Specifies that IPSec should use the 768-bit DH prime modulus group when performing the new DH exchange.

- **group2**—Specifies the 1024-bit DH prime modulus group.

The following shows a sample of the steps required to configure an IPSec profile on a router:

```
Router(config)# crypto ipsec profile vpnprof
Router(config-crypto-map)# set transform-set trans2
Router(config-crypto-map)# set identity
Router(config-crypto-map)# set security-association lifetime seconds 60
Router(config-crypto-map)# set pfs group2
```

Configure the Hub for DMVPN

After you have configured an IPSec profile name, you need to configure the hub router for mGRE and IPSec integration. This configuration process associates the tunnel with the IPSec profile that you configured in the previous section. To configure the hub for DMVPN, use the following steps:

Step 1 Use the **interface tunnel** command to configure a tunnel interface and enter interface configuration mode. The format of the command is as follows:

```
interface tunnel number
```

- *number*—Specifies the number of the tunnel interface that you want to create or configure. There is no limit to the number of tunnel interfaces that you can create.

Step 2 Use the **ip address** command to set a primary or secondary IP address for the tunnel interface. The format of the command is as follows:

```
ip address ip-address mask [secondary]
```

- *ip-address*—The IP address of the tunnel.

- *mask*—The associated subnet mask.

- **secondary** (Optional)—Specifies that the configured address is a secondary IP address. If this keyword is omitted, the configured address is the primary IP address.

Step 3 Use the **ip mtu** command to set the maximum transmission unit (MTU) size, in bytes, of IP packets sent on an interface. The format of the command is as follows:

```
ip mtu bytes
```

- *bytes*—The MTU size in bytes.

Step 4 Use the **ip nhrp authentication** command to configure the authentication string for an interface using NHRP. The format of the command is as follows:

```
ip nhrp authentication string
```

- *string*—Authentication string configured for the source and destination stations that controls whether NHRP stations allow intercommunication. The string can be up to eight characters long.

Step 5 Use the **ip nhrp map multicast dynamic** command to allow NHRP to automatically add spoke routers to the multicast NHRP mappings. The format of the command is as follows:

```
ip nhrp map multicast dynamic
```

Step 6 Use the **ip nhrp network-id** command to enable NHRP on an interface. The format of the command is as follows:

```
ip nhrp network-id number
```

- *number*—Specifies a globally unique 32-bit network identifier from a nonbroadcast multiaccess (NBMA) network. The range is from 1 to 4,294,967,295.

Step 7 Use the **tunnel source** command to set the source address for a tunnel interface. The format of the command is as follows:

```
tunnel source {ip-address | interface-type interface-number}
```

- *ip-address*—IP address to use as the source address for packets in the tunnel.

- *interface-type*—Interface type.

- *interface-number*—Port, connector, or interface card number. The numbers are assigned at the factory at the time of installation or when added to a system and can be displayed with the **show interfaces** command.

Step 8 Use the **tunnel key** command to enable an ID key for a tunnel interface. The format of the command is as follows:

```
tunnel key key-number
```

- *key-number*—Specifies a number from 0 to 4,294,967,295 that identifies the tunnel key.

Step 9 Use the **tunnel mode gre multipoint** command to set the encapsulation mode to mGRE for the tunnel interface. The format of the command is as follows:

```
tunnel mode gre multipoint
```

Step 10 Use the **tunnel protection ipsec-profile** command to associate a tunnel interface with an IPSec profile. The format of the command is as follows:

```
tunnel protection ipsec-profile name
```

- *name*—Specifies the name of the IPSec profile; this value must match the name specified in the **crypto ipsec profile name** command.

The following shows a sample of the steps required to configure the hub for DMVPN:

```
Router(config)# interface tunnel 5
Router(config-if)# ip address 10.0.0.1 255.255.255.0
Router(config-if)# ip mtu 1416
Router(config-if)# ip nhrp authentication donttell
Router(config-if)# ip nhrp map multicast dynamic
Router(config-if)# ip nhrp network-id 99
Router(config-if)# tunnel source Ethernet0
Router(config-if)# tunnel key 100000
Router(config-if)# tunnel mode gre multipoint
Router(config-if)# tunnel protection ipsec-profile vpnprof
```

Configure the Spoke for DMVPN

Use the following steps to configure each of the spoke routers for DMVPN:

Step 1 Use the **interface tunnel** command to configure a tunnel interface and enters interface configuration mode. The format of the command is as follows:

```
interface tunnel number
```

- *number*—Specifies the number of the tunnel interface that you want to create or configure. There is no limit on the number of tunnel interfaces you can create.

Step 2 Use the **ip address** command to set a primary or secondary IP address for the tunnel interface. The format of the command is as follows:

```
ip address ip-address mask [secondary]
```

- *ip-address*—IP address of the tunnel.

- *mask*—Associated subnet mask.

- **secondary** (Optional)—Specifies that the configured address is a secondary IP address. If this keyword is omitted, the configured address is the primary IP address.

Step 3 Use the **ip mtu** command to set the MTU size, in bytes, of IP packets sent on an interface. The format of the command is as follows:

```
ip mtu bytes
```

- *bytes*—MTU size in bytes.

Step 4 Use the **ip nhrp authentication** command to configure the authentication string for an interface using NHRP. The format of the command is as follows:

```
ip nhrp authentication string
```

- *string*—Authentication string configured for the source and destination stations that controls whether NHRP stations allow intercommunication. The string can be up to eight characters long.

Step 5 Use the **ip nhrp map** command to statically configure the IP-to-NBMA address mapping of IP destinations connected to an NBMA network. The format of the command is as follows:

```
ip nhrp map hub-tunnel-ip-address hub-physical-ip-address
```

- *hub-tunnel-ip-address*—Defines the NHRP server at the hub, which is permanently mapped to the static public IP address of the hub.

- *hub-physical-ip-address*—Defines the static public IP address of the hub.

Step 6 Use the **ip nhrp map multicast** command to enable the use of a dynamic routing protocol between the spoke and hub, and sends multicast packets to the hub router. The format of the command is as follows:

```
ip nhrp map multicast hub-physical-ip-address
```

- *hub-physical-ip-address*—Defines the static public IP address of the hub.

Step 7 Use the **ip nhrp nhs** command to configure the hub router as the NHRP next-hop server. The format of the command is as follows:

```
ip nhrp nhs hub-tunnel-ip-address
```

- *hub-tunnel-ip-address*—Address of the Next Hop Server being specified.

Step 8 Use the **ip nhrp network-id** command to enable NHRP on an interface. The format of the command is as follows:

```
ip nhrp network-id number
```

- *number*—Specifies a globally unique 32-bit network identifier from an NBMA network. The range is from 1 to 4294967295.

Step 9 Use the **tunnel source** command to set the source address for a tunnel interface. The format of the command is as follows:

```
tunnel source {ip-address | interface-type interface-number}
```

- *ip-address*— IP address to use as the source address for packets in the tunnel.

- *interface-type*— Interface type.

- *interface-number*— Port, connector, or interface card number. The numbers are assigned at the factory at the time of installation or when added to a system and can be displayed with the **show interfaces** command.

Step 10 Use the **tunnel key** command to enable an ID key for a tunnel interface. The format of the command is as follows:

```
tunnel key key-number
```

- *key-number*—Specifies a number from 0 to 4,294,967,295 that identifies the tunnel key.

Step 11 Use the **tunnel mode gre multipoint** command to set the encapsulation mode to mGRE for the tunnel interface. The format of the command is as follows:

```
tunnel mode gre multipoint
```

or use the **tunnel destination** command to specify the destination for a tunnel interface. Use this command if data traffic can use hub-and-spoke tunnels. The format of the command is as follows:

```
tunnel destination hub-physical-ip-address
```

- *hub-physical-ip-address*—Defines the static public IP address of the hub.

Step 12 Use the **tunnel protection ipsec-profile** command to associate a tunnel interface with an IPSec profile. The format of the command is as follows:

```
tunnel protection ipsec-profile name
```

- *name*—Specifies the name of the IPSec profile; this value must match the name specified in the **crypto ipsec profile name** command.

The following shows a sample of the steps required to configure a spoke for DMVPN:

```
Router(config)# interface tunnel 5
Router(config-if)# ip address 10.0.0.1 255.255.255.0
```

```
Router(config-if)# ip mtu 1416
Router(config-if)# ip nhrp authentication donttell
Router(config-if)# ip nhrp map 10.0.0.1 172.17.0.1
Router(config-if)# ip nhrp map multicast 172.17.0.1
Router(config-if)# ip nhrp nhs 10.0.0.1
Router(config-if)# ip nhrp network-id 99
Router(config-if)# tunnel source Ethernet0
Router(config-if)# tunnel key 100000
Router(config-if)# tunnel mode gre multipoint
Router(config-if)# tunnel protection ipsec-profile vpnprof
```

Verify DMVPN

You can verify that the DMVPN feature is working by performing the following optional steps:

Step 1   Use the **show crypto isakmp sa** command to display all current IKE SAs at a peer. The format of the command is as follows:

```
show crypto isakmp sa
```

The following shows a sample of the output you could expect to see when using this command:

```
Router# show crypto isakmp sa
dst state conn-id slot
172.17.63.19 172.16.175.76 QM_IDLE 2 0
172.17.63.19 172.17.63.20 QM_IDLE 1 0
172.16.175.75 172.17.63.19 QM_IDLE 3 0
```

Step 2   Use the **show crypto map** command to display the crypto map configuration. The format of the command is as follows:

```
show crypto map [interface interface | tag map-name]
```

- **interface** *interface* (Optional)—Displays only the crypto map set applied to the specified interface.

- **tag** *map-name* (Optional)—Displays only the crypto map set with the specified *map-name*.

The following shows a sample of the output you could expect to see when using this command:

```
Router# show crypto map
Crypto Map "Tunnel5-head-0" 10 ipsec-isakmp
Profile name: vpnprof
Security association lifetime: 4608000 kilobytes/3600 seconds
PFS (Y/N): N
Transform sets={trans2, }
Crypto Map "Tunnel5-head-0" 20 ipsec-isakmp
Map is a PROFILE INSTANCE.
```

```
Peer = 172.16.175.75
Extended IP access list
access-list permit gre host 172.17.63.19 host 172.16.175.75
Current peer: 172.16.175.75
Security association lifetime: 4608000 kilobytes/3600 seconds
PFS (Y/N): N
Transform sets={trans2, }
Crypto Map "Tunnel5-head-0" 30 ipsec-isakmp
Map is a PROFILE INSTANCE.
Peer = 172.17.63.20
Extended IP access list
access-list permit gre host 172.17.63.19 host 172.17.63.20
Current peer: 172.17.63.20
Security association lifetime: 4608000 kilobytes/3600 seconds
PFS (Y/N): N
Transform sets={trans2, }
Crypto Map "Tunnel5-head-0" 40 ipsec-isakmp
Map is a PROFILE INSTANCE.
Peer = 172.16.175.76
Extended IP access list
access-list permit gre host 172.17.63.19 host 172.16.175.76
Current peer: 172.16.175.76
Security association lifetime: 4608000 kilobytes/3600 seconds
PFS (Y/N): N
Transform sets={trans2, }
Interfaces using crypto map Tunnel5-head-0:
Tunnel5
```

Step 3   Use the **show ip nhrp** command to display the NHRP cache. The format of the command is as follows:

```
show ip nhrp [dynamic | static] [type number]
```

- **dynamic** (Optional)—Displays only the dynamic (learned) IP-to-NBMA address cache entries.

- **static** (Optional)—Displays only the static IP-to-NBMA address entries in the cache (configured through the **ip nhrp map** command).

- *type* (Optional)—Interface type about which to display the NHRP cache (for example, **atm** or **tunnel**).

- *number* (Optional)—Interface number about which to display the NHRP cache.

The following shows a sample of the output you could expect to see when using this command:

```
Router# show ip nhrp
10.10.1.75/32 via 10.10.1.75, Tunnel5 created 00:32:11, expire 00:01:46
```

```
Type: dynamic, Flags: authoritative unique registered
NBMA address: 172.16.175.75
10.10.1.76/32 via 10.10.1.76, Tunnel5 created 00:26:41, expire 00:01:37
Type: dynamic, Flags: authoritative unique registered
NBMA address: 172.16.175.76
10.10.1.77/32 via 10.10.1.77, Tunnel5 created 00:31:26, expire 00:01:33
Type: dynamic, Flags: authoritative unique registered
NBMA address: 172.17.63.20
```

Configuring IPSec for IKE Pre-Shared Keys

The use of IKE pre-shared keys for authentication of IPSec sessions is relatively easy to configure, yet does not scale well for a large number of IPSec clients.

The process of configuring IKE pre-shared keys in Cisco IOS software for Cisco routers consists of four major tasks, listed next. The sections following this list discuss each configuration task in more detail.

- **Task 1: Prepare for IKE and IPSec.** Determine the detailed encryption policy: identify the hosts and networks that you wish to protect, determine details about the IPSec peers, determine the IPSec features you need, and ensure that existing ACLs are compatible with IPSec.

- **Task 2: Configure IKE.** Enable IKE, create the IKE policies, and validate the configuration.

- **Task 3: Configure IPSec.** Define the transform sets, create crypto ACLs, create crypto map entries, and apply crypto map sets to interfaces.

- **Task 4: Test and verify IPSec.** Use **show**, **debug**, and related commands to test and verify that IPSec encryption works and to troubleshoot problems.

Task 1 to Configure IPSec Encryption: Preparing for IKE and IPSec

Successful implementation of an IPSec network requires advance planning before you begin configuration of individual routers.

Configuring IPSec encryption can be complicated. You must plan in advance if you want to configure IPSec encryption correctly the first time and minimize misconfiguration. You should begin this task by defining the IPSec policy based on the overall company security policy. Some planning steps are as follows:

Step 1   Check the current configuration.

Use the **show running-configuration**, **show crypto isakmp policy**, and **show crypto map** commands, and the many other **show** commands, to check whether the current configuration of the router has any existing IPSec configuration. If NAT is a requirement, plan to introduce it to the configuration here.

Step 2 Determine IKE (IKE phase 1) policy.

Determine the IKE policies between IPSec peers based on the number and location of the peers.

Step 3 Determine IPSec (IKE phase 2) policy.

Identify IPSec peer details, such as IP addresses, IPSec transform sets, and IPSec modes. You then configure crypto maps to gather all IPSec policy details together.

Step 4 Ensure that the network works without encryption (no excuses!).

Before you configure IPSec, ensure that basic connectivity using the desired IP services has been achieved between IPSec peers. You can use the **ping** command to check basic connectivity.

Step 5 Ensure that access control lists (ACLs) are compatible with IPSec.

Ensure that perimeter routers and the IPSec peer router interfaces permit IPSec traffic. In this step, you need to enter the **show access-lists** command.

Step 1: Checking the Current Configuration

The current Cisco router configuration should be checked to see if there are any IPSec policies already configured that are useful for, or may interfere with, the IPSec policies that you plan to configure. Previously configured IKE and IPSec policies and details can, and should, be used if possible to save configuration time. However, previously configured IKE and IPSec policies and details can make troubleshooting more difficult if problems arise.

You can see if any IKE policies have previously been configured by starting with the **show running-config** command. You can also use the variety of **show** commands specific to IPSec. For example, you can use the **show crypto isakmp policy** command as shown in Example 8-1 to examine IKE policies.

Example 8-1 *Using the* **show crypto isakmp policy** *Command to Examine IKE Policies*

```
RouterA# show crypto isakmp policy
Default protection suite
    encryption algorithm:   DES - Data Encryption Standard (56 bit keys)
    hash algorithm:            Secure Hash Standard
    authentication method:  Rivest-Shamir-Adleman Signature
    Diffie-Hellman Group:   #1 (768 bit)
    lifetime:               86400 seconds, no volume limit
```

The default protection suite seen here is available for use without modification. You can also use the other available **show** commands covered in other sections of this chapter to view IKE and IPSec configuration.

The **show crypto map** command is useful for viewing any previously configured crypto maps (Step 4: Creating Crypto Maps). Previously configured maps can, and should, be used to save configuration time. However, previously configured crypto maps can interfere with the IPSec policy that you are trying to configure. Example 8-2 shows the use of the **show crypto map** command.

Example 8-2 *Using the* **show crypto map** *Command*

```
RouterA# show crypto map
Crypto Map "mymap" 10 ipsec-isakmp
        Peer = 172.30.2.2
        Extended IP access list 102
             access-list 102 permit ip host 172.30.1.2 host 172.30.2.2
        Current peer: 172.30.2.2
        Security association lifetime: 4608000 kilobytes/3600 seconds
        PFS (Y/N): N
        Transform sets={ mine, }
```

You can also use the **show crypto ipsec transform-set** command to view previously configured transform sets. Previously configured transforms can, and should, be used to save configuration time. The following is a sample of the **show crypto ipsec transform-set** command:

```
RouterA# show crypto ipsec transform-set mine
Transform set mine: { esp-des  }
   will negotiate = { Tunnel,  },
```

Step 2: Determining IKE (IKE Phase 1) Policy

Configuring IKE is complicated. You should determine the IKE policy details to enable the selected authentication method, then configure it. Having a detailed plan lessens the chances of improper configuration. Some planning steps include the following:

- **Determine the key distribution method**—Determine the key distribution method based on the numbers and locations of IPSec peers. For a small network, you may wish to manually distribute keys. For larger networks, you may wish to use a certificate authority (CA) server to support scalability of IPSec peers. You must then configure the ISAKMP to support the selected key distribution method.

- **Determine the authentication method**—Choose the authentication method based on the key distribution method. Cisco IOS software supports either pre-shared keys, RSA-encrypted nonces, or RSA signatures to authenticate IPSec peers. This chapter focuses on using pre-shared keys.

- **Identify IPSec peer's IP addresses and host names**—Determine the details of all the IPSec peers that will use ISAKMP and pre-shared keys to establish SAs. You will use this information to configure IKE.

- **Determine ISAKMP policies for peers**—An ISAKMP policy defines a combination or suite of security parameters to be used during the ISAKMP negotiation. Each ISAKMP negotiation begins by each peer agreeing on a common (shared) ISAKMP policy. The ISAKMP policy suites must be determined in advance of configuration. You must then configure IKE to support the policy details you determined. Some ISAKMP policy details include:

    — Encryption algorithm

    — Hash algorithm

    — IKE SA lifetime

The goal of this planning step is to gather the precise data you will need in later steps to minimize misconfiguration.

IKE Phase 1: Defining Policy Parameters

An IKE policy defines a combination of security parameters used during the IKE negotiation. A group of policies makes up a protection suite of multiple policies that enable IPSec peers to establish IKE sessions and establish SAs with a minimal configuration. Table 8-3 shows which parameter values provide stronger security.

Table 8-3   *IKE Phase 1 Policy Parameters*

Parameter	Strong	Stronger
Encryption algorithm	DES	3-DES
Hash algorithm	MD5	SHA-1
Authentication method	Pre-shared	RSA encryption RSA signature
Key exchange	DH Group 1	DH Group 2
IKE SA lifetime	86,400 seconds	<86,400 seconds

Creating IKE Policies for a Purpose

IKE negotiations must be protected, so each IKE negotiation begins by each peer agreeing on a common (shared) IKE policy. This policy states which security parameters will be used to protect subsequent IKE negotiations.

After the two peers agree upon a policy, an SA established at each peer identifies the security parameters of the policy. These SAs apply to all subsequent IKE traffic during the negotiation.

You can create multiple, prioritized policies at each peer to ensure that at least one policy will match a remote peer's policy.

Defining IKE Policy Parameters

You can select specific values for each IKE parameter per the IKE standard. You choose one value over another based on the security level that you desire and the type of IPSec peer you will connect to.

There are five parameters to define in each IKE policy, as outlined in Table 8-3 and in Table 8-4. Table 8-3 shows the relative strength of each parameter, whereas Table 8-4 shows the default values.

Table 8-4   *IKE Phase 1 Defaults*

Parameter	Accepted Values	Keyword	Default
Message encryption algorithm	DES	**Des**	DES
	3-DES	**3des**	
Message integrity (hash) algorithm	SHA-1 (HMAC variant)	**sha**	SHA-1
	MD5 (HMAC variant)	**md5**	
Peer authentication method	Pre-shared keys	**pre-share**	RSA signatures
	RSA-encrypted nonces	**rsa-encr**	
	RSA signatures	**rsa-sig**	
Key exchange parameters (DH group ID)	768-bit Diffie-Hellman	**1**	768-bit DH
	1024-bit DH	**2**	
	1536-bit DH	**5**	
ISAKMP-established SA's lifetime	Can specify any number of seconds	—	86,400 seconds (one day)

You can select specific values for each ISAKMP parameter per the ISAKMP standard. You choose one value over another based on the security level you desire and the type of IPSec peer you will connect to. There are five parameters to define in each IKE policy, as presented in Table 8-3, which shows the relative strength of each parameter.

IKE Policy Example

You should determine IKE policy details for each peer before you configure IKE. Table 8-5 shows a summary of IKE policy details that will be configured in examples for this chapter that support the network of Figure 8-27. The authentication method of pre-shared keys was covered earlier in this chapter in the section "Origin Authentication."

Table 8-5   *IKE Policy Example*

Parameter	Site 1	Site 2
Encryption algorithm	DES	DES
Hash algorithm	MD5	MD5
Authentication method	Pre-shared keys	Pre-shared keys
Key exchange	DH Group 1	DH Group 1
IKE SA lifetime	86,400 seconds	86,400 seconds
Peer IP address	172.30.2.2	172.30.1.2

Figure 8-27   *IPSec Example Network*

Step 3: Determining IPSec (IKE Phase 2) Policy

An IPSec policy defines a combination of IPSec parameters used during the IPSec negotiation. Planning for IPSec (IKE phase 2) is another important step that you should complete before you actually configure IPSec on a Cisco router. Policy details to determine at this stage include the following:

Step 1   Select IPSec algorithms and parameters for optimal security and performance.

Determine what type of IPSec to use when securing interesting traffic. Some IPSec algorithms require you to make trade-offs between high performance and stronger security. Some algorithms have import and export restrictions that may delay or prevent implementation of your network.

Step 2   Select transforms and, if necessary, transform sets.

Use the IPSec algorithms and parameters previously decided upon to help select IPSec transforms, transform sets, and modes of operation.

Step 3   Identify IPSec peer details.

Identify the IP addresses and host names of all IPSec peers to which you will connect.

Step 4   Determine IP addresses and applications of hosts to be protected.

Decide which hosts' IP addresses and applications should be protected at the local peer and remote peer.

Step 5   Select manually initiated or IKE-initiated SAs.

Choose whether SAs are manually established or are established via IKE.

The goal of this planning step is to gather the precise data that you will need in later steps to minimize misconfiguration.

IPSec Transforms Supported in Cisco IOS Software

Cisco IOS software supports the IPSec transforms shown in Tables 8-6 and 8-7.

Table 8-6   *AH Transforms*

Transform	Description
ah-md5-hmac	AH-HMAC-MD5 transform
ah-sha-hmac	AH-HMAC-SHA transform

NOTE   AH is rarely used because authentication is now available with the **esp-sha-hmac** and **esp-md5-hmac** transforms. AH transport mode is also not compatible with NAT or PAT.

Table 8-7   *ESP Transforms*

Transform	Description
esp-aes	ESP with the 128-bit AES encryption algorithm
esp-aes 192	ESP with the 192-bit AES encryption algorithm
esp-aes 256	ESP with the 256-bit AES encryption algorithm
esp-des	ESP transform using DES cipher (56 bits)
esp-3des	ESP transform using 3DES (EDE) cipher (168 bits)
esp-md5-hmac	ESP transform with HMAC-MD5 authentication used with an **esp-des** or **esp-3des** transform to provide additional integrity of ESP packet
esp-sha-hmac	ESP transform with HMAC-SHA authentication used with an **esp-des** or **esp-3des** transform to provide additional integrity of ESP packet
esp-null	ESP transform without a cipher; may be used in combination with **esp-md5-hmac** or **esp-sha-hmac** if one wants ESP authentication with no encryption

CAUTION   Never use **esp-null** in a production environment because it does not protect data flows.

Examples of acceptable transforms that can be combined into sets are shown in Table 8-8.

Table 8-8   *Acceptable Transform Combinations*

Transform Type	Allowed Transform Combinations
AH transform (Pick up to one)	**ah-md5-hmac**—AH with the MD5 (HMAC variant) authentication algorithm **ah-sha-hmac**—AH with the SHA (HMAC variant) authentication algorithm
ESP encryption transform (Pick up to one)	**esp-des**—ESP with the 56-bit DES encryption algorithm **esp-3des**—ESP with the 168-bit DES encryption algorithm (3DES) **esp-null**—Null encryption algorithm
ESP authentication transform (Pick up to one)	**esp-md5-hmac**—ESP with the MD5 (HMAC variant) authentication algorithm **esp-sha-hmac**—ESP with the SHA (HMAC variant) authentication algorithm
IP compression transform	**comp-lzs**—IP compression with the LZS algorithm

The Cisco IOS command parser prevents you from entering invalid combinations; for example, after you specify an AH transform, it does not allow you to specify another AH transform for the current transform set.

IPSec Policy Example

Determining network design details includes defining a more detailed IPSec policy for protecting traffic. You can then use the detailed policy to help select IPSec transform sets and modes of operation. Your IPSec policy should answer the following questions:

- What protections are required or are acceptable for the protected traffic?
- Which IPSec transforms or transform sets should be used?
- What are the peer IPSec endpoints for the traffic?
- What traffic should or should not be protected?
- Which router interfaces are involved in protecting internal nets and external nets?
- How are SAs set up (manually or IKE negotiated) and how often should the SAs be renegotiated?

Table 8-9 shows a summary of IPSec encryption policy details for the network of Figure 8-27 that will be configured in examples in this chapter. Details about IPSec transforms are covered in Step 1: Configuring Transform Set Suites in this chapter. The example policy specifies that TCP traffic between the hosts should be encrypted by IPSec using DES.

Table 8-9   *IPSec Encryption Policy*

Policy	Site 1	Site 2
Transform set	ESP-DES, tunnel	ESP-DES, tunnel
Peer host name	RouterB	RouterA
Peer IP address	172.30.2.2	172.30.1.2
Hosts to be encrypted	10.0.1.3	10.0.2.3
Traffic (packet) type to be encrypted	TCP	TCP
SA establishment	**ipsec-isakmp**	**ipsec-isakmp**

Identify IPSec Peers

An important part of determining the IPSec policy is to identify the IPSec peer the Cisco router will communicate with. The peer must support IPSec as specified in the Request For Comments (RFCs) as supported by Cisco IOS. Many different types of peers are possible. Before configuration, identify all the potential peers and their VPN capabilities. Possible peers include, but are not limited to, the following:

- Other Cisco routers
- The Cisco PIX Firewall
- The Cisco VPN Client
- CA servers (if they are used)
- Other vendor's IPSec products that conform to IPSec RFCs

Step 4: Ensuring That the Network Is Functional

You must check basic connectivity between peers before you begin configuring IPSec. The router **ping** command can be used to test basic connectivity between IPSec peers. Although a successful Internet Control Message Protocol (ICMP) echo (ping) will verify basic connectivity between peers, you should ensure that the network works with any other protocols or ports that you want to encrypt, such as Telnet, FTP, or SQL*NET before you begin IPSec configuration. A sample of the **ping** command follows:

```
RouterA# ping 172.30.2.2
```

After IPSec is activated, basic connectivity troubleshooting can be difficult because the security configuration may mask a more fundamental networking problem. Previous security settings could result in no connectivity.

Step 5: Ensuring that ACLs Are Compatible with IPSec

You need to ensure that existing ACLs on perimeter routers, the PIX Firewall, or other routers do not block IPSec traffic. Perimeter routers typically implement a restrictive security policy with ACLs, where only specific traffic is permitted and all other traffic is denied. Such a restrictive policy blocks IPSec traffic, so you need to add specific **permit** statements to the ACL to allow IPSec traffic.

Ensure that your ACLs are configured so that ISAKMP, ESP, and AH traffic is not blocked at interfaces used by IPSec. IKE (implemented in Cisco products as ISAKMP) uses UDP port 500. ESP is assigned IP number 50, and AH is assigned IP number 51. In some cases, you might need to add a statement to router ACLs to explicitly permit this traffic. You may need to add the ACL statements to the perimeter router by performing the following steps:

Step 1 Examine the current ACL configuration at the perimeter router and determine whether it will block IPSec traffic:

> RouterA# **show access-lists**

Step 2 Add ACL entries to permit IPSec traffic, as follows:

(a) Copy the existing ACL configuration and paste it into a text editor.

(b) Add the ACL entries to the top of the list in the text editor.

(c) Delete the existing ACL with the **no access-list** *access-list number* command.

(d) Enter configuration mode and copy and paste the new ACL into the router.

(e) Verify the ACL is correct with the **show access-lists** command.

Example 8-3 is a concatenated example showing ACL entries permitting IPSec traffic for RouterA.

Example 8-3 *ACL Entries Permitting IPSec Traffic for RouterA*

```
RouterA# show running-config
!
interface Ethernet0/1
 ip address 172.30.1.2 255.255.255.0
 ip access-group 102 in
!
access-list 102 permit ahp host 172.30.2.2 host 172.30.1.2
access-list 102 permit esp host 172.30.2.2 host 172.30.1.2
access-list 102 permit udp host 172.30.2.2 host 172.30.1.2 eq isakmp
```

Note that the protocol keyword **esp** equals the ESP protocol (number 50), the keyword **ahp** equals the AH protocol (number 51), and the **isakmp** keyword equals UDP port 500.

Task 2 to Configure IPSec Encryption: Configuring IKE

The next major task in configuring Cisco IOS IPSec is to configure the IKE parameters that you gathered earlier. This section presents the steps used to configure IKE policies.

Configuring IKE consists of the following essential steps and commands, which are described further in the subsequent sections:

Step 1 Enable or disable IKE with the **crypto isakmp enable** command.

Step 2 Create IKE policies with the **crypto isakmp policy** commands.

Step 3 Configure pre-shared keys with the **crypto isakmp key** and associated commands.

Step 4 Verify the IKE configuration with the **show crypto isakmp policy** command.

Step 1: Enabling or Disabling IKE

The first step in configuring IKE is to enable or disable ISAKMP. ISAKMP is globally enabled and disabled with the **crypto isakmp enable** command. ISAKMP is enabled by default. Use the **no** form of the command to disable ISAKMP. A sample of the use of the command to configure the sample network of Figure 8-27 follows:

```
RouterA(config)# no crypto isakmp enable
RouterA(config)# crypto isakmp enable
```

ISAKMP does not have to be enabled for individual interfaces, but is enabled globally for all interfaces at the router. You may choose to block ISAKMP access on interfaces that are not used for IPSec to prevent possible DoS attacks by using an ACL statement that blocks User Data Protocol (UDP) port 500 on the interfaces.

Step 2: Creating IKE Policies

The next major step in configuring Cisco IOS ISAKMP support is to define a suite of ISAKMP policies. The goal of defining a suite of IKE policies is to establish ISAKMP peering between two IPSec endpoints. Use the IKE policy details that you gathered during the planning task.

Use the **crypto isakmp policy** command to define an IKE policy. IKE policies define a set of parameters used during the IKE negotiation. Use the **no** form of this command to delete an IKE policy. The command syntax is as follows:

```
crypto isakmp policy priority
```

- *priority*—Uniquely identifies the IKE policy and assigns a priority to the policy. Use an integer from 1 to 10,000, with 1 being the highest priority and 10,000 the lowest.

This command invokes the ISAKMP policy configuration (config-isakmp) command mode.

NOTE Assign the most secure policy the lowest priority number so that the most secure policy will find a match before any less-secure policies are configured.

Creating IKE Policies with the **crypto isakmp** Command

The **crypto isakmp policy** command invokes the ISAKMP policy configuration command mode (config-isakmp), in which you can set ISAKMP parameters. If you do not specify one of these commands for a policy, the default value will be used for that parameter. While in config-isakmp command mode, the keywords shown in Table 8-10 are available to specify the parameters in the policy.

Table 8-10   *ISAKMP Configuration Commands*

Keyword	Accepted Values	Default Value	Description
des	56-bit DES-CBC	des	Message encryption algorithm
sha **md5**	SHA-1 (HMAC variant) MD5 (HMAC variant)	Sha	Message integrity (hash) algorithm
rsa-sig **rsa-encr** **pre-share**	RSA signatures RSA-encrypted nonces Pre-shared keys	rsa-sig	Peer authentication method
1 **2** **5**	768-bit DH 1024-bit DH 1536-bit DH	1	Key exchange parameters (DH group ID)
–	Can specify any number of seconds	86,400 seconds (one day)	ISAKMP-established SA's lifetime; default value is usually fine
exit			Exits config-isakmp mode

You can configure multiple ISAKMP policies on each peer that is participating in IPSec. ISAKMP peers negotiate acceptable ISAKMP policies before agreeing upon the SA to be used for IPSec.

Example 8-4 shows how you might configure IKE policy 110 on RouterA of Figure 8-28.

Example 8-4   *Configuring IKE Policy 110 on RouterA*

```
RouterA(config)# crypto isakmp policy 110
RouterA(config-isakmp)# authentication pre-share
RouterA(config-isakmp)# encryption des
RouterA(config-isakmp)# group 1
RouterA(config-isakmp)# hash md5
RouterA(config-isakmp)# lifetime 86400
```

Figure 8-28 *Configuring IKE Policy 110*

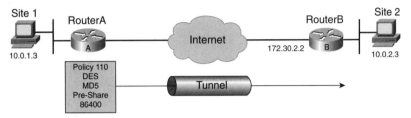

IKE Policy Negotiation

ISAKMP peers negotiate acceptable ISAKMP policies before agreeing upon the SA to be used for IPSec.

When the ISAKMP negotiation begins in IKE phase 1 Main Mode, ISAKMP looks for an ISAKMP policy that is the same on both peers. The peer that initiates the negotiation sends all its policies to the remote peer, and the remote peer tries to find a match with its policies. The remote peer looks for a match by comparing its own highest-priority policy against the other peer's received policies in its ISAKMP policy suite. The remote peer checks each of its policies in order of its priority (highest priority first) until a match is found.

A match is made when both policies from the two peers contain the same encryption, hash, authentication, and DH parameter values, and when the remote peer's policy specifies a lifetime less than or equal to the lifetime in the policy being compared. (If the lifetimes are not identical, the shorter lifetime from the remote peer's policy is used.) Assign the most secure policy the lowest priority number so that the most secure policy will find a match before any less secure policies that are configured find a match.

If no acceptable match is found, ISAKMP refuses negotiation and IPSec is not established. If a match is found, ISAKMP completes the Main Mode negotiation, and IPSec SAs are created during IKE phase 2 Quick Mode.

In Table 8-11, the first two policies for routers A and B match, while the third policy does not.

Table 8-11 *Matching IKE Policies*

RouterA Policies	Match	RouterB Policies
crypto isakmp policy 100 hash md5 authentication pre-share	Yes	crypto isakmp policy 100 hash md5 authentication pre-share
crypto isakmp policy 200 authentication rsa-sig hash sha	Yes	crypto isakmp policy 200 authentication rsa-sig hash sha

continues

Table 8-11 *Matching IKE Policies (Continued)*

RouterA Policies	Match	RouterB Policies

crypto isakmp policy 300
   authentication pre-share
   hash md5
	No	crypto isakmp policy 300
		   authentication rsa-sig
		   hash md5

Configuring ISAKMP Identity

IPSec peers authenticate each other during ISAKMP negotiations using the pre-shared key and the ISAKMP identity. The identity can be either the router's IP address or its host name. Cisco IOS software uses the IP address identity method by default. A command indicating the address mode does not appear in the router configuration.

If you choose to use the host name identity method, you must specify the method with the **crypto isakmp identity** global configuration command. Use the **no** form of this command to reset the ISAKMP identity to the default value (address). The command syntax is as follows:

```
crypto isakmp identity {address | hostname}
```

- **address**—Sets the ISAKMP identity to the IP address of the interface that is used to communicate to the remote peer during ISAKMP negotiations.

  The **address** keyword is typically used when there is only one interface that will be used by the peer for ISAKMP negotiations, and the IP address is known.

- **hostname**—Sets the ISAKMP identity to the host name concatenated with the domain name (for example, **myhost.domain.com**).

  The **hostname** keyword should be used if there is more than one interface on the peer that might be used for ISAKMP negotiations, or if the interface's IP address is unknown (such as with dynamically assigned IP addresses).

If you use the host name identity method, you may need to specify the host name for the remote peer if a DNS server is not available for name resolution. An example of this follows:

```
RouterA(config)# ip host RouterB.domain.com 172.30.2.1
```

Step 3: Configuring Pre-Shared Keys

Configure a pre-shared authentication key with the **crypto isakmp key** global configuration command. You must configure this key whenever you specify pre-shared keys in an ISAKMP policy. Use the **no** form of this command to delete a pre-shared authentication key. The command syntax is as follows:

```
crypto isakmp key keystring address peer-address
crypto isakmp key keystring hostname peer-hostname
```

- *keystring*—Specify the pre-shared key. Use any combination of alphanumeric characters up to 128 bytes. This pre-shared key must be identical at both peers.

- *peer-address*—Specify the IP address of the remote peer.
- *peer-hostname*—Specify the host name of the remote peer. This is the peer's host name concatenated with its domain name, such as **myhost.domain.com**.

NOTE   A given pre-shared key is shared between two peers. At a given peer, you could specify the same key to share with multiple remote peers; however, a more secure approach is to specify different keys to share between different pairs of peers.

Example 8-5 shows ISAKMP and pre-shared keys for RouterA and RouterB. Note that the keystring of *cisco1234* matches. The address identity method is specified. The ISAKMP policies are compatible. Default values do not have to be configured.

Example 8-5   *ISAKMP and Pre-shared Keys for RouterA and RouterB*

```
RouterA(config)# crypto isakmp key cisco1234 address 172.30.2.1
RouterA(config)# crypto isakmp policy 110
RouterA(config-isakmp)# hash md5
RouterA(config-isakmp)# authentication pre-share
RouterA(config-isakmp)# exit

RouterB(config)# crypto isakmp key cisco1234 address 172.30.1.1
RouterB(config)# crypto isakmp policy 110
RouterB(config-isakmp)# hash md5
RouterB(config-isakmp)# authentication pre-share
RouterB(config-isakmp)# exit
```

Step 4: Verifying the IKE Configuration

You can use the **show crypto isakmp policy** command to display configured and default policies. The resultant ISAKMP policy for RouterA is shown in the output listing of Example 8-6. RouterB's configuration is identical.

Example 8-6   *ISAKMP Policy for RouterA Output Listing*

```
RouterA# show crypto isakmp policy
Protection suite of priority 110
        encryption algorithm:   DES - Data Encryption Standard (56 bit keys).
        hash algorithm:         Message Digest 5
        authentication method:  Pre-Shared Key
        Diffie-Hellman group:   #1 (768 bit)
        lifetime:               86400 seconds, no volume limit
Default protection suite
        encryption algorithm:   DES - Data Encryption Standard (56 bit keys).
        hash algorithm:         Secure Hash Standard
        authentication method:  Rivest-Shamir-Adleman Signature
        Diffie-Hellman group:   #1 (768 bit)
        lifetime:               86400 seconds, no volume limit
```

Task 3 to Configure IPSec Encryption: Configuring IPSec

The next major task in configuring Cisco IOS IPSec is to configure the IPSec parameters that you previously gathered. This section presents the steps used to configure IPSec.

The general tasks and commands that are used to configure IPSec encryption on Cisco routers are summarized here, with detailed discussions of each step in the sections that immediately follow:

Step 1   Configure transform set suites with the **crypto ipsec transform-set** command.

Step 2   Configure global IPSec security association lifetimes with the **crypto ipsec security-association lifetime** command.

Step 3   Configure crypto ACLs with the **access-list** command.

Step 4   Configure crypto maps with the **crypto map** command.

Step 5   Apply the crypto maps to the terminating/originating interface with the **interface** and **crypto map** commands.

Step 1: Configuring Transform Set Suites

The first major step in configuring Cisco IOS IPSec is to use the IPSec policy to define a transform set.

A transform set is a combination of individual IPSec transforms designed to enact a specific security policy for traffic. During the ISAKMP IPSec SA negotiation that occurs in IKE phase 2 Quick Mode, the peers agree to use a particular transform set to protect a particular data flow. Transform sets combine the following IPSec factors:

- Mechanism for payload authentication: AH transform
- Mechanism for payload encryption: ESP transform
- IPSec mode (transport versus tunnel)

Transform sets equal a combination of an AH transform, an ESP transform, and the IPSec mode (either tunnel or transport mode). Transform sets are limited to one AH transform and one or two ESP transforms. Define a transform set with the **crypto ipsec transform-set** global configuration command. To delete a transform set, use the **no** form of the command. The command syntax is as follows:

```
crypto ipsec transform-set transform-set-name transform1 [transform2 [transform3]]
```

- *transform-set-name*—Specify the name of the transform set to create (or modify).
- *transform1, transform2, transform3*—Specify up to three transforms. These transforms define the IPSec protocol(s) and algorithm(s).

The command invokes the crypto-transform configuration mode. An example of the use of the command follows:

```
RouterA(config)# crypto ipsec transform-set mine des
```

You can configure multiple transform sets and then specify one or more of the transform sets in a crypto map entry. The transform set defined in the crypto map entry is used in the IPSec SA negotiation to protect the data flows specified by that crypto map entry's ACL. During the negotiation, the peers search for a transform set that is the same at both peers. When such a transform set is found, it is selected and applied to the protected traffic as part of both peers' IPSec SAs.

When ISAKMP is not used to establish SAs, a single transform set must be used. The transform set is not negotiated.

Editing Transform Sets

Use the following steps if you need to edit a transform set:

Step 1   Delete the transform set from the crypto map.

Step 2   Delete the transform set from the global configuration.

Step 3   Re-enter the transform set with corrections.

Step 4   Assign the transform set to a crypto map.

Step 5   Clear the SA database using the **clear crypto sa** command to clear all
         IPSec SAs on the router. You can use additional keywords to delete
         specific entries for peers. The **clear crypto sa** command has the following
         syntax:

```
clear crypto sa [peer [vrf fvrf-name] address | map map-name | entry
destination-address protocol spi | counters | vrf ivrf-name]
```

- **peer** [**vrf** *fvrf-name*] *address*—Deletes any IPSec SAs for the specified peer. The *fvrf-name* argument specifies the front-door VPN routing and forwarding (FVRF) of the peer address.

- **map**—Deletes any IPSec SAs for the named crypto map set.

- *map-name*—Specifies the name of a crypto map set.

- **entry**—Deletes the IPSec SA with the specified address, protocol, and SPI.

- *destination-address*—Specifies the IP address of the remote peer.

- *protocol*—Specifies either the ESP or AH.

- *spi*—Specifies an SPI (found by displaying the SA database).

- **counters**—Clears the traffic **counters** maintained for each SA;
  the **counters** keyword does not clear the SAs themselves.

- **vrf** *ivrf-name*—Clears all IPSec SAs that have inside virtual routing
  and forwarding (IVRF) with the name *ivrf-name*.

Step 6   Observe the SA negotiation and ensure it works properly.

Transforming Set Negotiation

Transform sets are negotiated during Quick Mode in IKE phase 2 by using the transform sets
that you previously configured. You can configure multiple transform sets and then specify one
or more of the transform sets in a crypto map entry. Configure the transforms from most to least
secure as per your policy. You can number your transform sets, and good practice calls for
numbering them from most secure to least secure so that the most secure transform sets have
the lower numbers. The transform set defined in the crypto map entry is used in the IPSec SA
negotiation to protect the data flows specified by that crypto map entry's ACL.

During the negotiation, the peers search for a transform set that is the same at both peers, as
shown in Figure 8-29. Each of RouterA's transform sets are compared against each of RouterB's
transform sets in succession. RouterA's transform sets 10, 20, and 30 are compared with
RouterB's transform set 40. The result is no match. All of RouterA's transform sets are then
compared against RouterB's transform sets. Ultimately, RouterA's transform set 30 matches
RouterB's transform set 60. When such a transform set is found, it is selected and is applied
to the protected traffic as part of both peers' IPSec SAs. IPSec peers agree on one transform
proposal per SA (unidirectional).

Figure 8-29   *Transform Set Negotiation*

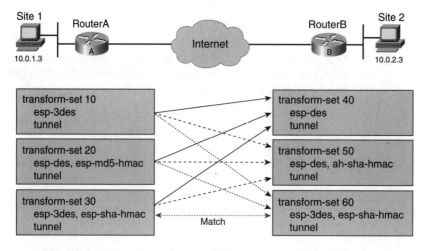

Table 8-12 describes the various types of allowed transform combinations for Cisco IOS
versions 12.2 and later.

Table 8-12   *Allowable Transform Combinations*

Transform Types	Allowed Combinations
AH transform	Select one of the following: **ah-md5-hmac**—AH with the MD5 (HMAC variant) authentication algorithm **ah-sha-hmac**—AH with the SHA (HMAC variant) authentication algorithm **ah-sha-hmac**—AH with the SHA (HMAC variant) authentication algorithm
ESP encryption transform	Select one of the following: **esp-des**—ESP with the 56-bit DES encryption algorithm **esp-3des**—ESP with the 168-bit DES encryption algorithm (3DES) **esp-null**—Null encryption algorithm
ESP authentication transform	Select one of the following: **esp-md5-hmac**—ESP with the MD5 (HMAC variant) authentication algorithm **esp-sha-hmac**—ESP with the SHA (HMAC variant) authentication algorithm
IP compression transform	**comp-lzs**—IP compression with the LZS algorithm

Step 2: Configuring Global IPSec SA Lifetimes

Both global and interface-specific SA lifetimes can be created. This section covers how to configure global SAs.

The IPSec SA lifetime determines how long IPSec SAs remain valid before they are renegotiated. Cisco IOS software supports a global lifetime value that applies to all crypto maps. The global lifetime value can be overridden within a crypto map entry. You can change global IPSec SA lifetime values by using the **crypto ipsec security-association lifetime** global configuration command. To reset a lifetime to the default value, use the **no** form of the command. The command syntax is as follows:

```
crypto ipsec security-association lifetime {seconds seconds | kilobytes kilobytes}
```

- **seconds** *seconds*—Specifies the number of seconds an SA will live before expiring. The default is 3600 seconds (one hour).

- **kilobytes** *kilobytes*—Specifies the volume of traffic that can pass between IPSec peers using a given SA before that SA expires. The default is 4,608,000 kilobytes.

Cisco recommends that you use the default lifetime values. Individual IPSec SA lifetimes can be configured using crypto maps, which are covered later in the section titled "Step 4: Creating Crypto Maps."

When an SA expires, a new one is negotiated without interrupting the data flow. Examples of setting global SA lifetimes follow. A new SA will be negotiated after 2700 seconds (45 minutes).

```
RouterA(config)# crypto ipsec security-association lifetime kilobytes 1382400
RouterA(config)# crypto ipsec security-association lifetime seconds 2700
```

Step 3: Configuring Crypto ACLs

Crypto ACLs are used to define which IP traffic is or is not protected by IPSec. This section covers how to configure crypto ACLs.

Purpose of Crypto ACLs

As shown in Figure 8-30, crypto ACLs perform the following functions:

- **Outbound**—Select outbound traffic to be protected by IPSec. Traffic that is not selected is sent in clear text.

- **Inbound**—Process inbound traffic to filter out and discard traffic that should have been protected by IPSec.

Figure 8-30 *Purpose of Crypto Access Control Lists*

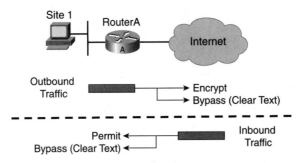

Extended IP ACLs for Crypto ACLs

The crypto ACLs identify the traffic flows to be protected. Extended IP ACLs select IP traffic to encrypt by protocol, IP address, network, subnet, and port. Although the ACL syntax is unchanged from extended IP ACLs, the meanings are slightly different for crypto ACLs—**permit** specifies that matching packets must be encrypted, and **deny** specifies that matching packets need not be encrypted. Crypto ACLs behave similar to an extended IP ACL applied to outbound traffic on an interface.

See the Cisco IOS Command Reference for a complete description of the **access-list** command. The command syntax for the basic form of extended IP access lists is as follows:

```
access-list access-list-number { permit | deny } protocol source source-wildcard
destination destination-wildcard [precedence precedence] [tos tos] [log]
```

- **permit**—Causes all IP traffic that matches the specified conditions to be protected by crypto, using the policy described by the corresponding crypto map entry.
- **deny**—Instructs the router to route traffic in the clear.
- *source* and *destination*—These are networks, subnets, or hosts.
- *protocol*—Indicates which IP packet type(s) to encrypt.

Any unprotected inbound traffic that matches a *permit* entry in the crypto ACL for a crypto map entry flagged as IPSec will be dropped, because this traffic was expected to be protected by IPSec.

If you want certain traffic to receive one combination of IPSec protection (authentication only) and other traffic to receive a different combination (both authentication and encryption), create two different crypto ACLs to define the two different types of traffic. These different ACLs are then used in different crypto map entries that specify different IPSec policies.

CAUTION   Cisco recommends that you avoid using the **any** keyword to specify source or destination addresses. The **permit any any** statement is strongly discouraged, because it will cause all outbound traffic to be protected (and cause all protected traffic to be sent to the peer specified in the corresponding crypto map entry) and will require protection for all inbound traffic. Then, all inbound packets that lack IPSec protection will be silently dropped, including packets for routing protocols, NTP, echo, echo response, and so on.

Try to be as restrictive as possible when defining which packets to protect in a crypto ACL. If you must use the **any** keyword in a **permit** statement, you must preface that statement with a series of **deny** statements to filter out any traffic (that would otherwise fall within that **permit** statement) that you do not want to be protected.

In the section "**crypto map** Commands Example," later in the chapter, you will associate a crypto ACL to a crypto map, which in turn is assigned to a specific interface.

Configuring Symmetrical Peer Crypto ACLs

You must configure mirror image crypto ACLs for use by IPSec. Both inbound and outbound traffic is evaluated against the same outbound IPSec ACL. The ACL's criteria is applied in the forward direction to traffic exiting your router, and in the reverse direction to traffic entering your router. When a router receives encrypted packets back from an IPSec peer, it uses the same ACL to determine which inbound packets to decrypt by viewing the source and destination addresses in the ACL in reverse order.

The example shown in Figure 8-31 illustrates why symmetrical ACLs are recommended.

Figure 8-31 *Configuring Mirror Image ACLs*

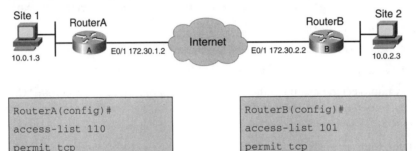

For site 1, IPSec protection is applied to traffic between hosts on the 10.0.1.0 network as the data exits RouterA's s0 interface en route to site 2 hosts on the 10.0.2.0 network. For traffic from site 1 hosts on the 10.0.1.0 network to site 2 hosts on the 10.0.2.0 network, the ACL entry on RouterA is evaluated as follows:

- source = hosts on 10.0.1.0 network
- dest = hosts on 10.0.2.0 network

For incoming traffic from site 2 hosts on the 10.0.2.0 network to site 1 hosts on the 10.0.1.0 network, that same ACL entry on RouterA is evaluated as follows:

- source = hosts on 10.0.2.0 network
- permit = hosts on 10.0.1.0 network

Step 4: Configuring Crypto Maps

Crypto map entries must be created for IPSec to set up SAs for traffic flows that must be encrypted. This section examines the purpose of crypto maps and the **crypto map** command, and considers example crypto maps.

Purpose of Crypto Maps

Crypto map entries created for IPSec set up SA parameters, tying together the various parts configured for IPSec, including:

- Which traffic should be protected by IPSec (crypto ACL)
- The granularity of the traffic to be protected by a set of SAs
- Where IPSec-protected traffic should be sent (who the remote IPSec peer is)

- The local address to be used for the IPSec traffic
- What IPSec type should be applied to this traffic (transform sets)
- Whether SAs are established manually or via IKE
- Other parameters that might be necessary to define an IPSec SA

Crypto Map Parameters

You can apply only one crypto map set to a single interface. The crypto map set can include a combination of Cisco Encryption Technology (CET), IPSec using IKE, and IPSec with manually configured SA entries. Multiple interfaces can share the same crypto map set if you want to apply the same policy to multiple interfaces.

If you create more than one crypto map entry for a given interface, use the sequence number (*seq-num*) of each map entry to rank the map entries: the lower the *seq-num*, the higher the priority. At the interface that has the crypto map set, traffic is evaluated against higher-priority map entries first.

Crypto maps define the following:

- The access list to be used
- Remote VPN peers
- Transform-set to be used
- Key management method
- SA lifetimes

You must create multiple crypto map entries for a given interface if any of the following conditions exist:

- If different data flows are to be handled by separate IPSec peers.
- If you want to apply different IPSec parameter values to different types of traffic (to the same or separate IPSec peers); for example, if you want traffic between one set of subnets to be authenticated, and traffic between another set of subnets to be both authenticated and encrypted. In this case, the different types of traffic should have been defined in two separate A CLs, and you must create a separate crypto map entry for each crypto ACL.
- If you are not using IKE to establish a particular set of SAs, and you want to specify multiple ACL entries, you must create separate ACLs (one per permit entry) and specify a separate crypto map entry for each ACL.

Configuring IPSec Crypto Maps

You must use the **crypto map** global configuration command to create or modify a crypto map entry and enter the crypto map configuration mode. Set the crypto map entries that reference dynamic maps to be the lowest-priority entries in a crypto map set (that is, to have the highest sequence numbers). Use the **no** form of this command to delete a crypto map entry or set. The command syntax is presented in Example 8-7.

Example 8-7 *Using the* **no** *Form of* **crypto map** *to Delete a Crypto Map Entry or Set*

```
crypto map map-name seq-num cisco
crypto map map-name seq-num ipsec-manual
crypto map map-name seq-num ipsec-isakmp [dynamic dynamic-map-name]
no crypto map map-name [seq-num]
```

- **cisco** (Default value.)—Indicates that CET will be used instead of IPSec to protect the traffic specified by this newly specified crypto map entry.

- *map-name*—The name you assign to the crypto map set.

- *seq-num*—The number you assign to the crypto map entry.

- **ipsec-manual**—Indicates that ISAKMP will not be used to establish the IPSec SAs to protect the traffic specified by this crypto map entry.

- **ipsec-isakmp**—Indicates that ISAKMP will be used to establish the IPSec SAs to protect the traffic specified by this crypto map entry.

- **dynamic** (Optional)—Specifies that this crypto map entry references a pre-existing static crypto map. If you use this keyword, none of the crypto map configuration commands are available.

- *dynamic-map-name* (Optional)—Specifies the name of the dynamic crypto map set that should be used as the policy template.

When you enter the **crypto map** command, you invoke the crypto map configuration mode with the available commands shown in Example 8-8.

Example 8-8 *Invoking Crypto Map Configuration Mode*

```
router(config-crypto-map)# help
    match address [access-list-id | name]
    peer [hostname | ip-address]
    transform-set [set_name(s)]
    security-association [inbound | outbound]
    set
    no
    exit
```

Some rules to keep in mind when using IPSec crypto maps include the following:

- Use a different sequence number for each peer.

- Multiple peers can be specified in a single crypto map for redundancy.

- Use one crypto map per interface.

crypto map Commands Example

You can configure crypto maps with two peers specified for redundancy. If the first peer cannot be contacted, the second peer is used. There is no limit to the number of redundant peers that can be configured, as shown in Figure 8-32.

Figure 8-32   **crypto map** *with Multiple Peers*

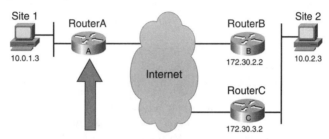

The configuration of a crypto map for RouterA in Figure 8-32 is shown in Example 8-9.

Example 8-9   *Configuration of a Crypto Map for RouterA*

```
RouterA(config)# crypto map mymap 110 ipsec-isakmp
RouterA(config-crypto-map)# match address 110
RouterA(config-crypto-map)# set peer 172.30.2.2
RouterA(config-crypto-map)# set peer 172.30.3.2
RouterA(config-crypto-map)# set pfs group1
RouterA(config-crypto-map)# set transform-set mine
RouterA(config-crypto-map)# set security-association lifetime 86400
```

The **crypto map** command has a crypto map configuration mode with the following commands and syntax:

- **set**—Used with the **peer**, **pfs**, **transform-set**, and **security-association** commands.
- **peer** [*hostname* | *ip-address*]—Specifies the allowed IPSec peer by IP address or host name.
- **pfs** [**group1** | **group2**]—Specifies DH Group 1 or Group 2.
- **transform-set** [*set_name(s)*]—Specifies the list of transform sets in priority order. For an **ipsec-manual** crypto map, you can specify only one transform set. For an **ipsec-isakmp** or **dynamic** crypto map entry, you can specify up to six transform sets.
- **security-association lifetime**—Sets SA lifetime parameters in seconds or kilobytes.
- **match address** [*access-list-id* | *name*]—Identifies the extended ACL by its name or number. The value should match the *access-list-number* or *name* argument of a previously defined IP-extended ACL being matched.
- **no**—Used to delete commands entered with the **set** command.
- **exit**—Exits crypto map configuration mode.

After you define crypto map entries, you can assign the crypto map set to interfaces by using the **crypto map** (interface configuration mode) command.

NOTE	ACLs for crypto map entries tagged as **ipsec-manual** are restricted to a single permit entry, and subsequent entries are ignored. The SAs established by that particular crypto map entry are only for a single data flow. To be able to support multiple manually established SAs for different kinds of traffic, define multiple crypto ACLs, and then apply each one to a separate **ipsec-manual** crypto map entry. Each ACL should include one **permit** statement that defines what traffic to protect.

Step 5: Applying Crypto Maps to Interfaces

The last step in configuring IPSec is to apply the crypto map set to an interface.

Apply the crypto map to the IPSec router's interface connected to the Internet with the **crypto map** command in interface configuration mode. Use the **no** form of the command to remove the crypto map set from the interface. A sample of the use of the **crypto map** command follows:

```
RouterA(config)# interface ethernet0/1
RouterA(config-if)# crypto map mymap
```

The command syntax is as follows:

crypto map *map-name*

- *map-name*—The name that identifies the crypto map set, and is the name assigned when the crypto map is created.

IPSec Configuration Examples

Consider the configuration example for RouterA and RouterB that has been used throughout this chapter. Example 8-10 presents the output of the **show running-config** command for RouterA to show the application of the commands discussed in this chapter. Example 8-10 has been concatenated to only show commands that are related to what has been covered in this chapter to this point.

Example 8-10 *Displaying the Output of the* **show running-config** *Command for RouterA*

```
RouterA# show running-config
crypto isakmp policy 100
 hash md5
 authentication pre-share
crypto isakmp key cisco1234 address 172.30.2.1
!
crypto ipsec transform-set mine esp-des
!
 !
 crypto map mymap 110 ipsec-isakmp
 set peer 172.30.2.1
 set transform-set mine
 match address 110
 !
```

Example 8-10 *Displaying the Output of the* **show running-config** *Command for RouterA (Continued)*

```
interface Ethernet0/1
 ip address 172.30.1.1 255.255.255.0
 ip access-group 101 in
 crypto map mymap
!
access-list 101 permit ahp host 172.30.2.1 host 172.30.1.1
access-list 101 permit esp host 172.30.2.1 host 172.30.1.1
access-list 101 permit udp host 172.30.2.1 host 172.30.1.1 eq isakmp
access-list 110 permit tcp 10.0.1.0 0.0.0.255 10.0.2.0 0.0.0.255
access-list 110 deny ip any any
!
!
!
RouterB# show running-config
crypto isakmp policy 100
 hash md5
 authentication pre-share
crypto isakmp key cisco1234 address 172.30.1.1
!
crypto ipsec transform-set mine esp-des
!
 !
 crypto map mymap 100 ipsec-isakmp
 set peer 172.30.1.1
 set transform-set mine
 match address 102
!
interface Ethernet0/1
 ip address 172.30.2.1 255.255.255.0
 ip access-group 101 in
 crypto map mymap
!
access-list 101 permit ahp host 172.30.1.1 host 172.30.2.1
access-list 101 permit esp host 172.30.1.1 host 172.30.2.1
access-list 101 permit udp host 172.30.1.1 host 172.30.2.1 eq isakmp
access-list 102 permit tcp 10.0.2.0 0.0.0.255 10.0.1.0 0.0.0.255
access-list 102 deny ip any any
```

Task 4 to Configure IPSec Encryption: Testing and Verifying IPSec and ISAKMP

Cisco IOS software contains a number of **show**, **clear**, and **debug** commands that are useful for testing and verifying IPSec and ISAKMP. These commands are presented in this section.

You can perform the following actions to test and verify that you have correctly configured the VPN using Cisco IOS:

- Display your configured IKE policies by using the **show crypto isakmp policy** command.

- Display your configured transform sets by using the **show crypto ipsec transform set** command.

- Display the current state of your IPSec SAs by using the **show crypto ipsec sa** command.

You can perform the following actions to test and verify that you have correctly configured VPN using Cisco IOS:

- View your configured crypto maps with the **show crypto map** command.

- Debug IKE and IPSec traffic through the Cisco IOS with the **debug crypto ipsec** and **debug crypto isakmp** commands.

show crypto isakmp policy Command

Use the **show crypto isakmp policy** EXEC command to view the parameters for each ISAKMP policy, as shown in Example 8-11 for RouterA of Figure 8-27.

Example 8-11 *Using the* **show crypto isakmp policy** *EXEC command to View the Parameters for Each ISAKMP Policy*

```
RouterA# show crypto isakmp policy
Protection suite of priority 110
        encryption algorithm:   DES - Data Encryption Standard (56 bit keys).
        hash algorithm:         Message Digest 5
        authentication method:  Rivest-Shamir-Adleman Encryption
        Diffie-Hellman group:   #1 (768 bit)
        lifetime:               86400 seconds, no volume limit
Default protection suite
        encryption algorithm:   DES - Data Encryption Standard (56 bit keys).
        hash algorithm:         Secure Hash Standard
        authentication method:  Rivest-Shamir-Adleman Signature
        Diffie-Hellman group:   #1 (768 bit)
        lifetime:               86400 seconds, no volume limit
```

show crypto ipsec transform-set Command

Use the **show crypto ipsec transform-set** EXEC command to view the configured transform sets. A sample use of the **show crypto ipsec transform-set** follows:

```
RouterA# show crypto ipsec transform-set
    Transform set mine: { esp-des  }
    will negotiate = { Tunnel,  },
```

The command has the following syntax:

```
show crypto ipsec transform-set [tag transform-set-name]
```

- **tag** *transform-set-name* (Optional)—Shows only the transform sets with the specified **transform-set-name**.

If no keyword is used, all transform sets configured at the router are displayed.

show crypto ipsec sa Command

Use the **show crypto ipsec sa** EXEC command to view the settings used by current SAs. If no keyword is used, all SAs are displayed. Example 8-12 shows an example of using the **show crypto ipsec sa** command.

Example 8-12 *Using the* **show crypto ipsec sa** *EXEC Command to View the Settings*

```
RouterA# show crypto ipsec sa
interface: Ethernet0/1
    Crypto map tag: mymap, local addr. 172.30.1.2
    local  ident (addr/mask/prot/port): (172.30.1.2/255.255.255.255/0/0)
   remote ident (addr/mask/prot/port): (172.30.2.2/255.255.255.255/0/0)
   current_peer: 172.30.2.2
     PERMIT, flags={origin_is_acl,}
    #pkts encaps: 21, #pkts encrypt: 21, #pkts digest 0
    #pkts decaps: 21, #pkts decrypt: 21, #pkts verify 0
    #send errors 0, #recv errors 0
     local crypto endpt.: 172.30.1.2, remote crypto endpt.: 172.30.2.2
     path mtu 1500, media mtu 1500
     current outbound spi: 8AE1C9C
```

The command syntax is as follows:

```
show crypto ipsec sa [map map-name | address | identity] [detail]
```

- **map** *map-name* (Optional)—Shows any existing SAs created for the crypto map.
- **address** (Optional)—Shows all the existing SAs, sorted by the destination address and then by protocol (AH or ESP).
- **identity** (Optional)—Shows only the flow information. It does not show the SA information.
- **detail** (Optional)—Shows detailed error counters. (The default is the high-level send/ receive error counters.)

show crypto map Command

Use the **show crypto map** EXEC command to view the crypto map configuration. If no keywords are used, all crypto maps configured at the router will be displayed.

Example 8-13 shows an example of using the **show crypto map** command.

Example 8-13 *Using the* **show crypto map** *EXEC Command to View the Crypto Map Configuration*

```
RouterA# show crypto map
Crypto Map "mymap" 10 ipsec-isakmp
        Peer = 172.30.2.2
        Extended IP access list 102
            access-list 102 permit ip host 172.30.1.2 host     172.30.2.2
        Current peer: 172.30.2.2
        Security association lifetime: 4608000 kilobytes/3600 seconds
        PFS (Y/N): N
        Transform sets={ mine, }
```

The command syntax is as follows:

```
show crypto map [interface interface | tag map-name]
```

- **interface** *interface* (Optional)—Shows only the crypto map set applied to the specified interface.

- **tag** *map-name* (Optional)—Shows only the crypto map set with the specified *map-name*.

debug crypto Commands

Use the **debug crypto ipsec** EXEC and the **debug crypto isakmp** commands to display IPSec and ISAKMP events. The **no** form of these commands disables debugging output.

NOTE   Because the **debug crypto ipsec** and the **debug crypto isakmp** commands generate a significant amount of output for every IP packet processed, use them only when traffic on the IP network is low, so that other activity on the system is not adversely affected.

Example 8-14, which demonstrates ISAKMP and IPSec debugging, shows normal IPSec setup messages. Note the inline comments (**!**).

Example 8-14 *ISAKMP and IPSec Debugging*

```
RouterA# debug crypto ipsec
Crypto IPSEC debugging is on
RouterA# debug crypto isakmp
Crypto ISAKMP debugging is on
RouterA#
*Feb 29 08:08:06.556 PST: IPSEC(sa_request): ,
  (key eng. msg.) src= 172.30.1.2, dest= 172.30.2.2,
    src_proxy= 10.0.1.0/255.255.255.0/0/0 (type=4),
    dest_proxy= 10.0.2.0/255.255.255.0/0/0 (type=4),
    protocol= ESP, transform= esp-des esp-md5-hmac ,
    lifedur= 3600s and 4608000kb,
    spi= 0x0(0), conn_id= 0, keysize= 0, flags= 0x4004
! Interesting traffic from Site1 to Site2 triggers ISAKMP Main Mode.
*Feb 29 08:08:06.556 PST: ISAKMP (4): beginning Main Mode exchange
*Feb 29 08:08:06.828 PST: ISAKMP (4): processing SA payload. message ID = 0
*Feb 29 08:08:06.828 PST: ISAKMP (4): Checking ISAKMP transform 1 against priority 100
    policy
*Feb 29 08:08:06.828 PST: ISAKMP:       encryption DES-CBC
*Feb 29 08:08:06.828 PST: ISAKMP:       hash MD5
*Feb 29 08:08:06.828 PST: ISAKMP:       default group 1
*Feb 29 08:08:06.832 PST: ISAKMP:       auth pre-share
*Feb 29 08:08:06.832 PST: ISAKMP (4): atts are acceptable. Next payload is 0
! The IPSec peers have found a matching ISAKMP policy
*Feb 29 08:08:06.964 PST: ISAKMP (4): SA is doing pre-shared key authentication
! Pre-shared key authentication is identified
```

Example 8-14 *ISAKMP and IPSec Debugging (Continued)*

```
*Feb 29 08:08:07.368 PST: ISAKMP (4): processing KE payload. message ID = 0
*Feb 29 08:08:07.540 PST: ISAKMP (4): processing NONCE payload. message ID = 0
*Feb 29 08:08:07.540 PST: ISAKMP (4): SKEYID state generated
*Feb 29 08:08:07.540 PST: ISAKMP (4): processing vendor id payload
*Feb 29 08:08:07.544 PST: ISAKMP (4): speaking to another IOS box!
*Feb 29 08:08:07.676 PST: ISAKMP (4): processing ID payload. message ID = 0
*Feb 29 08:08:07.676 PST: ISAKMP (4): processing HASH payload. message ID = 0
*Feb 29 08:08:07.680 PST: ISAKMP (4): SA has been authenticated with
172.30.2.2
! Main mode is complete. The peers are authenticated, and secret
! keys are generated. On to Quick Mode!
*Feb 29 08:08:07.680 PST: ISAKMP (4): beginning Quick Mode exchange, M-ID of
 -1079597279
*Feb 29 08:08:07.680 PST: IPSEC(key_engine): got a queue event...
*Feb 29 08:08:07.680 PST: IPSEC(spi_response): getting spi 3658276911d for SA
        from 172.30.2.2     to 172.30.1.2     for prot 3
*Feb 29 08:08:08.424 PST: ISAKMP (4): processing SA payload. message ID = -1079597279
*Feb 29 08:08:08.424 PST: ISAKMP (4): Checking IPSec proposal 1
*Feb 29 08:08:08.424 PST: ISAKMP: transform 1, ESP_DES
*Feb 29 08:08:08.424 PST: ISAKMP:   attributes in transform:
*Feb 29 08:08:08.424 PST: ISAKMP:      encaps is 1
*Feb 29 08:08:08.424 PST: ISAKMP:      SA life type in seconds
*Feb 29 08:08:08.424 PST: ISAKMP:      SA life duration (basic) of 3600
*Feb 29 08:08:08.428 PST: ISAKMP:      SA life type in kilobytes
*Feb 29 08:08:08.428 PST: ISAKMP:      SA life duration (VPI) of  0x0 0x46 0x50 0x0
*Feb 29 08:08:08.428 PST: ISAKMP:      authenticator is HMAC-MD5
*Feb 29 08:08:08.428 PST: ISAKMP (4): atts are acceptable.
*Feb 29 08:08:08.428 PST: IPSEC(validate_proposal_request): proposal part #1,
  (key eng. msg.) dest= 172.30.2.2, src= 172.30.1.2,
    dest_proxy= 10.0.2.0/255.255.255.0/0/0 (type=4),
    src_proxy= 10.0.1.0/255.255.255.0/0/0 (type=4),
    protocol= ESP, transform= esp-des esp-md5-hmac ,
    lifedur= 0s and 0kb,
    spi= 0x0(0), conn_id= 0, keysize= 0, flags= 0x4
*Feb 29 08:08:08.432 PST: ISAKMP (4): processing NONCE payload. message ID = -10
79597279
*Feb 29 08:08:08.432 PST: ISAKMP (4): processing ID payload. message ID = -1079597279
*Feb 29 08:08:08.432 PST: ISAKMP (4): processing ID payload. message ID = -1079597279
! A matching IPSec policy has been negotiated and authenticated.
! Next the SAs are set up.
*Feb 29 08:08:08.436 PST: ISAKMP (4): Creating IPSec SAs
*Feb 29 08:08:08.436 PST:        inbound SA from 172.30.2.2     to 172.30.1.2
        (proxy 10.0.2.0     to 10.0.1.0    )
*Feb 29 08:08:08.436 PST:        has spi 365827691 and conn_id 5 and flags 4
*Feb 29 08:08:08.436 PST:        lifetime of 3600 seconds
*Feb 29 08:08:08.440 PST:        lifetime of 4608000 kilobytes
*Feb 29 08:08:08.440 PST:        outbound SA from 172.30.1.2     to 172.30.2.2
        (proxy 10.0.1.0     to 10.0.2.0    )
*Feb 29 08:08:08.440 PST:        has spi 470158437 and conn_id 6 and flags 4
*Feb 29 08:08:08.440 PST:        lifetime of 3600 seconds
*Feb 29 08:08:08.440 PST:        lifetime of 4608000 kilobytes
```

continues

Example 8-14 *ISAKMP and IPSec Debugging (Continued)*

```
*Feb 29 08:08:08.440 PST: IPSEC(key_engine): got a queue event...
*Feb 29 08:08:08.440 PST: IPSEC(initialize_sas): ,
  (key eng. msg.) dest= 172.30.1.2, src= 172.30.2.2,
    dest_proxy= 10.0.1.0/255.255.255.0/0/0 (type=4),
    src_proxy= 10.0.2.0/255.255.255.0/0/0 (type=4),
    protocol= ESP, transform= esp-des esp-md5-hmac ,
    lifedur= 3600s and 4608000kb,
    spi= 0x15CE166B(365827691), conn_id= 5, keysize= 0, flags= 0x4
*Feb 29 08:08:08.444 PST: IPSEC(initialize_sas): ,
  (key eng. msg.) src= 172.30.1.2, dest= 172.30.2.2,
    src_proxy= 10.0.1.0/255.255.255.0/0/0 (type=4),
    dest_proxy= 10.0.2.0/255.255.255.0/0/0 (type=4),
    protocol= ESP, transform= esp-des esp-md5-hmac ,
    lifedur= 3600s and 4608000kb,
    spi= 0x1C060C65(470158437), conn_id= 6, keysize= 0, flags= 0x4
*Feb 29 08:08:08.444 PST: IPSEC(create_sa): sa created,
  (sa) sa_dest= 172.30.1.2, sa_prot= 50,
    sa_spi= 0x15CE166B(365827691),
    sa_trans= esp-des esp-md5-hmac , sa_conn_id= 5
*Feb 29 08:08:08.444 PST: IPSEC(create_sa): sa created,
  (sa) sa_dest= 172.30.2.2, sa_prot= 50,
    sa_spi= 0x1C060C65(470158437),
    sa_trans= esp-des esp-md5-hmac , sa_conn_id= 6
! IPSec SAs are set up and data can be securely exchanged.
RouterA#
```

ISAKMP Crypto System Error Messages

Cisco IOS software can generate many useful system error messages for ISAKMP. Two of the error messages follow:

- **%CRYPTO-6-IKMP_SA_NOT_AUTH: Cannot accept Quick Mode exchange from [IP_address] if SA is not authenticated!**—The ISAKMP SA with the remote peer was not authenticated, yet the peer attempted to begin a Quick Mode exchange. This exchange must only be done with an authenticated SA. The recommended action is to contact the remote peer's administrator to resolve the improper configuration.

- **%CRYPTO-6-IKMP_SA_NOT_OFFERED: Remote peer [IP_address] responded with attribute [chars] not offered or changed**—ISAKMP peers negotiate policy by the initiator offering a list of possible alternate protection suites. The responder responded with an ISAKMP policy that the initiator did not offer. The recommended action is to contact the remote peer's administrator to resolve the improper configuration.

Configuring IPSec Manually

You can configure your keys manually. This section provides a brief discussion of how to do this and also details why manual key use is not generally recommended.

Use the **set session-key** command in crypto map configuration mode to manually specify the IPSec session keys within a crypto map entry. Use the **no** form of this command to remove IPSec session keys from a crypto map entry. This command is only available for **ipsec-manual** crypto map entries. The command has the following syntax:

```
set session-key {inbound | outbound} ah spi hex-key-string
set session-key {inbound | outbound} esp spi cipher hex-key-string [authenticator
    hex-key-string]
```

- **inbound**—Sets the inbound IPSec session key. (You must set both inbound and outbound keys.)

- **outbound**—Sets the outbound IPSec session key.

- **ah**—Sets the IPSec session key for the AH protocol. Use when the crypto map entry's transform set includes an AH transform.

- **esp**—Sets the IPSec session key for the ESP protocol. Use when the crypto map entry's transform set includes an ESP transform.

- *spi*—Specifies the SPI, a number that is used to uniquely identify an SA. The SPI is an arbitrary number that you assign in the range of 256 to 4,294,967,295 (FFFF FFFF).

- *hex-key-string*—Specifies the session key entered in hexadecimal format. It is an arbitrary string of 8, 16, or 20 bytes. The crypto map entry's transform set includes:

  — A DES algorithm, which specifies at least 8 bytes per key.

  — An MD5 algorithm, which specifies at least 16 bytes per key.

  — An SHA algorithm, which specifies 20 bytes per key.

  — Keys longer than the above sizes are simply truncated.

- **cipher**—Indicates that the key string is to be used with the ESP encryption transform.

- **authenticator** (Optional)—Indicates that the key string is to be used with the ESP authentication transform. This argument is required only when the crypto map entry's transform set includes an ESP authentication transform.

If the crypto map entry's transform set includes an AH or ESP protocol, you must define IPSec AH or ESP keys for both inbound and outbound traffic. If your transform set includes an ESP authentication protocol, you must define IPSec keys for ESP authentication for inbound and outbound traffic. When ESP is used, the key length is 56 bits with DES and 168 bits with 3DES. When AH HMAC is used, the key length is 128 bits with MD5, 160 bits with SHA.

When you define multiple IPSec session keys within a single crypto map, you can assign the same SPI number to all the keys. The SPI is used to identify the SA used with the crypto map. However, not all peers have the same flexibility in SPI assignment. You should coordinate SPI assignment with your peer's operator, making certain that the same SPI is not used more than once for the same destination address and protocol combination.

Session keys at one peer must match the session keys at the remote peer. If you change a session key, the SA that is using the key is deleted and reinitialized.

Configuring IPSec manually is not recommended. You can configure IPSec SAs manually and not use ISAKMP to set up the SA. Cisco recommends that you use ISAKMP to set up the SAs because it is very difficult to ensure the SA values match between peers, and DH is a vastly more secure method to generate secret keys between peers. Other reasons not to configure IPSec manually included the following:

- Manual keying does not scale well and is often insecure due to difficulty in manually creating secure keying material.

- Manually established SAs do not expire.

- ACLs for crypto map entries tagged as **ipsec-manual** are restricted to a single permit entry and subsequent entries are ignored.

- The SAs established by a manual crypto map entry are only for a single data flow.

Configuring IPSec for RSA-Encrypted Nonces

This section provides a brief overview of configuring IPSec for RSA-encrypted nonces.

RSA-encrypted nonces provide a strong method of authenticating the IPSec peers and the DH key exchange. RSA-encrypted nonces provide repudiation—a quality that prevents a third party from being able to trace your activities over a network. A drawback is that they are somewhat more difficult to configure and, therefore, more difficult to scale to a large number of peers. RSA-encrypted nonces require that peers possess each other's public keys but do not use a CA. Instead, there are two ways for peers to get each other's public keys:

- You manually configure and exchange RSA keys.

- You use RSA signatures previously used during a successful ISAKMP negotiation with a remote peer.

NOTE   RSA-encrypted nonces must initially be exchanged via a secure method.

The IPSec configuration process for RSA encryption is very similar to the process of configuring IKE pre-shared keys, with the additional step of configuring RSA keys, summarized as follows:

- **Task 1: Prepare for IKE and IPSec.** Determine a detailed security policy for RSA encryption to include how to distribute the RSA public keys.

- **Task 2: Configure RSA keys.** Manually generate an RSA key-pair and configure the router for the RSA public keys.

- **Task 3**: **Configure IKE.** Configure ISAKMP for IPSec to select RSA encryption as the authentication method in an ISAKMP policy.
- **Task 4: Configure IPSec.** This is typically done in the same way that it is done when configuring IPSec for pre-shared keys.
- **Task 5: Test and verify IPSec.** You use additional commands to view and manage RSA public keys.

Task 2, configure RSA keys manually, is the only one of these tasks that is discussed in further detail. The other tasks mirror the activities required for pre-shared keys, as discussed earlier in the chapter in the section "Configuring IPSec for IKE Pre-Shared Keys."

Configuring RSA keys can be complex. To illustrate this fact, the following is a basic presentation of the steps and commands that are used in Task 2:

Step 1   Plan for RSA keys.

Step 2   Configure the router's host name and domain name (if they have not already been configured):

```
hostname name
ip domain-name name
```

Step 3   Generate the RSA keys:

```
crypto key generate rsa usage keys
```

Step 4   Enter peer RSA public keys.

There are several substeps necessary to enter the peers' public keys. Attention to detail is important, because any mistakes made entering the keys will cause them not to work. The following are the required commands:

```
crypto key pubkey-chain
crypto key pubkey-chain rsa
addressed-key key-address
named-key key-name
```

Step 5   Verify the key configuration.

It is easy to make mistakes when copying and pasting the RSA keys. Verifying the keys ensures that they match. Use these commands:

```
show crypto key mypubkey rsa
show crypto key pubkey-chain rsa
```

Step 6   Manage RSA keys.

Removing old keys is part of the configuration process. Old keys can consume much unnecessary space. The following command will help you manage RSA keys:

```
crypto key zeroize rsa
```

NOTE	For a complete discussion of all the tasks and steps that are necessary to configure RSA-encrypted nonces, see the "Configuring IKE Security Protocol" chapter in the *Cisco IOS Security Configuration Guide*, release 12.2, Part 4, "IP Security and Encryption."
	This section provides only a brief overview of the commands that are used for Task 2, because it is unique to RSA-encrypted nonces.

Using NAT with IPSec

NAT poses a special problem for IPSec. NAT was developed to forestall the move to IPv6 as IPv4 IP addresses were on the verge of being completely assigned. A NAT border device, such as a firewall or router, translates an internal network IP address into a public network IP address. This device saves addresses because businesses can now assign their own IP address series to internal hosts and permit only those that require a public network to reach the Internet through NAT.

NAT provides a one-to-one address translation. A single internal address gets translated into a single public address. With the rise in the use of web browsers and the availability of information on the web, NAT conversion quickly presented the problem of how to decide which hosts will be permitted to access the Internet.

Port Address Translation (PAT) solved that problem. A version of NAT, PAT is a many-to-one conversion scheme in which many internal network IP addresses are converted to a single public network IP address. A unique port number is mapped to each internal IP address and is included in the TCP/UDP header for each packet. The combination of the port number and public IP address is used to reverse the translation process for returning packets.

PAT was developed to work only with TCP, UDP, and ICMP messages. IPSec's predominant protocol, ESP, does not use ports, so PAT causes a problem for IPSec. Additionally, PAT devices are not able to map multiple SPIs, which would be a requirement in some IPSec installations.

IPSec NAT Transparency (also known as NAT Transversal) for the Cisco IOS Firewall solves the IPSec with NAT problem by making NAT IPSec-aware. It does this by encapsulating IPSec packets in a UDP wrapper to allow the IPSec packets to pass through NAT/PAT devices. Address translation can be applied to the encapsulating UDP header without affecting the encapsulated IPSec packet.

IKE Phase 1 and 2 Negotiation

Two types of NAT detection are accomplished before IKE Quick Mode begins during IKE phase 1 negotiation:

- **NAT Support**—IPSec endpoint devices send each other vendor identification strings that tell each other whether or not they support NAT Transparency.

- **NAT Existence**—IPSec endpoints now need to determine whether NAT devices exist along the path between the two devices.

  — Each peer sends NAT discovery (NAT-D) payloads containing hashes of the IP address and port of both the source and destination addresses from each end.

The first NAT-D payload sent by each peer contains a hash of the source IP address and port. The second payload contains a hash of the destination IP address and port. NAT-D payloads are sent in the third and fourth messages of IKE phase 1 Main Mode and in the second and third messages of IKE phase 1 Aggressive Mode.

— Each peer recalculates the hashes. Because of the order of transmission, the peer performs a hash of its local address first, and then a hash of its remote address.

— If the hashes match, no translation occurred along the route, so no NAT devices exist and normal IPSec protocols can be used.

— If the hashes do not match, then at least one NAT device exists in the path between the peers.

Once IKE phase 1 has determined the existence of NAT devices, IKE phase 2 decides whether or not the peers at both ends will use NAT Transparency.

UDP encapsulation with NAT Transparency resolves many of the problems that exist between NAT and IPSec. Because it permits IPSec packets to traverse NAT devices, NAT Transparency also eliminates the incompatibility between:

- ESP and PAT, by hiding the ESP packet behind the UDP header, allowing PAT to process the packet as a normal UDP packet.

- Checksums and NAT, by setting the checksum of the new UDP header to 0 to prevent intermediate devices from performing a checksum against the packet.

- Fixed IKE destination ports and PAT, by allowing PAT to use the port address in the new UDP header for translation functions.

NAT Transparency Packet Encapsulation

With NAT Transparency, additional fields are inserted into the packet, and the total packet length and checksum fields are changed to match the addition. A UDP header and a non-IKE marker are inserted before the ESP header. The non-IKE marker is 8 bytes in length.

Figure 8-33 shows the application of NAT Transparency to ESP packets using transport mode.

Figure 8-33 *ESP Transport Mode with NAT Transparency*

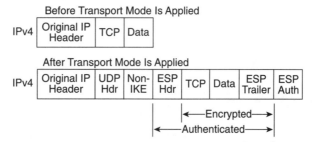

Figure 8-34 shows the application of NAT Transparency to ESP packets using tunnel mode.

Figure 8-34 *ESP Tunnel Mode with NAT Transparency*

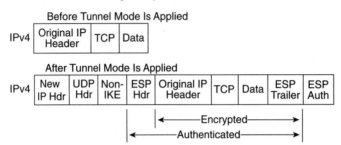

NAT keepalives must be enabled to keep the dynamic NAT mapping working properly during a connection between two IPSec peers using NAT Transparency. Keepalives are UDP packets with unencrypted payloads of 1 byte. Be sure to set the idle-timeout value to be shorter than the 20-second value of the NAT mapping expiration time. NAT keepalive packets are sent upon expiration of the idle-timeout value, which is adjustable from 5 to 3600 seconds. If the idle-timeout value is set too high, the fixed, 20-second NAT mapping expiration time could expire, causing the dynamic NAT mapping to time out.

Configuring IPSec to Work with NAT

Cisco IOS Firewall devices running Cisco IOS 12.2(13)T or later automatically detect and negotiate NAT Transparency. No configuration steps are required to implement this service.

In some instances, such as when your network devices already use some type of IPSec-aware NAT, you may want to disable NAT Transparency. In these cases, use the **no crypto ipsec nat-transparency udp-encapsulation** command.

To configure NAT keepalives, use the **crypto isakmp nat-keepalive** command. This command has the following format:

> **crypto isakmp nat-keepalive** *seconds*

- *seconds*—The number of seconds between keepalive packets; the range is 5 to 3600 seconds.

Example 8-15 shows an example of configuring NAT keepalives to be sent every 18 seconds.

Example 8-15 *Configuring NAT Keepalives*

```
crypto isakmp policy 1
authentication pre-share
crypto isakmp key 1234 address 56.0.0.1
crypto isakmp nat keepalive 18
!
crypto ipsec transform-set t2 esp-des esp-sha-hmac
!
crypto map test2 10 ipsec-isakmp
set peer 56.0.0.1
set transform-set t2
match address 101
```

Use the **show crypto ipsec sa** command to verify your configuration.

Chapter Summary

The following list summarizes what you learned in this chapter:

- Cisco supports the following IPSec standards: AH, ESP, DES, 3DES, MD5, SHA, RSA signatures, IKE (also known as ISAKMP), DH, and CAs.

- There are five steps to IPSec: identifying interesting traffic, IKE phase 1, IKE phase 2, IPSec encrypted traffic, and tunnel termination.

- IPSec SAs consist of a destination address, SPI, IPSec transform, mode, and SA lifetime value.

- Define the detailed crypto IKE and IPSec policy before you begin configuration.

- Ensure that router ACLs permit IPSec traffic.

- IKE policies define the set of parameters used during IKE negotiation.

- Transform sets determine IPSec transform and mode.

- Crypto ACLs determine the traffic to be encrypted.

- Use **show** and **debug** commands to test and troubleshoot IPSec connections.

- IPSec can also be configured manually or by using encrypted nonces.

Cisco IOS Commands Presented in This Chapter

Many Cisco IOS version 12.3 commands were discussed or referenced in this chapter. These commands can be found in the *Command Reference* online at http://www.cisco.com/univercd /cc/td/doc/product/software/ios123/123mindx/crgindx.htm.

Chapter Review Questions

The following review questions cover some of the key facts and concepts that were introduced in this chapter. Answers to these questions can be found in Appendix A, "Answers to Chapter Review Questions."

1. What are the two major types of VPN solutions that were discussed in this chapter?

2. What makes the DH public key exchange such a versatile tool?

3. What three peer authentication methods can be used with IPSec?

4. Which IPSec protocol provides both confidentiality and authentication?

5. What are the five steps of IPSec?

6. What is the purpose of a transform set?

7. What are the five IKE phase 1 policy parameters?

8 What command do you use to define an IKE policy?

9 What command would you use to define an IKE pre-shared key of Key1234 to use with a peer that has a host name of MyPeer567?

10 What command do you use to establish a crypto map on an interface?

11 What are five important **show** commands that you can use to verify your IKE and IPSec configurations?

12 What is the default lifetime for manually configured IPSec SAs?

13 What configuration tasks are required to enable NAT Transparency on Cisco IOS routers with Cisco IOS versions 12.2(13)T or later?

Case Study

The Future Corporation uses a VPN between Austin and London, as shown in Figure 8-35.

Figure 8-35 *Austin to London VPN*

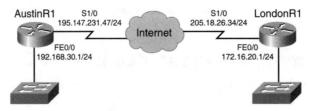

Scenario

Your task as network administrator is to configure router AustinR1 to support the VPN and to match the configuration already in place on router LondonR1. Use the following instructions for each of the tasks to configure the VPN. NAT is not being used for the purposes of this scenario.

Show all the configuration commands that you would need to execute to configure the IKE and IPSec policies outlined in Task 1. Also show all **show** and **debug** commands that you would use to check your configuration.

Use the following IKE policy:

- The key distribution method is manual.

- The authentication method will be through pre-shared keys. Use the host name of the peer when establishing the shared key. The pre-shared key is **AusLonVKey**.

- LondonR1's IP address and host name are shown in Figure 8-35.

- Use 3-DES, SHA-1, pre-shared keys, DH Group 2, and an IKE SA lifetime of 16 hours (57,600 seconds) for your ISAKMP policy.

Use the following IPSec policy:

- Use the **esp-sha-hmac** and **esp-3des** transforms and call your transform set **AusLon**.
- LondonR1 is the only host you will be connecting with through the VPN.
- The IPSec tunnel will protect all traffic from AustinR1 to LondonR1.
- SAs will be initiated by IKE. The IPSec SA lifetime will be 20 hours (72,000 seconds).

1 Task 1—Prepare for IKE and IPSec

Indicate the commands that you would use to perform these tasks:

- Check the current configuration.
- Ensure that the network works without encryption.
- Ensure that the ACLs are compatible with IPSec.

2 Task 2—Configure IKE

Indicate the commands that you would use to perform these tasks:

- Create the IKE policy.
- Configure the pre-shared key.
- Verify the IKE configuration.

3 Task 3—Configure IPSec

Indicate the commands that you would use to perform these tasks:

- Configure the transform set.
- Configure the global IPSec SA lifetime.
- Configure the crypto ACL.
- Configure the crypto map.
- Apply the crypto map to the interface.

4 Task 4—Test and Verify IPSec

Indicate the commands that you would use to perform these tasks:

- Display your configured IKE policies
- Display your configured transform sets
- Display the current state of your IPSec Sas
- View your configured crypto maps
- Debug IKE and IPSec traffic through the Cisco IOS

Solutions

The correct commands that can be used to configure the DallasR3 Cisco IOS Firewall router for IDS support follow.

Task 1: Prepare for IKE and IPSec

Indicate the commands that you would use to perform these tasks:

- Check the current configuration.
  - **show running-config**
  - **show crypto isakmp policy**
  - **show crypto map**
  - **show crypto ipsec transform-set**
- Ensure that the network works without encryption:
  - **ping 172.16.20.1**

    Ping the internal interface of the peer router, not the external interface. Once the IPSec tunnel is in place, you will no longer be able to ping the external interface.
- Ensure that the ACLs are compatible with IPSec.
  - **interface Serial1/0**
  - **ip address 195.147.231.47 255.255.255.0**
  - **ip access-group 102 in**
  - **access-list 102 permit ahp host 205.18.26.34 host 195.147.231.47**
  - **access-list 102 permit esp host 205.18.26.34 host 195.147.231.47**
  - **access-list 102 permit udp host 205.18.26.34 host 195.147.231.47 eq isakmp**

Task 2: Configure IKE

Indicate the commands that you would use to perform these tasks:

- Create the IKE policy.
  - **crypto isakmp policy 110**
  - **authentication pre-share**
  - **encryption 3des**
  - **group 2**
  - **hash sha**
  - **lifetime 57600**

- Configure the pre-shared key.
  - **crypto isakmp identity hostname**
  - **crypto isakmp key AusLonVKey hostname LondonR1**
- Verify the IKE configuration.
  - **show crypto isakmp policy**

Task 3: Configure IPSec

Indicate the commands that you would use to perform these tasks:

- Configure the transform set.
  - **crypto ipsec transform-set AusLon esp-sha-hmac esp-3des**
- Configure the global IPSec SA lifetime.
  - **crypto ipsec security-association lifetime seconds 72000**
- Configure the crypto ACL.
  - **access-list 110 permit ip 192.168.30.0 0.0.0.255 172.16.20.0 0.0.0.255**
  - **access-list 110 deny ip any any**
- Configure the crypto map.
  - **crypto map AusLon 110 ipsec-isakmp**
  - **match address 110**
  - **set peer 205.18.26.34**
  - **set pfs group2**
  - **set transform-set AusLon**
  - **set security-association lifetime 72000**
- Apply the crypto map to the interface.
  - **interface Serial1/0**
  - **crypto map AusLon**

Task 4: Test and Verify IPSec

Indicate the commands that you would use to perform these tasks:

- Display your configured IKE policies using the **show crypto isakmp policy** command.
- Display your configured transform sets using the **show crypto ipsec transform set** command.
- Display the current state of your IPSec SAs with the **show crypto ipsec sa** command.
- View your configured crypto maps with the **show crypto map** command.
- Debug IKE and IPSec traffic through the Cisco IOS with the **debug crypto ipsec** and **debug crypto isakmp** commands.

Upon completion of this chapter, you will be able to perform the following tasks:

- Describe the Cisco IOS CA Support Standards
- Describe the Simple Certificate Enrollment Protocol
- Identify the CA Vendor Products that Support Cisco VPN Products
- Prepare a Cisco Router for IKE and IPSec Configurations
- Configure a Cisco Router for CA Support
- Configure a Cisco Router for IKE Using RSA Signatures
- Configure a Cisco Router for IPSec Using RSA Signatures
- Test and Verify the IKE and IPSec Configurations

CHAPTER 9

Building Advanced IPSec VPNs Using Cisco Routers and Certificate Authorities

This chapter introduces configuration of Cisco IOS IPSec using a certificate authority (CA). After presenting an overview of the configuration process, the chapter shows you each major step of the configuration that is unique to CA support. It includes the following topics:

- Certificate authorities
- Configuring CA support tasks
- Preparing for IKE and IPSec
- CA support overview
- Configuring CA support
- Configuring IKE
- Configuring IPSec
- Testing and verifying IPSec

Certificate Authorities

The use of pre-shared keys is a straightforward process for device or user authentication. An administrator assigns a key to each host or user and then configures the server to respond only to those pre-shared keys. It is a simple process, but it does not scale well to large organizations where there may be hundreds or thousands of keys to keep track of.

Digital certificates were developed as a method of automating the assignment and maintenance of security keys and form the basis of the Public Key Infrastructure (PKI). Ronald Rivest, Adi Shamir, and Leonard Adleman developed the RSA public-key cryptosystem in 1977. In this system, a CA provides RSA digital certificates upon registration with that CA. These digital certificates permit stronger security than do pre-shared keys. Once the initial configuration has been completed, peers using RSA digital certificates can authenticate with one another without operator intervention.

CAs are trusted repositories for storing digital certificates and for attesting to the authenticity of those certificates. CAs are usually third-party agents, such as VeriSign or Entrust, but you could also set up your own CA using Windows 2000 Certificate Services.

The following outlines how CAs are used:

1 A client that wants to use digital certificates creates a pair of keys, one public and one private, using key-generating software. Next, the client prepares an unsigned certificate (X.509) that contains, among other things, the client's ID and the public key that was just created. This unsigned certificate is then sent to a CA electronically using a secure method.

2 The CA computes a hash of the unsigned certificate. The CA then takes that hash and encrypts it using the CA's private key. This encrypted hash is the digital signature, and the CA attaches it to the certificate and returns the signed certificate to the client. This certificate is called an identity certificate and will be stored on the client device until it expires or is deleted. The CA also sends the client the CA's digital certificate containing the public key of the CA. This CA certificate becomes the root certificate for the client.

3 The client now has a signed digital certificate that it can send to any other peer partner. If the peer partner wants to authenticate the certificate, it decrypts the signature using the CA's public key found in the root certificate.

It is important to note that a CA will send a client's certificate only to that client itself. If the client wants to establish IPSec VPNs with another client, for example, it will trade digital certificates with that client, thereby sharing public keys.

When a client wants to encrypt data to send to a peer, it uses the peer's public key from the digital certificate. The peer then decrypts the package with its own private key.

When a client wants to digitally sign a package, it uses its own private key to create a "signed" hash of the package. The receiving peer then uses the client's public key to create a comparison hash of the package. When the two hash values match, the signature has been verified.

Another function of a CA is to periodically generate a list of certificates that have expired or have been explicitly voided. The CA makes these Certificate Revocation Lists (CRLs) available to its customers. When a client receives a digital certificate, it checks the CRL to find out if the certificate is still valid.

Cisco IOS CA Support Standards

Cisco IOS supports the following open CA standards:

- **Internet Key Exchange (IKE)**—A hybrid protocol that implements Oakley and Skeme key exchanges inside the Internet Security Association and Key Management Protocol (ISAKMP) framework. Although IKE can be used with other protocols, its initial implementation is with the IPSec protocol. IKE provides authentication of the IPSec peers, negotiates IPSec keys, and negotiates IPSec SAs.

- **Public-Key Cryptography Standard #7 (PKCS #7)**—A standard from RSA Data Security, Inc. that is used to encrypt, sign, and package certificate enrollment messages.

- **Public-Key Cryptography Standard #10 (PKCS #10)**—A standard syntax from RSA Data Security, Inc. for certificate requests.

- **RSA keys**—RSA is the public key cryptographic system developed by Rivest, Shamir, and Adleman. RSA keys come in pairs: one public key and one private key.

- **X.509v3 certificates**—Certificate support that allows the IPSec-protected network to scale by providing the equivalent of a digital identification card to each device. When two devices wish to communicate, they exchange digital certificates to prove their identity (thus removing the need to manually exchange public keys with each peer or to manually specify a shared key at each peer). These certificates are obtained from a CA. X.509 is part of the X.500 standard.

- **CA interoperability**—CA interoperability permits Cisco IOS devices and CAs to communicate so that your Cisco IOS device can obtain and use digital certificates from the CA. Although IPSec can be implemented on your network without the use of a CA, using a CA with the Simple Certificate Enrollment Protocol (SCEP) provides manageability and scalability for IPSec.

Simple Certificate Enrollment Protocol

SCEP is a Cisco, VeriSign, Entrust, Microsoft, Netscape, and Sun Microsystems initiative that provides a standard way of managing the certificate lifecycle. SCEP is a transaction-oriented request and response protocol that is transport-mechanism independent. SCEP requires manual authentication during the enrollment process.

NOTE   The Certificate Enrollment Protocol (CEP) terminology used in some Cisco documentation is the same as the SCEP terminology used here.

This initiative is important for driving open development of certificate handling protocols that can otherwise be interoperable with many vendors' devices.

SCEP is described in the Internet Engineering Task Force (IETF) draft, which can be found at http://www.ietf.org/.

SCEP provides two authentication methods: manual authentication, and authentication based on a pre-shared secret. In manual mode, the end entity that is submitting the request is required to wait until the CA operator, using any reliable out-of-band method, can verify its identity. A message digest algorithm 5 (MD5) "fingerprint" generated on the PKCS #10 must be compared out-of-band between the server and the end entity. SCEP clients and CAs (or registration authority [RA], if appropriate) must display this fingerprint to a user to enable this verification, if manual mode is used.

When using a pre-shared secret scheme, the server should distribute a shared secret to the end entity, which can uniquely associate the enrollment request with the given end entity. The distribution of the secret must be private: only the end entity should know this secret. When creating the enrollment request, the end entity is asked to provide a challenge password.

When using the pre-shared secret scheme, the end entity must enter the redistributed secret as the password. In the manual authentication case, the challenge password is also required because the server may challenge an end entity with the password before any certificate can be revoked. Later on, this challenge password is included as a PKCS #10 attribute, and is sent to the server as encrypted data. The PKCS #7 envelope protects the privacy of the challenge password with Data Encryption Standard (DES) encryption.

CA Servers Interoperable with Cisco Routers

There are several CA vendors that interoperate with Cisco IOS software on Cisco routers. See Cisco.com for the latest information regarding supported CA servers for your version of Cisco IOS.

Several CA vendors support SCEP for enrolling Cisco routers. Cisco is using the Cisco Security Associate Program to test new CA and PKI solutions with the Cisco Security family of products. More information on the Security Associate Program can be found at Cisco.com.

The following subsections present several common CA servers that interoperate with Cisco IOS software:

- Entrust Technologies Entrust/PKI
- VeriSign OnSite
- Betrusted UniCERT
- Microsoft Windows Certificate Services

Entrust Technologies Entrust/PKI

Entrust uses software that is installed and administered by the user. Cisco IOS interoperates with the Entrust/PKI CA server. Entrust/PKI enables you to issue digital identifications to any device or application that supports the X.509 certificate standard, meeting the need for security, flexibility, and low cost by supporting all devices and applications from one PKI. Entrust/PKI has the following system requirements and standards support capabilities:

- **Requirements**—Entrust runs on the Microsoft Windows NT 4.0 (required for Cisco interoperability), Solaris 2.6, HP-UX 10.20, and AIX 4.3 operating systems. Entrust requires RSA usage keys on the routers. You must use Cisco IOS Release 11.(3)5T and later.

- **Standards supported**—Entrust supports CA services, and RA capability, SCEP, and PKCS #10.

Refer to the Entrust website at http://www.entrust.com for more information.

VeriSign OnSite

The VeriSign OnSite CA server is another CA that operates with Cisco routers. VeriSign administers the CA, providing the certificates as a service.

VeriSign's OnSite solution delivers a fully integrated enterprise PKI to control, issue, and manage IPSec certificates for Cisco PIX Firewalls and Cisco routers. VeriSign OnSite is a service that is administered by VeriSign. VeriSign OnSite has the following system requirements and standards support capabilities:

- **Requirements**—There are no local server requirements. Configure the router for CA mode with a high (greater than 60 seconds) retry count. You must use Cisco IOS Release 12.0(6.0.1)T or later. Cisco IOS 12.0(5)T is not supported because of a known bug in that release.

- **Standards supported**—Supports SCEP, X.509 certificate format, and PKCS #7, #10, #11, and #12.

Refer to the VeriSign website at http://www.verisign.com for more information.

Betrusted UniCERT

Betrusted, Incorporated has implemented support for SCEP in UniCERT (Betrusted's CA server), as well as the PKI Plus toolkit—these make it easy for customers to enable certificate within their environments. UniCERT has the following system requirements and standards support capabilities:

- **Requirements**—The current release of the UniCERT CA module is available for Windows NT. You must use Cisco IOS Release 12.0(5)T or later.

- **Standards supported**—The following standards are supported with this CA server: X.509v3, X.9.62, X.9.92, and X9.21-2; CRLv2 and RFC 2459; PKCS #1, #7, #10, #11, and #12; RFC 2510 and RFC 2511; SCEP, Lightweight Directory Access Protocol (LDAP) version 2, LDAPv3, DAP, SQL, TCP/IP, Post Office Protocol (POP) 3, Simple Mail Transfer Protocol (SMTP), HTTP, Online Certificate Status Protocol (OCSP), Federal Information Processing Standard (FIPS) 186-1, FIPS 180-1, FIPS 46-3, and FIPS 81 CBC.

Refer to the Baltimore website at http://www.baltimore.com for more information.

Microsoft Windows Certificate Services

Microsoft has SCEP add-on support available for the Windows 2000 Certificate Services server through the Microsoft Windows 2000 Server Resource Kit, and for the Windows 2003 Certificate Services server as a download from Microsoft's website. This support lets customers use SCEP to obtain certificates and certificate revocation information from Microsoft Certificate Services for all of Cisco's virtual private network (VPN) security solutions. Microsoft Windows Certificate Services has the following system requirements and standards support capabilities:

- **Requirements**—Compatible PC that is capable of running Windows 2000 or 2003 Server. You must use Cisco IOS Release 12.0(5)T or later.

- **Standards supported**—The following standards are supported with this CA server: X.509v3, CRLv2, PKCS family (PKCS #7, #10, #12), PKI X.509 (PKIX), Secure Sockets Layer (SSL) version 3, Kerberos v5 RFC 1510, 1964 tokens, Server-Gated Cryptography (SGC), IPSec, public key authentication PKinit, PC/SC, and IETF 2459.

To install the SCEP add-on, complete the following steps:

Step 1 Install the SCEP add-on for Certificate Services on a root (CA). Both enterprise root CAs and stand-alone root CAs are supported.

Step 2 Log on with the appropriate administrative privileges to the server on which the root CA is installed.

Step 3 Run the cepsetup.exe file located on the Windows 2000 Resource Kit CD-ROM.

Step 4 In the SCEP Add-on for Certificate Services Setup Wizard, complete the following substeps:

   (a) Select whether or not you want to require a challenge phrase for certificate enrollment. You may wish to use a challenge phrase for added security, especially if you configure the CA to automatically grant certificates. You later obtain the challenge phrase immediately before enrolling the IPSec client by accessing the CA's URL, http://*URLHostName*/certsrv/mscep/mscep.dll, and copying the phrase, replacing *URLHostName* with the real name of the CA server. The phrase is then entered upon IPSec client enrollment.

   (b) Enter information about who is enrolling for the RA certificate, which will later allow certificates to be requested from the CA on behalf of the router.

   (c) (Optional.) Select Advanced Enrollment Options if you want to specify the cryptographic service provider (CSP) and key lengths for the RA signature and encryption keys.

Step 5 The URL, http://*URLHostName*/certsrv/mscep/mscep.dll, is displayed when the SCEP Setup Wizard finishes and confirms a successful installation. *URLHostName* is the name of the server that hosts the CA's enrollment web pages (also referred to as certificate services web pages).

   You may need to update the mscep.dll with a later version.

Refer to the Microsoft website at http://www.microsoft.com for more information.

Enrolling a Device with CA

The following is the typical process for enrolling with a CA:

Step 1 Configure the router for CA support.

Step 2   Generate a public and private key pair on the router.

Step 3   The router authenticates the CA server:

   (a) Send the certificate request to the CA/RA.

   (b) Generate a CA/RA certificate.

   (c) Download a CA/RA certificate to a router.

   (d) Authenticate a CA/RA certificate via the CA/RA fingerprint.

Step 4   The router sends a certificate request to the CA.

Step 5   The CA generates and signs an identity certificate.

Step 6   The CA sends the certificates to the router and posts the certificates in its public repository (directory).

Step 7   The router verifies the identify certificate and posts the certificate.

Most of these steps have been automated by Cisco and the SCEP protocol that is supported by many CA server vendors. Each vender determines how long certificates are valid. Contact the relevant vendor to determine how long the certificates will be valid for your particular case.

Multiple RSA Key Pair Support

Beginning with Cisco IOS Release 12.2(8)T, Cisco introduced the capability to support multiple RSA key pairs. Up to that release, Cisco IOS permitted either one general-purpose key pair or a set of special-purpose key pairs (an encryption and a signing key pair).

Some network configurations require working with multiple CAs, which might have different requirements for general-purpose versus special-purpose key certificates or key length. Previously, because the router could only support one general-purpose or special-purpose set of keys, administrators were often forced to make compromises on which type of key to use.

With the capability to support multiple RSA key pairs, an administrator can configure a different key pair for each CA. Each key pair can be selected without compromising requirements for key length, key lifetime, or general-purpose versus special-purpose usage keys.

Configuration tasks remain unchanged from previous releases, although additional functionality has been added to some of the commands. As these commands are presented in the upcoming sections, multiple RSA key pair support features will be noted.

Configuring CA Support Tasks

This section presents an overview of the CA support tasks that you will perform in this chapter.

The configuration process for RSA signatures consists of five major tasks. This chapter discusses the CA configuration tasks and steps in detail. Tasks and steps identical to pre-shared keys are not covered in detail in this chapter. Refer to Chapter 8, "Building IPSec VPNs Using

Cisco Routers and Pre-Shared Keys," for a detailed explanation of these steps. The tasks to configure CA support that are covered in this chapter are as follows:

- **Task 1: Prepare for IKE and IPSec.** Determine the detailed encryption policy: identify the hosts and networks you wish to protect, determine IPSec peer details, determine the IPSec features you need, and ensure that existing access control lists (ACLs) are compatible with IPSec.

- **Task 2: Configure CA support.** Set the router's host name and domain name, generate the keys, declare a CA, and authenticate and request your own certificates.

- **Task 3: Configure IKE for IPSec.** Enable IKE, create the IKE policies, and validate its configuration.

- **Task 4: Configure IPSec.** Define the transform sets, create crypto ACLs, create crypto map entries, and apply crypto map sets to interfaces.

- **Task 5: Test and verify IPSec.** Use **show**, **debug**, and related commands to test and verify that IPSec encryption works, as well as to troubleshoot problems.

Task 1 to Configure CA Support: Prepare for IKE and IPSec

Successful implementation of an IPSec network requires advance planning before you begin configuration of individual routers.

You must plan in advance if you want to configure IPSec encryption correctly the first time and minimize misconfiguration. You should begin this task by defining the IPSec security policy based on the overall company security policy.

The steps to prepare for IKE and IPSec when using CA support are very similar to those steps used when performing this task when using pre-shared keys. There are six steps here, corresponding to the five steps shown in the section "Task 1 to Configure IPSec Encryption: Preparing for IKE and IPSec" in Chapter 8. Step 1 has been added to plan for CA support and the remaining steps renumbered, as shown below:

Step 1 Plan for CA support.

Determine the CA server details. This includes variables such as the type of CA server to be used, the IP address, and the CA administrator contact information.

Step 2 Check the current configuration.

Use the **show run**, **show crypto isakmp [policy]**, and **show crypto map** commands, and the many other **show** commands, which are covered later in this chapter in the section titled, "Task 5 to Configure CA Support: Testing and Verifying the IKE and IPSec Configurations."

Step 3 Determine IKE (IKE phase 1) policy.

Determine the IKE policies between IPSec peers based on the number and location of the peers.

Step 4   Determine IPSec (IKE phase 2) policy.

Identify IPSec peer details, such as IP addresses and IPSec modes. You then configure crypto maps to gather all IPSec policy details together.

Step 5   Ensure that the network works without encryption.

Before you configure IPSec, ensure that basic connectivity using the desired IP services has been achieved between IPSec peers. You can use the **ping** command to check basic connectivity.

Step 6   Ensure that ACLs are compatible with IPSec.

Ensure that perimeter routers and the IPSec peer router interfaces permit IPSec traffic. In this step, you need to enter the **show access-lists** command.

NOTE   Only steps 1 and 3 will be discussed further in this chapter. The remaining steps are identical to the corresponding steps used when configuring pre-shared keys. See the section "Task 1 to Configure IPSec Encryption: Preparing for IKE and IPSec" in Chapter 8 if you would like to review those steps. Remember that the step numbers are different, so use corresponding step titles for comparison.

Step 1: Planning for CA Support

Configuring a CA is complicated. Having a detailed plan lessens the chances of improper configuration. Some planning steps include the following:

- **Determine the type of CA server to use.** CA servers come in a multitude of configurations and capabilities. You must determine which one fits your needs in advance of configuration. Requirements include (but are not limited to) the RSA key type required, CRL capabilities, and support for RA mode.

- **Identify the CA server's IP address, host name, and URL.** This information is necessary if you use LDAP.

- **Identify the CA server administrator contact information.** You need to arrange for your certificates to be validated if the process is not automatic.

The goal is to be ready for CA support configuration.

Determining CA Server Details

Table 9-1 illustrates the minimum information needed to configure a CA server on a Cisco router like those shown in Figure 9-1. Depending on the CA server that you choose, other variables may also have to be identified and resolved.

Table 9-1 *CA Server Parameters*

Parameter	CA Server
Type of CA server	Windows 2000
Host name	vpnca
IP address	172.30.1.51
URL	vpnca.cisco.com
Administrator contact	1-800-555-1212

Figure 9-1 *Configuring a CA Server on a Cisco Router*

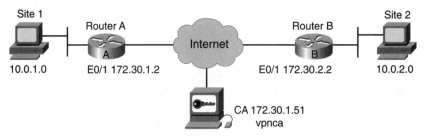

Step 3: Determining IKE (IKE Phase 1) Policy

Configuring IKE is complicated. You should determine the IKE policy details to enable the selected authentication method and then configure it. Having a detailed plan lessens the chances of improper configuration. Some planning steps include the following:

- **Determine the key distribution method**—Determine the key distribution method based on the numbers and locations of IPSec peers. For small networks, you may wish to manually distribute keys. For larger networks, you may wish to use a CA server to support scalability of IPSec peers. You must then configure ISAKMP to support the selected key distribution method.

> **NOTE** Remember that Cisco uses ISAKMP to perform IKE functions.

- **Determine the authentication method**—Choose the authentication method based on the key distribution method. Cisco IOS software supports either pre-shared keys, RSA encrypted nonces, or RSA signatures to authenticate IPSec peers. This chapter focuses on using RSA signatures.

- **Identify IPSec peers' IP addresses and host names**—Determine the details of all the IPSec peers that will use ISAKMP and RSA signature keys to establish security associations (SAs). You will use this information to configure IKE.

- **Determine IKE phase 1 policies for peers**—An ISAKMP policy defines a combination or suite of security parameters to be used during the ISAKMP negotiation. Each ISAKMP negotiation begins by each peer agreeing on a common (shared) ISAKMP policy. The ISAKMP policy suites must be determined in advance of configuration. You must then configure IKE to support the policy details you determined. Some ISAKMP policy details include the following:

  — Encryption algorithm

  — Hash algorithm

  — IKE SA lifetime

The goal of this planning step is to gather the precise data that you will need in later steps to minimize misconfiguration.

Examining Parameters

An IKE policy defines a combination of security parameters used during the IKE negotiation. A group of policies makes up a protection suite of multiple policies that enable IPSec peers to establish IKE sessions and establish SAs with a minimal configuration. Table 9-2 shows an example of possible combinations of IKE parameters into either a strong or stronger policy suite and the relative strength of each parameter.

Table 9-2   *IKE Policy Parameters*

Parameter	Strong	Stronger
Encryption algorithm	DES	3DES
Hash algorithm	MD5	SHA-1
Authentication method	Pre-shared	RSA encryption RSA signature
Key exchange	DH Group 1	DH Group 2
IKE SA lifetime	86,400 seconds	<86,400 seconds

Creating IKE Policies for a Purpose

IKE negotiations must be protected, so each IKE negotiation begins by each peer agreeing on a common (shared) IKE policy. This policy states which security parameters are used to protect subsequent IKE negotiations.

After the two peers agree upon a policy, an SA established at each peer identifies the security parameters of the policy, and these SAs apply to all subsequent IKE traffic during the negotiation.

You can create multiple, prioritized policies at each peer to ensure that at least one policy will match a remote peer's policy.

Defining IKE Policy Parameters

You can select specific values for each IKE parameter per the IKE standard. You choose one value over another based on the security level that you desire and the type of IPSec peer to which you will connect.

There are five parameters to define in each IKE policy, as outlined in Tables 9-2 and 9-3. Table 9-3 shows the default values.

Table 9-3   *IKE Policy Default Parameters*

Parameter	Accepted Values	Keyword	Default
Message encryption algorithm	DES 3DES	des 3des	DES
Message integrity (hash) algorithm	SHA-1 (HMAC variant) MD5 (HMAC variant)	sha md5	SHA-1
Peer authentication method	Pre-shared keys RSA encrypted nonces RSA signatures	pre-share rsa-encr rsa-sig	RSA signatures
Key exchange parameters (DH group ID)	768-bit DH or 1024-bit DH	1 2	768-bit DH
ISAKMP-established SA's lifetime	Can specify any number of seconds	—	86,400 seconds (one day)

You can select specific values for each ISAKMP parameter per the ISAKMP standard. You choose one value over another based on the security level you desire and the type of IPSec peer to which you will connect.

Determining IKE Policy Example

You should determine IKE policy details for each peer before you configure IKE. Table 9-4 shows a summary of IKE policy details that will be configured in examples for this chapter for the network shown in Figure 9-2. The authentication method of RSA signature keys is covered in this chapter, while the method of using pre-shared keys was covered in Chapter 8, "Origin Authentication."

Table 9-4   *IKE Policy Parameter Selection*

Parameter	Site 1	Site 2
Encryption algorithm	DES	DES
Hash algorithm	MD5	MD5
Authentication method	RSA signatures	RSA signatures
Key exchange	DH Group 1	DH Group 1
IKE SA lifetime	86,400 seconds	86,400 seconds
Peer IP address	172.30.2.2	172.30.1.2

Figure 9-2   *Example Network*

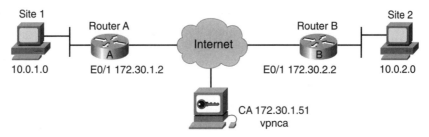

Task 2 to Configure CA Support: Configure CA Support

This section presents a detailed explanation of the steps necessary to configure CA support on Cisco routers.

Configuring Cisco IOS CA support is complicated. Having a detailed plan lessens the chances of improper configuration. The planning steps and their associated commands are shown in the following steps and described in detail in the sections that follow:

Step 1   (Optional.) Manage the NVRAM memory usage.

In some cases, storing certificates and CRLs locally does not present a problem. However, in other cases, memory might become an issue—particularly if your CA supports an RA and a large number of CRLs end up being stored on your router.

Step 2   Set the router's time and date.

The router must have an accurate time and date to enroll with a CA server. Use the **clock timezone** and **clock set** commands for this purpose. You could also use the Network Time Protocol (NTP) to keep your router's time and date synchronized with other network devices.

WARNING   Keep in mind that NTP is an insecure protocol that is frequently used in DoS attacks. Security best practices recommend that you disable NTP on critical devices.

If you elect to use NTP, be sure to set up a tight ACL that permits only specific NTP devices and use the **ntp access-group serve-only** or **ntp access-group peer** command to control NTP packet access to your system.

For further information on configuring NTP, see the Cisco Security Advisory: NTP Vulnerability at http://www.cisco.com/en/US/products/products_security_advisory09186a00800b13d9.shtml.

Step 3   Configure the router's host name and domain name.

The host name is used in prompts and default configuration filenames and is set with the **hostname** command. The domain name is used to define a default domain name that the Cisco IOS software uses to complete unqualified host names and is set with the **ip domain-name** command.

Step 4   Generate an RSA key pair.

RSA keys are used to identify the remote VPN peer. You can generate one general-purpose key or two special-purpose keys using the **crypto key generate rsa** command. Multiple RSA key pairs are supported since Cisco IOS Release 12.2(8)T.

Step 5   Declare a CA.

To declare the CA that your router should use, use the **crypto ca trustpoint** global configuration command. Use the **no** form of this command to delete all identity information and certificates associated with the CA.

Step 6   Authenticate the CA.

The router needs to authenticate the CA. It does this by obtaining the CA's self-signed certificate that contains the CA's public key. Use the **crypto ca authenticate name** command.

Step 7   Request your own certificate.

Complete this step to obtain your router's identity certificate from the CA using the **crypto ca enroll name** command.

Step 8   Save the configuration.

After configuring the router for CA support, the configuration should be saved with the **copy running-config startup-config** command.

Step 9   (Optional.) Monitor and maintain CA interoperability.

The following substeps are optional, depending on your particular requirements:

(a) Request a CRL using the **crypto ca crl request name** command.

(b) Delete your router's RSA keys with the **crypto key zeroize rsa** command.

(c) Delete both public and private certificates from the configuration with the **no certificate** and **no ca trustpoint** commands.

(d) Delete the peer's public keys using the **no named-key** or **no addressed-key** commands.

Step 10 Verify the CA support configuration.

The commands detailed in this section, **show crypto ca certificates**, **show crypto key mypubkey rsa**, and **show crypto key pubkey-chain rsa**, allow you to view any configured CA certificates.

Step 1 (Optional): Managing NVRAM Memory Usage

In some cases, storing certificates and CRLs locally will not present a problem. However, in other cases, memory might become an issue—particularly if your CA supports an RA and a large number of CRLs end up being stored on your router. These certificates and CRLs can consume a large amount of NVRAM space.

The following are the types of certificates stored on a router:

- The router's own identity certificate
- The CA's root certificate
- RA certificates (CA vendor-specific)

The number of CRLs stored on a router depends on whether or not the CA supports an RA. If the CA does not support an RA, one CRL is stored on the router. If the CA does support an RA, multiple CRLs are stored on the router.

To save NVRAM space, you can specify that certificates and CRLs should not be stored locally, but should be retrieved from the CA when needed. This saves NVRAM space but could have a slight performance impact.

To specify that certificates and CRLs should not be stored locally on your router, but should be retrieved when required, turn on query mode by using the **crypto ca certificate query** command in global configuration mode.

Step 2: Setting the Router's Time and Date

Ensure that the router's time zone, time, and date have been accurately set with the **show clock** commands in privileged EXEC mode. The clock must be accurately set before generating RSA key pairs and enrolling with the CA server because certificates are time-sensitive. On certificates, there is a valid from and to date and time. When the router validates the certificate, the router determines whether its system clock falls within the validity range. If it does, the certificate is valid. If not, the certificate is deemed invalid or expired.

To specify the router's time zone, use the **clock timezone** global configuration command. The command sets the time zone and an offset from Universal Time Code ([UTC], displayed by the router).

The syntax for the **clock timezone** command is as follows:

```
clock timezone zone hours [minutes]
```

- *zone*—Name of the time zone to be displayed when standard time is in effect.

- *hours*—Hours offset from UTC.

- *minutes* (Optional.)—Minutes offset from UTC.

The following example sets the time zone to Central Standard Time (CST) in the United States:

```
RouterA(config)# clock timezone cst -6
```

To set the router's time and date, use the **clock set** privileged EXEC command.

The syntax for the **clock set** command is as follows:

```
clock set hh:mm:ss day month year
clock set hh:mm:ss month day year
```

- *hh:mm:ss*—Current time in hours (military format), minutes, and seconds.

- *day*—Current day (by date) in the month.

- *month*—Current month (by name).

- *year*—Current year (no abbreviation).

The following example sets the time to one second before midnight, December 31, 2001:

```
RouterA(config)# clock set 23:59:59 31 december 2001
```

You can also optionally set your router to automatically update the calendar and time from an NTP server with the **ntp** series of commands, as long as you remember that it is a security risk and handle it accordingly.

Step 3: Configure the Router's Hostname and Domain Name

If the router's host name and domain name have not previously been configured, you need to configure them for CA support to work correctly.

To specify or modify the host name for the network server, use the hostname global configuration command. The host name is used in prompts and default configuration filenames. The setup command facility also prompts for a host name at startup.

The syntax for the **hostname** command is as follows:

```
hostname name
```

- *name*—New host name for the router.

To define a default domain name that the Cisco IOS software uses to complete unqualified host names (names without a dotted-decimal domain name), use the **ip domain-name** global configuration command. To disable use of the Domain Name System (DNS), use the **no** form of this command.

The command syntax for the **ip domain-name** command is as follows:

```
ip domain-name name
```

- *name*—Default domain name used to complete unqualified host names. Do not include the initial period that separates an unqualified name from the domain name.

The following shows an example of using the **ip domain-name** command:

```
RouterA(config)# ip domain-name futurecorp.com
```

Use the **ip host** global configuration command to define a static hostname-to-address mapping in the host cache. This is a necessary step if the domain name is not resolvable. To remove the name-to-address mapping, use the **no** form of this command.

The syntax for the **ip host** command is as follows:

```
ip host name address1 [address2...address8]
```

- *name*—Name of the host. The first character can be either a letter or a number.
- *address1*—Associated IP address.
- *address2...address8* (Optional.)—Additional associated IP address. You can bind up to eight addresses to a host name.

The following shows an example of using the **ip host** command:

```
RouterA(config)# ip host vpnex 192.168.10.20
```

Step 4: Generating an RSA Key Pair

Use the **crypto key generate rsa** global configuration command to generate RSA key pairs.

The syntax for the **crypto key generate rsa** command is as follows:

```
crypto key generate rsa [usage-keys | general-keys] [key-pair-label]
```

- **usage-keys** (Optional.)—Specifies that two RSA special-usage key pairs should be generated (that is, one encryption pair and one signature pair), instead of one general-purpose key pair.
- **general-keys** (Optional.)—Specifies that the general-purpose key pair should be generated. (This keyword was added with Multiple RSA Key Pair Support.)
- *key-pair-label* (Optional.)—Specifies the name of the key pair that router will use. (If this argument is enabled, you must specify either **usage-keys** or **general-keys**. This keyword was added with Multiple RSA Key Pair Support.)

By default, RSA key pairs do not exist. If **usage-keys** is not used in the command, general-purpose keys are generated. RSA keys are generated in pairs: one public RSA key and one private RSA key. If your router already has RSA keys with the same label when you issue this command, you are warned and prompted to replace the existing keys with new keys.

NOTE   Before issuing the command to generate RSA keys, make sure your router has a host name and IP domain name configured (with the **hostname** and **ip domain-name** commands). You will be unable to complete the **crypto key generate rsa** command without a host name and IP domain name.

The keys generated by the **crypto key generate rsa** command are saved in the private configuration in NVRAM, which is never displayed to the user or backed up to another device.

There are two mutually exclusive types of RSA key pairs: special-usage keys and general-purpose keys. When you generate RSA key pairs, you can indicate whether to generate special-usage keys or general-purpose keys. If you include the optional **usage-keys** keyword in the **crypto key generate rsa** command, the system will generate special-usage keys. If you omit the keyword, general-purpose keys will be created.

If you generate a named key pair using the *key-pair-label* argument, you must also specify the **usage-keys** keyword or the **general-keys** keyword. Named key pairs allow you to have multiple RSA key pairs, enabling the Cisco IOS software to maintain a different key pair for each identity certificate. If *key-pair-label* is not specified, the fully qualified domain name (FQDN) of the router is used as the name of the key pair.

Generating Special-Usage Keys

If you generate special-usage keys, two pairs of RSA keys are generated. One pair is used with any IKE policy that specifies RSA signatures as the authentication method, and the other pair is used with any IKE policy that specifies RSA encrypted nonces as the authentication method.

If you plan to have both types of RSA authentication methods in your IKE policies, you might prefer to generate special-usage keys. With special-usage keys, each key is not unnecessarily exposed. (Without special-usage keys, one key is used for both authentication methods, increasing that key's exposure.)

Generating General-Purpose Keys

If you generate general-purpose keys, only one pair of RSA keys is generated. This pair is used with IKE policies specifying either RSA signatures or RSA encrypted nonces. Therefore, a general-purpose key pair might get used more frequently than a special-usage key pair.

Generating RSA Keys Example

Key generation can be very time-consuming, depending on the router and length of the key chosen. Example 9-1 shows an example of generating a general-purpose key pair and then viewing the resultant key.

Example 9-1 *Generating a General-Purpose Key Pair and then Viewing the Resultant Key*

```
RouterA(config)# crypto key generate rsa
The name for the keys will be: router.cisco.com
Choose the size of the key modulus in the range of 360 to 2048 for your Signature Keys.
Choosing a key modulus greater than 512 may take a few minutes.

How many bits in the modulus [512]: 512
Generating RSA keys ...
[OK]
RouterA# show crypto key mypubkey rsa
% Key pair was generated at: 23:58:59 UTC Dec 31 2000
```

Example 9-1   *Generating a General-Purpose Key Pair and then Viewing the Resultant Key (Continued)*

```
Key name: RouterA.cisco.com
Usage: General Purpose Key
Key Data:
  305C300D 06092A86 4886F70D 01010105 00034B00 30480241 00A9443B 62FDACFB
  CCDB8784 19AE1CD8 95B30953 1EDD30D1 380219D6 4636E015 4D7C6F33 4DC1F6E0
  C929A25E 521688A1 295907F4 E98BF920 6A81CE57 28A21116 E3020301 0001
```

When you generate RSA keys, you are prompted to enter a modulus length. A longer modulus could offer stronger security, but takes longer to generate and takes longer to use. A modulus below 512 is normally not recommended. Cisco recommends using a minimum modulus of 1024. Table 9-5 shows examples of how long it takes to generate keys of different modulus lengths.

Table 9-5   *RSA Key Generation*

Router	360 bits	512 bits	1024 bits	2048 bits
Cisco 2500	11 seconds	20 seconds	4 minutes, 38 seconds	Longer than 1 hour
Cisco 4700	Less than 1 second	1 second	4 seconds	50 seconds

Step 5: Declaring a CA Using Commands

Note that in Cisco IOS Release 12.2(8)T, **crypto ca trustpoint** replaces the **crypto ca identity** command from previous Cisco IOS versions. This is done so that the router will try to enroll to the CA server automatically when its certificates expire.

Use the **crypto ca trustpoint** global configuration command to declare what CA your router will use. Use the **no** form of this command to delete all identity information and certificates associated with the CA.

The syntax for the **crypto ca trustpoint** command is as follows:

```
crypto ca trustpoint name
```

- *name*—Create a name for the CA. (If you previously declared the CA and just want to update its characteristics, specify the name you previously created.) The CA might require a particular name, such as its domain name.

NOTE   The **crypto ca trustpoint** command is only significant locally. It does not have to match the identity defined on any of the VPN peers.

Performing the **crypto ca trustpoint** command puts you into ca-trustpoint configuration mode, where you can specify characteristics for the CA.

The first command to use within ca-trustpoint configuration mode is the **enrollment** command. The following shows the syntax for the **enrollment** command:

```
enrollment [mode] [retry period minutes] [retry count number] url url
```

- **mode** (Optional.)—RA mode, if your CA system provides an RA.

- **retry period** *minutes* (Optional.)—Specifies the wait period between certificate request retries. The default is 1 minute between retries. (Specify between 1 to 60 minutes.)

- **retry count** *minutes* (Optional.)—Specifies the number of times a router will resend a certificate request when it does not receive a response from the previous request. The default is 10 retries. (Specify from 1 to 100 retries.)

- **url** *url*—URL of the CA where your router should send certificate requests.

  If you are using SCEP for enrollment, *url* must be in the form http://*CA_name*, where *CA_name* is the host DNS name or IP address of the CA.

  If you are using TFTP for enrollment, *url* must be in the form tftp://*certserver* /*file_specification*. (The *file_specification* is optional.)

The next command to use within ca-trustpoint configuration mode is the **crl** command. The following shows the syntax for the **crl** command:

```
crl {query url | optional | best-effort}
```

- **query** *url*—The LDAP URL published by the CA server is specified to query the CRL; for example, ldap://*another_server*.

- **optional**—CRL verification is optional.

- **best-effort**—CRL verification will be attempted, but if the CRL is unavailable, the certificate will be accepted.

Another command that you might use within ca-trustpoint configuration mode is **rsakeypair**. This command was added to support the Multiple RSA Key Pair Support feature. The following shows the syntax for the **rsakeypair** command:

```
rsakeypair key-label [key-size [encryption-key-size]]
```

- *key-label*—The name of the key pair, which is generated during enrollment if it does not already exist or if the **auto-enroll regenerate** command is configured.

- *key-size* (Optional.)—The size of the desired RSA key. If not specified, the existing key size is used. (The specified size must be the same as *encryption-key-size*.)

- *encryption-key-size* (Optional.)—The size of the second key, which is used to request separate encryption, signature keys, and certificates. (The specified size must be the same as *key-size*.)

Example 9-2 shows how these commands might be applied.

Example 9-2 *Applying Commands in ca-trustpoint Configuration Mode*

```
RouterA(config)# crypto ca trustpoint vpnca
RouterA(ca-trustpoint)# enrollment url http://bar.cisco.com
RouterA(ca-trustpoint)# crl query ldap://bar.cisco.com
RouterA(ca-trustpoint)# rsakeypair exampleCAkeys 1024 1024
```

Declaring a CA Example

Example 9-3 declares an Entrust CA and identifies characteristics of the CA. In this example, the name *vpnca* is created for the CA, which is located at http://vpnca. The example also declares a CA using an RA. The CA's scripts are stored in the default location, and the CA uses SCEP instead of LDAP. This is the minimum possible configuration required to declare a CA that uses an RA.

Example 9-3 *Declaring an Entrust CA and Identifying Characteristics of the CA*

```
RouterA(config)# crypto ca trustpoint vpnca
RouterA(ca-trustpoint)# enrollment mode url http://vpnca/certsrv/mscep/mscep.dll
RouterA(ca-trustpoint)# exit
```

Example 9-4 declares a Microsoft Windows 2000 CA. Note that the enrollment URL points to the MSCEP DLL.

Example 9-4 *Declaring a Microsoft Windows 2000 CA*

```
crypto ca trustpoint labca
 enrollment mode  url http://vpnca/certsrv/mscep/mscep.dll
 crl optional
```

Step 6: Authenticating the CA

The router needs to authenticate the CA to verify that it is valid. The router does this by obtaining the CA's self-signed certificate that contains the CA's public key. Because the CA's certificate is self-signed (the CA signs its own certificate), the CA's public key should be manually authenticated by contacting the CA administrator to compare the CA certificate's fingerprint when you perform this step. To get the CA's public key, use the **crypto ca authenticate** *name* command in global configuration mode. Use the same name that you used when declaring the CA with the **crypto ca trustpoint** command.

If you are using RA mode (using the **enrollment mode ra** command) when you issue the **crypto ca authenticate** command, the RA signing and encryption certificates are returned from the CA as well as the CA certificate.

Example 9-5 shows a CA authentication.

Example 9-5 *CA Authentication*

```
RouterA(config)# crypto ca authenticate labca
Certificate has the following attributes:
Fingerprint: 93700C31 4853EC4A DED81400 43D3C82C
% Do you accept this certificate? [yes/no]: y
```

Step 7: Requesting a Certificate

To obtain your router's identity certificate from the CA, use the **crypto ca enroll** global configuration command. Use the **no** form of this command to delete a current enrollment request.

The syntax for the **crypto ca enroll** command is as follows:

```
crypto ca enroll name
```

- *name*—Specifies the name of the CA. Use the same name as when you declared the CA using the **crypto ca trustpoint** command.

This command requests certificates from the CA for all of your router's RSA key pairs. This task is also known as "enrolling" with the CA.

During the enrollment process, you are prompted for a challenge password, which can be used by the CA administrator to validate your identity. Do not forget the password you use. (Technically, enrolling and obtaining certificates are two separate events, but they both occur when the **crypto ca enroll** command is issued.)

Your router needs a signed certificate from the CA for each of your router's RSA key pairs; if you previously generated general-purpose keys, this command obtains the one certificate corresponding to the one general-purpose RSA key pair. If you previously generated special-usage keys, this command obtains two certificates corresponding to each of the special-usage RSA key pairs.

If you already have a certificate for your keys, you will be unable to complete this command; instead, you are prompted to remove the existing certificate first. (You can remove existing certificates with the **no certificate** command.)

Example 9-6 shows a CA enrollment.

Example 9-6 *CA Enrollment*

```
RouterA(config)# crypto ca enroll labca
% Start certificate enrollment ..
% Create a challenge password. You will need to verbally provide this
    password to the CA Administrator in order to revoke your certificate.
    For security reasons, your password will not be saved in the configuration.
    Please make a note of it.

Password: <password>
Re-enter password: <password>

% The subject name in the certificate will be: r1.cisco.com
% Include the router serial number in the subject name? [yes/no]: no
% Include an IP address in the subject name? [yes/no]: no
Request certificate from CA? [yes/no]: yes
% Certificate request sent to Certificate Authority.
% The certificate request fingerprint will be displayed.
% The 'show crypto ca certificate' command will also show the fingerprint.

RouterA(config)#
    Signing Certificate Request Fingerprint:
    0EE481F1 CBB4AF30 5D757610 6A4CF13D
  Encryption Certificate Request Fingerprint:
    710281D4 4DE854C7 AA61D953 CC5BD2B9
```

CAUTION	The **crypto ca enroll** command is not saved in the router configuration. If your router reboots after you issue the **crypto ca enroll** command but before you receive the certificates, you must reissue the command.

Step 8: Saving the CA Support Configuration

After you configure the router for CA support, you should save the configuration to by NVRAM using the **copy running-config startup-config** command.

Step 9 (Optional): Monitoring and Maintaining CA Interoperability

The following steps are optional, depending on your particular requirements:

Step 1   Request a CRL.

A CRL is not always required. If the CA server requires a CRL, you need to request one from the CA server. To request immediate download of the latest CRL, use the **crypto ca crl request** command.

The syntax for the **crypto ca crl request** command is as follows:

```
crypto ca crl request name
```

- *name*—Specifies the name of the CA. Use the same name as when you declared the CA using the **crypto ca trustpoint** command.

When your router receives a certificate from a peer, it downloads a CRL from either the CA or a CRL distribution point as designated in the peer's certificate. Your router then checks the CRL to make sure that the certificate the peer sent has not been revoked. (If the certificate appears on the CRL, your router will not accept the certificate and will not authenticate the peer.)

With CA systems that support RAs, multiple CRLs exist and the peer's certificate indicates which CRL applies and should be downloaded by your router. If your router does not have the applicable CRL and is unable to obtain one, your router rejects the peer's certificate—unless you include the **crl optional** command in your configuration. If you use the **crl optional** command, your router will still try to obtain a CRL, but if it cannot obtain a CRL, it can still accept the peer's certificate.

When your router receives additional certificates from peers, your router continues to attempt to download the appropriate CRL, even if it was previously unsuccessful, and even if the **crl optional** command is enabled. The **crl optional** command only specifies that when the router cannot obtain the CRL, the router is not forced to reject a peer's certificate outright.

Step 2 Delete your router's RSA keys.

There might be circumstances in which you want to delete your router's RSA keys. For example, if you believe the RSA keys were compromised in some way and should no longer be used, you should delete the keys. To delete all of your router's RSA keys, use the **crypto key zeroize rsa** command in global configuration mode.

The syntax for the **crypto key zeroize rsa** command is as follows:

```
crypto key zeroize rsa [key-pair-label]
```

- *key-pair-label* (Optional)—Specifies the name of the key pair that router will delete. (This keyword was added with Multiple RSA Key Pair Support.)

Step 3 Delete certificates from the configuration.

After you delete a router's RSA keys, you should also delete the certificates from the configuration. Complete the following substeps to do this:

(a) Ask the CA administrator to revoke your router's certificates at the CA. You must supply the challenge password that you created when you originally obtained the router's certificates with the **crypto ca enroll** command.

(b) Manually remove the router's certificates from the router configuration. To delete your router's certificate or RA certificates from your router's configuration, use the following commands in global configuration mode:

- **show crypto ca certificates**—Views the certificates stored on your router. Note the serial number of the certificate you wish to delete.

- **crypto ca certificate chain** *name*—Enters certificate chain configuration mode.

- **no certificate** *certificate-serial-number*—Deletes the certificate. Use the serial number you noted in the first bullet.

NOTE To delete the CA's certificate, you must remove the entire CA trustpoint, which also removes all certificates associated with the CA: your router's certificate, the CA certificate, and any RA certificates. To remove a CA trustpoint, use the following command in global configuration mode: **no crypto ca trustpoint** *name*.

Step 4 Delete the peer's public keys.

There might be circumstances in which you want to delete other peers' RSA public keys from your router's configuration. For example, if you no longer

trust the integrity of a peer's public key, you should delete the key. To delete
the peer's public key, use the following commands:

- **crypto key pubkey-chain rsa**—Enter public key chain configuration mode.

- **no named-key** *key-name* [**encryption** I **signature**] or **no addressed-key** *key-address* [**encryption** I **signature**]—Delete a remote peer's RSA public key. Specify the peer's FQDN or the remote peer's IP address. You can optionally delete just the encryption key or the signature key by using the encryption or signature keywords.

Step 10: Verifying the CA Support Configuration

Example 9-7 illustrates the result of the **show crypto ca certificates** command.

Example 9-7   **show crypto ca certificates** *Command Result*

```
RouterA# show crypto ca certificates

Certificate
  Subject Name
    Name: myrouter.xyz.com
        IP Address: 172.30.1.2
    Status: Available
  Certificate Serial Number: 0123456789ABCDEF0123456789ABCDEF
  Key Usage: General Purpose

CA Certificate
  Status: Available
  Certificate Serial Number: 3051DF7123BEE31B8341DFE4B3A338E5F
  Key Usage: Not Set
```

Example 9-8 is sample output from the **show crypto key mypubkey rsa** command. Special-usage RSA keys were previously generated for this router using the **crypto key generate rsa** command.

Example 9-8   **show crypto key mypubkey rsa** *Command Sample Output*

```
% Key pair was generated at: 23:57:50 UTC Dec 31 2000
Key name: myrouter.xyz.com
  Usage: Signature Key
  Key Data:
    005C300D 06092A86 4886F70D 01010105 00034B00 30480241 00C5E23B 55D6AB22
    04AEF1BA A54028A6 9ACC01C5 129D99E4 64CAB820 847EDAD9 DF0B4E4C 73A05DD2
    BD62A8A9 FA603DD2 E2A8A6F8 98F76E28 D58AD221 B583D7A4 71020301 0001
% Key pair was generated at: 23:58:59 UTC Dec 31 2000
Key name: myrouter.xyz.com
  Usage: Encryption Key
  Key Data:
  00302017 4A7D385B 1234EF29 335FC973 2DD50A37 C4F4B0FD 9DADE748 429618D5
  18242BA3 2EDFBDD3 4296142A DDF7D3D8 08407685 2F2190A0 0B43F1BD 9A8A26DB
  07953829 791FCDE9 A98420F0 6A82045B 90288A26 DBC64468 7789F76E EE21
```

Example 9-9 is sample output from the **show crypto key pubkey-chain rsa** command.

Example 9-9 **show crypto key pubkey-chain rsa** *Command Sample Output*

```
Codes: M - Manually Configured, C - Extracted from certificate
Code      Usage         IP-address        Name
M         Signature     10.0.0.1          myrouter.domain.com
M         Encryption    10.0.0.1          myrouter.domain.com
C         Signature     172.30.1.2        RouterA.domain.com
C         Encryption    172.30.1.2        RouterA.domain.com
C         General       172.30.2.2        RouterB.domain1.com
```

This sample shows manually configured special-usage RSA public keys for the peer, myrouter. This sample also shows three keys obtained from peers' certificates: special-usage keys for peer RouterA and a general-purpose key for peer RouterB.

Certificate support is used in the previous example; if certificate support was not in use, none of the peers' keys would show *C* in the code column, but would all have to be manually configured.

Configuring CA Support Example

Example 9-10 displays the **running-config** command of a router that is properly configured for CA support.

Example 9-10 **running-config** *of a Router Properly Configured for CA Support*

```
RouterA# show running-config
!
hostname RouterA
!
ip domain-name cisco.com
!
crypto ca trustpoint mycaserver
enrollment mode url http://vpnca:80
 crl optional query url ldap://vpnca
 crypto ca certificate chain entrust
 certificate 37C6EAD6
  30820299 30820202 A0030201 02020437 C6EAD630 0D06092A
  864886F7 0D010105
  (certificates concatenated)
```

Task 3 to Configure CA Support: Configure IKE for IPSec

The next major task in configuring Cisco IOS IPSec is to configure the IKE parameters that you gathered earlier. This section presents the steps used to configure IKE policies.

NOTE The following steps are identical to the steps for configuring pre-shared keys, except for Step 2, which is described in detail in the next section. Refer to Chapter 8 under the section "Task 2 to Configure IPSec Encryption: Configuring IKE" for the detailed explanation of the other three steps that are not covered here.

Configuring IKE consists of the following essential steps and commands:

Step 1   Enable or disable IKE with the **crypto isakmp enable** command.

Step 2   Create IKE policies with the **crypto isakmp policy** command.

Step 3   Set the IKE identity to an address or host name with the **crypto isakmp identity** command.

Step 4   Test and verify the IKE configuration with the **show crypto isakmp policy** and **show crypto isakmp sa** commands.

Step 2: Cr

the ISAKMP policy configuration command
AKMP parameters. If you do not specify one of
is used for that parameter. Example 9-11 is a
policy command.

Exan

Table

words in Table 9-6 are available to specify the

		es	Default Value	Description
			des	Message encryption algorithm
			sha	Message integrity (hash) algorithm
	rsa-encr	RSA encrypted nonces	rsa-sig	Peer authentication method
	pre-share	Pre-shared keys		

continues

Table 9-6 *Keywords Specifying the Parameters in the Policy (Continued)*

Command	Keyword	Accepted Values	Default Value	Description
group	1	768-bit DH or	1	Key exchange parameters (DH group ID)
	2	1024-bit DH		
lifetime	—	Can specify any number of seconds	86,400 seconds (one day)	ISAKMP-established SA's lifetime; the default value usually is fine

You can configure multiple ISAKMP policies on each peer that is participating in IPSec. ISAKMP peers negotiate acceptable ISAKMP policies before agreeing upon the SA to be used for IPSec.

Task 4 to Configure CA Support: Configure IPSec

The next major task in configuring Cisco IOS IPSec is to configure the IPSec parameters that you previously gathered. This section presents the steps used to configure IPSec.

NOTE The following steps are identical to configuring pre-shared keys. Refer to the material in the section "Task 3 to Configure IPSec Encryption: Configuring IPSec" of Chapter 8 for the detailed explanation of each step.

The general steps and commands used to configure IPSec encryption on Cisco routers are summarized as follows:

Step 1 Configure transform set suites with the **crypto ipsec transform-set** command.

Step 2 Configure global IPSec SA lifetimes with the **crypto ipsec security-association lifetime** command.

Step 3 Configure crypto ACLs with the **access-list** command.

Step 4 Configure crypto maps with the **crypto map** command.

Step 5 Apply the crypto maps to the terminating or originating interface with the **interface** and **crypto map** commands.

Task 5 to Configure CA Support: Test and Verify IPSec

Cisco IOS software contains a number of **show**, **clear**, and **debug** commands that are useful for testing and verifying IPSec and ISAKMP, which are considered in this section. These commands do not need to be entered in the order listed. They each provide different usable data.

NOTE   While many of the test and verify commands are used the same as when configuring pre-shared keys, the commands shown in Step 7, **debug crypto key-exchange** and **debug crypto pki {messages | transactions}**, are unique to RSA signatures.

Complete the following steps to test and verify that you have correctly configured a VPN using Cisco IOS:

Step 1   Display your configured IKE policies by using the **show crypto isakmp policy** command.

Step 2   Display your configured transform sets by using the **show crypto ipsec transform set** command.

Step 3   Display the current state of your IPSec SAs by using the **show crypto ipsec sa** command.

Step 4   View your configured crypto maps by using the **show crypto map** command.

Step 5   Debug IKE and IPSec traffic through Cisco IOS with the **debug crypto ipsec** command.

Step 6   Debug IKE and IPSec traffic through Cisco IOS with the **debug crypto isakmp** command.

CAUTION   Use **debug** commands with caution. In general, it is recommended that these commands only be used under the direction of your router technical support representative when troubleshooting specific problems. Enabling debugging can disrupt operation of the router when internetworks are experiencing high load conditions.

Before you start a **debug** command, always consider the output that this command will generate and the amount of time this may take.

Before debugging, look at your CPU load by using the **show processes cpu** command. Verify that you have ample CPU available before beginning the debugs.

NOTE   When debugs are running, you do not usually see the router prompt, especially when the debug is intensive. However, in most cases, you can use the **no debug all or undebug all** command to stop the debugs.

Step 7 Debug CA events through the Cisco IOS with the **debug crypto key-exchange** and **debug crypto pki** {**messages** | **transactions**} commands.

Chapter Summary

The following list summarizes what you learned in this chapter:

- Define the detailed crypto CA, IKE, and IPSec security policy before beginning configuration.

- Ensure that you can contact your CA administrator before beginning configuration.

- Configure CA details before configuring IKE.

- Manually verify the CA certificate with the CA administrator. Each CA server supported by Cisco IOS software has a slightly different configuration process.

- Use the RSA signatures authentication method for IKE when using CA support.

- The IPSec configuration process is the same as that used for pre-shared and RSA encrypted nonces authentication.

Cisco IOS Commands Presented in This Chapter

Many Cisco IOS version 12.3 commands were discussed or referenced in this chapter. These commands can be found in the *Command Reference* online at http://www.cisco.com/univercd/cc/td/doc/product/software/ios123/123mindx/crgindx.htm.

Chapter Review Questions

The following review questions cover some of the key facts and concepts that were introduced in this chapter. Answers to these questions can be found in Appendix A, "Answers to Chapter Review Questions."

1 What is the purpose of the SCEP protocol?

2 Which CA servers provide interoperability with Cisco IOS software?

3 What three tasks must you perform as you prepare for CA support?

4 What Cisco IOS command would you use to generate an RSA key pair?

5 What command mode must you be in to enter the encryption, hash, authentication, group, and lifetime IKE policy commands.

6 You are setting up IPSec on an existing router and want to be sure that all previous RSA keys have been removed. What command would you use to delete all of your router's RSA keys?

7 What are the five steps required to complete Task 4, configuring IPSec on Cisco routers?

8 What command do you used to apply a crypto map to an interface on a Cisco router?

9 What command would you use to view IPSec SAs on your Cisco router?

10 What specific Cisco IOS **debug** commands are available to view CA events?

Case Study

The Future Corporation uses a VPN between Dallas and Plano, as shown in Figure 9-3.

Figure 9-3   *Dallas to Plano VPN*

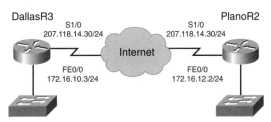

Scenario

Your task as network administrator is to configure router DallasR3 to support the VPN and to match the configuration already in place on router PlanoR2. Use the following instructions for each of the tasks to configure the VPN. Network Address Translation (NAT) is not being used for the purposes of this scenario.

Show all the configuration commands that you would need to execute to configure the IKE and IPSec policies outlined in Task 1. Also show all **show** and **debug** commands that you would use to check your configuration.

Use the following CA server details:

- The CA server is a Windows 2000 server.
- The host name is DalVPNCA.
- The CA's IP address is 172.16.10.167.
- The CA's URL is DalVPNCA.futurecorp.com.
- The administrator's phone number is 123-555-1212.

Use the following IKE policy:

- The key distribution method is via the CA server. No RA is being used.
- The authentication method will be through RSA signatures. Use a modulus of 1024 when generating the keys.

- PlanoR2's IP address and host name are shown in Figure 9-3.
- Use 3DES, SHA-1, pre-shared keys, DH Group 2, and an IKE SA lifetime of 16 hours (57,600 seconds) for your ISAKMP policy.

Use the following IPSec policy:

- Use the **esp-sha-hmac** and **esp-3des** transforms and call your transform set **DalPla**.
- LondonR1 is the only host you will be connecting with through the VPN.
- The IPSec tunnel will protect all traffic from DallasR3 to PlanoR2.
- SAs will be initiated by IKE. The IPSec SA lifetime will be 20 hours (72,000 seconds).

1   Task 1: Prepare for IKE and IPSec

Indicate the commands that you would use to perform these tasks:

- Check the current configuration.
- Ensure that the network works without encryption.
- Ensure that ACLs are compatible with IPSec.

2   Task 2: Configure a Cisco Router for CA Support

Indicate the commands that you would use to perform these tasks:

- Set the router's time and date.
- Configure the router's host name and domain name.
- Generate an RSA key pair.
- Declare a CA.
- Authenticate the CA.
- Request your own certificate.
- Verify the CA support configuration.

3   Task 3: Configure IKE

Indicate the commands that you would use to perform these tasks:

- Create the IKE policy.
- Verify the IKE configuration.

4   Task 4: Configure IPSec

Indicate the commands that you would use to perform these tasks:

- Configure the transform set.
- Configure the global IPSec security association lifetime.
- Configure the crypto ACL.

- Configure the crypto map.
- Apply the crypto map to the interface.

5 Task 5: Test and Verify IPSec

Indicate the commands that you would use to perform these tasks:

- Display your configured IKE policies.
- Display your configured transform sets.
- Display the current state of your IPSec SAs.
- View your configured crypto maps.
- Debug IKE and IPSec traffic through Cisco IOS.

Solutions

The correct commands that can be used to configure the DallasR3 Cisco IOS Firewall router for IDS support follow.

Task 1: Prepare for IKE and IPSec

Indicate the commands that you would use to perform these tasks:

- Check the current configuration.
    - **show running-config**
    - **show crypto isakmp policy**
    - **show crypto map**
    - **show crypto ipsec transform-set**
- Ensure that the network works without encryption.
    - **ping 172.16.12.2**
- Ensure that ACLs are compatible with IPSec.
    - **interface Serial1/0**
    - **ip address 207.118.14.30 255.255.255.0**
    - **ip access-group 102 in**
    - **!**
    - **access-list 102 permit ahp host 207.118.14.35 host 207.118.14.30**
    - **access-list 102 permit esp host 207.118.14.35 host 207.118.14.30**
    - **access-list 102 permit udp host 207.118.14.35 host 207.118.14.30 eq isakmp**

Task 2: Configure a Cisco Router for CA Support

Indicate the commands that you would use to perform these tasks:

- Set the router's time and date.
  - **clock timezone CST -6**
  - **clock set 10:33:42 July 5 2003**
- Configure the router's host name and domain name.
  - **hostname DallasR3**
  - **ip domain-name Futurecorp.com**
- Generate an RSA key pair.
  - **crypto key generate rsa**
  - **How many bits in the modulus [512]: 1024**
- Declare a CA.
  - **crypto ca trustpoint DalVPNCA**
  - **enrollment url http://DalVPNCA/certsrv/mscep/mscep.dll**
  - **crl optional**
- Authenticate the CA.
  - **crypto ca authenticate DalVPNCA**
- Request your own certificate.
  - **crypto ca enroll DalVPNCA**
- Verify the CA support configuration.
  - **show crypto ca certificates**
  - **show crypto key mypubkey rsa**
  - **show crypto key pubkey-chain rsa**

Task 3: Configure IKE

Indicate the commands that you would use to perform these tasks:

- Create the IKE policy.
  - **crypto isakmp policy 110**
  - **authentication rsa-sig**
  - **encryption 3des**
  - **group 2**
  - **hash sha**
  - **lifetime 57600**

- Verify the IKE configuration.
    - **show crypto isakmp policy**

Task 4: Configure IPSec

Indicate the commands that you would use to perform these tasks:

- Configure the transform set.
    - **crypto ipsec transform-set DalPla esp-sha-hmac esp-3des**
- Configure the global IPSec security association lifetime.
    - **crypto ipsec security-association lifetime seconds 72000**
- Configure the crypto ACL.
    - **access-list 110 permit ip 172.16.12.0 0.0.0.255 any**
    - **access-list 110 deny ip any any**
- Configure the crypto map.
    - **crypto map DalPla 110 ipsec-isakmp**
    - **match address 110**
    - **set peer 207.118.14.35**
    - **set pfs group2**
    - **set transform-set DalPla**
    - **set security-association lifetime 72000**
- Apply the crypto map to the interface.
    - **interface Serial1/0**
    - **crypto map DalPla**

Task 5: Test and Verify IPSec

Indicate the commands that you would use to perform these tasks:

- Display your configured IKE policies using the **show crypto isakmp policy** command.
- Display your configured transform sets using the **show crypto ipsec transform set** command.
- Display the current state of your IPSec SAs with the **show crypto ipsec sa** command.
- View your configured crypto maps with the **show crypto map** command.
- Debug IKE and IPSec traffic through Cisco IOS with the **debug crypto ipsec** and **debug crypto isakmp** commands.

Upon completion of this chapter, you will be able to perform the following tasks:

- Describe Cisco Easy VPN Server
- Describe Cisco Easy VPN Remote
- Configure Cisco Easy VPN Server
- Configure RADIUS Authentication for Group Profiles
- Install and Configure Cisco Easy VPN Remote Using Cisco VPN Client 3.5

CHAPTER 10

Configuring IOS Remote Access Using Cisco Easy VPN

This chapter covers the configuration of Cisco IOS remote access using Cisco Easy VPN and Cisco VPN Client.

This chapter covers the following topics:

- Introduction to Cisco Easy VPN
- Overview of Cisco Easy VPN Server
- Overview of the Cisco Easy VPN Remote feature
- Overview of Cisco VPN Client 3.5
- How Cisco Easy VPN works
- Configuring Cisco Easy VPN Server for extended authentication
- Cisco VPN Client 3.5 manual configuration tasks
- Working with Cisco VPN Client 3.5

Cisco Easy VPN Introduction

This section discusses Cisco Easy VPN and its two components, Cisco Easy VPN Remote and Cisco Easy VPN Server.

Cisco Easy VPN, a software enhancement for existing Cisco routers and security appliances, greatly simplifies VPN deployment for remote offices and telecommuters. Based on the Cisco Unified Client Framework, Cisco Easy VPN centralizes VPN management across all Cisco VPN devices, greatly reducing the complexity of VPN deployments. Cisco Easy VPN enables an integration of Easy VPN Remote devices—Cisco routers, Cisco PIX Firewalls, the Cisco VPN 3002 Hardware Client, or software clients— within a single deployment with a consistent policy and key management method that greatly simplifies remote-side administration.

Cisco Easy VPN Server

Cisco Easy VPN Server enables Cisco IOS routers, PIX Firewalls, and Cisco VPN 3000 Series Concentrators to act as VPN headend devices in site-to-site or remote access VPNs, where the remote-office devices are using the Cisco Easy VPN Remote feature. Using this feature, security policies defined at the headend are pushed to the remote VPN device, ensuring that those connections have up-to-date policies in place before the connection is established.

In addition, an Easy VPN Server–enabled device can terminate IPSec tunnels initiated by mobile remote workers running Cisco VPN Client software on PCs. This flexibility makes it possible for mobile and remote workers, such as sales people on the road or telecommuters, to access their headquarters' intranet where critical data and applications exist.

Cisco Easy VPN Remote

The Cisco Easy VPN Remote feature enables Cisco IOS routers, PIX Firewalls, and Cisco VPN 3002 Hardware Client, or software clients to act as remote VPN clients. As such, these devices can receive security policies from an Easy VPN Server, minimizing VPN configuration requirements at the remote location. This cost-effective solution is ideal for remote offices with little IT support, or large customer premises equipment (CPE) deployments where it is impractical to individually configure multiple remote devices. This feature makes VPN configuration as easy as entering a password, which increases productivity and lowers costs as the need for local IT support is minimized.

In the example in Figure 10-1, the VPN gateway is a Cisco IOS router running the Easy VPN Server feature. Remote Cisco IOS routers and VPN software clients connect to the Cisco IOS router Easy VPN Server for access to the corporate intranet.

See Cisco.com for a complete list of Cisco routers that support Cisco Easy VPN.

Figure 10-1   *Remote Access with Cisco Easy VPN*

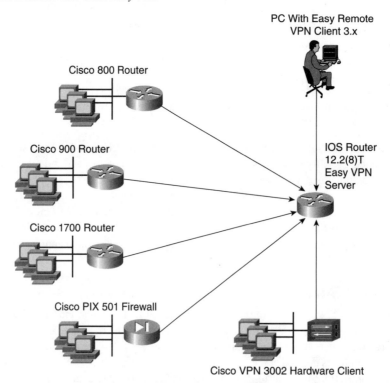

PC With Easy Remote
VPN Client 3.x

Cisco 800 Router

Cisco 900 Router

Cisco 1700 Router

IOS Router
12.2(8)T
Easy VPN
Server

Cisco PIX 501 Firewall

Cisco VPN 3002 Hardware Client

Cisco Easy VPN Server Overview

This section provides an overview of the Cisco Easy VPN Server features of Cisco IOS Release 12.2(8)T.

The Cisco IOS Release 12.2(8)T Easy VPN Server introduces server support for Cisco VPN Client release 3.x software clients and supported hardware clients. It allows remote end users to communicate using IPSec with supported Cisco IOS 12.2(8)T VPN gateways. Centrally managed IPSec policies are pushed to the clients by the server, minimizing configuration by the end users.

New Features of 12.2(8)T and Cisco Easy VPN

The Cisco IOS Release 12.2(8)T Easy VPN Server adds support for the following functions:

- **Mode Configuration version 6 support**—IKE Mode Configuration (MC) allows an IPSec server to download an IP address and other network level configurations to a VPN client as part of an IKE negotiation. The server gives an IP address to the VPN client to be used as an "inner" IP address encapsulated under IPSec. This provides a known IP address for the client, even though the client may be using a dynamic IP address obtained from its ISP. This technique allows a corporate IPSec server to negotiate VPN tunnels with clients from a variety of locations and control the tunnel parameters by passing policy information to the clients during IKE Mode Configuration.

- **Extended Authentication (XAUTH) version 6 support**—XAUTH allows a VPN server to request extended authentication via ISAKMP from a VPN client, forcing the client to respond with its extended authentication credentials. The VPN server will then respond with a failed or passed message.

  When the server requests extended authentication, it will specify the type of extra authentication and any parameters required for it. The extended authentication takes place as soon as IKE Phase 1 has finished and before any other processes have begun. If authentication fails, the IKE Phase 1 SA is terminated and the IPSec tunnel is not completed.

- **Internet Key Exchange Dead Peer Detection (DPD)**—Cisco VPN Client implements a new keepalives scheme—IKE DPD.

  DPD enables two IPSec peers to determine if the other is still "alive" during the lifetime of a VPN connection. DPD is useful because a host may reboot or the dialup link of a remote user may disconnect without notifying the peer that the VPN connection has gone away. When an IPSec host determines that a VPN connection no longer exists, it can notify a user, attempt to switch to another IPSec host, or clean up valuable resources that were allocated for the peer that no longer exists.

  A Cisco IOS VPN device can be configured to send and reply to DPD messages. DPD messages are sent if no other traffic is being passed through the IPSec tunnel. If a configured amount of time has lapsed since the last inbound data was received, DPD sends a message (DPD R-U-THERE). DPD messages are unidirectional and are automatically sent by Cisco VPN Clients. DPD must be configured on the router only if the router wishes to send DPD messages to the Cisco VPN Client to determine the health of the VPN client.

- **Split tunneling control**—Remote Cisco VPN Clients can support split tunneling, which enables a VPN client to have intranet and Internet access at the same time. If split tunneling is not configured, the VPN client directs all traffic through the tunnel, even traffic destined for the Internet.

- **Initial contact**—If a VPN client is suddenly disconnected, the gateway may not be notified. Consequently, removal of connection information (IKE and IPSec SAs) for that VPN client does not immediately occur. Thus, if the VPN client attempts to reconnect to the gateway, the gateway will refuse the connection because the previous connection information is still valid. To avoid this scenario, a new capability called initial contact has been introduced; all Cisco VPN products support it. If a Cisco VPN Client or router is connecting to another Cisco gateway for the first time, an initial-contact message is sent that tells the receiver to ignore and delete any old connection information that has been maintained for that newly connecting peer. Initial contact ensures that connection attempts are not refused because of SA synchronization problems, which are often identified via invalid security parameter index (SPI) messages and require devices to have their connections cleared.

- **Group-based policy control**—Policy attributes, such as IP addresses, DNS, and split-tunnel access, can be provided on a per-group or per-user basis.

Supported IPSec Attributes

Cisco Easy VPN supports the following IPSec options and attributes:

- Authentication algorithms:
  - HMAC-MD5
  - HMAC-SHA1
- Authentication types:
  - Pre-shared keys
  - RSA digital signatures (not supported by Cisco Easy VPN Remote Phase II)
- Diffie-Hellman (DH) groups:
  - 2
  - 5 (not supported by Cisco Easy VPN Remote Phase II)
- IKE encryption algorithms:
  - Data Encryption Standard (DES)
  - Triple DES (3DES)
- IPSec encryption algorithms:
  - DES
  - 3DES
  - NULL

- IPSec protocol identifiers:
  - — Enhanced Serial Port
  - — IP Payload Compression (IPCOMP)–Lempel-Ziv standard (LZS)
- IPSec protocol mode—tunnel mode

For information on these options and attributes, refer to the chapter "Configuring Internet Key Exchange Security Protocol" in the *Cisco IOS Security Configuration Guide*, Release 12.2 at, http://www.cisco.com/en/US/products/sw/iosswrel/ps1835 /products_configuration_guide_book09186a0080087df1.html.

Unsupported IPSec Attributes

The following IPSec attributes are not currently supported by Cisco Easy VPN and, therefore, should not be configured on the Easy VPN Server for these VPN clients:

- **Authentication types**—Authentication using Digital Signature Standard (DSS) is not supported.
- **DH group**—DH-1 is not supported.
- **IPSec protocol identifier**—IPSEC Authentication Header (AH) is not supported.
- **IPSec protocol mode**—Transport mode is not supported.
- **Miscellaneous**
  - — Manual keys are not supported.
  - — Perfect forward secrecy (PFS) is not supported.

Cisco Easy VPN Remote Overview

The Cisco Easy VPN Remote feature allows certain Cisco IOS routers, Cisco PIX Firewalls, and Cisco VPN 3002 Hardware or software clients to act as remote VPN clients.

In the example shown in Figure 10-1, remote offices or individual PCs may access corporate computing resources using various Cisco VPN Clients terminating at Cisco IOS 12.2(8)T routers.

Supported Cisco Easy VPN Remote Clients

The following list details Cisco VPN Clients that support the Cisco Easy VPN Remote feature:

- Cisco VPN Client 3.x or later
- Cisco VPN 3002 Hardware Client 3.x or later
- Cisco PIX Firewall 501 VPN Client
- Cisco PIX Firewall 506E
- Cisco Easy VPN Remote routers
  - — Cisco 800 series

— Cisco 900 series

— Cisco 1700 series

Visit Cisco.com for the latest listing of Cisco Easy VPN Remote devices and software clients.

Cisco VPN Client 3.x or Later

Simple to deploy and operate, Cisco VPN Client enables customers to establish secure, end-to-end encrypted tunnels to any Easy VPN Server. This thin design, IPSec implementation is available via Cisco.com for use with any Cisco central site, remote access VPN product and is included free of charge with the Cisco VPN 3000 Series Concentrator. The client can be preconfigured for mass deployments, and initial logins require very little user intervention. VPN access policies and configurations are downloaded from the Easy VPN Server and pushed to the client when a connection is established, allowing simple deployment and management, as well as high scalability. The Cisco VPN Client, shown in Figure 10-2, supports the Cisco Unity Client protocol.

Figure 10-2   *Cisco VPN Client Software Version Later than 3.x*

Cisco VPN Client provides support for the following computer operating systems:

- Microsoft Windows 95 (OSR2+), 98, Me, NT 4.0, 2000, XP
- Linux (Intel)
- Solaris (UltraSPARC, 32 and 64 bit)
- MAC OS X 10.1

Cisco VPN 3002 Hardware Client 3.x or Later

The Cisco VPN 3002 Hardware Client has the Cisco Unity Client software built into it, enabling the Hardware Client to emulate the Cisco VPN 3000 Series Concentrator software client. With the Hardware Client, you can plug remote-site PCs into the Hardware Client, instead of loading the VPN client software, or additional applications on all remote-site PCs.

There are two versions of the Hardware Client:

- **Cisco VPN 3002 Hardware Client**—One private and one public interface, as shown in Figure 10-3.

Figure 10-3 *Cisco VPN 3002 Hardware Client*

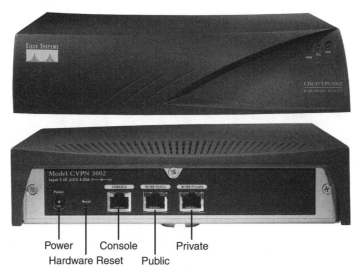

- **Cisco VPN 3002-8E Hardware Client**—One public interface, and the private interface is a built-in 8-port 10/100BASE-T Ethernet switch (100 full duplex is locked in, not configurable), as shown in Figure 10-4. It includes Auto MDIX, a technology that eliminates crossover cables.

Figure 10-4 *Cisco VPN 3002-8E Hardware Client*

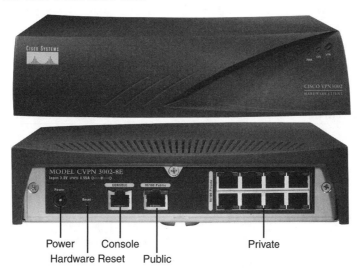

There are two modes of operation for the Hardware Client: client mode and network extension. These modes are configurable via the CLI or the GUI. They can be remotely managed via an IPSec tunnel or Secure Shell (SSH).

The Hardware Client is powered by an external power supply. It auto-senses the voltage, either 110V or 220V.

Cisco PIX Firewall 501 VPN Clients

The PIX Firewall 501, shown in Figure 10-5, delivers enterprise-class security for small offices and telecommuters. Ideal for securing high-speed, "always on" broadband environments, the PIX Firewall 501 provides small office networking features and powerful remote management capabilities in a compact, all-in-one solution.

Figure 10-5 *Cisco PIX Firewall 501 VPN Client*

The PIX Firewall 501 provides a convenient way for multiple computers to share a single broadband connection. In addition to its RS-232 (RJ-45) 9600-baud console port and its integrated 10BASE-T port for the outside interface, it features an integrated auto-sensing, auto-MDIX 4-port 10/100 switch for the inside interface. Auto-MDIX support eliminates the need to use crossover cables with devices connected to the switch.

The PIX Firewall 501 can also secure all network communications from remote offices to corporate networks across the Internet using its standards-based IKE/IPSec VPN capabilities. Users can also enjoy plug-and-play networking by taking advantage of the built-in DHCP server within the PIX Firewall, which automatically assigns network addresses to the computers when they are powered on. Additional features of the PIX Firewall 501 include:

- 7500 simultaneous connections
- 60-Mbps clear-text throughput
- 133-MHz processor
- 16 MB of SDRAM
- 3-Mbps 3DES throughput with ten simultaneous VPN peers
- Supports the Cisco Unity Client protocol

Cisco Easy VPN Remote Router Clients

Cable modems, xDSL routers, and other forms of broadband access provide high-performance connections to the Internet, but many applications also require the security of VPN connections that perform a high level of authentication and that encrypt the data between two particular endpoints. However, establishing a VPN connection between two routers can be complicated, and typically requires tedious coordination between network administrators to configure the two routers' VPN parameters.

The Easy VPN Remote feature eliminates much of this tedious work by implementing the Cisco Unity Client protocol, which allows most VPN parameters to be defined at a VPN remote access server. This server can be a dedicated VPN device, such as a Concentrator, a Cisco PIX Firewall, or a Cisco IOS router that supports the Cisco Unity Client protocol.

After the VPN remote access server has been configured, a VPN connection can be created with minimal configuration on an IPSec client, such as a Cisco uBR905 or Cisco uBR925 cable access router, as well as on the Cisco 806, Cisco 826, Cisco 827, Cisco 828, and Cisco 1700 series routers. When the IPSec client initiates the VPN connection, the VPN remote access server pushes the IPSec policies to the IPSec client and creates the corresponding IPSec tunnel.

The Cisco Easy VPN Remote feature provides for automatic management of the following details:

- Negotiating tunnel parameters—addresses, algorithms, lifetime, and so on
- Establishing tunnels according to the parameters
- Automatically creating the Network Address Translation (NAT)/Port Address Translation (PAT) and associated access lists that are needed, if any
- Authenticating users—ensuring that users are who they say they are by way of usernames, group names, and passwords
- Managing security keys for encryption and decryption
- Authenticating, encrypting, and decrypting data through the tunnel

The Cisco Easy VPN Remote feature was released in two phases, Phase I and Phase II. Phase I was introduced as part of Cisco IOS Release 12.2(4)YA and Phase II as part of Cisco IOS Release 12.2(8)YJ. Table 10-1 summarizes the major differences between the Cisco Easy VPN Remote Phase I and Phase II feature sets.

Table 10-1   *Cisco Easy VPN Remote Phase I and II Features*

Item	Phase I: 12.2(4)YA	Phase II: 12.2(8)YJ
IPSec tunnel	Tunnel is automatically connected only when a Cisco Easy VPN Remote feature is configured on an interface (automatic tunnel mode).	Establishes and terminates a tunnel on demand (manual tunnel control) or automatically (automatic tunnel mode).
Inside interface	Supports only the default inside interface.	Supports multiple inside interfaces.

continues

Table 10-1   *Cisco Easy VPN Remote Phase I and II Features (Continued)*

Item	Phase I: 12.2(4)YA	Phase II: 12.2(8)YJ
Outside interface	Supports only one tunnel for a single outside interface.	Supports multiple tunnels, one tunnel for each outside interface.
Default inside interface	The default inside interface is the FastEthernet0 interface for the Cisco 1700 series. The Ethernet0 interface is the default inside interface for the Cisco 800 and Cisco 900 series routers.	Cisco 1700 series routers no longer have a default inside interface. Inside interfaces must be configured manually. On Cisco 1700 series routers, the last inside interface of a tunnel can be unconfigured only after unconfiguring the outside interface. Default inside interfaces on the Cisco 800 and Cisco 900 series routers can be manually disabled if one other inside interface has been configured on the router.
Cable DHCP proxy enhancement	Not supported.	The **cable-modem dhcp-proxy** interface configuration command is enhanced to support the loopback interface for Cisco uBR905 and uBR925 cable access routers so that a public IP address is automatically assigned to the loopback interface.
NAT interoperability support	NAT configurations are not supported.	Supports a manually assigned NAT configuration on an interface.
Cisco IOS Firewall support	Cisco IOS Firewall configurations are not supported.	Works in conjunction with Cisco IOS Firewall configurations.
show crypto ipsec client ezvpn command	No inside or outside interfaces are shown.	Output shows the list of inside and outside interfaces for each channel.
Cisco Easy VPN Remote Web Manager	Not supported.	Web-based GUI device management tool for Cisco uBR905 and Cisco uBR925 cable access routers.

The remainder of this chapter discusses the Phase II features that are found in Cisco IOS versions 12.2(8)YJ and later.

Cisco Easy VPN Remote Phase II

This section covers Cisco Easy VPN Remote Phase II modes of operation, restrictions, and supported servers.

Modes of Operation

The Easy VPN Remote Phase II feature supports two modes of operation:

- **Client mode**—Specifies that NAT/PAT be configured, to allow PCs and hosts on the client side of the VPN connection to form a private network that does not use any IP addresses in the destination server's IP address space. In client mode, the Easy VPN Remote Phase II feature automatically configures the NAT/PAT translation and ACLs that are needed to implement the VPN connection. These configurations are automatically created when the VPN connection is initiated. When the tunnel is torn down, the NAT/PAT and ACL configurations are automatically deleted. The NAT/PAT configuration is created with the following assumptions:

  - The **ip nat inside** command is applied to all inside interfaces, including default inside interfaces. The default inside interface is the Ethernet0 interface (for the Cisco 806, Cisco 826, Cisco 827, and Cisco 828 routers, and for the Cisco uBR905 and Cisco uBR925 cable access routers).

  - The **ip nat outside** command is applied to the interface that is configured with the Easy VPN Remote Phase II configuration. On the Cisco uBR905 and Cisco uBR925 routers, this is always the Cable-modem0 interface. On the Cisco 800 series and Cisco 1700 series routers, this is the outside interface configured with the Easy VPN Remote Phase II configuration. On the Cisco 1700 series routers, multiple outside interfaces can be configured.

NOTE   The NAT/PAT translation and ACL configurations that are created by the Easy VPN Remote Phase II feature are not written to either the startup-configuration or running-configuration files. These configurations, however, can be displayed by using the **show ip nat statistics** and **show access-list** commands.

- **Network extension mode**—Specifies that the PCs and other hosts at the client end of the IPSec tunnel should be given IP addresses that are fully routable and reachable by the destination network over the tunneled network so that they form one logical network. PAT is not used, which allows the client PCs and hosts to have direct access to the PCs and hosts on the destination network.

Both modes of operation also optionally support split tunneling, which allows secure access to corporate resources through the IPSec tunnel while also allowing Internet access through a connection to an ISP or other service, thereby eliminating the corporate network from the path for web access.

Authentication can occur using XAUTH. In this situation, when the Easy VPN Server requests XAUTH, the following messages are displayed on the client router's console:

```
EZVPN: Pending XAuth Request, Please enter the following command:
EZVPN: crypto ipsec client ezvpn xauth
```

The user can then provide the necessary user ID, password, and other information by entering the **crypto ipsec client ezvpn xauth** command and responding to the prompts that follow, such as:

```
Router# crypto ipsec client ezvpn xauth
```

Client Mode

Figure 10-6 illustrates the Easy VPN Remote client mode of operation. In this example, the Cisco uBR905 cable access router provides access to two PCs, which have IP addresses in the 10.0.0.0 private network space. These PCs connect to the Ethernet interface on the Cisco uBR905 router, which also has an IP address in the 10.0.0.0 private network space. The Cisco uBR905 router performs NAT/PAT translation over the IPSec tunnel so that the PCs can access the destination network.

Figure 10-6 *Easy VPN Remote Phase II Client Mode*

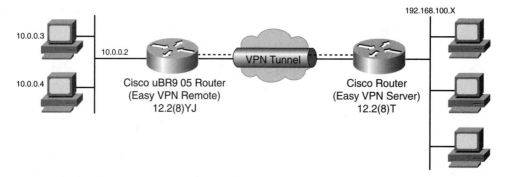

Figure 10-6 could also represent a split-tunneling connection, in which the client PCs can access public resources on the Internet without including the corporate network in the path for the public resources.

Network Extension Mode

Figure 10-7 illustrates the network extension mode of operation. In this example, the Cisco uBR905 cable access router and Cisco 1700 series router both act as Cisco Easy VPN Remote clients, connecting to an Easy VPN Server router.

The client hosts are given IP addresses that are fully routable by the destination network over the tunnel. These IP addresses could be either in the same subnet space as the destination network or in separate subnets, as long as the destination routers are configured to properly route those IP addresses over the tunnel. This provides a seamless extension of the remote network.

Figure 10-7 *Easy VPN Remote Phase II Network Extension Mode*

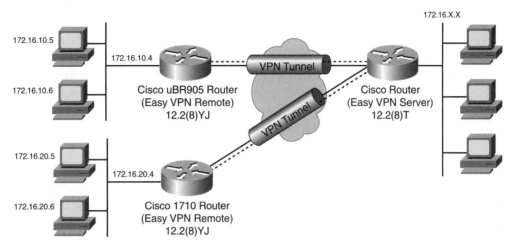

Restrictions

The following list details some restrictions inherent to Easy VPN Remote Phase II:

- **Subinterfaces are not supported**—Establishing Easy VPN Remote Phase II tunnels over subinterfaces is not supported in Cisco IOS Release 12.2(8)YJ.

- **The Cisco Cable Monitor web interface does not work**—The Cisco Easy VPN Remote Web Manager does not work with the Cisco Cable Monitor web interface in Cisco IOS Release 12.2(8)YJ. To access the Cable Monitor web interface, you must first disable the Easy VPN Remote Web Manager interface with the **no ip http ezvpn** command, and then enable the Cable Monitor with the **ip http cable-monitor** command.

- **Only one destination peer is supported**—The Easy VPN Remote Phase II feature supports the configuration of only one destination peer and tunnel connection. If your application requires the creation of multiple IPSec tunnels, you must manually configure the IPSec tunnel and NAT/PAT parameters on both the client and the server.

- **Digital certificates are not supported**—Authentication is supported using pre-shared keys and XAUTH only.

- **Only ISAKMP policy Group 2 is supported on IPSec servers**—The Cisco Unity Client protocol supports only ISAKMP policies that use Group 2 (1024-bit DH) IKE negotiation, so the IPSec server being used with the Easy VPN Remote Phase II feature must be configured for a Group 2 ISAKMP policy. The IPSec server cannot be configured for ISAKMP Group 1 or Group 5 when being used with a Cisco Easy VPN Remote client.

- **PFS is not supported**—The Easy VPN Remote Phase II feature does not support the PFS feature that is available on the Concentrator.

- **Only certain transform sets are supported**—To ensure a secure tunnel connection, the Easy VPN Remote Phase II feature does not support transform sets that provide encryption without authentication (ESP-DES and ESP-3DES) or transform sets that provide authentication without encryption (ESP-NULL ESP-SHA-HMAC and ESP-NULL ESP-MD5-HMAC).

- **Secondary IP address is used as NAT inside address by default**—The Ethernet0 LAN interface on the Cisco 800 series routers defaults to a primary IP address in the private network of 10.10.10.0. You can change this IP address to match the local network's configuration by using either the **ip address** CLI command or the Cisco Router Web Setup (CRWS) web interface. These two techniques differ slightly in how the new IP address is assigned. When the CLI command is used, the new IP address is assigned as the primary address for the interface. When the CRWS interface is used, the new IP address is assigned as the secondary address and the existing IP address is preserved as the primary address for the interface. This allows the CRWS interface to maintain the existing connection between the PC web browser and the Cisco 800 series router. Because of this behavior, the Easy VPN Remote Phase II feature assumes that if a secondary IP address exists on the Ethernet0 interface, the secondary address should be used as the IP address of the inside interface for the NAT/PAT configuration. If no secondary address exists, the primary IP address is used for the inside interface address, as is normally done on other platforms. If this behavior is not desired, use the **ip address** command to change the interface's address, instead of using the CRWS web interface.

Supported Cisco Easy VPN Servers

The Easy VPN Remote Phase II feature requires that the destination peer be a VPN gateway or Concentrator that supports the Easy VPN Server. At the time of publication, this includes the following platforms when running the indicated software releases:

- **Cisco 806, Cisco 826, Cisco 827, and Cisco 828 routers**—Cisco IOS Release 12.2(8)T or later release

- **Cisco 1700 series**—Cisco IOS Release 12.2(8)T or later release

- **Cisco 2600 series**—Cisco IOS Release 12.2(8)T or later release

- **Cisco 3620 Multiservice Platform**—Cisco IOS Release 12.2(8)T or later release

- **Cisco 3660 Multiservice Platform**—Cisco IOS Release 12.2(8)T or later release

- **Cisco 7100 series VPN routers**—Cisco IOS Release 12.2(8)T or later release

- **Cisco 7200 series routers**—Cisco IOS Release 12.2(8)T or later release

- **Cisco 7500 series routers**—Cisco IOS Release 12.2(8)T or later release

- **Cisco uBR905 and Cisco uBR925 cable access routers**—Cisco IOS Release 12.2(8)T or later release

- **Cisco VPN 3000 series**—Software Release 3.11 or later release

- **Cisco PIX 500 series**—Software Release 6.2 or later release

Cisco VPN Client 3.5 Overview

This section introduces you to Cisco VPN Client Release 3.5. Cisco VPN Client is software that enables you to establish secure, end-to-end encrypted tunnels to any Easy VPN Server. This thin design, which is an IPSec-compliant implementation, is available via Cisco.com for customers with SMARTnet support, and is included free of charge with the Concentrator.

Figure 10-2, earlier in the chapter, displays the Cisco VPN Client splash window. Users can preconfigure the connection entry (name of connection) and host name or IP address of remote Easy VPN Servers. Click **Connect** to initiate IKE phase 1.

Cisco VPN Client can be preconfigured for mass deployments, and initial logins require very little user intervention. VPN access policies and configurations are downloaded from the Easy VPN Server and pushed to Cisco VPN Client when a connection is established, allowing simple deployment and management.

Cisco VPN Client provides support for the following operating systems:

- Windows 95, 98, Me, NT 4.0, 2000, and XP
- Red Hat Linux v6.2 Kernel 2.2.12 only (Intel)
- Sun Solaris OS v2.6 only (UltraSPARC, 32-bit version)
- MAC OS X 10.1.x

Cisco VPN Client is compatible with the following Cisco products (Easy VPN Servers):

- Cisco IOS Software–based platforms version 12.2(8)T and later
- Cisco VPN 3000 Series Concentrator version 3.0 and later
- Cisco PIX Firewalls version 6.2 and later

Features and Benefits

Cisco VPN Client provides the following features and benefits:

- Intelligent peer availability detection
- Simple Certificate Enrollment Protocol (SCEP)
- Data compression (LZS)
- Command-line options for connecting, disconnecting, and connection status
- Configuration file with option locking
- Support for Microsoft network login (all platforms)
- DNS, Microsoft Windows Internet Name Service (WINS), and IP address assignment
- Load balancing and backup server support
- Centrally controlled policies
- Integrated personal firewall (stateful firewall): Zone Labs technology (Windows only)
- Personal firewall enforcement: ZoneAlarm and BlackICE (Windows only)

<table>
<tr><td>**NOTE**</td><td>Cisco VPN Client supports more features than the Cisco IOS Release 12.2(8)T Easy VPN Server can accommodate. Always compare the Cisco VPN Client specifications against the Easy VPN Server supported and unsupported feature lists. For example, although Cisco VPN Client supports Zone Labs and BlackICE personal firewall features, the 12.2(8)T version of the Easy VPN Server does not.</td></tr>
</table>

Specifications

This section provides a listing of specifications for the Cisco VPN Client 3.x product.

- Supported tunneling protocols
  - IPSec ESP
  - Transparent tunneling
    - ☐ IPSec over TCP (NAT or PAT)
    - ☐ IPSec over UDP (NAT, PAT, or a firewall)
- Supported encryption and authentication—IPSec (ESP) using DES or 3DES (56/168 bit) with MD5 or SHA
- Supported key management techniques
  - IKE—aggressive and main mode (digital certificates)
  - DH Groups 1, 2, and 7—Easy VPN Server supports neither DH-1PFS nor PFS
  - Rekeying
- Supported data compression technique—LZS compression
- Digital certificate support
  - Two supported enrollment mechanisms:
    - ☐ SCEP
    - ☐ Certificates enrolled with Microsoft Internet Explorer
  - Supported CAs:
    - ☐ Entrust Technologies
    - ☐ GTE Cybertrust
    - ☐ Netscape
    - ☐ Baltimore Technologies
    - ☐ RSA Keon
    - ☐ VeriSign
    - ☐ Microsoft
  - Support is provided for the Entrust Entelligence Client

— Smartcards—Supported via MS CAPI (CRYPT_NOHASHOID)

☐ Activcard (Schlumberger cards)

☐ eAladdin

☐ Gemplus

☐ Datakey

- Supported authentication methodologies

  — XAUTH

  — RADIUS with support for:

    ☐ State—or reply-message attributes (token cards)

    ☐ Security dynamics (RSA SecurID ready)

    ☐ Microsoft NT Domain authentication

    ☐ MSCHAPv2—NT password expiration

    ☐ X.509v3 digital certificates

- Profile management—Cisco VPN Client can be easily distributed with preconfigured Profile Configuration Files (PFCs)

- Policy management—ISAKMP

  — Keeps track of centrally controlled policies, such as the following:

    ☐ DNS information

    ☐ WINS information

    ☐ IP address

    ☐ Default domain name

  — Contains the ability to save connection attributes

Cisco Easy VPN Functionality

When an Easy VPN Remote client initiates a connection with an Easy VPN Server gateway, the "conversation" that occurs between the peers consists of the following major steps:

- Device authentication via IKE
- User authentication using IKE XAUTH
- VPN policy push (using MC)
- IPSec SA creation

Cisco Easy VPN Remote Connection Process

The following is a detailed step-by step description of the Cisco Easy VPN Remote connection process:

- **Task 1: Initiate the IKE phase 1 process.** The peers authenticate one another using pre-shared keys or digital signatures.

- **Task 2: Establish IKE SA.** The peers negotiate the parameters they will use to establish the IKE SA.

- **Task 3: Accept the SA proposal.** The peers agree on the IKE SA parameters.

- **Task 4: Initiate username/password challenge.** The server prompts for a username and password, the user supplies the information, and the server authenticates the user.

- **Task 5: Initiate the MC process.** The client requests the remaining VPN parameters from the server.

- **Task 6: Initiate the Reverse Route Injection RRI process.** The server creates a static route to each of the client's IP addresses.

- **Task 7: Initiate IKE quick mode.** IKE quick mode completes IPSec SA and the VPN connection.

Task 1 of Easy VPN Remote Connection Process: Initiating the IKE Phase 1 Process

Figure 10-8 shows the initiation of the IKE phase 1 process from a Cisco VPN Client. Because there are two ways to perform authentication, Cisco VPN Client must consider the following when initiating this phase:

- If a pre-shared key is to be used for authentication, Cisco VPN Client initiates aggressive mode (AM). When pre-shared keys are used, the accompanying group name entered in the configuration GUI (ID_KEY_ID) is used to identify the group profile associated with this VPN client.

- If digital certificates are to be used for authentication, Cisco VPN Client initiates main mode (MM). When digital certificates are used, the organizational unit (OU) field of a distinguished name (DN) is used to identify the group profile.

Figure 10-8 *Cisco VPN Client Initiates IKE Phase 1*

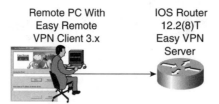

Remote PC With
Easy Remote
VPN Client 3.x

IOS Router
12.2(8)T
Easy VPN
Server

Because Cisco VPN Client may be configured for pre-shared key authentication, which initiates IKE AM, it is recommended that the administrator change the identity of the Cisco IOS VPN device via the **crypto isakmp identity hostname** command. This does not affect certificate authentication via IKE MM.

Task 2 of Easy VPN Remote Connection Process: Establishing IKE SA

As shown in Figure 10-9, Cisco VPN Client attempts to establish an SA between peer IP addresses by sending multiple IKE proposals to the Easy VPN Server. To reduce manual configuration on Cisco VPN Client, these IKE proposals include several combinations of the following:

- Encryption and hash algorithms
- Authentication methods
- DH group sizes

Figure 10-9 *Cisco VPN Client Establishes an IKE SA*

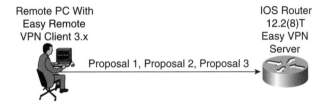

Task 3 of Easy VPN Remote Connection Process: Accepting the SA Proposal

IKE policy is global for the Easy VPN Server and can consist of several proposals. In the case of multiple proposals, the Easy VPN Server will use the first match (so you should always have your most secure policies listed first).

Shown in Figure 10-10, the IKE SA is successfully established, device authentication ends, and user authentication begins at this point.

Figure 10-10 *Easy VPN Server Accepts the SA Proposal*

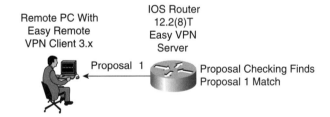

Task 4 of Easy VPN Remote Connection Process: Initiating Username/Password Challenge

If the Easy VPN Server is configured for XAUTH, Cisco VPN Client waits for a username/ password challenge, as shown in Figure 10-11:

- The user enters a username/password combination.
- The information that is entered is checked against authentication entities using authentication, authorization, and accounting (AAA) protocols, such as RADIUS and TACACS+. Token cards may also be used via AAA proxy, using an internal database for local authentication.

Figure 10-11 *Easy VPN Server Initiates Username/Password Challenge*

VPN devices that are configured to handle remote VPN clients should always be configured to enforce user authentication.

Task 5 of Easy VPN Remote Connection Process: Initiating the MC Process

As shown in Figure 10-12, if the Easy VPN Server indicates successful authentication, Cisco VPN Client requests the remaining configuration parameters from the Easy VPN Server:

- MC starts.
- The remaining system parameters (IP address, DNS, split-tunneling information, and so on) are downloaded to Cisco VPN Client using MC.

Figure 10-12 *MC Process Is Initiated*

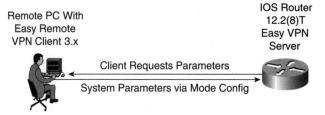

Remember that the IP address is the only required parameter in a group profile; all other parameters are optional.

Task 6 of Easy VPN Remote Connection Process: Initiating the RRI Process

After the Easy VPN Server knows the VPN client's assigned IP address, it must determine how to route packets through the appropriate VPN tunnel, as shown in Figure 10-13.

Figure 10-13 *RRI Process Is Initiated*

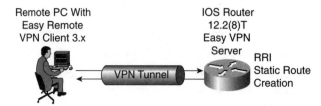

Reverse Route Injection (RRI) ensures that a static route is created on the Easy VPN Server for each VPN client's internal IP address.

NOTE   It is recommended that you enable RRI on the crypto map (static or dynamic) for the support of VPN clients, unless the crypto map is being applied to a generic routing encapsulation (GRE) tunnel that is already being used to distribute routing information.

Task 7 of Easy VPN Remote Connection Process: Initiating IKE Quick Mode

After the VPN client has successfully received the configuration parameters, IKE quick mode is initiated to negotiate IPSec SA establishment, as shown in Figure 10-14.

Figure 10-14 *IKE Quick Mode Completes Connection*

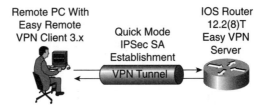

After IPSec SAs are created, the VPN connection is complete.

Configuring Cisco Easy VPN Server for XAUTH

This section examines the general tasks used to configure a Easy VPN Server to support XAUTH for Easy VPN Remote client access.

In this section, you will complete the following tasks to configure an Easy VPN Server for XAUTH with Easy VPN Remote clients:

- **Task 1: Configure XAUTH.** Establish secure authentication processes.

- **Task 2: Create an IP address pool.** Identify the pool of IP addresses available to connecting clients.

- **Task 3: Configure group policy lookup.** Configure the server to use both a RADIUS server and a local database for authorizing Easy VPN Remote clients.

- **Task 4: Create an ISAKMP policy for remote VPN client access.** Identify the ISAKMP policy parameters to be used by all Easy VPN Remote clients.

- **Task 5: Define a group policy for a MC push.** Create group policies for various groups that can connect to the server.

- **Task 6: Create a transform set.** Build a transform set that lists preference of acceptable transforms to be used by clients.

- **Task 7: Create a dynamic crypto map with RRI.** Create a dynamic crypto map that can adjust to individual clients and populate routing information with RRI.

- **Task 8: Apply a MC to the dynamic crypto map.** Configure the router to respond to MC requests from clients.

- **Task 9: Apply a dynamic crypto map to the router's outside interface.** After the dynamic crypto map has been configured, the next step is to apply the crypto map to a router interface.

- **Task 10: Enable IKE DPD.** (Optional task.) Set up Dead Peer Detection so that IKE tunnels can be torn down when no longer needed.

Task 1 to Configure Easy VPN Server: Configuring XAUTH

Complete the following steps to configure XAUTH on your Easy VPN Server router:

Step 1 Enable AAA login authentication.

Step 2 Set the XAUTH timeout value.

Step 3 Enable IKE XAUTH for the dynamic crypto map.

Step 1: Enabling AAA Login Authentication

Enable AAA login authentication by using the **aaa authentication login** command in global configuration mode.

The following shows an example of using the **aaa authentication login** command:

```
vpngate1(config)# aaa authentication login vpnusers local
```

The syntax for the **aaa authentication login** command is as follows:

```
aaa authentication login list-name method1 [method2...]
```

- *list-name*—Character string used to name the list of authentication methods activated when a user logs in. The list name must match the list name defined during AAA configuration.

- *method*—Keyword used to describe the authentication method used.

Step 2: Setting the XAUTH Timeout Value

Set the XAUTH timeout value by using the **crypto isakmp xauth timeout** command.

The following shows an example of using the **crypto isakmp xauth timeout** command:

```
vpngate1(config)# crypto isakmp xauth timeout 20
```

The syntax for the **crypto isakmp xauth timeout** command is as follows:

```
crypto isakmp xauth timeout seconds
```

seconds—The XAUTH timeout value in seconds.

Step 3: Enabling IKE XAUTH for the Dynamic Crypto Map

Enable IKE XAUTH for the dynamic crypto map by using the **crypto map** command.

The following shows an example of using the **crypto map client authentication list** command:

```
vpngate1(config)# crypto map dynmap client authentication list vpnusers
```

The syntax for the **crypto map** command is as follows:

```
crypto map map-name client authentication list list-name
```

- *map-name*—Name that you assign to the crypto map set.

- *list-name*—Character string used to name the list of authentication methods activated when a user logs in. The list name must match the list name defined during AAA configuration.

Task 2 to Configure Easy VPN Server: Creating an IP Address Pool

Figure 10-15 shows an example of a remote client connection to an Easy VPN server (in this case a router) through the Internet cloud. This figure is the model for the remainder of this section.

Figure 10-15 *Remote Client Connection Example*

If you are using a local IP address pool, you also need to configure that pool using the **ip local pool** command. Creating a local address pool is optional if you are using an external DHCP server. The following shows an example of using the **ip local pool** command:

```
vpngate1(config)# ip local pool remote-pool 10.0.1.100 10.0.1.150
```

The syntax for this command is as follows:

```
ip local pool {default | poolname} [low-ip-address [high-ip-address]] [group
    group-name] [cache-size size]
```

- **default**—Creates a default local IP address pool that is used if no other pool is named.

- *poolname*—Name of the local IP address pool.

- *low-IP-address* [*high-IP-address*]—First and, optionally, last address in an IP address range.

- **group** *group-name*—(Optional) Creates a pool group.

- **cache-size** *size*—(Optional) Sets the number of IP address entries on the free list that the system checks before assigning a new IP address. Returned IP addresses are placed at the end of the free list. Before assigning a new IP address to a user, the system checks the number of entries from the end of the list (as defined by the cache-size size option) to determine that there are no returned IP addresses for that user. The range for the cache size is 0 to 100. The default cache size is 20.

Task 3 to Configure Easy VPN Server: Configuring Group Policy Lookup

Configure group policy lookup by using two steps:

Step 1 Establish an AAA section in the configuration file using the **aaa new-model** command in global configuration mode. The syntax for this command is as follows:

```
aaa new-model
```

Step 2 Enable group policy lookup using the **aaa authorization network** command. A local and RADIUS server may be used together and will be tried in the order listed.

The syntax for the **aaa authorization network** command is as follows:

```
aaa authorization network list-name local group radius
```

- *list-name*—Character string used to name the list of authorization methods.

The following shows an example of using the **aaa new-model** and **aaa authorization network** commands:

```
vpngate1(config)# aaa new-model
vpngate1(config)# aaa authorization network vpn-remote-access local
```

Task 4 to Configure Easy VPN Server: Creating ISAKMP Policy for Remote VPN Client Access

Complete this task to configure the ISAKMP policy for all Easy VPN Remote clients that are attaching to this router. Use the standard ISAKMP configuration commands to accomplish this task. Example 10-1 shows how to configure the ISAKMP policy starting in global configuration mode.

Example 10-1 *Configure the ISAKMP Policy Starting in Global Configuration Mode*

```
vpngate1(config)# crypto isakmp enable
vpngate1(config)# crypto isakmp policy 1
vpngate1(config-isakmp)# authentication pre-share
vpngate1(config-isakmp)# encryption 3des
vpngate1(config-isakmp)# group 2
vpngate1(config-isakmp)# exit
```

Task 5 to Configure Easy VPN Server: Defining a Group Policy for a MC Push

Complete this task to define a group policy to be pushed during MC. Although users can belong to only one group per connection, they may belong to specific groups with different policy requirements.

Use the following steps, beginning in global configuration mode, to define the policy attributes that are pushed to VPN client via MC:

Step 1   Add the group profile to be defined.

Step 2   Configure the IKE pre-shared key.

Step 3   (Optional) Specify the DNS servers.

Step 4   (Optional) Specify the WINS servers.

Step 5   (Optional) Specify the DNS domain.

Step 6   Specify the local IP address pool.

Step 1: Adding the Group Profile to Be Defined

Use the **crypto isakmp client configuration group** command to specify group policy information that needs to be defined or changed.

The syntax for the **crypto isakmp client configuration group** command is as follows:

```
crypto isakmp client configuration group {group-name | default}
```

- *group-name*—Group definition that identifies which policy is enforced for users.

- **default**—Policy that is enforced for all users who do not offer a group name that matches a *group-name* argument. The default keyword can only be configured locally.

The following shows an example of using the **crypto isakmp client configuration group** command:

```
vpngate1(config)# crypto isakmp client configuration group vpn-remote-access
vpngate1(config-isakmp-group)#
```

Step 2: Configuring the IKE Pre-Shared Key

Use the **key** command to specify the IKE pre-shared key when defining group policy information for the MC push. You must use this command if the VPN client identifies itself to the router with a pre-shared key.

Use the **key** command in ISAKMP group configuration mode to specify the IKE pre-shared key for the group policy attribute definition. The following shows an example of using the **key** command:

```
vpngate1(config-isakmp-group)# key myvpnkey
```

The syntax for the **key** command is as follows:

```
key name
```

- *name*—IKE pre-shared key that matches the password entered on the VPN client. This value must match the "password" field defined in the Cisco VPN Client 3.x configuration user interface.

Step 3 (Optional): Specifying DNS Servers

Specify the primary and secondary DNS servers by using the **dns** command in ISAKMP group configuration mode.

NOTE   You must enable the **crypto isakmp configuration group** command, which specifies group policy information that needs to be defined or changed, before using the **dns** command.

The following shows examples of using the **dns** command:

```
vpngate1(config-isakmp-group)# dns DNS1 DNS2
vpngate1(config-isakmp-group)# dns 172.26.26.120 172.26.26.130
```

The syntax for the **dns** command is as follows:

```
dns primary-server secondary-server
```

- *primary-server*—Name or IP address of the primary DNS server.
- *secondary-server*—Name or IP address of the secondary DNS server.

Step 4 (Optional): Specifying WINS Servers

Specify the primary and secondary WINS servers by using the **wins** command in ISAKMP group configuration mode.

The following shows examples of using the **wins** command:

```
vpngate1(config-isakmp-group)# wins WINS1 WINS2
vpngate1(config-isakmp-group)# wins 172.26.26.160 172.26.26.170
```

The syntax for the **wins** command is as follows:

```
wins primary-server secondary-server
```

- *primary-server*—Name or IP address of the primary WINS server.
- *secondary-server*—Name or IP address of the secondary WINS server.

Step 5 (Optional): Specifying the DNS Domain

Specify the DNS domain to which a group belongs by using the **domain** command in ISAKMP group configuration mode.

The following shows an example of using the **domain** command:

```
vpngate1(config-isakmp-group)# domain cisco.com
```

The syntax for the **domain** command is as follows:

```
domain name
```

- *name*—Name of the DNS domain.

Step 6: Specifying the Local IP Address Pool

Use the **pool** command to refer to an IP local pool address, which defines a range of addresses that will be used to allocate an internal IP address to a VPN client.

Use the **pool** command in ISAKMP group configuration mode to define a local pool address.

The following shows an example of using the **pool** command:

```
vpngate1(config-isakmp-group)# pool remote-pool
```

The syntax for the **pool** command is as follows:

```
pool name
```

- *name*—Name of the local pool.

Task 6 to Configure Easy VPN Server: Creating a Transform Set

This task creates a transform set for the Easy VPN Remote clients to use when they attempt to build an IPSec tunnel to this router. Use the standard method for creating a transform set.

Here is an example of how to create a transform set for Easy VPN Remote client access:

```
vpngate1(config)# crypto ipsec transform-set vpntransform esp-3des esp-sha-hmac
vpngate1(cfg-crypto-trans)# exit
```

Task 7 to Configure Easy VPN Server: Creating a Dynamic Crypto Map with RRI

This task creates a dynamic crypto map to be used when building IPSec tunnels to Easy VPN Remote clients. In this example, RRI is used to ensure that returning data destined for a particular IPSec tunnel can find that tunnel.

Complete the following steps to create the dynamic crypto map with RRI:

Step 1   Create a dynamic crypto map.

Step 2   Assign a transform set to the crypto map.

Step 3   Enable RRI.

Step 1: Creating a Dynamic Crypto Map

Create a dynamic crypto map entry, and enter the crypto map configuration mode by using the **crypto dynamic-map** command.

The following shows an example of using the **crypto dynamic-map** command:

```
vpngate1(config)# crypto dynamic-map dynmap 1
vpngate1(config-crypto-map)#
```

The syntax for the **crypto dynamic-map** command is as follows:

```
crypto dynamic-map dynamic-map-name dynamic-seq-num
```

- *dynamic-map-name*—Specifies the name of the dynamic crypto map set.
- *dynamic-seq-num*—Specifies the number of the dynamic crypto map entry.

A dynamic crypto map entry is essentially a crypto map entry without all the parameters configured. It acts as a policy template in which the missing parameters are later dynamically configured (as the result of an IPSec negotiation) to match a remote peer's requirements. This allows remote peers to exchange IPSec traffic with the router even if the router does not have a crypto map entry specifically configured to meet all of the remote peer's requirements.

Dynamic crypto maps are not used by the router to initiate new IPSec security associations with remote peers. Dynamic crypto maps are used when a remote peer tries to initiate an IPSec SA with the router. Dynamic crypto maps are also used in evaluating traffic.

Step 2: Assigning a Transform Set to the Dynamic Crypto Map

Specify which transform sets are allowed for the crypto map entry by using the **set transform-set** command. When using this command, be sure to list multiple transform sets in order of priority (highest priority first). Note that this is the only configuration statement required in dynamic crypto map entries.

The following shows an example of using the **set transform-set** command:

```
vpngate1(config-crypto-map)# set transform-set vpntransform
vpngate1(config-crypto-map)#
```

The syntax for the **set transform-set** command is as follows:

```
set transform-set transform-set-name [transform-set-name2...transform-set-name6]
```

- *transform-set-name*—Name of the transform set:
  - For an IPSec-manual crypto map entry, you can specify only one transform set.
  - For an IPSec-ISAKMP or dynamic crypto map entry, you can specify up to six transform sets.

Step 3: Enabling RRI

Enable RRI by using the **reverse-route** command. Figure 10-16 depicts the process.

Figure 10-16 *Enable RRI*

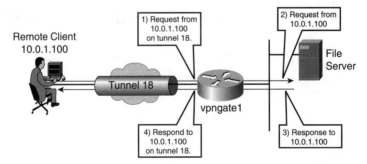

The following shows an example of using the **reverse-route** command:

```
vpngate1(config-crypto-map)# reverse-route
vpngate1(config-crypto-map)# exit
```

The syntax for the **reverse-route** command is as follows:

```
reverse-route
```

This command has no arguments or keywords.

Task 8 to Configure Easy VPN Server: Applying MC to Dynamic Crypto Map

Use this task to apply MC to a dynamic crypto map by using the following steps in global configuration mode:

Step 1   Configure the router to respond to MC requests.

Step 2   Enable IKE queries for group policy lookup.

Step 3   Apply changes to the dynamic crypto map.

Step 1: Configuring the Router to Respond to MC Requests

Configure the router to initiate or reply to MC requests. Note that Cisco VPN Clients require the **respond** keyword to be used. The **initiate** keyword was used with older Cisco VPN Clients but is no longer used with the 3.x version Cisco VPN Clients.

The following shows an example of using the **crypto map** *map-name* **client configuration** command:

```
vpngate1(config)# crypto map dynmap client configuration address respond
```

The syntax for the **crypto map** *map-name* **client configuration** command is as follows:

```
crypto map map-name client configuration address {initiate | respond}
```

- *map-name*—Name that identifies the crypto map.

- **initiate**—Indicates the router will attempt to set IP addresses for each peer (no longer used with Cisco VPN Client 3.x and later).

- **respond**—Indicates the router will accept requests for IP addresses from any requesting peer.

Step 2: Enabling IKE Querying for Group Policy Lookup

Enable IKE querying for group policy when requested by the VPN client. AAA uses the *list-name* argument to determine which storage is used to find the policy (local or RADIUS) as defined in the **aaa authorization network** command.

The following shows an example of using the **crypto map isakmp authorization list** command:

```
vpngate1(config)# crypto map dynmap isakmp authorization list vpn-remote-access
```

The syntax for the **crypto map isakmp authorization list** command is as follows:

```
crypto map map-name isakmp authorization list list-name
```

- *map-name*—Name that you assign to the crypto map set.
- *list-name*—Character string used to name the list of authorization methods activated when a user logs in. The list name must match the list name defined during AAA configuration.

Step 3: Applying Changes to the Dynamic Crypto Map

Apply changes to the dynamic crypto map by using the **crypto map** command in global configuration mode.

The following shows an example of using the **crypto map ipsec-isakmp dynamic** command:

```
vpngate1(config)# crypto map dynmap 1 ipsec-isakmp dynamic dynmap
```

The syntax for the **crypto map** command is as follows:

```
crypto map map-name seq-number ipsec-isakmp dynamic dynamic-map-name
```

- *map-name*—Name that you assign to the dynamic crypto map.
- *dynamic-map-name*—Name that you assign to the dynamic crypto map.
- *seq-number*—Specifies the number of the dynamic crypto map entry.

Task 9 to Configure Easy VPN Server: Applying a Dynamic Crypto Map to the Router's Outside Interface

This task is used to apply the new dynamic crypto map to the Easy VPN Server router's outside interface.

Example 10-2 shows an example of how to apply the new dynamic crypto map to the outside interface beginning in global configuration mode.

Example 10-2 *Apply the New Dynamic Crypto Map to the Outside Interface*

```
vpngate1(config)# interface ethernet0/1
vpngate1(config-if)# crypto map dynmap
vpngate1(config-if)# exit
```

Task 10 to Configure Easy VPN Server: Enabling IKE DPD (Optional)

Use the **crypto isakmp keepalive** command in global configuration mode to enable a Cisco IOS VPN gateway (instead of the VPN client) to send IKE DPD messages, as shown in Figure 10-17.

Figure 10-17 *Enable IKE DPD*

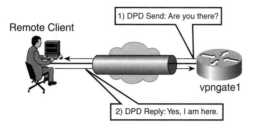

The following shows an example of using the **crypto isakmp keepalive** command:

```
vpngate1(config)# crypto isakmp keepalive 20 10
```

The syntax for the **crypto isakmp keepalive** command is as follows:

```
crypto isakmp keepalive secs retries
```

- *secs*—Specifies the number of seconds between DPD messages. The range is between 1–3,600 seconds.

- *retries*—Specifies the number of seconds between retries if DPD messages fail. The range is 2 to 60 seconds.

RADIUS Authentication for Group Profiles

You can store group policy information in a group profile that is defined and stored locally on the Cisco IOS VPN router, or on an AAA server that your router can access. When using the RADIUS authentication protocol, you need to configure the group policy on the RADIUS server and permit the Cisco IOS VPN router to send authentication requests to that server.

Perform the following tasks to set up group policy attributes on your RADIUS server:

- **Define a username**—This name must be the same as the group name used in Cisco VPN Client. If your VPN clients are set to use the group name "Intranet," for example, then you need to define an "Intranet" user on the RADIUS server. When using digital certificates, you must define the username to match the OU field from the DN in the client's certificate.

- **Set the user's password**—Always use the password "cisco," which identifies the password as a special one used for RADIUS purposes.

- **Add a user to group**—Policies are defined at the group level, so you must add your new user to a group. Cisco recommends using a group name that matches the username to keep things simple.

Use the **radius-server host** command to specify the RADIUS server and to allow the Cisco IOS VPN router to send requests to the RADIUS server. The syntax for the **radius-server host** command is as follows:

```
radius-server host {hostname | ip-address} [auth-port port-number]
    [acct-port port-number] [timeout seconds] [retransmit retries] [key string]
    [alias{hostname | ip-address}]
```

- *hostname*—DNS name of the RADIUS server host.

- *ip-address*—IP address of the RADIUS server host.

- **auth-port** (Optional)—Specifies the UDP destination port for authentication requests.

- *port-number* (Optional)—Port number for authentication requests; the host is not used for authentication if set to 0. If unspecified, the port number defaults to 1645.

- **acct-port** (Optional)—Specifies the UDP destination port for accounting requests.

- *port-number* (Optional)—Port number for accounting requests; the host is not used for accounting if set to 0. If unspecified, the port number defaults to 1646.

- **timeout** (Optional)—The time interval (in seconds) that the router waits for the RADIUS server to reply before retransmitting. This setting overrides the global value of the **radius-server timeout** command. If no timeout value is specified, the global value is used. Enter a value in the range 1 to 1000.

- *seconds* (Optional)—Specifies the **timeout** value. Enter a value in the range 1 to 1000. If no **timeout** value is specified, the global value is used.

- **retransmit** (Optional)—The number of times a RADIUS request is re-sent to a server, if that server is not responding or responding slowly. This setting overrides the global setting of the **radius-server retransmit** command.

- *retries* (Optional)—Specifies the retransmit value. Enter a value in the range 1 to 100. If no retransmit value is specified, the global value is used.

- **key** (Optional)—Specifies the authentication and encryption key used between the router and the RADIUS daemon running on this RADIUS server. This key overrides the global setting of the **radius-server key** command. If no key string is specified, the global value is used.

  The key is a text string that must match the encryption key used on the RADIUS server. Always configure the key as the last item in the **radius-server host** command syntax, because the leading spaces are ignored, but spaces within and at the end of the key are used. If you use spaces in the key, do not enclose the key in quotation marks unless the quotation marks themselves are part of the key.

- *string* (Optional)—Specifies the authentication and encryption key for all RADIUS communications between the router and the RADIUS server. This key must match the encryption used on the RADIUS daemon. All leading spaces are ignored, but spaces within and at the end of the key are used. If you use spaces in your key, do not enclose the key in quotation marks unless the quotation marks themselves are part of the key.

- **alias** (Optional)—Allows up to eight aliases per line for any given RADIUS server.

Cisco VPN Client 3.5 Installation and Configuration Tasks

This section contains information regarding the installation and configuration of Cisco VPN Client release 3.5.

In this section, you will complete the following tasks to install and Cisco VPN Client 3.5:

- Task 1: Install Cisco VPN Client 3.x.
- Task 2: Create a new connection entry.
- Task 3 (optional): Modify Cisco VPN Client options.
- Task 4: Configure Cisco VPN Client general properties.
- Task 5: Configure Cisco VPN Client authentication properties.
- Task 6: Configure Cisco VPN Client connections properties.

Task 1 to Install and Configure Cisco VPN Client 3.5: Installing Cisco VPN Client 3.x

Installation of Cisco VPN Client varies slightly based on the type of operating system. Always review the installation instructions that come with Cisco VPN Client before you attempt any installation.

Generally, installation of Cisco VPN Client 3.5 involves the following steps (this example is based on installing Cisco VPN Client on a Microsoft Windows 2000 PC):

Step 1   Obtain a copy of the Cisco VPN Client application. The application can be downloaded from the Cisco website or by obtaining a Cisco VPN 3000 Series Concentrator CD-ROM.

Step 2   Locate and run the Cisco VPN Client **setup.exe** executable. If this is the first time Cisco VPN Client is installed, a window opens and displays the following message: Do you want the installer to disable the IPSec Policy Agent?

Step 3   Click **Yes** to disable the IPSec policy agent. The Welcome window opens.

Step 4   Read the Welcome window, and click **Next**. The License Agreement window opens.

Step 5   Read the license agreement, and click **Yes**. The Choose Destination Location window opens.

Step 6   Click **Next**. The Select Program Folder window opens.

Step 7   Accept the defaults by clicking **Next**. The Start Copying Files window opens.

Step 8   The files are copied to the hard disk drive of the PC and the InstallShield Wizard Complete window opens.

Step 9   Choose **Yes, I Want to Restart My Computer Now** and click **Finish**. The PC restarts.

This completes the installation of the Cisco VPN Client.

Task 2 to Install and Configure Cisco VPN Client 3.5: Creating a New Connection Entry

Cisco VPN Client enables users to configure multiple connection entries. Multiple connection entries enable the user to build a list of possible network connection points. For example, a corporate telecommuter may want to connect to the Sales office in Boston for sales data (the first connection entry), and then they may want to connect to the Austin factory for inventory data (a second connection entry). Each connection contains a specific entry name and remote server host name or IP address.

Generally, creating a new connection entry involves the following steps (this example is based on creating new connection entries on a Windows 2000 PC):

Step 1 Choose **Start > Programs > Cisco Systems VPN Client > VPN Dialer**. The Cisco Systems VPN Client window opens.

Step 2 Click **New**. The New Connection Entry Wizard opens.

Step 3 Enter a name for the new connection entry in the Name of the New Connection Entry field (for example, Boston Sales).

Step 4 Click **Next**.

Step 5 Enter the public interface IP address or host name of the remote Easy VPN Server in the Remote Server field.

Step 6 Click **Next**.

Step 7 Choose **Group Access Information** and complete the following substeps. The following entries are always case sensitive:

    (a) Enter a group name that matches a group on the Easy VPN Server.

    (b) Enter the group password.

    (c) Confirm the password.

Step 8 Click **Next**.

Step 9 Click **Finish**, and leave the Cisco Systems VPN Client window open.

You have successfully configured the network parameters for Cisco VPN Client and created a new VPN connection entry, as shown earlier in Figure 10-2.

Task 3 to Install and Configure Cisco VPN Client 3.5 (Optional): Modifying Cisco VPN Client Options

Several configuration options are available from the Options menu. Figure 10-18 shows how to choose the Options menu from the splash window.

Figure 10-18 *Modify Cisco VPN Client Options*

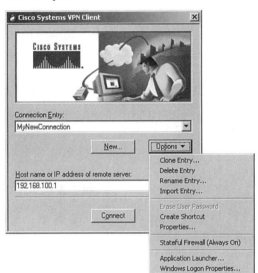

The Options drop-down menu enables you to configure or change optional parameters. By clicking the Options button, the following options become available:

- **Clone Entry**—Enables you to copy a connection entry with all its properties.

- **Delete Entry**—Enables you to delete a connection entry.

- **Rename Entry**—Enables you to rename a connection entry (not case sensitive).

- **Import Entry**—Provides a preconfigured PCF file that will load the Cisco VPN Client parameters.

- **Erase User Password**—Eliminates a saved password. Erase User Password is available only when you have enabled Allow Password Storage under the MC parameters for this group.

- **Create Shortcut**—Enables you to create a shortcut for your desktop.

- **Properties**—Enables you to configure or change the properties of the connection.

- **Stateful Firewall (Always On)**—Blocks all inbound traffic to Cisco VPN Client that is not related to an outbound session. After the remote user enables the stateful firewall, it is always on.

- **Application Launcher**—Enables you to launch an application before establishing a connection. This is used in conjunction with Microsoft Windows Login Properties, which enables Cisco VPN Client to make the connection to the Concentrator before the user logs in.

If you want to know what version of Cisco VPN Client you have installed on your PC, right-click the Cisco VPN Dialer icon in the system tray to view the Cisco VPN Client version.

Task 4 to Install and Configure Cisco VPN Client 3.5: Configuring Cisco VPN Client General Properties

From the Options menu, choose **Properties**. The following three tabs are found in the Properties window:

- **General tab**—Enables IPSec through NAT, displays the status of the local LAN access feature, and selects Microsoft network logon options.

- **Authentication tab**—Configures the Cisco VPN Client's group or digital certificate information.

- **Connections tab**—Enables backup connections, and links the VPN connection to Dialup Networking phonebook entries.

There are two versions of the General tab, depending on the operating system you are using: one version for Windows 95, 98, and Me and another version for Windows NT 4.0, 2000, and XP. The Windows 95, 98, and Me version provides options for transparent tunneling, local LAN access, and Microsoft login options. The Windows NT 4.0, 2000, and XP version provides transparent tunneling and local LAN access only.

Figure 10-19 displays both versions of the General tab.

Figure 10-19 *Configure Cisco VPN Client General Properties*

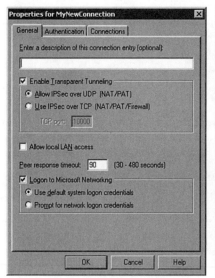
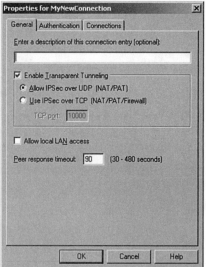

Windows 95, 98, and ME   Windows NT 4, 2000, and XP

The functions of the General tab are as follows:

- **Enable Transparent Tunneling**—Works with Windows 95, 98, NT 4.0, 2000, and XP.

- **Allow IPSec over UDP (NAT/PAT)**—Enables you to use Cisco VPN Client to connect to the Easy VPN Server via UDP through a firewall or router that is running NAT. Both Cisco VPN Client and Easy VPN Server must be enabled for this feature to work.

- **Use IPSec over TCP (NAT/PAT/Firewall)**—Enables you to use Cisco VPN Client to connect to the Easy VPN Server via TCP through a firewall or router that is running NAT. Both Cisco VPN Client and Easy VPN Server must be enabled for this feature to work.

- **Allow Local LAN Access**—For security purposes, the user can disable local LAN access when using an insecure local LAN, such as in a hotel. This option is not available when using a Cisco IOS–based Easy VPN Server or PIX Firewall as the VPN gateway.

- **Peer Response Timeout**—Specifies the number of seconds to wait before Cisco VPN Client decides that the peer is no longer active. Cisco VPN Client continues to send DPD requests until it reaches the Peer Response Timeout value.

- **Logon to Microsoft Network**—Works with Windows 95, 98, and Me only.

- **Use Default System Logon Credentials**—Use the logon username and password resident on your PC to log on to the Microsoft network, such as student4.

- **Prompt for Network Logon Credentials**—If your logon username and password differ from the enterprise network, the enterprise network prompts you for the username and password.

Task 5 to Install and Configure Cisco VPN Client 3.5: Configuring Cisco VPN Client Authentication Properties

The Easy VPN Server and the Cisco VPN Client connection can be authenticated with either the group name and password or digital certificates. The Authentication tab enables you to set your authentication information. You need to choose one method, group or certificates, via the radio buttons.

Within the Group Access Information area of the Authentication tab, enter the group name and password in the appropriate fields. The group name and password must match what is configured for this group within Cisco Easy VPN Server. Entries are case sensitive. Figure 10-20 shows an example of the Authentication tab.

For certificates to be exchanged, the Certificate radio button must be selected. In the Name drop-down menu, any personal certificates loaded on your PC are listed. Choose the certificate to be exchanged with the Easy VPN Server during connection establishment. If no personal certificates are loaded in your PC, the drop-down menu is blank. Use the Validate Certificate button to check the validity of the Cisco VPN Clients' certificate.

Figure 10-20 *Configure Cisco VPN Client Authentication Properties*

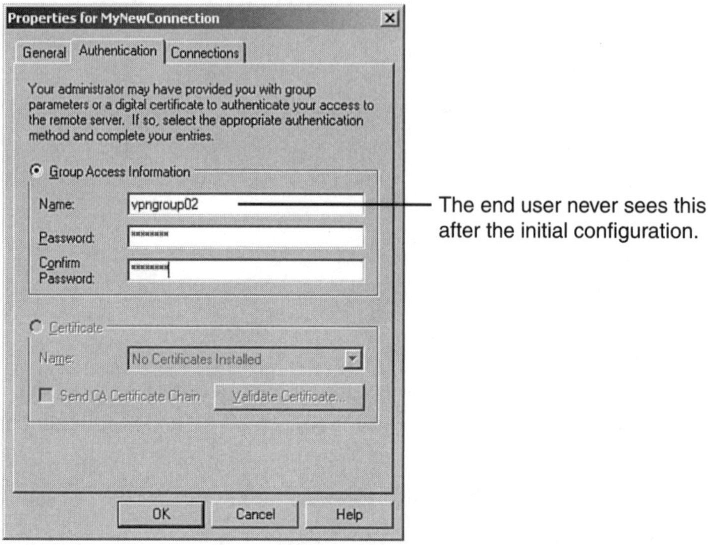

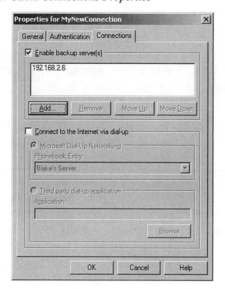

Task 6 to Install and Configure Cisco VPN Client 3.5: Configuring Cisco VPN Client Connection Properties

The Connections tab, shown in Figure 10-21, defines backup networks and connection to the Internet via dialup networking.

Figure 10-21 *Configure Cisco VPN Client Connections Properties*

An enterprise network may include one or more backup Easy VPN Servers to use if the primary Easy VPN Server gateway is not available. To enable this feature, choose the **Enable backup server(s)** check box and then click **Add** to enter the IP address of the backup Easy VPN Server.

Cisco VPN Client attempts to connect to the primary Easy VPN Server first. If it cannot be reached, Cisco VPN Client accesses the backup list for the addresses of available backup Easy VPN Server.

Connecting to an enterprise network using a dialup connection is typically a two-step process:

Step 1   Use a dialup connection to your ISP.

Step 2   Use Cisco VPN Client to connect to the enterprise network.

Connecting to the Internet via dialup automatically launches the connection before making the VPN connection. It makes connecting to the ISP and Easy VPN Server an easy, one-step process. Click **Connect to the Internet via Dial-Up Networking** to enable the option.

Working with Cisco VPN Client 3.5

This section contains information regarding the Cisco VPN Client program menus, log viewer, and status displays.

Program Menu

Figure 10-22 displays the Cisco VPN Client program menu as viewed on a Windows 2000 PC.

Figure 10-22 *Cisco VPN Client Program Menu*

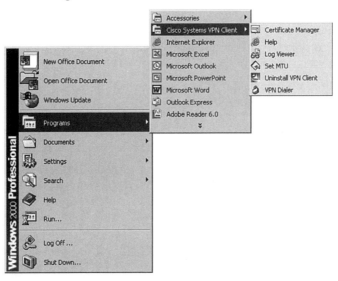

After Cisco VPN Client is installed, access the Cisco VPN Client program menu by choosing **Start > Programs > Cisco Systems VPN Client**. Under the Cisco VPN Client menu, a number of options are available:

- **Certificate Manager**—Enables you to enroll, import, export, verify, and view certificates.

- **Help**—Accesses the Cisco VPN Client help text. Help is also available by doing the following:

  — Press **F1** at any window while using the Cisco VPN Client.

  — Click the **Help** button.

  — Choose **Help > Help VPN Client**.

- **Log Viewer**—Displays the Cisco VPN Client event log.

- **Set Maximum Transmission Unit (MTU)**—Cisco VPN Client automatically sets the MTU size to approximately 1420 bytes. For unique applications, Set MTU can change the MTU size to fit a specific scenario.

- **Uninstall VPN Client**—Only one Cisco VPN Client can be loaded at a time. When upgrading, the old Cisco VPN Client must be uninstalled before the new Cisco VPN Client is installed. Choose **Uninstall VPN Client** to remove the old Cisco VPN Client.

- **Cisco VPN Dialer**—Initiates the Cisco VPN Client connection process by displaying the Cisco VPN Client splash window.

Log Viewer

Examining the event log can help a network administrator diagnose problems with an IPSec connection between a Cisco VPN Client and an Easy VPN Server. The Log Viewer application collects event messages from all processes that contribute to the Cisco VPN Client–Easy VPN Server connection.

Figure 10-23 displays the Log Viewer window with a sample Cisco VPN Client log file. From the toolbar, you can perform the following:

- Save the log file
- Print the log file
- Capture event messages to the log
- Filter the events
- Clear the event log
- Search the event log

Figure 10-23 *Cisco VPN Client Log Viewer*

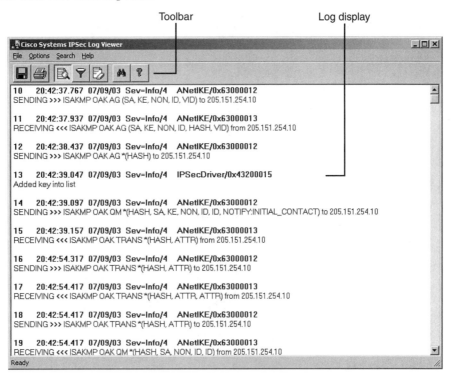

Setting MTU Size

Figure 10-24 displays the SetMTU window, which is where you set the MTU size.

Figure 10-24 *Setting MTU Size*

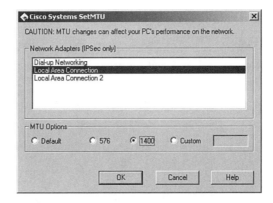

Cisco VPN Client automatically sets the MTU size to approximately 1420 bytes. For unique applications in which fragmentation is still an issue, Set MTU can change the MTU size to fit the specific scenario. In the Network Adapters (IPSec only) field, choose the network adapter. In the example in Figure 10-24, Local Area Connection is selected. In the MTU Options group box, set the MTU option size by choosing the appropriate radio button. You must reboot for MTU changes to take effect.

Client Connection Status: General Tab

The Cisco Systems VPN Client Connection Status window contains up to three tabs: General, Statistics, and Firewall (Firewall is not shown in Figure 10-25 because it is not currently supported by Cisco IOS 12.2(8)T Cisco Easy VPN). Figure 10-25 displays the General tab.

Figure 10-25 *Cisco VPN Client Connection Status—General Tab*

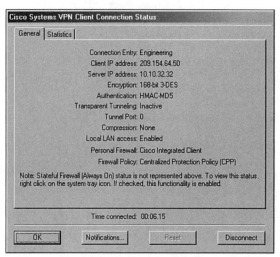

The General tab provides IP security information, listing the IPSec parameters that govern this IPSec tunnel. The following information is available within the General tab:

- **Client IP Address**—The IP address assigned to Cisco VPN Client for the current session.

- **Server IP Address**—The IP address of the Easy VPN Server device to which Cisco VPN Client is connected.

- **Encryption**—The data encryption method for traffic through this tunnel.

- **Authentication**—The data or packet authentication method used for traffic through this tunnel.

- **Transparent Tunneling**—The status of transparent tunnel mode in Cisco VPN Client (either active or inactive).

- **Tunnel Port**—If transparent mode is active, the tunnel port through which packets are passing is displayed. This field also identifies whether Cisco VPN Client is sending packets through UDP or TCP. If Transparent Tunneling is inactive, then the value of Tunnel Port is 0.

- **Compression**—Displays whether data compression is in effect, as well as the type of compression in use. Currently, the type of compression is LZS.

- **Local LAN Access**—Displays whether this parameter is enabled or disabled.

- **Personal Firewall**—Displays the name of the firewall in use on the Cisco VPN Client PC, such as the Cisco Integrated Client, Zone Labs ZoneAlarm or ZoneAlarm Pro, BlackICE Defender, and so on. This feature is not currently supported in Cisco IOS Release 12.2(8)T Cisco Easy VPN.

- **Firewall Policy**—Displays the firewall policy in use:

  - Are You There (AYT)—Not currently supported in Cisco IOS Release 12.2(8)T Cisco Easy VPN.

  - Centralized Protection Policy (CPP) or "policy pushed" as defined on the VPN gateway—Not currently supported in Cisco IOS Release 12.2(8)T Cisco Easy VPN.

Client Connection Status: Statistics Tab

Figure 10-26 displays the Statistics tab.

Figure 10-26 *Client Connection Status—Statistics Tab*

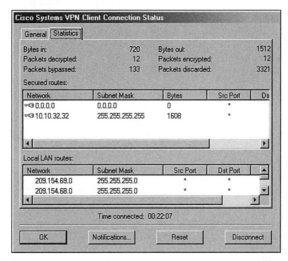

The Statistics tab in the Connection Status window shows statistics for data packets that Cisco VPN Client has processed during the current session, or since the statistics were reset. The following information is available in this window:

- **Bytes In**—The total amount of data received after a secure packet has been successfully decrypted.

- **Bytes Out**—The total amount of encrypted data transmitted through the tunnel.

- **Packets Decrypted**—The total number of data packets received on the port.

- **Packets Encrypted**—The total number of secured data packets transmitted out of the port.

- **Packets Bypassed**—The total number of data packets that Cisco VPN Client did not process because they did not need to be encrypted. Local Acknowledge Response Protocols (ARPs) and DHCP fall into this category.

- **Packets Discarded**—The total number of data packets that Cisco VPN Client rejected because they did not come from the secure Easy VPN Server gateway.

- **Secured Routes**—The IP address of the private network with which this Cisco VPN Client has a secure connection.

- **Local LAN Routes**—If present, this check box shows the network addresses of the networks you can access on your local LAN while you are connected to your organization's private network.

Upcoming Cisco VPN Client Changes

The descriptions of the Cisco VPN Client contained in this chapter are based on version 3.x of the Cisco VPN Client. Release 4.0.2.A is currently available.

The first thing you will notice is that the Microsoft Windows Start menu has changed for the client. The options for Certificate Manager and Log Viewer are gone and the name of the main application has changed from VPN Dialer to the more intuitive name of VPN Client. The remaining options on the Start menu are Help, Set MTU, and Uninstall VPN Client.

Other new features of Release 4.0 of Cisco VPN Client are described in the following sections.

Virtual Adapter

To help solve protocol incompatibility problems, Cisco has included a virtual adapter in the new release of the Cisco VPN Client. This virtual adapter appears in the network properties list and acts just like a physical adapter.

Windows 2000 system users will see a warning message when installing Release 4.0 of the Cisco VPN Client. The message warns that no digital signature was found and asks whether it is okay to continue the installation. Simply accept the message to continue with the installation. The Windows 2000 warning message looks like this:

The Microsoft digital signature affirms that software has been tested with Windows and that the software has not been altered since it was tested.

The software you are about to install does not have a Microsoft digital signature. Therefore, there is no guarantee that this software works correctly with Windows.

Cisco Systems VPN Adapter

If you want to search for Microsoft digitally signed software, visit the Windows Update Web site at http://windowsupdate.microsoft.com to see if one is available.

Do you want to continue the installation?

Common GUI for Windows and Mac VPN Clients

Earlier releases of the Cisco VPN Client provided a different GUI, depending upon the version of the operating system hosting the client. Release 4.0 changes that and provides a consistent GUI environment regardless of the operating system. There may be different capabilities between operating systems, so there will be differences in the GUI to accommodate those functionality differences.

The Certificates Manager and Log Viewer have been pulled into the Cisco VPN Client application so that you can view everything from one common interface. Figure 10-27 shows the new interface. The toolbar buttons change depending upon the tab selected.

Figure 10-27 *Common GUI of Release 4.0 of the Cisco VPN Client*

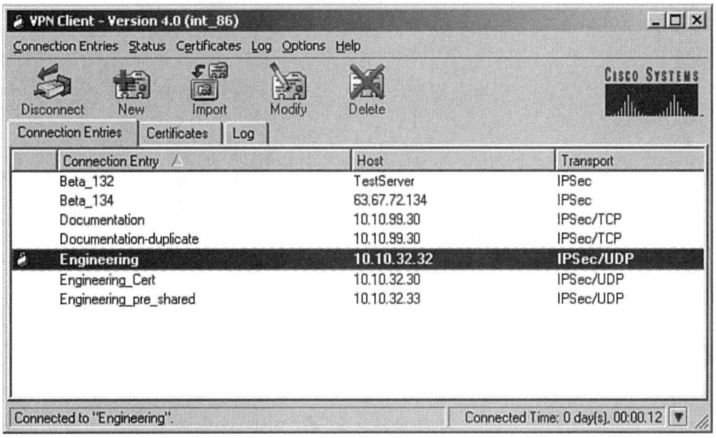

Deleting Alerts (Within Reason)

Release 4.0 Cisco VPN Clients that connect to a VPN 3000 Concentrator can display alerts from the concentrator to show why a VPN connection has disconnected. These alerts are shown in a pop-up window and describe the reason why an IPSec tunnel has been torn down. The client also logs a message in the Notifications log and in the IPSec log files. If an IPSec delete does not tear down the connection, the alert will be written to the log files, but will not appear in a pop-up window.

The alert feature is not configurable on Cisco VPN Client. The system administrator enables the alert feature on the VPN 3000 Concentrator. Cisco VPN Client and the Concentrator negotiate whether or not to display these messages during tunnel initiation.

Single IPSec-SA

Release 4.0 of Cisco VPN Client creates a single VPN tunnel with a single SA pair for split-tunneling connections. All appropriate network traffic uses this same tunnel, regardless of whether or not split tunneling is in use. This host-to-all approach eliminates the need to build separate tunnels and SAs for each network participating in a split-tunnel network.

Personal Firewall Enhancements

In Release 4.0, Cisco has added support for the Sygate Personal Firewall and Sygate Personal Firewall Pro, Version 5.0, Build 1175 and higher to Cisco VPN Client. Release 4.0 of Cisco VPN Client supports the following personal firewalls:

- ZoneAlarm Pro 2.6.3.57 and more recent
- ZoneAlarm 2.6.3.57 and more recent
- Zone Labs Integrity 1.0 and more recent
- BlackICE Agent and BlackICE Defender 2.5 and more recent
- Sygate Personal Firewall and Sygate Personal Firewall Pro, Version 5.0, Build 1175 and more recent

The new release also includes support for these features:

- The ability to enable or disable stateful firewalls from the command line.
- Configurable ICMP permissions.

Third-Party VPN Vendor Compatibility

Release 4.0 of Cisco VPN Client provides the ability to use other VPN products while Cisco VPN Client is installed on a user's system. Compatibility with VPN clients from Microsoft, Nortel, Checkpoint, Intel, and others is now supported.

RADIUS SDI XAUTH Request Handling

RADIUS SDI XAUTH handling has been improved, which may result in better performance when using Cisco VPN Client, Release 4.0 with that capability. Administrators use the PCF or INI files to configure this capability.

ISO-Standard Format for Log Filenames

In prior releases, log files generated by the Cisco VPN Client GUI used the naming convention of MMM-dd-yyy-hh-mm-ss.log for log files. The ISO 8601 extended specification for representing dates and times calls for a convention of LOG-yyyy-MM-dd-hh-mm-ss.txt for these filenames. Release 4.0 of Cisco VPN Client now adheres to the ISO standard format.

An added benefit of this name change is that the chronological order of the log files will now be the same as the alphanumeric order, making it easier to locate important log information.

Enhancements to GINA

Release 4.0.2 of Cisco VPN Client includes an improved application launch verification mechanism. This enhancement affects the Graphical Identification and Authentication (GINA) DLL used by Windows NT 4.0, Windows 2000, and Windows XP platforms.

Chapter Summary

The following list summarizes what you have learned in this chapter:

- Cisco Easy VPN features greatly enhance deployment of remote access solutions for Cisco IOS customers.
- The Easy VPN Server adds several new commands to Cisco IOS in 12.2(8)T.
- Cisco VPN Client 3.5 can be configured manually by users or automatically by using preconfiguration files.

Cisco IOS Commands Presented in This Chapter

Many Cisco IOS version 12.3 commands were discussed or referenced in this chapter. These commands can be found in the *Command Reference* online at http://www.cisco.com/univercd /cc/td/doc/product/software/ios123/.

Chapter Review Questions

The following review questions cover some of the key facts and concepts that were introduced in this chapter. Answers to these questions can be found in Appendix A, "Answers to Chapter Review Questions."

1 If a VPN client is suddenly disconnected, what feature of Cisco Easy VPN Server lets clients reconnect without having to wait for previous SAs to timeout or be deleted?

2 Which Cisco hardware devices can act as Cisco Easy VPN Servers?

3 Which IPSec protocol does Cisco Easy VPN Server support?

4 Which Cisco products support the Cisco Easy VPN Remote feature?

5 What are the two modes of operation that can be used with Cisco Easy VPN Remote Phase II devices?

6 Which Cisco Easy VPN Remote mode of operation is not compatible with PAT?

7 The first task in configuring a Cisco IOS router for Cisco Easy VPN Server usage is to create an IP address pool. When might you not have to create this pool?

8 What elements make up a group policy that will be pushed from a Cisco IOS router to a Cisco Easy VPN Remote client?

9 What command would you use to enable IKE DPD on a Cisco IOS Easy VPN Server to check every 60 seconds with 5 second retries?

10 What feature of Cisco VPN Client blocks all inbound traffic to Cisco VPN Client that is not related to an outbound session?

11 What three tabs are available from the Properties window that is activated from the Options menu of a Cisco VPN Client connection?

12 Where would you configure a Cisco VPN Client to connect to a Cisco Easy VPN Server via TCP through a firewall or router that is running NAT?

Case Study

The Future Corporation's network structure is shown in Figure 10-28.

Figure 10-28 *The Future Corporation*

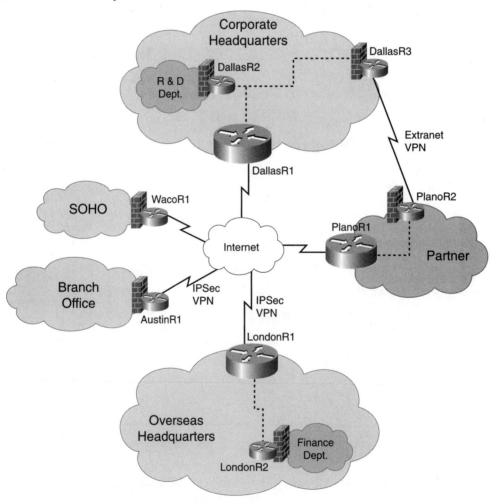

Scenario

The Future Corporation provides laptop computers for its mobile sales force, executives, and managers. The laptops are configured with the Cisco VPN Client.

Your task is to configure the Cisco Easy VPN router DallasR1 for XAUTH to support these users. Based on the following specifications, show all the commands you would need to issue on the router to configure DallasR1 for XAUTH support:

1 The pool of addresses that has been set aside for these users is 172.16.10.200 through 172.16.10.250. Name the address pool **futureco-remote-pool**.

2 The ISAKMP policy for VPN clients is priority 1 and establishes the use of a pre-shared key (JQ8brD907yZ), 3DES encryption, and DH Group 2.

3 The IKE group policy is called futureco-remote-access.

4 DNS servers are at 172.16.10.41 and 172.16.10.51.

5 WINS servers are at 172.16.10.42 and 172.16.10.52.

6 The Future Corporation's domain name is futureco.com.

7 Use **esp-3DES** and **esp-sha-hmac** in your IPSec transform set, which will be called vpnremotes.

8 Create a dynamic crypto map called **vpnremotes-map**.

9 Send IKE DPD messages every 30 seconds with retries 3 seconds apart.

10 Set the XAUTH timeout to 30 seconds.

Solutions

The correct steps and commands to use to configure Easy VPN router DallasR1 for XAUTH based on the configuration specifications are as follows:

Task 1: Configure XAUTH

Step 1   Enable AAA login authentication:

```
DallasR1(config)# aaa authentication login futureco-remote-access local
```

Step 2   Set the XAUTH timeout value:

```
DallasR1(config)# crypto isakmp Xauth timeout 30
```

Step 3   Enable IKE XAUTH for the dynamic crypto map:

```
DallasR1(config)# crypto map vpnremotes-map client authentication list
    futureco-remote-access
```

Task 2: Create an IP Address Pool

```
DallasR1(config)# ip local pool futureco-remote-pool 172.16.10.200 172.16.10.250
```

Task 3: Configure Group Policy Lookup

Step 1 Establish an AAA section in the configuration file:

```
aaa new-model
```

Step 2 Enable group policy lookup:

```
DallasR1(config)# aaa authorization network futureco-remote-access local
```

Task 4: Create an ISAKMP Policy for Remote VPN Client Access

Example 10-3 Shows the ISAKMP policy for remote VPN client access.

Example 10-3 *ISAKMP Policy for Remote VPN Client Access*

```
DallasR1(config)# crypto isakmp enable
DallasR1(config)# crypto isakmp policy 1
DallasR1(config-isakmp)# authen pre-share
DallasR1(config-isakmp)# encryption 3des
DallasR1(config-isakmp)# group 2
DallasR1(config-isakmp)# exit
```

Task 5: Define a Group Policy for a MC Push

Step 1 Add the group profile to be defined:

```
DallasR1(config)# crypto isakmp client configuration group
    futureco-remote-access
```

Step 2 Configure the IKE pre-shared key:

```
DallasR1(config-isakmp-group)# key JQ8brD907yZ
```

Step 3 Specify the DNS servers:

```
DallasR1(config-isakmp-group)# dns 172.16.10.41 172.16.10.51
```

Step 4 Specify the WINS servers:

```
DallasR1(config-isakmp-group)# wins 172.16.10.42 172.16.10.52
```

Step 5 Specify the DNS domain:

```
DallasR1(config-isakmp-group)# domain futureco.com
```

Step 6 Specify the local IP address pool.

```
DallasR1(config-isakmp-group)# pool futureco-remote-pool
```

Task 6: Create a Transform Set

```
DallasR1(config)# crypto ipsec transform-set vpnremotes esp-3des esp-sha-hmac
```

Task 7: Create a Dynamic Crypto Map with RRI

Step 1   Create a dynamic crypto map:

```
DallasR1(config)# crypto dynamic-map vpnremotes-map 1
```

Step 2   Assign a transform set to the crypto map:

```
DallasR1(config-crypto-map)# set transform-set vpnremotes
```

Step 3   Enable RRI:

```
DallasR1(config-crypto-map)# reverse route
DallasR1(config-crypto-map)# exit
```

Task 8: Apply a MC to the Dynamic Crypto Map

Step 1   Configure the router to respond to MC requests:

```
DallasR1(config)# crypto map vpnremotes-map client configuration address
   respond
```

Step 2   Enable IKE queries for group policy lookup:

```
DallasR1(config)# crypto map vpnremotes-map isakmp authorization list
   futureco-remote-access
```

Step 3   Apply changes to the dynamic crypto map:

```
DallasR1(config)# crypto map vpnremotes-map 1 ipsec-isakmp dynamic
   vpnremotes-map
```

Task 9: Apply a Dynamic Crypto Map to the Router Outside Interface

Example 10-4 shows how to apply a dynamic crypto map to the router interface.

Example 10-4 *Apply a Dynamic Crypto Map to the Router Interface*

```
DallasR1(config)# interface FastEthernet4/0
DallasR1(config-if)# crypto map vpnremotes-map
DallasR1(config-if)# exit
```

Task 10: Enable IKE DPD

```
DallasR1(config)# crypto isakmp keepalive 30 3
```

Upon completion of this chapter, you will be able to perform the following tasks:

- Install Cisco SDM on a Cisco Router
- Use SDM Wizards to Configure VPN Policies on a Cisco Router
- Use SDM Wizards to Configure Cisco IOS Firewall Policies on a Cisco Router

CHAPTER 11

Securing Cisco Routers Using Security Device Manager

This chapter introduces and explains Cisco Security Device Manager (SDM). This chapter includes the following topics:

- SDM overview
- SDM software
- Using the Startup Wizard
- Introducing the SDM user interface
- Using SDM to configure a WAN
- Using SDM to configure a firewall
- Using SDM to configure a VPN
- Using SDM to perform security audits
- Using the Reset to Factory Default Wizard
- Using SDM Advanced, Wizard, and Monitor Modes

Understanding Security Device Manager

SDM is an easy-to-use, browser-based device management tool that is used to configure single Cisco IOS routers. It is embedded within the Cisco IOS 800 through 3700 series routers at no additional cost. The SDM software files reside in the router's Flash Memory alongside other router operating system files.

SDM simplifies router and security configuration through the use of several intelligent wizards to enable efficient configuration of key router VPN and Cisco IOS Firewall parameters. This capability permits administrators to quickly and easily deploy, configure, and monitor Cisco access routers.

SDM is designed for resellers and network administrators of small- to medium-sized businesses who are proficient in LAN fundamentals and basic network design, but have little or no experience with the Cisco IOS CLI or may not be a security expert.

SDM is designed to help you secure your Cisco routers and their associated networks without having to memorize multiple CLI commands or having to be an expert in network security. For more advanced users, SDM provides several time-saving tools, such as an ACL Editor, a VPN Crypto Map Editor, and a preview of Cisco IOS CLI commands.

SDM Features

SDM contains a unique Security Audit Wizard that provides a comprehensive router security audit. SDM uses security configurations recommended by the Cisco Technical Assistance Center (TAC) and International Computer Security Association (ICSA) as its basis for comparisons and default settings.

SDM also provides:

- An Autodetect Wizard for finding misconfigurations and for proposing fixes.
- Strong security defaults and configuration entry checks.
- Router- and interface-specific defaults that reduce configuration time.

SDM wizards help to provide faster VPN and firewall deployments. SDM contains a suggested workflow (located in the lower part of the browser pages) to guide untrained users through router configuration.

A typical process flow proceeds as follows:

1 Configure LAN parameters.

2 Configure WAN parameters.

3 Configure firewall parameters.

4 Configure VPN parameters.

5 Perform a security audit.

Although SDM is designed for users with little to no CLI experience, it is just as useful to advanced users. Advanced CLI users use SDM to quickly fine-tune configurations (using the ACL Editor) or to diagnose problems (using the VPN tunnel quality monitor).

In addition to the configuration wizards already mentioned, you can use SDM to discover and configure existing LAN and WAN interfaces.

SDM contains an intuitive embedded online help system.

Security Configuration Intelligence

SDM contains embedded parameter-checking intelligence to help you accurately configure router VPN and firewall settings.

If SDM detects a configuration conflict, the SDM software will generate a warning window describing the condition, as shown in Figure 11-1.

Figure 11-1 *SDM Warning Message*

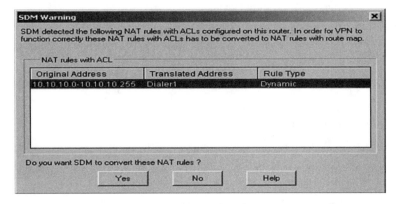

You should always read SDM warning messages and consider following the recommendations to repair the original condition. Warnings messages usually allow you to choose either to let SDM fix the configuration conflict automatically or to fix the conflict manually yourself.

SDM User Profiles

SDM was designed with the following users in mind:

- **Small office/home office (SOHO)** — These SDM users usually have a working knowledge of networking and security, but no significant Cisco IOS CLI experience. SOHO users typically use the Cisco Router Web Setup (CRWS) tool for general router configuration tasks, and then use SDM for router security configuration.

- **Small-to-medium business (SMB) and branch office** — These SDM users typically possess basic technical system administrator level knowledge. These users may have a rudimentary knowledge of networks and security, but no significant Cisco IOS CLI experience.

- **Enterprise branch office** — These SDM users are typically network site administrators with a modest knowledge of the Cisco IOS CLI and basic security.

- **Enterprise headquarters** — These SDM users are typically very knowledgeable of the Cisco IOS CLI and are capable in both networking and security.

All of these users can benefit from SDM features.

SDM Feature Details

SDM 1.0 comes with the following main features:

- Security configuration:
  - SDM contains an ACL Editor to configure both standard and extended ACLs. You can add, edit, and delete an ACL and the entries within a list.

— SDM allows you to configure Network Address Translation (NAT) and Port Address Translation (PAT).

— SDM allows you to configure Context-Based Access Control (CBAC) for both simple and advanced firewalls (including firewalls with demilitarized zones [DMZs]).

— SDM contains a VPN Wizard and advanced configuration for:

— Site-to-site VPNs

— Easy VPN Phase II (remote client only)

— Generic routing encapsulation (GRE) tunneling

- SDM contains interface configuration for Ethernet, T1/E1 (serial only), and DSL (Point-to-Point Protocol over Ethernet [PPPoE]) router interfaces.

- SDM contains system configuration tools for Dynamic Host Configuration Protocol (DHCP), Telnet setup, and passwords.

- SDM allows you to enable static or dynamic routing for Routing Information Protocol (RIP), Open Shortest Path First (OSPF), and Enhanced Interior Gateway Routing Protocol (EIGRP).

- SDM contains several help options, including online help, "how to?" help, and tooltips.

- SDM includes a security audit tool for defining "at risk" problems and for suggesting how to lock down the router.

- SDM contains a "one-click" router lockdown feature.

- SDM contains both graphical monitoring and logging configuration.

Understanding SDM Software

This topic provides an overview of SDM software functions. This section discusses the supported Cisco IOS releases and devices. For supported systems that are not preloaded with SDM, this section explains where to obtain SDM, how to install the application, and how to verify installation on the router. This section also discusses the software requirements for interacting with SDM from a management workstation and talk about the communication protocols used.

Supported Cisco IOS Releases and Devices

SDM 1.0 supports Cisco routers and their associated Cisco IOS software versions, as shown Table 11-1.

Table 11-1   *Supported Cisco Routers and Cisco IOS Software Releases*

SDM Supported Platforms	Supported Cisco IOS Versions
831, 836, and 837	• 12.2(13)ZH or later
1710, 1721, 1751, and 1760	• 12.2(13)ZH or later • 12.2(13)T3 or later • 12.3(1)M or later
1711 and 1712	• 12.2(15)ZL or later
2610XM, 2611XM, 2620XM, 2621XM, 2650XM, 2651XM, and 2691	• 12.2(11)T6 or later • 12.3(1)M or later • 12.2(15)ZJ
3620, 3640, 3640A, 3661, and 3662	• 12.2(11)T6 or later • 12.3(1)M or later
3725 and 3745	• 12.2(11)T6 or later • 12.3(1)M or later

NOTE   For the 1710, 1721, 1751, and 1760 series of routers, release 12.2(11)T6 is not supported because of a missing Cisco IOS CLI command that is required for SDM to operate correctly.

Always consult the latest documentation on Cisco.com for information on SDM device and Cisco IOS software version support.

Obtaining SDM

SDM comes preinstalled on all Cisco 1700, 2600XM, 3600, and 3700 routers that were manufactured in June 2003 or later and were purchased with the VPN bundle.

SDM is also available as a separate option on all supported routers with Cisco IOS software security features manufactured in June 2003 or later.

If you have a router that does not have SDM installed and you would like to use SDM on that router, you must download SDM from Cisco.com and install it on your router.

Installing SDM on Existing Routers

If you choose to install SDM on an existing (SDM-supported) Cisco router, you must obtain the sdm-vXX.zip file from Cisco.com and copy its unzipped contents to your router Flash Memory file system.

When you install SDM on an existing router, use the "Downloading and Installing Cisco Security Device Manager (SDM)" document.

Follow the procedure for your specific router to download the SDM files. SDM contains two procedures for accomplishing this, depending on the type of Cisco router you have:

- Cisco 1700, 2600, 3600, or 3700 series router procedure.

- Cisco 831, 836, or 837 router-specific procedures. This procedure is slightly different because these routers use the CRWS tool as the default device manager. Reference the "Switching Between Cisco Security Device Manager (SDM) and Cisco Router Web Setup Tool (CRWS) on Cisco 83x Series Routers" document for more detailed information.

Once you download the SDM files, there are two processes to replace the router configuration in Flash Memory:

- You can retain your existing configuration file and configure the router to be an HTTP/ HTTP Secure (HTTPS) router using local authentication. Configure a local user with a privilege level of 15. Configure vty connections to use local login with a privilege level of 15. An optional recommended step is to turn on local logging.

  If you use your existing configuration file, SDM will not display the Startup Wizard the first time you run SDM. It is assumed that you have already done basic network configuration.

- If the router does not contain a preexisting configuration and you want to start from a fresh (SDM-provided) default configuration file, you can copy one of the default configuration files included in the zipped bundle that you downloaded from Cisco.com. The packaged files contain a default configuration file for each type of supported router.

  If you use the SDM default configuration file, SDM will display the Startup Wizard, letting you enter basic network configuration information, the first time you run SDM.

NOTE   SDM requires approximately 2.3 MB of free router Flash Memory.

Displaying Router Flash Memory

If you are not sure if SDM is loaded into Flash Memory or need to know how much Flash Memory is available, use the **show flash** CLI command.

SDM contains several **show** commands. The **show flash** command is executed as shown in Figure 11-2. This SDM command displays the same information as the CLI command but in a GUI window.

In the example shown in Figure 11-2, you can see the Cisco IOS image and other files, including the sdm.tar and sdm.shtml required files. Also, you can see how much Flash Memory is used and how much is available.

Figure 11-2 *Executing SDM* **show** *Commands*

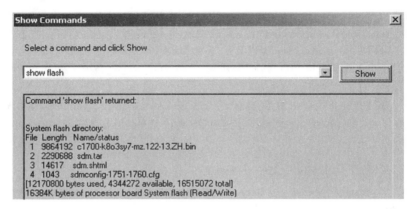

SDM Software Requirements

SDM uses an industry-standard Java client application to minimize the impact of the SDM application on router performance.

You access SDM by executing an HTML file in the router, which then loads the SDM Java file. Always use a supported browser to launch SDM from a PC. SDM currently supports the following browsers:

- Netscape Navigator version 4.79 or later.
- Microsoft Internet Explorer version 5.5 or later.

NOTE   Java and JavaScript must be enabled on the selected browser. The supported browsers contain Java plug-ins with Java Virtual Machine (JVM). SDM also supports Java Runtime Engine (JRE) versions 1.3.1 or later.

The SDM client is compatible with the Microsoft Windows operating system, including Windows 98, NT 4.0 (SP4), 2000, XP, and Me.

SDM Router Communications

SDM communicates with the router when accessing the SDM application for download to the PC, when reading and writing the router configuration, and when checking router status.

SDM uses different communications methods based on the Cisco IOS software version of the target routers:

- For Cisco IOS Software Releases 12.3M or later and 12.2(13)ZH or later, SDM uses a secure HTTP transport method (HTTPS). For earlier Cisco IOS versions, SDM uses HTTP as the transport method. In both cases, SDM relies on Telnet access for communication to the routers.

NOTE Because SDM can deny certain types of traffic, and lock down router access, it is very important for you to know how SDM communicates with your router. If you lock the router down too tightly, you may not be able to use SDM to administer the router.

- For Cisco IOS Software Releases 12.2(11)T, 12.2(13)T, and 12.2(15)T, SDM uses Secure Shell (SSH) and Telnet:
    — When configuration changes are made in SDM, Cisco IOS commands are transferred to the router's Flash Memory as a temporary file using RCP.
    — The temporary file is copied to the router's running configuration and then is deleted.
    — SDM uses a "squeeze" process to reclaim router Flash Memory. You use the squeeze function in two instances:
        — Whenever you are removing an older SDM version and adding a newer one
        — Whenever SDM prompts you to perform a "squeeze"

Using the SDM Startup Wizard

SDM is a tool for configuring, managing, and monitoring a single Cisco access router.

Each Cisco access router is accessible by its own copy of SDM, which is located in the router's Flash Memory.

A common scenario that SDM supports is to have one user monitoring the router while another user is simultaneously using SDM to modify the configuration of the router. It is *not* recommended that multiple users use SDM to modify the configuration at the same time. Although SDM will permit this scenario, it does not assure consistent or predictable results.

Users now have the flexibility to configure the router with both SDM and the CLI. Because the SDM user interface does not support all the Cisco IOS software functionality (for example, QoS), you can augment the SDM-generated configuration with some CLI commands.

For unsupported interfaces, such as ISDN interfaces, SDM automatically detects whether the interfaces support security features, such as firewalls, crypto maps, and NAT. If the security features are supported, users can use SDM to configure the security features to the unsupported interfaces. However, the user still needs to configure the unsupported interface parameters directly through the CLI.

First-Time SDM Access

Use the following process when you access SDM for the first time. This procedure assumes that either an out-of-box router with SDM was installed or a default SDM configuration was loaded into Flash Memory.

Step 1   Connect a PC to the router's lowest-numbered LAN Ethernet port using a crossover cable.

Step 2   Assign a static IP address to the PC. Cisco recommends using **10.10.10.2** with a **255.255.255.0** subnet mask.

Step 3   Launch a supported browser.

Step 4   Enter the URL **https://10.10.10.1/flash/sdm.shtml**. You will be prompted to log in.

Step 5   Log in using the default user account:

- Username: **sdm**
- Password: **sdm**

The SDM Startup Wizard opens, the Welcome page of which is shown in Figure 11-3, requiring you to enter a basic network configuration.

Figure 11-3   *SDM Startup Wizard Welcome Page*

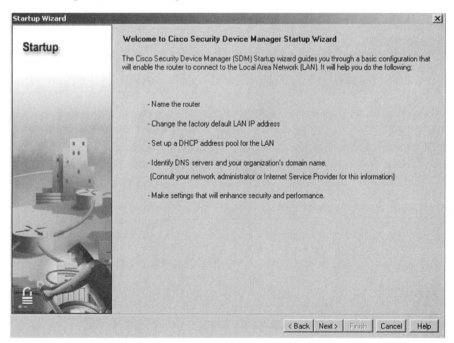

NOTE   The Startup Wizard information needs to be entered only once and will appear only when a default configuration is detected.

Step 6   Click **Next**. The Basic Configuration window opens, as shown in Figure 11-4.

Figure 11-4 *SDM Startup Wizard—Basic Configuration*

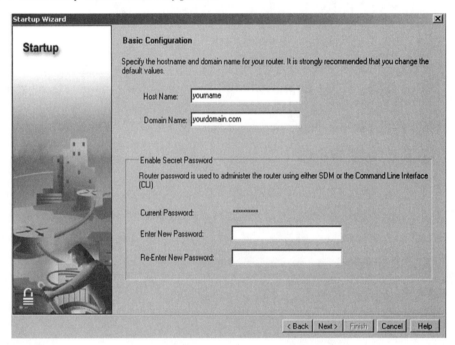

Basic Configuration and Changing Default Username and Password

On the Basic Configuration window, shown in Figure 11-4, you should enter the router Host Name and Domain Name. These fields are optional but it is recommended that you change the defaults.

Step 1   (Optional) Enter the router host name in the Host Name field.

Step 2   (Optional) Enter the router domain name in the Domain Name field.

   The user must enter a new enable secret password with a minimum length of six characters. SDM will not allow you to proceed until a valid password is entered and reentered.

Step 3   Enter a new enable secret password using a minimum length of six characters (Cisco recommends using passwords of no less than ten characters) in the Enter New Password field.

Step 4   Enter the new password, once more, in the Re-Enter New Password field.

NOTE   SDM will not allow you to proceed until a valid password is
            entered and reentered.

Step 5   Click **Next**. The Change Default Username and Password window opens.

          You must change the SDM default username (which is sdm) and password (also sdm).
          This username and password combination is too well known and permits privileged
          EXEC access to your router.

Step 6   Enter a new username in the Enter New User Name field.

Step 7   Enter a new password in the Enter New Password field.

Step 8   Enter the new password, once more, in the Re-Enter New Password field.

Step 9   Click **Next**. The LAN Interface Configuration window opens, as shown in
          Figure 11-5.

Figure 11-5   *SDM Startup Wizard—LAN Interface Configuration*

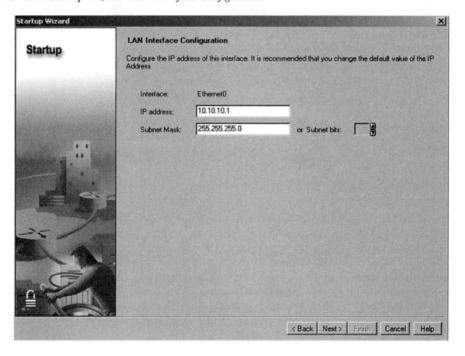

Configuring the LAN Interface

The default LAN interface configuration includes an IP address of 10.10.10.1 with a
subnet mask of 255.255.255.0 preconfigured on the lowest-numbered Ethernet port, as
shown in Figure 11-5. You can keep this address assignment while you complete the initial

configuration, or you can change the address configuration to match the interface's final installation address.

Step 1   (Optional) Enter the IP address of the router interface connected to the LAN network in the IP Address field.

Step 2   (Optional) Enter an appropriate subnet mask in the Subnet Mask field.

Step 3   Click **Next**. The DHCP Server Configuration window opens, as shown in Figure 11-6.

Figure 11-6   *SDM Startup Wizard—DHCP Server Configuration*

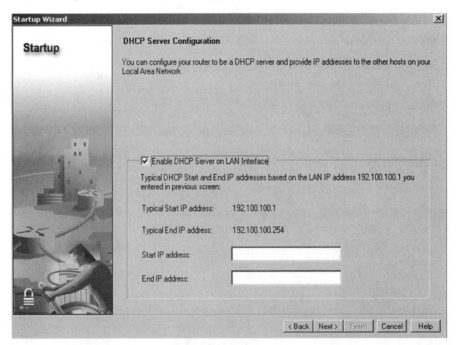

Configuring DHCP

You can configure the router as a DHCP server, as shown in Figure 11-6. If you check the Enable DHCP Server on LAN Interface box, the router can assign private IP addresses to devices on the LAN. If you do check this box, then you must enter a start and end IP address for the DHCP pool.

Step 1   (Optional) Check the **Enable DHCP Server on LAN Interface** check box.

NOTE   For 8*xx* routers, the check box is selected by default.

Step 2   (Optional) Enter the DHCP pool starting IP address in the Start IP Address field.

Step 3   (Optional) Enter the DHCP pool ending IP address in the End IP Address field.

NOTE   The address pool must be based on the LAN IP address and subnet mask that you entered in the LAN Interface Configuration window.

Step 4   Click **Next**. The Domain Name Server window opens.

Configuring DNS

You may optionally want to enter the IP addresses of your primary and secondary DNS servers to permit the router to perform IP domain lookups. If so, complete the following steps:

Step 1   Enter a primary DNS server IP address in the Primary DNS field.

Step 2   Enter a secondary DNS server IP address in the Secondary DNS field.

Step 3   Click **Next**. The Security Configuration window opens, shown in Figure 11-7.

Figure 11-7   *SDM Startup Wizard—Security Configuration*

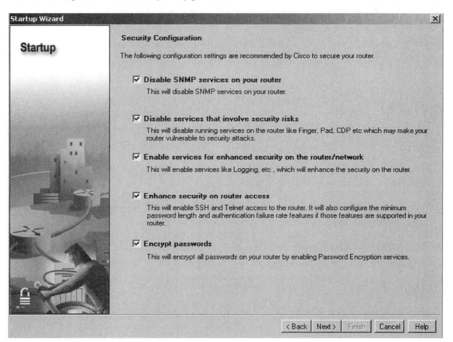

Configuring Security

SDM lets you disable some features that are on by default in Cisco IOS software. When enabled, these features can create security risks or use up valuable memory in the router. SDM also enables basic security features to protect the router and the surrounding networks.

Generally, you should leave the check boxes in the Security Configuration window selected, unless you know that your requirements are different. If you decide later to enable a feature listed here, you can use SDM Advanced Mode to reenable it.

Step 1   Check or uncheck the check boxes according to your security requirements:

- **Disable SNMP Services on Your Router**—Disables SNMP services on your router.

- **Disable Services That Involve Security Risks**—Disables services that are considered security risks, such as the finger service, TCP and UDP small servers, Cisco Discovery Protocol (CDP), and others.

- **Enable Services for Enhanced Security on the Router/Network**— Enables TCP SYN wait time, logging, a basic firewall on all outside interfaces, and other services.

- **Enhance Security on Router Access**—Secures vty (Telnet) access, passwords and parameters, banner settings, and other settings.

- **Encrypt Passwords**—Enables password encryption within the router configuration.

Step 2   Click **Next**. The Wizard Summary window opens.

Viewing Summary Window

The Wizard Summary window, shown in Figure 11-8, displays a summary of the configuration changes that you have made. All SDM wizards provide a summary page.

You should review the basic configuration you gave the router and make any changes (to do so, click **Back**) before leaving the wizard.

In the Startup Wizard, the summary is provided using descriptive sentences versus command-line instructions. In other wizards, you can choose how you want this presented.

You also have the option to click Cancel to abort the startup, click Help to get help, or click Next to proceed to accept the changes.

Step 1   Review the contents of the summary window.

Step 2   Click **Next**. The Startup Wizard Completed window opens, as shown in Figure 11-9.

Figure 11-8 *SDM Startup Wizard—Summary Window*

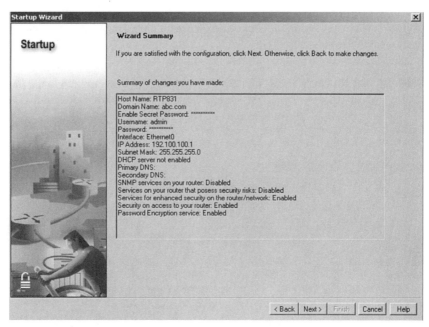

Figure 11-9 *SDM Startup Wizard Completed Window*

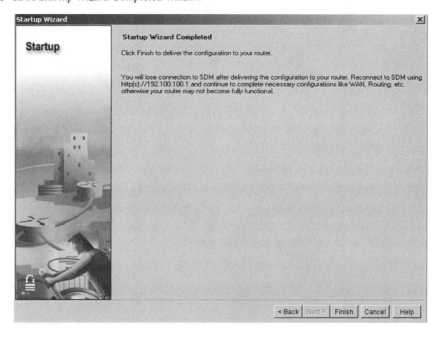

Configuration Delivery

In Figure 11-9, you can see that the Startup Wizard Completed window tells you the new IP address that must be used to reconnect to the router and relaunch SDM. At this point, SDM is ready to load the new configuration to the startup configuration of your router. Once the copy is complete, SDM will reboot the router to activate the new configuration.

Step 1   Click **Finish**, which is now active, to deliver the configuration to the router's Flash Memory. The SDM Startup Wizard Configuration Delivery message box opens, as shown in Figure 11-10.

Figure 11-10 *SDM Startup Wizard Configuration Delivery Message*

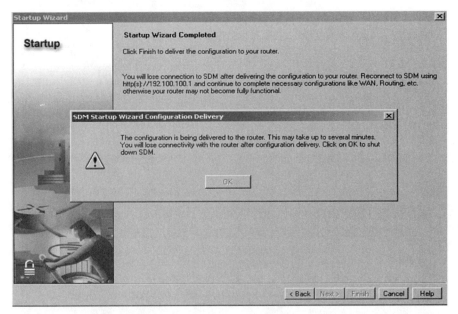

Loading the configuration may take a few minutes, and the OK button is disabled during the transfer process. Once the configuration is delivered, the OK button becomes enabled.

Step 2   Click **OK** to shut down SDM and terminate the connection.

To access SDM after the initial Startup Wizard is completed, type in the URL of the router's SDM application in the address window of your browser. You can use either http: or https:, followed by the router IP address, then /flash/sdm.shtml, as shown in the following example using the IP address configured with the SDM Startup Wizard:

```
https://192.100.100.1/flash/sdm.shtml
```

Entering https specifies that the Secure Sockets Layer (SSL) protocol be used for a secure connection. If SSL is not available, use http: to access the router.

Once you have your WAN interface configured, you can access SDM through a LAN or WAN interface.

Troubleshooting SDM Problems

Use the following steps to troubleshoot SDM access problems:

Step 1 Determine whether there is a browser problem by checking the following:

- Are Java and JavaScript enabled on the browser? If not, enable them.

- Are popup windows being blocked? Disable popup blockers on the PC (SDM requires popup windows).

- Are there any unsupported Java plug-ins installed and running? Disable them using the Windows Control Panel.

Step 2 Determine whether the router might be preventing access. Remember that certain configuration settings are required for SDM to work. Check the following settings:

- Did you use one of the default configurations, or did you use an existing router configuration? Sometimes new configurations disable SDM access.

- Is the HTTP server enabled on the router? If it is not, enable it and check that other SDM prerequisite parameters are configured as well.

- Did SDM access work before, but now does not? Ensure that your PC is not being blocked by a new ACL. Remember, SDM requires HTTP, SSH, Telnet access, and/or RCP access to the router, which could have been inadvertently disabled in a security lockdown.

- Determine whether SDM is installed on the router.

Step 3 Connect to the router through the console port and use the **show flash** command to view the Flash Memory file system and make sure the required SDM files are present. Flash Memory must contain the **sdm.shtml** file and the **sdm.tar** file before SDM can function properly.

Introducing the SDM User Interface

This topic explains the various elements of the SDM user interface beginning with a discussion of the features of the SDM main window. Additional topics within this section of the chapter include discussions of the SDM menu bar and toolbar and a discussion of the various wizard mode options of SDM.

SDM Main Window Features

SDM uses an intelligent configuration reader. When SDM is launched, it reads the existing router configuration and presents the features that are available for SDM configuration. An example of this overview window is shown in Figure 11-11.

Figure 11-11 *System and Configuration Overview*

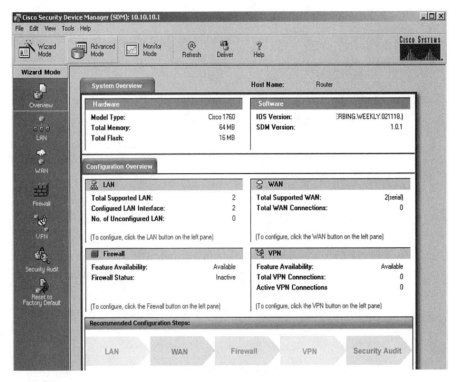

The SDM main window contains the following elements:

- **Menu bar**—Provides the standard File, Edit, View, Tools, and Help menus.
- **Toolbar**—Provides access to SDM wizards and operating modes.
- **Current mode indicator**—Located to the left, just below the toolbar, the current mode indicator displays the current mode you are in.

NOTE   The menu, toolbar, and current mode are always displayed at the top of each window. The other parts of the window change based upon the mode and the function you are performing.

- **Category bar**—Located just beneath the current mode indicator, this column displays the options available in the present window. The selection changes to reflect the options available for the current mode.

When you first log in to SDM, the Overview window opens. This window displays a summary of the router configuration settings. It displays the router model, total amount of installed memory and Flash Memory, Cisco IOS and SDM versions, the hardware installed, and a summary of some security features, such as the state of the firewall and the number of active VPN connections.

SDM Menu Bar

The SDM menu bar contains the following elements:

- **File**—Contains the common file functions, such as save the running configuration to the PC, deliver SDM configuration changes to the router, write the running configuration to the startup configuration, and reset the router to the SDM factory default configuration.
- **Edit > Preferences**—Contains the following two options:
  - **Preview Commands Before Sending to Router in Wizard Mode**—Click this option if you would like SDM to display a list of the configuration commands generated in Wizard Mode before the commands are sent to the router. The default is to not display the commands.
  - **Confirm Before Exiting from SDM**—Click this option if you want SDM to display a dialog box asking for confirmation (Are you sure?) when you exit SDM. The default is to display the message.

NOTE Each time you log in, SDM remembers these preferences.

- **View**—Allows you to switch modes, view router running configurations, use common router **show** commands, display SDM default rules, or perform a refresh (removes all undelivered SDM configurations).
- **Tools**—Allows you to use extended ping, Telnet into the router, or perform a router security audit.
- **Help**—Provides access to common online help methods and the current SDM and router software versions.

SDM Toolbar

Navigating the SDM user interface is done through the toolbar.

SDM contains the following three modes:

- **Wizard Mode**—Designed for the novice, this mode can be used to guide you through common SDM tasks.

- **Advanced Mode**—This mode is designed for more experienced SDM users who prefer to perform tasks in any order. In this mode, you can freely view existing configurations and configure features within and outside of the wizards.

- **Monitor Mode**—This mode is used to view the following:
  — Router status
  — Interface status
  — Firewall status
  — VPN status
  — Logging status

To select a mode, click its button in the toolbar. For each mode, the category bar of SDM changes, showing the options available for that mode.

The toolbar also contains three other buttons:

- **Refresh**—Reloads information from the router and updates the SDM display. This removes all undelivered SDM configurations.

- **Deliver**—Displays the SDM Deliver Configuration to Router dialog box, which lets you send the configuration commands you have generated with SDM to the router. Your router is not configured until you complete this step. This is the last step that is done automatically when you use a wizard.

  You may choose to save the router configuration as a file on your PC. When you click Save to File, SDM creates an sdm-cli-*timestamp*.txt file to a specified directory on your PC's hard drive.

NOTE   When in Advanced Mode, you must manually deliver the configuration.

- **Help**—Displays the online help.

SDM Wizard Mode Options

To get to the Wizard Mode window, click the Wizard Mode icon. This opens the window to the default Overview window. If there is a configuration change within SDM and you attempt to enter Wizard Mode, a dialog box appears. It states that you must perform a Refresh or Deliver before entering Wizard Mode. Click either button to perform one of those functions.

When the page appears, the wizards are displayed on the left in the category bar. SDM contains several wizard options, as shown in the following list:

- **Overview**—This is not truly a wizard. The Overview function lets you view the Cisco IOS version, the hardware installed, and configuration summary for the router. The Overview contains links to several functions, including most of the other wizards that follow in this list.

- **LAN**—Used to configure the LAN interfaces and DHCP.

- **WAN**—Used to configure PPP, Frame Relay, and High-Level Data Link Control (HDLC) WAN interfaces.

- **Firewall**—Contains two options:
  - A simple inside/outside firewall wizard
  - A more complex inside/outside/DMZ with multiple interfaces wizard

- **VPN**—Contains three options:
  - A secure site-to-site VPN wizard
  - An Easy VPN wizard
  - A GRE tunnel with IPSec wizard

- **Security Audit**—Contains two options:
  - The router security audit wizard
  - An easy one-step router security lockdown wizard

- **Reset to Factory Default**—Resets the router configuration back to the SDM factory default configuration settings.

NOTE   At the end of each wizard procedure, all changes are automatically delivered to the router using SDM-generated CLI commands. You may choose whether or not to preview the commands to be sent. The default is to not preview the commands.

Configuring a WAN Using the WAN Wizard

This topic explains how to configure a WAN using SDM WAN Wizard. If your router does not have a WAN interface, this wizard will not function. Begin configuring a WAN connection from the SDM Wizard Mode window, discussed in the previous section, "SDM Wizard Mode Options."

Creating a New WAN Connection

The WAN Wizard takes you through the processes required to set up a WAN interface for supported interface types: PPP, Frame Relay, and HDLC.

Step 1   Click the **WAN** button in the Wizard Mode column. The WAN—Create a New WAN Connection window opens, as shown in Figure 11-12. If you are not sure what to do, select a "How Do I" topic at the bottom of the window, or click Help in the menu bar.

Figure 11-12 *Create a New WAN Connection*

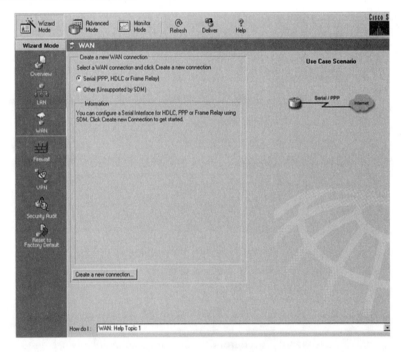

This window allows you to create new WAN connections and to view existing WAN connections.

Step 2   Click a WAN connection type radio button from the list in the upper part of the window. The types shown in this list are based on the physical interfaces installed on the router that have not yet been configured. A Use Case Scenario diagram for the selected interface type appears to the right to provide you with a visual representation of the physical connections.

NOTE	If your router has interfaces that are not supported by SDM, such as an ISDN interface, or a supported interface that has an unsupported configuration that was created using the CLI, the interface will not appear in this window. If you need to configure another type of connection, you can do that by using the CLI.

Step 3   Click the **Create a New Connection** button below the selection window, which opens the Serial Wizard window. The example used in this and the following WAN Wizard steps will configure a serial Frame Relay WAN.

Running the Serial Wizard

The SDM Serial Wizard first reviews the different types of WAN connections supported by SDM. All pages of the WAN Wizard have a common navigation interface at the bottom of the window that includes Back, Next, Finish, Cancel, and Help buttons.

Step 1   Click **Next**. The Select Interface window opens.

Step 2   Select the interface that you want to use for this connection from the Available Interfaces list box. This list contains the available unconfigured interfaces.

Step 3   Click **Next**. The Configure Encapsulation window opens.

Configuring Encapsulation and IP Address

The next few windows of the WAN Wizard require you to select the protocol you will be using and to configure the IP address and subnet mask.

Step 1   Click the appropriate Encapsulation type radio button. Choose from:

- Frame Relay
- PPP
- HDLC

Step 2   Click **Next**. The Enter the IP Address for the Connection window opens.

Step 3   Click the **Static IP Address** radio button. If you do not choose to configure a static IP address, your only other choice is to configure an IP unnumbered interface by sharing the IP address of a configured LAN interface.

Step 4   Enter a static IP address in the IP Address field.

Step 5   Enter a subnet mask in the Subnet Mask field in xxx.xxx.xxx.xxx notation. You could also click the subnet up/down arrows to select the number of bits you want in the mask and let SDM enter the correct subnet.

Step 6   Click **Next**. The Configure LMI and DLCI window opens, as shown in Figure 11-13.

Figure 11-13 *Configure LMI and DLCI*

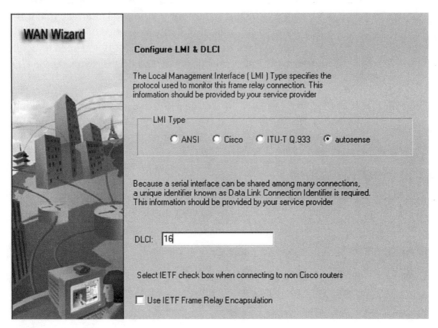

Configuring LMI and DLCI

The Configure LMI and DLCI window opens because you selected to use Frame Relay across this interface and must configure the Local Management Interface (LMI) type, the data-link connection identifier (DLCI), and the encapsulation type. Had you used one of the other protocols, this window would not have appeared.

Step 1 Click a radio button from the LMI Type list. You can click ANSI, Cisco, ITU-T Q.933, or Autosense.

Step 2 Enter in the DLCI field the DLCI that your Frame Relay service provider provided for this interface.

Step 3 Cisco is the default type of Frame Relay encapsulation used. If the remote end of the WAN terminates on a non-Cisco router, check the **Use IETF Frame Relay Encapsulation** check box.

Step 4 Click **Next**. The Advanced Options window opens.

Configuring Advanced Options

The WAN Wizard Advanced Options window lets you set up PAT for one of the router's LAN interfaces and connected subnet. This is an optional configuration.

Step 1 (Optional) Click the **PAT** radio button.

Step 2 (Optional) Select the LAN interface to be translated from the list box.

Step 3 Click **Next**. The WAN Wizard Summary window opens.

Completing the WAN Interface Configuration

The WAN Wizard Summary window gives you a chance to review all the proposed configuration settings that you have chosen for this WAN interface before delivering them to the router.

Step 1 Examine the summary. Go back and make any changes if required.

Step 2 Click **Finish**. The SDM Commands Delivery Status Message window opens. A status bar indicates the progress of delivering the configuration settings to the router. Once the delivery is completed, an OK button becomes active.

Step 3 Use Telnet or a console connection to verify that the configuration was successfully copied to the router and click **OK**. The WAN Wizard main window opens.

Viewing and Editing Existing WAN Connections

The new WAN connection appears in the Current WAN Connection(s) list of the WAN Wizard main window, as shown in Figure 11-14.

Figure 11-14 *Viewing Current WAN Connections*

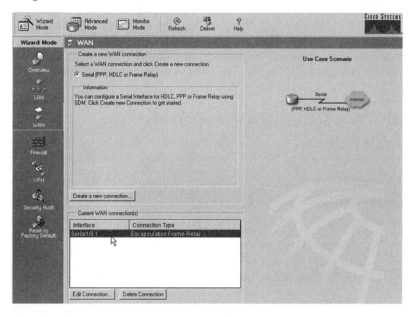

At this point, you could select the connection for editing or deletion.

Verifying Interface Status Using Advanced Mode

SDM automatically enables the new WAN interface by issuing the **no shutdown** CLI command. You can check the status of your router's interfaces from the Interfaces and Connections window of Advanced Mode, as shown in Figure 11-15.

Figure 11-15 *Advanced Mode—Interfaces and Connections*

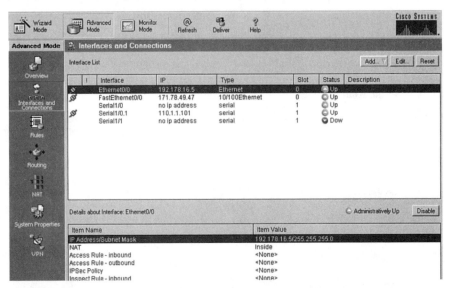

Choose **Advanced Mode > Interfaces and Connections** to verify the interface status. This window displays all the router connections and their states (Up = green, Down = red). You can also use this window to change the status of a router connection from down to up or from up to down.

Using SDM to Configure a Firewall

If your router has the Cisco IOS Firewall feature set, you can use SDM firewall wizards to configure a firewall for your LAN. This section discusses the SDM Firewall Wizard.

Step 1 Click **Firewall** on the Wizard Mode category bar. The Firewall Wizard main window opens, as shown in Figure 11-16.

Step 2 Choose the type of firewall that you want to create:

- **Basic Firewall**—Click this radio button if you want SDM to create a firewall using SDM default rules. This one-step firewall wizard configures only one outside interface and one or more inside interfaces. It does not support configuring a DMZ or custom inspection rules. The Use Case Scenario diagram represents a typical network configuration for this type of firewall. This is a basic firewall used in telecommuter or SOHO scenarios.

- **Advanced Firewall**—Click this radio button if you want SDM to lead you through the con-figuration of a firewall with a DMZ interface. This wizard allows you to configure the router to connect to the Internet and configure hosts off a DMZ interface to be accessible to outside users. This wizard also lets you specify an inspection rule for the firewall.

Step 3 Click **Launch the Selected Task**. The selected firewall wizard starts.

Figure 11-16 *Starting the Firewall Wizard*

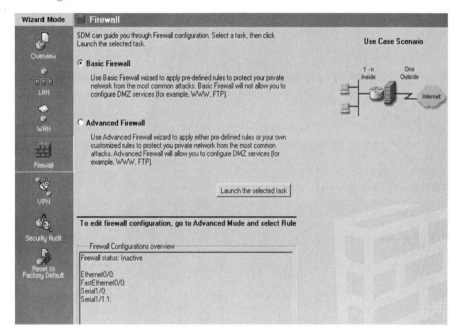

Creating a Basic Firewall

If you chose to create a basic firewall, the Basic Firewall Configuration Wizard starts and presents the Welcome to the One-Step Firewall Configuration Wizard window. This window is an informational window that describes the process that SDM will use to create your firewall.

SDM will apply a default inspection rule to the outbound direction of the outside interface, and apply necessary access rules to the inside/outside interfaces to protect your network. SDM performs three actions during the One-Step Firewall Configuration Wizard process:

- Applies access rules to the inside and outside interfaces.
- Applies inspection rules to the outside interface.
- Turns on IP unicast reverse-path forwarding on the outside interface.

Step 1 Click **Next**. The Basic Firewall Interface Configuration window opens.

Step 2 Specify the following:

- The outside (untrusted) interface is connected to the Internet or to your organization's WAN.

- The inside (trusted) interfaces connect to the LAN. You can select multiple interfaces.

NOTE When making firewall settings, keep in mind which interface you are using to access SDM through. If you select as the outside (untrusted) interface the interface through which you access SDM, it will cause you to lose your connection to SDM because it is now protected by a firewall. This means you will not be able to launch SDM from the outside interface after the Firewall Wizard completes. There is a warning window that reminds you of this possibility. If you should inadvertently lock yourself out, you will need to access the router using the console and modify the firewall access lists before you can log in to SDM again.

Step 3 Check the **Add Log Option to Anonymously Denied Access Rule Entries** radio button if you want to log all failed network access attempts caused by unauthorized users or protocols that are specified in the firewall access rules.

Step 4 Click **Next**. The One-Step Firewall Configuration Summary window opens.

The One-Step Firewall Configuration Summary window summarizes the firewall information. You can review the information and use the Back button to return to windows in the wizard to make changes.

SDM lists the router's interfaces that you designated as the interfaces in this wizard session, along with their IP addresses. SDM describes in descriptive sentences versus CLI syntax the access and inspection rules that will be associated with these interfaces if these changes are applied.

For the inside (trusted) interface(s), SDM will apply access rules with these characteristics:

- To the inbound direction to deny spoofing traffic.
- To the inbound direction to deny traffic sources from outside the trusted network.
- To the inbound direction to permit all other traffic.

For the outside (untrusted) interface(s), SDM will apply access rules with these characteristics:

- To the inbound direction to permit IPSec tunnel traffic.
- To the inbound direction to deny spoofing traffic.
- To the inbound direction to deny traffic sourced from any of the router's trusted networks.
- To the inbound direction to deny all other traffic.

Additional measures taken for the outside (untrusted) interface(s) include:

- Applying a default inspection rule to the outbound direction.
- Turning on unicast reverse path forwarding checking.

Step 5 Read the Firewall Wizard Summary window and determine whether the types of settings described are what you want.

NOTE   At the bottom of the window, you may also select to save the configuration to the router's startup configuration.

Step 6 Click **Finish**. The SDM Commands Delivery Status message box opens to display a running status of the process of configuring the firewall settings on your router.

NOTE   The SDM Preferences menu has a Preview option. If you select that option, the SDM Commands Delivery Status message box will display the commands that SDM is sending to the router's configuration.

Step 7 Click **OK** to complete the Firewall Wizard.

Building an Advanced Firewall

If you chose to create an advanced firewall, the Advanced Firewall Configuration Wizard starts and presents an informational window that describes the process that SDM will use to create your firewall.

The configuration tasks are very similar to the Basic Firewall Wizard configuration tasks, except that the wizard also offers configuration protection for a DMZ interface so that you can permit access to managed DMZ services from the Internet. Typical DMZ services include DNS servers, Internet web servers, FTP servers, and SMTP mail servers.

SDM performs three actions during the Advanced Firewall configuration process:

- Applies access rules to the inside (trusted), outside (untrusted), and DMZ interfaces.
- Applies inspection rules to the inside (trusted), outside (untrusted), and DMZ interfaces.
- Enables IP unicast reverse-path forwarding on the outside (untrusted) interfaces.

After reading the introductory information, continue with the following steps:

Step 1 Click **Next**. The Advanced Firewall Interface Configuration window opens.

Step 2 Specify the following:

- The outside (untrusted) interface is connected to the Internet or to your organization's WAN. You can select multiple interfaces.

NOTE	Be sure not to select the interface you use to access SDM as the outside (untrusted) interface, because you will not be able to use SDM through that interface once the firewall has been configured.

- The inside (trusted) interfaces connect to the LAN. You can select multiple interfaces.

- Select a DMZ interface.

Step 3 Click **Next**. The Advanced Firewall DMZ Service Configuration window opens.

Configuring DMZ Services

The Advanced Firewall DMZ Service Configuration window is shown in Figure 11-17.

Figure 11-17 *Configuring DMZ Services*

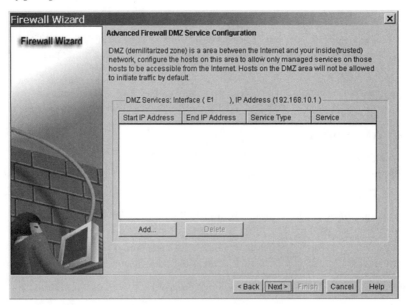

This window identifies which services inside the DMZ will be made available through the router's outside interfaces. You can add multiple hosts and services to this window.

Step 1 Click **Add**. The DMZ Service Configuration window opens, as shown in Figure 11-18.

Step 2 Configure the DMZ network hosts by specifying the address range with start and end IP addresses.

NOTE	To specify an individual host, just enter a start IP address with no end IP address.

Figure 11-18 *Configuring DMZ Services*

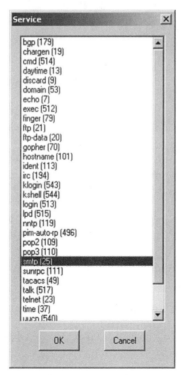

Step 3 Click either the **TCP** or **UDP** radio button.

Step 4 Click the **Service** button. The Service window opens, as shown in Figure 11-19.

Figure 11-19 *Identifying Hosts and Services*

Step 5 Select a service from the list and click **OK**. Figure 11-19 shows the selection of SMTP at port 25 as the service to permit.

Step 6 Repeat Steps 4 through 8 to add additional services to the DMZ service list.

Step 7 When you have finished adding services, click **Next**. The Internet Firewall Inspection Rule Configuration window opens.

Configuring Inspection Rules

CBAC inspection rules permit specific return traffic onto the network. These rules cause the router to examine outgoing packets for specified types of traffic. Traffic arriving at the outside interface is compared against the traffic types in the inspection rule, and is allowed onto the network if it is associated with a session that was started on the LAN and is also a type specified in the inspection rules.

You can use the SDM default inspection rule, as shown in Figure 11-20, which uses common traffic types and is defaulted to alert and to not log errors when this type of traffic is encountered.

Figure 11-20 *Default Inspection Rule*

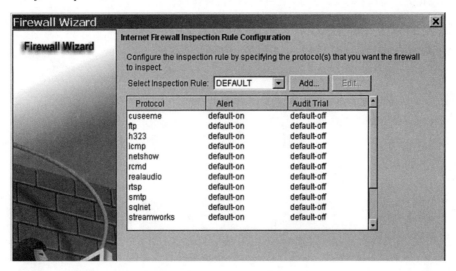

Step 1 Use the default SDM inspection rule or click **Add** to build a new inspection rule.

Step 2 Click **Next**. The Internet Firewall Configuration Summary window opens.

NOTE The Firewall Wizard takes into consideration any preexisting VPNs configured for the router. The Firewall Wizard will not create a rule that will block valid VPN users.

Step 3 Click **Finish**. The configuration changes are sent to the router.

The inspection rule is applied to the inside interface in the inbound direction and to the DMZ interface in the outbound direction. If you decide later to change the inspection rule, you can use the Advanced Mode rules option to make the changes.

Using SDM to Configure a VPN

You can let SDM guide you through a simple VPN configuration by using the VPN Wizard:

Step 1   Click **VPN** on the Wizard Mode category bar. The VPN Wizard main window opens, as shown in Figure 11-21.

Figure 11-21 *VPN Wizard*

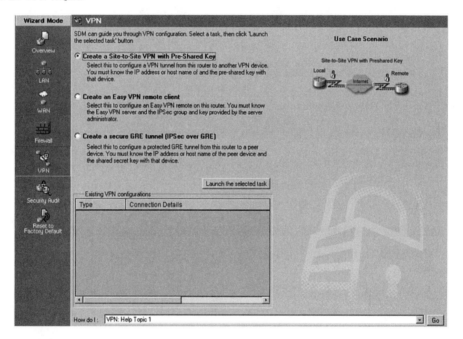

Step 2   Click one of the three VPN Wizard radio buttons:

- **Create a Site-to-Site VPN with Pre-Shared Key**—Creates a router-to-router VPN using pre-shared keys.

- **Create an Easy VPN Remote Client**—Configures the router's VPN client for connection to a VPN server (Easy VPN Remote Phase II support only).

- **Create a Secure GRE Tunnel (IPSec over GRE)**—Configures a protected GRE tunnel between this router and a peer system.

Step 3   Click **Launch the Selected Task**. The following steps will use the example of creating a site-to-site VPN with pre-shared keys. The Site-to-Site VPN with Pre-Shared Key window opens.

Creating a Site-To-Site VPN with Pre-Shared Key

You can choose to let SDM perform a Quick Setup or to open a Step-by-Step Wizard to configure the VPN.

Quick Setup uses SDM-generated defaults. Quick Setup uses a default Internet Key Exchange (IKE) policy for authentication, a default transform set to control the encryption of data, and a default IPSec rule that will encrypt all traffic between the router and the remote device. You can view the default IKE settings by selecting View Defaults.

The Step-by-Step Wizard provides more configuration flexibility. You can create IKE policies as part of this wizard.

Step 1 Click one of the two wizard option radio buttons:

- **Quick Setup**—Uses SDM-generated defaults.

- **Step by Step Wizard**—Allows you to create custom policies.

NOTE Quick Setup is best used when both the local and remote routers are Cisco routers using SDM.

Step 2 Click **Next**. The VPN Connection Information window opens, as shown in Figure 11-22.

Figure 11-22 *VPN Connection Configuration*

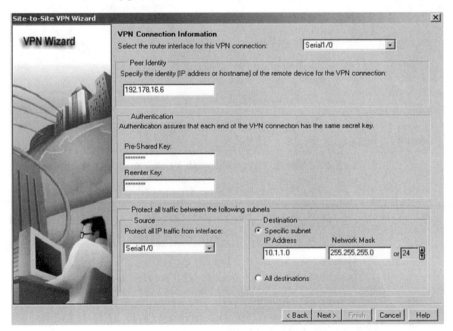

Step 3 Select from the drop-down list box the router interface used for the VPN connection.

Step 4 Enter the remote VPN router IP address or host name in the Peer Identity field.

Step 5 Enter a pre-shared key in the Pre-Shared Key field. Both sides must agree on the pre-shared key that is used to authenticate each other.

NOTE   The key can be up to 128 characters with any combination of letters and numbers, but question marks and spaces are not allowed. The key is displayed in asterisks to protect its secrecy.

Step 6 Reenter the pre-shared key in the Reenter Key field.

Step 7 Select the source (inside) interface that will be used for traffic on the VPN connection in the Protect All IP Traffic from Interface drop-down list box.

Step 8 Click one of the two destination radio buttons:

- **Specific Subnet**—Enables you to specify a remote subnet as the destination to enter the VPN tunnel.

    - Enter the IP address in the IP Address field.

    - Enter a network mask in the Network Mask field, or select a predefined mask using the list box.

- **All Destinations**—Permits all destinations to enter the VPN tunnel.

NOTE   SDM creates an access list that permits IP traffic between the source and destination as specified in this record.

Step 9 Click **Next**. The summary of the configuration window opens, where you can review the peer address, IKE policy, transform set, and IPSec rule before they are delivered to the router.

Step 10 Click **Finish** to deliver the configuration to the router. The SDM Commands Delivery Status window opens.

Step 11 Click **OK** when the OK button becomes active. The VPN Wizard main window appears, listing the new VPN configuration in the Existing VPN Configurations field.

Viewing or Changing VPN Settings

Use SDM Advanced Mode to view, add, or edit VPN rules, policies, and global settings.

You can also view the status of your interface by clicking **Interfaces and Connections**. If you highlight your VPN interface, SDM Advanced Mode will provide a summary of the entire configuration, including the IPSec policy number, assigned access list, and inspection rules.

Using SDM to Perform Security Audits

The SDM security audit feature compares router configurations to a predefined checklist of "best practices" using ICSA and Cisco TAC recommendations.

Examples of what the audit performs includes, but is not limited to, the following:

- Shuts down unneeded servers on the router (BOOTP, finger, and TCP/UDP small servers)
- Shuts down unneeded services on the router (CDP, IP source-route, and IP classless)
- Applies a firewall to the outside interfaces
- Disables Simple Network Management Protocol (SNMP) or enables it with hard-to-guess community strings
- Shuts down unused interfaces using **no ip proxy-arp**
- Forces passwords for the router console and vty lines
- Forces the use of an enable secret password
- Enforces the use of ACLs

Performing a Security Audit

Security Audit contains two modes:

- **Perform Security Audit**—Examines the router configuration and then displays the report card window, which shows a list of possible security problems. You can pick and choose which vulnerabilities you would like to lock down.
- **One-Step Lockdown**—Initiates the automatic lockdown using recommended settings.

Perform the following steps to perform a security audit:

Step 1 Click **Security Audit** on the Wizard Mode category bar to open the Security Audit welcome window, shown in Figure 11-23.

Step 2 Click one of the two available Security Audit Wizard buttons. In the example shown in Figure 11-23, the Perform Security Audit button is chosen. The Inside and Outside Interfaces dialog box opens.

Step 3 Identify the inside and outside interfaces from the list of available interfaces.

Step 4 Click **Next**. The Security Audit test window opens, as shown in Figure 11-24.

Figure 11-23 *Security Audit*

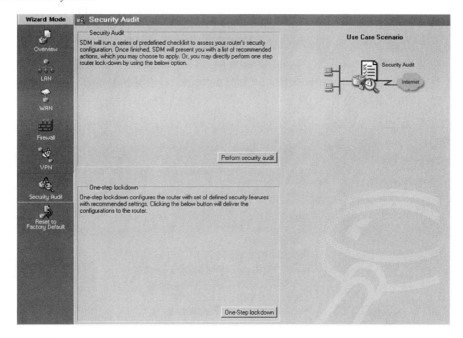

Figure 11-24 *Security Audit Tests*

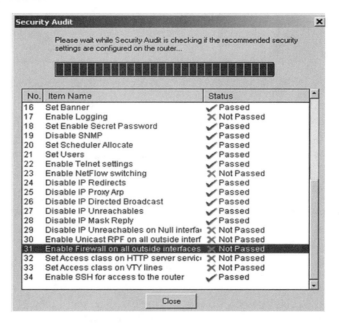

The Security Audit Wizard tests your router configuration to determine whether any security vulnerabilities exist. The Security Audit window, shown in Figure 11-24, shows each of the tests being performed and whether or not the router passed the test. Vulnerable items are marked with a red *X*.

Step 5   Click **Close**. The Security Audit report card window opens, as shown in Figure 11-25, presenting a list of potential security vulnerabilities found during the audit.

Figure 11-25 *Security Audit Report Card*

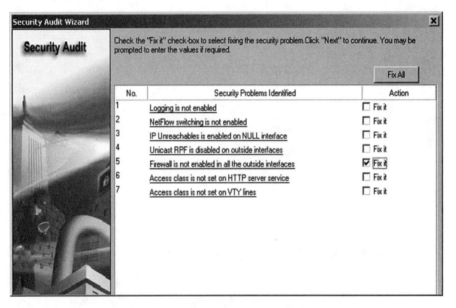

Step 6   Check the **Fix It** check box next to each problem that you want SDM to fix.

NOTE   For a description of the problem and a list of the Cisco IOS commands that will be added to your configuration, click the problem description hyperlinks. A help page describing the selected problem will open.

Step 7   Click **Next**. Additional windows may appear requiring your input, such as a password.

NOTE   You can also click Fix All to automatically secure all vulnerabilities found with a "best practice" solution.

Pay special attention to any warning messages that appear. Make sure that you do not "fix" a potential security breach and lock yourself out of the router, too. Upon completion of all configuration fixes, the Security Audit Summary window opens.

Step 8 Review the changes that will be delivered to the router.

Step 9 Click **Finish**. The changes are sent to the router.

One-Step Lockdown

Choosing the One-Step lockdown button from the screen, shown in Figure 11-23, initiates a wizard that provides an easy one-step router lockdown for many security features.

This option tests your router configuration for any potential security problems and automatically makes any necessary configuration changes to correct any problems found. The conditions checked for and, if needed, corrected are as follows (a partial list of these conditions is shown in Figure 11-24):

- Disable Finger Service
- Disable Packet Assembler/Disassembler (PAD) Service
- Disable TCP Small Servers Service
- Disable UDP Small Servers Service
- Disable IP BOOTP Server Service
- Disable IP Identification Service
- Disable CDP
- Disable IP Source Route
- Enable Password Encryption Service
- Enable TCP Keepalives for Inbound Telnet Sessions
- Enable TCP Keepalives for Outbound Telnet Sessions
- Enable Sequence Numbers and Time Stamps on Debugs
- Enable IP Cisco Express Forwarding (CEF)
- Disable IP Gratuitous Address Resolution Protocols (ARPs)
- Set Minimum Password Length to Less Than 6 Characters
- Set Authentication Failure Rate to Less Than 3 Retries
- Set TCP Synwait Time
- Set Banner
- Enable Logging
- Set Enable Secret Password
- Disable SNMP
- Set Scheduler Interval
- Set Scheduler Allocate

- Set Users
- Enable Telnet Settings
- Enable NetFlow Switching
- Disable IP Redirects
- Disable IP Proxy ARP
- Disable IP Directed Broadcast
- Disable MOP Service
- Disable IP Unreachables
- Disable IP Mask Reply
- Disable IP Unreachables on Null Interface
- Enable Unicast Reverse Path Forwarding (RPF) on Outside Interfaces
- Enable Firewall on All of the Outside Interfaces
- Set Access Class on HTTP Server Service
- Set Access Class on Virtual Type Terminal (VTY) Lines
- Enable SSH for Access to the Router

The One-Step Lockdown process will present a warning window saying:

```
"This will lock down your router. If you later want to undo some of the settings,
you will need to go to System Properties in Advanced Mode. Are you sure?"
```

Clicking Yes to the question begins the lockdown process. There are no additional windows for this process. SDM does everything automatically for you.

NOTE Remember that you can use the Advanced Mode—System Properties function to undo specific settings.

Using the Factory Reset Wizard

You can reset your Cisco router to the factory defaults by using the SDM Reset to Factory Default Wizard.

Access the wizard by clicking **Reset to Factory Default** on the Wizard Mode category bar. The Reset to Factory Default Wizard window opens.

This wizard contains two steps:

- **Save Running Config to PC**—This function copies the router running configuration to the SDM host PC. SDM verifies that this step is completed before allowing you to continue with the reset (or erase) procedure.
- **Reset Router**—Performs the actual reset procedure.

Step 1   Click **Save Running Config to PC**. SDM prompts you to select a directory
on your local PC where it will store the configuration file.

NOTE   Before you proceed with Step 2, make sure that you understand how to
reconnect to your router following the reset procedure. The wizard
window gives the following steps for reconnecting after reset:

   1   Configure the PC with the static IP address **10.10.10.2** and the
       subnet mask **255.255.255.0**.

   2   Point your web browser to **http(s)://10.10.10.1/flash/sdm.shtml**.

   3   Log in to SDM again, using the username **sdm**, and the password **sdm**.

   Write down these instructions, or print them for later reference.

Step 2   Click **Reset Router**. You will lose your connection to SDM. Wait a few
minutes while the router resets and then reloads with the default settings.

Now you may reconnect SDM to the router by using the router's lowest-numbered LAN
interface.

Using SDM Advanced Mode

SDM Advanced Mode, which is accessed by clicking the corresponding icon on the SDM
toolbar, is designed for more experienced users who prefer to jump to desired configuration
functions rather than use the wizards.

This is also where you can edit, add, or delete configuration settings that were specified when
using any of the wizards identified in the previous sections of this chapter.

A selection of areas of interest displays in the Advanced Mode category bar to the left of
the window. You can jump to any of the following configuration areas by clicking the appropriate icon:

- Overview
- Interfaces and Connections
- Rules
- Routing
- NAT
- System Properties
- VPN

Advanced Mode—Overview

The first Advanced Mode page is the Overview page, shown in Figure 11-26, which displays basic information about your router hardware, software versions, and some high-level configuration information.

Figure 11-26 *Advanced Mode Overview Window*

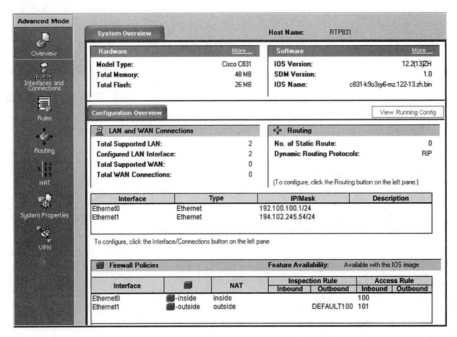

The Overview page in Advanced Mode shows more detailed configuration information than does the Overview page in Wizard Mode. This page contains the following information:

- **System Overview**—Contains the following information:
  - **Host Name**—The configured name of the router.
  - **Hardware Group**—Shows basic information about your router hardware, and contains the following fields and link:
    - **Model Type**—Shows the router model number.
    - **Total Memory**—Shows the amount of RAM installed on the router.
    - **Total Flash**—Shows the amount of Flash Memory installed on the router.
    - **More**—Click this link to display additional information about the hardware.
  - **Software Group**—Shows basic information about the software running on the router, and contains the following fields and link:
    - **IOS Version**—The version of Cisco IOS software currently running on the router.

- **SDM Version**—The version of Cisco SDM software currently running on the router.

- **IOS Name**—The filename of the Cisco IOS software currently running.

- **More**—Click this link to display detailed information about the Cisco IOS image that is running on the router.

- **Configuration Overview**—Contains the following information:

  - **View Running Config**—Click this link to view the configuration the router is using.

  - **LAN and WAN Connections Group**—Shows information about the LANs configured on your router, and contains the following fields:

    - **Total Supported LAN**—The total number of LAN interfaces that are present in the router.

    - **Configured LAN Interfaces**—The number of supported LAN interfaces currently configured on the router.

    - **Total Supported WAN**—The number of SDM-supported WAN interfaces that are present on the router.

    - **Total WAN Connections**—The total number of SDM-supported WAN connections that are present on the router.

  - **Routing Group**—Shows basic information about the routing configuration, and contains the following fields:

    - **No. of Static Route**—The number of static routes configured on the router.

    - **Dynamic Routing Protocols**—Lists any dynamic routing protocols that are configured on the router.

  - **Interface Table**—Shows a list of all the interfaces installed on the router, with each interface shown as one row in the table. This table contains the following fields:

    - **Interface**—The interface name.

    - **Type**—The type of network interface.

    - **IP/Mask**—The IP address and subnet mask of the interface.

    - **Description**—The description of the interface as entered during configuration. If no description has been entered, indicate whether the interface connects inside or outside your local network.

- **Firewall Policies Group**—Shows information about the firewall configured on the router, and contains the following fields:

  - **Feature Availability**—Indicates whether or not the Cisco IOS software that you are currently running on the router contains the Cisco IOS Firewall feature set.

— **Firewall Policies Table**—Shows a list of all the interfaces installed on the router, with each interface shown as one row in the table, and shows the firewall policies configured for each interface. This table contains the following fields:

- **Interface**—The interface name.
- **Brick-wall icon**—Appears if a firewall is currently configured on the interface.
- **NAT**—Indicates whether or not NAT is configured on the interface and, if it is, whether it is configured for inbound or outbound traffic on the interface.
- **Inspection Rule**—Lists the name of any rule that inspects either inbound or outbound traffic.
- **Access Rule**—Lists the name or number of any ACL that filters either inbound or outbound traffic.

Advanced Mode—Interfaces and Connections

Clicking the Interfaces and Connections icon on the Advanced Mode category bar opens the Interfaces and Connections window, shown in Figure 11-27.

Figure 11-27 *Advanced Mode Interfaces and Connections Window*

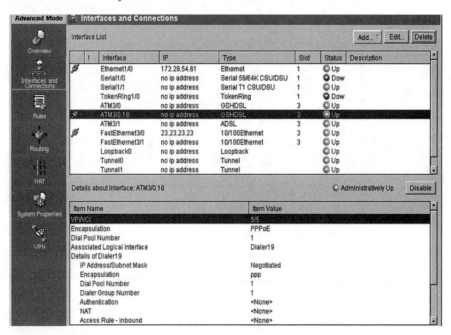

The upper portion of the window shows logical and physical interfaces that are present in the router, giving details about the interface name, IP address, interface type, and the physical slot the interface occupies. It also shows the current status of the interfaces as Up (green) or Down (red).

NOTE   The status for an interface could also be Wait (yellow), meaning that a connection for this interface has been configured but not yet delivered to the router. This could occur when another administrator is making a configuration change while you are viewing the Interfaces and Connections window.

The buttons in the top portion of the window enable you to add new interfaces, edit existing interfaces, or delete logical interfaces.

The lower portion of the window shows details about the selected interface (NAT, ACL, crypto associations, and so on). You can toggle the interface states by administratively disabling and reenabling them using the Disable/Enable button.

Advanced Mode—Rules

Clicking the Rules icon on the Advanced Mode category bar opens the Rules window, shown in Figure 11-28, where you define how the router should behave when it encounters a particular kind of traffic.

Figure 11-28 *Advanced Mode Rules Window*

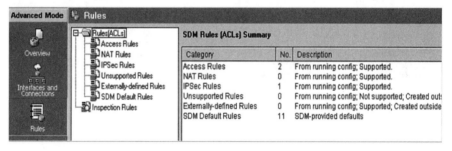

SDM provides default rules that are used in the wizards. You can create custom rules, which can also be used in the wizards or in Advanced Mode configurations.

The different types of rules include the following:

- **Access Rules**—Specify the traffic that can enter and leave the network. These rules include both standard and extended ACLs.

- **NAT Rules**—Determine how private IP addresses are translated into valid Internet IP addresses.

- **IPSec Rules**—Determine which traffic will be encrypted on secure connections.

- **Unsupported Rules**—Rules that were not created using SDM and are not supported by SDM. These rules are read-only and cannot be modified using SDM. You must use the CLI to edit these rules directly.

- **Externally-Defined Rules**—Rules that were not created using SDM but are supported by SDM. These rules cannot be assigned to a router interface using SDM. You must use the CLI to assign these rules to router interfaces.

- **SDM Default Rules**—Rules that are predefined in the SDM software and can be applied in both Wizard Mode and Advanced Mode.

- **Inspection Rules**—CBAC firewall inspection rules.

Use the online help to learn how to use SDM to configure these rules. It is assumed that you have a basic understanding of these common rules before you alter them in Advanced Mode.

Advanced Mode—Routing

Clicking the Routing icon on the Advanced Mode category bar opens the Routing window, shown in Figure 11-29, where you configure static routes and dynamic routing (including RIP, OSPF, and EIGRP routes).

Figure 11-29 *Advanced Mode Routing Window*

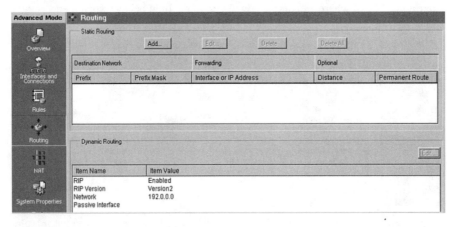

From this window, you can review the routes, add new routes, edit existing routes, and delete routes.

NOTE   Routing can be configured only in Advanced Mode.

The Static Routing section of the Routing window contains the following sections:

- **Destination Network**—This is the network to which the static route provides a path. This portion of a static route is identified by a network prefix and prefix mask.

- **Forwarding**—This is the interface or IP address through which packets must be sent to reach the destination network.

- **Optional**—This area shows whether a distance metric has been entered, and whether or not the route has been designated as a permanent route.

NOTE   If SDM detects a previously configured static route entry that has the next-hop interface configured as the "Null" interface, then the static route entry will be read-only. In addition, if SDM detects a previously configured static route entry with "tag" or "name" options, that entry will be read-only. Read-only entries cannot be edited or deleted using SDM.

The Dynamic Routing section of the Routing window allows you to configure RIP, OSPF, and EIGRP dynamic routes. This section displays item names and item values for the various parameters associated with each routing protocol enabled on the router. You can add, edit, or delete any of the three allowable dynamic routing protocols from this window.

Advanced Mode—NAT

Clicking the NAT icon on the Advanced Mode category bar opens the NAT window, shown in Figure 11-30, which lets you view NAT rules, designate interfaces as inside or outside, view address pools, and set translation timeouts.

Figure 11-30 *Advanced Mode NAT Window*

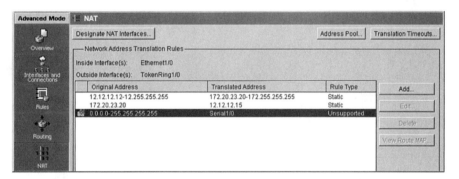

The NAT main page shows a list of all the translation rules. You can create, modify, and delete NAT rules using this page. Rules that are not supported by SDM are marked as read-only with a special icon, as shown in Figure 11-30. These rules were created using the CLI.

Click **Designate NAT Interfaces** to designate the inside and outside interfaces that you want to use for NAT translations. NAT uses the inside/outside designations as reference points when interpreting translation rules. Inside interfaces are those interfaces connected to private networks. Outside interfaces connect to the WAN or to the Internet. The designated inside and outside interfaces are listed above the NAT rule list.

Click **Address Pool** to configure or edit address pools. Address pools are used with dynamic address translation. The router can dynamically assign addresses from the pool as they are needed. When an address is no longer needed, it is returned to the pool.

Click **Translation Timeouts** to configure the timeout values for NAT translation entries and other values. When dynamic NAT is configured, translation entries have a timeout period after which they expire and are purged from the translation table.

Advanced Mode—System Properties

Clicking the System Properties icon on the Advanced Mode category bar opens the System Properties window, shown in Figure 11-31, which enables you to define the overall attributes of the router, such as the router name, domain name, password, SNMP status, DNS server address, user accounts, router log attributes, vty settings, SSH settings, and other router access security settings.

Figure 11-31 *Advanced Mode System Properties Window*

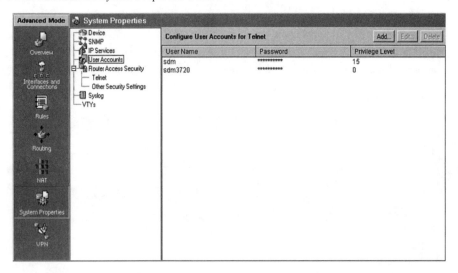

The System Properties window lets you configure the following properties:

- **Device**—Contains the following tabs:
  - **Device Name**—Contains the following fields:
    - **Host**—Enter the router's name.
    - **Domain**—Enter the domain name for your organization.
    - **Enter the New Text Banner**—Enter text for the router banner.

- **Password**—Contains the following fields:
  - **Enable Secret Password**—Enter the enable secret password used for router administration.
  - **Current Password**—If a password has already been set, this area contains asterisks (*).
  - **Enter New Password**—Enter the new enable password in this field.
  - **Reenter New Password**—Reenter the password exactly as you entered it in the Enter New Password field.
- **SNMP**—Contains the following fields:
  - **Enable SNMP**—Check this box to enable SNMP support. Uncheck this box to disable SNMP support. SNMP is enabled by default.
  - **Community String**—The community string table lists all the configured community strings and their types.
  - **Trap Receiver**—Enter the IP addresses and community strings of the hosts where trap information should be sent.
  - **SNMP Server Location**—Enter the SNMP server location. This field is a notation field and does not affect the SNMP configuration.
  - **SNMP Server Contact**—Enter contact information for a person managing the SNMP server. This field is a notation field and does not affect the SNMP configuration.
- **IP Services**—Use this window to enable the use of DNS servers for host name to address translation. This section contains the following fields:
  - **Enable DNS-based Hostname to Address Translation**—Check this box to enable the router to use DNS. Uncheck this box if you do not want to use DNS.
  - **DNS IP Address**—Enter the IP addresses of the DNS servers that you want the router to send DNS requests to.
- **User Accounts**—Contains the following fields:
  - **User Name**—A user account name for HTTP, HTTPS, Telnet, PPP, or other types of access to the router.
  - **Password**—The user account password, displayed as asterisks (*).
  - **Privilege Level**—Administrative level this user is permitted to access.

NOTE   The user password is not the same as the enable secret password configured in the System Properties Password window. The user password enables the specified user to log on to the router and enter a limited set of commands.

- **Other Security Settings**—The parameter settings for the router security configurations contain the following fields:
    - **Variable**—The configuration item, such as CDP and TCP SYN wait time.
    - **Value**—The configuration value for that parameter.
- **Syslog**—Syslog configuration fields include the following:
    - **Logging IP Address/Hostname**—Click Add and enter the IP address or host name of a network host to which you want the router to send logging messages for storage.
    - **Logging to Buffer**—If you want system messages to be logged to the router's buffer, enter the buffer size in this field.
- **VTYs**—Contains the following vty configuration fields:
    - **Line Range**—Displays the range of vty connections to which the rest of the settings in the row apply.
    - **Input Protocols Allowed**—Shows the protocols configured for input. Can be Telnet, SSH, or both Telnet and SSH.
    - **Output Protocols Allowed**—Shows the protocols configured for output. Can be Telnet, SSH, or both Telnet and SSH.
    - **EXEC Timeout**—The number of seconds of inactivity after which a session will be terminated.
    - **Inbound Access-Class**—The name or number of the access rule applied to the inbound direction of the line range.
    - **Outbound Access-Class**—The name or number of the access rule applied to the outbound direction of the line range.
    - **ACL**—If configured, shows the ACL associated with the vty connections.

NOTE   To use SSH as an input or output protocol, you must enable it by clicking SSH in the System Properties tree and generating a RSA key.

Advanced Mode—VPN

Clicking the VPN icon on the Advanced Mode category bar opens the VPN window, shown in Figure 11-32 with an IKE Policies window open.

The VPN window is used to configure IPSec policies and IKE policies and to assign global settings such as IKE keepalives and IPSec security association (SA) lifetime settings.

Figure 11-32 *Advanced Mode VPN Window*

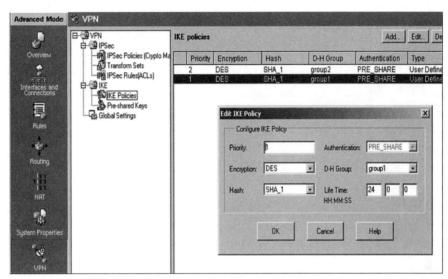

An example of how to edit an IKE policy is shown below, using Figure 11-32 as a reference:

Step 1 Expand the VPN tab (press the + key).

Step 2 Click the IKE Policies tab.

Step 3 Select the policy you want to edit from the list.

Step 4 Click the **Edit** button. The Edit IKE Policy window opens.

Step 5 Make modifications to the policy.

Step 6 Click **OK**.

NOTE   Whenever you make a change in Advanced Mode, the configuration changes are not made
to the router until you click the Deliver button. Only after the delivery function is complete
will the configuration changes reside in the router running configuration.

Understanding Monitor Mode

The Monitor Mode window, shown in Figure 11-33, is accessed by clicking the Monitor Mode
button on the SDM toolbar.

Monitor Mode lets you view information about your router, the router interfaces, the firewall,
and any active VPN connections. You can also view any messages in the router event log.

Figure 11-33 *Viewing Monitor Mode*

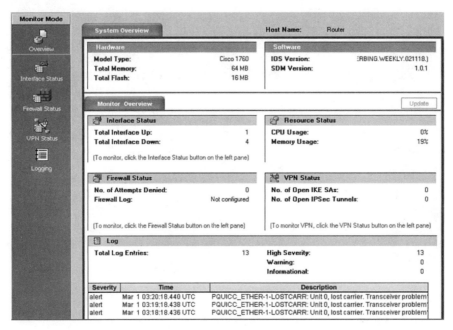

Monitor Mode includes the following elements, which are accessed through its category bar:

- **Overview**—Displays the router status, including a list of the error log entries.

- **Interface Status**—Used to select the interface to monitor and the conditions (for example, packets and errors, in or out) to view.

- **Firewall Status**—Displays a log showing the number of entry attempts that were denied by the firewall.

- **VPN Status**—Displays statistics about active VPN connections on the router.

- **Logging**—Displays an event log categorized by severity level.

Chapter Summary

The following list summarizes what you have learned in this chapter:

- Cisco SDM is a useful tool for configuring Cisco access routers.

- SDM contains several easy-to-use wizards for efficient configuration of Cisco access routers.

- SDM allows you to customize Cisco access router configurations using advanced features.

Cisco IOS Commands Presented in This Chapter

Many Cisco IOS version 12.3 commands were discussed or referenced in this chapter. These commands can be found in the *Command Reference* online at http://www.cisco.com/univercd /cc/td/doc/product/software/ios123/123mindx/crgindx.htm.

You can find additional information on the Security Device Manager at Cisco.com.

Chapter Review Questions

The following review questions cover some of the key facts and concepts that were introduced in this chapter. Answers to these questions can be found in Appendix A, "Answers to Chapter Review Questions."

1   What is the suggested workflow presented by SDM to help guide untrained users through an initial router configuration?

2   Which router platforms support SDM?

3   Where is the SDM application installed so that it can be accessed from a supported web browser?

4   When using SDM for the first time, what is the default administrative username and password?

5   During initial router configuration using the SDM Startup Wizard, what are the default security configuration settings?

6   When you open the Wizard Mode window, you are presented with an overview of the router features and configuration. What actual configuration wizards are available from the Wizard Mode window?

7   What types of serial interface encapsulation can be configured using the SDM WAN Wizard?

8   Once you have configured router settings using one of the wizards, what SDM feature would you use to modify or remove those configuration settings?

9   Why might you choose to run the Security Audit Wizard instead of the One-Step Security Lockdown Wizard?

10   What elements are monitored with SDM Monitor Mode?

Case Study

The Future Corporation's network structure is shown in Figure 11-34.

Scenario

As The Future Corporation's network administrator, you are replacing the WacoR1 1721 router in the Waco office with a new 1760 router running Cisco IOS Release 12.3(1)M. SDM was already installed on the router when you received it.

Figure 11-34 *The Future Corporation*

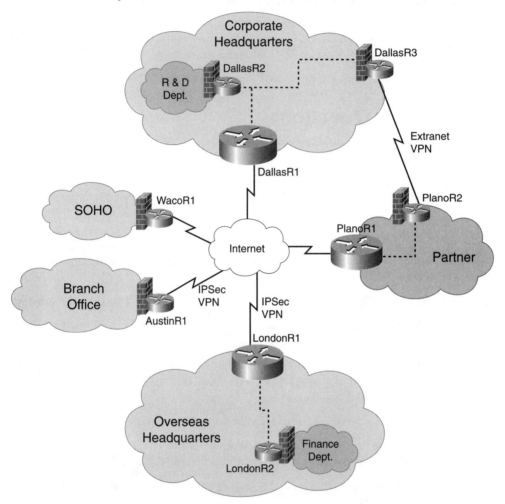

The external serial 1/0 interface will have an IP address of 193.122.19.82 using a subnet mask of 255.255.255.0. The internal Fast Ethernet 0/0 interface will have an IP address of 192.168.20.1 using a subnet mask of 255.255.255.0. The DNS server is at IP address 203.14.17.13.

Perform all the steps required to use the SDM Startup Wizard to perform an initial configuration of the router. Use SDMFCAdmin and SDMFCPass as the new SDM administrator account and password.

Solutions

The following is the list of steps required to configure router WacoR1 using the SDM Startup Wizard:

Step 1 Connect a PC to Fast Ethernet port 0/0 using a crossover cable.

Step 2   Assign a static IP address of **10.10.10.2** with a **255.255.255.0** subnet mask to the PC.

Step 3   Launch a supported browser.

Step 4   Use URL **https://10.10.10.1/flash/sdm.shtml**.

Step 5   Log in using the default username of **sdm** with a password of **sdm**.

Step 6   Click **Next** to open the Basic Configuration window.

Step 7   Enter **WacoR1** in the Host Name field.

Step 8   Enter **FutureCorp.com** in the Domain Name field.

Step 9   Enter **BlueH20** in the Enter New Password field.

Step 10   Enter **BlueH20**, once more, in the Re-Enter New Password field.

Step 11   Click **Next** to open the Change Default Username and Password window.

Step 12   Enter **SDMFCAdmin** in the Enter New User Name field.

Step 13   Enter **SDMFCPass** in the Enter New Password field.

Step 14   Enter **SDMFCPass**, once more, in the Re-Enter New Password field.

Step 15   Click **Next** to open the LAN Interface Configuration.

Step 16   Enter **192.168.20.1** in the IP Address field.

Step 17   Enter **255.255.255.0** in the Subnet Mask field.

Step 18   Click **Next** to open the DHCP Server Configuration window.

Step 19   Check the **Enable DHCP Server on LAN Interface** check box.

Step 20   Enter **192.168.20.2** in the Start IP Address field.

Step 21   Enter **192.168.20.100** in the End IP Address field.

Step 22   Click **Next** to open the Domain Name Server window.

Step 23   Enter **203.14.17.13** in the Primary DNS field.

Step 24   Click **Next** to open the Security Configuration window.

Step 25   Check all five check boxes.

Step 26   Click **Next** to open the Wizard Summary window.

Step 27   Review the contents of the Summary window.

Step 28   Click **Next** to open the Startup Wizard Completed window.

Step 29   Click **Finish** to deliver the configuration to the router's Flash Memory.

Step 30   Click **OK** to shut down SDM and terminate the connection.

Upon completion of this chapter, you will be able to perform the following tasks:

- Define Key Features and Concepts of Router MC
- Install Router MC
- Import and Manage Router Policies
- Configure Cisco IOS VPN Policies
- Deploy Cisco IOS VPN Policies
- Configure Cisco IOS Firewall Policies
- Deploy Cisco IOS Firewall Policies

CHAPTER 12

Managing Enterprise VPN Routers

This chapter introduces and explains Management Center for VPN Routers (Router MC) release 1.2.1. The following topics are covered in this chapter:

- Introducing Router MC 1.2.1
- Installing Router MC
- Using Router MC
- Creating workflows and activities
- Configuring general Cisco IOS Firewall settings
- Building access rules
- Using building blocks
- Using upload

Router MC 1.2.1 Introduction

Router MC is a web-based application that is designed for large-scale management of VPN and firewall configurations on Cisco routers. Figure 12-1 shows a typical Router MC installation.

Figure 12-1 *Network Management with Router MC*

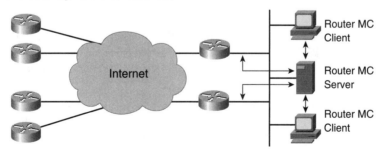

Router MC 1.2.1 enables you to do the following:

- Set up and maintain VPN connections among multiple Cisco VPN routers, in a hub-and-spoke topology.

- Provision the critical connectivity, security, and performance parameters of a site-to-site VPN, quickly and easily.

- Efficiently migrate from leased-line connections to Internet or intranet-based VPN connections.

- Overlay a VPN over a Frame Relay network for added security.

- Configure Cisco IOS routers to function as firewalls.

Router MC is scalable to a large number of routers. Its hierarchical router grouping and policy inheritance features enable the configuration of multiple like routers simultaneously, instead of having to configure each router individually. Router MC enables deployment of VPN or firewall configurations to groups of routers or individual routers. It translates the configurations into CLI commands and deploys them either directly to the routers in the network or to a configuration file for each router. It also uses reusable policy components that can be referenced across multiple connections.

Understanding Router MC Concepts

The following topics are key concepts in Router MC:

- **Hub-and-spoke topology**—In a hub-and-spoke VPN topology, multiple remote devices (spokes) communicate securely with a central device (hub). A separate, secured tunnel extends between the centralized hub and each of the individual spokes.

- **VPN settings and policies**—In Router MC, VPN configurations are divided into the following:

  - **VPN settings**—VPN configurations that provide a framework for network behavior and VPN policy implementation. Settings include selection of a failover method and routing protocol, packet fragmentation settings, specification of internal networks and inside interfaces for hubs and spokes, and hub assignment for spokes.

  - **IKE policies**—Define the combination of security parameters to be used during IKE negotiation between two IPSec peers, including the encryption and authentication algorithms, the Diffie-Hellman (DH) group identifier, and the lifetime of the security association (SA).

  - **Tunnel policies**—Define what data will be securely transmitted via the tunnel (crypto ACL) and which authentication and encryption algorithms will be applied to the data to ensure its authenticity, integrity, and confidentiality (transform set).

NOTE	In Router MC, tunnel policies are defined on spokes. Router MC generates the relevant CLI commands for the spoke and also automatically adds matching policies on the spoke's corresponding hub so that the VPN connection between the peers can be established. As long as you always deploy to both peers of the VPN connection together, Router MC will ensure compatible policy configuration.

- **Transform sets**—A combination of security protocols, algorithms, and other settings that specify exactly how the data in the IPSec tunnel will be encrypted and authenticated.
- **Network groups**—Named collections of networks and/or hosts. A network group name can be referenced during the definition of VPN settings and policies, instead of having to specify each network or host individually for each policy definition.
- **Network Address Translation (NAT) policies**—Enable the devices in the secured private network to access outside networks for nonconfidential purposes without monopolizing the resources required for VPN connections.

- **Device hierarchy and inheritance**—Router MC provides a default two-level device hierarchy in which all devices are contained within a global group. Router MC allows you to create device groups to facilitate efficient management of a large number of devices by enabling you to define VPN configurations on multiple devices simultaneously, rather than having to configure each device individually.

Policy inheritance in the device hierarchy is implemented in a top-down fashion. The global group is the highest-level object.

- All devices in the device inventory inherit VPN configurations defined on the global level.
- All the groups and devices contained within the groups inherit VPN configurations defined on a device group, and override any global configurations for those devices.
- VPN configurations defined on an individual device apply to that device only, and override any configurations inherited from global or group configurations.

- **Activities**—Activities are temporary proposals used to change or create VPN configurations on specific devices. The activity must be approved before its configuration changes are committed to the Router MC database, at which point they are ready for deployment to the relevant devices or files.

Before you make any configuration changes, you must create a new activity or open an existing activity. An activity can be opened by only one person at a time but can be accessed by several people in sequence; therefore, before the activity is approved, another user can open it and make further configuration changes to the selected objects.

- **Jobs**—A job is a deployment task in which you specify the devices to which VPN configurations should be deployed. Router MC generates the CLI commands for the devices specified in the job, based on the VPN policies you defined. These commands can be previewed before deployment takes place. Within the context of the job, you can specify whether to deploy the commands directly to the devices in the network or to a file.

- **Building blocks**—Building blocks in Router MC refer to network groups and transform sets. Building blocks are reusable, named, global components that can be referenced by multiple policies. When referenced, a building block is incorporated as an integral component of the policy. If you change the definition of a building block, this change is reflected in all policies that reference that building block.

  Building blocks aid in policy definition by eliminating the need to define that component each time a policy is defined. For example, although transform sets are integral to tunnel policies, you can define several transform sets independently of the tunnel policy definitions. These transform sets are always available for selection when creating tunnel policies, on the object on which you defined them and its descendants.

- **Device import**—In Router MC, importing devices means bringing information about the devices you want to manage into the device inventory. Router MC imports devices either by querying the physical devices for information or by reading device information from a file or multiple files in a specified directory on the server. Devices can be imported individually or in groups.

- **Upload of existing VPN configurations**—Upload refers to the process of transferring into Router MC VPN settings and policies that were previously configured on a device. This means that you do not have to redefine all the VPN configurations when using Router MC to manage the VPN, or when copying VPN settings or policies from one device to other devices.

  Router MC supports only the upload of VPN configurations that are not peer-specific. These include transform sets, pre-shared keys, dynamic pre-shared keys, certificate authority (CA) policies, routing policies, and Internet Key Exchange (IKE) policies.

- **Predefined device groups and policies**—Router MC provides predefined device groups, IKE policies, and transform sets that you can use if they meet your requirements. Their purpose is to save time and help you get up and running quickly with Router MC.

  The predefined device groups are device type specific, as reflected in their names. They are contained in the device hierarchy, under the global group. VPN settings and policies have been predefined on the device groups so that you can simply import devices into the group and they will inherit the policies defined on the group level.

  The predefined IKE policy and transform sets are defined on the global level and are available for selection when configuring any device groups or devices.

Router MC Components

Router MC is integrated with CiscoWorks Common Services, which supplies core server-side components that are required by Router MC, such as Apache Web server, Secure Sockets Layer (SSL) libraries, Secure Shell (SSH) libraries, embedded SQL database, Tomcat servlet engine, the CiscoWorks desktop, and others.

Before installing Router MC 1.2.1, you must ensure that CiscoWorks Common Services 2.2 is installed and operational. CiscoWorks Common Services provides centralized management of certain functions for all the CiscoWorks VPN/Security Management Solution (VMS) products that you have installed. These functions include:

- Backing up and restoring data
- Integration with Access Control Server (ACS) or Common Management Framework (CMF) for user authentication and permissions
- Licensing
- Starting/stopping the database
- Logging of administration tasks

NOTE   These functions are not performed from within the Router MC user interface, but are accessed using the CiscoWorks user interface.

Once you have installed CiscoWorks Common Services 2.2, you may install the Router MC 1.2.1 VMS module and other modules, such as CiscoWorks Management Center for Firewalls (Firewall MC), CiscoWorks Management Center for IDS Sensors (IDS MC), and CiscoWorks Management Center for Cisco Security Agents (CSA MC).

Router MC 1.2.1 Supported Devices

Table 12-1 provides information about the Cisco IOS routers and minimum Cisco IOS software versions supported by Router MC 1.2.1. Support for additional routers and Cisco IOS software releases might be added at a later stage. You can find information about new router support at Cisco.com.

NOTE   Table 12-1 shows the minimum Cisco IOS software release supported by Router MC on a given router. However, to take advantage of the latest IPSec features, Cisco IOS Software Release 12.2 or later is recommended. In order for routers to support Dynamic Multipoint VPN (DMVPN) configuration, as provided by Router MC 1.2, the minimum Cisco IOS software requirements are higher. As displayed in the table, Cisco IOS Software Release 12.2(13)T or later is required for all router types, except for the 83*x* router family, which requires Cisco IOS Software Release 12.2(13)ZH.

Table 12-1   *Supported Router Types and Cisco IOS Software Releases*

Router Type	Minimum Cisco IOS Release	Minimum Cisco IOS Release (DMVPN Support)
1710, 1720, 1721, 1750, 1751, and 1760 (spoke)	12.2	12.2(13)T and above
XM series: 2610, 2611, 2620, 2621, 2650, and 2651	12.2	12.2(13)T and above
2691	12.2	12.2(13)T and above
3620, 3640, and 3660 (hub)	12.2	12.2(13)T and above
3620, 3640, and 3660 (spoke)	12.2	12.2(13)T and above
3725 and 3745	12.2	12.2(13)T and above
C7400 (hub)	12.1(9)YE	12.2(13)T and above
C7100 and C7200 (hub)	12.1(9)E	12.2(13)T and above
71*xx*, 72*xx*, and 74*xx* (spoke)	12.1(9)E	12.2(13)T and above
803 (spoke)	12.2	
806 (spoke)	12.2	
826, 827, and 828 (spoke)	12.2	
831, 836, and 837		12.2(13)ZH
C6sup2_rp (Catalyst 6500 with VPN Services Module) (hub)	12.2(9)YO1	

Router MC Communications

Router MC communications are handled by both SSL and SSH, as shown in Figure 12-2.

Figure 12-2 *Router MC Communications*

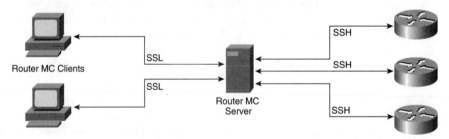

This ensures that the information passed between the Router MC components is secure. SSL processes all communications between the Router MC server and the Router MC clients. SSH processes all communications between the Router MC server and the managed Cisco routers.

NOTE	You must configure SSH on your Cisco routers before attempting to manage them using Router MC.

Supported Tunnel Technologies

Router MC supports the following tunneling technologies:

- **IPSec**—IPSec is a framework of open standards that provides data confidentiality, data integrity, and data origin authentication between peers that are connected over unprotected networks, such as the Internet.

- **IPSec with generic routing encapsulation (GRE)**—GRE is a tunneling protocol that can encapsulate a variety of protocol packet types inside IP tunnels, creating a virtual point-to-point link to devices at remote points over an IP internetwork.

- **IPSec with GRE over a Frame Relay network**—This option provides all the advantages of using IPSec with GRE and the ability to create secure VPN tunnels over a Frame Relay network. Router MC supports a Frame Relay topology in which the hub acts only as a VPN endpoint, while each spoke acts as both a VPN endpoint and a Frame Relay endpoint. This means that there must be a device in the hub subnet before the VPN endpoint at the hub that acts as the second Frame Relay endpoint.

- **IPSec with GRE and DMVPN**—DMVPN combines GRE tunnels, IPSec encryption, and Next Hop Resolution Protocol (NHRP). It allows for the management of devices with dynamically assigned IP addresses. It also enables direct spoke-to-spoke communication, without the need to go through the hub.

Installing Router MC

This section provides an overview of the entire installation process.

Router MC requires Virtual Memory System (VMS) Common Services 2.2. VMS Common Services provides the CiscoWorks 2000 Server–based components, software libraries, and software packages developed for Router MC. You can find additional information on VMS at Cisco.com.

NOTE	CiscoWorks VMS Common Services 2.2 and Router MC 1.2.1 may also be installed on a Solaris 2.8 server system. See Cisco.com for more detailed information regarding the installation of Router MC on Solaris server and client systems.

Installation Requirements

Before you begin to install Router MC, verify that the server on which you plan to install Router MC meets the requirements shown in Table 12-2.

Table 12-2 *Router MC 1.2 Minimum Server Requirements*

Requirement Type	Microsoft Windows 2000	Sun Solaris
Hardware	IBM PC–compatible computer with 1-GHz or faster Pentium processor Color monitor with video card capable of 16-bit color CD-ROM drive 100BASE-T or faster network connection	Either Sun Ultra SPARC 60 MB with 440 MHz or faster processor or Sun Ultra SPARCIII (Sun Blade 2000 Workstation or Sun Fire 280R Workgroup Server) 17-inch color monitor CD-ROM drive
Memory (RAM)	1 GB	1 GB
Available Disk Drive Space	9 GB minimum on the drive on which you install the product 2 GB virtual memory NTFS file system (recommended)	9 GB on the partition on which you install the product (the default is /opt)
System Software	ODBC Driver Manager 3.5.10 or later Microsoft Windows 2000 or Professional or Server with Service Pack 3 Microsoft Windows Advanced Server without enabling terminal services	Solaris 2.8 with these patches: • 109742 has been replaced by 108528-13 • 109322 has been replaced by 108827-15 • 109279 has been replaced by 108528-13 • 108991 has been replaced by 108827-15
Additional Software— Browsers (Optional)	Microsoft Internet Explorer 6.0 Microsoft IE 6.0 with Service Pack 1 Sun Java plug-in version 1.3.1-b24 Netscape Navigator 7.1	Netscape Navigator 7.0 (if you are using the desktop on the server system); use Netscape Navigator downloaded from Sun site only

NOTE CiscoWorks Common Services is required for Router MC to work. CiscoWorks Common Services provides the CiscoWorks 2000 Server base components and software developed specifically for Router MC, including the necessary software libraries and packages. For more information, see the *Quick Start Guide for the VPN/Security Management Solution.*

Client Access Requirements

Before you log in to Router MC, verify that the client machine used to log in to Router MC meets the requirements shown in Table 12-3.

Table 12-3   *Router MC Minimum Client Workstation Requirements*

Requirement Type	Microsoft Windows Operating Systems	Sun Solaris Operating Systems
System Hardware and Software	IBM PC–compatible computer with 300-MHz or faster Pentium processor, running Microsoft Windows 2000 with Service Pack 3 (Professional or Server), or Microsoft Windows XP SPI with Microsoft VM Color monitor with video card set to 256 colors	Sun SPARCstation running Solaris 2.8 or Sun SPARC Ultra 10 running Solaris 2.8 Color monitor with video card set to 24 bits color depth
Available Disk Drive Space	400 MB virtual memory	400 MB virtual memory Swap space equal to double the amount of RAM (for example, if your system has 256 MB of RAM, you need 512 MB of swap space)
Memory (RAM)	256 MB	256 MB
Sun Java Virtual Machine (JVM)	Sun Java plug-in version 1.3.1-b24	Sun Java plug-in version 1.3.1-b24
Browser	Microsoft Internet Explorer 6.0 with Service Pack 1 or Netscape Navigator 7.1	Netscape Navigator 7.0 for Solaris 2.8

NOTE   CiscoWorks Common Services requires the Java plug-in from Sun Microsystems Java Runtime Environment (JRE) 1.3.1. CiscoWorks Common Services is not compatible with the Java plug-in from JRE versions 1.2.x or 1.4.x, or any maintenance releases of JRE 1.3.1 (such as 1.3.1_01, 1.3.1_02, and so on). If the required JRE is not present on the client system, CiscoWorks Common Services downloads and installs it automatically; you do not need to install the JRE before accessing CiscoWorks Common Services. However, if an incompatible version of the JRE is present on the client system, you must remove it before accessing CiscoWorks Common Services. If you do not, some features of CiscoWorks Common Services may not function properly.

Installation Process

Router MC is automatically installed in the CiscoWorks Common Services installation folder. The default folder location is C:\Program Files\CSCOpx\MDC\iosmdc, where C:\ is the drive of installation. A typical installation of Router MC on a Windows 2000 platform that already has VMS Common Services 2.2 installed takes about 10 minutes.

Complete the following steps to install Router MC:

Step 1   Insert the Cisco Router MC CD-ROM into the CD-ROM drive. If autorun is enabled, the CD-ROM should start the installation process automatically. If autorun is not enabled, locate the setup.exe file on the CD-ROM and execute it.

Step 2   The Extracting Files dialog box appears. After the progress bar indicates that all files have been extracted, the InstallShield Wizard preparation dialog box appears.

Step 3   Click **Next**. The Router MC Installation window displays, requesting a password for the Router MC database.

Step 4   Enter a password in the Password field and confirm the password in the Confirm Password field.

Step 5   Click **Next**. The Start Copying Files window is displayed.

Step 6   Click **Next**. The Setup Status window is displayed with an installation status bar that shows the installation progress. After the installation completes, the InstallShield Wizard Complete window is displayed.

Step 7   Click the **Yes, I Want to Restart My Computer Now** radio button, and click **Finish**. The computer will restart to complete the installation of Router MC.

Configure Routers for SSH

Communication between the routers and Router MC requires SSH. You need to configure each of the routers for SSH before you can use Router MC with them.

Installing SSH on a router is a two-step process:

Step 1   Configure a domain name

Step 2   Generate RSA usage keys using a modulus of at least 1024.

Example 12-1 shows a sample of the configuration steps required on each router:

Example 12-1 *Configuring Routers for SSH Support*

```
Router(config)# ip domain-name cisco.com
Router(config)# crypto key generate rsa usage-keys modulus 1024
Router(config)# ip ssh time-out 60
Router(config)# ip ssh authentication 2
```

Using Router MC

This section explains how to start using Router MC. It covers how to log in to CiscoWorks and what roles are responsible for delegation of tasks. When you are logged in to CiscoWorks, you can create accounts based upon the authorization roles that CiscoWorks uses, and then launch Router MC. Additionally, a description of the Router MC interface is covered to help familiarize you with the product.

CiscoWorks Login

Complete the following steps to launch Router MC. First log in to the CiscoWorks server:

Step 1   Open a browser and point the browser to the CiscoWorks server with a port number of 1741. Cisco recommends using the server name and letting DNS resolve the IP address—for example, http://*Server-name*:1741. If the CiscoWorks server is local, type the following address in the browser to open the CiscoWorks Login window:

```
http://127.0.0.1:1741
```

Step 2   If this is the first time that you are using CiscoWorks, enter the username **admin** and the password **admin**.

CiscoWorks User Authorization Roles

The username and password must be authenticated to log in to Router MC. After authentication, Router MC establishes your authorization level from the CiscoWorks user authorization roles.

Types of Authorization Roles

There are five types of user authorization roles that are pertinent to Router MC. These roles can be used to delegate different responsibilities to users who log in to Router MC. For example, you can specify who can generate configurations or who can approve configurations. The five types of user authorization roles are as follows:

- **Help Desk**—Read-only for the entire system
- **Approver**—Can review policy changes and accept or reject changes
- **Network operator**—Can create and submit jobs
- **Network administrator**—Can perform administrative tasks on Router MC
- **System administrator**—Can perform all tasks on Router MC

Table 12-4 shows a more detailed description of tasks that are permitted for each of the user authorization roles. Users can be assigned multiple authorization roles.

Table 12-4   *Router MC Permissions and Associated Roles*

Router MC Permission	Permitted Router MC Tasks
View Config Help Desk = **Yes** Approver = **Yes** Net Op = **Yes** Sys Admin = **Yes** Net Admin = **Yes**	Activity and job workflow: • View activities. • View jobs. • Create a job to generate configurations. • View job status. VPN and firewall settings and policies: • View settings and policies in the Configuration tab.

continues

Table 12-4 *Router MC Permissions and Associated Roles (Continued)*

Router MC Permission	Permitted Router MC Tasks
View Admin Help Desk = **Yes** Approver = **Yes** Net Op = **Yes** Sys Admin = **Yes** Net Admin = **Yes**	View administrative settings for the Router MC application, in the Admin tab.
View CLI Help Desk = **No** Approver = **Yes** Net Op = **Yes** Sys Admin = **Yes** Net Admin = **Yes**	View CLI commands for policy definitions, per activity, in the Configuration tab. View the CLI commands generated for the devices in a deployment job, in the Deployment tab.
Modify Config Help Desk = **No** Approver = **No** Net Op = **Yes** Sys Admin = **No** Net Admin = **Yes**	Device management: • Specify device credentials. • Import devices (also need Modify Device-List permission). • Reimport devices. • Edit devices. • Move and delete devices (also need Modify Device-List permission). • Create device groups (also need Modify Device-List permission). • Delete device groups (also need Modify Device-List permission). Activity and job workflow: • Create and submit activity. • Delete activity. VPN and firewall settings and policies: • Define/modify general, hub, and spoke settings. • Create/modify IKE and VPN tunnel policies. • Create/modify access rules. • Create/modify transform sets. • Create/modify translation rules. • Create/modify network groups. • Upload policies to target device.

Table 12-4   *Router MC Permissions and Associated Roles (Continued)*

Router MC Permission	Permitted Router MC Tasks
Modify Device-List Help Desk = **No** Approver = **No** Net Op = **No** Sys Admin = **Yes** Net Admin = **Yes**	Device management: • Import devices (also need Modify Config permission). • Move and delete devices (also need Modify Config permission). • Create device groups (also need Modify Config permission). • Delete device groups (also need Modify Config permission). • Add unmanaged spoke. Activity workflow: • Create activity. • Submit activity. • Delete activity.
Modify Admin Help Desk = **No** Approver = **No** Net Op = **No** Sys Admin = **Yes** Net Admin = **Yes**	Administration: • Modify administrative settings for the Router MC application. Activity workflow: • Close an activity opened by another user.
Approve Activity Help Desk = **No** Approver = **Yes** Net Op = **No** Sys Admin = **No** Net Admin = **Yes**	Approve a submitted activity, thereby committing its policy configurations to the database. Reject a submitted activity.
Approve Job Help Desk = **No** Approver = **Yes** Net Op = **No** Sys Admin = **No** Net Admin = **Yes**	Approve a job so that it can be deployed.
Deploy Help Desk = **No** Approver = **No** Net Op = **Yes** Sys Admin = **No** Net Admin = **Yes**	Deploy job to devices or files. Redeploy job. Rollback job.

Adding Users in CiscoWorks

Prior to logging in to Router MC, you might want to add some users based on your organization's security policy. After logging in to CiscoWorks, complete the following steps to add users based upon CiscoWorks user authorization roles:

Step 1   Choose **Server Configuration > Setup > Security > Add Users**. The Add User page is displayed.

Step 2   Complete the following substeps to add a user to the CiscoWorks database:

(a) (Required) Enter the user's name in the User Name field.

(b) (Required) Enter the user password in the Local Password field.

(c) (Required) Reenter the password in the Confirm Password field.

(d) (Optional) Enter the user's e-mail address.

(e) (Optional) Enter the user's Cisco Connection Online (CCO) login name in the CCO Login field.

(f) (Optional) Enter the password that is associated with the CCO login in the CCO Password field. Confirm this password by entering it in the Confirm Password field.

(g) (Optional) Enter the username for the proxy server login if a proxy server exists on the network.

(h) (Optional) Enter the password associated with the proxy server login. Confirm this password by entering it in the Confirm Password field.

(i) (Optional) Locate the Roles section on the lower-left side of the Add User page. Use the check boxes to select the appropriate roles the user will fulfill.

Step 3   Click **Add** to complete the addition of the user to the CiscoWorks database. The Add User page will refresh to indicate that the change was received.

Launching Router MC

Complete the following steps to launch Router MC:

Step 1   Choose **VPN/Security Management Solution > Management Center**. The folder will expand to reveal the VPN Routers icon, as shown in Figure 12-3.

Step 2   Click **VPN Routers**. A Security Alert window is displayed.

Step 3   Click **Yes** to accept the security certificate. Router MC will display in background.

Step 4   Minimize the CiscoWorks desktop to the background to avoid confusion.

Figure 12-3 *Router MC Launch*

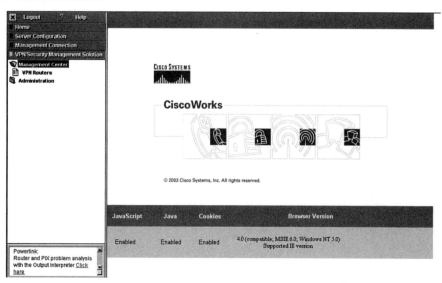

Using the Router MC Main Window

The Router MC main window, shown in Figure 12-4, is the first window you encounter when you enter Router MC.

Figure 12-4 *Router MC Main Window*

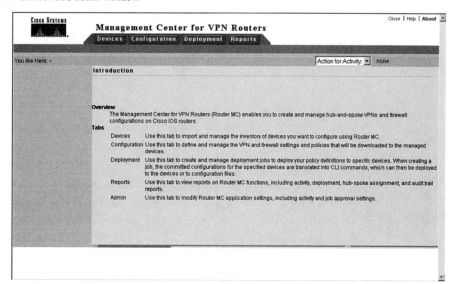

The Router MC user interface contains five tabs, four of which are shown in Figure 12-4:

- **Devices**—Use this tab to import and manage the inventory of routers that you want to configure using Router MC.

- **Configuration**—Use this tab to define and manage the VPN and firewall settings and policies that will be downloaded to the managed routers.

- **Deployment**—Use this tab to create and manage deployment jobs to deploy your policy definitions to specific routers. When creating a job, the committed configurations for the specified routers are translated into CLI commands, which can then be deployed to the routers or to a configuration file.

- **Reports**—Use this tab to view reports on Router MC functions, including activity, deployment, hub-spoke assignment, and audit trail reports.

- **Admin**—The Admin tab is not shown in Figure 12-4 but does appear in subsequent figures. Use this tab to modify Router MC application settings, including activity and job approval settings.

Using the Router MC Interface

Figure 12-5 shows the user interface of Router MC. This is the main work area of the application.

Figure 12-5 *Router MC Interface*

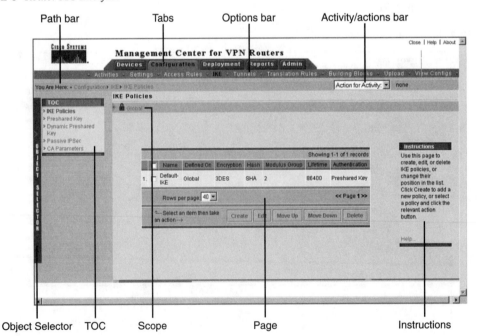

The common elements of the Router MC interface are as follows:

- **Path bar**—Provides a context for the displayed page. Shows the selected tab, option, and then the current page.
- **Options bar**—Displays the options available for the selected tab.
- **Tabs**—Provide access to the Router MC features. Click a tab to access its options.
- **Activity and actions bar**—Displays activity and action icons that change, depending upon what state the activity is in; it can be viewed from the Devices and Configuration tabs only. Options are as follows:
  - **Create**—Creates a new activity.
  - **Open**—Opens a new or existing activity. A popup window opens from which you make your selection.
  - **Close**—Closes the activity shown by the activity bar.
  - **Lock Current Object**—Reserves selected objects for your activity so that they cannot be selected for any other activity.
  - **Submit**—Submits an activity for approval.
  - **Approve**—Commits the activity's configurations to the database.
  - **Reject**—Prevents the activity's configurations from being applied to the database.
  - **Delete**—Discards the activity shown by the activity bar.
  - **View Details**—Displays the details of the current changes.
- **Instructions**—Provides a brief overview of how to use the page.
- **Page**—Displays the area used to perform application tasks.
- **Scope**—Displays the object or objects selected in the Object Selector. Scope is also refered to as the Object Bar.
- **Object Selector**—Shows a hierarchy of objects, such as devices and device groups, and lets you select objects to configure.
- **TOC**—The table of contents (TOC) appears whenever you enable one of Router MC's wizards. The TOC lists the steps in the wizard and allows quick navigation to a specific wizard step.

Using the Devices Tab

The Devices tab is used to import and manage the inventory of routers that you want to configure using Router MC.

The Devices tab includes the following options:

- **Device Hierarchy**—Use this option to view your device hierarchy and to manage your routers within the hierarchy by creating device groups, moving or deleting devices/groups, editing router parameters, and adding unmanaged spokes.

- **Device Import**—Use this option to import the routers you want to configure into Router MC, and to reimport routers when necessary.
- **Credentials**—Use this option to edit router credentials or synchronize the credentials of multiple routers from a comma-separated value (CSV) file.

NOTE   Device credentials include the username, password, and enable password.

Using the Configuration Tab

Use the options in the Configuration tab, shown in Figure 12-6, to configure VPN and firewall settings and policies for deployment to your routers. You can configure settings and policies globally for all routers, for groups of routers, or for individual routers. Select your configuration context using the Object Selector along the left side of the page.

Figure 12-6   *Configuration Tab*

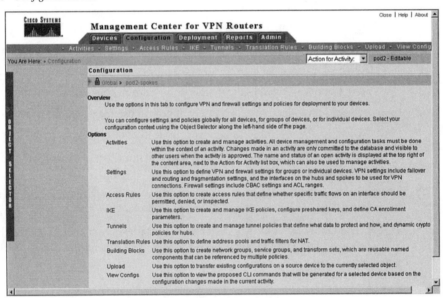

The Configuration tab includes the following options:

- **Activities**—Use to create and manage activities. All router management and configuration tasks must be done within the context of an activity. Changes made in an activity are committed to the database and visible to other users only when the activity is approved. The name and status of an open activity is displayed at the top right of the context area, next to the Action for Activity list box, which can also be used to manage activities.
- **Settings**—Use to define VPN and firewall settings for groups or individual routers. VPN settings include failover, routing, and fragmentation settings, and interfaces on the hubs

and spokes to be used for VPN connections. Firewall settings include Context-Based Access Control (CBAC) settings and ACL ranges.

- **Access Rules**—Use to create access rules that define whether specific traffic flows on an interface should be permitted, denied, or inspected.

- **IKE**—Use to create and manage IKE policies, configure pre-shared keys, and define CA enrollment parameters.

- **Tunnels**—Use to create and manage tunnel policies that define what data to protect and how, and dynamic crypto policies for hubs.

- **Translation Rules**—Use to define address pools and traffic filters for NAT.

- **Building Blocks**—Use to create network groups, service groups, and transform sets, which are reusable named components that can be referenced by multiple policies.

- **Upload**—Use to transfer existing configurations on a source router to the currently selected object.

- **View Configs**—Use to view the proposed CLI commands that will be generated for a selected router based on the configuration changes made in the current activity.

Using the Deployment Tab

Deployment of VPN and firewall configurations is always done within the context of a deployment job. When you create a job, you specify the routers or router groups to which you want to deploy configurations. Router MC translates the committed policy configurations for each router into CLI commands. These CLI commands can be previewed and deployed either directly to the routers in the network or to output files in a specified directory and are configured in Router MC from the Deployment tab.

The Deployment tab includes the following options:

- **Jobs**—Use to create and manage jobs. The name and status of an open job is displayed at the top right of the context area, next to the Action for Job list box, which can also be used to manage jobs.

- **View Configs**—Use to view the CLI commands generated for a specific router in the open job.

- **Status**—Displays the status of the routers targeted for deployment in the open job.

Using the Reports Tab

The Reports tab is used to view reports on various Router MC functions.

The Reports tab includes the following options:

- **Deployment**—Use to view the deployment status of all managed routers.

- **Activities**—Use to view the status of existing activities, including the objects locked by each activity.

> **NOTE** Router MC uses a locking model, in which the objects for the policies that are being defined and all their descendants in the object hierarchy are locked to other users until the activity is approved or deleted. This is important in large networks where several people have the authority to configure routers. It prevents a potential situation where two or more people are making configuration changes to the same objects at the same time.

- **Audit**—Use to define a query to generate an audit log of user interaction with Router MC that can include information about routers, activities, policies, deployments, and so forth.

- **Hub-Spoke Assignment**—Use to generate a report that shows the primary and failover assignment of spokes to selected hubs, or to all hubs in the device hierarchy.

Using the Admin Tab

Administrators use the Admin tab to define various Router MC application settings, and to define Auto Update Server (AUS) settings.

The Admin tab includes the following options:

- **Application Settings**—Use to define various general application settings, such as activity and job approval settings, settings for historical jobs and activities, GRE routing range, and others.

- **Auto Update Server Settings**—Use to define the AUS settings that enable Router MC to communicate with AUS when managing routers with dynamic IP addresses.

Creating Workflows and Activities

This section introduces and explains the concepts of the user workflow within Router MC, along with activities and jobs.

Workflow Tasks

In Router MC, all device management and configuration tasks must be done within the context of an activity. The basic user workflow tasks for most functions are as follows:

- **Task 1: Create an activity**—All router management and VPN configuration must be done within the context of an activity. When you create an activity, you prepare a proposal to create or change VPN configurations on specific devices. This proposal must be approved before configurations can be deployed to the routers.

- **Task 2: Create device groups**—Organize your routers in a hierarchy. When you create device groups, you divide your router inventory strategically to facilitate management and deployment. All routers within a device group can share common policies, which can be deployed to a set of routers at the same time, rather than individually. Device groups help you to keep a clear picture of the relationships between the routers in your network.

- **Task 3: Import devices**—When you import devices, bring their router information into the device inventory, allowing you to manage the devices by using Router MC. You can import device information by having Router MC query the routers directly or by importing router information that is contained in a file.

- **Task 4: Define VPN and/or firewall settings**—There are two ways to complete this task:
  - If you are configuring a VPN, you must specify the inside interfaces and internal networks on the hub and spoke, and the VPN interface on the spokes and the hubs to which the spokes are assigned. You can also choose the method to be used for resiliency, either IKE Keepalive or GRE. Additional VPN settings not covered in the basic user workflow include more advanced configurations for GRE, and packet fragmentation.
  - If you are configuring firewall policies to be deployed to your routers, you must define the parameters required for implementing CBAC and for defining access rules, such as fragmentation, timeouts, half-open connections, logging, and ACL ranges.

- **Task 5: Define VPN policies and/or firewall ACLs**—There are two ways to complete this task:
  - For VPN policy configuration, you must define an IKE policy and a tunnel policy. The IKE policy defines a combination of security parameters to be used during IKE negotiation and authentication of peers. A tunnel policy defines the VPN connection from a spoke to its assigned hub. Tunnel policies that you define on the spoke are then implemented on the hub. You can select the authentication and encryption algorithms that will be used to secure the traffic.
  - To define your network security policy for firewall policy configuration, you must use ACLs. ACLs provide traffic filtering by enabling the implementation of ACLs and CBAC inspection rules on the routers' interfaces.

- **Task 6: Approve the activity**—Upon completing the VPN configurations, the activity must be approved before the configurations are committed to the database and deployed.

- **Task 7: Create and deploy a job**—When you create a job, specify the devices or device groups to which you want to deploy configurations and choose whether to deploy directly to the devices or to files. CLI commands are generated according to the configurations and can be viewed before deployment.

Task 1: Creating an Activity

All actions must be performed within the context of an activity. For example, to import a device, the activity must be editable. After configuring a device or group, submit the activity for approval to be committed to the Router MC database.

An activity can have the following status:

- **Editable**—Configuration changes can be made to the objects selected for the activity. An activity remains editable until it is approved, submitted for approval, or deleted. An activity can be opened and closed and edited any number of times while it is in the editable status. The objects being configured in the activity are locked; they cannot be configured within the context of another activity. The configuration changes can be seen only in the context of the current activity.

- **Submitted**—Available only if the activity submission step is enabled in the Application Settings page in the Admin tab. It indicates that the activity was submitted for approval. The activity is no longer editable, so no further configuration changes can be made within the activity. The objects selected for the activity are still locked to other activities. The approver can open the activity in read-only mode and approve or reject the activity. An approved activity moves to the approved status. A rejected activity becomes editable again.

- **Approved**—The activity was approved by a person with approval permissions. The configurations defined within the activity are now committed policy configurations and are ready to be deployed to the devices or to a file. The locks are lifted from the activity's objects, and they can be configured within the context of another activity.

Activity Actions

Activities are temporary proposals where VPN configuration changes are made to specific objects, such as global objects, device groups, or devices. The activity must be approved before its configuration changes are committed to the Router MC database, at which point they are ready for deployment to the relevant devices or files.

You can perform any of the following functions on activities:

- **Create**—Enables you to create a new activity.

- **Open**—Enables you to open an existing activity.

- **Lock Current Object**—Locks the object selected in the Object Selector and all its descendants, effectively reserving them for the current activity only.

NOTE **Locking an Object for the Activity**—When you are creating or opening an activity, the objects selected in the Object Selector are locked to other users only when you actually start making configuration changes. Simply selecting objects in the Object Selector does not lock them; other users working in other activities can select them. To avoid this, lock the currently selected object and its descendents for the activity. In effect, those objects are being reserved for an activity so that they cannot be selected by any other activity.

- **Close**—Closes the open activity.
- **Submit**—Submits the open activity for approval.

NOTE   By default, the submission of activities for approval is disabled in Router MC under the Admin tab. The submission step is not required and you can approve the activity yourself if you have the appropriate permissions. Only an administrator can change activity approval settings in the Admin tab if the organization requires one set of users to define configurations and another set to approve and commit them.

- **Approve**—Approves the activity and commits its configurations.

NOTE   By default, using Approve submits the activity and commits it to the Router MC database in one move.

- **Reject**—Rejects the activity and returns it to the editable status so that further changes can be made. This button is not present if activity submission is disabled.
- **Delete**—Deletes the activity and removes it from the list of activities on the Activities page. Only an editable activity can be deleted; submitted activities have already been committed to the Router MC database.
- **View Details**—Displays details of the open activity. The View Details option launches the activity details in a separate window that gives the name, description, status, creation date, and an historical report that details the users and their actions.

From the Configuration > Activities page, you can choose any of the following options:

- **Create**—Enables you to create a new activity.
- **Close**—Closes the open activity.
- **Open**—Opens an existing activity.
- **Approve**—Approves the activity and commits its configurations.

NOTE   By default, using Approve submits the activity and commits it to the Router MC database in one move.

- **Delete**—Deletes the activity and removes it from the list of activities on the Activities page. Only an editable activity can be deleted; submitted activities have already been committed to the Router MC database.

Activity Creation

Before you make any configuration changes, you must create a new activity or open an existing activity. An activity can be opened by only one person at a time but can be worked on by several people in sequence. This means that before the activity is approved, another user can open it and make further configuration changes to the selected objects. The objects being configured within the activity, and all their descendants in the hierarchy, are locked until the activity is approved or deleted. No other activity can have the same objects or any of their descendants selected for configuration. This ensures that there is no overlap between users, which might result in configuration discrepancies.

Before importing any routers or making any configuration changes, you must create an activity. Complete the following steps to create an activity:

Step 1   Select **Create** from the Activity/Job list drop-down menu. The Create New Activity window is displayed.

Step 2   Enter a unique name for this activity in the Name field.

Step 3   (Optional) Enter a description for this activity in the Description field.

Step 4   Click **Create**. The new activity is created and the name appears next to the Action for Activity list box.

Another way to create an activity would be from the Activities page. Complete the following steps to create an activity:

Step 1   Choose **Configuration > Activities**. The Activities page is displayed.

Step 2   Click **Create**. The Create New Activity window is displayed.

Step 3   Enter a name in the Name field and an optional description in the Description field.

Step 4   Click **OK**. The new activity is created and the name appears next to the Action for Activity list box.

Configuration Tab After Activity Creation

The updated Configuration tab will show the name of the activity listed next to the Action for Activity list box.

Notice that the new activity is marked as editable. When an activity is in this editable state, configuration changes can be made to the objects selected for the activity. An activity remains editable until it is approved (or submitted for approval) or deleted. An activity can be opened and closed and edited any number of times while it is in the editable state. The objects being configured in the activity are locked, meaning they cannot be configured within the context of another activity. The configuration changes can only be seen in the context of the current activity.

At this point, you could choose one of several configuration options (see the section of this chapter titled "Using the Configuration Tab" for a complete description of these options:

- Activities
- Settings
- Access Rules
- IKE
- Tunnels
- Translation Rules
- Building Blocks
- Upload
- View Configs

Task 2: Creating Device Groups

The next major task or function that must be performed is the creation of device groups. This section explains how to create device groups using Router MC.

Router MC provides a default two-level device hierarchy in which all routers are contained within a global group. Router MC allows you to create additional levels in the hierarchy by grouping your devices within the global group. Using device groups facilitates efficient management of a large number of devices by enabling you to define VPN or firewall policies on multiple devices simultaneously, rather than having to configure each device individually.

Policy inheritance in the device hierarchy is implemented in a top-down fashion. The global group is the highest-level object. Policy inheritance uses the following guidelines:

- All devices in the device inventory inherit policies defined on the global level.
- All the groups inherit policies defined on a device group and devices contained within that group, and override the global configurations (if any) for those devices.
- Policies defined on an individual device apply to that device only, and override any policies inherited from higher-level objects in the hierarchy.

Grouping routers provides an easy and scalable mechanism for assigning common policies simultaneously to a set of routers, rather than doing so individually and in sequence. Device groups allow you to divide your network by any strategy you choose, including geographic locale, organizational function, corporate priority, or schedule of deployment.

NOTE   It is best to group your routers according to the policies that should apply to them. The primary benefits of grouping relate to managing policies across multiple similar routers simultaneously. A group that contains a combination of hubs and spokes will disperse its policies to those routers in ways that apply appropriately to them.

Device Group Creation

Complete the following steps to create a new device group:

Step 1   Click the **Devices** tab.

Step 2   Select **Device Hierarchy**. The Device Hierarchy page opens.

Step 3   Enter a unique name for your device group in the Name field.

Step 4   Select the type of group you want to create, either a standard device group or a High Availability (HA) group. In this example, a standard device group type is selected.

> **NOTE**   An HA group consists of two or more hub routers that use Hot Standby Routing Protocol (HSRP) and Reverse Route Injection (RRI) to provide transparent, automatic router failover.

Step 5   Go to the Create In area and select the parent object in which the device group will be created.

> **NOTE**   Router MC contains three predefined device groups called Default-1710-eth0, Default-17x0-serial0, and Default-806-spokes. These predefined device groups are based on the Cisco router models used most frequently in VPN environments and on the configurations most commonly used for those VPNs. Each configuration contains a specific IKE policy and two transform sets. Additionally, the inside interfaces and VPN interfaces are also predefined.

Step 6   Click **Create**. The Device Hierarchy page refreshes. The new device group appears within the Global folder along with the three predefined device groups.

Viewing Device Hierarchy

In a hub-and-spoke VPN topology, multiple remote routers (spokes) communicate securely with a central router (hub). A separate, secured tunnel extends between the centralized hub and each of the individual spokes.

You have several options available to you from within the **Devices > Device Hierarchy** page:

- **Edit**—Select a device folder (to select all devices in the group) or individual routers and click **Edit** to perform the following subtasks:
  - Rename the device group (only when the device group is selected)

      — Change router roles (hub or spoke)

      — Change router Cisco IOS versions (the list starts with Software Release 12.2)

- **Move**—Click **Move** to move devices or groups from one position to another within the device hierarchy.

- **Delete**—Select one or more routers or groups in the tree and click **Delete** to remove them from your hierarchy. If you delete a group, you will also delete all of its routers, subgroups, and associated policies unless you first move them elsewhere.

- **Add Unmanaged Spoke**—Click this button to add an unmanaged spoke to your inventory. Unmanaged spokes are VPN routers in your inventory that are unavailable for direct Router MC configuration. Router MC uses the policy settings of an unmanaged spoke only to configure—by inference—its associated hub. You must use the CLI to configure unmanaged spokes.

- **Create Group**—Click this button to add a new device group.

The Device Hierarchy page contains a small tab called All. This tab displays the entire device hierarchy found in the Router MC database.

Task 3: Importing Devices

This section explains how to import device identity information using Router MC.

Device import brings into Router MC a range of identifying information for the router, such as its domain name, its interfaces and subinterfaces, and the IP addresses of its interfaces and subinterfaces. Router MC imports devices either by querying the physical devices for information or by reading device information from a file or multiple files in a specified directory on the server. Devices can be imported individually or in groups.

NOTE   The device import function is not the same as the configuration upload function. Configuration upload gathers information about the actual configuration of the router, including policies such as transform sets, pre-shared keys, dynamic pre-shared keys, CA policies, routing policies, and IKE policies. You will learn more about the configuration upload function later in this lesson.

The Router MC device import feature allows you to update the Router MC device inventory database with information from the following sources:

- Preexisting router configuration files
- Physical router configuration files
- CSV files

To access the Device Import window, shown in Figure 12-7, choose **Devices > Device Import**.

Figure 12-7 *Device Import*

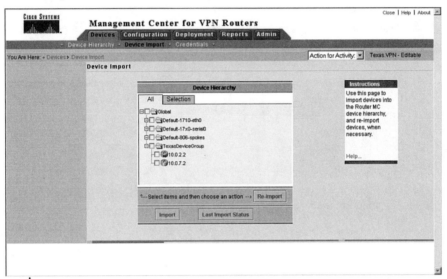

You have several options available to you from within this window:

- **Import**—Click this button to access the import wizard to import routers into Router MC.

- **Last Import Status**—Click this button to display the import status of the routers in the most recent import operation.

- **Re-import**—Click this button to reimport the selected router or device group. This is useful if router information has changed and you want to bring the new router information into the Router MC database.

The Device Import page contains two small tabs:

- **All**—Displays the entire device hierarchy.

- **Selection**—Displays only the routers you selected for import.

Choosing the Device Import Method

Complete the following steps to choose the device import method to begin the process of importing device configurations into the Router MC database:

Step 1   Choose **Devices > Device Import**. The Device Import page opens, as shown in Figure 12-7.

Step 2 Click **Import**. The Choose Method page opens, as shown in Figure 12-8.

Figure 12-8 *Choose Import Method*

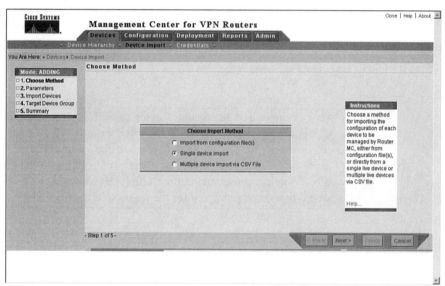

NOTE	Notice the tabs at the bottom of the window in Figure 12-8. The Back, Next, Finish, and Cancel buttons, along with the Instruction pane along the right side of the window, indicate the use of one of Router MC's many task wizards. The instructions give you information and advice and explain the processes you need to accomplish on each page of the wizard. When the last task has been completed, the Finish button becomes available for you to indicate the completion of the task.

Step 3 Select the appropriate import method radio button from the following list:

- **Import from Configuration File(s)**—(Default) Click this radio button to import router configuration information from either a preexisting directory or a single router configuration file. By default, configuration files must be named primary-device-name.cfg. The Router MC administrator may change the required suffix for the configuration files in the Admin tab.

- **Single Device Import**—Click this radio button to import the configuration of a single router using an SSH session. For routers using dynamic IP addressing, the IP address is retrieved from AUS.

- **Multiple Device Import via CSV File**—Click this radio button to import configurations from multiple routers using SSH and a CSV reference file. To use this import option, you must first create a CSV reference file containing the IP addresses, and administrative passwords of the routers you wish to import configurations from. See the Router MC online help function for more information on how to create the CSV file for multiple device import.

Step 4   Click **Next**. The Parameters page opens.

NOTE   This example uses the Single Device Import option, which means that you now need to inform Router MC exactly which router to communicate with using SSH. If you had chosen to import from a configuration file, you 'would have been prompted for the location of the file. If you had chosen to import multiple devices using a CSV file, you would have been prompted for the location of the CSV file.

Step 5   Select one of the following two radio buttons:

- **Device IP/Name**—Click this radio button if you are importing a configuration from a router with a fixed IP address (preferably the IP address of the external router interface). Then, enter the fixed IP address in the adjacent field.

- **Dynamic IP Hostname**—Click this radio button if you are importing a configuration from a spoke router with a dynamic IP address assigned by a DHCP server. Then, enter the host name of the router you wish to import the configuration from (not the DNS server) in the adjacent field.

Step 6   Enter the login name for an administrative account on the router in the Username field.

Step 7   Enter the password associated with the above login name (administrative account) in the Password field.

Step 8   Enter the enable password for the router in the Enable Password field.

Step 9   Click **Next**. The Import Devices page opens, as shown in Figure 12-9, where you can select the router's role.

Step 10   Select the router role from the Role list box. Your choices include the following:

- **Hub**—Select this role if the router serves as a primary or secondary hub in a VPN. On deployment, only hub-specific VPN configurations are deployed to this router.

Figure 12-9 *Device Role*

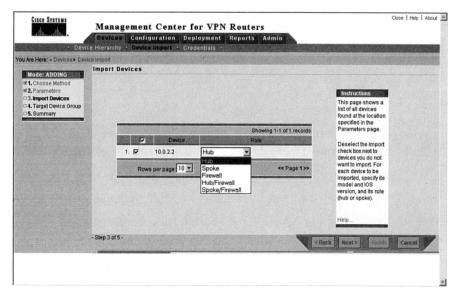

- **Spoke**—Select this role if the router serves as a spoke in a VPN. On deployment, only spoke-specific VPN configurations are deployed to this router.

- **Firewall**—Select this role if the router serves as firewall router only and does not participate in a VPN. On deployment, only firewall configurations will be deployed to this router.

- **Hub/Firewall**—Select this role if the router serves as hub in a VPN and will also provide firewall functionality. On deployment, both hub-related VPN configurations and firewall configurations will be deployed to this router.

- **Spoke/Firewall**—Select this role if the router serves as a spoke in a VPN and will also provide firewall functionality. On deployment, both spoke-related VPN configurations and firewall configurations will be deployed to this router.

NOTE   This example imports the router as a hub.

Step 11 Click **Next**. The Target Device Group page opens.

Step 12 In the **Import To** area, select the device group of which you want the imported router to become a member.

Step 13 Click **Next**. The Device Import Summary page opens.

Step 14 Review the information in the Device Import Summary page. This page
identifies each router selected for import, by listing its name, role, and parent
device group. For routers imported from a preexisting configuration file, it
also lists the router model and Cisco IOS version.

Step 15 Click **Finish**, which is now available, to start the import process. The Last
Import Status dialog box opens.

Step 16 View the Last Import Status dialog box. The device status updates as the import
process proceeds. There are four possible indicators for the import status:

- **Pending**—Displayed while awaiting the import procedure to begin.

- **In Progress**—Displayed during the import procedure.

- **Completed**—Displayed following a successful import procedure.

- **Failed**—Displayed whenever an error occurs during the import procedure.
  Failures also contain an error field, which provides basic error information.

The Import Status page displays the progress of the device import. It refreshes
every 10 seconds with a device import status update.

NOTE Most device import and management actions occur in the context of an
activity, and do not take effect until that the activity has been approved.
The only exceptions to this rule are changes to device names, changes to
device credentials, and changes to hub assignments—all of which take
effect immediately regardless of the current activity's approval state.

Step 17 Click **Close**. You are returned to the Device Import Device Hierarchy page,
shown in Figure 12-10.

Step 18 View the updated Device Hierarchy page. Note that the newly imported
router appears in the All tab.

Understanding Reimport Method

The Reimport option on the Devices page allows you to connect to routers that have been defined
in Router MC and reimport their configurations. This is important when dealing with routers that
have been configured by a command line and the configurations need to be updated in Router MC.

Regardless of the method that was originally used to populate Router MC, you will be asked
for reimport parameters.

Figure 12-10 *Updated Device Hierarchy*

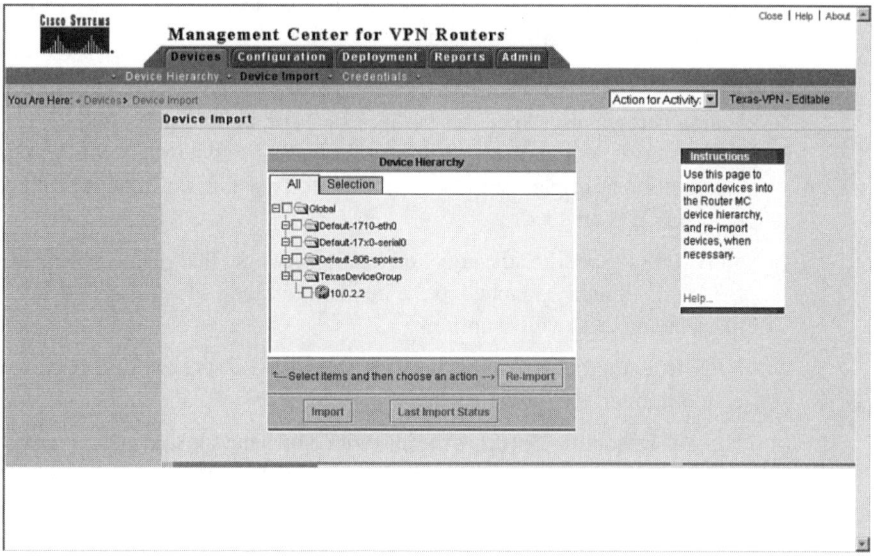

Task 4: Defining VPN Settings

Router MC permits configuring VPN settings using the Settings wizard from the Configuration tab. The Settings wizard has the following sections:

- **General**—Settings that apply to hub-and-spoke routers, unlike the specific settings that apply to specific router types.

  - **Failover and Routing**—Specifies whether to use IKE or GRE for failover and routing. IKE is the default with a Keepalive of 10 seconds.

  - **Fragmentation**—Specifies the method to use when trying to avoid packet loss over a VPN connection, by a preferred method of maximum transmission unit (MTU) handling. Options include end-to-end MTU discovery or local MTU handling.

- **Hub**—Settings that apply to hub routers.

  - **Inside Interfaces**—Specifies the physical or subinterfaces that connect the hub with all other networks attached to the hub. This is used by Router MC to create ACLs for filter options.

NOTE   You cannot choose an inside interface that has already been assigned to a spoke as the tunnel endpoint interface.

> — **Networks**—Specifies the attached inside networks that reside behind the hub but are not directly attached to the inside interfaces. This is used by Router MC to create ACLs for filter options.

- **Spoke**—Settings that apply to spoke routers.

  > — **Inside Interfaces**—Specifies the interfaces or subinterfaces with all other spoke side networks. Router MC creates ACLs for filter options. It also uses this information to implement NAT and to specify which traffic will be secured when GRE is enabled.

  > — **Networks**—Specifies the attached inside networks that reside behind the spoke but are not directly attached to the inside interfaces. This is used by Router MC to create ACLs for filter options.

  > — **VPN Interfaces**—Specifies the VPN interface on spokes. This is the tunnel endpoint interface on the spoke.

  > — **Hub Assignment**—Specifies the hub with which the spoke will be communicating and the VPN interface on the hub. This is the tunnel endpoint interface on the hub.

General—Failover and Routing

For failover and routing in the VPN hierarchy, use either IKE Keepalive or IPSec with GRE.

Configuring IKE Keepalive

Complete the following steps to configure IKE Keepalive:

Step 1 Choose **Configuration > Settings**. The Settings page is displayed.

Step 2 Select **Failover and Routing** from the TOC. The Failover and Routing page is displayed.

Step 3 Click the **IKE Keepalive** radio button in the Failover section.

Step 4 Click **Apply**. The Failover and Routing page refreshes to indicate that Router MC received the changes.

Router MC supports a Frame Relay topology in which each hub acts only as a VPN endpoint and each spoke acts as both a VPN endpoint and a Frame Relay endpoint. There must be a device in the hub subnet that acts as the second Frame Relay endpoint and is positioned before the VPN endpoint at the hub.

NOTE If you specify that you want to use GRE, Router MC automatically determines whether you use Frame Relay, and configures the devices accordingly. Using Router MC is never required to specify whether Frame Relay exists in the network.

Configuring GRE

Complete the following steps to configure GRE:

Step 1   Choose **Configuration > Settings**. The Settings page is displayed.

Step 2   Select **Failover and Routing** from the TOC. The Failover and Routing page is displayed.

Step 3   Click the **GRE** radio button in the Failover section.

Step 4   Select **EIGRP** or **OSPF** from the (GRE) Routing Protocol drop-down menu.

Step 5   Enter the GRE process number in the (GRE) Process Number (110-120) field.

Step 6   Enter the loopback address in the (GRE) Loopback Address Range field.

Step 7   Click **Apply**. The Failover and Routing page refreshes to indicate that Router MC received the changes.

Consider the following prerequisites before using GRE on a network:

- To use GRE, identify the inside interfaces on the devices and specify these in the Router MC Settings configuration area. Inside interfaces are the physical interfaces on the device that connects to its internal subnets and networks.

- In Router MC, select a routing protocol, known as an Interior Gateway Protocol (IGP), to enable GRE. The following are the available routing protocols in Router MC:

  — **Enhanced Interior Gateway Routing Protocol (EIGRP)**—Allows the exchange of routing information within an autonomous system and addresses some of the more difficult issues associated with routing in large, heterogeneous networks. Compared to other protocols, EIGRP provides superior convergence properties and operating efficiency, and combines the advantages of several different protocols.

  — **Open Shortest Path First (OSPF)**—A link-state, hierarchical protocol that features least-cost routing, multipath routing, and load balancing.

- In Router MC, specify an IGP process number. The IGP process number identifies the IGP process to which the inside interface on the device belongs. When GRE is implemented, this will be the secured IGP. For secure communication, the inside interfaces on the devices in the VPN must use the same IGP process. The IGP process number must be within the range specified in the application settings under the Admin tab. If an IGP process exists on the device that is within this range, but is different from the IGP process number specified in the GRE settings, Router MC will remove the existing IGP process. If the existing IGP process matches the one specified in the GRE settings, any networks included in the existing IGP process that do not match the specified inside interfaces will be removed.

- When inside interfaces on the devices are configured to use an IGP process other than the IGP process specified in the GRE settings (which means that the interfaces belong to unsecured IGPs):

  — **Spokes**—Manually remove the inside interfaces from the unsecured IGP via the device CLI before configuring GRE with Router MC.

  — **Hubs**—If the hub inside interface is used as a network access point for Router MC, then on deployment, the interface will be published in both secured and unsecured IGPs. To ensure that the spoke peers use only the secured IGP, manually add the **auto-summary** command for the unsecured IGP or remove the unsecured IGP from that inside interface.

- In Router MC, provide a subnet that is unique and not globally routable for loopback. This subnet must be used only to support the implementation of loopback for GRE. The loopback interfaces are created, maintained, and used only by Router MC. Do not use them for any other purpose.

- If using static routes and not unsecured IGP, make sure to configure static routes on the spokes for the hub inside interfaces.

- **For 7100 and 7400 routers**—In general, it is recommended that Router MC have its own network access interface, separate from the inside interfaces on the device. However, if a device does not have interfaces that can be reserved for management only, and the external interface on the device is an Ethernet interface, Router MC can be connected to the network via an additional Ethernet hub that is attached to the hub's external Ethernet interface.

General—Fragmentation: Configuring End-to-End MTU Discovery

Router MC instructs routers to fragment packets prior to encryption so that network performance is not decreased. It can instruct the device to handle packets that are larger than the MTU either with end-to-end MTU discovery or by setting the MTU locally on the device.

- **MTU discovery**—End-to-end MTU discovery uses Internet Control Message Protocol (ICMP) messages to determine the maximum MTU that a host can use to send a packet through the VPN tunnel without causing fragmentation. The MTU setting for each link in a transmission path is checked to ensure that no transmitted packet exceeds the smallest MTU in that path. The discovered MTU decides whether fragmentation is necessary.

- **Local MTU handling**—Typically used when ICMP is blocked. If the local MTU handling option is selected, Router MC sets the MTU size on the device to 1420 bytes.

NOTE   The recommended best practice is to use end-to-end MTU discovery.

Complete the following steps to configure end-to-end MTU discovery:

Step 1   Choose **Configuration > Settings**. The Settings page is displayed.

Step 2   Choose **General > Failover and Routing** from the TOC. The Fragmentation page is displayed.

Step 3   Click the **End-to-End MTU Discovery** radio button.

Step 4   Click **Apply**. The Fragmentation page will refresh to indicate that Router MC received the changes.

Configuring Hub Inside Interfaces

A hub's inside interfaces are physical interfaces or subinterfaces on the hub that connect the hub with the hub side networks. There are two types of subnets that connect to the hub's inside interface:

- **Attached networks**—Subnets that are directly connected to the hub's inside interfaces, with no intermediary network device.

- **Internal networks**—Subnets located beyond the attached networks that are connected to the attached networks through an intermediary.

NOTE   You cannot choose an inside interface that has already been assigned to a spoke as the tunnel endpoint interface.

The inside interface definitions have the following purposes in Router MC:

- Inside interfaces can be included in the tunnel policy filter definition to specify what traffic to secure in the IPSec tunnel. For example, secure all traffic between the inside interfaces on the hub and the inside interfaces on the spoke. Router MC uses the inside interface specifications to create the required ACLs for the filter options that include inside interfaces.

- When GRE is enabled, the inside interface definitions specify what traffic will be secured in the GRE tunnels. Only traffic from the networks attached to the inside interfaces is included in the tunnels.

Complete the following steps to manually configure the hub router's inside interfaces:

Step 1   Choose **Configuration > Settings**. The Settings page is displayed.

Step 2   Expand the **Object Selector**, then select the folder for the device group you wish to configure.

Step 3   Choose **Hub > Inside Interfaces** from the TOC. The Inside Interfaces page is displayed, as shown in Figure 12-11.

Figure 12-11 *Hub Inside Interfaces*

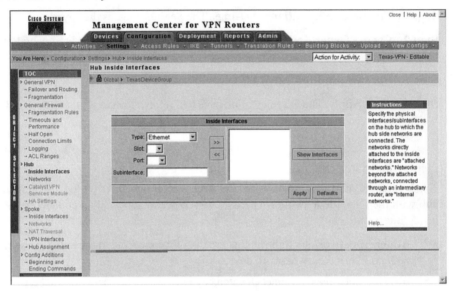

Step 4 Click **Show Interfaces**. The Show Interfaces dialog box opens.

NOTE Clicking Show Interfaces displays all the interfaces for the router type in the device group. Alternatively, you may select a Slot, Port, and Subinterface and then use the >> button to add that interface to the list. Use the << button to remove an interface from the list.

Step 5 Check the check box for the inside interface of the hub router.

Step 6 Click **Select**. The Show Interfaces dialog box closes, and the name of the selected interface appears in the selection confirmation area.

Step 7 Click **Apply**. Upon deployment, each hub in the device group will be configured with the selected interface as the inside interface.

Networks

A hub's internal networks are a group of subnets that reside behind the hub but are not directly connected to the hub's inside interfaces. There is an intermediary router located between the internal networks and the networks directly attached to the hub's inside interfaces, which are attached networks.

Internal networks can be included in the tunnel policy filter definition to specify what traffic to secure in the IPSec tunnel. For example, secure all traffic between the internal networks on the hub and the internal networks on the spoke. Router MC uses the internal network specifications to create the required ACLs for the filter options that include the internal networks.

Complete the following steps to configure internal networks on the hub router:

Step 1 Choose **Configuration > Settings**. The Settings page is displayed.

Step 2 Choose **Hub > Networks** from the TOC. The Hub Side Networks page is displayed.

Step 3 Enter an IP address of a network or host in the Add a Host/Network field, and click the >>> button to add it to the list of Hub Side Networks.

NOTE	When adding an IP address of a host or network, it has to be in a specific format. For example, if you are adding network 192.168.1.0 with a subnet mask of 255.255.255.0, the entry would be 192.168.1.0/ 255.255.255.0.

Step 4 Select a network group from the Add Networks Groups list, and click the >>> button to add it to the list of Hub Side Networks.

NOTE	Network groups are a part of the building blocks that Router MC uses. To access the network groups, choose **Configuration > Building Blocks > Network Groups**. Building blocks will be covered in the "Using Building Blocks" section.

Step 5 Click **Apply**. The Hub Side Networks page refreshes to indicate that Router MC received the changes.

Configuring Spoke Inside Interfaces

The settings for the spoke's inside interfaces are the same as those for the hub's inside interfaces. The exception is that you cannot choose an inside interface that has already been assigned to a spoke as the tunnel endpoint interface.

Complete the following steps to manually configure the spoke router's inside interfaces:

Step 1 Choose **Spoke > Inside Interfaces** from the TOC. The Inside Interfaces page is displayed.

Step 2 Click **Show Interfaces**. The Show Interfaces dialog box opens.

Step 3 Check the check box for the inside interface of the spoke routers.

Step 4 Click **Select**. The Show Interfaces dialog box closes, and the name of the selected interface appears in the selection confirmation area. Now you need to select the spoke VPN interfaces.

Step 5 Choose **Spoke > VPN Interfaces** from the TOC. The Spoke VPN Interface page opens.

Step 6 Click **Show Interfaces**. The Show Interfaces page appears.

Step 7 Click the radio button for the spoke VPN interface.

Step 8 Click **Select**. The Spoke VPN Interface page updates.

Step 9 Click **Apply**. The Spoke VPN Interface page updates.

Step 10 Optionally, you may want to validate which routers have the selected interface by completing the following:

(a) Click **Validate**. The Validate Interface page appears.

(b) Check whether the VPN interface you selected earlier is available on all the spoke routers.

(c) Click **Close**.

Now you need to assign a hub for the spokes.

Step 11 Choose **Spoke > Hub Assignment** from the TOC. The Hub Assignment page appears.

Step 12 Select the primary hub from the Primary Hub list box.

Step 13 Select the primary interface from the Primary Interface list box.

Step 14 Select the failover hub from the Failover Hub list box.

Step 15 Select the failover interface from the Failover Interface list box.

Step 16 Click **Apply**. The Hub Assignment page updates.

Configuring Spoke Networks

The settings for the spoke side network are the same as the settings for the hub side networks. Complete the following steps to configure internal networks on the hub router:

Step 1 Choose **Configuration > Settings**. The Settings page is displayed.

Step 2 Choose **Spoke > Networks** from the TOC. The Spoke Side Networks page is displayed.

Step 3 Enter an IP address of a network or host in the Add a Host/Network field, and click the **>>>** button to add it to the list of Spoke Side Networks.

Step 4   To add an existing network group to the spoke side networks, select it from the Add Network Groups list, and click the **>>>** button. For more information, take a look at the Working with Network Groups link to understand network groups.

NOTE	When adding an IP address of a host or network, it must be in a specific format. For example, if you are adding network 192.168.1.0 with a subnet mask of 255.255.255.0, the entry would be 192.168.1.0/ 255.255.255.0.

Step 5   Select a network group from the Add Network Groups list and click the **>>>** button to add it to the list of Spoke Side Networks.

Step 6   Click **Apply**. The Spoke Side Networks page refreshes to indicate that Router MC received the changes.

Task 5: Defining VPN Policies

This section explains Router MC's use of IKE policies with hub-and-spoke VPN routers.

Router MC enables you to define IKE policies on multiple devices, rather than having to define them on each device individually. Using Router MC, you can define IKE policies that specify:

- Encryption algorithm
  - Data Encrypted Standard (DES)
  - Triple DES (3DES)
- Hash algorithm
  - Secure Hash Algorithm (SHA)
  - Message digest algorithm 5 (MD5)
- Authentication method
  - Dynamic pre-shared key
  - Pre-shared key
  - CA enrollment

NOTE	If you select the authentication method of CA enrollment (RSA Signature) for a Router MC IKE policy, or if your device was previously configured with RSA Signature, you must deploy configurations directly to your device, not to a file.

- DH group
  - **Group 1**—768 bit
  - **Group 2**—1024 bit
  - **Group 5**—2048 bit
- **Key lifetime**—value range of 60 to 86,400 seconds.

The following predefined IKE policy will be used if you do not define any other IKE policies:

- **Encryption algorithm**—DES
- **Hash algorithm**—SHA
- **Authentication method**—Pre-shared key
- **Diffie-Hellman group**—Group 1 (768 bit)
- **Lifetime**—86,400 seconds, no volume limit

NOTE   When configuring objects underneath groups, you have the option to inherit default policies from the parent container. If you wish to define your own policies for the objects, you must uncheck the Inherit Default Policies check box.

Defining IKE Policies

Complete the following steps to configure an IKE policy with a pre-shared key for the global group:

Step 1   Choose **Configuration > IKE**. The IKE page is displayed.

Step 2   If you need to, expand the Object Selector and select the device group for which you want to configure an IKE policy.

NOTE   Router MC remembers the last device group you worked with and presents that device group as you move through other tabs and menus.

Step 3   Select **IKE Policies** from the TOC. The IKE Policies page is displayed, as shown in Figure 12-12.

You have several options available to you from within this page:

- **Create**—Click this button to create a new IKE policy.
- **Edit**—Click this button to edit an existing IKE policy.
- **Move Up**—Click this button to move an IKE policy up one row in the list (increasing the priority of the IKE policy).

Figure 12-12 *IKE Policies*

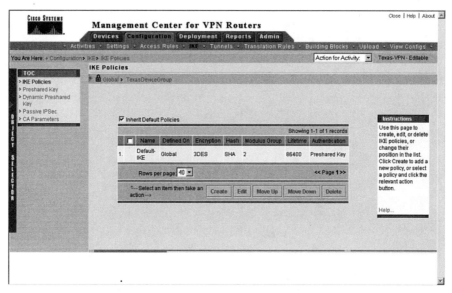

- **Move Down**—Click this button to move an IKE policy down one row in the list (decreasing the priority of the IKE policy).

- **Delete**—Click this button to delete the selected IKE policy.

Step 4 Click **Create**. The Name and Comment page appears.

Step 5 Enter an appropriate name for the new IKE policy in the Name field.

Step 6 (Optional) Enter an optional comment describing the new IKE policy in the Comment field.

Step 7 Click **Next**. The Algorithms page is displayed.

Step 8 Select an appropriate encryption algorithm from the Encryption Algorithm list box.

Step 9 Select an appropriate hash algorithm from the Hash Algorithm list box.

Step 10 Select an appropriate modulus group from the Modulus Group list box.

Step 11 Click **Next**. The Parameters page is displayed.

Step 12 Enter an appropriate lifetime (in seconds) in the Lifetime field.

Step 13 Select an appropriate authentication method (either Preshared Key or RSA Signature) from the drop-down Authentication field menu.

Step 14 Click **Next**. The IKE Policy Summary page is displayed.

Step 15 Review the IKE Policy Summary page to verify that the information listed on this page is correct.

Step 16 Click **Finish**. The IKE Policies page is displayed with the new IKE policy, as shown in Figure 12-13.

Figure 12-13 *Update IKE Policies List*

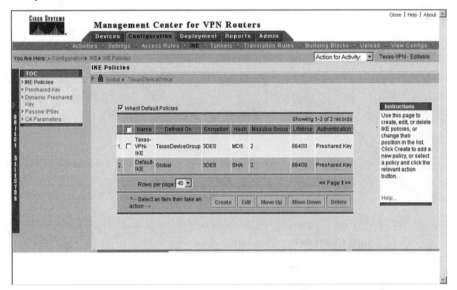

NOTE   The authentication parameters you define apply to all the IKE policies on the selected object. For example, if you have selected a device group and you define a pre-shared key, all IKE policies on all devices in that device group that use the pre-shared key as the authentication method will use the key you defined.

Step 17 View the updated IKE policies list for the selected device group.

Step 18 (Optional) If appropriate, check the check box next to an IKE policy and use the Move Up and Move Down buttons to either increase or decrease the selected IKE policy's priority.

Using Pre-Shared Keys

If you want to use the pre-shared key as your authentication method, the peers that will be participating in VPN communications must be configured with a specific key that will be their shared secret for authenticating the connection. You can decide on a specific key to use, or you can let Router MC automatically allocate a random key to the participating peers. Router MC allocates a different key for each hub-spoke connection. If all the connections in a VPN use the same pre-shared key, security can be compromised. Therefore, it is advisable to use automatically generated keys.

Like IKE policies, pre-shared key parameters are specific to the object you selected in the Object Selector, and are inherited by lower-level objects, unless you override them. Complete the following steps to configure an autogenerated pre-shared key for the default-1710-eth0 group:

Step 1   Choose **Configuration > IKE**. The IKE page is displayed.

Step 2   Use the Object Selector to select the **Default-1710-eth0** group. The IKE page will refresh to display the Default-1710-eth0 group on the Object Bar.

Step 3   Select **Preshared Key** from the TOC. The Preshared Key page is displayed.

Step 4   Click the **Auto-Generate** radio button from the Key field.

Step 5   Check the **Regenerate** check box to have Router MC generate a new key for the next deployment to devices.

NOTE   As soon as you click Apply, the Regenerate check box is cleared. It does not remain checked because the new key will be generated only for the upcoming deployment, not for subsequent deployments, unless you check it again before the subsequent deployments.

Step 6   Click **Apply**. The Preshared Key page is refreshed to indicate that Router MC received the changes.

Creating Dynamic Pre-Shared Keys

Router MC enables you to create dynamic, wildcard, pre-shared keys on a hub, to be used for communication with any device in a specified network, even if the IP address of the device is unknown, such as a device that gets a dynamic IP address and configuration from the DHCP server on startup. If you can specify the network segment to which the device belongs, you can define a wildcard pre-shared key to be used if a device from the specified network segment initiates IKE negotiation. In such a case, a dynamic crypto map entry is created on the hub, and the remote peer's missing parameters are dynamically configured when the IKE and IPSec SAs are established.

Complete the following steps to configure a dynamic pre-shared key for the default-806-spokes group:

Step 1   Choose **Configuration > IKE**. The IKE page is displayed.

Step 2   Use the Object Selector to select the **Default-806-spokes** group. The IKE page will refresh to display the Default-806-spokes group on the Object Bar.

Step 3   Select **Dynamic Preshared Key** from the TOC. The Dynamic Preshared Key page is displayed.

Step 4   Click **Create**. The Create Dynamic Preshared Key window is displayed.

Step 5   Enter a network address in the Network field and a key string in the Key field.

Step 6   Click **OK**. The Create Dynamic Preshared Key window disappears, and the Dynamic Preshared Key page refreshes to display the new Dynamic Preshared Key.

Step 7   Click **Apply** to apply your definitions. Your new dynamic shared key is added to the list of dynamic shared keys.

NOTE   When you add an IP address of a network, it must be in a specific format. For example, if you are adding network 192.168.1.0 with a subnet mask of 255.255.255.0, the entry would be 192.168.1.0/255.255.255.0.

CA Enrollment

When RSA Signature is used as the authentication method, the peers are configured to obtain digital certificates from a CA. This CA manages certificate requests and issues certificates to the participating IPSec network devices. Define CA enrollment parameters to determine how the CA manages certificate requests from devices.

CA enrollment can be defined only at the global level and for one CA system only. You must specify the single CA server to which your routers will send certificate requests.

NOTE   Router MC supports the Microsoft, VeriSign, and Entrust CAs. If you use the Microsoft CA, be sure to specify during installation that challenge passwords should not be requested.

Complete the following steps to configure CA enrollment globally:

Step 1   Choose **Configuration > IKE**. The IKE page is displayed.

Step 2   Use the Object Selector to select the **Global** group. The IKE page will refresh to display the global group on the Object Bar.

Step 3   Select **CA Enrollment** from the TOC. The CA Enrollment page is displayed.

Step 4 Complete the following substeps to configure CA enrollment:

(a) Enter the enrollment URL in the Enrollment URL field.

NOTE The enrollment URL must be in the form of http://*IP_address*, where *IP_address* is the address of the CA enrollment server. If the CA cgi-bin script location is not the default /cgi-bin/pkiclient.exe at the CA, you must also include the nonstandard script location in the URL, in the form of http://*CA_name/script_location*, where *script_location* is the full path to the CA scripts.

(b) Enter the retry period for CA enrollment in the Enrollment Retry Period (minutes) field. The range of time that is useable is 1 to 60 minutes with a default of 1 minute.

(c) Enter the retry count for enrollment in the Enrollment Retry Count field. The range of retires that is useable is 1 to 100 with a default of 10 retries. If you put 0 in this field, the number of retries is infinite.

(d) Check the **Include Router Serial Number** check box if you want to have the router's serial number associated with the CA certificate.

(e) Check the **Re-Enroll** check box to select new certificates from the CA server.

Step 5 Click **Apply**. The CA Enrollment page refreshes to indicate that Router MC received the changes.

Configuring Tunnel Policies

Tunnel policies define what data will be securely transmitted via the tunnel (crypto ACL) and which authentication and encryption algorithms will be applied to the data to ensure its authenticity, integrity, and confidentiality (transform set).

NOTE In Router MC, tunnel policies are defined on spokes. Router MC generates the relevant CLI commands for the spoke and also automatically adds matching policies on the spoke's corresponding hub so that the VPN connection between the peers can be established. If you always deploy to both peers of the VPN connection together, Router MC will ensure compatible policy configuration.

To configure a tunnel policy, use the following steps:

Step 1 Choose **Configuration > Tunnels**. The Tunnels page opens.

Step 2 Choose an appropriate tunneling option from the TOC:

- **Tunnel Policies**—Select this option if you wish to define a VPN connection between two predetermined peers.

- **Dynamic Crypto Policies**—Select this option if you wish to define a VPN for environments where the peers are not always predetermined.

Step 3 Click **Create**. The Name and Comment page opens.

Step 4 Enter an appropriate name in the Name field.

Step 5 (Optional) Enter an appropriate comment in the Comment field.

Step 6 Click **Next**. The Traffic Filter page opens.

Step 7 View the predefined access control entries (ACEs).

An ACL is an ordered list of rules, known as ACEs, that describe how an entire subnet or specific network host interacts with another to permit or deny a specific service, protocol, or both. By default, Router MC allows automatic generation of supplementary ACEs for your jobs.

Each ACE describes network traffic based on source IP address, destination IP address, protocol, and possibly ports. Each ACE has an action to permit or deny. When a packet arrives at a router, the ACEs in the ACL are scanned for the first one that matches the packet. When the router finds a matching ACE, it executes the associated permit or deny action. If no ACE match is found, the packet is denied. At deployment, Router MC compares the settings on your selected routers to all four of the predefined ACEs. Router MC applies the ACEs under circumstances where they match the configuration of your routers.

NOTE   The recommended best practice is to leave all the predefined ACEs in the list. If there are any conflicts with your selected routers, you will be notified at deployment.

You could, at this point, click Create and specify a new ACE, or click Edit to edit an existing ACE. You could also choose to move an ACE up or down in the list to change its priority.

NOTE   If you leave all the predefined ACEs, you will secure all internal traffic on the selected hub and spokes.

Step 8 Click **Next**. The Transform Sets page opens.

Step 9   Click **Create**. The Name and Comment page opens.

Step 10   Enter an appropriate name in the Name field.

Step 11   (Optional) Enter an appropriate comment in the Comment field.

Step 12   Click **Next**. The Transform Set Protocols page opens, as shown in Figure 12-14.

Figure 12-14   *Transform Set Protocols*

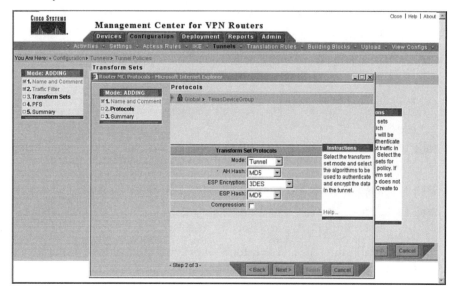

Step 13   Select the appropriate IPSec mode of operation from the Mode list box. Your choices are as follows:

- Transport
- Tunnel

Step 14   Select an appropriate AH hash method from the AH Hash list box. Your choices are as follows:

- MD5
- SHA

NOTE   If you do not want to use AH authentication, do not make a selection in this field.

Step 15 Select an appropriate Encapsulating Security Payload (ESP) encryption method from the ESP Encryption list box. Your choices are as follows:

- DES
- 3DES
- ESP-AES
- ESP-AES 128
- ESP-AES 192
- ESP-AES 256

Step 16 Select an appropriate ESP hash method from the ESP Hash list box. Your choices are as follows:

- MD5
- SHA

Step 17 If you want the data in the IPSec tunnel to be compressed using the Lempel-Ziv-STAC (LZS) algorithm, check the **Compression** check box.

Step 18 Click **Next**. The Summary page opens.

Step 19 Verify that the new transform set parameters are correct. If they are not correct, click **Back** and correct the mistake.

Step 20 Click **Finish**. The new transform set policy is created. Now you need to assign the new policy to a transform set.

Step 21 Select the new transform set policy from the Transform Set 1 list box.

Router MC provides you with two predefined transform sets:

- **Default-Strong-TS**—Offers high security using the following parameters:
  - **Mode**—Tunnel
  - **AH hash**—None
  - **Encryption algorithm**—3DES
  - **Hash algorithm**—SHA
  - **Compression**—None
- **Default-Weak-TS**—Offers lower security using the following parameters:
  - **Mode**—Tunnel
  - **AH hash**—None
  - **Encryption algorithm**—DES

— **Hash algorithm**—SHA

— **Compression**—None

NOTE   You can select up to three transform sets per tunnel policy. If you are defining the policy on a spoke or group of spokes, selecting more than one transform set usually is not necessary, because the spoke's assigned hub would typically be a higher-performance router that is capable of supporting any transform set that the spoke supports. However, if you are defining the policy on a hub for a dynamic crypto environment, you should select more than one transform set to ensure that there will be a transform set match between the hub and the unknown spoke.

Step 22 Click **Next**. The Perfect Forward Secrecy (PFS) page opens.

Step 23 If you wish to use PFS, check the PFS check box and select an appropriate DH group from the Modulus Group list box.

Perfect forward secrecy (PFS) generates a new key by carrying out a DH exchange every time a new quick-mode SA requires a new key to be generated. With PFS, if one key is compromised, previous and subsequent keys are not compromised, because subsequent keys are not derived from previous keys. This option increases the level of security but at the cost of increased processor overhead. You should use PFS only if the sensitivity of the data mandates it.

You need to select the strength of the DH exchange by selecting one of the following from the Modulus Group list box:

- **Group 1**—768 bits
- **Group 2**—1024 bits
- **Group 5**—2048 bits

NOTE   DH Group 2 is recommended because Group 5 is not supported on some smaller Cisco routers, such as the Cisco 800, 2500, or 1700 Series.

Step 24 Click **Next**. The Summary of Tunnel Policy page opens.

Step 25 Verify the tunnel policy information in the Summary of Tunnel Policy page.

Step 26 Click **Finish**. The tunnel policy is created and the main Tunnel Policies page opens.

Upon deployment, the tunnel policy will be applied to the selected device group.

Dynamic Crypto Policies

Dynamic crypto policies are recommended for use in networks where the peers are not always predetermined and are only relevant for hub routers. They allow remote peers to exchange IPSec traffic with a local hub even if the hub does not know the remote peer's identity.

A dynamic crypto map policy created in Router MC essentially creates a crypto map entry without all the parameters configured. The missing parameters are later dynamically configured, as the result of an IPSec negotiation, to match a remote peer's requirements.

Dynamic crypto map entries are used when an unknown remote peer tries to initiate an IPSec SA with the local hub. The hub cannot be the initiator of the SA negotiation.

Complete the following steps to configure a dynamic crypto policy for the global group's hub routers:

Step 1 Choose **Configuration > Tunnels**. The Tunnels page is displayed.

Step 2 Use the Object Selector to select the **Global** group. The Tunnels page will refresh to display the global group on the Object Bar.

Step 3 Choose **Dynamic Crypto Policies** from the TOC. The Dynamic Crypto Policies page is displayed.

Step 4 Click **Create**. The Create Dynamic Crypto Policy window is displayed.

Step 5 Complete the following substeps to configure the dynamic crypto policy settings:

    (a) Select the **Ethernet**, **Fast Ethernet**, **Gigabit Ethernet**, or **Serial interface** type from the Interface drop-down menu.

    (b) Select the slot of the interface from the Slot drop-down menu.

    (c) Select the port of the interface from the Port drop-down menu.

NOTE If you click **Show Interfaces**, a list of available interfaces is displayed.

    (d) Enter the subinterface address, if it exists, in the Subinterface field.

NOTE When entering a subinterface address, enter an integer from 0 to 4294967295.

    (e) Select the transform set from the Transform Set drop-down menu.

Step 6 Click **OK**. The Dynamic Crypto Policies page is displayed with the new dynamic crypto policy.

If necessary, you may edit or delete any dynamic crypto policy in the list.

Task 6: Approving Activities

This section explains how to approve activities using Router MC.

An activity must be approved before its configurations are committed and can be deployed.

NOTE   By default, Router MC allows any user who creates an activity to approve that activity. Later in the chapter, the section "Job Actions" explains how to use the Admin tab to require submission of activities for approval by a user with appropriate permissions.

Complete the following steps to approve your new activity:

Step 1   Select **Approve** from the Actions for Activity list box. The Approve Activity dialog box opens.

Step 2   (Optional) Enter a description for your activity approval.

NOTE   It is recommended that you develop a system by which approval comments are entered. At a minimum, users should enter their initials for later tracking purposes.

Step 3   Click **OK**. The activity is approved and your configurations are committed to the Router MC database. The Activities page is updated to indicate that the activity was approved, as shown in Figure 12-15.

Figure 12-15   *Approved Activities List*

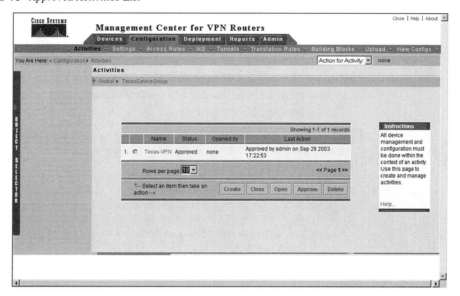

Task 7: Creating and Deploying Jobs

This section explains how to create and deploy jobs using Router MC.

A job is a deployment task in which you specify the routers to which VPN and firewall configurations should be deployed. Router MC generates the CLI commands for the routers specified in the job, based on the policies you defined. These commands can be previewed before deployment takes place. Within the context of the job, you can specify whether to deploy the commands directly to the routers in the network or to a file.

Complete the following steps to create and deploy a Router MC job:

Step 1   Choose **Deployment > Jobs**. The Jobs page opens.

Step 2   Click **Create**. The Name and Description page opens.

Step 3   Enter a unique name for the job in the Name field.

Step 4   (Optional) Enter an appropriate description of the job in the Description field.

Step 5   Click **Next**. The Select Devices page opens.

> **NOTE**   Because Router MC automatically selects routers on which policy changes have been made but have not yet been deployed, in most cases, you will not need to make any device selections.

Step 6   If not already selected by Router MC, select the device group or individual routers from the All tab.

Step 7   Click **Next**. If Router MC has added routers to the job, a dialog box opens listing the names of the added routers and the reason they were added.

Step 8   Click **Close**. The Deployment Options page opens, as shown in Figure 12-16.

Step 9   Select an appropriate deployment method from the following list:

- **Deploy To: Device**—Click this radio button if you want Router MC to deploy the configurations directly to the selected routers by sending CLI commands over an SSH connection.

- **Deploy To: File**—Click this radio button if you want Router MC to deploy the configurations to an output file for each router in the job and place the files in the directory of your choice.

> **NOTE**   If you deploy configurations to a file, you must transfer the configurations from the file to your routers at a later stage. Deploying configurations to a file is useful when the routers are not yet in place in the physical network (also known as greenfield deployment), or if you wish to delay deployment.

Figure 12-16 *Job Deployment Options*

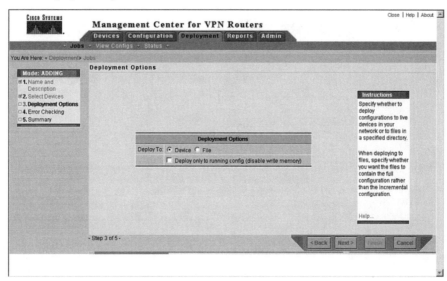

Step 10 If you want to deploy the configurations to your router running configuration only, check the **Deploy Only to Running Config (Disable Write Memory)** check box.

Step 11 Click **Next**. The Error Checking page opens.

NOTE   Errors prevent deployment, whereas warnings do not prevent deployment. If any errors are issued, you must go back and resolve them before deployment may proceed.

Step 12 Click **Next**. The Summary page opens.

Step 13 Review the job creation summary.

Step 14 Click **Finish**. A dialog box opens asking if you want to deploy the job immediately.

Step 15 Click **Yes** to deploy the job now. The Job Deployment Status page opens, as shown in Figure 12-17.

In this page, you can view the deployment status of your job, and of each router in the job relative to the job status.

Jobs proceed through the following states:

* **Generating**—Status displayed while CLI commands are being generated.

* **Deployed**—Status displayed after the job has been deployed.

Figure 12-17   *Job Deployment Status*

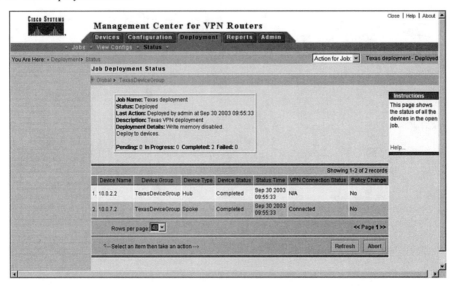

Devices proceed through the following states:

- **Pending**—Status displayed just before deployment starts.

- **Deploying**—Status displayed during deployment.

- **Completed**—Status displayed after the configuration of the router has been deployed.

Step 16 Click **Refresh** to obtain an updated view of job and router states.

Step 17 Choose **Deployment > View Configs**. The Current page opens, as shown in Figure 12-18.

Step 18 Scroll through the Current Configuration window to see the configuration deployed to the router device group.

Step 19 Select **Incremental Tftp** from the TOC. The Incremental Tftp page opens.

Step 20 Scroll through the Incremental TFTP Configuration page to view the CLI commands generated by Router MC.

You have several options available to you in the TOC for viewing configurations:

- **Incremental Telnet**—Displays the CLI commands generated by Router MC for the router, in the current activity or job, in Telnet format. This includes the **do** and **undo** commands required to implement the policies defined for the router in Router MC.

- **Incremental Tftp**—Displays the CLI commands generated by Router MC for the router, in the current activity or job, in TFTP format. This includes the **do** and **undo** commands required to implement the policies defined for the router in Router MC.

Figure 12-18 *Device Group Current Configuration*

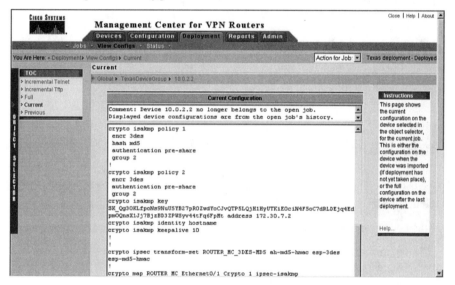

- **Full**—Displays the proposed complete configuration on the router after deployment, including the incremental configuration and the previous configuration of the router.

- **Current**—Displays the current configuration on the router. If deployment has not yet taken place, the current configuration reflects the configuration on the router at the time it was imported. If configurations were previously deployed to the router, the current configuration reflects the full configuration of the router after the last deployment, including the commands that were on the router previously and the commands that Router MC generated for the router to implement the policy definitions.

- **Previous**—Displays the configuration on the router prior to the last successful deployment. If you perform a "rollback" on the job, this will be the configuration that will be restored on the router. If the router has not previously been included in a deployed job, no previous configuration will be available.

Configuring General Cisco IOS Firewall Settings

This section explains how to configure general Cisco IOS Firewall settings using Router MC.

Router MC lets you configure your router to function as a firewall by using CBAC and access rules. General firewall settings include the parameters that are required for implementing CBAC and defining ACL ranges for access rules:

- Fragmentation rules
- Timeouts and performance
- Half-open connection limits
- Logging settings
- ACL ranges

Fragmentation Rules

Fragmentation rules protect hosts from DoS attacks that involve fragmented IP packets. Fragmentation rules are configured by choosing **Configuration > Settings > General Firewall > Fragmentation Rules** to open the Fragmentation Rules window.

Fragmentation rules contain the following elements:

- **Maximum Packets**—Enter the maximum number of packets that will be inspected in the fragmentation rule (Range: 50 to 10,000 packets).
- **Timeout**—Enter the maximum time (in seconds) that a connection for a given protocol in the fragmentation rule can remain active without any traffic passing through the router (Range: 1 to 1000 seconds).
- **Interface**—Select the router interface that you wish to assign the fragmentation rule to.
- **Direction**—Select the direction on the router interface (In or Out) where the fragmentation rule is to be applied.

Timeouts and Performance

CBAC uses timeout and threshold values to manage session state information, to determine when to drop sessions that do not become fully established. These timeouts apply to all sessions that are inspected. Timeouts and performance settings are configured by choosing **Configuration > Settings > General Firewall > Timeouts and Performance** to open the Timeouts and Performance window, shown in Figure 12-19.

The Timeouts and Performance window contains the following elements:

- **TCP SYN Wait**—Enter the length of time (in seconds) the firewall will wait for a TCP session to reach the established state before dropping that session (Cisco IOS default: 30 seconds).
- **TCP FIN Wait**—Enter the length of time (in seconds) a TCP session will continue to be managed after the firewall detects the exchange has ended (Cisco IOS default: 5 seconds).

Figure 12-19 *Timeouts and Performance*

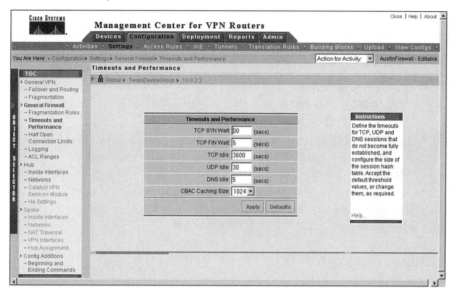

- **TCP Idle**—Enter the length of time (in seconds) a TCP session will continue to be managed after no activity is detected (Cisco IOS default: 3600 seconds).

- **UDP Idle**—Enter the length of time (in seconds) a UDP session will continue to be managed after no activity is detected (Cisco IOS default: 5 seconds).

- **DNS Idle**—Enter the length of time (in seconds) a DNS name lookup session will continue to be managed after no activity is detected (Cisco IOS default: 5 seconds).

- **CBAC Caching Size**—Select a number that specifies the size of the hash table in terms of buckets. Possible values for the hash table are 1024, 2048, 4096, and 8192 (Cisco IOS default: 1024).

Half-Open Connection Limits

Half-open connections occur when a network attacker floods a server with a barrage of requests for connection and does not complete the connection. The resulting volume of half-open connections can overwhelm the server, causing it to deny service to valid requests. Half-open connection limits are configured by choosing **Configuration > Settings > General Firewall > Half-Open Connection Limits** to open the Half-Open Connection Limits window, which contains the following elements:

- **Maximum Incomplete: High**—Enter the number of existing half-open sessions that will cause the firewall to start deleting half-open sessions, to accommodate new connection requests (Cisco IOS default: 500).

- **Maximum Incomplete: Low**—Enter the number of existing half-open sessions that will cause the firewall to stop deleting half-open sessions (Cisco IOS default: 400).

- **Rate Per One Minute: High**—Enter the rate of new session connection attempts (detected in the last one-minute sample period) that will cause the firewall to start deleting half-open sessions, to accommodate new session attempts (Cisco IOS default: 500).

- **Rate Per One Minute: Low**—Enter the rate of new session connection attempts (detected in the last one-minute sample period) that will cause the firewall to stop deleting half-open session (Cisco IOS default: 400).

- **Maximum Incomplete Per Host: Number**—Enter the number of existing half-open sessions with the same destination host address that will cause the firewall to start dropping half-open sessions to that destination host address (Cisco IOS default: 50).

- **Maximum Incomplete Per Host: Block Time**—Enter the length of time (in minutes) for the firewall to block a host that tried to open more than the specified number of connections per minute (Cisco IOS default: 0 minutes).

Logging

The Logging window allows you to enable or disable the configuration of the audit trail and alert features on the selected routers. By default, the Alert option is selected in Cisco IOS software. Logging options are set by choosing **Configuration > Settings > General Firewall > Logging** to open the Logging window.

NOTE   Deselecting the Audit or Alert options disables these actions in the inspection rules and fragmentation rules upon deployment, for new policies only. Access rules that previously enabled these logging features will not be changed automatically.

The Logging window contains the following options:

- **Audit**—Check this check box if you want inspection rules to configure audit trails to be generated on the selected routers (Cisco IOS default: enabled).

- **Alert**—Check this check box if you want inspection rules to configure alert messages on the selected routers.

ACL Ranges

Both standard and extended type ACLs may be used when configuring CBAC on an outbound ACL (at an external interface) or an inbound ACL (at an internal interface). Only extended ACLs can be used to deny CBAC return traffic from entering the network through the firewall. This means, when CBAC creates temporary openings in an ACL, the ACL must be an extended type ACL.

Each ACL on a router has a unique name or number that is used to identify it. Although names are usually used to identify ACLs, specific cases require ACLs to be identified by numbers, such as when using Java blocking in an HTTP inspection rule. When a number is used to identify an ACL, the number must be within the specific range of numbers that is valid for the protocol.

NOTE   When uploading ACLs from a router, the uploaded ACLs might be numbered. The values of the ACL ranges will distinguish between Router MC ACLs and non–Router MC ACLs.

In the ACL Ranges record, you define the ranges of standard and extended ACL numbers. Because only 99 numbers are available for each type of ACL, Router MC provides an extended range of numbers for each of the standard and extended ACL types. ACL ranges are set by choosing **Configuration > Settings > General Firewall > ACL Ranges** to open the ACL Ranges window, shown in Figure 12-20.

Figure 12-20 *ACL Ranges*

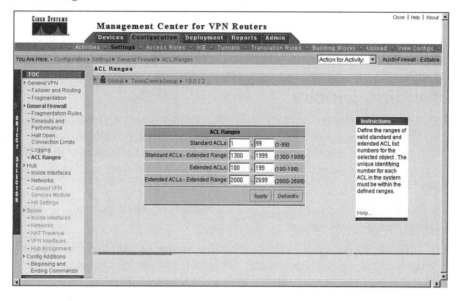

Building Access Rules

This section explains how to build access rules using Router MC.

Router MC uses access rules to define your network security policy. When you configure firewall policies that will be deployed to devices, access rules provide traffic filtering by enabling the implementation of ACLs and CBAC inspection rules on the devices' interfaces.

In Router MC, access rules are defined as either mandatory or default, and can be applied on the global level, device group level, or on an individual router. Begin access rule configuration by choosing **Configuration > Access Rules** to open the Access Rules window, which has the following options:

- **Mandatory**—Mandatory rules are obligatory for descendant objects and cannot be overridden. Mandatory rules are listed first, so they take precedence over any rules that come later.

- **Default**—Default rules can be overridden on descendant objects, because of the first-match nature of access rules. Default rules take effect if no relevant mandatory rules apply.

Access rules are used to build ACLs and CBAC inspection rules for your router interfaces.

Access rules contain the following elements:

- Source address
- Destination address
- Service (protocol)
- Action (permit, deny, and inspect)
- Assigned interface
- Enable (true or false)

Using Building Blocks

This section explains how to use building blocks with Router MC. Building blocks are reusable, named, global components that can be referenced by name by multiple policies. When referenced, a building block is incorporated as an integral component of the policy. If you change the definition of a building block, this change is reflected in all policies that reference that building block.

Building blocks are defined by choosing Configuration > Building Blocks to open the Building Blocks window.

Building blocks aid in policy definition by eliminating the need to define that component each time you define a policy. For example, although transform sets are integral to tunnel policies, you can define several transform sets independently of the tunnel policy definitions. These transform sets are always available for selection when you create tunnel policies (on the objects on which you defined them and its descendants). Each transform set can be referenced by multiple tunnel policies.

NOTE	If you change the definition of a building block, this change is reflected in all policies that reference that building block.

Building blocks are referenced by name. A building block defined on a lower-level object with the same name as a building block defined on the parent object will override the building block on the parent object.

You can define the following types of building blocks:

- **Network groups**—Named collections of networks and/or hosts. A network group name can be referenced during the definition of policies, instead of having to specify each network or host individually for each policy definition.

- **Transform sets**—A combination of security protocols, algorithms, and other settings that specify exactly how the data in the IPSec tunnel will be encrypted and authenticated. During the IPSec SA negotiation, the peers agree to use a particular transform set when protecting a particular data flow.

- **Service groups**—Named collections of protocol and port definition mappings that describe specific network services. Service groups can be referenced during the definition of access rules.

Network Groups

Transform sets are configured by choosing Configuration > Building Blocks > Network Groups to open the Network Groups window.

Network groups contain the following elements:

- **Name**—Enter a name for the new network group.
- **Defined On**—Enter a network for the new network group.

Transform Sets

Transform sets are configured by choosing Configuration > Building Blocks > Transform Sets to open the Transform Sets window.

Transform sets contain the following elements:

- **Name**—Enter a name for the new transform set.
- **Mode**—Select the mode for the new transform set.
- **Defined On**—Select the object group or object that the new transform set applies to.
- **AH Hash**—Select AH Hash if AH is being used for the new transform set.
- **ESP Encryption**—Select the ESP encryption method for the new transform set.
- **ESP Hash**—Select the ESP hash method for the new transform set.
- **Compression**—Select whether or not compression is used for the new transform set.

Service Groups

Router MC 1.2.1 contains 97 redefined service groups. Service groups are viewed and configured by choosing Configuration > Building Blocks > Service Groups to open the Service Groups window.

Figure 12-21 shows the process of creating a new service group.

Figure 12-21 *Creating Service Groups*

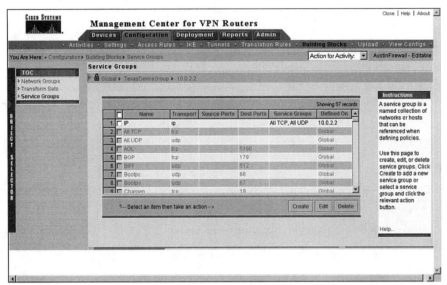

Service groups contain the following elements:

- **Name**—Enter a name for the new service group.
- **Transport**—Select the transport protocol for the new service group.
- **Source Ports**—Select the source ports for the new service group.
- **Destination Ports**—Select the destination ports for the new service group.
- **Service Groups**—Select the services to be part of the new service group.
- **Defined On**—Select the object on which the new service group is to be defined.

Network Address Translation Rules

This section discusses the configuration of NAT rules using Router MC. NAT permits a router or other edge device to translate private network addresses into public network addresses. Although this feature adds a small amount of protection to the addresses, the real significance of NAT is that it limits the requirement for organizations to purchase public addresses.

Address Pool

Router MC supports dynamic NAT only and applies to it an overload feature that permits what is known as port-level NAT or Port Address Translation (PAT). Router MC uses PAT if the addressing requirements of the network exceed the available addresses in the dynamic NAT pool.

PAT can associate thousands of private NAT addresses with a small group of public IP addresses, through the use of port addressing.

Router MC automatically applies these overload features to the range of addresses in the NAT pool. No user intervention is required to enable or configure PAT.

Complete the following steps to configure an address pool on a spoke router:

Step 1   Choose **Configuration > Translation Rules**. The Translation Rules page is displayed.

Step 2   Use the Object Selector to select a spoke router. The Translation Rules page will refresh to display the spoke router on the Object Bar.

Step 3   Choose **Address Pool** from the TOC. The Address Pool page is displayed.

Step 4   Enter the starting IP address of the address pool in the From field.

Step 5   Enter the ending IP address of the address pool in the To field.

Step 6   Enter the subnet mask of the address pool in the Pool Subnet field.

Step 7   Click **Apply**. The Address Pool page refreshes to indicate that Router MC received the changes.

Traffic Filter

Router MC allows you to configure traffic flows to use NAT. Complete the following steps to configure a traffic filter for a spoke router:

Step 1   Choose **Configuration > Translation Rules**. The Translation Rules page is displayed.

Step 2   Use the Object Selector to select a spoke router. The Translation Rules page will refresh to display the spoke router on the Object Bar.

Step 3   Choose **Traffic Filter** from the TOC. The Traffic Filter page is displayed.

Step 4   Click **Create**. The Create Filter window is displayed.

Step 5   Enter a source IP address in the IP Address field or choose a network group from the Network Group drop-down menu.

Step 6   Enter a destination IP address in the IP Address field or choose a network group from the Network Group drop-down menu.

> **NOTE** When adding an IP address of a host or network, it has to be in a specific format. For example, if you are adding network 192.168.1.0 with a subnet mask of 255.255.255.0, the entry would be 192.168.1.0/ 255.255.255.0.

Step 7 Check the **Permit** check box to allow traffic to use NAT.

Step 8 Click **Apply**. The Create Filter window disappears and the Traffic Filter page is refreshed to indicate that Router MC received the changes.

You may move traffic filters up and down in the list as processed by the VPN router by using the Move Up and Move Down buttons. Additionally, you may edit or delete existing traffic filters.

Managing Configurations

This section introduces and explains managing configuration files for VPN routers.

Upload

If you have used a CLI in the past to create and manage VPN policies on your devices, there is no reason to duplicate your efforts simply because you have installed Router MC.

It is important to use the upload function strategically. Uploading is not intended to bring the policies or settings for every individual device in your entire existing network into Router MC. You should upload from only those few devices whose settings are most desirable and most appropriately applied to other devices in your inventory.

Router MC supports the uploading of some, but not all, VPN configuration commands that you have entered at a device CLI. Generally, you can upload VPN configurations that are not peer-specific and that are reusable. These include transform sets, pre-shared keys, dynamic pre-shared keys, CA policies, routing policies, and IKE policies.

VPN configurations must comply with the following conditions to upload successfully:

- You cannot upload a routing policy unless it contains information regarding resiliency, specifying either IKE Keepalive or OSPF/EIGRP. If both resiliency types are present, Router MC does not upload the routing policy. If the source device has more than one routing policy available for upload, Router MC uploads only the first one it encounters. An error occurs if the autonomous number for the routing process is outside the defined autonomous number range for Router MC.

- When uploading a CA policy, the CA identity must be identical to the device domain name or no upload occurs.

- Router MC supports one pre-shared key per object.
- Router MC uploads IKE policies only when they use either a pre-shared key or rsa-sig as the credential type.
- Router MC ignores any CLI commands that it does not support.

Complete the following steps to upload a router's configuration to Router MC:

Step 1 Choose **Configuration > Upload**. The Upload page is displayed, as shown in Figure 12-22.

Figure 12-22 *Upload*

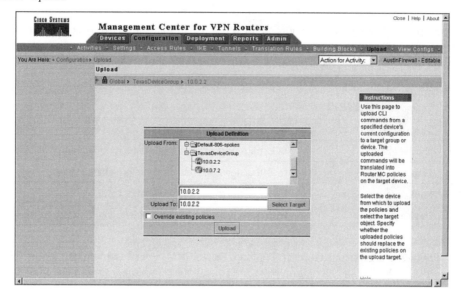

Step 2 Select the source device or group that contains the configuration files you would like to upload from the Upload Definition list.

Step 3 Use the Object Selector to select a target router or group where you would like to have policies uploaded. The Upload page will refresh to display the router on the Object Bar.

NOTE If you select a group as your target, the policies you upload later will apply to every device and subgroup within that group. If you select a single device, the uploaded policy will apply to that device only. You can upload policies only to the object types that support them.

Step 4 Check the **Override Existing Policies** check box to replace existing routing policies, pre-shared keys, or CA policies on the target device or group.

NOTE	Routing policies, pre-shared keys, and CA policies cannot exist in multiple instances on any one device or group in your inventory. If you check the Override Existing Policies check box, policies of these three types from the source device will override all policies currently set on the selected target. Pre-shared keys can exist in multiple instances for a single object in your inventory. GRE policies and CA policies can exist in single instances only, and you can upload them only to the global level in your VPN device hierarchy.

Step 5 Click **Upload**. Support policy types will upload successfully and the Upload page will refresh with an Upload Completed message. If the upload is not successful, the Upload page will refresh with an error message.

Table 12-5 outlines the supported target policy types:

Table 12-5   *Supported Target Policy Types*

Target Object	Supported Policy Type
Global group	IKE, transform set, CA policy, and routing policy
Hub router	IKE, transform set, and dynamic pre-shared keys
Spoke router	IKE, transform set, and pre-shared keys
Device group	IKE, transform set, pre-shared keys, and dynamic pre-shared keys

Following a valid and successful upload, Router MC generates an upload report. This report replaces the Upload Definition page and is available at no other time. The report shows:

- The policies that were uploaded, such as transform set or IKE policy
- Any error messages or warnings encountered
- The actual CLI syntax of the uploaded policies

Viewing Configurations

Router MC enables you to view the CLI commands that will be written to the devices or to configuration files to implement the VPN definitions. You can preview device configurations before you submit an activity or before deployment, or you can confirm the configurations after deployment.

When viewing configurations for devices within the context of an activity, in the Configure tab, you will see commands for the policies in the activity, even if the activity has not been approved and the configurations have not been committed to the database. This enables you to preview the commands that will be generated and, if necessary, to edit the policies in the activity. You will also see commands for previously committed policies.

When viewing configurations for devices within the context of a job, in the Deployment tab, you will see only commands generated for committed policies. You will not see configurations for policies in activities that have not been approved and whose configurations have not been committed to the database.

Within the context of an open activity or job, you have the following options for viewing a device's configurations:

- **Incremental**—Shows the CLI commands generated by Router MC for the device, in the current activity or job. These includes the **do** and **undo** commands required to implement the VPN configurations defined for the device in Router MC but does not include the rest of the device's configurations. You can view the incremental device configurations in Telnet or Trivial File Transfer Protocol (TFTP) format.

- **Full**—Shows the proposed complete configuration on the device after deployment, including the incremental configuration and the previous configuration on the device.

- **Current**—Shows the current configuration on the device. If deployment has not yet taken place, the current configuration reflects the configuration on the device when the device was imported. If configurations have previously been deployed to the device, the current configuration reflects the full configuration on the device after the last deployment, including the commands that were on the device previously and the commands that Router MC wrote to the device to implement the VPN policy definitions.

- **Previous (under Deployment tab only)**—Shows the configuration that was last deployed to the device. If you do the rollback operation for the job, this is the configuration that will be restored on the device. If the device has not previously been included in a deployed job, no previous configuration will be available.

NOTE   When previewing proposed configurations for a hub in an activity, you will not see the commands that will be written to the hub as a result of VPN configurations on a peer spoke. You can preview these commands only within the context of a job.

Complete the following steps to view the current configuration of a spoke router:

Step 1   Choose **Configuration > View Configs**. The View Configs page is displayed.

Step 2   Use the Object Selector to select a spoke router. The View Configs page will refresh to display the spoke router on the Object Bar.

Step 3   Choose **Current** from the TOC. The View Configs page will refresh to display the current configuration of the spoke router.

You may also view configurations of devices by choosing **Deployment > View Configs**.

Router MC Deployment Options

The VPN settings and policies you define in Router MC must be deployed to the devices so that they can be implemented in the network. When you deploy the configurations, you must create a job that contains the previously approved activities. In addition, these jobs will contain devices for which activities have been approved.

Router MC has two deployment options:

- **Direct to device**—You can deploy the configurations directly to the devices in the network. In this case, Router MC is responsible for writing the CLI commands to the devices via SSH.

- **Files**—You can deploy the configurations to an output file. Router MC creates a configuration file for each device in the job and places the files in a directory of your choice. If you deploy configurations to a file, you must transfer the configurations from the file to your devices at a later stage. Deploying configurations to a file is useful when the devices are not yet in place in your network (known as greenfield deployment), if you have your own mechanisms in place to transfer configurations to your devices, or if you want to delay deployment.

NOTE   Router MC generates and deploys committed policy configurations only, meaning the configurations from approved activities. Configurations defined in activities that have not yet been approved cannot be deployed because they have not yet been committed.

Job Actions

You can manage jobs from the Jobs page or from the Jobs list box in the top-right corner of pages in the Deployment tab. The following topics provide information about managing jobs:

- **Creating a job**—Create a job to deploy the VPN policy configurations to your network. When creating a job, specify the devices to which you want to deploy the configurations and whether you want to deploy directly to the devices or to an output file.

- **Opening a job**—You can open a job from the Jobs page in the Deployment tab or from the Action for Job list box located in the top-right corner of pages in the Deployment tab. Opening a job allows you to view the following:

  — The CLI commands that were generated for the devices in the job.

  — Details about the deployment status of devices in a job.

- **Approving a job**—In some organizations, jobs must be approved by a user with the appropriate permissions before they can be deployed. By default, jobs do not have to be approved; however, this setting can be changed in the Application Settings page under the Admin tab. If the job approval stage is enabled, the approver can preview the proposed configurations for the devices in a job and then either approve or reject the job.

- **Deploying a job**—When you deploy a job, you transfer the configurations generated for the devices in the job to the devices in the network directly or to files in a specified output directory (depending on the option you chose when creating the job). When a job has been deployed, its devices become available for inclusion in other jobs. You can deploy a job from the Jobs page in the Deployment tab.

  If you have opened a job, you can deploy the job by selecting Deploy from the Action for Job list box located in the top-right corner of pages in the Deployment tab. When you deploy a job, the Job Deployment Status page appears, indicating the status of the devices in the job.

- **Redeploying a job**—You can redeploy a job if necessary. For example, if the previous deployment failed, correct the problems that caused the deployment to fail and then redeploy the job or change the directory to which configurations are deployed. During redeployment, configurations are written only to devices for which the previous deployment failed. You can redeploy a job from the Jobs page in the Deployment tab, as described in the following procedure. Alternatively, if you have opened a job, you can redeploy the job by selecting Redeploy from the Action for Job list box located in the top-right corner of the pages in the Deployment tab.

- **Rejecting a job**—You can reject a job if necessary and if you have the permissions to do so. For example, if you see problems in the proposed configurations generated for the devices in the job, you can reject the job so that those configurations never reach the devices. When you reject a job, the devices in the job immediately become available for inclusion in other jobs. A rejected job cannot be deployed but it can be opened to view its generated configurations. You can reject a job from the Jobs page in the Deployment tab. Alternatively, if you have opened a job, you can reject the job by selecting Reject from the Action for Job list box located in the top-right corner of the pages in the Deployment tab.

- **Rollback**—After deployment, you can revert to the device's previous configuration, meaning the device configuration prior to deployment. This is known as rollback. You can choose whether to roll back the configuration on all the devices in the job or on only the devices for which deployment failed. Rollback will be implemented only on devices that are not currently included in another job. You can view the configuration that will be restored upon rollback. If a device has been included in multiple jobs, its previous configuration is the configuration prior to the deployment of the last job in which the device was included. When you perform rollback on a job, the device's previous configuration becomes the current configuration and the device no longer has a previous configuration. Therefore, you can perform successful rollback for a device only once. If you roll back another job in which the same device was included, no current configurations will be available for that device when you select View Configs under the Deployment tab.

NOTE Rollback is not done to live devices. The previous configuration is copied to a specified directory, even if you originally deployed directly to your devices.

You can do rollback from the Jobs page in the Deployment tab. Alternatively, if you have opened a job, you can do rollback by selecting **Roll Back** from the Action for Job list box located in the top-right corner of pages in the Deployment tab.

NOTE   You can do rollback only on jobs with a status of Deployed or Redeployed. If the job status is Redeployed, the configurations from the most recent deployment will be restored.

Job Creation

Complete the following steps to create a job for deployment directly to the device:

Step 1   Choose **Deployment > Jobs**. The Jobs page is displayed.

Step 2   Click **Create**. The Name and Description page is displayed.

Step 3   Enter a name and description in the Name and Description fields, respectively.

Step 4   Click **Next**. The Select Devices page is displayed.

Step 5   Select the devices to deploy the configuration changes by using the check boxes.

NOTE   If the global routing policy has changed, it will be necessary to deploy the configuration to all devices, then create another job to deploy individual device configuration changes.

Step 6   Click **Next**. The Deployment Options page is displayed.

Step 7   Select **Device** from the Deploy To drop-down menu and click **Next**. The Error Checking page is displayed. If any errors are encountered, resolve them before continuing with the deployment.

NOTE   The Error Checking page of the Job wizard enables you to view errors and warnings pertaining to the proposed deployment of configurations to the devices in the job.

Step 8   Click **Next**. The Summary page is displayed.

Step 9   Verify that the information displayed on the Summary page is correct and click **Finish**.

Job Status

When you view the job status, by choosing **Deployment > Status**, the job can have the following status:

- **Generating**—Configurations for the devices in the job are currently being generated. You can monitor the generation progress for specific devices in the Status section of the Deployment tab and in the Job Details page, accessed by clicking the job's name in the list.

- **Generated**—Configurations for all the devices in the job have been generated. The configurations can now be viewed in the View Configs section of the Deployment tab.

- **Rejected**—The job, including all its generated configurations, has been rejected. When a job is rejected, its devices immediately become available for inclusion in other jobs. No actions can be performed on a rejected job but you can view the configurations generated for the job and the status of the job, accessed from the Status option under the Deployment tab.

- **Deploying**—The configurations generated for the job are currently being deployed to the devices or to an output directory, depending on the option selected during job creation. You can monitor the generation progress for specific devices in the Status section of the Deployment tab and in the Job Details page, accessed by clicking the job's name in the list.

- **Deployed**—The configurations for all the devices in the job have been deployed to the devices or to output files.

- **Rollback in Progress**—The configurations that were on the devices prior to deployment are currently being restored to a specified directory.

- **Rollback Complete**—The configurations that were on the devices prior to deployment have been restored.

- **Failed**—Deployment to one or more devices in the job failed. You can see the reasons for the deployment failure in the Job Deployment Status page.

Administration

This section explains viewing and generating reports and administering the server.

Deployment Reports

The Deployment Report provides information about the deployment status of every device that you are managing with Router MC. Access the Deployment Report by selecting the **Deployment** option from the Reports tab.

The Job Status column can have the following job statuses:

- **Generating**—Configurations for the devices in the job are currently being generated.

- **Generated**—Configurations for all the devices in the job have been generated.

- **Generation Failed**—Generation of CLI commands for one or more devices in the job failed.

- **Approved**—The job has been approved by a user with the appropriate permissions and is ready for deployment. This status is valid only if job approval is enabled in the Admin tab, meaning that jobs must be approved before they can be deployed.

- **Rejected**—The job, including all its generated configurations, has been rejected.

- **Deploying**—The configurations generated for the job are currently being deployed to the devices or to files in an output directory, depending on the option selected during job creation.

- **Deployed**—The configurations for all the devices in the job have been deployed to the devices or to files.

- **Rollback in Progress**—The configurations that were on the devices prior to deployment are currently being restored to a specified directory.

- **Rollback Complete**—The configurations that were on the devices prior to deployment have been restored.

- **Failed**—Deployment to one or more devices in the job failed.

Activities Reports

The Activities report lists all existing active activities and provides information for each one, such as its status, who has it open, and which objects are selected in the activity.

Choose **Reports > Activities** to view the activities report.

NOTE   Approved or deleted activities are not shown in the activities report.

Audit Trail Reports

You can generate an audit trail report to track past events that occurred in Router MC, such as inventory or policy changes, job and activity history, and so on. When a query is created, specify exactly what information you want and the time period. Router MC generates a report based on your specifications.

Complete the following steps to generate and view an audit trail report:

Step 1   Choose **Reports > Audit Trail**. The Audit Trail page is displayed.

Step 2   Select the component used to generate an audit report for changes by using the check boxes.

Step 3   Enter the login name you wish to filter for an audit report.

Step 4   Select an activity to filter from the Activity Name drop-down menu.

Step 5   Enter a Start Date to filter the date, either by entering it manually or by clicking ... to display a pop-up window that enables you to select a date.

Step 6   Enter an End Date to filter the date, either by entering it manually or by clicking ... to display a pop-up window that enables you to select a date.

Step 7   Use the check boxes to select the fields you want to display on the audit report.

Step 8   Select the field in the Sort By columns to sort the data by time, login name, component, item, activity, and description.

Step 9   Click **Apply**. The Audit Trail page will refresh with the audit report displayed on the page.

Administration

Settings under the Administration tab allow you to configure the performance and behavior of the Router MC application.

If you have Administrator permissions, you can change the settings for the Router MC application. Application settings include activity and job approval settings, settings for historical jobs and activities, and the IGP process range available for GRE.

- **Activity approval**—Checking the Disable Submission of Activities for Approval check box indicates that activities do not need to be submitted for approval. The Submit option is not available for activities. In general, submission of activities for approval is not necessary if the same user typically has the authority to define configurations and commit them to the database.

- **Job approval**—Checking the Disable Approval of Jobs check box indicates that jobs do not need approval before they are deployed.

- **GRE Routing Range fields**—Enter an IGP process range for GRE. The default range is 110 to 120.

- **Maximum Historical Jobs Saved field**—Enter a number of jobs that Router MC discards when the historical jobs exceed this value. The default value is 10.

- **Maximum Historical Activities Saved field**—Enter a number of activities that Router MC discards when the historical activities exceed this value. The default value is 10.

- **Clear Audit Records Date field**—Specify a date in the format MM/DD/YYYY, or click the ... button to select a date from a calendar. Router MC retains only those audit records that were created on or after the specified date.

- **... button**—Click to open a calendar from which you can select the date of the oldest Router MC audit record you want to keep. Click OK to confirm your selection and close the calendar or click Cancel to close the calendar without selecting a date.

- **Config File Suffix field**—Enter the filename suffix required for device configuration files being imported into Router MC. In most cases, the suffix should be .cfg.

- **Apply button**—Click to confirm your selections and apply them.

Chapter Summary

This following list summarizes what Router MC allows you to do, as described in this chapter:

- Deploy VPN configurations to devices or groups of devices.
- Import router VPN settings directly from a device or file.
- Support large installations of VPN routers for ease of administration and support.
- Centralize the configuration of IKE and tunnel policies for multiple devices.

Chapter Review Questions

The following review questions cover some of the key facts and concepts that were introduced in this chapter. Answers to these questions can be found in Appendix A, "Answers to Chapter Review Questions."

1 Which tunnel technologies are supported by the Management Center for VPN Routers (Router MC)?

2 What are building blocks as used in Router MC?

3 The Management Center for VPN Routers is not a standalone application. What host applications are required before you can install Router MC?

4 What are the five types of user authorization roles that can be used in Router MC?

5 What are the names of the five tabs across the top of the Router MC common interface?

6 What menu options would you choose to open the window in which you would identify the VPN interfaces for a spoke router?

7 What deployment options are available for the VPN settings and policies you define in Router MC?

8 What are the options for job status that might be displayed on Status window when you choose **Deployment > Status**?

9 What report types are available from the Reports tab of Router MC?

10 What is the default value of historical jobs saved by the Router MC?

Case Study

The Future Corporation's network structure is shown in Figure 12-23.

Figure 12-23 *The Future Corporation*

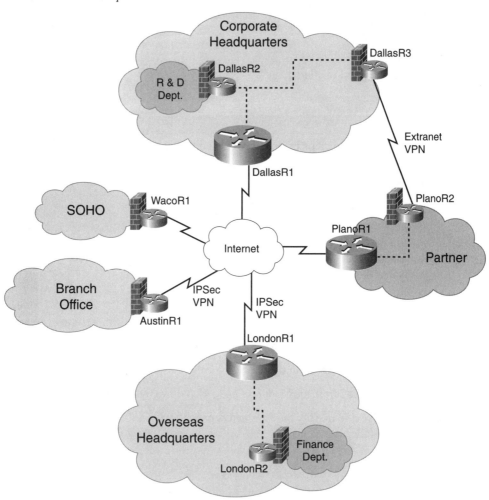

Scenario

You have just installed the Management Center for VPN Routers at your corporate facility in Dallas. You would like to begin using Router MC to configure and manage your VPN routers.

You want to configure the IKE policy for the Austin router. What steps would you follow to configure the IKE policy for AustinR1 to implement these requirements:

- Policy Name: VPNAustin
- Policy Description: VPN to London
- Encryption Algorithm: 3DES
- Hash Algorithm: SHA
- Modulus Group: 2
- SA Lifetime: 86400
- Authentication: Pre-shared key

Solutions

Complete the following steps in Router MC to configure an IKE policy with a pre-shared key for the global group:

Step 1   Choose **Configuration > IKE**.

Step 2   Use the Object Selector to select the **Global** group.

Step 3   Select **IKE Policies** from the TOC.

Step 4   Enter the name **VPNAustin** with a description of **VPN to London** in the Name and Description fields.

Step 5   Click **Next** to bring up the Algorithms page.

Step 6   Complete the following substeps to configure the algorithm settings:

   (a) Select **3DES** from the Encryption Algorithm drop-down menu.

   (b) Select **SHA** from the Hash Algorithm drop-down menu.

   (c) Select **2** from the Modulus Group drop-down menu to select DH Group 2.

Step 7   Click **Next** to display the Parameters page.

Step 8   Enter the lifetime of **86400** in the Lifetime (seconds) field.

Step 9   Select **Preshared Key** from the drop-down menu.

Step 10   Click **Next** to display the Summary page.

Step 11   Verify that the information listed on this page is correct, and then click **Finish**. The IKE Policies page is displayed with the new IKE policy.

CHAPTER 13

Case Study

The following case study will allow you to put together most of the security elements discussed throughout this book. Read through the "Introduction" and "Requirements" sections carefully and then apply what you have learned as you create a solution for The Future Corporation.

Introduction

The Future Corporation recently acquired a facility in Seattle, Washington, in an effort to gain market penetration in the Pacific Northwest. The Seattle facility has connectivity to the Internet through an ISP using a Cisco 3600 router with Cisco IOS Firewall software.

The current administrator has implemented several facilities locally that you will use through the conversion of the facility into The Future Corporation network. Those facilities include Cisco Secure Access Control Server (ACS), DNS, and logging servers.

Your task will be to impose The Future Corporation's security policy onto the Cisco 3600 router in Seattle according to the requirements given in the following section. Additionally, you will be required to establish an IPSec VPN between the SeattleR1 router and the DallasR1 router, as shown in Figure 13-1.

Figure 13-1 *Seattle to Dallas Connection*

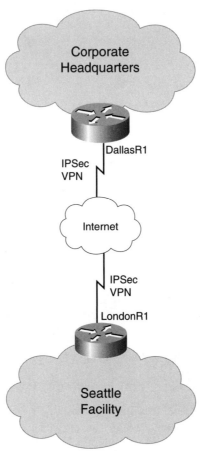

Requirements

Table 13-1 contains the interface and host name information for the Seattle router.

Table 13-1 *Router Interfaces and Host Name*

Router Parameter	Value
FastEthernet 0/0 IP address and mask	192.168.60.1/24
Serial 1/0 IP address and mask	167.221.126.1/30
Host name	SeattleR1

Table 13-2 supplies the specific security policy parameters that have been assigned to the new Seattle router.

Table 13-2 *Basic Security Requirements*

Security Parameter	Value
Enable password	Egr87np0sr
Enable secret password	ESm33qsun2
VTY password	V9344qznrs
AUX password	A6jkbrffh1
CON and AUX inactivity timeout	5 minutes 30 seconds
Password encryption	Enabled
Message of the day (MOTD) banner	WARNING: You are attempting to enter The Future Corporation network. Unauthorized access and use of this network will be vigorously prosecuted.
SNMP read-only community string	RO77SNMP
SNMP read-write community string	RW34SNMP
Admin workstations permitted full access to SNMP data	192.168.60.190, 192.168.60.194, and 192.168.60.227

Table 13-3 specifies the AAA requirements for SeattleR1.

Table 13-3 *AAA Requirements*

Security Parameter	Value
AAA service type	TACACS+
AAA authentication	TACACS+, then local username and password = aaalocal/aaaisdown
TACACS+ server	192.168.60.44
TACACS+ key	aaa345qyb3
Console port login	TACACS+, then enable password
AAA accounting	Record ACS server start and stop times for EXEC and network processes

Table 13-4 specifies generic security settings that are required on all of The Future Corporation's routers.

The Future Corporation employs Context-Based Access Control (CBAC) to help protect applications from intrusion. Table 13-5 shows the CBAC requirements that must be implemented on SeattleR1.

Table 13-4   *Additional General Security Requirements*

Security Parameter	Value
Timestamp	Time-stamp all debug and log messages using local time. Record debug times to the millisecond to assist troubleshooting efforts.
Disable unnecessary services	BOOTP CDP on public interface IP classless routing IP domain lookups Finger service HTTP service IP directed broadcasts on all interfaces IP mask replies on all interfaces IP redirects on the public interface IP source routing IP unreachable messages on the public interface NTP service on all interfaces Proxy ARP Small servers
DNS server	192.168.60.47
Logging server	192.168.60.48
Logging	Enable
Audit trail	Enable
Alerts	Enable

Table 13-5   *CBAC Security Requirements*

Security Parameter	Value
CBAC	Synwait = 50 seconds Finwait = 8 seconds TCP idle = 3300 seconds (55 minutes) UDP idle = 35 seconds DNS timeout = 8 seconds Incomplete high = 750 Incomplete low = 400 One minute high = 500 One minute low = 400

Table 13-6 provides the information you need to create the IPSec configuration required on SeattleR1.

Table 13-6   *IPSec Requirements*

Security Parameter	Value
IPSec	Use CA support and RSA signatures
	Use 1024-bit modulus when generating keys
	CA server = DalVPNCA
	IKE encryption = 3DES
	Group = DH Group 2
	Hash = SHA
	IKE SA lifetime = 57600
	IPSec transforms = esp-sha-hmac and esp-3des
	IPSec SA lifetime = 72000
	IPSec traffic = all traffic to and from DallasR1

Look through the requirements carefully and record the CLI commands that you would be required to execute on SeattleR1 to implement all of The Future Corporation's security policy elements. After you have finished, compare your answers to the proposed solutions provided in the next section.

Solutions

In some cases, your answers may differ from the solutions shown here. Cisco devices may have several different methods of accomplishing the intended results. Access lists, policy names, and other elements local to the Seattle router may vary without affecting the overall solution.

Beginning Router Configuration

The following listing shows the configuration of the new Seattle router at initial installation:

```
Router# show config
Current configuration:
!
Version 12.3
service tcp-small-servers
service udp-small-servers
no service password-encryption
!
hostname Router
!
```

```
interface FastEthernet0/0
 no ip address
 shutdown
!
interface Serial1/0
 no ip address
 shutdown
!
line console 0
line aux 0
line vty 0 4
!
end
```

Solution Configuration Steps

To accomplish the requirements of the scenario, execute the following commands on router SeattleR1:

- Basic security configuration:
  - Set the enable password:

    SeattleR1(config)#**enable password Egr87np0sr**
  - Set the enable secret password:

    SeattleR1(config)#**enable secret ESm33qsun2**
  - Set up vty lines 0 to 4 to use passwords and set the password:

    SeattleR1(config)#**line vty 0 4**

    SeattleR1(config-line)#**login**

    SeattleR1(config-line)#**password V9344qznrs**
  - Set up the auxiliary port to use passwords and set the password:

    SeattleR1(config)#**line aux 0**

    SeattleR1(config-line)#**login**

    SeattleR1(config-line)#**password A6jkbrffh1**
  - Set the inactivity timeout on the console port to 5 minutes and 30 seconds:

    SeattleR1(config)#**line console 0**

    SeattleR1(config-line)#**exec-timeout 5 30**
  - Set the inactivity timeout on the auxiliary port to 5 minutes and 30 seconds:

    SeattleR1(config)#**line aux 0**

    SeattleR1(config-line)#**exec-timeout 5 30**
  - Set up password encryption for all passwords:

    SeattleR1(config)#**service password-encryption**

— Set up the message of the day banner:

SeattleR1(config)#**banner motd #**

WARNING: You are attempting to enter The Future Corporation network. Unauthorized access and use of this network will be vigorously prosecuted. #

— Set the read-only community string:

SeattleR1(config)#**snmp-server community RO77SNMP ro**

— Create the standard ACL containing the permissible IP addresses of the administrative workstations:

NOTE   IP address 192.168.64.123 is located in the overseas headquarters.

SeattleR1(config)#**access-list 88 permit 192.168.60.190**

SeattleR1(config)#**access-list 88 permit 192.168.60.194**

SeattleR1(config)#**access-list 88 permit 192.168.60.227**

— Set the read/write SNMP community string and provide the list of allowable device addresses:

SeattleR1(config)#**snmp-server community RW34SNMP rw 88**

- Configure AAA

— Enable AAA service:

SeattleR1(config)#**aaa new-model**

— Set the default login method to TACACS+ with local authentication for backup:

SeattleR1(config)#**aaa authentication login default group tacacs+ local**

— Establish a local username and password:

SeattleR1(config)#**username aaalocal password aaaisdown**

— Provide the location of the AAA server:

SeattleR1(config)#**tacacs-server host 192.168.60.44**

— Define the key to use with TACACS+ traffic:

SeattleR1(config)#**tacacs-server key aaa345qyb3**

— Create a new authentication entry for the console port:

SeattleR1(config)#**aaa authentication login console-in group tacacs+ enable**

— Set up the console port to use the new authentication entry:

SeattleR1(config)#**line console 0**

SeattleR1(config-line)#**login authentication console-in**

— Set up AAA accounting to record all start and stop times for EXEC processes and network processes on ACS:

SeattleR1(config)#**aaa accounting exec start-stop tacacs+**

SeattleR1(config)#**aaa accounting network start-stop tacacs+**

— Set up the router to time-stamp logging and debug entries using local time; record debug times to the millisecond:

SeattleR1(config)#**service timestamps debug datetime localtime msec**

SeattleR1(config)#**service timestamps log datetime localtime**

- Disable unnecessary services

— Disable BOOTP server:

SeattleR1(config)#**no ip bootp server**

— Disable CDP server:

SeattleR1(config)#**no cdp run**

SeattleR1(config)#**interface s1/0**

SeattleR1(config-if)#**ip address 167.221.126.1 255.255.255.250**

SeattleR1(config-if)#**exit**

— Restrict DNS service:

SeattleR1(config)#**ip name-server 192.168.60.47**

SeattleR1(config)#**no ip domain-lookup**

— Disable finger service

SeattleR1(config)#**no ip finger**

SeattleR1(config)#**no service finger**

— Disable HTTP service:

SeattleR1(config)#**no ip http server**

— Disable IP directed broadcasts:

SeattleR1(config)#**interface s1/0**

SeattleR1(config-if)#**no ip directed-broadcast**

SeattleR1(config-if)#**exit**

SeattleR1(config)#**interface fe0/0**

SeattleR1(config-if)#**ip address 192.168.60.1 255.255.255.0**

SeattleR1(config-if)#**no ip directed-broadcast**

SeattleR1(config-if)#**exit**

— Disable IP mask replies:

SeattleR1(config)#**interface s1/0**

SeattleR1(config-if)#**no ip mask-reply**

SeattleR1(config-if)#**exit**

SeattleR1(config)#**interface fe0/0**

SeattleR1(config-if)#**no ip mask-reply**

SeattleR1(config-if)#**exit**

— Disable IP redirects:

SeattleR1(config)#**interface s1/0**

SeattleR1(config-if)#**no ip redirect**

SeattleR1(config-if)#**exit**

— Disable IP source routing:

SeattleR1(config)#**no ip source-route**

— Disable IP unreachable messages (for interfaces connected to untrusted networks):

SeattleR1(config)#**interface s1/0**

SeattleR1(config-if)#**no ip unreachable**

SeattleR1(config-if)#**exit**

— Disable NTP service:

SeattleR1(config)#**interface s1/0**

SeattleR1(config-if)#**ntp disable**

SeattleR1(config-if)#**exit**

SeattleR1(config)#**interface fe0/0**

SeattleR1(config-if)#**ntp disable**

SeattleR1(config-if)#**exit**

— Disable proxy ARP:

SeattleR1(config)#**interface s1/0**

SeattleR1(config-if)#**no ip proxy-arp**

SeattleR1(config-if)#**exit**

— Disable small servers:

SeattleR1 (config)#**no service tcp-small-servers**

SeattleR1 (config)#**no service udp-small-servers**

— Turn on logging and enable audit trail and alert:

SeattleR1(config)#**logging on**

SeattleR1(config)#**logging 192.168.60.48**

SeattleR1(config)#**ip inspect audit-trail**

SeattleR1(config)#**no ip inspect alert-off**

- Configure CBAC

  — Configure CBAC to wait 50 seconds for a TCP session to reach the established state before dropping the session:

  SeattleR1(config)#**ip inspect tcp synwait-time 50**

  — Configure CBAC to manage TCP sessions for 8 seconds after the firewall detects a FIN exchange:

  SeattleR1(config)#**ip inspect tcp finwait-time 8**

  — Configure CBAC to manage TCP sessions for 55 minutes after no activity:

  SeattleR1(config)#**ip inspect tcp idle-time 3300**

  — Configure CBAC to manage UDP sessions for 35 seconds after no activity:

  SeattleR1(config)#**ip inspect udp idle-time 35**

  — Configure CBAC to manage DNS name lookup session for 8 seconds after no activity:

  SeattleR1(config)#**ip inspect dns-timeout 8**

  — Configure CBAC to permit 600 existing half-opened sessions before starting to delete half-opened sessions:

  SeattleR1(config)#**ip inspect max-incomplete high 750**

  — Configure CBAC to stop deleting half-opened sessions when the number of half-opened sessions reaches 350:

  SeattleR1(config)#**ip inspect max-incomplete low 400**

  — Configure CBAC to start deleting half-opened sessions when the number of new unestablished TCP sessions reaches 450:

  SeattleR1(config)#**ip inspect one-minute high 500**

  — Configure CBAC to stop deleting half-opened sessions when the number of new unestablished TCP sessions reaches 350:

  SeattleR1(config)#**ip inspect one-minute low 400**

- Configure IPSec with CA support

  — Check the current configuration:

  SeattleR1(config)#**show running-config**

  SeattleR1(config)#**show crypto isakmp policy**

SeattleR1(config)#**show crypto map**

SeattleR1(config)#**show crypto ipsec transform-set**

— Ensure that the network works without encryption:

SeattleR1(config)#**ping 172.16.10.1**

— Ensure that ACLs are compatible with IPSec:

SeattleR1(config)#**interface Serial1/0**

SeattleR1(config-if)#**ip access-group 102 in**

SeattleR1(config)#**access-list 102 permit ahp host 203.14.17.1 host 167.221.126.1**

SeattleR1(config)#**access-list 102 permit esp host 203.14.17.1 host 167.221.126.1**

SeattleR1(config)#**access-list 102 permit udp host 203.14.17.1 host 167.221.126.1 eq isakmp**

— Set the router's time and date:

SeattleR1(config)#**clock timezone PST -8**

SeattleR1(config)#**clock set 18:04:16 July 31 2003**

— Configure the router's host name and domain name:

SeattleR1(config)#**hostname SeattleR1**

SeattleR1(config)#**ip domain-name Futurecorp.com**

— Generate an RSA key pair:

SeattleR1(config)#**crypto key generate rsa**

SeattleR1(config)#**How many bits in the modulus [512]: 1024**

— Declare a CA:

SeattleR1(config)#**crypto ca trustpoint DalVPNCA**

SeattleR1(ca-trustpoint)#**enrollment url http://DalVPNCA/certsrv/ mscep/mscep.dll**

SeattleR1(ca-trustpoint)#**crl optional**

SeattleR1(ca-trustpoint)#**exit**

— Authenticate the CA:

SeattleR1(config)#**crypto ca authenticate DalVPNCA**

— Request your own certificate:

SeattleR1(config)#**crypto ca enroll DalVPNCA**

— Verify the CA support configuration:

SeattleR1(config)#**show crypto ca certificates**

SeattleR1(config)#**show crypto key mypubkey rsa**

SeattleR1(config)#**show crypto key pubkey-chain rsa**

— Create the IKE policy:

SeattleR1(config)#**crypto isakmp policy 110**

SeattleR1(config)#**authentication rsa-sig**

SeattleR1(config)#**encryption 3des**

SeattleR1(config)#**group 2**

SeattleR1(config)#**hash sha**

SeattleR1(config)#**lifetime 57600**

— Verify the IKE configuration:

SeattleR1(config)#**show crypto isakmp policy**

— Configure the transform set:

SeattleR1(config)#**crypto ipsec transform-set SeaDal esp-sha-hmac esp-3des**

— Configure the global IPSec SA lifetime:

SeattleR1(config)#**crypto ipsec security-association lifetime seconds 72000**

— Configure the crypto ACL:

SeattleR1(config)#**access-list 110 permit ip 192.168.60.0 0.0.0.255 172.16.10.0 0.0.0.255**

SeattleR1(config)#**access-list 110 deny ip any any**

— Configure the crypto map:

SeattleR1(config)#**crypto map Seadal 110 ipsec-isakmp**

SeattleR1(config)#**match address 110**

SeattleR1(config)#**set peer 203.14.17.1**

SeattleR1(config)#**set transform-set SeaDal**

SeattleR1(config)#**set security-association lifetime 72000**

— Apply the crypto map to the interface:

SeattleR1(config)#**interface Serial1/0**

SeattleR1(config-if)#**crypto map SeaDal**

This scenario did not address IDSs, which are more frequently enabled on interior routers, not on bastion routers, such as SeattleR1. Additionally, the CiscoWorks Management Center for VPN Routers was not included in this scenario because of the difficulty in demonstrating proper implementation of policy parameters through the tool.

Ending Router Configuration

The following listing shows the configuration of the new Seattle router following the application of the solution configuration steps:

```
Router# show config
Current configuration:
!
Version 12.3
no service tcp-small-servers
no service udp-small-servers
no service finger
service timestamps debug datetime localtime msec
service timestamps log datetime localtime
service password-encryption
!
hostname SeattleR1
!
aaa new-model
!
aaa authentication login default group tacacs+ local
aaa authentication login console-in group tacacs+ enable
aaa accounting exec start-stop tacacs+
aaa accounting network start-stop tacacs+
!
username aaalocal password aaaisdown
!
enable secret 5 $1$hMKt$TpsKRGG4P/Ov.KdJ.Nl7b/
enable password 7 0874145D0210001181D
!
ip subnet-zero
!
no ip source-route
no ip finger
no ip domain-lookup
no ip bootp server
no cdp run

ip domain-name Futurecorp.com
ip name-server 192.168.60.47
!
clock timezone PST -8
clock set 18:04:16 July 31 2003
!
ip inspect audit-trail
no ip inspect alert-off
ip inspect tcp synwait-time 50
ip inspect tcp finwait-time 8
ip inspect tcp idle-time 3300
ip inspect udp idle-time 35
ip inspect dns-timeout 8
ip inspect max-incomplete high 750
ip inspect max-incomplete low 400
ip inspect one-minute high 500
```

```
            ip inspect one-minute low 400
            !
            crypto isakmp policy 110
             authentication rsa-sig
             encryption 3des
             group 2
             hash sha
             lifetime 57600
            !
            crypto ca trustpoint DalVPNCA
             enrollment url http://DalVPNCA/certsrv/mscep/mscep.dll
             crl optional
            !
            crypto ipsec transform-set SeaDal esp-sha-hmac esp-3des
            crypto ipsec security-association lifetime seconds 72000
            !
            crypto map Seadal 110 ipsec-isakmp
             match address 110
             set peer 203.14.17.1
             set transform-set SeaDal
             set security-association lifetime 72000
            !
            interface FastEthernet0/0
             ip address 192.168.60.1 255.255.255.0
             no ip directed-broadcast
             no ip mroute-cache
             no ip mask-reply
             ntp disable
            !
            interface Serial1/0
             ip address 167.221.126.1 255.255.255.250
             ip access-group 102 in
             crypto map SeaDal
             no ip proxy-arp
             no ip directed-broadcast
             no ip mroute-cache
             no ip mask-reply
             no ip redirect
             no ip unreachable
             ntp disable
            !
            ip classless
            no ip http server
            !
            logging on
            logging 192.168.60.48
            access-list 88 permit 192.168.60.190
            access-list 88 permit 192.168.60.194
            access-list 88 permit 192.168.60.227
            access-list 102 permit ahp host 203.14.17.1 host 167.221.126.1
            access-list 102 permit esp host 203.14.17.1 host 167.221.126.1
            access-list 102 permit udp host 203.14.17.1 host 167.221.126.1 eq isakmp
            access-list 110 permit ip 192.168.60.0 0.0.0.255 172.16.10.0 0.0.0.255
            access-list 110 deny ip any any
```

```
snmp-server community RO77SNMP ro
snmp-server community RW34SNMP rw 88
!
tacacs-server host 192.168.60.44
tacacs-server key aaa345qyb3
!
banner motd #
WARNING: You are attempting to enter The Future Corporation network. Unauthorized
  access and use of this network will be vigorously prosecuted.
#
!
line console 0
 login authentication console-in
 exec-timeout 5 30
!
line aux 0
 login
 password 7 106D01491542065A0F0F
 exec-timeout 5 30
!
line vty 0 4
 login
 password 7 14341A5B1C513E7A2723
!
```

Answers to Chapter Review Questions

Chapter 1

1. List three reasons that explain why network security is becoming more important.

Answer: Network security is becoming more important because of the increased use of e-business, the requirement to do business safely in unsafe environments, and the need to implement the requirements of network security policies.

2. What is the Cisco SAFE Blueprint?

Answer: The Cisco SAFE Blueprint is a loosely structured guide, based on Cisco and Cisco partner products, that can be used when designing the security elements of a network. SAFE builds layered security by developing and deploying mitigating defenses in depth against expected threats.

3. What are the four types of security threats?

Answer: The four general threats to network security are unstructured threats, structured threats, external threats, and internal threats.

4. List four common attack methods or techniques used by attackers.

Answer: Attackers may use one or more of the following attack methods or techniques to compromise your network: packet sniffers, IP weaknesses, password attacks, DoS or DDoS attacks, man-in-the-middle attacks, application layer attacks, trust exploitation, port redirection, virus attacks, Trojan horses, worms, and, probably most commonly, operator error.

5. What four methods can be used to mitigate the use of packet sniffers by network intruders?

Answer: The use of packet sniffers can be mitigated by using strong authentication, switched infrastructures, antisniffer tools, and cryptography.

6. List four key components of a complete security policy.

Answer: Complete security policies contain most of the following: statement of authority and scope, acceptable use policy, identification and authentication policy,

Internet access policy, campus access policy, remote access policy, and incident handling procedures.

7. What four types of hardware are included in Cisco offerings of network security products?

Answer: Cisco network hardware security products include Cisco IOS Firewalls, Cisco PIX Firewalls, Cisco VPN 3000 Series Concentrators, and Cisco IDSs.

8. Which of the Cisco network security management applications was designed specifically to manage VPNs on Cisco 7100 and 7200 routers?

Answer: Cisco VDM was designed specifically to manage VPNs on Cisco 7100 and 7200 routers.

9. What is the biggest security issue with using syslog servers to record system messages from network devices?

Answer: Syslog messages are sent as clear text between the managed device and the management host. Syslog has no packet-level integrity checking to ensure that the packet contents have not been altered in transit. An attacker may alter syslog data to confuse a network administrator during an attack.

10. What are the three most common methods for implementing NAT?

Answer: NAT is most commonly implemented as static NAT, dynamic NAT, or as NAPT (also called Port Address Translation).

Chapter 2

1. What are the four general classifications used to group physical threats to network security?

Answer: Physical threats to network security can be grouped into these four general classifications: hardware, environmental, electrical, and maintenance.

2. List four methods that can be used to mitigate hardware threats to mission-critical routing and switching equipment located in a telecommunications room.

Answer: Threats to hardware located in telecommunications rooms can be mitigated by doing the following:

- Lock the room and limit access to authorized personnel.
- Ensure that the room is accessible only through secured access points.
- Use electronic access controls with logging of all entry attempts.
- Use security cameras monitored by security personnel at entry points.

3. What is the biggest difference between the enable password and the enable secret password?

   Answer: The enable secret password is always hashed using the MD5 hashing algorithm for storage in the router configuration. Enable passwords are stored in the router configuration as clear text by default.

4. Assuming that all network ports have been connected, configured, and enabled properly, what must be present to permit Telnet access to a router?

   Answer: You must configure a vty user-level password to access a router with Telnet.

5. What Cisco IOS command can you use to encrypt vty passwords?

   Answer: The **service password-encryption** command will encrypt all passwords on a Cisco router except for the enable secret password, which is automatically encrypted.

6. What three services are provided by AAA servers, such as the Cisco Secure ACS system?

   Answer: AAA servers provide authentication, authorization, and accounting services for supported devices.

7. What are the two predominant security server protocols used for AAA with Cisco devices?

   Answer: TACACS+ and RADIUS are the two predominant security server protocols used for AAA with Cisco devices.

8. What three elements are required in S/Key systems?

   Answer: S/Key systems require a client, a host, and a password calculator.

9. What command is used to globally enable the AAA service on a Cisco IOS router?

   Answer: The **aaa new-model** command is used to globally enable the AAA service on a Cisco IOS router.

10. What AAA command would you use to establish local authentication as the default method to use in case the AAA server is not reachable via the network?

    Answer: The **aaa authentication login default local** command establishes local authentication as the default method to use when the AAA server is not reachable.

11. After you have configured AAA authentication and authorization commands globally, what must you do to complete the AAA configuration process?

    Answer: Once you have globally configured AAA authentication and authorization, you need to apply the authentication commands to specific lines and interfaces.

12. List the three **debug** commands that you can use to troubleshoot AAA activities on your Cisco IOS router.

    Answer: The three AAA **debug** troubleshooting commands are **debug aaa authentication**, **debug aaa authorization**, and **debug aaa accounting**.

Chapter 3

1. What authentication protocols are supported by Cisco Secure ACS for Windows?

    Answer: The authentication protocols that Cisco Secure ACS for Windows supports are PAP, CHAP, MS-CHAP, MS-CHAP V2, LEAP, EAP-CHAP, EAP-TLS, and ARAP.

2. Cisco Secure ACS for Windows can communicate with other ACS servers as masters, clients, or peers to enable what three strong distributed system features?

    Answer: The master, client, and peer roles that Cisco Secure ACS for Windows can assume permit authentication forwarding, fallback on failed connections, and remote and centralized accounting.

3. Which Windows NT service module has the primary responsibility for determining whether access should be granted and for defining the privileges associated with each user?

    Answer: The CSAuth Windows NT service module has the primary responsibility for authenticating and authorizing user requests.

4. List the six steps required to install Cisco Secure ACS for Windows?

    Answer: The six steps of the Cisco Secure ACS for Windows installation process are as follows:

    Step 1 Configure the Windows NT or Windows 2000 server to work with Cisco Secure ACS for Windows.

    Step 2 Verify a basic network connection from the Windows NT or Windows 2000 server to the network access server using ping and Telnet.

    Step 3 Install Cisco Secure ACS for Windows on the Windows NT or Windows 2000 server following the Windows NT or Windows 2000 installation shield.

    Step 4 Initially configure Cisco Secure ACS for Windows via the web browser interface.

    Step 5 Configure the network access server for AAA.

    Step 6 Verify correct installation and operation.

5. What protocol must you use to perform the configuration of Cisco Secure ACS for Windows?

    Answer: Cisco Secure ACS for Windows 0 supports only HTML; a web browser is the only way to configure it.

6. When you want to configure reusable sets of authorization components to apply to one or more users or groups of users, which option from the Cisco Secure ACS for Windows main menu would you choose?

    Answer: The Shared Profile Components option from the Cisco Secure ACS for Windows main menu allow you to configure reusable sets of authorization components to apply to one or more users or groups of users.

7. What system administration capabilities does the Cisco Secure ACS for UNIX enable for UNIX 2.3 DSM?

Answer: The DSM function of Cisco Secure ACS for UNIX 2.3 allows system administrators to do the following:

- Limit the number of concurrent sessions that are available to a specific user, group, or VPDN.

- Set per-user session limits for individual users or groups of users.

8. What operating system supports Cisco Secure ACS for Unix 2.3?

Answer: Cisco Secure ACS for Unix 2.3 requires Sun Microsystems' Solaris operating system, release 2.6 or 2.5.1 that has current patches installed.

9. What are the first steps that are required to configure a Cisco IOS router to use TACACS+ with a Cisco Secure ACS for Windows server?

Answer: The first steps that are required to configure a Cisco IOS router to use TACACS+ with a Cisco Secure ACS for Windows server are to enable TACACS+, specify the list of Cisco Secure ACS for Windows servers that will provide AAA services for the router, and configure the encryption key that is used to encrypt the data transfer between the router and the Cisco Secure ACS for Windows server.

10. You will be configuring your Cisco IOS router for access to three different Cisco Secure ACS for Windows servers using TACACS+. What must you keep in mind as you prepare to configure the router for AAA service?

Answer: When configuring a TACACS+ key for use on multiple TACACS+ servers, remember that the key must be the same for all TACACS+ servers listed for a given router.

11. Which Cisco IOS command can you use to get a more meaningful output from debug commands?

Answer: You can use the **service timestamps** command to get a more meaningful output from debug commands on Cisco IOS devices.

Chapter 4

1. List six network services that you might want to disable on your Cisco IOS Firewall router.

Answer: For security reasons, you might want to disable some or all of the following services: BOOTP service, CDP, classless routing behavior, configuration auto-loading, DNS, finger, HTTP service, IP directed broadcasts, IP mask reply, IP redirects, IP source routing, IP unreachable notifications, NTP service, proxy ARP, SNMP, TCP small servers, and UDP small servers.

2. What command would you use to disable BOOTP service on your Cisco IOS Firewall, and where would the command be applied?

Answer: You can disable BOOTP service on your Cisco IOS Firewall by using the **no ip bootp server** global command.

3. You can disable CDP either globally or by individual interface on a Cisco IOS device. What global and interface commands would you use in each case?

Answer: To disable CDP globally on a Cisco IOS device, use the **no cdp run** global command. To disable CDP for an interface, use the **no cdp enable** command in interface configuration mode.

4. What are the major differences between a standard IP ACL and an extended IP ACL on a Cisco IOS device?

Answer: Standard IP ACLs on Cisco IOS devices can permit or deny packets based on the source IP address only. Extended IP ACLs can permit or deny packets based on any combination of the following: source IP address, destination IP address, source TCP/UDP port, destination TCP/UDP port, ICMP and IGMP message types, and protocol type.

5. What is the key feature of the Turbo ACL feature of Cisco IOS Firewalls?

Answer: The Cisco IOS Firewall Turbo ACL feature compiles the ACLs into a set of lookup tables, while maintaining the first match requirements.

6. What are the four types of enhanced ACLs within the Cisco IOS Firewall product?

Answer: The enhanced ACL types of the Cisco IOS Firewall product are dynamic, time-based, reflexive, and CBAC.

7. You have created a standard ACL with the following entry:

access-list 84 permit 168.41.0.0 0.0.255.255

You have applied the list to inbound traffic on your Cisco IOS Firewall's external interface. What will be the effect of this ACL?

Answer: ACL 84 will permit all outbound traffic, but will only allow inbound traffic from network 168.41.0.0. All other inbound network traffic will be dropped by the implicit deny all entry inherent as the last entry in every standard or extended ACL.

8. Create a standard named ACL and apply it to serial interface 3/4 on your Cisco IOS Firewall, AustinHQ1, for inbound traffic. The ACL should permit all addresses from network 203.43.18.0 except for hosts 203.43.18.47 and 203.43.18.123. Additionally, this ACL should prevent traffic from all other sources. Name the ACL EastAustin. Show the commands that would be required to complete this assignment.

Answer: To create and apply the standard named ACL described in the question, enter the following commands:

```
AustinHQ1# config t
AustinHQ1 (config)# ip access-list standard EastAustin
AustinHQ1 (config-std-nacl)# deny 203.43.18.47
AustinHQ1 (config-std-nacl)# deny 203.43.18.123
AustinHQ1 (config-std-nacl)# permit 203.43.18.0 0.0.0.255
AustinHQ1 (config-std-nacl)# exit
AustinHQ1 (config)# interface s3/4
AustinHQ1 (config-if)# ip access-group EastAustin in
AustinHQ1 (config-if)# end
```

9. What are the three basic rules that you should follow when developing ACLs?

   Answer: When you are developing ACLs you should follow these three basic rules:

   Rule #1: Write it out.

   Rule #2: Set up a development system.

   Rule #3: Test.

10. What are the two ways to control access to router services?

    Answer: You can control access to router services by disabling the service itself or by restricting access to the service by using ACLs.

11. Configure an ACL and apply it to the appropriate line(s) to restrict Telnet access to router AustinHQ3 to the management workstations at 172.17.19.44 and 172.17.19.73.

    Answer: Your ACL number or name may differ, but the following example of an extended ACL applied to vty lines 0 to 4 will limit Telnet access to the management workstations 172.17.19.44 and 172.17.19.73:

```
AustinHQ3# config t
AustinHQ3(config)# access-list 123 permit host 172.17.19.44 eq 23 any log
AustinHQ3(config)# access-list 123 permit host 172.17.19.73 eq 23 any log
AustinHQ3(config)# access-list 123 deny any log
AustinHQ3(config)# line vty 0 4
AustinHQ3(config-line)# access-class 123 in
AustinHQ3(config-line)# end
```

12. Why might you want to filter ICMP messages on your Cisco IOS Firewall router?

    Answer: You might want to filter ICMP messages because ICMP Echo packets can be used to discover subnets and hosts on the protected network and can also be used to generate DoS floods. ICMP redirect messages can be used to alter host routing tables. Both ICMP echo and redirect messages should be blocked inbound by the router.

13. When you set up logging on your Cisco IOS device, you can send the log message to one or more facilities. What are the five most common facilities that can be used for this purpose?

    Answer: When you set up logging on your Cisco IOS device, you can send the log messages to the console, to terminal lines, to the memory buffer, to SNMP traps, or to a syslog device.

14. Cisco router log messages fall into one of eight levels from 0 to 7. Which of these level numbers indicates the most severe error condition?

    Answer: Cisco log message level 0 indicates the most severe error condition. Level 0 messages indicate that the router is unusable.

15. You have set up a syslog server at 172.16.19.47. You want to begin sending log messages to that device for error messages indicating a critical condition on router AustinHQ7. What commands would you enter on the router to set up this new logging requirement?

    Answer: Enter the following commands to begin logging critical messages to the syslog device at 172.16.19.47:

    ```
    AustinHQ7# config t
    AustinHQ7(config)# logging 172.16.19.47
    AustinHQ7(config)# logging trap critical
    AustinHQ7(config)# logging on
    AustinHQ7(config)# end
    ```

Chapter 5

1. What three features does the Cisco IOS Firewall feature set add to Cisco IOS routers to provide network protection on multiple levels?

   Answer: The Cisco IOS Firewall feature set adds CBAC, authentication proxy, and intrusion detection to Cisco IOS routers to provide network protection on multiple levels.

2. What is the key feature of CBAC?

   Answer: The key feature of CBAC is that it intelligently filters TCP and UDP packets based on application layer protocol session information.

3. What is the key feature of the Cisco IOS Firewall authentication proxy?

   Answer: The Cisco IOS Firewall authentication proxy enables network administrators to apply specific security policies on a per-user basis.

4. When the Cisco IOS Firewall IDS detects a signature match on a packet, what are the three configurable actions that can be taken?

   Answer: When the Cisco IOS Firewall IDS detects a signature match on a packet, the firewall can send an alarm, drop the packet, or send TCP resets to terminate the session.

5. CBAC guards against DoS attacks by keeping track of which three thresholds?

   Answer: CBAC guards against DoS attacks by keeping track of these three thresholds:

   • The total number of half-opened TCP or UDP sessions

   • The number of half-opened sessions based on time

   • The number of half-opened TCP-only sessions per host

6. How does CBAC keep track of session information?

Answer: CBAC uses a state table to maintain session state information. Whenever a packet is inspected, a state table is updated to include information about the state of the packet's connection. Return traffic id permitted back through the firewall only if the state table contains information indicating that the packet belongs to a permissible session.

7. List six application layer protocols that can be configured for CBAC.

Answer: CBAC can be configured to manage any of these TCP/UDP application layer protocols: RPC, Microsoft RPC, FTP, TFTP, UNIX R-commands, SMTP, HTTP, Java, SQL*Net, RTSP, H.323, Microsoft NetShow, StreamWorks, and VDOLive.

8. What device does CBAC use to control the flow of allowable session traffic through an interface?

Answer: CBAC uses dynamic ACLs to control the flow of allowable session traffic through an interface. ACL entries are dynamically created and deleted. CBAC dynamically creates and deletes ACL entries at the firewall interfaces, according to the information maintained in the state tables. These ACL entries are applied to the interfaces to examine traffic that is flowing back into the internal network. These entries create temporary openings in the firewall to permit only traffic that is part of a permissible session.

9. What six basic tasks are required to configure CBAC on a Cisco IOS Firewall router?

Answer: The six basic tasks that are required to configure CBAC on a Cisco IOS Firewall router are as follows:

- Set audit trails and alerts.
- Set global timeouts and thresholds.
- Define PAM.
- Define inspection rules.
- Apply inspection rules and ACLs to interfaces.
- Test and verify.

10. What command would you use to specify how long the software will wait for a TCP session to reach the established state before dropping the session?

Answer: To specify how long the software will wait for a TCP session to reach the established state before dropping the session, use the **ip inspect tcp synwait-time** command.

11. You want to specify the number of allowable half-opened sessions that your Cisco IOS Firewall router will maintain before it begins to drop sessions at 350 half-opened sessions. What command would you use to accomplish this requirement?

Answer: To set the number of existing half-opened sessions that will cause the Cisco IOS Firewall software to start deleting half-opened sessions at 350, use the **ip inspect max-incomplete high 350** command.

12. What command would you use to define a set of CBAC inspection rules on a Cisco IOS Firewall?

Answer: Use the **ip inspect name** command in global configuration mode to define a set of CBAC inspection rules on a Cisco IOS Firewall.

Chapter 6

1. What is the key feature of the Cisco IOS Firewall authentication proxy?

Answer: The key feature of the Cisco IOS Firewall authentication proxy is that it enables network administrators to apply specific security policies on a per-user basis.

2. When using the Cisco IOS Firewall authentication proxy to apply per-user policies, where are the policies for the users stored?

Answer: When using the Cisco IOS Firewall authentication proxy to apply per-user policies, the policies for the users are stored on ACS servers.

3. How does a Cisco IOS Firewall apply policies from each user's profile when performing authentication proxy functions?

Answer: When performing authentication proxy services for users, the Cisco IOS Firewall uses the information from each user's profile to create dynamic access control entries (ACEs) and add them to the inbound (input) ACL of an input interface, and to the outbound (output) ACL of an output interface if an output ACL exists at the interface. By doing this, the firewall allows authenticated users access to the network as permitted by the authorization profile.

4. How does the authentication proxy handle failed login attempts?

Answer: The Cisco IOS Firewall authentication proxy has a failed-attempt lockout function. If the authentication fails, the authentication proxy reports the failure to the user and prompts the user with multiple retries. If the user fails to authenticate after five attempts, the user must wait two minutes and initiate another HTTP session to trigger the authentication proxy.

5. What happens when the idle timer expires for a user of authentication proxy services?

Answer: If the idle timer expires, the authentication proxy removes the user's profile information and dynamic ACL entries. When this happens, traffic from the client host is blocked. The user must initiate another HTTP connection to trigger the authentication proxy.

6. Which TACACS+ AAA protocols and servers does the Cisco IOS Firewall authentication proxy support?

Answer: The Cisco IOS Firewall authentication proxy supports the following TACACS+ AAA protocols and servers:

- Cisco Secure ACS for Windows NT/2000 (Cisco Secure ACS-NT/2000)
- Cisco Secure ACS for UNIX (Cisco Secure ACS-UNIX)
- TACACS+ Freeware

7. Which RADIUS AAA protocols and servers does the Cisco IOS Firewall authentication proxy support?

   Answer: The Cisco IOS Firewall authentication proxy supports the following RADIUS AAA protocols and servers:

   - Cisco Secure ACS for Windows
   - Cisco Secure ACS for UNIX
   - Lucent Technologies Ascend RADIUS server
   - Lucent Technologies Livingston RADIUS server

8. List the tasks that are required to configure the authentication proxy.

   Answer: The following are the tasks required to configure the authentication proxy:

   - Task 1—Configure the AAA server.
   - Task 2—Configure AAA on the router:
     - Enable AAA.
     - Specify AAA protocols.
     - Define AAA servers.
     - Allow AAA traffic.
     - Enable the router's HTTP server for AAA.
   - Task 3—Authenticate the proxy configuration on the router:
     - Set the default idle time.
     - Create and apply authentication proxy rules.
   - Task 4—Verify the configuration.

9. What commands would you use to enable the HTTP server service on your router and then force AAA authentication for this service?

   Answer: To use the authentication proxy, use the **ip http server** command to enable the HTTP server on the router and use the **ip http authentication aaa** command to make the HTTP server use AAA for authentication.

Chapter 7

1. What are two important issues to consider when implementing Cisco IOS IDS?

   Answer: When implementing Cisco IOS IDS, you need to consider the performance impact of memory usage and the limited signature coverage.

2. What are the two types of signature implementations used by Cisco IOS IDS?

   Answer: Cisco IOS IDSs use atomic and compound signatures. Atomic signatures are those that trigger on a single packet. Compound signatures are those that trigger on multiple packets.

3. What three response options are available when using Cisco IOS IDS?

   Answer: Routers that are equipped with Cisco IOS IDS can take three possible actions when the packets of a session match a signature: send an alarm to alert administrators; reset TCP sessions; or immediately drop packets. These methods can be used by themselves or in combination with each other.

4. What five steps must be completed to initialize Cisco IOS IDS?

   Answer: To initialize Cisco IOS IDS, complete these five steps:

   - Set the notification type.
   - Set the router's PostOffice parameters.
   - Set Security Monitor's PostOffice parameters.
   - Set the protected network definition.
   - Set the router's maximum queue size for holding alarms.

5. What command would you use on a Cisco IOS IDS to set 134.14.15.0 through 134.14.37.0 as addresses on protected networks?

   Answer: On a Cisco IOS IDS, to set 134.14.15.0 through 134.14.37.0 as addresses on protected networks, use the following command:

   ip audit po protected 134.14.15.0 to 134.14.37.254

6. What command would you use to set the spam attack threshold to 120 messages on a Cisco IOS IDS?

   Answer: To set the spam attack threshold to 120 messages on a Cisco IOS IDS, use the following command:

   ip audit smtp spam 120

7. You have set up your Cisco IOS IDS router to discard packets for certain types of attack activities. You would still like to be notified when the router sees the specific attack profiles. Where would you place the audit rule and what direction of traffic would you monitor to see alarms for these attack profiles?

   Answer: You have set up your Cisco IOS IDS router to discard packets for certain types of attack activities. You would still like to be notified when the router sees the specific attack profiles. Place the audit rule on the inbound direction of the interface that handles the incoming traffic.

8. Create an audit rule named AUDIT5 that presents alarms for information and attack signatures. The rule should also drop offending attack packets and reset TCP sessions when they present an attack profile.

   Answer: The following commands will create an audit rule named AUDIT5 that presents alarms for information and attack signatures, as well as specify that attack signature packets should be dropped and attack TCP sessions should be reset:

ip audit name AUDIT5 info action alarm

ip audit name AUDIT5 attack action alarm drop reset

9. Which **show** command would you use to display the interface settings for the interfaces of your Cisco IOS IDS router?

   Answer: Use the command **show ip audit interface** to display the interface settings for the interfaces of your Cisco IOS IDS router.

10. Which command would you use to configure you Cisco IOS IDS router to send alarm notifications to a syslog server?

   Answer: To configure your Cisco IOS IDS router to send alarm notifications to a syslog server, use the **ip audit notify log** global configuration command.

11. When using PostOffice to send alerts from your Cisco IOS IDS router to your Security Monitor, what additional information must you supply that is not required when using syslog?

   Answer: When using PostOffice to send alerts from your Cisco IOS IDS router to your Security Monitor, you need to supply the following information (not required with syslog):

   (a) Host ID

   (b) Organization name

   (c) Organization ID

   (d) PostOffice port

   (e) Heartbeat interval

Chapter 8

1. What are the two major types of VPN solutions that were discussed in this chapter?

   Answer: Remote access VPNs and site-to-site VPNs are the two major types of VPN solutions that were discussed in this chapter.

2. What makes the DH public key exchange such a versatile tool?

   Answer: The DH key agreement is a public key exchange method that provides a way for two peers to establish a shared secret key, which only they know, over an insecure channel.

3. What three peer authentication methods can be used with IPSec?

   Answer: Pre-shared keys, RSA signatures, and RSA-encrypted nonces are the three peer authentication methods that can be used with IPSec.

4. Which IPSec protocol provides both confidentiality and authentication?

   Answer: The ESP protocol provides both confidentiality and authentication. AH provides only authentication.

5. What are the five steps of IPSec?

   Answer: The five steps of IPSec are:

   (a) Interesting traffic is identified.

   (b) Peers negotiate a basic set of security services that will be used to protect all subsequent communications between the peers.

   (c) Peers negotiate IPSec SA parameters.

   (d) Data is transferred between IPSec peers based on the IPSec parameters and keys stored in the SA database.

   (e) IPSec SAs terminate through deletion or by timing out.

6. What is the purpose of a transform set?

   Answer: A transform set is a combination of algorithms and protocols that enacts a security policy for traffic.

7. What are the five IKE phase 1 policy parameters?

   Answer: The five IKE phase 1 policy parameters are the encryption algorithm, the hash algorithm, the authentication method, the key exchange method, and the security association lifetime.

8. What command do you use to define an IKE policy?

   Answer: You use the **crypto isakmp policy** command to define an IKE policy.

9. What command would you use to define an IKE pre-shared key of Key1234 to use with a peer that has a host name of MyPeer567?

   Answer: To define an IKE pre-shared key of Key1234 to use with a peer that has host name of MyPeer567, use the command **crypto isakmp key Key1234 hostname MyPeer567**.

10. What command do you use to establish a crypto map on an interface?

    Answer: You use the **crypto map** *map-name* command to establish a crypto map on an interface.

11. What are five important **show** commands that you can use to verify your IKE and IPSec configurations?

    Answer: Five important **show** commands that you can use to verify your IKE and IPSec configurations are as follows:

    - **show running-configuration**

- **show crypto isakmp policy**
- **show crypto ipsec transform set**
- **show crypto ipsec sa**
- **show crypto map**

12. What is the default lifetime for manually configured IPSec SAs?

Answer: Manually configured IPSec SAs never expire. This is just one of several factors that make the manual configuration of IPSec SAs a poor choice.

13. What configuration tasks are required to enable NAT Transparency on Cisco IOS routers with Cisco IOS versions 12.2(13)T or later?

Answer: NAT Transparency is enabled by default on Cisco IOS versions 12.2(13)T or later. No configuration tasks are required.

Chapter 9

1. What is the purpose of the SCEP protocol?

Answer: The purpose of the SCEP protocol is to provide a standard way of managing the certificate lifecycle.

2. Which CA servers provide interoperability with Cisco IOS software?

Answer: The following CA servers interoperate with Cisco IOS software:

- Entrust Technologies Entrust/PKI
- VeriSign OnSite
- Betrusted UniCERT
- Microsoft Windows Certificate Services

3. What three tasks must you perform as you prepare for CA support?

Answer: As you prepare for CA support, you need to:

- Determine the type of CA server to use.
- Identify the CA server's IP address, host name, and URL.
- Identify the CA server administrator contact information.

4. What Cisco IOS command would you use to generate an RSA key pair?

Answer: To generate an RSA key pair, use the Cisco IOS **crypto key generate rsa** command.

5. What command mode must you be in to enter the encryption, hash, authentication, group, and lifetime IKE policy commands.

Answer: To enter the encryption, hash, authentication, group, and lifetime IKE policy commands, you must be in **config-isakmp** command mode. Use the **crypto isakmp policy** command to enter this command mode.

6. You are setting up IPSec on an existing router and want to be sure that all previous RSA keys have been removed. What command would you use to delete all of your router's RSA keys?

    Answer: To delete all of your router's RSA keys, use the **crypto key zeroize rsa** command in global configuration mode.

7. What are the five steps required to complete Task 4, configuring IPSec on Cisco routers?

    Answer: The following five steps are used to configure IPSec encryption on Cisco routers:

    (a) Configure transform set suites.

    (b) Configure global IPSec SA lifetimes.

    (c) Configure crypto ACLs.

    (d) Configure crypto maps.

    (e) Apply the crypto maps to the terminating or originating interface.

8. What command do you used to apply a crypto map to an interface on a Cisco router?

    Answer: To apply a crypto map to an interface on a Cisco router, use the **crypto map** command in **config-if** command mode.

9. What command would you use to view IPSec SAs on your Cisco router?

    Answer: To view IPSec SAs on your Cisco router, use the **show crypto ipsec sa** command.

10. What specific Cisco IOS **debug** commands are available to view CA events?

    Answer: Debug CA events through Cisco IOS with the **debug crypto key-exchange** and **debug crypto pki** commands.

Chapter 10

1. If a VPN client is suddenly disconnected, what feature of Cisco Easy VPN Server lets clients reconnect without having to wait for previous SAs to timeout or be deleted?

    Answer: The initial-contact capability of Cisco Easy VPN Server permits disconnected clients to reconnect without having to wait for previous SAs to timeout or be deleted. If a VPN client or router is connecting to another Cisco gateway for the first time, an initial-contact message is sent that tells the receiver to ignore and delete any old connection information that has been maintained for that newly connecting peer.

2. Which Cisco hardware devices can act as Cisco Easy VPN Servers?

    Answer: Cisco IOS routers, PIX Firewalls, and Cisco VPN 3000 Series Concentrators can act as Cisco Easy VPN Servers.

3. Which IPSec protocol does Cisco Easy VPN Server support?

Answer: Cisco Easy VPN Server supports the ESP IPSec protocol. The AH IPSec protocol is not supported.

4. Which Cisco products support the Cisco Easy VPN Remote feature?

Answer: The following list details Cisco VPN Clients that support the Cisco Easy VPN Remote feature:

- Cisco VPN Client 3.x or later
- Cisco VPN 3002 Hardware Client 3.x or later
- Cisco PIX Firewall 501 and 506 VPN client
- Cisco Easy VPN Remote routers
  - Cisco 800 series
  - Cisco 900 series
  - Cisco 1700 series

5. What are the two modes of operation that can be used with Cisco Easy VPN Remote Phase II devices?

Answer: Cisco Easy VPN Remote Phase II devices support client mode and network extension mode.

6. Which Cisco Easy VPN Remote mode of operation is not compatible with PAT?

Answer: The Cisco Easy VPN Remote network extension mode is not compatible with PAT.

7. The first task in configuring a Cisco IOS router for Cisco Easy VPN Server usage is to create an IP address pool. When might you not have to create this pool?

Answer: Creating a local address pool is optional if you are using an external DHCP server.

8. What elements make up a group policy that will be pushed from a Cisco IOS router to a Cisco Easy VPN Remote client?

Answer: The IKE pre-shared key, DNS server addresses, WINS server addresses, DNS domain name, split tunneling, and the local IP address pool are the elements that make up a group policy that will be pushed from a Cisco IOS router to a Cisco Easy VPN Remote client.

9. What command would you use to enable IKE DPD on a Cisco IOS Easy VPN Server to check every 60 seconds with 5 second retries?

Answer: The command to use to enable IKE DPD on a Cisco IOS Easy VPN Server to check every 60 seconds with 5 second retries is **crypto isakmp keepalive 60 5**.

10. What feature of Cisco VPN Client blocks all inbound traffic to Cisco VPN Client that is not related to an outbound session?

Answer: The Stateful Firewall (Always On) feature of Cisco VPN Client blocks all inbound traffic to Cisco VPN Client that is not related to an outbound session.

11. What three tabs are available from the Properties window that is activated from the Options menu of a Cisco VPN Client connection?

Answer: General, Authentication, and Connections tabs are available from the Properties window activated from the Options menu of a Cisco VPN Client connection.

12. Where would you configure a Cisco VPN Client to connect to a Cisco Easy VPN Server via TCP through a firewall or router that is running NAT?

Answer: You would configure a Cisco VPN Client to connect to a Cisco Easy VPN Server via TCP through a firewall or router that is running NAT by clicking the appropriate radio button on the General tab of the connection.

Chapter 11

1. What is the suggested workflow presented by SDM to help guide untrained users through an initial router configuration?

Answer: The suggested workflow presented by SDM to help guide untrained users through an initial router configuration is:

(a) Configure LAN parameters.

(b) Configure WAN parameters.

(c) Configure firewall parameters.

(d) Configure VPN parameters.

(e) End with a security audit

2. Which router platforms support SDM?

Answer: SDM is supported on a variety of Cisco IOS routers, including Cisco 800, 1700, 2600XM, 3600, and 3700 series routers.

3. Where is the SDM application installed so that it can be accessed from a supported web browser?

Answer: SDM is installed in the router's Flash Memory for access from supported web browsers.

4. When using SDM for the first time, what is the default administrative username and password?

Answer: When SDM is accessed for the first time, the default username and password are both lowercase sdm.

5. During initial router configuration using the SDM Startup Wizard, what are the default security configuration settings?

   Answer: The default security configuration settings employed by the SDM Startup Wizard are:

   - Disable SNMP on your router
   - Disable services that involve security risks
   - Enable services for enhanced security on the router/network
   - Enhance security on router access
   - Encrypt passwords

6. When you open the Wizard Mode window, you are presented with an overview of the router features and configuration. What actual configuration wizards are available from the Wizard Mode window?

   Answer: The wizards available from the Wizard Mode window are the following:

   - **LAN Wizard**—Used to configure the LAN interfaces and DHCP.
   - **WAN Wizard**—Used to configure PPP, Frame Relay, and HDLC WAN interfaces.
   - **Firewall wizards**—Used to configure simple or complex firewall settings.
   - **VPN wizards**—Used to configure site-to-site VPNs, Easy VPNs, and GRE tunnels with IPSec.
   - **Security Audit wizards**—Used to perform a security audit of the router or to perform a one-step router security lockdown.
   - **Reset to Factory Default Wizard**—Resets the router configuration back to the SDM factory default configuration settings.

7. What types of serial interface encapsulation can be configured using the SDM WAN Wizard?

   Answer: The SDM WAN Wizard lets you configure PPP, Frame Relay, and HDLC encapsulation from serial interfaces.

8. Once you have configured router settings using one of the wizards, what SDM feature would you use to modify or remove those configuration settings?

   Answer: The SDM Advanced Mode feature allows you to view, add, edit, or delete router configurations.

9. Why might you choose to run the Security Audit Wizard instead of the One-Step Security Lockdown Wizard?

   Answer: One of the biggest differences between the Security Audit Wizard and the One-Step Security Lockdown Wizard is that the Security Audit Wizard presents you with a list of possible security vulnerabilities and lets you decide which ones to fix. The One-Step Security Lockdown Wizard is an automated process that configures strict security settings on your router without giving you any choice in the selected settings.

10. What elements are monitored with SDM Monitor Mode?

Answer: Monitor Mode includes the following elements:

- **Overview**—Displays the router status, including a list of the error log entries.
- **Interface Status**—Used to select the interface to monitor and the conditions (for example, packets and errors, in or out) to view.
- **Firewall Status**—Displays a log showing the number of entry attempts that were denied by the firewall.
- **VPN Status**—Displays statistics about active VPN connections on the router.
- **Logging**—Displays an event log categorized by severity level.

Chapter 12

1. Which tunnel technologies are supported by the Management Center for VPN Routers (Router MC)?

Answer: The tunnel technologies supported by Router MC are IPSec, IPSec with GRE, and IPSec over GRE over a Frame Relay network.

2. What are building blocks as used in Router MC?

Answer: In Router MC, building blocks refer to network groups and transform sets. Building blocks are reusable, named, global components that can be referenced by multiple policies. When referenced, a building block is incorporated as an integral component of the policy.

3. The Management Center for VPN Routers is not a standalone application. What host applications are required before you can install Router MC?

Answer: Router MC requires VMS 2.1 Common Services or CiscoWorks 2000. VMS Common Services provides the CiscoWorks 2000 Server–based components, software libraries, and software packages developed for Router MC.

4. What are the five types of user authorization roles that can be used in Router MC?

Answer: The five types of user authorization roles that can be used in Router MC are Help Desk, Approver, Network Operator, Network Administrator, and System Administrator.

5. What are the names of the five tabs across the top of the Router MC common interface?

Answer: The names of the five tabs across the top of the Router MC common interface are Devices, Configuration, Deployment, Reports, and Admin.

6. What menu options would you choose to open the window in which you would identify the VPN interfaces for a spoke router?

Answer: To bring up the window in which you would identify the VPN interfaces for a spoke router, choose **Configuration > Settings > Spoke > VPN Interfaces**.

7. What deployment options are available for the VPN settings and policies you define in Router MC?

Answer: Router MC has two deployment options for the VPN settings and policies you define:

- You can deploy the configurations directly to the devices in the network to activate the configuration immediately.
- You can deploy the configurations to an output file to save the configuration settings for use at a later time.

8. What are the options for job status that might be displayed on Status window when you choose **Deployment > Status**?

Answer: The options for job status that might be displayed on the Status window are Generating, Generated, Rejected, Deploying, Deployed, Rollback in Progress, Rollback Complete, and Failed.

9. What report types are available from the Reports tab of Router MC?

Answer: You can view Deployment, Activities, and Audit Trail reports from the Reports tab of Router MC.

10. What is the default value of historical jobs saved by the Router MC?

Answer: The default value of historical jobs saved by the Router MC is 10.

Sample Network Security Policy

This appendix contains an example of a network security policy for The Future Corporation's network. The policy statements contained in this appendix cover the major issues of enterprise network security for The Future Corporation. It is not intended to be a critique of, or a standard for, a security policy for a real enterprise. You may want to view additional network security policy examples, such as those from the SysAdmin, Audit, Network, Security (SANS) Institute at the following web address: http://www.sans.org/resources/policies/.

Statement of Authority and Scope

As an authorized user of The Future Corporation's internal network, each employee has access to information with a wide range of sensitivity levels. Familiarity with and observance of The Future Corporation's Network Security Policy ("the policy") is important so that every employee can contribute to ensuring network security and information integrity. The Future Corporation follows the "need to know" principle by deliberately avoiding disclosure of information that the employee does not need to know for job performance.

Audience

The policy was written for the following audience:

- Network users who are expected to comply with the policy
- System support personnel who implement and support the policy
- Managers who are concerned about protection of data and the associated cost of the policy
- Company executives who want to ensure network integrity balanced with ease of use and cost of implementation
- Company lawyers and auditors who are concerned about the company's reputation and responsibility to clients and customers

Scope of the Network Security Policy

The policy is a part of "The Future Corporation's Commitment to Security," a top-level document outlining The Future Corporation's commitment to security of all types. The policy outlines the network security guidelines for online access to The Future Corporation's corporate information by company employees and subcontractors and by any other business, including (but not limited to) business partners, vendors, and customers.

Legal Authority of The Future Corporation's Network Security Policy

The Future Corporation's board of directors and senior executive staff have been empowered by the company shareholders to create, implement, enforce, and maintain the policy in accordance with applicable local, national, and international laws. The Future Corporation's chief information officer (CIO) and corporate attorney are responsible for enforcing the policy.

Network Security Policy Stakeholders

It is the responsibility of all The Future Corporation's users, system administrators, and information system operations and maintenance personnel to help ensure that the integrity of corporate network and computing resources, as well as the integrity and confidentiality of information processed and stored on those resources, is protected in accordance with sound security practices as outlined in this Network Security Policy.

The following personnel are responsible for drafting, maintaining, and enforcing the policy:

- Vice president of information systems (IS) and chief information officer (CIO)
- Vice president of central engineering
- Vice president of sales and marketing
- Information security officer
- Director of networking and telecommunications in the IS organization
- Senior manager of IS operations
- Corporate controller
- Corporate attorney

System Administrator Responsibilities

System administrators for network equipment and multiuser hosts are responsible for ensuring compliance with the following guidelines:

- Assign accounts only to individuals.
- Ensure that within The Future Corporation, account names and other machine-based representations of a user's account, such as UNIX user IDs, are globally unique. For example, throughout the entire company, only one individual must be associated with the login ID jdoe. If any given account name appears on multiple hosts, that name should always represent the same person.
- Install security patches and updated network equipment images, recommended by the information security officer or designee, on a priority basis agreed upon for the severity of each patch.

- Implement username and password management as outlined in the policy.
- Deactivate user accounts upon termination.
- Store system configuration files on a secure Trivial File Transfer Protocol (TFTP) server. Do not share the files or make them publicly available. Consider the use of kerberized RCP between Cisco routers and the TFTP host.
- Review the system log files on a daily basis. Report signs of a possible major security incident to the information security officer or designee immediately. Send a report of minor security breaches, such as multiple failed login attempts, to the information security officer on a weekly basis as appropriate.
- Run on a regular basis network security management tools that are designed to help system administrators find weak passwords and network vulnerabilities and check file integrity and system configurations (such as CiscoSecure Scanner, CiscoSecure Intrusion Detection System, Cisco Netsys, Crack, COPS, Tiger, or Tripwire).

Network Security Policy Maintenance Procedure

The company stakeholders shall review and update the policy at least once a year.

The IS department must conduct random system audits with little or no advance notice under the direction of the information security officer and document the results of the audit checks.

Implementation Procedure

The director of networking and telecommunications shall create a network design that specifies the exact network topology and network equipment that will be used to implement the policy.

Audits shall be conducted when new network equipment and host systems are connected to the network to establish a baseline of operation and to ensure that it conforms to the policy.

User Education

Policy awareness must be incorporated as part of employee orientation. Users are required to read and sign the Network Use Policy annually as a condition of employment.

Social Engineering Awareness Prevention

Employees shall use discretion when discussing business matters with nonemployees. Establish a need to know before discussing anything that might be used to construct a concept of how the company manages its affairs.

Vulnerability Audit Policy

The Future Corporation shall employ the facilities of NetAudit, LLC, to perform annual and random vulnerability audits of network resources and procedures. The purpose of these audits is to determine if network security policies are consistently implemented and enforced across the enterprise and to ascertain any areas of security vulnerability that need to be addressed.

Acceptable Use

This policy is applicable to all components of The Future Corporation and all employees shall provide full cooperation to the NetAudit staff in the performance of these audits.

Frequency

NetAudit shall perform a full security audit of all network facilities, services, and procedures during the month of May each calendar year. NetAudit shall perform at its discretion random security audits of smaller portions of the network throughout the year, but not less than six random audits per year.

Audit Targets

All network assets will be subjected to these vulnerability audits. Network assets include, but are not limited to, workstations, servers, hubs, switches, routers, firewalls, wireless access devices, transmission devices, intrusion detection devices, physical circuits, and virtual circuits.

Additionally, all personnel may become the subject of security vulnerability audits at any time, with or without their knowledge or prior consent. All employees are expected to fully support and implement The Future Corporation's network security policies at all times.

The security vulnerability audits shall include an audit of unsecured physical or electronic access points to the network, such as hubs, switches, or active wall drops in unused areas. Physical security of data resource devices shall be studied with every audit.

Audits performed on configurable devices, such as computers or routers, shall include a comprehensive list of all installed operating systems, service patches, and applications as well as a review of configuration and security files to verify adherence to network policies.

Reporting

NetAudit shall document all security vulnerability audits and present the findings to the vice president of IS and CIO for their review and subsequent actions.

Network Use Policy

The Network Use Policy defines what the company will and will not tolerate regarding internal and external access, use of software and hardware, and any additional constraints required by federal, state, or local laws, regulations, or ordinances.

Acceptable Use

Individuals and groups within The Future Corporation who are responsible for establishing or maintaining connections between The Future Corporation's network and other businesses should take appropriate measures to minimize the risk of these connections being used to compromise The Future Corporation's information security.

Unacceptable Use

Users are not allowed to access or make copies of system configuration files from network equipment or network servers, such as /etc/passwd or router configuration files, unless they are system administrators.

Users are not allowed to gain, or attempt to gain, EXEC or root access or the equivalent to network equipment and hosts that make up The Future Corporation's network and IS infrastructure, unless their job tasks permit such access.

Compliance Requirements

Users must comply with the directives contained in the Network Use Policy and any revisions or modifications made to it. Access to the company's infrastructure and data that it contains is a privilege associated with employment; it is not a right. As such, the company may change a user's access privileges at its discretion at any time. Failure to comply with the company's requirements regarding use of its data infrastructure may result in disciplinary action up to and including dismissal.

Identification and Authentication Policy

The Identification and Authentication Policy defines the technical and procedural methods used for identification and authorization.

Acceptable Use

The Identification and Authentication Policy applies to all The Future Corporation employees and will be implemented and enforced by The Future Corporation's IS department. The Training and Development department will develop training regarding the importance of password security and will provide that training to all employees on no less than an annual basis.

Password Management

The following guidelines govern the selection and use of passwords:

- Passwords, if possible, should use a mixture of dictionary-based words containing uppercase and lowercase letters, should use a mixture of special and numeric characters, and should be at least eight characters long (for example, deltA9Cog, china&fish, or run7w00deN).
- Change passwords quarterly (every three months).
- Create unique passwords for each account a user possesses.
- Do not record passwords in written form.
- Do not disclose passwords to anyone, even to coworkers.

Authentication Management

The Future Corporation will use a remote security database running the TACACS+ protocol for policy enforcement of authentication.

Internet Access Policy

The Future Corporation realizes that a connection to the Internet is important to company business, yet having such a connection creates security risks. The Internet Access Policy defines guidelines for accessing the Internet.

Acceptable Use

The Future Corporation employees may openly use outbound access to the Internet for company research. Dial-in users may gain outbound access to the Internet. Reasonable constraints on total logon time and idle time should be determined and implemented.

Firewall Usage

A firewall system consisting of a perimeter router and bastion host, at a minimum, must be used to prevent unauthorized access to the campus network from the Internet. Packet filtering rules should be developed to control access to and through the perimeter, with logging of violations of the rules to a syslog server.

Public Services Usage

Inbound access from the Internet to the campus network will be severely restricted unless network layer encryption is employed over the Internet. Inbound Internet access shall be restricted to the bastion host for e-mail, HTTP, FTP, and other required Internet traffic.

Campus Access Policy

The Campus Access Policy defines the process of assigning levels of access to each user.

Acceptable Use

The Campus Access Policy applies to all The Future Corporation employees requiring access to network hosts and facilities and to those employees charged with maintaining the network hosts and facilities.

Trust Relationship

Access to campus hosts is permitted to all company employees based on the trust level assigned by the employee's manager. The Future Corporation seeks to balance transparent user access with network security. The Future Corporation has established five trust levels as follows:

- **Department User**—Requires full access to department data stores and read access to common corporate information.

- **Department Manager**—Requires full access to department data stores, read access to peer department data stores, read access to common corporate information, and full access to managerial information stores.

- **Executive Manager**—Requires full access to executive information data stores, full access to managerial information stores, and read access to all other data stores.

- **System/Network Administrator**—Requires Department User rights to IS information stores, and administrative access to specific servers, hosts, or devices.

- **IS Administrator**—Requires administrative access to all network servers, hosts, and devices, including full access to all data stores.

Each employee is assigned a trust level based on the person's need to access network services to perform job tasks. Technical controls shall be established and enforced to ensure that trust relationships are maintained.

Access to campus hosts by external parties is denied unless specifically authorized by the IS department and the affected department manager.

Network Equipment Security

EXEC or root access to network equipment is denied except to IS department employees specified by the senior manager of IS operations. Employ network layer encryption to secure vital traffic flows between internal servers.

Remote Access Policy

Personnel who access The Future Corporation's corporate network from home-based offices or via dialup lines must clearly understand and accept the security responsibilities that accompany remote access privileges.

Remote access is a literal extension of The Future Corporation's internal network, providing a potential path to the company's most sensitive information. It is therefore of paramount importance that people with remote access privileges take extreme care in ensuring that only employees and authorized contractors can gain access to the internal network.

Any computer used to access The Future Corporation's internal network shall be password-protected or shall be configured in such a way that an unauthorized user cannot launch the communications software package that initiates a connection to The Future Corporation network. The Future Corporation IS department shall specify which type of machine or file protection utility is used, and it should not be possible for password protection to be easily bypassed (for example, by rebooting the machine).

Remote access connections must be authenticated with TACACS+ or token cards and servers.

Acceptable Use

The Remote Access Policy applies to any of The Future Corporation's employees or business partners who require remote access to The Future Corporation's network hosts and facilities.

Mobile Computing

The Future Corporation employees who have a need shall be allowed to gain access to the campus network only via network access servers controlled by the IS department. Employees must use IS-supported Microsoft Windows 95, Microsoft Windows 98, Microsoft Windows 2000, Microsoft Windows XP, or Apple Macintosh computers with remote access software approved by the IS department.

The Future Corporation employees and authorized third parties, such as customers and vendors, may use dialup connections to gain access to the corporate network. Dialup access should be strictly controlled using one-time password authentication.

It is the responsibility of employees with dialup access privileges to ensure that nonemployees do not use dialup connections to gain access to The Future Corporation's company information system resources.

Home Access

The Future Corporation employees who want to set up home-based offices may use remote connections to link their home computers to the corporate network. When possible, remote connections to the corporate network must use Challenge Handshake Authentication Protocol (CHAP).

Telecommuter Agreement

Users who are granted remote access privileges are required to sign a document that indicates their understanding of the importance of protecting The Future Corporation's information from unauthorized disclosure. The document shall also indicate their acceptance of the security requirements set forth in this document and in the top-level Network Security Policy.

Branch Office Access

The IS department must approve all remote branch office access to the campus network to ensure network security.

Business Partner (Extranet) Access

The IS department must approve all remote business partner access to the campus network to ensure network security. A firewall must be employed to control such access.

Encryption

An encryption program shall be used for all remote access transactions. The encryption algorithm chosen shall balance the security needs of the transaction in question against the required data throughput.

Incident-Handling Policy

The Future Corporation's Network Security Policy stakeholders must develop a detailed Incident-Handling Policy that contains contingency plans designed to handle all possible security incidents. The incident-handling procedure must be written in a "cookbook" approach to ensure that incidents can be managed in a predictable way by on-duty IS personnel at any time. The incident-handling procedure must address the points in this section.

Intrusion Detection Requirements

IDS software, such as Cisco Secure IDS, should be deployed to provide vital information about the status of the security perimeter. A real-time, enterprise-scale IDS designed to detect, report, and terminate unauthorized activity in the demilitarized zone (DMZ) portion of the perimeter network should include the following capabilities:

- The IDS must have scalability and performance to allow the administrators to centrally monitor network activity at the DMZ.

- The IDS must be implemented in a multitiered hierarchy, allowing the administrators to quickly add IDS monitor systems as the network grows.

- The central management station also must remotely control the configuration of the remote IDSs via an intuitive GUI integrated into a network management system, allowing the organization to monitor the security of its connections from one centralized location. This ensures consistent security policy enforcement enterprise-wide.

- The management station must also feed alarm information into an adjacent database archive. Information such as the origin, type, destination, and time of attacks must be logged for trend analysis.

Incident Response Procedure

A detailed Incident Response Procedure must be written as an operational document by the senior manager of IS operations and must be reviewed and updated quarterly or within one week after a major incident. The vice president of IS and the information security officer must approve the procedure document. The Incident Response Procedure must structure the company's response to an attack so that, when an incident occurs, the available resources are applied to solving the problem instead of deciding how to solve it. The procedure must address the following requirements:

1 **Prepare and plan for incidents**—IS operations personnel must receive a minimum of 16 hours of training per year on how to identify incidents and how to implement the Incident Response Procedure. The procedure document must specify the type and duration of training.

2 **Identify an incident**—System administrators must monitor the IDS throughout the day to identify incidents. System log files should be monitored hourly and analyzed at the end of the day. The senior system administrator on duty at the time of an incident is responsible for identifying an incident. The Incident Response Procedure must specify priority levels of incidents, as suggested in RFC 2196, "Site Security Handbook."

3 **Handle the incident**—The Incident Response Procedure must specify how system administrators must handle an incident. The following procedure is an outline of the steps to take and document:

   — Identify the attack's type and priority.

   — Identify the attack's start and stop times.

- Identify the attack's point of origin.

- Specify the impacted computer or network systems.

- Trace the attack back to its origin without trespassing on other networks or computer systems.

- Attempt to thwart the attack or mitigate damage. Isolate the system under attack.

- Notify appropriate points of contact.

- Protect evidence of the attack, such as log files.

- Restore IS services when appropriate.

4 Document and apply lessons learned—An incident report should be written under the guidance of the senior manager of IS operations and should address the following points:

- An inventory should be taken of the attacked system's assets.

- A description of lessons learned should be written.

- The Network Security Policy should be revised if required.

- The attack perpetrators should be investigated and prosecuted.

Points of Contact

Table B-1 lists the members of the incident response team, which is responsible for implementing the company's security policy when an incident occurs.

Table B-1   *Members of the Incident Response Team*

Point of Contact	Roles
Senior system administrator on duty when an incident occurs	• Primary point of contact to identify and respond to an incident • Immediately alerts senior manager of IS operations and the incident response team of the incident and requests support, if needed • Implements required corrective actions detailed in the Incident-Handling Policy • Documents the incident in a report and delivers it to the senior manager of IS operations • Provides after-action feedback on the accuracy and usability of the Incident-Handling Policy to senior manager of IS operations

continues

Table B-1   *Members of the Incident Response Team (Continued)*

Point of Contact	Roles
Senior manager of IS operations	• Primary management point of contact • Determines how to respond to the incident • Coordinates system administrators during serious incidents • Available by pager or cell phone 24 hours a day • Contacts the next person in the chain of command • Provides after-action reporting to senior management, information and security officers, and IS staff with detailed steps taken or required to prevent similar incidents from occurring in the future
Information security officer	• Escalates the incident to a computer incident response team, such as CERT • Involves law enforcement, if required • Reviews appropriate security policies and system configurations to determine weaknesses that may have permitted the incident
Director of networking and telecommunications in the IS organization	• Supports IS staff in responding to the incident as required by the Incident-Handling Policy • Determines if additional network assets or human resources are required to prevent similar incidents in the future • Acquires appropriate funding for additional equipment or personnel required as a result of the incident
Vice president of central engineering	• Analyzes effect of incident to see if critical corporate product information may have been compromised • Determines corrective actions required in response to incident to secure engineering resources against future attacks of a similar nature
Vice president of sales and marketing	• Analyzes effect of incident to see if critical corporate sales information may have been compromised • Determines corrective actions required in response to incident to secure sales resources against future attacks of a similar nature

Table B-1   *Members of the Incident Response Team (Continued)*

Point of Contact	Roles
Corporate controller	• Analyzes effect of incident to see if critical corporate financial information may have been compromised • Determines corrective actions required in response to incident to secure financial resources against future attacks of a similar nature
Vice president of IS and CIO	• Works with the executive team to handle communications inside and outside the company • Is the only person authorized to talk to news agencies and any entities external to the company • Ensures that the incident response is documented and that appropriate changes in procedures are implemented to prevent further occurrences
Corporate attorney	• Coordinates the prosecution of perpetrators • Approves external communications

Configuring Standard and Extended Access Lists

This appendix presents an overview of configuring standard and extended IP access lists in Cisco IOS Software. This appendix is included in this book because many Cisco security features in Cisco IOS Software use standard or extended IP access lists, and you might need a refresher or reference on access list fundamentals.

An *IP access list* is a sequential collection of permit and deny conditions that apply to IP addresses and optionally to IP protocols and TCP and UDP ports. Access lists permit or deny packets from entering or leaving specified interfaces. Cisco IOS Software supports the following types of access lists for IP:

- Standard IP access lists use source addresses for matching operations.

- Extended IP access lists use source and destination addresses for matching. They also allow optional matching of IP protocol and TCP or UDP port, allowing finer granularity of control.

- Dynamic extended IP access lists grant per-user access from a specific source to a specific destination through a user authentication process.

- Reflexive access lists allow IP packets to be filtered based on session-backflow information.

IP access lists provide two primary uses for implementing network security: packet filtering and traffic selection.

Packet filtering helps control packet movement through the network, helping limit network traffic and restricting network use by certain IP addresses or networks across Cisco router interfaces. For example, packet filtering is useful on a perimeter router to allow only traffic from the public Internet to access a bastion host, or to prevent IP address spoofing. Packet filtering using access lists can also be used to control access to the network and to network equipment. For example, a standard IP access list can control which remote IP addresses can perform router or Ethernet switch administration via Telnet access.

Traffic selection determines "interesting" traffic that will invoke a desired security operation. For example, extended IP access lists are used in crypto maps to determine interesting traffic that will be encrypted with Cisco Encryption Technology (CET) and IPSecurity (IPSec) in Cisco IOS Software.

The types of access lists and the available list numbers for IP are described in Table C-1.

Table C-1   *Types of Access Lists and Their Numbers*

Type of Access List	List Number Range
IP standard	1 to 99
IP extended	100 to 199
Bridging access list for filtering protocol type code	200 to 299
AppleTalk access list	600 to 699
Bridging access list for filtering 48-bit MAC address or vendor code	700 to 799
IPX standard	800 to 899
IPX extended	900 to 999
IPX SAP	1000 to 1099
Extended bridging access list for filtering 48-bit MAC address or vendor code	1100 to 1199
IPX summary address access list	1200 to 1299
IP standard access list (expanded range)	1300 to 1999
IP extended access list (expanded range)	2000 to 2699
Simple rate-limit access list for quality of service policies uses **access-list rate limit** command.	1 to 99 or 100 to 199

IP Addressing and General Access List Concepts

This section presents a review of IP addressing and network and subnet masks. It also covers concepts common to both standard and extended IP access lists, such as wildcard masks, explicit deny all masks, implicit masks, and general access list configuration and design principles. This review section is included because you should thoroughly understand IP addressing in order to create effective access lists.

IP Addressing

An IP address is 32 bits in length and is divided into two parts. The first part designates the network portion of the address, and the second part designates the host address portion. The host address can optionally be partitioned into a subnet address and a host address. A subnet address lets a network address be divided into smaller networks.

IP addresses use dotted-decimal notation to represent a binary number up to 32 bits in length. Each decimal digit represents an 8-bit binary number, or an octet. An example of an address is 192.168.20.204, which represents the binary number 11000000.10101000.00010100.11001100.

Each of the 8 bits in an octet has an equivalent decimal weight, as shown in Table C-2. Going from right to left, the bit weight is 1, 2, 4, 8, 16, 32, 64, 128. The minimum value for an octet is 0; it contains all 0s. The maximum value for an octet is 255; it contains all 1s. If a value of 255 occurs in the host portion of an IP address, it is reserved for broadcast messages to all hosts on a network.

Table C-2   *Decimal Weight of Each Bit in an Octet*

Bit Weight	128	64	32	16	8	4	2	1	Decimal Equivalent
Bits in Octet	0	0	0	0	0	0	0	0	0
Bits in Octet	1	1	1	1	1	1	1	1	255

The allocation of IP addresses is managed and administered by the Internet Network Information Center (InterNIC), a central authority. InterNIC is also the main repository for Requests For Comments (RFCs), which specify how Internet protocols work.

Network Classes

IP addressing supports five different network classes. The far leftmost bits of an IP address indicate the network class, which can be one of the following:

- Class A networks are intended mainly for use with a few very large networks because they provide only 7 bits for the network address field. Each Class A network can have over 16 million hosts. All Class A IP addresses have been assigned.

- Class B networks allocate 14 bits for the network address field and 16 bits for the host address field. This address class offers a good compromise between network and host address space.

- Class C networks allocate 22 bits for the network address field. Class C networks provide only 8 bits for the host field, however, so the number of hosts per network might be a limiting factor.

- Class D addresses are reserved for multicast groups, as described formally in RFC 1112. In Class D addresses, the four highest-order bits are set to 1, 1, 1, and 0.

- Class E addresses are also defined by IP but are reserved for future use. In Class E addresses, the four highest-order bits are all set to 1.

Table C-3 summarizes address ranges and standard network masks for Class A, B, and C networks, which are the most commonly used. The high-order bits of the first octet determine the address range for each class.

Figure C-1 shows the address formats for Class A, B, and C IP networks. Each network address in the overall IP address consists of one or more octets, and each network address falls on an even octet boundary. The rest of the IP address consists of the host octets, which specify addresses for individual hosts in the network address.

Table C-3 *Class A, B, and C Subnets and Addresses*

Class	High-Order Bits	First Octet	Standard Mask
A	0	1.0.0.0 to 126.0.0.0	255.0.0.0
B	10	128.1.0.0 to 191.254.0.0	255.255.0.0
C	110	192.0.1.0 to 223.255.254.0	255.255.255.0

Figure C-1 *Network and Host Fields for Class A, B, and C Networks*

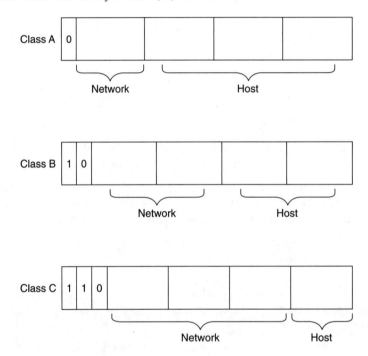

Subnet Addresses

IP networks can also be divided into smaller units, called *subnets*. Subnets allow you to "carve up" your assigned IP schema into smaller units within your enterprise. Subnets are created by borrowing bits from the leftmost (higher-order) bits in the host field of the IP address and using them as a subnet field, as shown in Figure C-2. A subnetted IP address consists of an address field, a subnet field, and a host ID field. If you chose to use 8 bits of subnetting in a Class B IP address, the third octet provides the subnet number. Subnets are useful for dividing up an organization's network structure, for hiding the internal complexity of an organization from the open Internet, and for making more efficient use of the host ID field of IP addresses. A subnet mask is used to differentiate the host address from the network address.

Figure C-2   *Example of Subnetting a Class B Network Address, in Which 8 Bits Borrowed from the Host Field Enables up to 16 Subnets of the Network Address*

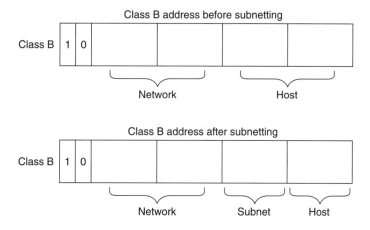

Subnet bits come from the high-order bits of the host field. To determine a subnet mask for an address, add up the decimal values of each position that has a 1 in it. Here's an example:

224 = 128 + 64 + 32 = 11100000

Because the subnet mask is not defined by the octet boundary but by bits, you need to convert dotted-decimal addresses to binary and back into dotted-decimal. Table C-4 is a handy reference for converting a binary octet to its decimal equivalent.

Table C-4   *Decimal Weight of Each Bit in a Subnet Mask*

Bit Weight	128	64	32	16	8	4	2	1	Decimal Equivalent
Bits in Octet	1	0	0	0	0	0	0	0	128
Bits in Octet	1	1	0	0	0	0	0	0	192
Bits in Octet	1	1	1	0	0	0	0	0	224
Bits in Octet	1	1	1	1	0	0	0	0	240
Bits in Octet	1	1	1	1	1	0	0	0	248

continues

Table C-4   *Decimal Weight of Each Bit in a Subnet Mask (Continued)*

Bit Weight	128	64	32	16	8	4	2	1	Decimal Equivalent
Bits in Octet	1	1	1	1	1	1	0	0	252
Bits in Octet	1	1	1	1	1	1	1	0	254
Bits in Octet	1	1	1	1	1	1	1	1	255

Table C-5 contains a reference to help you determine subnet addresses for Class B and Class C addresses. Subnetting Class A networks is especially useful to make the most use of the large host field (three octets) of Class A networks.

Table C-5   *Class B and C Subnets and Hosts*

Class B Subnetting		
Subnet Mask	Number of Subnets	Number of Hosts
255.255.192.0	2	16,382
255.255.224.0	6	8,190
255.255.240.0	14	4,094
255.255.248.0	30	2,046
255.255.252.0	62	1,022
255.255.254.0	126	510
255.255.255.0	254	254
255.255.255.128	510	126
255.255.255.192	1,022	62
255.255.255.224	2,046	30
255.255.255.240	4,094	14
255.255.255.248	8,190	6
255.255.255.252	16,382	2
Class C Subnetting		
Subnet Mask	Number of Subnets	Number of Hosts
255.255.255.192	2	62
255.255.255.224	6	30
255.255.255.240	14	14
255.255.255.248	30	6
255.255.255.252	62	2

Network administrators create subnet addresses by subdividing part of the host field of an IP address with a subnet mask. Network administrators decide the size of subnets based on organization and growth needs. The subnet mask is coded into the network equipment involved with creating the network. Network devices use subnet masks to identify which part of the address is considered network and which part to use for host addressing. The network equipment compares the IP address of packets with the subnet mask to determine the network, subnetwork, and host fields when receiving or transmitting packets. The lengths of the network, subnet, and host fields are all variable.

Wildcard Masks

Both standard IP and extended IP access lists use wildcard masks to determine if a packet matches an access list entry. Wildcard masks are like network and subnet masks in that they are written in 32-bit dotted-decimal format.

A wildcard mask works as follows: A 0 in a bit position of the wildcard mask indicates that the corresponding bit in the address is checked against the rules in the access list; a 1 in a bit position of the wildcard mask indicates that the corresponding bit in the address is not "interesting" and can be ignored.

For this reason, the 0 bits in the mask are sometimes called "do-care" bits, and the 1 bits are called "don't-care" bits. Table C-6 contains examples of wildcard masks in decimal and binary form.

Table C-6 *Examples of Wildcard Masks*

Octet Bit Position								
Decimal Octet	**128**	**64**	**32**	**16**	**8**	**4**	**2**	**1**	**Example**
0	0	0	0	0	0	0	0	0	Check all address bits
15	0	0	0	0	1	1	1	1	Check the first four address bits
252	1	1	1	1	1	1	0	0	Check the last two address bits
255	1	1	1	1	1	1	1	1	Do not check the address

By carefully setting wildcard masks, an administrator can select a single or several IP addresses for permit or deny tests.

An access list can contain an indefinite number of actual and wildcard addresses. A wildcard address has a nonzero address mask and thus potentially matches more than one actual address. Remember that the order of the access list statements is important because the access list is not processed further after a match is found. Table C-7 contains examples of IP addresses and corresponding access list masks and the resulting matches for each example. When considering Tables C-6 and C-7, remember the following rules used to find a matching address with a wildcard mask:

- 0 bit = must match bits in addresses
- 1 bit = no need to match bits in addresses

Table C-7 *Examples of Access List Wildcard Masks and Matches*

Address	Wildcard Mask	Matches
0.0.0.0	255.255.255.255	Any address
131.108.0.0	0.0.255.255	Network 131.108.0.0
131.108.7.8	0.0.0.0	Host or subnet address
255.255.255.255	0.0.0.0	Local broadcast
131.120.121.5	0.0.7.255	Only subnet 131.120.121.0, assuming a subnet mask of 255.255.248.0

General Access List Configuration Tasks

You need to complete two general tasks to create standard IP or extended IP access lists—create the access list and apply the access list to an interface or terminal line:

1 Create an access list in global configuration mode by specifying an access list number and access conditions. Refer to Table C-1 for the access list number.

   Define a standard IP access list using a source address and wildcard.

   Define an extended IP access list using source and destination addresses, a protocol identifier, and optional port-type information on some protocols for finer granularity of control.

   Use the context-sensitive help feature by entering **?** in the Cisco IOS user interface to verify available names and proper command syntax.

2 Apply the access list to interfaces or terminal lines in interface configuration mode.

   After an access list is created, you can apply it to one or more interfaces or terminal lines. Access lists can be applied on either outbound or inbound interfaces.

Access List Configuration Principles

Following these general principles helps ensure that the access lists you create have the intended results:

- **Top-down processing**—Organize your access list so that more-specific references in a network or subnet appear before more-general ones. For example, filter on IP addresses from specific to general: hosts first, then subnets, then specific networks, then any networks. If a specific entry appears after a general entry and they are related conditions, the specific entry will never be processed. For example, if you want to filter a specific host address and then permit all other addresses, make sure your entry about the specific host appears first.

- **Occurrence precedence**—Place more frequently occurring conditions before less-frequent conditions so that less CPU processing is done by the access list, but do not violate the specific-to-general rule.

- **Implicit deny any**—Unless you end your access list with an explicit permit any, it will deny by default all traffic that fails to match any of the access list lines.

- **New lines added to the end**—Subsequent additions are always added to the end of the access list. You cannot selectively insert or delete lines when using numbered access lists, but you can selectively delete lines when using IP named access lists. (This is a Cisco IOS Release 11.2 feature that is discussed further in the "Named IP Access Lists" section of this appendix.) You can use a text editor to edit, delete, and then reapply an access list, or you can use the Access List Manager software from Cisco Systems to manage complex access lists.

- **Undefined access list equals permit any**—If you apply an access list to an interface with the **ip access-group** command before any access list lines have been created, the result is to permit any traffic. The list goes "live" when you apply the access to an interface. If you were to enter only one host-specific permit line, the list would go from a permit any to a "deny most" (because of the implicit deny any) as soon as you press Enter. For this reason, you should create your complete access list before you apply it to an interface.

Configuring Standard IP Access Lists

This section covers how to configure standard IP access lists. Standard IP access lists permit or deny packets based only on the packet's source IP address. The access list number range for defining standard IP access lists is 1 to 99. Standard IP access lists are easier to configure than extended IP access lists, yet they are less powerful because they cannot be used to filter on traffic types or destination addresses. Figure C-3 shows that a standard IP access list could be used to deny access to a network based on the source address.

Figure C-3 *Standard IP Access Lists Permit or Deny Packets Based on the Packet's Source IP Address—The Access List Here Denies Access to a Network*

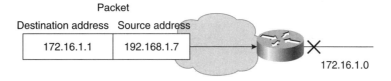

| **CAUTION** | Cisco IOS Software Release 11.1 and later have introduced substantial changes to IP access lists. The extensions in Release 11.1 and later are compatible with previous releases; migrating from a release earlier than Release 11.1 to the current image converts your access lists automatically. However, previous releases are not upwardly compatible with these changes. Thus, if you save an access list with the current image and then use older software, the resulting access list will not be interpreted correctly. This could cause severe security problems. Save your old configuration file before booting Release 11.1 or later images. |

Standard IP Access List Processing

A standard IP access list is a sequential collection of permit and deny conditions that apply to source IP addresses. The router tests addresses against the conditions in an access list one by one. The first match determines whether the router accepts or rejects the packet. Because the router stops testing conditions after the first match, the order of the conditions is critical. If no conditions match, the router rejects the packet. Standard IP access lists process packets differently for inbound and outbound traffic filtering, which is considered next.

Inbound Traffic Processing

Let's discuss processing for standard IP access lists intended to filter inbound traffic. This process is illustrated in Figure C-4. Upon receiving a packet, the router checks the packet's source address against entries in the access list. If the access list permits the source address, the router exits the access list and continues processing the packet according to the router configuration. If the access list rejects the address, the router discards the packet and returns an ICMP Host Unreachable message.

Figure C-4 *Inbound Traffic Processing for Standard IP Access Lists*

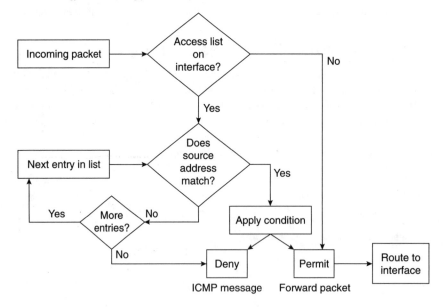

Note that, if no more entries are found in the access list, the packet is denied. This highlights an important rule to remember when creating access lists. The last entry in an access list is known as an *implicit deny any*. It is embedded in Cisco IOS Software and is not listed in the router configuration. All traffic not explicitly permitted is implicitly denied. The implicit deny any rule is useful in implementing a security policy because access lists default to a closed security policy, and you do not have to specify every deny condition. Make sure you have explicit permit statements for traffic you want to allow across the interface, or you will cut off desired traffic. The implicit deny any rule applies to both standard and extended IP access lists.

Outbound Traffic Processing

Next, let's consider processing for standard IP access lists intended to filter outbound traffic. This process is illustrated in Figure C-5. For standard IP access lists applied to outbound traffic, after receiving and routing a packet to a controlled interface, the router checks the packet's source address against the access list. If the access list permits the address, the router transmits the packet. If the access list denies the address, the router discards the packet and returns an ICMP Host Unreachable message.

Figure C-5   *Outbound Traffic Processing for Standard IP Access Lists*

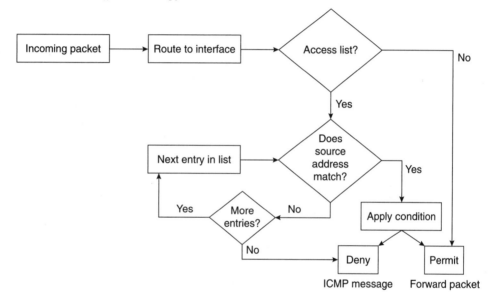

NOTE   The primary difference between a standard IP access list and an extended IP access list is that the latter checks information other than the source address in the packet against the access list.

Standard IP Access List Commands

You use the **access-list** command to create an entry in a standard traffic filter list. The command syntax for the **access-list** command used in a standard IP access list is as follows:

```
access-list access-list-number {deny | permit} {source [source-wildcard] | [log]}
```

The following are the parameters for this syntax:

Command Parameter	Description
access-list-number	Identifies the list to which the entry belongs. A number from 1 to 99.
**deny	permit**	Indicates whether this entry allows or blocks traffic from the specified address.

continues

Command Parameter	Description
source	Identifies the source IP address.
source-wildcard	(Optional) Indicates the wildcard bits to be applied to *source*, as follows: • Use a 32-bit quantity in four-part dotted-decimal format. Place 1s in the bit positions to be ignored by the access list entry. • Use the keyword **any** as an abbreviation for *source* and a *source-wildcard* of 0.0.0.0 255.255.255.255. • If this field is omitted, the mask 0.0.0.0 is assumed.
log	(Optional) Generates an informational syslog message about the packet that matches the entry to be sent to the console or to a syslog server. (The level of messages logged to the console is controlled by the **logging console** command.)

You use the **ip access-group** command in interface configuration mode to apply an existing access list to an interface. Each interface may have both an inbound and an outbound access list (provided that they are both standard or extended). The command syntax for the **ip access-group** command is as follows:

```
ip access-group access-list-number {in | out}
```

The following are the parameters for this syntax:

Command Parameter	Description
access-list-number	Identifies the list to which the entry belongs. A number from 1 to 99.
in	Filters on inbound packets.
out	Filters on outbound packets.

You can delete the entire list from the configuration by entering the **no access-list** *access-list-number* command in global configuration mode. You can remove the application of an access list to an interface or line with the **no ip access-group** *access-list-number* command in interface configuration mode.

Implicit Masks

You can use the implicit mask feature of standard IP access lists to reduce typing and simplify configuration. The implicit mask makes it easier to enter a large number of individual addresses. You use implicit masks by not coding a wildcard mask into the access list entry. You apply an implicit wildcard mask of 0.0.0.0 to the IP address entered as source, and all bits of the address are used to permit or deny traffic. One restriction of implicit masks is that the source IP address must specify a host address, not a network or subnet address. Consider the following three examples of standard IP access lists with implicit masks:

```
access-list 1 permit 10.1.1.3
access-list 1 permit 172.16.21.3
access-list 1 permit 192.168.244.196
```

The first line is an example of a specific host configuration for a Class A IP address. Because no mask is specified, the mask is assumed or implied to be 0.0.0.0 so that all bits in the IP address are used in the access list. The implicit mask makes it seem as if the access list entry is really **access-list 1 permit 10.1.1.3 0.0.0.0**. The second and third lines are examples of implicit masks for a Class B and a Class C address.

Location of Standard Access Lists

Access list location can be complex, but you should generally place standard IP access lists as close to the destination router as possible to exercise the most security control while enabling the greatest flexibility of access. Some general guidelines that are useful for access list placement are shown in the sample configuration in Figure C-6.

Figure C-6 *Sample Topology Showing Where Standard IP Access Lists Should Be Placed*

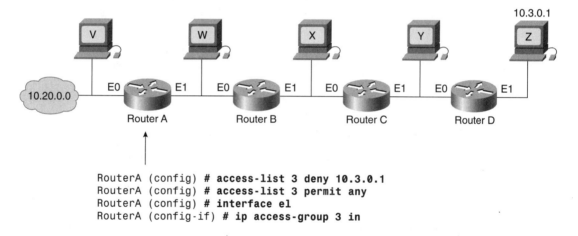

```
RouterA (config) # access-list 3 deny 10.3.0.1
RouterA (config) # access-list 3 permit any
RouterA (config) # interface el
RouterA (config-if) # ip access-group 3 in
```

If the policy goal is to deny Host Z access to Host V and not to change any other access policy, on which router should the access list shown be configured and on which interface of that router? The access list would be placed on Router A. The reason is that the standard IP access list can specify only the source address. Wherever in the path the traffic is denied, no hosts beyond can connect.

The access list could be configured as an outbound list on E0, but it would most likely be configured as an inbound list on E1 so that packets to be denied would not have to be routed first.

What would be the effect of placing the access list on other routers? The answer follows:

- **Router B**—Host Z could not connect with Hosts V and W.
- **Router C**—Host Z could not connect with Hosts V, W, and X.
- **Router D**—Host Z could not connect with hosts V, W, X, and Y.

Common Errors in Standard IP Access Lists

Consider the example of errors in coding standard IP access lists in the following lines:

```
access-list 1 permit 172.16.129.231
!
access-list 1 permit 0.0.0.0
access-list 1 permit 192.168.0.0
!
access-list 1 deny 0.0.0.0 255.255.255.255
access-list 1 deny any
```

This example of standard IP access lists contains the following errors:

- The IP address in the first line is actually a subnetted address with a subnet mask of 255.255.240.0, so a wildcard mask of 0.0.15.255 should have been used instead of the implicit mask of 0.0.0.0 (see Table C-7).

- **permit 0.0.0.0** would exactly match the address 0.0.0.0 and then permit it. In most cases, this address is illegal, so this list would prevent all traffic from getting through (the implicit deny any).

- **permit 192.168.0.0** is probably a configuration error. The intention is probably 192.168.0.0 0.0.255.255. The exact address 192.168.0.0 is reserved to refer to the network and would never be assigned to a host. Network and subnets are represented by explicit masks. As a result, no traffic would get through with this list, again due to the implicit deny any.

- **deny 0.0.0.0 255.255.255.255** and **deny any** are unnecessary to configure from a strictly technical standpoint because they duplicate the function of the implicit deny any that occurs when a packet fails to match all the configured lines in an access list. Denying any is the same as configuring 0.0.0.0 255.255.255.255. It is considered good configuration practice for system administrators to include a **deny any** statement at the end of an access list, so the last line is actually not in error!

Standard IP Access List Example

Consider the sample configuration for the network shown in Figure C-7. The access list configuration for Router A is shown.

Who can connect to Host A? Can Host B communicate with Host A? Yes. This is permitted by the first line, which uses an implicit host mask.

Can host C communicate with host A? No. Host C is in the subnet denied by the second line.

Can host D communicate with host A? Yes. Host D is on a subnet that is explicitly permitted by the third line.

Can users on the Internet communicate with host A? No. Users outside this network are not explicitly permitted, so they are denied by the **access-list 2 deny any** command.

Figure C-7   *Standard Access List Example for Router A*

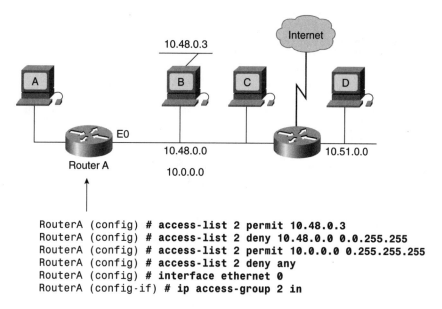

```
RouterA (config) # access-list 2 permit 10.48.0.3
RouterA (config) # access-list 2 deny 10.48.0.0 0.0.255.255
RouterA (config) # access-list 2 permit 10.0.0.0 0.255.255.255
RouterA (config) # access-list 2 deny any
RouterA (config) # interface ethernet 0
RouterA (config-if) # ip access-group 2 in
```

Configuring Extended IP Access Lists

This section considers how to configure extended IP access lists, which allow more granular control of traffic filtering and selection than do standard IP access lists. After presenting an overview of extended IP access lists, this section examines how extended IP access lists are processed in Cisco IOS Software. This section examines the commands used to configure extended IP access lists, and it then presents several examples. It concludes by discussing where to place extended IP access lists.

Standard IP access lists offer quick configuration and low overhead in limiting traffic based on the source address within a network. Extended IP access lists provide a higher degree of control by enabling filtering based on the transport layer protocol, destination address, and application port number. These features make it possible to limit traffic based on the uses of the network, as illustrated in Figure C-8. In the figure, the perimeter router can control access to internal servers and applications using extended IP access lists on traffic from the Internet. Alternatively, extended IP access lists can be used on internal routers to control access to servers and applications inside the network.

Figure C-8   *Extended IP Access Lists Enable Filtering Based on the Transport Layer Protocol, Source and Destination Address, and Application Port Number*

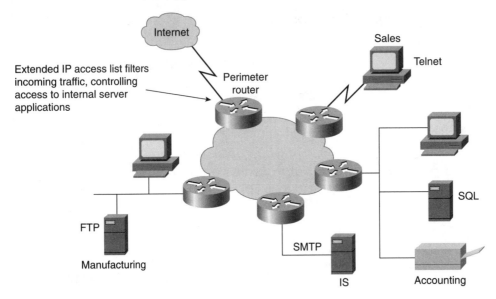

Extended IP Access List Processing

Access list statements operate in sequential, logical order. They evaluate packets from the top down. If a packet header and access list statement match, the packet skips the rest of the statements. If a condition match is true, the packet is permitted or denied. As soon as one parameter or condition fails, the next line in the access list is tested until the end of the access list is reached.

You can use extended IP access lists to check the source address, protocol, and destination address. Depending on the network configuration and protocols used, extended IP access lists provide more protocol-dependent options available for filtering. For example, TCP or UDP ports can be checked, which allows routers to filter at the application layer.

Let's consider packet processing for extended IP access lists, which is illustrated in Figure C-9. The router checks each packet for matches in source address, destination address, protocol, and protocol options. If the conditions are met and the access list is a permit statement, the packet is forwarded. If the conditions are met and the access list is a deny statement, the router discards the packet and returns an ICMP Host Unreachable message.

Extended IP Access List Commands

You use the **access-list** command to create an entry in a complex traffic filter access list.

The command syntax for the **access-list** command used in an extended IP access list is as follows:

```
access-list access-list-number [dynamic dynamic-name [timeout minutes]]
  {deny | permit} protocol source source-wildcard destination destination-wildcard
  [precedence precedence] [tos tos] [log]
```

Figure C-9 *The Extended IP Access List Checks Source Address, Protocol, and Destination Address in the Order Shown*

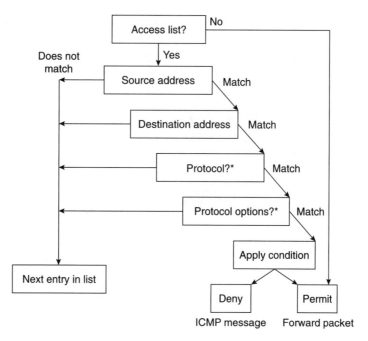

* If present in access list

The following are the parameters for this syntax:

Command Parameter	Description
access-list-number	Identifies the list to which the entry belongs. A number from 100 to 199.
dynamic *dynamic-name*	(Optional) Identifies this access list as a dynamic access list used for lock-and-key security.
timeout *minutes*	(Optional) Specifies the absolute length of time (in minutes) that a temporary access list entry can remain in a dynamic access list used for lock-and-key security. The default is an infinite length of time and allows an entry to remain permanently.
deny | permit	Indicates whether this entry is used to allow or block the specified address(es).
protocol	Specifies the name or number of an IP protocol. It can be one of the protocol keywords: **ahp, eigrp, esp, gre, icmp, igmp, igrp, ip, ipinip, nos, ospf, pcp, tcp,** or **udp,** or an integer in the range 0 to 255 representing an IP protocol number. To match any Internet protocol (including ICMP, TCP, and UDP), use the keyword **ip**. Protocol keywords **icmp, tcp,** and **udp** define alternative syntax with protocol-specific options.

continues

Command Parameter	Description
source and *destination*	Specify the number of the network or host as a 32-bit quantity in dotted-decimal notation. You can use the keywords **any** and **host** to simplify configuration.
source-wildcard	Specifies the wildcard bits to be applied to *source*. 0s indicate bits that must match, and 1s are "don't-care" bits. There are three alternative ways to specify the source wildcard: • Use a 32-bit quantity in four-part dotted-decimal format. Place 1s in the bit positions you want to ignore. • Use the keyword **any** as an abbreviation for *source* and a *source-wildcard* of 0.0.0.0 255.255.255.255. • Use **host** *source* as an abbreviation for *source* and a *source-wildcard* of *source* 0.0.0.0.
destination-wildcard	Specifies the wildcard bits to be applied to the *destination*. 0s indicate bits that must match, and 1s are "don't-care" bits. There are three alternative ways to specify the destination wildcard: • Use a 32-bit quantity in four-part dotted-decimal format. Place 1s in the bit positions you want to ignore. • Use the keyword **any** as an abbreviation for *destination* and a *destination-wildcard* of 0.0.0.0 255.255.255.255. • Use **host** *destination* as an abbreviation for *destination* and a *destination-wildcard* of *destination* 0.0.0.0.
precedence *precedence*	(Optional) Specifies the packets that can be filtered by precedence level. Specified by a number from 0 to 7 or by name: • **critical (5)** • **flash (3)** • **flash-override (4)** • **immediate (2)** • **internet (6)** • **network (7)** • **priority (1)** • **routine (0)**
tos *tos*	(Optional) Specifies the packets that can be filtered by type of service (ToS) level, as specified by a ToS name or number: • **max-reliability (2)** • **max-throughput (4)** • **min-delay (8)** • **min-monetary-cost (1)** • **normal (0)**

Command Parameter	Description
log	(Optional) Generates an informational syslog message about the packet that matches the entry to be sent to the console or to a syslog server. (The level of messages logged to the console is controlled by the **logging console** command.) Exercise caution when using this keyword because it consumes CPU cycles.

Extended Mask Keywords

The keyword **any** in either the source or destination position matches any address and is equivalent to configuring 0.0.0.0 255.255.255.255, as illustrated in the following example:

```
access-list 101 permit ip  0.0.0.0  255.255.255.255  0.0.0.0  255.255.255.255
! alternate configuration follows:
access-list 101 permit ip any any
```

The keyword **host** in either the source or destination position causes the address that immediately follows it to be treated as if it were specified with a mask of 0.0.0.0, as illustrated in the following example:

```
access-list 101 permit ip  0.0.0.0  255.255.255.255 172.16.6.3 0.0.0.0
! alternate configuration follows:
access-list 101 permit ip any host 172.16.6.3
```

ICMP Command Syntax

You use the **access-list icmp** command to create an entry in a complex traffic filter list. The protocol keyword **icmp** indicates that an alternative syntax is being used for this command and that protocol-specific options are available.

The command syntax for the **access-list icmp** command used in an extended IP access list is as follows:

```
access-list access-list-number [dynamic dynamic-name [timeout minutes]]
{deny | permit} icmp source source-wildcard destination
destination-wildcard [icmp-type [icmp-code] | icmp-message]
[precedence precedence] [tos tos] [log]
```

The following are the parameters for this syntax:

Command Parameter	Description
icmp	Specifies the ICMP protocol.
icmp-type	(Optional) Specifies the packets that can be filtered by ICMP message type. The type is a number from 0 to 255.
icmp-code	(Optional) Specifies the packets that have been filtered by ICMP message type that can also be filtered by ICMP message code. The code is a number from 0 to 255.
icmp-message	(Optional) Specifies the packets that can be filtered by a symbolic name representing an ICMP message type or a combination of ICMP message type and ICMP message code.

ICMP Message Names, Types, and Codes

Cisco IOS Release 10.3 and later provide symbolic message names that make configuration and reading of complex access lists easier. With symbolic names, it is not critical to understand the meaning of message 8 and message 0 in order to filter the **ping** command. Instead, the configuration would use **echo** and **echo-reply**.

Table C-8 summarizes the ICMP message names in alphabetical order, showing the ICMP type and, where applicable, the ICMP codes.

Table C-8   *ICMP Message Names, Types, and Codes*

ICMP Message Name	ICMP Type	ICMP Code	Description
administratively-prohibited	3	13	Communication administratively prohibited.
alternate-address	6	None	Alternative address.
conversion-error	31	None	Datagram conversion error.
dod-host-prohibited	3	10	Host prohibited.
dod-net-prohibited	3	9	Net prohibited.
echo	8	None	Echo (**ping**).
echo-reply	0	None	Echo reply.
general-parameter-problem	12	0	Parameter problem. Pointer indicates the error.
host-isolated	3	8	Source host isolated.
host-precedence-unreachable	3	14	Host unreachable for precedence.
host-redirect	5	1	Host redirect.
host-tos-redirect	5	3	Host redirect for ToS.
host-tos-unreachable	3	12	Host unreachable for ToS.
host-unknown	3	7	Host unknown.
host-unreachable	3	1	Host unreachable.
information-reply	16	None	Information replies.
information-request	15	None	Information requests.
log-input	None	None	Log matches against any ICMP message name and associated type, code, or parameter.
mask-reply	18	None	Mask replies.
mask-request	17	None	Mask requests.

Table C-8   *ICMP Message Names, Types, and Codes (Continued)*

ICMP Message Name	ICMP Type	ICMP Code	Description
mobile-redirect	32	None	Mobile host redirect.
net-redirect	5	0	Redirect datagram for network.
net-tos-redirect	5	2	Net redirect for ToS.
net-tos-unreachable	3	11	Network unreachable for ToS.
net-unreachable	3	0	Network unreachable.
network-unknown	3	6	Network unknown.
no-room-for-option	12	2	Parameter required but no room. Bad length.
option-missing	12	1	Parameter required but not present.
packet-too-big	3	4	Fragmentation needed and data fragmentation (DF) bit set.
parameter-problem	12	None	All parameter problems.
port-unreachable	3	3	Port unreachable.
precedence-unreachable	3	15	Precedence cutoff in effect.
protocol-unreachable	3	2	Protocol unreachable.
reassembly-timeout	11	1	Fragment reassembly time exceeded.
redirect	5	None	All redirects.
router-advertisement	9	None	Router discovery advertisements.
router-solicitation	10	None	Router discovery solicitations.
source-quench	4	None	Source quenches.
source-route-failed	3	5	Source route failed.
time-exceeded	11	None	All time-exceeded messages.
timestamp-reply	14	0	Timestamp replies.
timestamp-request	13	0	Timestamp requests.
traceroute	30	None	Traceroute.
ttl-exceeded	11	0	TTL exceeded in transit.
unreachable	3	None	All destination unreachables.

NOTE	You can log packets that match an ICMP message code with the **log-input** keyword. For example, the following sample access list logs packets of ICMP message type 3 and code 4 (ICMP unreachable, packet too big) for any IP address:

```
router(config)# access-list 101 permit icmp any any log-input 3 4
router# show access-lists 101
Extended IP access list 101
    permit icmp any any packet-too-big log-input
```

TCP Syntax

You use the **access-list tcp** command to create an entry in a complex traffic filter list. The protocol keyword **tcp** indicates that an alternative syntax is being used for this command and that protocol-specific options are available.

The command syntax for the **access-list tcp** command is as follows:

```
access-list access-list-number [dynamic dynamic-name [timeout minutes]]
{deny | permit} tcp source source-wildcard [operator port [port]]
destination destination-wildcard [operator port [port]] [established]
[precedence precedence] [tos tos] [log]
```

The parameters that are unique to this syntax are as follows:

Command Parameter	Description
tcp	Specifies TCP.
operator	(Optional) Specifies a qualifying condition that compares source and destination ports. The keyword can be **lt**, **gt**, **eq**, **neq**, or **range**.
port	(Optional) Specifies a decimal number from 0 to 65535 or a name that represents a TCP port number. TCP port names can be used only when filtering TCP.
established	(Optional) Establishes a Telnet or another activity in one direction only. A match occurs if the TCP datagram has the ACK or RST bits set.

Reserved TCP Port Keywords and Numbers

IP and TCP extended IP access lists can filter on source and/or destination port number. Cisco IOS Software allows you to filter on any TCP port with the **access-list** command. You can enter either the port number or a keyword in the **access-list** command. Cisco IOS contains convenient keywords you can use in place of the port number. You can use the **?** in place of the port number when entering the command in order to verify the port numbers associated with these protocol names.

Table C-9 lists the TCP keywords, brief descriptions of the TCP ports, and the port numbers for keywords supported in the **access-list** command. See the Assigned Numbers RFC (RFC 1700) for a complete list of assigned ports.

Table C-9   *TCP Well-Known Port Key Names and Numbers*

Keyword	Description	Port Number
bgp	Border Gateway Protocol	179
chargen	Character generator	19
cmd	Remote commands (**rcmd**)	514
daytime	Daytime	13
discard	Discard	9
domain	Domain Name Service	53
echo	Echo	7
exec	Exec (**rsh**)	512
finger	Finger	79
ftp	File Transfer Protocol	21
ftp-data	FTP data connections (used infrequently)	20
gopher	Gopher	70
hostname	NIC host name server	101
ident	IDENT protocol	113
irc	Internet Relay Chat	194
klogin	Kerberos login	543
kshell	Kerberos shell	544
login	Login (**rlogin**)	513
lpd	Printer service	515
nntp	Network News Transport Protocol	119
pim-auto-rp	PIM Auto-RP	496
pop2	Post Office Protocol version 2	109
pop3	Post Office Protocol version 3	110
smtp	Simple Mail Transport Protocol	25
sunrpc	Sun Remote Procedure Call	111
syslog	Syslog	514
tacacs	TAC Access Control System	49
talk	Talk	517
telnet	Telnet	23

continues

Table C-9 *TCP Well-Known Port Key Names and Numbers (Continued)*

Keyword	Description	Port Number
time	Time	37
uucp	UNIX-to-UNIX copy program	540
whois	Nickname	43
www	World Wide Web (HTTP)	80

UDP Syntax

The **access-list udp** command creates an entry in a complex traffic filter list. The protocol keyword **udp** indicates that an alternative syntax is being used for this command and that protocol-specific options are available.

The command syntax for the **access-list udp** command is as follows:

```
access-list access-list-number [dynamic dynamic-name [timeout minutes]]
    {deny | permit} udp source source-wildcard [operator port [port]]
    destination destination-wildcard [operator port [port]]
    [precedence precedence] [tos tos] [log]
```

The parameters that are unique to this syntax are as follows:

Command Parameter	Description
udp	Specifies UDP.
operator	(Optional) Specifies a qualifying condition that compares source and destination ports. The keyword can be **lt**, **gt**, **eq**, **neq**, or **range**.
port	(Optional) Specifies a decimal number from 0 to 65535 or a name that represents a UDP port number. UDP port names can be used only when filtering UDP.

Reserved UDP Port Keywords and Numbers

IP and UDP extended access lists can filter on source or destination port number. Cisco IOS allows you to filter on any UDP port with the **access-list** command. You can enter either the port number or a keyword in the **access-list** command. Cisco IOS contains convenient keywords you can use in place of the port numbers. You can use the **?** in place of the port number when entering the command in order to verify the port numbers associated with these protocol names. Table C-10 lists the UDP keywords, a brief description of the UDP port, and the port numbers for keywords supported in the **access-list** command. See the Assigned Numbers RFC (RFC 1700) for a complete list of assigned ports.

Table C-10   *Extended IP Access List Fields for Reserved UDP*

Keyword	Description	Port Number
biff	Biff (mail notification, comsat)	512
bootpc	Bootstrap protocol (BOOTP) client	68
bootps	BOOTP server	67
discard	Discard	9
dnsix	DNSIX security protocol auditing	195
domain	Domain Name Service (DNS)	53
echo	Echo	7
isakmp	Internet Security Association and Key Management Protocol	500
mobile-ip	Mobile IP registration	434
nameserver	IEN116 name service (obsolete)	42
netbios-dgm	NetBIOS datagram service	138
netbios-ns	NetBIOS name service	137
ntp	Network Time Protocol	123
pim-auto-rp	PIM Auto-RP	496
rip	Routing Information Protocol (**router** UDP keyword)	520
snmp	Simple Network Management Protocol	161
snmptrap	SNMP Traps	162
sunrpc	Sun Remote Procedure Call	111
syslog	System Logger	514
tacacs	Terminal Access Controller Access Control System	49
talk	Talk	517
tftp	Trivial File Transfer Protocol	69
time	Time	37
who	Who service (**rwho**)	513
xdmcp	X Display Manager Control Protocol	177

Location of Extended IP Access Lists

Because extended IP access lists can filter on more than source address, location is no longer a constraint. Frequently, policy decisions and goals are the driving force behind extended IP access list placement.

If your goal is to minimize traffic congestion and maximize performance, you might want to deploy access lists on the network's perimeter routers to minimize cross traffic and host unreachable messages. If your goal is to maintain tighter control of access to specific internal hosts as part of your network security policy, you might want to place your access lists on routers closest to the protected hosts. You should avoid placing access lists on core or backbone routers because this can cause additional latency. Notice how changing network goals affects access list configuration.

Here are some suggestions and considerations regarding access list placement:

- Minimize the distance traveled by traffic that will be denied (and ICMP unreachable messages).
- Keep denied traffic off the backbone.
- Size the router to handle the CPU overhead from access lists.
- Place access lists on the correct interfaces to protect traffic as efficiently as possible.
- Complex access lists can be difficult to maintain. Carefully review changes to access lists before applying them to your production network.
- Consider network growth impacts on access list maintenance.

Extended IP Access List Example 1

Consider an example of an extended IP access list designed to enable and protect Internet mail traffic. Figure C-10 illustrates the network and contains the partial configuration of Router B.

Figure C-10 *Using an Extended IP Access List in Router A Enables Yet Protects Internet Mail Traffic*

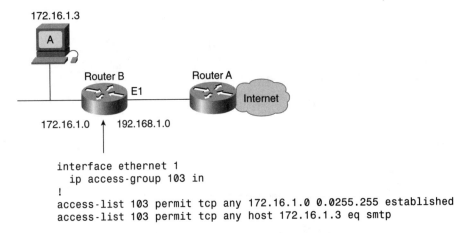

```
interface ethernet 1
  ip access-group 103 in
!
access-list 103 permit tcp any 172.16.1.0 0.0255.255 established
access-list 103 permit tcp any host 172.16.1.3 eq smtp
```

In this example, Ethernet interface 1 is part of a Class B network at 172.16.0.0, and the mail host's address is 172.16.1.3. The keyword **established** is used only for the TCP protocol to indicate an established connection. A match occurs if the TCP packet has the ACK or RST bits set, which indicates that the packet belongs to an existing connection. If the SYN bit is set, indicating session initialization, the packet does not match and is discarded.

NOTE   TCP hosts must establish a connection-oriented session with one another. To ensure reliable transport services, connection establishment is performed by using a *three-way handshake* mechanism. The three-way handshake is accomplished using two flag bits in the TCP packet header. The synchronization (SYN) bit is used to initiate the connection, and the acknowledge (ACK) bit is used to acknowledge the SYN. The three-way handshake proceeds in the following manner:

1 The first host (Router A in Figure C-10) initiates a connection by sending a packet with the SYN bit set to indicate a connection request.

2 The second host (Router B) receives the SYN and replies by acknowledging the SYN with an ACK bit.

3 The first host (Router A) replies with an ACK bit also. Data transfer can then begin.

Extended IP Access List Example 2

Consider the example of an extended IP access list that permits name/domain server packets and ICMP echo and echo-reply packets. Figure C-11 illustrates this network and contains the partial configuration of Router B.

Figure C-11 *An Extended IP Access List That Permits Name/Domain Server Packets and ICMP Echo and Echo-Reply Packets*

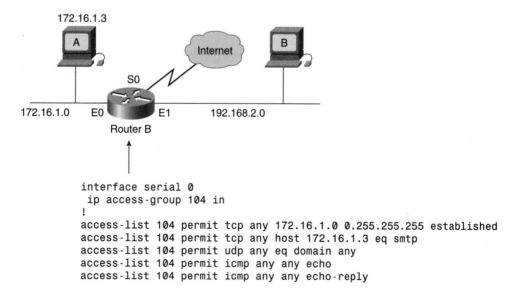

```
interface serial 0
 ip access-group 104 in
!
access-list 104 permit tcp any 172.16.1.0 0.255.255.255 established
access-list 104 permit tcp any host 172.16.1.3 eq smtp
access-list 104 permit udp any eq domain any
access-list 104 permit icmp any any echo
access-list 104 permit icmp any any echo-reply
```

Verifying Access List Configuration

This section covers how to verify access list configuration. A variety of commands useful for verifying access list configuration are at your disposal. They include the **show access-lists**, **clear access-list counters**, and **show line** commands. The **show running-config** command is very useful for displaying currently configured access lists. Each of these commands is entered in privileged EXEC mode.

You use the **show access-lists** command to display access lists from all protocols. You use the **show ip access-list** command to display all configured IP access lists. You use the **show ip access-list** [*access-list-number* | *name*] command to examine a specific access list. You can also use the **show running-config** command to display the access lists that you have created.

The system counts how many packets pass each line of an access list; the counters are displayed by the **show access-lists** command. These counters are useful for troubleshooting an access list to determine which line of the list is causing a packet to be permitted or denied. They are also useful for maintenance to determine which lines of an access list are used the most. You use the **clear access-list counters** command in EXEC mode to clear an access list's counters. You use the **clear access-list counters** {*access-list-number* | *name*} command to clear a specific access list.

You use the **show line** command to display information about terminal lines.

The output from the **show ip access-list** command displays the contents of currently defined IP access lists. Consider the following example of the **show access-lists** command, noting the matches shown for the access list:

```
p1r1#show access-lists
Extended IP access "list" 100
    deny tcp host 10.1.1.2 host 10.1.1.1 eq telnet (3 matches)
    deny tcp host 10.1.2.2 host 10.1.2.1 eq telnet
    permit ip any any (629 matches)
```

Named IP Access Lists

You use the **ip access-list** command to configure a named IP access list as opposed to a numbered IP access list. Named access lists are used to configure reflexive access lists and context-based access control. Named access lists are entered in global configuration mode. The **ip access-list** command first appeared in Cisco IOS Release 11.2.

The **ip access-list** command takes you into access-list configuration mode, where you must define the denied or permitted access conditions with **deny** and **permit** commands. Specifying **standard** or **extended** with the **ip access-list** command determines the prompt and options you get when you enter access list configuration mode.

You use the **ip access-group** command to apply the access list to an interface.

The command syntax for the **ip access-list** command is as follows:

```
ip access-list {standard | extended} name
```

The parameters of this syntax are as follows:

Command Parameter	Description
standard	Specifies a standard IP access list.
extended	Specifies an extended IP access list.
name	Specifies the name of the access list. Names cannot contain a space or quotation mark, and they must begin with an alphabetic character to prevent ambiguity with numbered access lists.

NOTE

Named access lists are not recognized by or compatible with any software release prior to Cisco IOS Release 11.2.

Consider the following captured session, which shows **ip extended access-list** command options:

```
p2r1(config)#ip access-list extended AccessList
p2r1(config-ext-nacl)#?
Ext Access List configuration commands:
  default   Set a command to its defaults
  deny      Specify packets to reject
  dynamic   Specify a DYNAMIC list of PERMITs or DENYs
  evaluate  Evaluate an access list
  exit      Exit from access-list configuration mode
  no        Negate a command or set its defaults
  permit    Specify packets to forward
  remark    Access list entry comment

p2r1(config-ext-nacl)#permit ?
  <0-255>   An IP protocol number
  ahp       Authentication Header Protocol
  eigrp     Cisco's EIGRP routing protocol
  esp       Encapsulation Security Payload
  gre       Cisco's GRE tunneling
  icmp      Internet Control Message Protocol
  igmp      Internet Gateway Message Protocol
  igrp      Cisco's IGRP routing protocol
  ip        Any Internet Protocol
  ipinip    IP in IP tunneling
  nos       KA9Q NOS compatible IP over IP tunneling
  ospf      OSPF routing protocol
  pcp       Payload Compression Protocol
  pim       Protocol Independent Multicast
  tcp       Transmission Control Protocol
  udp       User Datagram Protocol

p2r1(config-ext-nacl)#permit ip ?
  A.B.C.D  Source address
  any      Any source host
  host     A single source host
```

```
p2r1(config-ext-nacl)#permit ip any any ?
  log           Log matches against this entry
  log-input     Log matches against this entry, including input interface
  precedence    Match packets with given precedence value
  reflect       Create reflexive access list entry
  time-range    Specify a time-range
  tos           Match packets with given TOS value

p2r1(config-ext-nacl)#permit tcp ?
  A.B.C.D  Source address
  any      Any source host
  host     A single source host

p2r1(config-ext-nacl)#permit tcp any any ?
  ack           Match on the ACK bit
  eq            Match only packets on a given port number
  established   Match established connections
  fin           Match on the FIN bit
  gt            Match only packets with a greater port number
  log           Log matches against this entry
  log-input     Log matches against this entry, including input interface
  lt            Match only packets with a lower port number
  neq           Match only packets not on a given port number
  precedence    Match packets with given precedence value
  psh           Match on the PSH bit
  range         Match only packets in the range of port numbers
  reflect       Create reflexive access list entry
  rst           Match on the RST bit
  syn           Match on the SYN bit
  time-range    Specify a time-range
  tos           Match packets with given TOS value
  urg           Match on the URG bit

p2r1(config-ext-nacl)#permit tcp any any eq ?
  <0-65535>  Port number
  bgp        Border Gateway Protocol (179)
  chargen    Character generator (19)
  cmd        Remote commands (rcmd, 514)
  daytime    Daytime (13)
  discard    Discard (9)
  domain     Domain Name Service (53)
  echo       Echo (7)
  exec       Exec (rsh, 512)
  finger     Finger (79)
  ftp        File Transfer Protocol (21)
  ftp-data   FTP data connections (used infrequently, 20)
  gopher     Gopher (70)
  hostname   NIC hostname server (101)
  ident      Ident Protocol (113)
  irc        Internet Relay Chat (194)
  klogin     Kerberos login (543)
  kshell     Kerberos shell (544)
  login      Login (rlogin, 513)
  lpd        Printer service (515)
  nntp       Network News Transport Protocol (119)
```

```
pim-auto-rp  PIM Auto-RP (496)
pop2         Post Office Protocol v2 (109)
pop3         Post Office Protocol v3 (110)
smtp         Simple Mail Transport Protocol (25)
sunrpc       Sun Remote Procedure Call (111)
syslog       Syslog (514)
tacacs       TAC Access Control System (49)
talk         Talk (517)
telnet       Telnet (23)
time         Time (37)
uucp         Unix-to-Unix Copy Program (540)
whois        Nickname (43)
www          World Wide Web (HTTP, 80)
```

Summary

This appendix presented a review of standard and extended IP access lists supported in Cisco IOS Software for controlling traffic and identifying interesting traffic on Cisco routers.

References

The topics considered in this appendix are complex and should be studied further to more fully understand them and put them to use. You can use the following references to learn more about the topics in this appendix.

Configuring IP Access Lists

Refer to the *Cisco IOS Release 12.0 Network Protocols Configuration Guide, Part 1*, in the "Filter IP Packets" section of the "Configuring IP Services" chapter, for more information on configuring IP access lists.

Refer to the *Cisco IOS Release 12.0 Network Protocols Command Reference, Part 1*, in the "IP Services Commands" chapter, for information on specific IP access list commands.

IP Protocol and Addressing Information

Cisco Connection CD, "Technology Information" section, Internetworking Technology Overview, "Internet Protocols" section. Cisco Systems, Inc., 1999.

RFC 950, J. Postel and J. Mogul, "Internet Standard Subnetting Procedure," August 1985. This RFC describes how to subnet IP addresses.

RFC 1700, J. Postel and N. Haller, "Assigned Numbers," October 1994. This RFC is a summary of the ongoing process of the assignment of protocol parameters for the Internet protocol suite.

GLOSSARY

The following terms were introduced in this book or have special significance to the topics within this book:

A

acceptable use policy. Defines what the company will and will not tolerate regarding internal and external access, use of software and hardware, and any additional constraints required by federal, state, or local laws, regulations, or ordinances.

Adaptive Security Algorithm (ASA). Examines all traffic flowing into and out of PIX Firewalls and maintains a database of session state information for each connection. Any packet that does not match its recorded entry in the ASA's session state database is rejected immediately. Additionally, ASA defines levels of security for ports and only permits traffic to flow from a higher-security port to a lower-security port unless a specific rule has been defined permitting otherwise.

antireplay. A security service that enables the receiver to reject old or duplicate packets to protect itself against replay attacks. IPSec provides this optional service by use of a sequence number combined with the use of data authentication.

Are You There (AYT). A process through which Cisco VPN Client enforces firewall policy defined on the local firewall by monitoring that firewall to make sure it is running. The client sends periodic "Are you there?" messages to the firewall. If no response is received, Cisco VPN Client terminates the connection to the Cisco VPN Series Concentrator.

authentication. In security, the verification of the identity of a person, device, application, or process.

Authentication Header (AH). A security protocol that provides data authentication and optional antireplay services. AH is embedded in the data to be protected (a full IP datagram).

B

bastion host. A secure server (typically UNIX, Windows NT, or Linux based) that provides essential services to the outside world.

Anonymous FTP server, World Wide Web server services, Domain Name System services, incoming e-mail (SMTP) services to deliver e-mail to the company, and Internet proxy services for internal hosts are all examples of the types of services provided by bastion hosts.

C

Certificate Revocation List (CRL). Data structure that enumerates digital certificates that have been invalidated by their issuer prior to when they were scheduled to expire.

certificate authority (CA). Entity that issues digital certificates (especially X.509 certificates) and vouches for the binding between the data items in a certificate.

Cisco Encryption Technology (CET). A 40- and 56-bit Data Encryption Standard (DES) network layer encryption available since Cisco IOS Software Release 11.2.

Cisco Unified Client Framework. A consistent connection, policy, and key management method across Cisco routers, security appliances, and Cisco VPN Clients.

classless interdomain routing (CIDR). Technique supported by Border Gateway Protocol version 4 (BGP4) and based on route aggregation. CIDR allows routers to group routes together to reduce the quantity of routing information carried by the core routers. With CIDR, several IP networks appear to networks outside the group as a single, larger entity. With CIDR, IP addresses and their subnet masks are written as four octets, separated by periods, followed by a forward slash and a two-digit number that represents the subnet mask.

Context-Based Access Control (CBAC). System that provides internal users with secure access control for each application and for all traffic across network perimeters. CBAC enhances security by scrutinizing both source and destination addresses and by tracking each application's connection status.

cookie. A piece of information sent by a web server to a web browser that the browser is expected to save and send back to the web server whenever the browser makes additional requests of the web server. The main purpose of cookies is to identify users and possibly prepare customized web pages for them. This information is packaged into a cookie and sent to your web browser, which stores it for later use. The next time you go to the same website, your browser will send the cookie to the web server. The server can use this information to present you with custom web pages. So, for example, instead of seeing just a generic welcome page, you might see a welcome page with your name on it.

D

data authentication. Process of verifying that data has not been altered during transit (data integrity) or that the data came from the claimed originator (data origin authentication).

data confidentiality. A security service where the protected data cannot be observed.

Data Encryption Standard (DES). Standard cryptographic algorithm developed by the U.S. National Bureau of Standards.

data flow. A grouping of traffic, identified by a combination of source address/mask, destination address/mask, IP next protocol field, and source and destination ports, where the protocol and port fields can have the values of any. In effect, all traffic matching a specific combination of these values is logically grouped together into a data flow. A data flow can represent a single TCP connection between two hosts, or it can represent all the traffic between two subnets. IPSec protection is applied to data flows.

demilitarized zone (DMZ). Network that is isolated from a corporation's production environment. The DMZ is often used as a location for public-access servers, where the effects of successful intrusion attempts can be minimized and controlled.

denial of service (DoS). The intended result of certain system attacks. These attacks typically send useless traffic to a particular host or port. While they may not compromise or damage hosts, well-executed DoS attacks can prevent any legitimate traffic from getting through, effectively denying the services from intended users.

Diffie-Hellman (DH) key exchange. A public key cryptography protocol that allows two parties to establish a shared secret over insecure communications channels. DH is used within Internet Key Exchange (IKE) to establish session keys. DH is a component of Oakley key exchange. Cisco IOS software supports 768-bit and 1024-bit DH groups.

Digital Signal Processor (DSP). Segments the voice signal into frames and stores them in voice packets.

Digital Signature Standard (DSS). The digital signature algorithm (DSA) developed by the U.S. National Security Agency (NSA) to generate a digital signature for the authentication of electronic documents.

Directory System Agent (DSA). Software that provides the X.500 directory service for a portion of the directory information base. Generally, each DSA is responsible for the directory information for a single organization or organizational unit.

Distributed Denial of Service (DDoS). An especially malicious form of DoS attack that compromises multiple hosts and enslaves them to send vast amounts of traffic to a target host. These "zombie" attack hosts often reside on unsuspecting public networks such as those found in universities. Network administrators are often unaware that their hosts have become zombies because they only watch for incoming attacks. RFC 2267 specifies ingress and egress filters that can prevent your routers and hosts from becoming the source of a DoS attack.

Domain Name System (DNS). System used on the Internet to translate names of network nodes into addresses.

Dynamic Host Configuration Protocol (DHCP). Provides a mechanism for allocating IP addresses dynamically so that addresses can be reused when hosts no longer need them.

E

Elliptic Curve Cryptography (ECC). A public-key encryption technique based on elliptic curve theory that can be used to create faster, smaller, and more efficient cryptographic keys. ECC generates keys through the properties of the elliptic curve equation instead of using the traditional method of generation as the product of large prime numbers. The technology can be used in conjunction with most public-key encryption methods, such as RSA and Diffie-Hellman.

Encapsulating Security Payload (ESP). Security protocol that provides data privacy services, optional data authentication, and antireplay services. ESP encapsulates the data to be protected.

encryption. Application of a specific algorithm to data to alter the appearance of the data, making it incomprehensible to those who are not authorized to see the information.

Enhanced Interior Gateway Routing Protocol (EIGRP). Advanced version of IGRP developed by Cisco that provides superior convergence properties and operating efficiency, and combines the advantages of link state protocols with those of distance-vector protocols.

Extended Authentication (XAUTH). Permits Cisco VPN Client systems to be authenticated by TACACS+ or RADIUS external servers during IKE phase 1 negotiations when establishing an IPSec secure tunnel. When XAUTH is configured on the Cisco VPN Client, the user of that device is prompted for a username and password, which must be authenticated by the remote authentication server before the IPSec tunnel can be established.

Extensible Markup Language (XML). A standard maintained by the World Wide Web Consortium (W3C) that defines a syntax that lets you create markup languages to specify information structures.

F - G

failover. Allows two separate devices on a network to provide redundancy to the security infrastructure. If one unit fails, the other picks up.

File Transfer Protocol (FTP). Application protocol, part of the TCP/IP protocol stack, used for transferring files between network nodes. FTP is defined in RFC 959.

firewall. Device or software package designated as a buffer between any connected public networks and a private network. A firewall uses access lists and other methods to ensure the security of the private network.

generic routing encapsulation (GRE). Tunneling protocol developed by Cisco that can encapsulate a variety of protocol packet types inside IP tunnels, creating a virtual point-to-point link to Cisco routers at remote points over an IP internetwork. By connecting multiprotocol subnetworks in a single-protocol backbone environment, IP tunneling using GRE allows network expansion across a single-protocol backbone environment.

H

hash. The result of transforming, or hashing, a string of characters into a usually shorter, fixed-length value or key that represents the original string.

Hashed Message Authentication Codes (HMAC). A mechanism for message authentication using cryptographic hash functions. HMAC can be used with any iterative cryptographic hash function, for example, MD5 or SHA-1, in combination with a secret shared key. The cryptographic strength of HMAC depends on the properties of the underlying hash function.

headend. Endpoint of a broadband network. All stations transmit toward the headend, which then transmits toward the destination stations.

hold-down routes. Routes used to make a remote VPN connection appear to be active even when there is no current tunnel established.

Hot Standby Router Protocol (HSRP). Provides high network availability and transparent network topology changes. HSRP creates a hot standby router group with a lead router that services all packets sent to the hot standby address. The lead router is monitored by other routers in the group, and if it fails, one of these standby routers inherits the lead position and the Hot Standby group address.

Hypertext Transfer Protocol (HTTP). The protocol used by web browsers and web servers to transfer files, such as text and graphics files.

I

Internet Assigned Numbers Authority (IANA). Organization operated under the auspices of the Internet Society (ISOC) as a part of the Internet Architecture Board (IAB). IANA delegates authority for IP address-space allocation and domain-name assignment to the InterNIC and other organizations. IANA also maintains a database of assigned protocol identifiers used in the TCP/IP stack, including autonomous system numbers.

Internet Control Message Protocol (ICMP). Network layer Internet protocol that reports errors and provides other information relevant to IP packet processing. Documented in RFC 792.

Internet Engineering Task Force (IETF). Task force consisting of over 80 working groups responsible for developing Internet standards. The IETF operates under the auspices of ISOC.

Internet Key Exchange (IKE). Establishes a shared security policy and authenticates keys for services (such as IPSec) that require keys. Before any IPSec traffic can be passed, each router/firewall/host must verify the identity of its peer. This can be done by manually entering pre-shared keys into both hosts or by a CA service.

Internet Security Association and Key Management Protocol (ISAKMP). Internet IPSec protocol (RFC 2408) that negotiates, establishes, modifies, and deletes security associations. It also exchanges key generation and authentication data (independent of the details of any specific key generation technique), a key establishment protocol, an encryption algorithm, or an authentication mechanism.

intrusion detection system (IDS). Security service that monitors and analyzes system events for the purpose of finding (and providing real-time or near real-time warning of) attempts to access system resources in an unauthorized manner.

IP Security (IPSec). A framework of open standards that provides data confidentiality, data integrity, and data authentication between participating peers. IPSec provides these security services at the IP layer. IPSec uses IKE to handle the negotiation of protocols and algorithms based on local policy and to generate the encryption and authentication keys to be used by IPSec. IPSec can protect one or more data flows between a pair of hosts, between a pair of security gateways, or between a security gateway and a host.

J - L

JavaScript. Interpreted programming language from Netscape that is used on websites for such things as popup windows and image change during mouse rollover.

Kerberos. Standard for authenticating network users. Kerberos offers two key benefits: it functions in a multivendor network, and it does not transmit passwords over the network.

LAN Extension mode. A mode used on a concentrator that does not rely upon NAT. Each individual device behind the VPN 3002 Hardware Client retains its IP address when seen at the headend network. This is the opposite of PAT mode.

Layer 2 Forwarding Protocol (L2FP). Protocol that supports the creation of secure virtual private dial-up networks over the Internet.

Layer 2 Tunneling Protocol (L2TP). An Internet Engineering Task Force (IETF) standards-track protocol defined in RFC 2661 that provides tunneling of PPP. Based on the best features of L2FP and PPTP, L2TP provides an industry-wide interoperable method of implementing virtual private dial-up networks (VPDNs).

load balancing. Distributing processing and communications activity evenly across a network to prevent a single device or circuit from being overwhelmed. Network load balancing is especially important because it is difficult to predict the number of requests or packets that will need to be processed at any given point in time. Load balancing can be used on a wide variety of network devices, including data servers, web servers, routers, firewalls, access servers, authentication servers, and data circuits.

lock-and-key security. An improved security solution in Cisco IOS Release 11.1 and later that uses dynamic access lists that grant access per user to a specific source/destination host through a user authentication process. You can allow user access through a firewall dynamically without compromising security restrictions.

M

Management Information Base (MIB). Database of network management information that is used and maintained by a network management protocol, such as SNMP or Common Management Information Protocol (CMIP). The value of a MIB object can be changed or retrieved using SNMP commands, usually through a GUI network management system. MIB objects are organized in a tree structure that includes public (standard) and private (proprietary) branches.

message digest algorithm 5 (MD5). A one-way hashing algorithm that produces a 128-bit hash. Both MD5 and Secure Hash Algorithm (SHA) are variations on MD4 and are designed to strengthen the security of the MD4 hashing algorithm. Cisco uses hashes for authentication within the IPSec framework. Also used for message authentication in SNMPv2. MD5 verifies the integrity of the communication, authenticates the origin, and checks for timeliness.

Microsoft Point-to-Point Compression (MPPC). A compression protocol used to compress Point-to-Point Protocol (PPP) packets between Cisco and Microsoft client devices. This protocol optimizes bandwidth usage to support multiple simultaneous connections.

Microsoft Point-to-Point Encryption (MPPE). An encryption technology that was developed to encrypt point-to-point links over dial-up lines or VPN tunnels. MPPE works as a subfeature of MPPC.

N

Network Access Server (NAS). Cisco platform (or collection of platforms, such as an AccessPath system) that interfaces between the packet world (for example, the Internet) and the circuit world (for example, the PSTN).

Network Address Translation (NAT). Mechanism for reducing the need for globally unique IP addresses. NAT allows an organization with addresses that are not globally unique to connect to the Internet by translating those addresses into globally routable address space. Also known as Network Address Translator.

Network Autodiscovery. A process used on Cisco VPN 3000 Series Concentrators to discover networks connected to the remote concentrator. Network Autodiscovery relies on RIP to discover networks.

Network Time Protocol (NTP). Protocol built on top of TCP that ensures accurate local time-keeping with reference to radio and atomic clocks located on the Internet. This protocol is capable of synchronizing distributed clocks within milliseconds over long time periods.

nonvolatile random-access memory (NVRAM). RAM that retains its contents when a unit is powered off.

O - P

Open Shortest Path First (OSPF). Link-state, hierarchical IGP routing algorithm proposed as a successor to RIP in the Internet community. OSPF features include least-cost routing, multipath routing, and load balancing. OSPF was derived from an early version of the Intermediate System–to–Intermediate System (IS-IS) Protocol.

PAT mode. A mode used on a concentrator where all the devices behind that concentrator have their IP addresses translated to the IP address of the outside interface of the VPN 3002 Hardware Client. This is the opposite of LAN Extension mode.

peer. In the context of this book, a router, firewall, VPN concentrator, or other device that participates in IPSec.

perfect forward secrecy (PFS). A cryptographic characteristic associated with a derived shared secret value. With PFS, if one key is compromised, previous and subsequent keys are not compromised, because subsequent keys are not derived from previous keys.

perimeter router. A general-purpose router (usually) with a serial connection to the Internet and an Ethernet connection to a DMZ. The perimeter router primarily uses packet-filtering rules to restrict access to TCP/IP services and applications.

Point-to-Point Tunneling Protocol (PPTP). Enables secure data transfer between remote clients and enterprise servers by creating on-demand, multiprotocol VPNs across TCP/IP-based public data networks, such as the Internet.

Port Address Translation (PAT). A specific form of NAT in which multiple private IP addresses are translated to use the same public IP address, using port numbers to differentiate the conversations. In PAT, the TCP or UDP port is translated in addition to the IP source or destination address. Also known as Port Address Translator.

Public Key Cryptography Standards (PKCS). Series of specifications published by RSA Laboratories for data structures and algorithm usage for basic applications of asymmetric cryptography.

Public Key Infrastructure (PKI). System of CAs (and optionally, RAs and other supporting servers and agents) that performs some set of certificate management, archive management, key management, and token management functions for a community of users in an application of asymmetric cryptography.

Q - R

quality of service (QoS). Measure of performance for a transmission system that reflects its transmission quality and service availability.

registration authority (RA). Optional PKI entity (separate from the CAs) that does not sign either digital certificates or CRLs but has responsibility for recording or verifying some or all of the information (particularly the identities of subjects) needed by a CA to issue certificates and CRLs and to perform other certificate management functions.

Remote Authentication Dial-In User Service (RADIUS). A standards-based protocol for authentication, authorization, and accounting (AAA) that is used for remote access users and other secure network access requirements.

Reverse Route Injection (RRI). Used to populate the routing table of an internal router running OSPF or RIP for remote VPN clients or LAN-to-LAN sessions.

Rivest, Shamir, and Adelman (RSA). The inventors of the technique of a public-key cryptographic system that can be used for encryption and authentication.

S

Scalable Encryption Processing (SEP). VPN concentrator modules that perform hardware-based cryptographic functions, including random number generation, hash transforms (MD5 and SHA-1) for authentication, and encryption and decryption (DES, Triple-DES, and AES).

Secure Hash Algorithm-1 (SHA-1). Algorithm that takes a message of less than 2^{64} bits in length and produces a 160-bit message digest. The large message digest provides security against brute-force collision and inversion attacks. SHA-1 (NIS94c) is a revision to SHA that was published in 1994.

Secure Shell (SSH). Sometimes called Secure Socket Shell, a UNIX-based command interface and protocol for gaining access to a remote computer securely.

Secure Sockets Layer (SSL). Encryption technology for the web used to provide secure transactions, such as the transmission of credit card numbers for e-commerce.

security association (SA). An IPSec SA is a description of how two or more entities use security services in the context of a particular security protocol (AH or ESP) to communicate securely on behalf of a particular data flow. It includes things such as the transform and the shared secret keys to be used for protecting the traffic.

Security Dynamics International Authentication (SDI). Third-party authentication services using token cards.

security parameter index (SPI). A number that, together with an IP address and security protocol, uniquely identifies a particular SA. When using IKE to establish the SAs, the SPI for each SA is a pseudo-randomly derived number. Without IKE, the SPI is manually specified for each SA.

Simple Network Management Protocol (SNMP). Network management protocol used almost exclusively in TCP/IP networks. SNMP provides a means to monitor and control network devices, and to manage configurations, statistics collection, performance, and security.

Simple Certificate Enrollment Protocol (SCEP). A CA interoperability protocol that permits compliant IPSec peers and CAs to communicate so that the IPSec peer can obtain and use digital certificates from the CA. Using IPSec peers and CA servers that support SCEP provides manageability and scalability for CA support.

split tunneling. The ability to direct packets over the Internet in clear text while simultaneously encrypting other packets through an IPSec tunnel. The VPN server provides either a list of networks whose traffic must be tunneled or a list of networks whose traffic must not be tunneled. You enable split tunneling on the Cisco VPN Client and configure the network list on the VPN server, such as the VPN concentrator.

stateful firewall. Denies or permits WAN traffic based on a session's state. Packets relating to dialogs initiated from within the firewall are permitted passage through the firewall, while those initiating from outside the firewall are denied passage through the firewall.

T

Telnet. Standard terminal-emulation protocol in the TCP/IP protocol stack. Telnet is used for remote terminal connection, enabling users to log in to remote systems and use resources as if they were connected to a local system. Telnet is defined in RFC 854.

Terminal Access Controller Access Control System Plus (TACACS+). A Cisco proprietary protocol for authentication, authorization, and accounting (AAA).

transform. Lists a security protocol (AH or ESP) with its corresponding algorithms. For example, one transform is the AH protocol with the HMAC-MD5 authentication algorithm; another transform is the ESP protocol with the 56-bit DES encryption algorithm and the HMAC-SHA authentication algorithm.

Trivial File Transfer Protocol (TFTP). Simplified version of FTP that allows files to be transferred from one computer to another over a network, usually without the use of client authentication (for example, username and password).

tunnel. In the context of this book, a secure communication path between two peers, such as two routers. It does not refer to using IPSec in tunnel mode.

Tunnel Endpoint Discovery (TED). An enhancement to IPSec that allows Cisco routers configured with dynamic crypto maps to initiate IPSec sessions with peers that are not preconfigured.

U - W

Uniform Resource Locator (URL). Type of formatted identifier that describes the access method and the location of an information resource object on the Internet.

virtual private network (VPN). Enables IP traffic to travel securely over a public TCP/IP network by encrypting all traffic from one network to another. A VPN uses "tunneling" to encrypt all information at the IP level.

Virtual Router Redundancy Protocol (VRRP). In installations of two or more VPN concentrators in a parallel, redundant configuration, provides automatic switchover to a backup system in case the primary system is out of service, thus ensuring user access to the VPN.

Wired Equivalent Privacy (WEP). An encryption protocol used on data signals transmitted between wireless LAN (WLAN) devices.

INDEX

A

B

C

D

E

F

G

H

J-K

L

N

Q-R

T

U

V

W

X-Y-Z

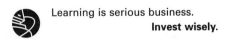

learn

NOW
I HAVE THE POWER TO MAKE
YOU MORE PRODUCTIVE ON THE JOB.
I CAN PREPARE YOU TO MEET
NEW CHALLENGES.

I AM A CISCO CAREER CERTIFICATION.
ADD ME TO YOUR TOOLBOX WITH
AUTHORIZED TRAINING FROM
CISCO LEARNING PARTNERS...
PAY EASILY WITH CISCO
LEARNING CREDITS.

It is the power to acquire new skillsets, and expand your capabilities. Only Cisco Learning Partners can put you ahead of the curve. Visit **www.cisco.com/go/learningpartners.**

THIS IS THE POWER OF THE NETWORK. now.

CISCO SYSTEMS

CCSP

CCSP Secure Exam Certification Guide

1-58720-072-4 • Available Now

This title is primarily intended for networking professionals pursuing the CCSP certification and preparing for the SECUR 642-501 exam, one of five CCSP component exams. The materials, however, appeal to an even broader range of networking professionals seeking a better understanding of the policies, strategies, and techniques of network security. The exam and course, Securing Cisco IOS Networks (SECUR), cover a broad range of networking security topics, providing an overview of the critical components of network security. The other component exams of CCSP then focus on specific areas within that overview, like PIX and VPNs, in even greater detail.

CCSP SECUR Exam Certification Guide (CCSP Self-Study) combines leading edge coverage of security concepts with all the proven learning and exam preparation features of the Exam Certification Guide series from Cisco Press, including the CD-ROM testing engine with more than 200 questions, pre- and post-chapter quizzes and a modular book and CD organization that breaks concepts down into smaller, easy-to-absorb blocks of information.

CCSP CSI Exam Certification Guide

1-58720-089-9 • Available Now

CCSP CSI Exam Certification Guide is a best-of-breed Cisco exam study guide that focuses specifically on the objectives for the CSI exam. Inside, you'll find preparation hints and test-taking tips to help you identify areas of weakness and improve both your conceptual and hands-on knowledge of network security.

CCSP CSI Exam Certification Guide presents you with an organized test preparation routine through the use of proven series elements and techniques. "Do I Know This Already?" quizzes open each chapter and allow you to decide how much time you need to spend on each section. Foundation Summary lists and tables make referencing easy and give you a quick refresher whenever you need it. Challenging chapter-ending review questions reinforce key concepts. An entire chapter of scenarios helps you place the exam objectives in real-world situations, thus increasing recall during exam time.

The companion CD-ROM contains a powerful testing engine that allows you to focus on individual topic areas or take a complete, timed exam. The assessment engine tracks your performance and provides feedback on a module-by-module basis, presenting links to the text for further review and helping you devise a complete study plan.

CCSP

CCSP Cisco Secure VPN Exam Certification Guide

1-58720-070-8 • Available Now

Becoming a CCSP distinguishes you as part of an exclusive group of experts, ready to take on today's most challenging security tasks. Installation and configuration of Cisco VPN 3000 Series concentrators and Cisco VPN 3002 Hardware Clients are critical tasks in today's network environments, especially as reliance on the public Internet as an extension of business networks increases. Whether you are seeking a Cisco VPN Specialist Certification or the full-fledged CCSP Certification, learning what you need to know to pass the CSVPN (Cisco Secure Virtual Private Networks) exam qualifies you to keep your company's network safe while meeting its business needs.

CCSP Cisco Secure VPN Exam Certification Guide is a comprehensive study tool that enables you to master the concepts and technologies required for success on the CSVPN exam. Each chapter of the *CCSP Cisco Secure VPN Exam Certification Guide* tests your knowledge of the exam subjects through sections that detail exam topics to master and areas that highlight essential subjects for quick reference and review. Challenging chapter-ending review questions and exercises test your knowledge of the subject matter, reinforce key concepts, and provide you with the opportunity to apply what you've learned in the chapter. In addition, a final chapter of scenarios pulls together concepts from all the chapters to ensure you can apply your knowledge in a real-world environment. The companion CD-ROM testing engine enables you to take practice exams that mimic the real testing environment, focus on particular topic areas, and refer to the electronic text for review.

CCSP Self-Study: Cisco Secure PIX Firewalls Advanced (CSPFA)

1-58705-149-4 • Available Now

The use of firewalls-devices residing at the network perimeter to protect against intrusion-is an essential building block to even the most basic security program. Cisco Systems has continued the support and development of the PIX OS to provide networks top-notch security while maintaining compatibility with the latest standards and protocols. Now offered in many models, the PIX Firewall is perfectly suited to meet the requirements of small offices (501 model), medium to large businesses (506E, 515E, and 525 models), and large enterprise and service provider customers (525 and 535 models and the Firewall Services Module). *CCSP Self-Study: Cisco Secure PIX Firewall Advanced (CSPFA)*, Second Edition, offers in-depth configuration and deployment information for this popular and versatile firewall solution.

CCSP Self-Study: Cisco Secure PIX Firewall Advanced (CSPFA), Second Edition, teaches you the skills needed to configure and operate the PIX Firewall product family. Chapter overviews bring you quickly up to speed and help you get to work right away. Lab exercises and scenario-based solutions allow you to adapt configurations to your network for rapid implementation, helping you make the most of your PIX Firewall. Chapter-ending review questions test your knowledge. PIX Device Manager (PDM) configuration procedures are presented to complement extensive coverage of traditional CLI commands.

Whether you are looking for a reference guide on working with the various PIX Firewall models or seeking a study tool for the CSPFA 642-521 exam, *CCSP Self-Study: Cisco Secure PIX Firewall Advanced (CSPFA)*, Second Edition, supports your effective use of the PIX Firewall.

Learning is serious business. **Invest wisely.**

CCSP

CCSP Self-Study: Cisco Secure Intrusion Detection System (CSIDS), Second Edition

ISBN: 1-58705-144-3 • Available Now

In addition to firewalls and other security appliances intended to limit outsider access to a network, intrusion detection and targeted countermeasures are a critical component of a complete network security plan. The Cisco Intrusion Detection Sensors and Management options work as a united system to provide detection, notification, and aggressive lockdown to malicious network breaches. *CCSP Self-Study: Cisco Secure Intrusion Detection System (CSIDS)*, Second Edition, offers in-depth configuration and deployment information for the reliable and intensive intrusion detection solutions from Cisco Systems.

CCSP Self-Study: Cisco Secure Intrusion Detection System (CSIDS), Second Edition, is a Cisco authorized, self-paced learning tool that helps you gain mastery over the use of both the host-based and network-based IDS options (as well as the Cisco Threat Response functionality) by presenting a consolidated all-inclusive reference on all of the current Cisco IDS sensor platforms and management platforms. Chapter overviews bring you quickly up to speed and help you get to work right away. Configuration examples are designed to show you how to make the most of your IDS system, and unique chapter-ending review questions test your knowledge.

Whether you are seeking a reference guide to working with the CIDS sensor and management platforms or a study guide for the 642-531 exam, *CCSP Self-Study: Cisco Secure Intrusion Detection System (CSIDS)*, Second Edition, supports your effective use of the Cisco IDS.

□ **YES!** I'm requesting a **free** subscription to *Packet*™ magazine.

□ No. I'm not interested at this time.

□ Mr.
□ Ms.

First Name (Please Print) _____ Last Name _____

Title/Position (Required) _____

Company (Required) _____

Address _____

City _____ State/Province _____

Zip/Postal Code _____ Country _____

Telephone (Include country and area codes) _____ Fax _____

E-mail _____

Signature (Required) _____ Date _____

□ I would like to receive additional information on Cisco's services and products by e-mail.

1. Do you or your company:
- A □ Use Cisco products   C □ Both
- B □ Resell Cisco products   D □ Neither

2. Your organization's relationship to Cisco Systems:
- A □ Customer/End User   E □ Integrator   J □ Consultant
- B □ Prospective Customer F □ Non-Authorized Reseller K □ Other (specify):
- C □ Cisco Reseller   G □ Cisco Training Partner _____
- D □ Cisco Distributor   I □ Cisco OEM

3. How many people does your entire company employ?
- A □ More than 10,000   D □ 500 to 999   G □ Fewer than 100
- B □ 5,000 to 9,999   E □ 250 to 499
- C □ 1,000 to 4,999   F □ 100 to 249

4. Is your company a Service Provider?
- A □ Yes   B □ No

5. Your involvement in network equipment purchases:
- A □ Recommend   B □ Approve   C □ Neither

6. Your personal involvement in networking:
- A □ Entire enterprise at all sites   F □ Public network
- B □ Departments or network segments at more than one site D □ No involvement
- C □ Single department or network segment   E □ Other (specify):
- _____

7. Your Industry:
- A □ Aerospace   G □ Education (K–12)   K □ Health Care
- B □ Agriculture/Mining/Construction   U □ Education (College/Univ.) L □ Telecommunications
- C □ Banking/Finance   H □ Government—Federal   M □ Utilities/Transportation
- D □ Chemical/Pharmaceutical   I □ Government—State   N □ Other (specify):
- E □ Consultant   J □ Government—Local   _____
- F □ Computer/Systems/Electronics

CPRESS

PACKET™

Packet magazine serves as the premier publication linking customers to Cisco Systems, Inc. Delivering complete coverage of cutting-edge networking trends and innovations, *Packet* is a magazine for technical, hands-on users. It delivers industry-specific information for enterprise, service provider, and small and midsized business market segments. A toolchest for planners and decision makers, *Packet* contains a vast array of practical information, boasting sample configurations, real-life customer examples, and tips on getting the most from your Cisco Systems' investments. Simply put, *Packet* magazine is straight talk straight from the worldwide leader in networking for the Internet, Cisco Systems, Inc.

We hope you'll take advantage of this useful resource. I look forward to hearing from you!

Cecelia Glover
Packet Circulation Manager
packet@external.cisco.com
www.cisco.com/go/packet

PACKET™